Selected Papers on

Computer Languages

Selected Papers on Computer Languages

DONALD E. KNUTH

CSLI was founded early in 1983 by researchers from Stanford University, SRI International, and Xerox PARC to further research and development of integrated theories of language, information, and computation.

CSLI headquarters and the publication offices are located in Ventura Hall, Stanford CA 94305.

Library of Congress Cataloging-in-Publication Data

```
Knuth, Donald Ervin, 1938-
    Selected papers on computer languages / Donald E. Knuth.
    xvi,594 p. 23 cm. -- (CSLI lecture notes ; no. 139)
Includes bibliographical references and index.
    ISBN 1-57586-382-0 (pbk. : alk. paper) --
    ISBN 1-57586-381-2 (hardback : alk. paper)
    1. Programming languages (Electronic computers) I. Title.
II. Series.

    QA76.7 .K63 2002
    005.13--dc21
                                        2002012119
```

Internet page
    http://www-cs-faculty.stanford.edu/~knuth/cl.html
contains further information and links to related books.

to Ole-Johan Dahl (1931–2002),
who taught me much about computation,

and to Louise Marie Bohning Knuth (1912–2002),
who taught me my mother tongue

Contents

vii

Preface

This book is devoted to the topic that got me hooked on computers in
the first place: the languages by which people are able to communicate
with machines.

Rules of grammar have always fascinated me. In retrospect I think
that the most exciting days of my elementary school education came
during the seventh grade, when I was taught how to make diagrams
of English-language sentences in order to see how the various parts of

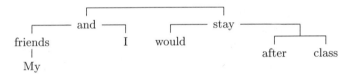

speech fit together. My friends and I would stay after class, trying to put
more and more sentences into diagrammatic form — and getting totally
confused by poetry, which seemed to break most of the rules.

During the summer of 1957, after I had just written my first computer programs for numerical problems like factoring numbers and for
fun problems like playing tic-tac-toe, an amazing program called IT —
the "Internal Translator" — arrived at the Case Tech Computing Center, where I had been working as a college freshman. IT would look at a
card that contained an algebraic equation, then the machine would flash
its lights for a few seconds and go punch-punch-punch; out would come
a deck of cards containing a machine-language program to compute the
value of the equation. Mystified by the fact that a mere computer could
understand algebra well enough to create its own programs, I got hold
of the source code for IT and spent two weeks poring over the listing.
Lo, the secrets were revealed, and several friends helped me in 1958 to
extend IT even further.

Of course in those days we had only a vague notion of what we were doing; our work was almost totally disorganized, with very few principles to guide us. But researchers in linguistics were beginning to formulate rules of grammar that were considerably more mathematical than before. And people began to realize that such methods are highly relevant to the artificial languages that were becoming popular for computer programming, even though natural languages like English remained intractable.

I found the mathematical approach to grammar immediately appealing — so much so, in fact, that I must admit to taking a copy of Noam Chomsky's *Syntactic Structures* along with me on my honeymoon in 1961. During odd moments, while crossing the Atlantic in an ocean liner and while camping in Europe, I read that book rather thoroughly and tried to answer some basic theoretical questions. Here was a marvelous thing: a mathematical theory of language in which I could use a computer programmer's intuition! The mathematical, linguistic, and algorithmic parts of my life had previously been totally separate. During the ensuing years those three aspects became steadily more intertwined; and by the end of the 1960s I found myself a Professor of Computer Science at Stanford University, primarily because of work that I had done with respect to languages for computer programming.

The present book begins with an account of what was happening all over the world before I myself had ever heard about programming languages. Chapter 1 tells the story of more than twenty pioneering efforts to design and implement notations and languages that could help programmers cope with the first computers. These intriguing and instructive developments represent the first creative steps in the evolution of "software," forming a parallel thread to the better-known history of hardware development.

ALGOL 60, the international algebraic language that profoundly influenced all subsequent work, is the concern of Chapters 2–8. Brief introductory remarks in Chapters 2 and 3 about ALGOL's basic concepts, especially about the important way in which the grammatical rules of ALGOL were presented, are followed by Chapter 4, a brash and somewhat hastily written article in which I recorded the initial reactions that my colleagues and I were having to ALGOL's more controversial innovations. Chapter 5 describes SMALGOL-61, a subset of ALGOL 60 intended to respect the limitations of modest-size machines. One of the most subtle aspects of the full language, known as "call-by-name recursion" and "up-level addressing," is considered briefly in Chapter 6. Then Chapter 7 presents a (short-lived yet interesting) proposal for expressing input and output operations at a high level, without changing the underlying language, although ALGOL 60 itself did not provide any such facilities. The preparation of that proposal gave me first-hand experience with the process of design-by-committee; it also led to a simple concept called a *list procedure* that deserves to be more widely known. Chapter 8 surveys the "remaining trouble spots" of ALGOL, which turn out to be remarkably few.

My own first attempt at designing a computer language — SOL, the Simulation Oriented Language — is the subject of Chapters 9 and 10. Shortly after doing that work I drafted some notes about the general principles of language design, intending to include them as part of a survey paper that I had been asked to write. Those notes, never before published, still seem surprisingly relevant, so I have included them as Chapter 11.

Chapter 12 points out that programming languages can be used for theoretical purposes to study abstract computers, just as they are used on real machines. Chapter 13 is a purely theoretical paper for which I have fond memories, because it solves a problem that had stumped me for several weeks during the 1960s. Finally I had decided that it was too tough for me, and resumed working on other things ... but when I awoke the next day, aha! The solution had somehow magically popped into my head. Although the problem itself is mathematically elegant, it is rather technical and has no known practical application; yet I found the work extremely instructive, and the things I learned while seeking a solution proved to be valuable in many subsequent investigations. Thus I came to appreciate the benefits that theory brings to practice.

The focus shifts in Chapter 14 to questions of *parsing*, namely to the study of methods by which a computer can efficiently recognize the grammatical structure of sentences that it reads. Volume 5 of my books on *The Art of Computer Programming* (*TAOCP*) is scheduled to be largely about parsing, and the material on "top-down parsing" in Chapter 14 of the present book is based largely on the draft manuscript of *TAOCP* as it existed in 1964. (I didn't publish any of those elementary ideas at the time, because I was optimistic that *TAOCP* would soon be in print.) Shortly after completing that draft, I realized that many of the ideas I had been reading about and discussing could be unified and extended, and that the resulting "bottom-up" approach would be quite powerful. This new approach seemed too advanced for my book, so I took time out to submit it for publication in 1965. The result, called LR(k) parsing because it involves "translation from left to right by looking k characters ahead," appears in Chapter 15. (Many people went on to refine and simplify the associated theory, which then became integrated into software practice; so I shall certainly have to discuss it in depth when I finally do finish the manuscript of Volume 5.)

Chapter 16 comes from the draft of Volume 6. It contains basic ideas about the theory of languages that I developed in 1964 but didn't publish until 1992, namely that the theory becomes even better if we think of languages as *multisets* of sentences, not just as ordinary sets.

Once a language can be parsed, we can attach *meaning* to its phrases, thereby complementing syntax with semantics. Chapters 17–19 deal with my favorite approach to this important subject, which is now popularly known as the study of *attribute grammars*.

The next few chapters contain background material that is largely of historical interest. Chapter 20 portrays the problems of parsing and translation as they were viewed in 1962; it explains why I was so delighted in later years to help develop a solid theoretical basis by which compiler techniques could be systematically understood and improved. Chapter 21 — my very first paper about computing, written when I was an undergraduate — provides an excellent contrast to the more "mature" efforts that followed, and contains an incredibly complicated flowchart. Flowcharts are the subject of Chapter 22; the experiments discussed in that chapter led to the method of exposition that I subsequently decided to adopt in *TAOCP*. Some early thoughts about "structured programming," as an alternative to flowcharts, appear in Chapter 23.

The emphasis shifts again in Chapter 24, towards the generation of efficient low-level machine code from high-level source language input. This chapter launched the empirical study of "typical" user programs, and recommended *profiling* tools that help speed programs up.

Finally, Chapter 25 — my most recent paper — considers another sort of optimization that curiously has not been addressed before, based on the transformation of *coroutines*. This chapter demonstrates that computer languages still contain fundamental aspects that are not well understood; I suspect that a thorough study of coroutine transformation will lead to further discoveries of important ideas.

I'm dedicating this book to my mother, Louise Knuth, whose deep love of language proved to be contagious. She encouraged me to read at a very early age, and continued to inspire me with her boundless energy. On the occasion of her 80th birthday in October, 1992, I began my after-dinner remarks as follows:

> Four score and zero years ago, my grandparents brought forth
> on this continent a new baby, conceived in Ohio, and dedicated

to prepositions, adjectives, nouns, adverbs, and all other kinds of words.

I'm also dedicating this book to my dear friend Ole-Johan Dahl, whose deep insights into computational processes led to the important notion of object-oriented languages. When I learned in 1966 of the SIMULA language that he developed together with Kristen Nygaard, it was love at first sight, and I immediately abandoned any further work with SOL. Ole-Johan has written some of the most elegant computer programs that I have ever seen. He gave me the opportunity to work with him for a year in Norway, where I learned many things that inspired my subsequent work. Fate decreed, alas, that he and my mother would both die during the same week, last summer; but the memory of their productive lives has sustained me as I prepared this book for publication.

I'm grateful too for having been able to work jointly with coauthors Richard Bigelow, Bob Floyd, John McNeley, Jack Merner, Frank Ruskey, and Luis Trabb Pardo. My research was generously supported by Burroughs Corporation, by IBM Corporation, and by various agencies of the U.S. government.

The present book has been made possible by the skills of Max Etchemendy, Tony Gee, Lauri Kanerva, Kimberly Lewis Brown, and Christine Sosa, who helped to convert hundreds of pages published long, long ago into a modern electronic format. Dan Eilers, Mark Ward, and Udo Wermuth gave invaluable help with the nitty-gritty details of proofreading. Papers on computer languages surely rank among the most difficult challenges that printers have ever had to face, from a typographic standpoint, so it gives me great pleasure to see this material finally typeset in the way I originally intended. (Perhaps even better.)

The process of compiling this book has given me the incentive to improve some of the original wording. Indeed, I first wrote nearly all of these chapters long before the copy editors of *TAOCP* taught me how to write better sentences. I cannot be happy now with stylistic errors that I would no longer tolerate in the writing of my students, so I have tried to remove them, together with all of the technical errors that have come to my attention. On the other hand I have attempted to retain the essence of the original exposition, and to avoid injecting any hindsight into the texts, so as not to imply falsely that I was clairvoyant or that I had anticipated certain ideas or trends sooner than other people did.

The only place where I found it necessary to change my original notation and terminology significantly was in Chapter 15, which was written when the theory of context-free languages was still in a state of flux: I've changed the term "intermediate symbol" to the now-standard term "nonterminal symbol" throughout that article. Moreover, Chapter 15 was written during a period when I still had not decided how to draw the tree diagrams in *TAOCP*; should they have the root at the bottom, as in nature, or at the top, as many of my friends were drawing them? [See Figure 2–17 in Volume 1.] I experimented for awhile with a return to nature, but I soon realized that common terms like "top-down parsing" gave me no choice. Thus, the nature-oriented tree diagrams in my original paper on LR(k) grammars are needlessly confusing today.

Nearly all of the illustrations in this book — more than 75 of them — have, incidentally, been redrawn using John Hobby's METAPOST, a computer language that continues to give me great joy.

Most of the chapters now also have an Addendum, in which I try to bring everything up to date by discussing the most important sequels to the original work, as far as I know them. And I have tried to put all of the bibliographies into a consistent format, so that they will be as useful as possible to everyone who pursues the subject.

This book is number five in a series that Stanford's Center for the Study of Language and Information (CSLI) plans to publish containing archival forms of the papers I have written. The first volume, *Literate Programming*, appeared in 1992; the second, *Selected Papers on Computer Science*, appeared in 1996; the third, *Digital Typography*, in 1999; and the fourth, *Selected Papers on Analysis of Algorithms*, in 2000. Three additional volumes are in preparation containing selected papers on Discrete Mathematics, Design of Algorithms, Fun and Games.

> *Donald E. Knuth*
> *Stanford, California*
> *March 2003*

Acknowledgments

"The early development of programming languages" originally appeared in *Encyclopedia of Computer Science and Technology* **7** (New York: Marcel Dekker, Inc., 1977), pp. 419–493. Copyright ©1977 by Marcel Dekker, Inc. Reprinted by permission.

"Backus Normal Form versus Backus Naur Form" originally appeared in *Communications of the ACM* **7**, (December 1964), pp. 735–736. (New York: Association for Computing Machinery, Inc.) Copyright presently held by the author.

"Teaching ALGOL 60" originally appeared in *Algol Bulletin* **19** (Amsterdam: Mathematisch Centrum, January 1965), pp. 4–6. Copyright presently held by the author.

"ALGOL 60 Confidential" originally appeared in *Communications of the ACM* **4** (June 1961), pp. 268–272. (New York: Association for Computing Machinery, Inc.) Copyright presently held by the author.

"SMALGOL-61" originally appeared in *Communications of the ACM* **4** (November 1961), pp. 499–502. (New York: Association for Computing Machinery, Inc.) Copyright presently held by the author.

"Man or boy?" originally appeared in *Algol Bulletin* **17** (Amsterdam: Mathematisch Centrum, July 1964), p. 7; **19** (January 1965), pp. 8–9. Copyright presently held by the author.

"A proposal for input-output conventions in ALGOL 60" originally appeared in *Communications of the ACM* **7** (May 1964), pp. 273–283. (New York: Association for Computing Machinery, Inc.) Copyright presently held by the author.

"The remaining trouble spots in ALGOL 60" originally appeared in *Communications of the ACM* **10** (October 1967), pp. 611–618. (New York: Association for Computing Machinery, Inc.) Copyright presently held by the author.

"SOL — A symbolic language for general purpose systems simulation" originally appeared in *IEEE Transactions on Electronic Computers* **EC-13** (1964), pp. 401–408. Copyright ©1964 by The Institute of Electrical and Electronics Engineers, Inc. Reprinted by permission.

"A formal definition of SOL" originally appeared in *IEEE Transactions on Electronic Computers* **EC–13** (1964), pp. 409–414. Copyright ©1964 by The Institute of Electrical and Electronics Engineers, Inc. Reprinted by permission.

"Programming languages for automata" originally appeared in *Journal of the ACM* **14** (October 1967), pp. 615–635. (New York: Association for Computing Machinery, Inc.) Copyright presently held by the author.

"A characterization of parenthesis languages" originally appeared in *Information and Control* **11** (1967), pp. 269–289. Copyright ©1967 by Academic Press. All rights reserved. Reprinted by permission.

Lou Knuth with half of her clan, January 2002
(photo by Diana Baxter)

Chapter 1

The Early Development of Programming Languages

[Written with Luis Trabb Pardo. Originally published in Encyclopedia of Computer Science and Technology, edited by Jack Belzer, Albert G. Holzman, and Allen Kent, Volume 7 (New York: Marcel Dekker, 1977), 419–493.]

This paper surveys the evolution of "high-level" programming languages during the first decade of computer programming activity. We discuss the contributions of Zuse in 1945 (the "Plankalkül"), Goldstine and von Neumann in 1946 ("Flow Diagrams"), Curry in 1948 ("Composition"), Mauchly et al. in 1949 ("Short Code"), Burks in 1950 ("Intermediate PL"), Rutishauser in 1951 ("Klammerausdrücke"), Böhm in 1951 ("Formules"), Glennie in 1952 ("AUTOCODE"), Hopper et al. in 1953 ("A-2"), Laning and Zierler in 1953 ("Algebraic Interpreter"), Backus et al. in 1954–1957 ("FORTRAN"), Brooker in 1954 ("Mark I AUTOCODE"), Kamynin and Lıûbimskiĭ in 1954 ("ПП-2"), Ershov in 1955 ("ПП"), Grems and Porter in 1955 ("BACAIC"), Elsworth et al. in 1955 ("Kompiler 2"), Blum in 1956 ("ADES"), Perlis et al. in 1956 ("IT"), Katz et al. in 1956–1958 ("MATH-MATIC"), Bauer and Samelson in 1956–1958 (U.S. Patent 3,047,228).

The principal features of each contribution are illustrated and discussed. For purposes of comparison, a particular fixed algorithm has been encoded as far as possible in each of the languages.

This summary of early work is based primarily on unpublished source materials, and the authors hope that they have been able to compile a fairly complete picture of the pioneering developments in this area.

Introduction

It is interesting and instructive to study the history of a subject not only because it helps us to understand how the important ideas were born —

and to see how the "human element" entered into each development —
but also because it helps us to appreciate the amount of progress that
has been made. This is especially striking in the case of programming
languages, a subject that has long been undervalued by computer scientists. After learning a high-level language, a person often tends to
think mostly of improvements that he or she would like to see, since all
languages can be improved, and it is very easy to underestimate the difficulty of creating that language in the first place. In order to perceive
the real depth of this subject, we need to realize how long it took to
develop the important concepts that we now regard as self-evident. The
ideas were by no means obvious a priori, and many years of work by
brilliant and dedicated people were necessary before our current state of
knowledge was reached.

The goal of this paper is to give an adequate account of the early
history of high-level programming languages, covering roughly the first
decade of their development. Our story will take us up to 1957, when
the practical importance of algebraic compilers was first being demon-
strated, and when computers were just beginning to be available in large
numbers. We will see how people's fundamental conceptions of algorithms and of the programming process evolved during the years — not
always in a forward direction — culminating in languages such as FOR-
TRAN I. The best languages we shall encounter are, of course, very
primitive by today's standards, but they were good enough to touch
off an explosive growth in language development; the ensuing decade
of intense activity has been detailed in Jean Sammet's 785-page book
[SA 69]. We shall be concerned with the more relaxed atmosphere of
the "pre-Babel" days, when people who worked with computers foresaw
the need for important aids to programming that did not yet exist. In
many cases these developments were so far ahead of their time that they
remained unpublished, and they are still largely unknown today.

Altogether we shall be considering about 20 different languages;
therefore we will have neither the space nor the time to characterize
any one of them completely. Besides, it would be rather boring to re-
cite so many technical rules. The best way to grasp the spirit of a
programming language is to read example programs, so we shall adopt
the following strategy: A certain fixed algorithm — which we shall call
the "TPK algorithm" for want of a better name[1] — will be expressed as
a program in each language we discuss. Informal explanations of this

---

[1] Consider "Grimm's law" in comparative linguistics, and/or the word "typical," and/or the names of the authors of this article.

program should then suffice to capture the essence of the corresponding language, although the TPK algorithm will not, of course, exhaust that language's capabilities. Once we have understood a program for TPK, we'll be able to discuss the most important language features that it does not reveal.

Note that the same algorithm will be expressed in each language, in order to provide a simple means of comparison. A serious attempt has been made to write each program in the style originally used by the authors of the corresponding languages. If comments appear next to the program text, they attempt to match the terminology used at that time by the original authors. Our treatment will therefore be something like a recital of "Chopsticks" as it would have been played by Bach, Beethoven, Brahms, and Brubeck. The resulting programs are not truly authentic excerpts from the historic record, but they will serve as fairly close replicas; the interested reader can pursue each language further by consulting the bibliographic references to be given.

The exemplary TPK algorithm that we shall be using so frequently can be written as follows in a dialect of ALGOL 60:

```
01      TPK: begin integer i;  real y;  real array a[0:10];
02             real procedure f(t);  real t;  value t;
03               f := sqrt(abs(t)) + 5 × t ↑ 3;
04             for i := 0 step 1 until 10 do read(a[i]);
05             for i := 10 step −1 until 0 do
06               begin y := f(a[i]);
07                 if y > 400 then write(i, 'TOO LARGE')
08                            else write(i, y);
09               end
10           end TPK.
```

[Actually ALGOL 60 is not one of the languages we shall be discussing, since it was a later development, but the reader ought to know enough about it to understand TPK. If not, here is a brief run-down on what the program means: Line *01* says that i is an integer-valued variable, whereas y takes on floating point approximations to real values; and a_0, a_1, ..., a_{10} also are real-valued. Lines *02* and *03* define the function $f(t) = \sqrt{|t|} + 5t^3$ for use in the algorithm proper, which starts on line *04*. Line *04* reads in eleven input values a_0, a_1, ..., a_{10}, in this order; then line *05* says to do lines *06*, *07*, *08*, *09* (delimited by **begin** and **end**) for $i = 10$, 9, ..., 0, in *that* order. The latter lines cause y to be set to $f(a_i)$, and then one of two messages is written out. The message is either the current value of i followed by the words 'TOO LARGE', or the current values of i and y, according as $y > 400$ or not.]

Of course this algorithm is quite useless; but for our purposes it will be helpful to imagine ourselves vitally interested in the process. Let us pretend that the function $f(t) = \sqrt{|t|} + 5t^3$ has a tremendous practical significance, and that it is extremely important to print out the function values $f(a_i)$ in the opposite order from which the a_i are received. This will put us in the right frame of mind to be reading the programs below. (If a truly useful algorithm were being considered here, it would need to be much longer in order to illustrate as many different features of the programming languages.)

Many of the programs we shall discuss will have italicized line numbers in the left-hand margin, as in the ALGOL code above. Such numbers are not really part of the programs; they appear only so that the accompanying text can refer easily to any particular line.

It turns out that most of the early high-level languages were not able to handle the TPK algorithm exactly as presented above; therefore we must make some modifications. In the first place, when a language deals only with integer variables, we shall assume that all inputs and outputs are integer valued, and that '$sqrt(x)$' denotes the largest integer not exceeding $\sqrt{x}$. Second, if the language does not provide for alphabetic output, the string 'TOO LARGE' will be replaced by the number 999. Third, some languages do not provide for input and output at all; in such a case, we shall assume that the input values $a_0, a_1, \ldots, a_{10}$ have somehow been supplied by an external process, and that our job is to compute 22 output values $b_0, b_1, \ldots, b_{21}$. Here $b_0, b_2, \ldots, b_{20}$ will be the respective "i values" 10, 9, $\ldots$, 0, and the alternate positions b_1, b_3, $\ldots, b_{21}$ will contain the corresponding $f(a_i)$ values and/or 999 codes. Finally, if a language does not allow programmers to define their own functions, the statement '$y := f(a[i])$' will essentially be replaced by its expanded form '$y := sqrt(abs(a[i])) + 5 \times a[i] \uparrow 3$'.

Prior Developments

Before getting into real programming languages, let us try to set the scene by reviewing the background very quickly. How were algorithms described prior to 1945?

The earliest known written algorithms come from ancient Mesopotamia, about 2000 B.C. In this case the written descriptions contained only sequences of calculations on particular sets of data, not an abstract statement of a particular procedure. It is clear that strict procedures were being followed (since, for example, multiplications by 1 were explicitly performed), but they never seem to have been written down. Iterations like 'for $i := 0$ **step** 1 **until** 10' were rare, but when present they would consist of a fully expanded sequence of calculations. (See [KN 72] for a survey of Babylonian algorithms.)

By the time of Greek civilization, several nontrivial abstract algorithms had been studied rather thoroughly. For example, see [KN 69, §4.5.2] for a paraphrase of Euclid's presentation of "Euclid's algorithm." The description of algorithms was always informal, however, rendered in natural language.

Mathematicians never did invent a good notation for dynamic processes during the ensuing centuries, although of course notations for (static) functional relations became highly developed. When a procedure involved nontrivial sequences of decisions, the available methods for precise description remained informal and rather cumbersome.

Example programs written for early computing devices, such as those for Babbage's calculating engine, were naturally presented in "machine language" rather than in a true programming language. For example, the three-address code for Babbage's machine was planned to consist of instructions such as '$V_4 \times V_0 = V_{10}$', where operation signs like '$\times$' would appear on an operation card and subscript numbers like (4, 0, 10) would appear on a separate variable card. The most elaborate program developed by Babbage and Lady Lovelace for this machine was a routine for calculating Bernoulli numbers; see [BA 61, pages 68 and 286–297]. An example Mark I program given in 1946 by Howard Aiken and Grace Hopper (see [RA 73, pages 216–218]) shows that its machine language was considerably more complicated.

Although all of these early programs were in a machine language, it is interesting to note that Babbage had noticed already on 9 July 1836 that machines as well as people could produce programs as output [RA 73, page 349]:

This day I had for the first time a general but very indistinct conception of the possibility of making an engine work out *algebraic* developments. I mean without *any* reference to the *value* of the letters. My notion is that as the cards (Jacquards) of the Calc. engine direct a series of operations and then recommence with the first so it might perhaps be possible to cause the same cards to punch others equivalent to any given number of repetitions. But there hole [*sic*] might perhaps be small pieces of formulae previously made by the first cards.

In 1914, Leonardo Torres y Quevedo used natural language to describe the steps of a short program for his hypothetical automaton. Helmut Schreyer gave an analogous description in 1939 for the machine that he had helped Konrad Zuse to build (see [RA 73, pages 95–98 and 167]).

To conclude this survey of prior developments, let us take a look at A. M. Turing's famous mathematical paper of 1936 [TU 36], where the concept of a universal computing machine was introduced for theoretical purposes. Turing's machine language was more primitive, not having a built-in arithmetic capability, and he defined a complex program by presenting what amounts to macroexpansions or open subroutines. For example, here was his program for making the machine move to the leftmost 'a' on its working tape:

m-config.	symbol	behavior	final m-config.
$\mathfrak{f}(\mathfrak{C}, \mathfrak{B}, a)$	$\begin{cases} \text{ə} \\ \text{not ə} \end{cases}$	L L	$\mathfrak{f}_1(\mathfrak{C}, \mathfrak{B}, a)$ $\mathfrak{f}(\mathfrak{C}, \mathfrak{B}, a)$
$\mathfrak{f}_1(\mathfrak{C}, \mathfrak{B}, a)$	$\begin{cases} a \\ \text{not } a \\ \text{None} \end{cases}$	 R R	$\mathfrak{C}$ $\mathfrak{f}_1(\mathfrak{C}, \mathfrak{B}, a)$ $\mathfrak{f}_2(\mathfrak{C}, \mathfrak{B}, a)$
$\mathfrak{f}_2(\mathfrak{C}, \mathfrak{B}, a)$	$\begin{cases} a \\ \text{not } a \\ \text{None} \end{cases}$	 R R	$\mathfrak{C}$ $\mathfrak{f}_1(\mathfrak{C}, \mathfrak{B}, a)$ $\mathfrak{B}$

[In order to carry out this operation, one first sends the machine to state $\mathfrak{f}(\mathfrak{C}, \mathfrak{B}, a)$; it will immediately begin to scan left on the tape (L) until first passing the symbol ə. Then it moves right until either encountering the symbol a or two consecutive blanks; in the first case it enters into state $\mathfrak{C}$ while still scanning the a, and in the second case it enters state $\mathfrak{B}$ after moving to the right of the second blank. Turing used the term "m-configuration" for state.]

Such "skeleton tables," as presented by Turing, represented the highest-level notations for precise algorithm description that had been developed before our story begins — except, perhaps, for Alonzo Church's "λ-notation" [CH 36], which represents an entirely different approach to calculation. Mathematicians would traditionally present the control mechanisms of algorithms informally, and the necessary computations would be expressed by means of equations. There was no concept of assignment (that is, of replacing the value of some variable by a new value); instead of writing $s \leftarrow -s$ one would write $s_{n+1} = -s_n$, giving a new name to each quantity that would arise during a sequence of calculations.

Zuse's "Plancalculus"

Near the end of World War II, Allied bombs destroyed nearly all of the sophisticated relay computers that Konrad Zuse had been building in Germany since 1936. Only his Z4 machine could be rescued, in what Zuse describes as a hair-raising [*abenteuerlich*] way; and he moved the Z4 to a little shed in a small Alpine village called Hinterstein.

> It was unthinkable to continue practical work on the equipment; my small group of twelve co-workers disbanded. But it was now a satisfactory time to pursue theoretical studies. The Z4 Computer that had been rescued could barely be made to run, and no especially algorithmic language was really necessary to program it anyway. [Conditional commands had consciously been omitted; see [RA 73, page 181].] Thus the PK [*Plankalkül*] arose purely as a piece of desk-work, without regard to whether or not machines suitable for PK's programs would be available in the foreseeable future. [ZU 72, page 6].

Zuse had previously come to grips with the lack of formal notations for algorithms while working on his planned doctoral dissertation [ZU 44]. Here he had independently developed a three-address notation remarkably like that of Babbage. For example, to compute the roots x_1 and x_2 of $x^2 + ax + b = 0$, given $a = V_1$ and $b = V_2$, he prepared the following *Rechenplan* [page 26]:

$$V_1 : 2 = V_3$$
$$V_3 \cdot V_3 = V_4$$
$$V_4 - V_2 = V_5$$
$$\sqrt{V_5} = V_6$$
$$V_3(-1) = V_7$$
$$V_7 + V_6 = V_8 = x_1$$
$$V_7 - V_6 = V_9 = x_2$$

He realized that this notation was limited to straight line programs [so-called *starre Pläne*], and he had concluded his previous manuscript with the following remark [ZU 44, page 31]:

Unstarre Rechenpläne constitute the true discipline of higher combinatorial computing; however, they cannot yet be treated in this place.

The completion of this work was the theoretical task Zuse set himself in 1945, and he pursued it very energetically. The result was an amazingly comprehensive language that he called the *Plankalkül* [program calculus], an extension of Hilbert's *Aussagenkalkül* [propositional calculus] and *Prädikatenkalkül* [predicate calculus]. Before laying this project aside, Zuse had completed an extensive manuscript containing programs far more complex than anything written before. Among other things, there were algorithms for sorting into order; for testing the connectivity of a graph represented as a list of edges; for integer arithmetic (including square roots) in binary notation; and for floating-point arithmetic. He even developed algorithms to test whether or not a given logical formula is syntactically well formed, and whether or not such a formula contains redundant parentheses — assuming six levels of precedence between the operators. To top things off, he also included 49 pages of algorithms for playing chess. Who would have believed that such pioneering developments could emerge from the solitary village of Hinterstein? His plans to include algorithms for matrix calculations, series expansions, etc., had to be dropped since the necessary contacts were lacking in that place. Furthermore, his chess playing program treated "en passant captures" incorrectly, because he could find nobody who knew chess any better than he did [ZU 72, pages 32 and 35]!

Zuse's 1945 manuscript unfortunately lay unpublished until 1972, although brief excerpts appeared in 1948 and 1959 [ZU 48, ZU 59]; see also [BW 72], where his work was brought to the attention of English speaking readers for the first time. It is interesting to speculate about what would have happened if he had published everything at once; would many people have been able to understand such radical new ideas?

The monograph [ZU 45] on Plankalkül begins with the following statement of motivation:

Aufgabe des Plankalküls ist es, beliebige Rechenvorschriften rein formal darzustellen. [The mission of the Plancalculus is to give a purely formal description of any computational procedure.]

So, in particular, the Plankalkül should be able to describe the TPK algorithm; and we had better turn now to this program, before we forget what TPK is all about. Zuse's notation may appear somewhat frightening at first, but we will soon see that it is really not difficult to understand.

$$01 \quad S2 = (S1.4, S\Delta1)$$

$$
\begin{array}{lll}
02 & P1 & \left| \begin{array}{cc} R(V) & \Rightarrow R \end{array} \right. \\
03 & & V \quad 0 \qquad 0 \\
04 & & S \quad \Delta1 \qquad \Delta1 \\[4pt]
05 & & \left| \begin{array}{ccc} \sqrt{|V|} + 5 \times V^3 & \Rightarrow R \end{array} \right. \\
06 & & V \quad 0 \qquad\qquad 0 \qquad 0 \\
07 & & S \quad \Delta1 \qquad\quad\; \Delta1 \quad \Delta1 \\[4pt]
08 & P2 & \left| \begin{array}{cc} R(V) & \Rightarrow \quad R \end{array} \right. \\
09 & & V \quad 0 \qquad\quad 0 \\
10 & & S \quad 11 \times \Delta1 \quad 11 \times 2
\end{array}
$$

$$
\begin{array}{lll}
11 & & \left| W2(11) \left[\begin{array}{c} R1(V) \Rightarrow Z \end{array} \right. \right. \\
12 & & V \qquad\qquad\quad 0 \;\; 0 \qquad 0 \\
13 & & K \qquad\qquad\qquad\quad i \\
14 & & S \qquad\qquad\qquad\quad\;\; \Delta1 \quad \Delta1 \\[4pt]
15 & & \left| \qquad\quad Z > 400 \dashrightarrow (i, +\infty) \Rightarrow R \;\ulcorner(10 - i) \right. \\
16 & & V \qquad\quad 0 \qquad\qquad\qquad\qquad\;\; 0 \\
17 & & K \\
18 & & S \qquad\quad \Delta1 \qquad\quad 1.4 \qquad\quad 2 \\[4pt]
19 & & \left| \qquad\quad \overline{Z > 400} \dashrightarrow (i,\; Z) \Rightarrow R \;\ulcorner(10 - i) \right. \\
20 & & V \qquad\quad 0 \qquad\qquad\quad 0 \quad 0 \\
21 & & K \\
22 & & S \qquad\quad \Delta1 \qquad\quad 1.4 \;\; \Delta1 \quad 2
\end{array}
$$

Line *01* of this code is the declaration of a compound data type, and before we discuss the remainder of the program we should stress the richness of data structures provided by Zuse's language (even in its early form [ZU 44]). This feature is, in fact, one of the greatest strengths of the Plankalkül; none of the other languages we shall discuss had such a perceptive notion of data, yet Zuse's proposal was simple and elegant. He started with data of type S0, a single bit [*Ja-Nein-Wert*] whose value is either '−' or '+'. From any given data types $\sigma_0, \ldots, \sigma_{k-1}$, a programmer could define the compound data type $(\sigma_0, \ldots, \sigma_{k-1})$, and individual components of this compound type could be referred to by applying the subscripts $0, \ldots, k-1$ to any variable of that type. Arrays could also be defined by writing $m \times \sigma$, meaning m identical components of type σ; this idea could be repeated, in order to obtain arrays of any desired dimension. Furthermore m could be '□', meaning a list of *variable* length, and Zuse made good use of such list structures in his algorithms dealing with graphs, algebraic formulas, and chess play.

Thus the Plankalkül included the important concept of hierarchically structured data, going all the way down to the bit level. Such advanced data structures did not enter again into programming languages until the late 1950s in IBM's Commercial Translator. The idea eventually appeared in many other languages, such as FACT, COBOL, PL/I, and extensions of ALGOL 60; see [CL 61] and [SA 69, page 325].

Binary n-bit numbers in the Plankalkül were represented by type S1.n. Another special type was used for *floating-binary numbers*, namely,

$$S\Delta 1 = (S1.3,\ S1.7,\ S1.22).$$

The first three-bit component here was for signs and special markers — indicating, for example, whether the number was real or imaginary or zero; the second was for a seven-bit exponent in two's complement notation; and the final 22 bits represented the 23-bit fraction part of a normalized number, with the redundant leading '1' bit suppressed. Thus, for example, the floating point number +400.0 would have appeared as

$$(-+-,\ ---+---,\ -----------------------+--+),$$

and it also could be written

$$(LO,\ LOOO,\ LOOLOOOOOOOOOOOOOOOOOOOOO).$$

[The $+$ and $-$ notation has its bits numbered 0, 1, ..., from left to right, while the L and O notation corresponds to binary numbers as we now know them, having their most significant bits at the left.] There was a special representation for "infinite" and "very small" and "undefined" quantities; for example,

$$+\infty = (LLO,\ LOOOO,\ O).$$

Our TPK program uses $+\infty$ instead of 999 on line *15*, since such a value seems an appropriate way to render the concept 'TOO LARGE'.

Let us return now to the program itself. Line *01* introduces the data type S2, namely, an ordered pair whose first component is a 4-bit integer (type S1.4) and whose second component is floating point (type SΔ1). This data type will be used later for the eleven outputs of the TPK algorithm. Lines *02–07* define the function $f(t)$, and lines *08–22* define the main TPK program.

The hardest thing to get used to about Zuse's notation is the fact that each operation spans several lines; for example, lines *11–14* must be read as a unit. The second line of each group (labeled 'V') is used to identify the subscripts for quantities named on the top line; thus

$$\begin{array}{ccc} R, & V, & Z \\ 0 & 0 & 0 \end{array}$$ stands for the variables R_0, V_0, Z_0.

Operations are done primarily on output variables [*Resultatwerte*] R_k, input variables [*Variablen*] V_k, and intermediate variables [*Zwischenwerte*] Z_k. The 'K' line is used to denote components of a variable, so that, in our example,

$$\begin{array}{l} V \\ 0 \\ i \end{array}$$ means component i of the input variable V_0.

(A completely blank 'K' line is normally omitted.) Complicated subscripts can be handled by making a zigzag bar from the K line up to the top line, as in line *17* of the program where the notation indicates component $10 - i$ of R_0. The bottom line of each group is labeled A or S, and it is used to specify the type of each variable. Thus the '2' in line *18* of our example means that R_0 is of type S2; the '$\Delta 1$' means that Z_0 is floating point (type S$\Delta 1$); and the '1.4' means that i is being represented as a 4-bit binary number (type S1.4).

Zuse remarked [ZU 45, page 10] that the number of possible data types was so large that it would be impossible to indicate a variable's type simply by using typographical conventions as in classical mathematics; thus he realized the importance of apprehending the type of each variable at each point of a program, although such information is usually redundant. This is probably one of the main reasons he introduced the peculiar multiline format. Incidentally, a somewhat similar multiline notation has been used in recent years to describe musical notes [SM 73]; it is interesting to speculate whether musical notation will evolve in the same way that programming languages have.

We are now ready to penetrate further into the meaning of the code above. Each plan begins with a specification part [*Randauszug*], stating the types of all inputs and outputs. Thus, lines *02–04* mean that P1 is a procedure that takes an input V_0 of type S$\Delta 1$ (floating point) and produces R_0 of the same type. Lines *08–10* say that P2 maps V_0 of type $11 \times$ S$\Delta 1$ (namely, a vector of 11 floating-point numbers, the array $a[0{:}10]$ of our TPK algorithm) into a result R_0 of type $11 \times$ S2 (namely, a vector of 11 ordered pairs as described earlier).

The double arrow $\Rightarrow$, which Zuse called the *Ergibt-Zeichen* (yields sign), was introduced for the assignment operation; thus the meaning of lines *05–07* should be clear. As we have remarked, mathematicians had never used such an operator before; in fact, the systematic use of assignments constitutes a distinct break between computer-science thinking and mathematical thinking. Zuse consciously introduced a new symbol for the new operation, remarking [ZU 45, page 15] that

$$\underset{3}{Z} + 1 \Rightarrow \underset{3}{Z}$$

was analogous to the equation

$$\underset{3.i}{Z} + 1 = \underset{3.i+1}{Z}$$

of traditional mathematics. (Incidentally, the publishers of [ZU 48] used the sign $\succcurlyeq$ instead of $\Rightarrow$, but Zuse never actually wrote $\succcurlyeq$ himself.) Notice that the variable receiving a new value appears on the right, while most present-day languages have it on the left. We shall see that there was a gradual "leftist" trend as languages developed.

It remains to understand lines *11–22* of the example. The notation 'W2(n)' represents an iteration, for $i = n - 1$ down to 0, inclusive; hence W2(11) stands for the second **for** loop in the TPK algorithm. (The index of such an iteration was always denoted by i, or $i.0$; if another iteration were nested inside, its index would be called $i.1$, etc.) The notation

$$\underset{0}{R1}(x)$$

on line *11* stands for the result R_0 of applying procedure P1 to input x. Lines *15–18* of the program mean

$$\textbf{if } Z_0 > 400 \textbf{ then } R_0[10 - i] := (i, +\infty);$$

notice Zuse's new notation $\rightarrow$ for conditionals. Lines *19–22* are similar, with a bar over '$Z_0 > 400$' to indicate the negation of that relation. There was no equivalent of '**else**' in the Plankalkül, nor were there **go to** statements. Zuse did, however, have the notation 'Fin' with superscripts, to indicate a jump out of a given number of iteration levels and/or to the beginning of a new iteration cycle (see [ZU 72, page 28; ZU 45, page 32]); this idea has recently been revived in the BLISS language [WR 71].

The reader should now be able to understand all of the code given above. In the text accompanying his programs in Plankalkül notation,

Zuse made it a point to state also the mathematical relations between the variables that appeared. He called such a relation an *impliziten Ansatz*; we would now call it an "invariant." This was yet another fundamental idea about programming. Like Zuse's data structures, it disappeared from programming languages during the 1950s, waiting to be enthusiastically received when the time was ripe [HO 71].

Zuse had visions of using the Plankalkül someday as the basis of a programming language that could be translated by machine (see [ZU 72, pages 5, 18, 33, 34]). But in 1945 he was considering first things first — namely, he needed to decide what concepts should be embodied in a notation for programming. We can summarize his accomplishments by saying that the Plankalkül introduced many extremely important ideas, but it lacked the "syntactic sugar" for expressing programs in a readable and easily writable format.

Zuse says he made modest attempts in later years to have the Plankalkül implemented within his own company, "but this project necessarily foundered because the expense of implementing and designing compilers outstripped the resources of my small firm." He also mentions his disappointment that more of the ideas of the Plankalkül were not incorporated into ALGOL 58, since some of ALGOL's original designers knew of his work [ZU 72, page 7]. Such an outcome was probably inevitable, because the Plankalkül was far ahead of its time from the standpoint of available hardware and software development. Most of the other languages we shall discuss started at the other end, by asking what was possible to implement rather than what was possible to write; it naturally took many years for these two approaches to come together and to achieve a suitable synthesis.

Flow Diagrams

On the other side of the Atlantic, Herman H. Goldstine and John von Neumann were wrestling with the same sort of problem that Zuse had faced: How should algorithms be represented in a precise way, at a higher level than the machine's language? Their answer, which was due in large measure to Goldstine's analysis of the problem together with suggestions by von Neumann, Adele Goldstine, and Arthur W. Burks [GO 72, pages 266–268], was quite different from the Plankalkül: They proposed a pictorial representation involving boxes joined by arrows, and they called it a "flow diagram." During 1946 and 1947 they prepared an extensive and carefully worked out treatise on programming based on the idea of flow diagrams [GV 47], and it is interesting to compare their work to that of Zuse. There are striking differences, such as an emphasis on numerical calculation rather than on data structures; and there also are striking parallels, such as the use of the term "Plan" in the titles of both documents. Although neither work was published in contemporary journals, perhaps the most significant difference was that the treatise of Goldstine and von Neumann was beautifully "varityped" and distributed in quantity to the vast majority of people involved with computers at that time. This fact, coupled with the high quality of presentation and von Neumann's prestige, meant that their report had an enormous impact, forming the foundation for computer programming techniques all over the world. The term "flow diagram" became shortened to "flow chart" and eventually it even became "flowchart" — a word that has entered our language as both noun and verb.

We all know what flowcharts are, but comparatively few people nowadays have seen an authentic original flow diagram. In fact, it is very instructive to go back to the original style of Goldstine and von Neumann, since their inaugural flow diagrams represent a transition point between the mathematical "equality" notation and the computer-science "assignment" operation. Figure 1 shows how the TPK algorithm would probably have looked if Goldstine and von Neumann had been asked to deal with it in 1947.

Several things need to be explained about this original notation. The most important consideration is probably the fact that the boxes containing '$10 \rightarrow i$' and '$i-1 \rightarrow i$' were *not* intended to specify any computation; the viewpoint of Goldstine and von Neumann was significantly different from what we are now accustomed to, and readers will find it worthwhile to ponder this conceptual difference until they are able to understand it. The box '$i-1 \rightarrow i$' represents merely a change in *notation*, as the flow of control passes that point, rather than an action to be performed by the computer. For example, box VII has done the computation necessary to place $2^{-39}(i-1)$ into storage position C.1; so after we pass the box '$i-1 \rightarrow i$' and go through the subsequent junction point to box II, location C.1 now contains $2^{-39}i$. The external notation has changed but location C.1 has not! This distinction between external and internal notations occurs throughout, the external notation being problem-oriented while the actual contents of memory are machine-oriented. The numbers attached to each arrow in the diagram indicate so-called "constancy intervals," where all memory locations have constant contents and all bound variables of the external notation have constant meaning. A "storage table" is attached by a dashed line to the constancy intervals, to show the relevant relations between external and internal values at that point. Thus, for example, we

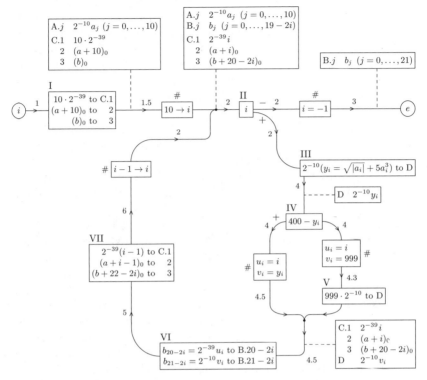

FIGURE 1. A flow diagram in the original Goldstine–von Neumann style.

note that the box '$10 \to i$' does not specify any computation but it provides the appropriate transition from constancy interval 1.5 to constancy interval 2. (See [GV 47, §7.6 and §7.7].)

Such flow diagrams generally contained four kinds of boxes: (a) Operation boxes, marked with a Roman numeral; this is where the computer program was supposed to make appropriate transitions in storage. (b) Alternative boxes, also marked with a Roman numeral, and having two exits marked + and −; this is where the computer control was to branch, depending on the sign of the named quantity. (c) Substitution boxes, marked with a # and using the '$\to$' symbol; this is where the external notation for a bound variable changed, as explained above. (d) Assertion boxes, also marked with a #; this is where important relations between external notations and the current state of the control were specified. The example shows three assertion boxes, one that says '$i = -1$', and two asserting that the outputs u_i and v_i (in a problem-oriented notation) now have certain values. Like substitution boxes, assertion boxes did not indicate any action by the computer; they merely stated relationships that helped to prove the validity of the program and that might help a programmer to write code for the operation boxes.

The next most prominent feature about original flow diagrams is the fact that programmers were required to be conscious of the *scaling* (that is, the binary point location) of all numbers in the computer memory. A computer word was 40 bits long, and its value was to be regarded as a binary fraction x in the range $-1 \leq x < 1$. Thus, for example, the flowchart in Figure 1 assumes that $2^{-10}a_j$ is initially present in storage position A.j, not the value a_j itself; the outputs b_j are similarly scaled.

The final mystery that needs to be revealed is the meaning of notations such as $(a + i)_0$, $(b)_0$, etc. In general, 'x_0' was used when x was an integer machine address; it represented the number $2^{-19}x + 2^{-39}x$, namely, a binary word with x appearing twice, in bit positions 9 to 20 and 29 to 40 (counting from the left). Such a number could be used in their machine to modify the addresses of 20-bit instructions that appeared in either half of a 40-bit word.

Once a flow diagram such as this had been drawn up, the remaining task was to prepare so-called "static coding" for boxes marked with Roman numerals. In this task programmers would use their problem-solving ability, together with their knowledge of machine language and the information from storage tables and assertion boxes, to make the required transitions. For example, in box VI one should use the facts that $u_i = i$, that storage D contains $2^{-10}v_i$, that storage C.1 contains $2^{-39}i$, and that storage C.3 contains $(b + 20 - 2i)_0$ (a word corresponding to the location of variable B.$20-2i$) to carry out the specified assignments. The job of box VII is slightly trickier: One of the tasks, for example, is to store $(b + 22 - 2i)_0$ in location C.3; the programmer was supposed to resolve this by adding $2 \cdot (2^{-19} + 2^{-39})$ to the previous contents of C.3. In general, the job of static coding required a fairly high level of problem-solving ability, and it was far beyond the state of the art in those days to get a computer to do such a thing. As with the Plankalkül, the notation needed to be simplified if it was to be suitable for machine implementation.

Let us make one final note about flow diagrams in their original form: Goldstine and von Neumann did not suggest any notation for subroutine calls, hence the function $f(t)$ in the TPK algorithm has been written in-line. In [GV 47, §12] there is a flow diagram for the algorithm that a loading routine must follow in order to relocate subroutines from a library, but there is no example of a flow diagram for a driver program that calls a subroutine. An appropriate extension of flow diagrams to subroutine calls could surely be made, but such a change would have made our example less "authentic."

A Logician's Approach

Let us now turn to the proposals made by Haskell B. Curry, who was working at the Naval Ordnance Laboratory in Silver Spring, Maryland; his activity was partly contemporaneous with that of Goldstine and von Neumann, since the last portion of [GV 47] was not distributed until 1948.

Curry wrote two lengthy memoranda [CU 48, CU 50] that have never been published; the only appearance of his work in the open literature has been the brief and somewhat cryptic summary in [CU 50']. He had prepared a rather complex program for ENIAC in 1946, and this experience led him to suggest a notation for program construction that is more compact than flowcharts.

His aims, which correspond to important aspects of what we now call "structured programming," were quite laudable [CU 50, paragraph 34]:

> The first step in planning the program is to analyze the computation into certain main parts, called here divisions, such that the program can be synthesized from them. Those main parts must be such that they, or at any rate some of them, are independent computations in their own right, or are modifications of such computations.

But in practice his proposal was not especially successful, because the way he factored a problem was not very natural. His components tended to have several entrances and several exits, and perhaps his mathematical abilities tempted him too strongly to pursue the complexities of fitting such pieces together. As a result, the notation he developed was somewhat eccentric, and the work was left unfinished. Here is how he might have represented the TPK algorithm:

$$F(t) = \{\sqrt{|t|} + 5t^3 : A\}$$
$$I = \{10 : i\} \to \{t = L(a + i)\} \to F(t) \to \{A : y\}$$
$$\to II \to It_7(0, i) \to O_1 \,\&\, I_2$$
$$II = \{x = L(b + 20 - 2i)\} \to \{i : x\} \to III$$
$$\to \{w = L(b + 21 - 2i)\} \to \{y : w\}$$
$$III = \{y > 400\} \to \{999 : y\} \,\&\, O_1$$

The following explanations should suffice to make the example clear, although they do not reveal the full generality of his language:

$\{E : x\}$ means "compute the value of expression E and store it in location x."

A denotes the accumulator of the machine.

$\{x = L(E)\}$ means "compute the value of expression E as a machine location and substitute it for all appearances of 'x' in the following instruction groups."

X $\to$ Y means "substitute instruction group Y for the first exit of instruction group X."

I_j denotes the jth entrance of this routine, namely, the beginning of its jth instruction group.

O_j denotes the jth exit of this routine (he used the words "input" and "output" for entrance and exit).

$\{x > y\} \to O_1 \,\&\, O_2$ means "if $x > y$, go to O_1, otherwise to O_2."

$It_7(m, i) \to O_1 \,\&\, O_2$ means "decrease i by 1, then if $i \geq m$ go to O_2, otherwise to O_1." (Here "It" stands for "iterate.")

Actually the main feature of interest in Curry's early work is not this programming language, but rather the algorithms he discussed for converting parts of it into machine language. He gave a recursive description of a procedure to convert fairly general arithmetic expressions into code for a one-address computer, thereby being the first person to describe the code-generation phase of a compiler. (Syntactic analysis was not specified; he gave recursive reduction rules analogous to well-known constructions in mathematical logic, assuming that any formula could be parsed properly.) His motivation for doing this was stated in [CU 50', page 100]:

> Now von Neumann and Goldstine have pointed out that, as programs are made up at present, we should not use the technique of program composition to make the simpler sorts of programs — these would be programmed directly — but only to avoid repetitions in forming programs of some complexity. Nevertheless, there are three reasons for pushing clear back to formation of the simplest programs from the basic programs [that is, from machine language instructions], viz.: (1) Experience in logic and in mathematics shows that an insight into principles is often best obtained by a consideration of cases too simple for practical use — e.g., one gets an insight into the nature of a group by considering the permutations of three letters, etc.... (2) It is quite possible that the technique of program composition can completely replace the elaborate methods of Goldstine and von

Neumann; while this may not work out, the possibility is at least worth considering. (3) The technique of program composition can be mechanized; if it should prove desirable to set up programs, or at any rate certain kinds of them, by machinery, presumably this may be done by analyzing them clear down to the basic programs.

The program that his algorithm would have constructed for $F(t)$, if the expression t^3 were replaced by $t \cdot t \cdot t$, is

$$\{|t| : A\} \to \{\sqrt{A} : A\} \to \{A : w\} \to \{t : R\} \to \{tR : A\} \to \{A : R\}$$
$$\to \{tR : A\} \to \{A : R\} \to \{5R : A\} \to \{A + w : A\}.$$

Here w is a temporary storage location, and R is a register used in multiplication.

An Algebraic Interpreter

The three languages we have seen so far were never implemented; they served purely as conceptual aids during the programming process. Such conceptual aids were obviously important, but they still left the programmer with a lot of mechanical things to do, and there were many chances for errors to creep in.

The first "high-level" programming language actually to be implemented was the Short Code, originally suggested by John W. Mauchly in 1949. William F. Schmitt coded it for the BINAC at that time. Later in 1950, Schmitt recoded Short Code for the UNIVAC, with the assistance of Albert B. Tonik, and J. Robert Logan revised the program in January 1952. Details of the system have never been published, and the earliest extant programmer's manual [RR 55] seems to have been written originally in 1952.

The absence of data about the early Short Code indicates that it was not an instant success, in spite of its eventual historic significance. This lack of popularity is not surprising when we consider the small number of scientific users of UNIVAC equipment in those days; in fact, the most surprising thing is that an algebraic language such as this was not developed first at the mathematically oriented centers of computer activity. Perhaps the reason is that mathematicians were so conscious of efficiency considerations that they could not imagine wasting any extra computer time for something that a programmer could do by hand. Mauchly had greater foresight in this regard; and J. R. Logan put it this way [RR 55]:

By means of the Short Code, any mathematical equations may be evaluated by the mere expedient of writing them down. There is a simple symbological transformation of the equations into code as explained by the accompanying write-up. The need for special programming has been eliminated.

In our comparisons of computer time with respect to time consumed by manual methods, we have found so far a speed ratio of at least fifty to one. We expect better results from future operations.

... It is expected that future use of the Short Code will demonstrate its power as a tool in mathematical research and as a checking device for some large-scale problems.

We cannot be certain how UNIVAC Short Code looked in 1950, but it probably was closely approximated by the 1952 version, when TPK could have been coded in the following way:

Memory equivalents: $i \equiv$ W0, $t \equiv$ T0, $y \equiv$ Y0.

Eleven inputs go respectively into words U0, T9, T8, ..., T0.

Constants: Z0 = 000000000000
Z1 = 010000000051   [1.0 in floating-decimal form]
Z2 = 010000000052   [10.0]
Z3 = 040000000053   [400.0]
Z4 = ΔΔΔTOOΔLARGE   ['TOO LARGE']
Z5 = 050000000051   [5.0]

Equation number recall information [labels]:

0 = line *01*,   1 = line *06*,   2 = line *07*

Short code:

	Equations	*Coded representation*
00	$i = 10$	00 00 00 W0 03 Z2
01	0: $y = (\sqrt{\ } $ abs $t) + 5$ cube t	T0 02 07 Z5 11 T0
02		00 Y0 03 09 20 06
03	y 400 if$\leq$to 1	00 00 00 Y0 Z3 41
04	i print, 'TOO LARGE' print-and-return	00 00 Z4 59 W0 58
05	0 0 if=to 2	00 00 00 Z0 Z0 72
06	1: i print, y print-and-return	00 00 Y0 59 W0 58
07	2: T0 U0 shift	00 00 00 T0 U0 99
08	$i = i - 1$	00 W0 03 W0 01 Z1
09	0 i if$\leq$to 0	00 00 00 Z0 W0 40
10	stop	00 00 00 00 ZZ 08

Each UNIVAC word consisted of twelve 6-bit bytes, and the Short Code equations were "symbologically" transliterated into groups of six 2-byte packets using the following equivalents (among others):

01 $-$	06 abs	$1n$ $(n+2)$nd power	59 print and return carriage
02)	07 $+$	$2n$ $(n+2)$nd root	$7n$ if=to n
03 $=$	08 pause	$4n$ if$\leq$to n	99 cyclic shift of memory
04 /	09 (	58 print and tab	$Sn, Tn, \ldots, Zn$ quantities

Thus, '$i = 10$' would be encoded as the word '00 00 00 W0 03 Z2' shown; packets of 00s could be used at the left to fill a word. Multiplication was indicated simply by juxtaposition (see line *01*).

The system was an *algebraic interpreter*, namely, an interpretive routine that repeatedly scanned the coded representation and performed the appropriate operations. The interpreter processed each word from right to left, so that it would see the '$=$' sign of an assignment operation last. This fact needed to be understood by the programmer, who had to break long equations appropriately into several words (see lines *01* and *02*). See also the print instructions on lines *04* and *06*, where the codes run from right to left.

This explanation should suffice to explain the TPK program above, except for the 'shift' on line *07*. Short Code had no provision for subscripted variables, but it did have a 99 order, which performed a cyclic shift in a specified block of memory. For example, line *07* of the example program means

$$temp = T0, \quad T0 = T1, \quad \ldots, \quad T9 = U0, \quad U0 = temp;$$

and fortunately this facility is all that the TPK algorithm needs.

The following press release from Remington Rand appeared in the *Journal of the Association for Computing Machinery* **2** (1955), page 291:

Automatic programming, tried and tested since 1950, eliminates communication with the computer in special code or language. ... The Short-Order Code is in effect an engineering "electronic dictionary" ... an interpretive routine designed for the solution of one-shot mathematical and engineering problems.

(Several other automatic programming systems, including "B-zero" — which we shall discuss later — were also announced at that time.) This is one of the few places where Short Code has been mentioned in the open literature. Grace Hopper referred to it briefly in [HO 52, page 243] (calling it "short-order code"), [HO 53, page 142] ("short-code"), and

[HO 58, page 165] ("Short Code"). In [HM 53, page 1252] it is stated that the "short code" system was "only a first approximation to the complete plan as originally conceived." This is probably true, but several discrepancies between [HM 53] and [RR 55] indicate that the authors of [HM 53] were not fully familiar with UNIVAC Short Code as it actually existed.

The Intermediate PL of Burks

Independent efforts to simplify the job of coding were being made at this time by Arthur W. Burks and his colleagues at the University of Michigan. The overall goal of their activities was to investigate the process of going from the vague "ordinary business English" description of some data-processing problem to the "internal program language" description of a machine-language program for that problem; and, in particular, to break this process up into a sequence of smaller steps [BU 51, page 12]:

> This has two principal advantages. First, smaller steps can more easily be mechanized than larger ones. Second, different kinds of work can be allocated to different stages of the process and to different specialists.

In 1950, Burks sketched a so-called "intermediate program language" that was to be the step one notch above the internal program language. Instead of spelling out complete rules for this intermediate language, he took portions of two machine programs previously published in [BU 50] and showed how they could be expressed at a higher level of abstraction. From these two examples it is possible to make a reasonable guess at how he might have written the TPK algorithm at that time:

$$1.\ 10 \to i$$

To 10

From 1,35

10. $A + i \to 11$	Compute location of a_i
11. $[A + i] \to t$	Look up a_i and transfer to storage
12. $|t|^{1/2} + 5t^3 \to y$	$y_i = \sqrt{|a_i|} + 5a_i^3$
13. $400, y;\ 20, 30$	Determine if $v_i = y_i$

To 20 if $y > 400$

To 30 if $y \le 400$

From 13

20. $999 \to y$	$v_i = 999$

To 30

From 13, 20

30. $(B + 20 - 2i)' \to 31$	Compute location of b_{20-2i}
31. $i \to [B + 20 - 2i]$	$b_{20-2i} = i$
32. $(B + 20 - 2i) + 1 \to 33$	Compute location of b_{21-2i}
33. $y \to [(B + 20 - 2i) + 1]$	$b_{21-2i} = v_i$
34. $i - 1 \to i$	$i \to i + 1$
35. $i, 0; \ 40, 10$	Repeat cycle until i negative

To 40 if $i < 0$

To 10 if $i \geq 0$

From 35

    40. F   Stop execution

Comments at the right of this program attempt to imitate Burks's style of writing comments at that time; they succeed in making the program almost completely self-explanatory. Notice that the assignment operation is well established by now; Burks used it also in the somewhat unusual form '$i \to i+1$' shown in the comment to instruction 34 [BU 50, page 41].

The prime symbol that appears within instruction 30 meant that the computer was to save this intermediate result, as it was a common subexpression that could be used without recomputation. Burks mentioned that several of the ideas embodied in this language were due to Janet Wahr, Don Warren, and Jesse Wright. He also made some comments about the feasibility of automating the process [BU 51, page 13]:

> Methods of assigning addresses and of expanding abbreviated commands into sequences of commands can be worked out in advance. Hence the computer could be instructed to do this work. ... It should be emphasized, however, that even if it were not efficient to use a computer to make the translation, the Intermediate PL would nevertheless be useful to the human programmer in planning and constructing programs.

At the other end of the spectrum, nearer to ordinary business language, Burks and his colleagues later proposed an abstract form of description that may be of independent interest, even though it does not relate to the rest of our story. The accompanying example suffices to give the flavor of their "first abstraction language," proposed in 1954. On the first line, c denotes the customer's name and address, and d^* is '1 inst', the first of the current month. The symbol $\mathrm{L}_i(x_1, \ldots, x_n)$ was used to denote a list of all n-tuples $(x_1, \ldots, x_n)$ of category i, sorted into increasing order by the first component x_1, and the meaning of the

$$\boxed{\text{XI}}$$

$$c, d^* \,(= 1\,\text{inst})$$

$$\underset{1\,\text{ult}\le d<d^*}{\rightthreetimes}\ \big(d, [k,s,u], [a,r]\big)$$

$$\sum_{d<1\,\text{ult}} (s-r) \qquad\qquad \sum_{d<1\,\text{ult}} (s-r) + \sum_{1\,\text{ult}\le d<d^*} (s-r)$$

Form XI: Customer's Statement

second line is "a listing, in order of the date d, of all invoices and all remittances for the past month." Here $[k, s, u]$ was an invoice, characterized by its number k, its dollar amount s, and its discount u; similarly, $[a, r]$ was a remittance of r dollars, identified by number a; and '1 ult' means the first of the previous month. The bottom gives the customer's old balance from the previous statement, and the new balance on the right. "The notation is so designed as to leave unprejudiced the method of the statement's preparation" [BC 54]. Such notations have not won over the business community, however, perhaps for reasons explained by Grace Hopper in [HO 58, page 198]:

> I used to be a mathematics professor. At that time I found there were a certain number of students who could not learn mathematics. I then was charged with the job of making it easy for businessmen to use our computers. I found it was not a question of whether they could learn mathematics or not, but whether they would. ... They said, "Throw those symbols out — I do not know what they mean, I have not time to learn symbols." I suggest a reply to those who would like data processing people to use mathematical symbols that they make them first attempt to teach those symbols to vice-presidents or a colonel or admiral. I assure you that I tried it.

Rutishauser's Contribution

Now let us shift our attention once again to Europe, where the first published report on methods for machine code generation was about to appear. Heinz Rutishauser was working with the Z4 computer, which by then had been rebuilt and moved to the Swiss Federal Institute of Technology [Eidgenössische Technische Hochschule (ETH)] in Zurich; and plans were afoot to build a brand new machine there. The background of Rutishauser's contribution can best be explained by quoting from a letter he wrote some years later [RU 63]:

> I am proud that you are taking the trouble to dig into my 1952 paper. On the other hand it makes me sad, because it reminds me of the premature death of an activity that I had started hopefully in 1949, but could not continue after 1951 because I had to do other work — to run practically singlehanded a fortunately slow computer as mathematical analyst, programmer, operator and even troubleshooter (but not as an engineer). This activity forced me also to develop new numerical methods, simply because the ones then known did not work in larger problems. Afterwards when I would have had more time, I did not come back to automatic programming but found more taste in numerical analysis. Only much later I was invited — more for historical reasons, as a living fossil so to speak, than for actual capacity — to join the ALGOL venture. The 1952 paper simply reflects the stage where I had to give up automatic programming, and I was even glad that I was able to put out that interim report (although I knew that it was final).

Rutishauser's comprehensive treatise [RU 52] described a hypothetical computer and a simple algebraic language, together with complete flowcharts for two compilers for that language. One compiler expanded all loops completely, while the other produced compact code using index registers. His source language was somewhat restrictive, since there was only one nonsequential control structure (the **for** statement); but that control structure was in itself an important contribution to the later development of programming languages. Here is how he might have written the TPK algorithm:

01	Für $i = 10(-1)0$
02	$a_i \ggcurly t$
03	$(\text{Sqrt Abs } t) + (5 \times t \times t \times t) \ggcurly y$
04	$\text{Max}(\text{Sgn}(y - 400), 0) \ggcurly h$
05	$\text{Z } 0_i \ggcurly b_{20-2i}$
06	$(h \times 999) + ((1 - h) \times y) \ggcurly b_{21-2i}$
07	Ende Index i
08	Schluss

Since no '**if** ... **then**' construction — much less **go to** — was present in Rutishauser's language, the computation of "y if $y \leq 400$, or 999 if $y > 400$" has been done here in terms of the Max and Sgn functions he did have, plus appropriate arithmetic; see lines *04* and *06*. (The function Sgn(x) is 0 if $x = 0$, or $+1$ if $x > 0$, or -1 if $x < 0$.) Another problem was that he gave no easy mechanism for converting between indices and other variables; indices (that is, subscripts) were completely tied to Für–Ende loops. Our program therefore invokes a trick to get i into the main formula on line *04*: 'Z 0_i' is intended to use the Z instruction, which transferred an indexed address to the accumulator in Rutishauser's machine [RU 52, page 10], and we have used that instruction in such a way that his compiler would produce the correct code. It is not clear whether or not he would have approved of this trick; if not, we could have introduced another variable, maintaining its value equal to i. But since he wrote a paper several years later [RU 61] entitled "Interference with an ALGOL procedure," there is some reason to believe he would have enjoyed the trick very much.

As with Short Code, the algebraic source code symbols had to be transliterated before the program was amenable to computer input, and the programmer had to allocate storage locations for the variables and constants. Here is how our TPK program would have been converted to a sequence of (floating-point) numbers on punched paper tape, using the memory assignments $a_i \equiv 100 + i$, $b_i \equiv 200 + i$, $0 \equiv 300$, $1 \equiv 301$, $5 \equiv 302$, $400 \equiv 303$, $999 \equiv 304$, $y \equiv 305$, $h \equiv 306$, $t \equiv 307$:

	Für	i	= 10	(−1)	0		
01	10^{12},	50,	10,	−1,	0,	Q,	

	begin stmt	a	sub i	⤜	t		
02	010000,	100,	.001,	200000,	307,	Q,	

	begin stmt	(	t	Abs	dummy	Sqrt
03	010000,	010000,	307,	110000,	0,	350800,

dummy	)	+	(	5	×	t
0,	200000,	020000,	010000,	302,	060000,	307,

×	t	×	t	)	⤜	y
060000,	307,	060000,	307,	200000,	200000,	305, Q,

	begin stmt	(	(	y	−	400	)
04	010000,	010000,	010000,	305,	030000,	303,	200000,

Sgn	dummy	)	Max	0	⤜	h
100000,	0,	200000,	080000,	300,	200000,	306, Q,

	begin stmt	Z	0 sub i	⤜	b_{20}	sub $-2i$
05	010000,	0, 230000,	0, .001,	200000,	220,	−.002, Q,

	begin stmt	(	h	×	999	)	+
06	010000,	010000,	306,	060000,	304,	200000,	020000,

$$(\qquad (\qquad 1 \qquad - \qquad h \qquad) \qquad \times \qquad y$$
$$010000, \, 010000, \, 301, \, 030000, \, 306, \, 200000, \, 060000, \, 305,$$
$$) \qquad \ggeq \qquad b_{21} \quad \text{sub} \ -2i$$
$$200000, \, 200000, \, 221, \, -.002, \, Q,$$

Ende

07   Q, Q,

Schluss

08   Q, Q.

Here Q represents a special flag that was distinguishable from all numbers. The transliteration is straightforward, except that unary operators such as 'Abs x' have to be converted to binary operators 'x Abs 0'. An extra left parenthesis is inserted before each formula, to match the $\ggeq$ (which has the same code as right parenthesis). Subscripted variables whose address is $\alpha + \Sigma c_j i_j$ are specified by writing the base address α followed by a sequence of values $c_j 10^{\ 3j}$; this scheme allows multiple subscripts to be treated in a simple way. The operator codes were chosen to make life easy for the compiler; for example, 020000 was the machine operation 'add' as well as the input code for $+$, so the compiler could treat almost all operations alike. The codes for left and right parentheses were the same as the machine operations to load and store the accumulator, respectively.

Since his compilation algorithm is published and reasonably simple, we can exhibit exactly the object code that would be generated from the source input above. The output is fairly long, but we shall consider it in its entirety in view of its importance from the standpoint of compiler history. Each word in Rutishauser's machine held two instructions, and there were 12 decimal digits per instruction word. The machine's accumulator was called Op.

Machine instructions		Symbolic form	
230010	200050	$10 \to \text{Op},$	$\text{Op} \to i,$
230001	120000	$1 \to \text{Op},$	$-\text{Op} \to \text{Op},$
200051	230000	$\text{Op} \to i',$	$0 \to \text{Op}$
200052	220009	$\text{Op} \to i'',$	$* + 1 \to \text{IR}_9$
239001	200081	$1 + \text{IR}_9 \to \text{Op},$	$\text{Op} \to \text{L}_1$
000000	230100	no-op,	loc $a_0 \to \text{Op}$
200099	010050	$\text{Op} \to \text{T},$	$i \to \text{Op}$
020099	210001	$\text{Op} + \text{T} \to \text{Op},$	$\text{Op} \to \text{IR}_1$
011000	200307	$(\text{IR}_1) \to \text{Op},$	$\text{Op} \to t$
010307	110000	$t \to \text{Op},$	$\lvert \text{Op} \rvert \to \text{Op}$
220009	350800	$* + 1 \to \text{IR}_9,$	go to Sqrt
000000	000000	no-op,	no-op

200999 010302	$\text{Op} \to \text{P}_1,\quad 5 \to \text{Op}$	
060307 060307	$\text{Op} \times t \to \text{Op},\quad \text{Op} \times t \to \text{Op}$	
060307 200998	$\text{Op} \times t \to \text{Op},\quad \text{Op} \to \text{P}_2$	
010999 020998	$\text{P}_1 \to \text{Op},\quad \text{Op} + \text{P}_2 \to \text{Op}$	
200305 010305	$\text{Op} \to y,\quad y \to \text{Op}$	
030303 200999	$\text{Op} - 400 \to \text{Op},\quad \text{Op} \to \text{P}_1$	
010999 100000	$\text{P}_1 \to \text{Op},\quad \text{Sgn Op} \to \text{Op}$	
200998 010998	$\text{Op} \to \text{P}_2,\quad \text{P}_2 \to \text{Op}$	
080300 200306	$\text{Max}(\text{Op}, 0) \to \text{Op},\quad \text{Op} \to h,$	
230000 200099	$0 \to \text{Op},\quad \text{Op} \to \text{T}$	
010050 020099	$i \to \text{Op},\quad \text{Op} + \text{T} \to \text{Op}$	
210001 230220	$\text{Op} \to \text{IR}_1,\quad \text{loc } b_{20} \to \text{Op}$	
200099 230002	$\text{Op} \to \text{T},\quad 2 \to \text{Op}$	
120000 060050	$-\text{Op} \to \text{Op},\quad \text{Op} \times i \to \text{Op}$	
020099 210002	$\text{Op} + \text{T} \to \text{Op},\quad \text{Op} \to \text{IR}_2$	
010000 231000	$(0) \to \text{Op},\quad \text{IR}_1 \to \text{Op}$	
202000 230221	$\text{Op} \to (\text{IR}_2),\quad \text{loc } b_{21} \to \text{Op}$	
200099 230002	$\text{Op} \to \text{T},\quad 2 \to \text{Op}$	
120000 060050	$-\text{Op} \to \text{Op},\quad \text{Op} \times i \to \text{Op}$	
020099 210001	$\text{Op} + \text{T} \to \text{Op},\quad \text{Op} \to \text{IR}_1$	
010301 030306	$1 \to \text{Op},\quad \text{Op} - h \to \text{Op}$	
200999 010306	$\text{Op} \to \text{P}_1,\quad h \to \text{Op}$	
060304 200998	$\text{Op} \times 999 \to \text{Op},\quad \text{Op} \to \text{P}_2$	
010999 060305	$\text{P}_1 \to \text{Op},\quad \text{Op} \times y \to \text{Op}$	
200997 010998	$\text{Op} \to \text{P}_3,\quad \text{P}_2 \to \text{Op}$	
020997 201000	$\text{Op} + \text{P}_3 \to \text{Op},\quad \text{Op} \to (\text{IR}_1)$	
010081 210009	$\text{L}_1 \to \text{Op},\quad \text{Op} \to \text{IR}_9$	
010050 220008	$i \to \text{Op},\quad * + 1 \to \text{IR}_8$	
030052 388003	$\text{Op} - i'' \to \text{Op},\quad \text{to } (\text{IR}_8 + 3) \text{ if } \text{Op} = 0$	
010050 020051	$i \to \text{Op},\quad \text{Op} + i' \to \text{Op}$	
200050 359000	$\text{Op} \to i,\quad \text{go to } (\text{IR}_9)$	
000000 999999	no-op, stop	
999999	stop	

(Several bugs on pages 39–40 of [RU 52] need to be corrected in order to produce this code, but Rutishauser's original intent is reasonably clear. The most common error made by a person who first tries to write a compiler is to confuse compilation time with object-code time, and Rutishauser gets the honor of being first to make this error!)

The code above has the interesting property that it is completely relocatable — even if we move all instructions up or down by half a word. Careful study of the output shows that index registers were treated rather awkwardly; but after all, this was 1951, and many compilers even nowadays produce far more disgraceful code than this.

Rutishauser published slight extensions of his source language notation in [RU 55] and [RU 55'].

Böhm's Compiler

An Italian graduate student, Corrado Böhm, developed a compiler at the same time and in the same place as Rutishauser, so it is natural to assume — as many people have — that they worked together. But in fact, their methods had essentially nothing in common. Böhm (who was a student of Eduard Stiefel) developed a language, a machine, and a translation method of his own, during the latter part of 1950, knowing only of [GV 47] and [ZU 48]; he learned of Rutishauser's similar interests only after he had submitted his doctoral dissertation in 1951, and he amended the dissertation at that time in order to clarify the differences between their approaches.

Böhm's dissertation [BO 52] was especially remarkable because he not only described a complete compiler, he also defined that compiler in its own language! And the language was interesting in itself, because *every* statement (including input statements, output statements, and control statements) was a special case of an assignment statement. Here is how TPK looks in Böhm's language:

A. Set $i = 0$ (plus the base address 100 for the input array a).

$$\pi' \to A$$
$$100 \to i$$
$$B \to \pi$$

B. Let a new input a_i be given. Increase i by unity, and proceed to C if $i > 10$, otherwise repeat B.

$$\pi' \to B$$
$$? \to \downarrow i$$
$$i + 1 \to i$$
$$[(1 \cap (i \dot{-} 110)) \cdot C] + [(1 \dot{-} (i \dot{-} 110)) \cdot B] \to \pi$$

C. Set $i = 10$.

$$\pi' \to C$$
$$110 \to i$$

D. Call x the number a_i, and prepare to calculate its square root r (using subroutine R), returning to E.

$$\pi' \to D$$
$$\downarrow i \to x$$
$$E \to X$$
$$R \to \pi$$

E. Calculate $f(a_i)$ and attribute it to y. If $y > 400$, continue at F, otherwise at G.

$$\pi' \to E$$
$$r + 5 \cdot \downarrow i \cdot \downarrow i \cdot \downarrow i \to y$$
$$[(1 \cap (y \dot{-} 400)) \cdot F] + [(1 \dot{-} (y \dot{-} 400)) \cdot G] \to \pi$$

F. Output the actual value $\qquad\qquad \pi' \to F$
  of i, then the value $\qquad\qquad\quad i \dot- 100 \to ?$
  999 ("too large"). $\qquad\qquad\qquad\quad 999 \to ?$
  Proceed to H. $\qquad\qquad\qquad\qquad\quad H \to \pi$

G. Output the actual $\qquad\qquad\qquad \pi' \to G$
  values of i and y. $\qquad\qquad\quad i \dot- 100 \to ?$
  $\qquad\qquad\qquad\qquad\qquad\qquad\quad y \to ?$
  $\qquad\qquad\qquad\qquad\qquad\qquad\quad H \to \pi$

H. Decrease i by unity, $\qquad\qquad\qquad \pi' \to H$
  and return to D if $i \geq 0$. $\qquad\qquad i \dot- 1 \to i$
  Otherwise stop. $\qquad [(1 \dot- (100 \dot- i)) \cdot D] + [(1 \cap (100 \dot- i)) \cdot \Omega] \to \pi$

Comments in an approximation to Böhm's style appear here on the left while the program itself is on the right. As remarked earlier, everything in Böhm's language appears as an assignment. The statement '$B \to \pi$' means "go to B," that is, set the program counter π to the value of variable B. The statement '$\pi' \to B$' means "this is label B"; a loading routine preprocesses the object code, using such statements to set the initial value of variables like B rather than to store an instruction in memory. The symbol '?' stands for the external world; hence the statement '? $\to x$' means "input a value and assign it to x", and the statement '$x \to$?' means "output the current value of x." An arrow '$\downarrow$' is used to indicate indirect addressing (restricted to one level); thus, '? $\to \downarrow i$' in part B means "read one input into the location whose value is i," namely, into a_i.

Böhm's machine operated only on *nonnegative integers* of 14 decimal digits. As a consequence, his operation $x \dot- y$ was the logician's "saturating subtraction,"

$$x \dot- y = \begin{cases} x - y, & \text{if } x > y; \\ 0, & \text{if } x \leq y. \end{cases}$$

He also used the notation $x \cap y$ for $\min(x, y)$. Thus it can be verified that

$$1 \cap (i \dot- j) = \begin{cases} 1, & \text{if } i > j; \\ 0, & \text{if } i \leq j; \end{cases}$$

$$1 \dot- (i \dot- j) = \begin{cases} 0, & \text{if } i > j; \\ 1, & \text{if } i \leq j. \end{cases}$$

Because of these identities, the complicated formula at the end of part B is equivalent to a conditional branch,

$$C \to \pi \qquad \text{if } i > 110;$$
$$B \to \pi \qquad \text{if } i \leq 110.$$

It is easy to read Böhm's program with these notational conventions in mind. Notice that part C doesn't end with '$D \to \pi$', although it could have; similarly we could have deleted '$B \to \pi$' after part A. (Böhm omitted a redundant go-to statement only once, out of six chances that he had in [BO 52].)

Part D shows how subroutines are readily handled in his language, although he did not explicitly mention them. The integer square root subroutine can be programmed as follows, given the input x and the exit location X:

R. Set $r = 0$ and $t = 2^{46}$.

$$\pi' \to R$$
$$0 \to r$$
$$70368744177664 \to t$$
$$S \to \pi$$

S. If $r + t \leq x$, go to T,
   otherwise go to U.

$$\pi' \to S$$
$$r + t \div x \to u$$
$$[(1 \div u) \cdot T] + [(1 \cap u) \cdot U] \to \pi$$

T. Decrease x by $r + t$,
   divide r by 2,
   increase r by t,
   and go to V.

$$\pi' \to T$$
$$x \div r \div t \to x$$
$$r : 2 + t \to r$$
$$V \to \pi$$

U. Divide r by 2.

$$\pi' \to U$$
$$r : 2 \to r$$

V. Divide t by 4.
   If $t = 0$, exit to X,
   otherwise return to S.

$$\pi' \to V$$
$$t : 4 \to t$$
$$[(1 \div t) \cdot X] + [(1 \cap t) \cdot S] \to \pi$$

(This algorithm is equivalent to the classical pencil-and-paper method for square roots, adapted to binary notation. It was given in hardware-oriented form as example P9.18 by Zuse in [ZU 45, pages 143–159]. To prove its validity, one can verify that the following invariant relations hold when we reach part S:

$$t \text{ is a power of 4};$$
$$r \text{ is a multiple of } 4t;$$
$$r^2/4t + x \text{ is the initial value of } x;$$
$$0 \leq x < 2r + 4t.$$

At the conclusion of the algorithm these conditions hold with $t = 1/4$; so r is the integer square root and x is the remainder.)

Böhm's one-pass compiler was capable of generating instructions rapidly, as the input was being read from paper tape. Unlike Rutishauser, Böhm recognized operator precedence in his language; for example, $r : 2 + t$ was interpreted as $(r : 2) + t$, because the division operator ':' took precedence over addition. However, Böhm did not allow parentheses to be mixed with precedence relations: If an expression began with a left parenthesis, the expression had to be *fully* parenthesized even when associative operators were present; on the other hand, if an expression did *not* begin with a left parenthesis, precedence was considered but no parentheses were allowed within it. The complete program for his compiler consisted of 114 assignments, broken down as follows:

    i) 59 statements to handle formulas with parentheses:

    ii) 51 statements to handle formulas with operator precedence;

    iii) 4 statements to decide between (i) and (ii).

There was also a loading routine, described by 16 assignment statements. So the compiler amounted to only 130 statements in all, including 33 statements that were merely labels ($\pi' \to \cdots$). Such brevity is especially surprising when we realize that a good deal of the program was devoted solely to checking the input for correct syntax; this check was not complete, however. (It appears to be necessary to add one more statement in order to fix a bug in his program, caused by overlaying information when a left parenthesis follows an operator symbol; but even with this "patch" the compiler is quite elegant.)

Rutishauser's parsing technique often required order n^2 steps to process a formula of length n. His idea was to find the leftmost pair of parentheses that has the highest level, so that they enclose a parenthesis-free formula α, and to compile the code for '$\alpha \to P_q$'; then the subformula '(α)' was simply replaced by 'P_q', q was increased by 1, and the process was iterated until no parentheses remained. Böhm's parsing technique, on the other hand, was of order n, generating instructions in what amounts to a linked binary tree, while the formula was being read in. To some extent, his algorithm anticipated modern list-processing techniques, which were first made explicit by Newell, Shaw, and Simon about 1956 (see [KN 68, §2.6]).

The table on the following page indicates briefly how Böhm's algorithm would have translated the statement $((a : (b \cdot c)) + ((d \cap e) \dot{-} f)) \to g$, assuming that the bug referred to above had been removed. After the operations shown in the table, the contents of the tree would be punched

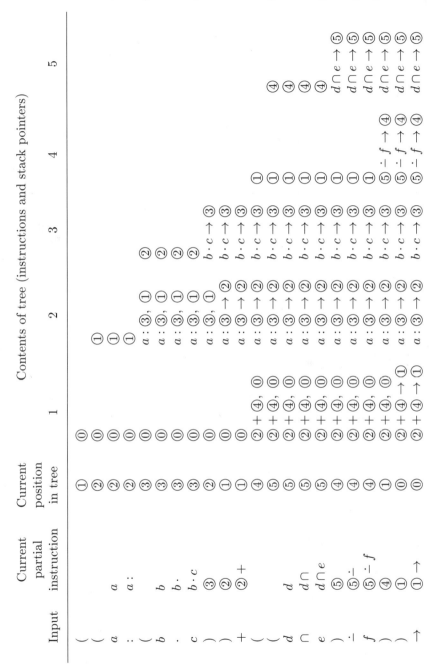

Contents of tree (instructions and stack pointers)

out, in reverse preorder:

$$d \cap e \rightarrow ⑤$$
$$⑤ \div f \rightarrow ④$$
$$b \cdot c \rightarrow ③$$
$$a : ③ \rightarrow ②$$
$$② + ④ \rightarrow ①$$

and the following symbol 'g' would evoke the final instruction '$① \rightarrow g$.'

Böhm's compiler assumed that the source code input would be transliterated into numeric form, but in an Italian patent filed in 1952 he proposed that it should actually be punched on tape using a typewriter with the keyboard shown in Figure 2 [BO 52′, Figure 9]. (His operation '$a \div b$' stood for $|a - b| = (a \div b) + (b \div a)$.) Constants in the source program were to be assigned a variable name and input separately. Although Böhm's programs were typeset with square brackets and curly braces as well as parentheses, he noted that only one kind of parenthesis was actually needed.

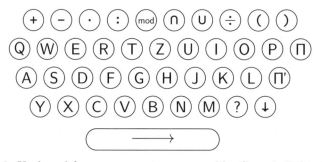

FIGURE 2. Keyboard for program entry, proposed by Corrado Böhm in 1952.

Of all the authors we shall consider, Böhm was the only one who gave an argument that his language was *universal*, namely, capable of computing any computable function.

Meanwhile, in England

Our story so far has introduced us to many firsts: the first algebraic interpreter, the first algorithms for parsing and code generation, the first compiler in its own language, etc. Now we come to the first *real* compiler, in the sense that it was really implemented and used; it really took algebraic statements and translated them into machine language.

The unsung hero of this development was Alick E. Glennie of Fort Halstead, the Royal Armaments Research Establishment. We may justly say "unsung" because it is very difficult to deduce the identity of the person responsible for this pioneering work from the published literature. When Christopher Strachey referred favorably to it in [ST 52, pages 46–47], he did not mention Glennie's name, and it was inappropriate for Glennie to single out his own contributions when he coauthored an article with J. M. Bennett at the time [BG 53, pages 112–113]. In fact, there are apparently only two published references to Glennie's authorship of this early compiler; one of these was a somewhat cryptic remark inserted by an anonymous referee into a review of Böhm's paper [TA 56] while the other appeared in a comparatively inaccessible publication [MG 53].

Glennie called his system AUTOCODE; and it may well have helped to inspire many other "AUTOCODE" routines, of increasing sophistication, developed during the late 1950s. Strachey said that AUTOCODE was beginning to come into use in September 1952. The Manchester Mark I machine language was particularly abstruse — see [WO 51] for an introduction to its complexities, including the intricacies of teleprinter code (used for base-32 arithmetic, backwards) — and its opaqueness may have been why this particular computer witnessed the world's first compiler. Glennie stated his motivations as follows, at the beginning of a lecture that he delivered at Cambridge University in February 1953 [GL 52]:

> The difficulty of programming has become the main difficulty in the use of machines. Aiken has expressed the opinion that the solution of this difficulty may be sought by building a coding machine, and indeed he has constructed one. However it has been remarked that there is no need to build a special machine for coding, since the computer itself being general purpose should be used. ... *To make it easy, one must make coding comprehensible.* This may be done only by improving the notation of programming. Present notations have many disadvantages, all are incomprehensible to the novice, they are all different (one for each machine) and they are never easy to read. It is quite difficult to decipher coded programmes even with notes and even if you yourself made the programme several months ago.

> Assuming that the difficulties may be overcome, it is obvious that the best notation for programmes is the usual mathematical notation because it is already known. ... Using a familiar notation for programming has very great advantages, in the elimination of errors in programmes, and the simplicity it brings.

His reference to Aiken should be clarified here, especially because Glennie stated several years later [GL 65] that "I got the concept from a reported idea of Professor Aiken of Harvard, who proposed that a machine be built to make code for the Harvard relay machines." Aiken's coding machine for the Harvard Mark III was cited also by Böhm [BO 52, page 176]; it is described in [HA 52, pages 36–38 and 229–263, illustrated on pages 20, 37, 230]. By pushing appropriate buttons on the console of this proposed device, one or more appropriate machine codes would be punched on tape for the equivalent of three-address instructions such as '$-b3 \times |ci| \rightarrow ai$' or '$1/\sqrt{x9} \rightarrow r0$'; there was a column of keys for selecting the first operand's sign, its letter name, and its (single) subscript digit, then another column of keys for selecting the function name, etc. (Incidentally, Heinz Rutishauser is listed as one of the 56 authors of the Harvard report [HA 52]; his visit to America in 1950 is one of the reasons he and Böhm did not work jointly together.)

Our TPK algorithm can be expressed in Glennie's AUTOCODE in the following way:

```
01    c@VA t@IC x@½C y@RC z@NC
02    INTEGERS +5→c
03    →t
04    +t TESTA Z
05    -t
06    ENTRY Z
07    SUBROUTINE 6 →z
08    +tt →y →x
09    +tx →y →x
10    +z +cx    CLOSE WRITE 1

11    a@/½ b@MA c@GA d@OA e@PA f@HA i@VE x@ME
12    INTEGERS +20→b +10→c +400→d +999→e +1→f
13    LOOP 10n
14    n →x
15    +b -x →x
16    x →q
17    SUBROUTINE 5 →aq
18    REPEAT n
19    +c →i
20    LOOP 10n
21    +an SUBROUTINE 1 →y
22    +d -y TESTA Z
23    +i SUBROUTINE 3
```

```
24    +e SUBROUTINE 4
25    CONTROL X
26    ENTRY Z
27    +i SUBROUTINE 3
28    +y SUBROUTINE 4
29    ENTRY X
30    +i -f →i
31    REPEAT n
32    ENTRY A CONTROL A WRITE 2 START 2
```

Although this language was much simpler than the Mark I machine code, it was still very machine oriented, as we shall see. (Rutishauser and Böhm had had a considerable advantage over Glennie in that they had designed their own machine language from scratch.) Lines *01–10* of this program represent a subroutine for calculating $f(t)$; 'CLOSE WRITE 1' on line *10* says that the preceding lines constitute subroutine number 1. The remaining lines yield the main program; 'WRITE 2 START 2' on line *32* says that the preceding lines constitute subroutine number 2, and that execution starts with number 2.

Let's begin at the beginning of this program and try to give a play-by-play account of what it means. Line *01* is a storage assignment for variables c, t, x, y, and z, in terms of absolute machine locations represented in the beloved teleprinter code. Line *02* assigns the value 5 to c; like all early compiler writers, Glennie shied away from including constants in formulas. Actually his language has been extended here: He had only the statement 'FRACTIONS' for producing constants between $-\frac{1}{2}$ and $\frac{1}{2}$, assuming that a certain radix point convention was being used on the Manchester machine. Since scaling operations were so complicated on that computer, it would be inappropriate for our purposes to let such considerations mess up or distort the TPK algorithm; thus the INTEGERS statement (which is quite in keeping with the spirit of his language) has been introduced to simplify our exposition.

Upon entry to subroutine 1, the subroutine's argument was in the machine's lower accumulator; line *03* assigns it to variable t. Line *04* means "go to label Z if t is positive"; line *05* puts $-t$ in the accumulator; and line *06* defines label Z. Thus the net effect of lines *04–06* is to put $|t|$ into the lower accumulator. Line *07* applies subroutine 6 (integer square root) to this value, and stores it in z. On line *08* we compute the product of t by itself; this fills both upper and lower accumulators, and the upper half (assumed zero) is stored in y, the lower half in x. Line *09* is similar; now x contains t^3. Finally line *10* completes the calculation of $f(t)$ by leaving $z + 5x$ in the accumulator. The 'CLOSE' operator causes the compiler to forget the meaning of label Z, but the machine addresses of variables c, x, y, and z remain in force.

Line *11* introduces new storage assignments, and in particular it reassigns the addresses of c and x. New constant values are defined on line *12*. Lines *13–18* constitute the input loop, enclosed by LOOP 10n ... REPEAT n; here n denotes one of the index registers (the famous Manchester B-lines), the letters k, l, n, o, q, r being reserved for this purpose. Loops in Glennie's language were always done for *decreasing* values of the index, down to and including 0; and in our case the loop was performed for $n = 20, 18, 16, \ldots, 2, 0$. These values are twice what might be expected, because the Mark I addresses were for half-words. Lines *14–16* set index q equal to $20 - n$; this needs to be done in stages (first moving from n to a normal variable, then doing the arithmetic, and finally moving the result to the index variable). The compiler recognized conversions between index variables and normal variables by insisting that all other algebraic statements begin with a + or − sign. Line *17* says to store the result of subroutine 5 (an integer input subroutine) into variable a_q.

Lines *20–31* constitute the output loop. Again n has the value $2i$, so the true value of i has been maintained in parallel with n (see lines *19* and *30*). Line *21* applies subroutine 1, namely our subroutine for calculating $f(t)$, to a_n and stores the result in y. Line *22* branches to label Z if $400 \geq y$; line *25* is an unconditional jump to label X. Line *23* outputs the integer i using subroutine 3, and subroutine 4 on line *24* is assumed to be similar except that a carriage return and line feed are also output. Thus the output is correctly performed by lines *22–29*.

The operations 'ENTRY A CONTROL A' on line *32* define an infinite loop 'A: **go to** A'; this was the so-called *dynamic stop* used to terminate a computation in those good old days.

Our analysis of the sample program is now complete. Glennie's language was an important step forward, but of course it still remained very close to the machine itself. And it was intended for the use of experienced programmers. As he said at the beginning of the user's manual [GL 52′], "The left hand side of the equation represents the passage of information to the accumulator through the adder, subtractor, or multiplier, while the right hand side represents a transfer of the accumulated result to the store." The existence of two accumulators complicated matters; for example, after the multiplication in lines *08* and *09* the upper accumulator was considered relevant (in the notation $\rightarrow y$), while elsewhere only the lower accumulator was used. The expression '$+a+bc$'

meant "load the *lower* accumulator with a, then add it to the double length product bc," whereas '$+bc + a$' meant "form the double-length product bc, then add a into the *upper* half of the accumulator." Expressions like $+ab + cd + ef$ were allowed, but not products of three or more quantities; and there was no provision for parentheses. The language was designed to be used with the 32-character teleprinter code, where there was no distinction between uppercase and lowercase letters. The symbols '+', '−', and '→' were punched as the teleprinter codes 'p', 'm', and '"', respectively.

We have remarked that Glennie's papers have never been published; this may be due to the fact that his employers in the British atomic weapons project were in the habit of keeping documents classified. Glennie's work was, however, full of choice quotes, so it is interesting to repeat several more remarks that he made at the time [GL 52]:

> There are certain other rules for punching that are merely a matter of common sense such as not leaving spaces in the middle of words or misspelling them. I have arranged that such accidents will cause the input programme to exhibit symptoms of distress. ... This consists of the programme coming to a stop and the machine making no further moves.
>
> [The programme] is quite long but not excessively long, about 750 orders. ... The part that deals with the translation of the algebraic notation is the most intricate programme that I have ever devised ... [but the number of orders required] is a small fraction of the total, about 140.
>
> My experience of the use of this method of programming has been rather limited so far, but I have been much impressed by the speed at which it is possible to make up programmes and the certainty of gaining correct programmes. ... The most important feature, I think, is the ease with which it is possible to read back and mentally check the programme. And of course on such features as these will the usefulness of this type of programming be judged.

At the beginning of the user's manual [GL 52'], he mentioned that "the loss of efficiency (in the sense of the additional space taken by routines made with AUTOCODE) is no more than about 10%." This remark appeared also in [BG 53, page 113], and it may well be the source of the oft-heard opinion that compilers are "90% efficient."

On the other hand, Glennie's compiler actually had very little tangible impact on other users of the Manchester machine. For this reason,

Brooker did not even mention it in his 1958 paper entitled "The Auto-code programs developed for the Manchester University computers" [BR 58]. This lack of influence may be due in part to the fact that Glennie was not resident at Manchester, but the primary reason was probably that his system did little to solve the really severe problems that programmers had to face in those days of small and unreliable machines. An improvement in the coding process was not regarded then as a breakthrough of any importance, since coding was often the simplest part of a programmer's task. When one had to wrestle with problems of numerical analysis, scaling, and two-level storage, meanwhile adapting one's program to the machine's current state of malfunction, coding itself was quite insignificant.

Thus when Glennie mentioned his system in the discussion following [MG 53], it met with a very cool reception. For example, Stanley Gill's comment reflected the prevailing mood [MG 53, page 79]:

> It seems advisable to concentrate less on the ability to write, say
>
> $$+ a + b + ab \to c$$
>
> as it is relatively easy for the programmer to write
>
> $$\begin{aligned} &\text{A}\, a\\ &\text{A}\, b\\ &\text{H}\, a\\ &\text{V}\, b\\ &\text{T}\, c\,. \end{aligned}$$

Nowadays we would say that Gill had missed a vital point, but in 1953 his remark was perfectly valid.

Some 13 years later, Glennie had the following reflections [GL 65]:

> [The compiler] was a successful but premature experiment. Two things I believe were wrong: (a) Floating-point hardware had not appeared. This meant that most of a programmer's effort was in scaling his calculation, not in coding. (b) The climate of thought was not right. Machines were too slow and too small. It was a programmer's delight to squeeze problems into the smallest space. ...
>
> I recall that automatic coding as a concept was not a novel concept in the early fifties. Most knowledgeable programmers knew of it, I think. It was a well known possibility, like the

possibility of computers playing chess or checkers. ... [Writing the compiler] was a hobby that I undertook in addition to my employers' business: they learned about it afterwards. The compiler ... took about three months of spare time activity to complete.

Early American "Compilers"

None of the authors we have mentioned so far actually used the word "compiler" in connection with what they were doing; the terms were *automatic coding, codification automatique, Rechenplanfertigung.* In fact it is not especially obvious to programmers today why a compiler should be so called. We can understand this best by considering briefly the other types of programming aids that were in use during those early days.

The first important programming tools to be developed were, of course, general-purpose subroutines for such commonly needed processes as input–output conversions, floating-point arithmetic, and transcendental functions. Once a library of such subroutines had been constructed, people began to think of further ways to simplify programming, and two principal ideas emerged: (a) Coding in machine language could be made less rigid, by using blocks of relocatable addresses [WH 50]. This idea was extended by M. V. Wilkes to the notion of an "assembly routine," able to combine a number of subroutines and to allocate storage [WW 51, pages 27–32]; and Wilkes later [WI 52, WI 53] extended the concept further to include general symbolic addresses that weren't simply relative to a small number of origins. For many years such symbols were called "floating addresses." Similar developments in assembly systems occurred in America and elsewhere (see [RO 52]). (b) An artificial machine language or *pseudocode* was devised, usually providing easy facilities for floating-point arithmetic as if it had been built into the hardware. An "interpretive routine" (sometimes called "interpretative" in those days) would process those instructions, emulating the hypothetical computer. The first interpretive routines appeared in the first textbook about programming, by Wilkes, Wheeler, and Gill [WW 51, pages 34–37, 74–77, 162–164]; the primary aim of their book was to present a library of subroutines and the methodology of subroutine usage. Shortly afterward a refined interpretive routine for floating-point calculation was described by Brooker and Wheeler [BW 53], including a stack by which subroutines could be nested to any depth. Interpretive routines in their more familiar compact form were introduced by J. M. Bennett (see [WW 51, Preface and pages 162–164], [BP 52]); the most influential was perhaps John Backus's IBM 701 Speedcoding System [BA 54, BH 54]. As we have already remarked, Short Code was a different sort of interpretive routine. The early history of library subroutines, assembly routines, and interpretive routines remains to be written; we have just reviewed it briefly here in order to put the programming language developments into context.

During the latter part of 1951, Grace Murray Hopper developed the idea that pseudocodes need not be interpreted; pseudocodes could also be expanded out into direct machine language instructions. She and her associates at UNIVAC proceeded to construct an experimental program that would do such a translation, and they called it a *compiling routine* [MO 54, page 15].

> To compile means to compose out of materials from other documents. Therefore, the compiler method of automatic programming consists of assembling and organizing a program from programs or routines or in general from sequences of computer code which have been made up previously.

(See also [HO 55, page 22].) The first "compiler" in this sense, named A-0, was in operation in the spring of 1952, when Hopper spoke on the subject at an early ACM National Meeting [HO 52]. Incidentally, M. V. Wilkes came up with a very similar idea, and called it the method of "synthetic orders" [WI 52]; we would now call this a macroexpansion.

The A-0 "compiler" was improved to A-1 (January 1953) and then to A-2 (August 1953); the original implementors were Richard K. Ridgway and Margaret H. Harper. Quite a few references to A-2 appeared in the literature of those days [HM 53, HO 53, HO 53', MO 54, WA 54], but the authors of those papers gave no examples of the language itself. Therefore it will be helpful to discuss here the state of A-2 as it existed late in 1953, when it was first released to UNIVAC customers for testing [RR 53]. As we shall see, the language was quite primitive by comparison with the ones we have been studying; hence we choose to credit Glennie with the first compiler, although A-0 was completed first. The main point, however, is to understand what was called a "compiler" in 1954, so that we can best appreciate the historical development of programming languages.

Here is how TPK would have looked in A-2 at the end of 1953.

Use of working storage:

00	02	04	06	08	10	12	14..34	36	38	40	42..58
10	5	400	-1	∞	4	3	$a_0..a_{10}$	i	y, y', y''	t, t', t''	buffer

Program:

0.	GMI000 000002	
	ITEM01 WS.000	Read input and necessary constants from tape 2
	SERVQ2 BLQCKA	
	1RG000 000000	
1.	GMM000 000001	
	000180 020216	$10.0 = i$
	1RG000 001000	
2.	AM0034 034040	$a_{10}^2 = t$
3.	RNA040 010040	$\sqrt[4]{t} = t'$
4.	APN034 012038	$a_{10}^3 = y$
5.	AM0002 038038	$5y = y'$
6.	AA0040 038038	$t' + y' = y''$
7.	AS0004 038040	$400 - y'' = t''$
8.	QWNΔCQ DEΔ003	
	K00000 K00000	
	F00912 E001RG	if $t'' \geq 0$, go on to Op. 10
	000000 Q001CN	
	1RG000 008040	
	1CN000 000010	
9.	GMM000 000001	
	000188 020238	'ΔΔΔTQQ ΔLARGE ΔΔΔΔΔΔ ΔΔΔΔΔΔ' $= y''$
	1RG000 009000	
10.	YTQ036 038000	Print i, y''
11.	GMM000 000001	
	000194 200220	Move 20 words from WS14 to WS40
	1RG000 011000	
12.	GMM000 000001	
	000220 200196	Move 20 words from WS40 to WS16
	1RG000 012000	
13.	ALL012 F000T⌿	
	1RG000 013036	Replace i by $i + (-1)$
	2RG000 000037	and go to Op. 2 if $i > -1$,
	3RG000 000006	otherwise go to Op. 14
	4RG000 000007	
	5RG000 000006	
	6RG000 000007	
	1CN000 000002	
	2CN000 000014	
	1RS000 000036	
	2RS000 000037	
14.	QWNΔCQ DEΔ002	
	810000 820000	Rewind tapes 1 and 2, and halt.
	900000 900000	
	1RG000 014000	
	⌿ØENDΔ INFQ.⌿	

There were 60 words of working storage, and each floating-point number used two words. These working storages were usually addressed by numbers 00, 02, ..., 58, except in the GMM instruction (move generator) when they were addressed by 180, 182, ..., 238, respectively; see operations 1, 9, 11, and 12. Since there was no provision for absolute value, operations 2 and 3 of this program find $\sqrt{|a_{10}|}$ by computing $\sqrt[4]{a_{10}^2}$. (The A-2 compiler would replace most operators by a fully expanded subroutine, in line; this subroutine would be copied anew each time it was requested, unless it was one of the four basic floating-point arithmetic operations.) Since there was no provision for subscripted variables, operations 11 and 12 shift the array elements after each iteration.

Most arithmetic instructions were specified with a three-address code, as shown in operations 2–7. But at this point in the development of A-2 there was no way to test the relation '$\geq$' without resorting to machine language; only a test for equality was built in. So operation 8 specifies the necessary UNIVAC instructions. (The first word in operation 8 says that the following 003 lines contain UNIVAC code. Those three lines extract (E) the sign of the first numeric argument (1RG) using a system constant in location 912, and if it was positive they instruct the machine to go to program operator 1CN. The next two lines say that 1RG is to be t'' (working storage 40), and that 1CN is to be the address of operation 10. The '008' in the 1RG specification tells the compiler that this is operation 8; such redundant information was checked at compile time. The compiler would substitute appropriate addresses for 1RG and 1CN in the machine language instructions. Since there was no notation for '1RG + 1', the programmer had to supply ten different parameter lines to the increment-and-test routine in operation 13.)

By 1955 A-2 had become more streamlined, and the necessity for 'QWN CQDE' in TPK had disappeared; operations 7–14 could now become

```
 7.  QT0038 004000   To Op. 9 if y″ > 400
     1CN000 000009
 8.  QU0038 038000   Go to Op. 10
     1CN000 000010
 9.  MV0008 001038
10.  YTQ036 038000
11.  MV0014 010040
12.  MV0040 010016
13.  AAL036 006006   Same meaning as before, but new syntax.
     1CN000 000002
     2CN000 000014
14.  RWS120 000000
     ENDΔCQ DINGΔΔ
```

(A description of A-2 coding, vintage 1955, appears in [PR 55], and also in [TH 55], which presented the same example program.)

Laning and Zierler

Grace Hopper was particularly active as a spokesperson for automatic programming during the 1950s; she went barnstorming throughout the country, significantly helping to accelerate the rate of progress. One of the most important things she accomplished was to help organize two key symposia on the topic, in 1954 and 1956, under the sponsorship of the Office of Naval Research. These symposia brought together many people and ideas at an important time. (On the other hand, it must be remarked that the contributions of Zuse, Curry, Burks, Mauchly, Böhm, and Glennie were not mentioned at either symposium, and Rutishauser's work was cited only once — not quite accurately [GO 54, page 76]. Communication was not rampant!)

In retrospect, the biggest event of the 1954 symposium on automatic programming was the announcement of a system that J. Halcombe Laning, Jr., and Niel Zierler had recently implemented for the Whirlwind computer at MIT. However, the significance of that announcement is not especially evident from the published proceedings [NA 54], 97% of which are devoted to enthusiastic descriptions of assemblers, interpreters, and 1954-style "compilers." We know of the impact mainly from Grace Hopper's introductory remarks at the 1956 symposium, discussing the past two years of progress [HO 56]:

> A description of Laning and Zierler's system of algebraic pseudo-coding for the Whirlwind computer led to the development of Boeing's BACAIC for the 701, FORTRAN for the 704, AT-3 for the UNIVAC, and the Purdue System for the Datatron and indicated the need for far more effort in the area of algebraic translators.

A clue to the importance of Laning and Zierler's contribution can also be found in the closing pages of a paper by John Backus and Harlan Herrick at the 1954 symposium. After describing IBM 701 Speedcoding and the tradeoffs between interpreters and "compilers," they concluded by speculating about the future of automatic programming [BH 54]:

> A programmer might not be considered too unreasonable if he were willing only to produce the formulas for the numerical solution of his problem, and perhaps a plan showing how the data was to be moved from one storage hierarchy to another, and then

demand that the machine produce the results for his problem. No doubt if he were too insistent next week about this sort of thing he would be subject to psychiatric observation. However, next year he might be taken more seriously.

After listing numerous advantages of high-level languages, they said: "Whether such an elaborate automatic-programming system is possible or feasible has yet to be determined." As we shall soon see, the system of Laning and Zierler proved that such a system is indeed possible.

Brief mention of their system was made by Charles Adams at the symposium [AL 54]; but the full user's manual [LZ 54] ought to be reprinted someday because their language went so far beyond what had been implemented before. The programmer no longer needed to know much about the computer at all, and the user's manual was (for the first time) addressed to a complete novice. Here is how TPK would look in their system:

01		$v\|N = \langle\text{input}\rangle,$
02		$i = 0,$
03	1	$j = i + 1,$
04		$a\|i = v\|j,$
05		$i = j,$
06		$e = i - 10.5,$
07		CP 1,
08		$i = 10,$
09	2	$y = F^1(F^{11}(a\|i)) + 5(a\|i)^3,$
10		$e = y - 400,$
11		CP 3,
12		$z = 999,$
13		PRINT $i, z.$
14		SP 4,
15	3	PRINT $i, y.$
16	4	$i = i - 1,$
17		$e = -0.5 - i,$
18		CP 2,
19		STOP

The program was typed on a Flexowriter, a machine that punched paper tape and had a fairly large character set (including both uppercase and lowercase letters); at MIT they also had superscript digits ^{0}, ^{1}, ..., ^{9} and a vertical line $|$. The language used the vertical line to indicate *subscripts*; thus the '$5(a\|i)^3$' on line *09* means $5a_i^3$.

A programmer would insert eleven input values for the TPK algorithm into the place shown on line *01*; those values would be converted to binary notation and stored on the magnetic drum as variables v_1, v_2, ..., v_{11}. If the numbers had a simple arithmetic pattern, an abbreviation could also be used; for example,

$$v|N = 1\,(.5)\,2\,(.25)\,3.5\,(1)\,5.5$$

would set $(v_1, \ldots, v_{11}) \leftarrow (1, 1.5, 2, 2.25, 2.5, 2.75, 3, 3.25, 3.5, 4.5, 5.5)$. If desired, a special code could be punched on the Flexowriter tape in line *01*, allowing the operator to substitute a data tape at that point before reading in the rest of the source program.

Lines *02–07* are a loop that moves the variables v_1, ..., v_{11} from the drum to variables a_0, ..., a_{10} in core. (All variables were in core unless specifically assigned to the drum by an ASSIGN or $|N$ instruction. This was an advanced feature of the system not needed in small problems.) The only thing that isn't self-explanatory about lines *02–07* is line *07*; 'CP k' means, "if the last expression computed was negative, go to the instruction labeled k."

In line *09*, F^1 denotes square root and F^{11} denotes absolute value. In line *14*, 'SP' denotes an unconditional jump. (CP and SP were the standard mnemonics for jumps in Whirlwind machine language.) Thus, except for control statements — for which there was no existing mathematical convention — Laning and Zierler's notation was quite easy to read. Their expressions featured normal operator precedence, as well as implied multiplication and exponentiation; and they even included a built-in Runge–Kutta mechanism for integrating a system of differential equations if the programmer wrote formulas such as

$$\mathrm{D}x = y + 1,$$
$$\mathrm{D}y = -x,$$

where D stands for d/dt! Another innovation, designed to help debugging, was to execute statement number 100 after any arithmetic error message, if 100 was a PRINT statement.

According to [LM 70], Laning first wrote a prototype algebraic translator in the summer of 1952. He and Zierler had extended it to a usable system by May 1953, when the Whirlwind had only 1024 16-bit words of core memory in addition to its drum. The version described in [LZ 54] utilized 2048 words and drum, but earlier compromises due to such extreme core limitations caused it to be quite slow. The source code was translated into blocks of subroutine calls, stored on the drum, and after being transferred to core storage (one equation's worth at a time) these subroutines invoked the standard floating-point interpretive routines on the Whirlwind [AL 54, page 64].

> The use of a small number of standard closed subroutines has certain advantages of logical simplicity; however, it also often results in the execution of numerous unnecessary operations. This fact, plus the frequent reference to the drum required in calling in equations, results in a reduction of computing speed of the order of magnitude of ten to one from an efficient computer program.

From a practical standpoint, those were damning words. Laning recalled, eleven years later [LA 65], that

> This was in the days when machine time was king, and people-time was worthless (particularly since I was not even on the Whirlwind staff). ... [The program] did perhaps pay for itself a few times when a complex problem required solutions with a twenty-four hour deadline.

In a recent search of his files, Laning found a listing of the Whirlwind compiler's first substantial application [LA 76]:

> The problem addressed is that of a three-dimensional lead pursuit course flown by one aircraft attacking another, including the fire control equations. What makes this personally interesting to me is tied in with the fact that for roughly five years previous to this time the [MIT Instrumentation] Lab had managed and operated the MIT Rockefeller Differential Analyzer with the principal purpose of solving this general class of problem. Unfortunately, the full three dimensional problem required more integrators than the RDA possessed.
>
> My colleagues who formulated the problem were very skeptical that it could be solved in any reasonable fashion. As a challenge, Zierler and I sat down with them in a $2\frac{1}{2}$ hour coding session, at least half of which was spent in defining notation. The tape was punched, and with the usual beginner's luck it ran successfully the first time! Although we never seriously capitalized on this capability, for reasons of cost and computer availability, my own ego probably never before or since received such a boost.

The lead-pursuit source program consisted of 79 statements, including 29 that merely assigned initial data values. The remaining statements included seven uses of the differential equation feature.

Laning describes his original parsing technique as follows [LA 76]:

> Nested parentheses were handled by a sequence of generated branch instructions (SP). In a one-pass operation the symbols were read and code generated a symbol at a time; the actual execution sequence used in-line SP orders to hop about from one point to another. The code used some rudimentary stacks, but was sufficiently intricate that I didn't understand it without extreme concentration even when I wrote it. ... Structured programs were not known in 1953!
>
> The notion of operator precedence as a formal concept did not occur to me at the time; I lived in fear that someone would write a perfectly reasonable algebraic expression that my system would not analyze correctly.

Plans for a much expanded Whirlwind compiler were dropped when the MIT Instrumentation Lab acquired its own computer, an IBM 650. Laning and his colleagues Philip C. Hankins and Charles P. Werner developed a compiler called MAC for this machine in 1957 and 1958. Although MAC falls out of the time period covered by our story, it deserves brief mention here because of its unusual three-line format proposed by R. H. Battin circa 1956, somewhat like Zuse's original language. For example, the statement

```
E  |                              3
M  |  Y = SQRT(ABS(A    )) + 5 A
S  |                I+1          I+1
```

would be punched on three cards. Although this language has not become widely known, it was very successful locally: MAC compilers were ultimately developed for use with IBM 704, 709, 7090, and 360 computers, as well as the Honeywell H800 and H1800 and the CDC 3600. (See [LM 70].) "At the present time, MAC and FORTRAN have about equal use at CSDL," according to [LA 76], written in 1976; here CSDL means C. S. Draper Laboratory, the successor to MIT's Instrumentation Lab.

But we had better get back to our story of the early days.

FORTRAN 0

During the first part of 1954, John Backus began to assemble a group of people within IBM Corporation to work on improved systems of

automatic programming (see [BA 76]). Shortly after learning of the
Laning and Zierler system at the ONR meeting in May, Backus wrote
to Laning that "our formulation of the problem is very similar to yours:
however, we have done no programming or even detailed planning."
Within two weeks, Backus and his co-workers Harlan Herrick and Irving
Ziller visited MIT in order to see the Laning–Zierler system in operation.
The big problem facing them was to implement such a language with
suitable efficiency [BH 64, page 382]:

> At that time, most programmers wrote symbolic machine in-
> structions exclusively (some even used absolute octal or decimal
> machine instructions). Almost to a man, they firmly believed
> that any mechanical coding method would fail to apply that
> versatile ingenuity which each programmer felt he possessed
> and constantly needed in his work. Therefore, it was agreed,
> compilers could only turn out code which would be intolera-
> bly less efficient than human coding (intolerable, that is, unless
> that inefficiency could be buried under larger, but desirable,
> inefficiencies such as the programmed floating-point arithmetic
> usually required then). ...
>
> [Our development group] had one primary fear. After work-
> ing long and hard to produce a good translator program, an
> important application might promptly turn up which would con-
> firm the views of the skeptics: ... its object program would
> run at half the speed of a hand-coded version. It was felt that
> such an occurrence, or several of them, would almost completely
> block acceptance of the system.

By November 1954, Backus's group had specified "The IBM Mathematical FORmula TRANslating system, FORTRAN." (Almost all the
languages we shall discuss from now on had acronyms.) The first paragraph of their report [IB 54] emphasized that previous systems had
offered the choice of easy coding and slow execution or laborious coding
and fast execution, but FORTRAN would provide the best of both worlds.
It also placed specific emphasis on the IBM 704; machine independence
was not a primary goal, although a concise mathematical notation that
"does not resemble a machine language" was definitely considered important. Furthermore they stated that "each future IBM calculator should
have a system similar to FORTRAN accompanying it" [IB 54].

> It is felt that FORTRAN offers as convenient a language for
> stating problems for machine solution as is now known. ...

> After an hour course in FORTRAN notation, the average pro-
> grammer can fully understand the steps of a procedure stated
> in FORTRAN language without any additional comments.

They went on to describe the considerable economic advantages of programming in such a language.

Readers of the present account probably imagine that they know
FORTRAN already, because FORTRAN is certainly the earliest high-level
language that is still in use. But comparatively few people have seen the
original 1954 version of the language, so it is instructive to study TPK
as it might have been expressed in "FORTRAN 0":

```
01              DIMENSION A(11)
02              READ A
03         2    DO 3,8,30 J=1,11
04         3    I = 11-J
05              Y=SQRT(ABS(A(I+1)))+5*A(I+1)**3
06              IF (400 >= Y) 8,4
07         4    PRINT I,999.
08              GO TO 2
09         8    PRINT I,Y
10        30    STOP
```

The READ and PRINT statements here do not mention any formats, although an extension to format specification was contemplated [page 26];
programmer-defined functions were also under consideration [page 27].
The DO statement in line *03* means, "Do statements 3 thru 8 and then
go to statement 30"; the abbreviation 'DO 8 J =1,11' was also allowed
at that time, but the original general form is shown here for fun. Notice
that the IF statement was originally only a two-way branch (line *06*);
the relation could be =, >, or >=. On line *05* we note that function names
need not end in F; they were required to be at least three characters long,
and there was no maximum limit (except that expressions could not be
longer than 750 characters). Conversely, the names of variables were restricted to be at most *two* characters long at this time; but this in itself
was an innovation: FORTRAN was the first algebraic language in which
a variable's name could be longer than one letter, contrary to established
mathematical conventions. Note also that mixed mode arithmetic was
allowed; the compiler would convert '5' to '5.0' in line *05*. A final curios-
ity about this program is the GO TO on line *08*; this statement did not
begin the DO loop all over again, it merely initiated the next iteration.

Several things besides mixed mode arithmetic were allowed in FOR-
TRAN 0 but withdrawn during implementation, notably: (a) one level

of subscripted subscripts, such as A(M(I,J),N(K,L)) were allowed; (b) subscripts of the form N*I+J were permitted, provided that at least two of the variables N, I, J were declared to be "relatively constant" (that is, infrequently changing); (c) a RELABEL statement was intended to permute array indices cyclically without physically moving the array in storage. For example, 'RELABEL A(3)' was to be like setting $(A_1, A_2, A_3, \ldots, A_n) \leftarrow (A_3, \ldots, A_n, A_1, A_2)$.

Incidentally, statements were called *formulas* throughout the 1954 document. There were arithmetic formulas, DO formulas, GO TO formulas, etc. Similar terminology had been used by Böhm, while Laning and Zierler and Glennie spoke of "equations"; Grace Hopper called them "operations." Furthermore, the word "compiler" is never used in [IB 54]; there is a FORTRAN language and a FORTRAN system, but not a FORTRAN compiler.

The FORTRAN 0 document represents the first attempt to define the syntax of a programming language rigorously. Backus's important notation [BA 59], which eventually became 'BNF' [KN 64], can be seen in embryonic form here.

With the FORTRAN language defined, it "only" remained to implement the system. It is clear from reading [IB 54] that considerable plans had already been made toward the implementation during 1954; but the full job took 2.5 more years (18 person-years) [BA 79], so we shall leave the IBM group at work while we consider other developments.

Brooker's AUTOCODE

Back in Manchester, R. A. Brooker introduced a new type of AUTO-CODE for the MARK I machine. This language was much "cleaner" than Glennie's, being nearly machine-independent and using programmed floating-point arithmetic. But it allowed only one operation per line, there were few mnemonic names, and there was no way for a user to define subroutines. The first plans for this language, as of March 1954, appeared in [BR 55], and the language eventually implemented was almost the same [BR 56, pages 155–157]. Brooker's emphasis on economy of description when defining the rules of AUTOCODE was especially noteworthy: "What the author aimed at was two sides of a foolscap sheet with possibly a third side to describe an example" [BR 55].

The floating-point variables in Brooker's language were called $v1$, $v2$, ..., and the integer variables — which may be used also as indices (subscripts) — were called $n1$, $n2$, ... The AUTOCODE for TPK is easily readable with only a few auxiliary comments, given the memory assignments $a_i \equiv v_{1+i}$, $y \equiv v_{12}$, $i \equiv n_2$:

6	$n1 = 1$	sets $n_1 = 1$
1	$vn1 = I$	reads input into v_{n_1}
	$n1 = n1 + 1$	
	$j1, 11 \geq n1$	jumps to 1 if $n_1 \leq 11$
	$n1 = 11$	
2	$*n2 = n1 - 1$	prints $i = n_1 - 1$
	$v12 = vn1$	
	$j3, v12 \geq 0{\cdot}0$	
	$v12 = 0{\cdot}0 - v12$	sets $v_{12} = |v_{12}|$
3	$v12 = F1(v12)$	$(v_{12} = \sqrt{|a_i|})$
	$v13 = 5{\cdot}0 \otimes vn1$	
	$v13 = vn1 \otimes v13$	
	$v13 = vn1 \otimes v13$	$(v_{13} = 5a_i^3)$
	$v12 = v12 + v13$	$(y = f(a_i))$
	$j4, v12 > 400{\cdot}0$	
	$*v12 = v12$	prints y
	$j5$	
4	$*v12 = 999{\cdot}0$	prints 999
5	$n1 = n1 - 1$	
	$j2, n1 > 0$	tests for last cycle
	H	halts
	$(j6)$	starts programme

The final instruction illustrates an interesting innovation: An instruction or group of instructions in parentheses was obeyed immediately, rather than added to the program. Thus '$(j6)$' jumps to statement 6.

This language is not at a very high level, but Brooker's main concern was simplicity and a desire to keep information flowing smoothly to and from the electrostatic high-speed memory. Mark I's electrostatic memory consisted of only 512 20-bit words, and it was necessary to make frequent transfers from and to the 32K-word drum; floating-point subroutines could compute while the next block of program was being read in. Thus two of the principal difficulties facing a programmer — scaling and coping with the two-level store — were removed by his AUTO-CODE system, and it was heavily used. For example [BR 58, page 16]:

> Since its completion in 1955 the Mark I AUTOCODE has been used extensively for about 12 hours a week as the basis of a computing service for which customers write their own programs and post them to us.

George E. Felton, who developed the first AUTOCODE for the Ferranti Pegasus, says in [FE 60] that its specification "clearly owes much to Mr. R. A. Brooker." Incidentally, Brooker's next AUTOCODE — for the Mark II or "Mercury" computer, first delivered in 1957 — was considerably more ambitious; see [BR 58, BR 58', BR 60].

Russian Programming Programs

Work on automatic programming began in Russia at the Mathematical Institute of the Soviet Academy of Sciences, and at the Academy's computation center, which originally was part of the Institute of Exact Mechanics and Computing Technique. The early Russian systems were appropriately called programming programs [Programmiruĭoshchye Programmy] — or ПП for short. An experimental program ПП-1 for the STRELA computer was constructed by E. Z. Lĩubimskiĭ and S. S. Kamynin during the summer of 1954; and these two authors, together with M. R. Shura-Bura, É. S. Lukhovitskaĩa, and V. S. Shtarkman, completed a production compiler called ПП-2 in February 1955. Their compiler is described in [KL 58]. Meanwhile, A. P. Ershov began in December 1954 to design another programming program, for the BESM computer, with the help of L. N. Korolev, L. D. Panova, V. D. Podderĩugin, and V. M. Kurochkin; their compiler, called simply ПП, was completed in March 1956, and it is described in Ershov's book [ER 58]. A review of these developments appears in [KO 58].

In both of these cases, and in the later system ПП-C completed in 1957 (see [ER 58']), the language was based on a notation for expressing programs developed by A. A. Lĩapunov in 1953. Lĩapunov's operator schemata [LJ 58] provide a concise way to represent program structure in a linear manner; in some ways this approach is analogous to the ideas of Curry that we have already considered, but it is somewhat more elegant and it became widely used in Russia.

Let us consider first how the TPK algorithm (exclusive of input-output) can be described in ПП-2. The overall operator scheme for the program would be written

$$A_1 \underset{13}{\rfloor} Z_2 A_3 R_4 \overset{6}{\lceil} A_5 \overset{4}{\rceil} A_6 R_7 \underset{10}{\lfloor} A_8 N_9 \overset{11}{\lceil} \underset{7}{\rfloor} A_{10} \overset{9}{\rceil} A_{11} F_{12} R_{13} \underset{2}{\lfloor} N_{14}.$$

Here the operators are numbered 1 through 14; the notations

$$\overset{n}{\lceil} \quad \text{and} \quad \underset{m}{\lfloor}$$

mean "go to operator n if true" and "go to operator m if false," respectively, while

$$\overset{i}{\rceil} \quad \text{and} \quad \underset{i}{\rfloor}$$

are the corresponding notations for "coming from operator i." This operator scheme was not itself input to the programming program explicitly; it would be kept by the programmer as documentation in lieu of a flowchart. The details of operators would be written separately and input to ПП-2 after dividing them into operators of types R (relational), A (arithmetic), Z (dispatch), F (address modification), O (restoration), and N (nonstandard, that is, machine language). In our example the details are essentially this:

$R_4.$ $p_1; 6, 5$	[if p_1 is true go to 6 else to 5]
$R_7.$ $p_2; 8, 10$	[if p_2 is true go to 8 else to 10]
$R_{13}.$ $p_3; 14, 2$	[if p_3 is true go to 14 else to 2]
$p_1.$ $c_3 < v_2$	[$0 < x$]
$p_2.$ $c_4 < v_3$	[$400 < y$]
$p_3.$ $v_6 < c_3$	[$i < 0$]
$A_1.$ $c_6 = v_6$	[$10 = i$, that is, set i equal to 10]
$A_3.$ $v_1 = v_2$	[$a_i = x$]
$A_5.$ $c_3 - v_2 = v_2$	[$0 - x = x$]
$A_6.$ $(\sqrt{v_2}) + (c_5 \cdot v_1 \cdot v_1 \cdot v_1) = v_3$	[$\sqrt{x} + (5 \cdot a_i \cdot a_i \cdot a_i) = y$]
$A_8.$ $v_6 = v_4,\ c_2 = v_5$	[$i = b_{20-2i},\ 999 = b_{21-2i}$]
$A_{10}.$ $v_6 = v_4,\ v_3 = v_5$	[$i = b_{20-2i},\ y = b_{21-2i}$]
$A_{11}.$ $v_6 - c_1 = v_6$	[$i - 1 = i$]
$Z_2.$ $v_1; 3, 6$	[dispatch a_i to special cell, in operators 3 thru 6]
$F_{12}.$ $v_6; 2, 10$	[modify addresses depending on parameter i, in operators 2 thru 10]
$N_9.$ BP 11	[go to operator 11]
$N_{14}.$ OST	[stop]
Dependence on parameter v_6.	$v_1, v_1, -1;\quad v_4, v_5, +2$ [when i changes, v_1 goes down by 1, and v_4 thru v_5 go up by 2]
$c_1.$ $.1 \cdot 10^1$	[1]
$c_2.$ $.999 \cdot 10^3$	[999]
$c_3.$ 0	[0]
$c_4.$ $.4 \cdot 10^3$	[400]
$c_5.$ $.5 \cdot 10^1$	[5]
$c_6.$ $.1 \cdot 10^2$	[10]
Working cells: 100, 119	[the compiled program can use locations 100–119 for temporary storage]

v_1.   130   [initial address of a_i]
v_2.   131   [address of x]
v_3.   132   [address of y]
v_4.   133   [initial address of b_{20-2i}]
v_5.   134   [initial address of b_{21-2i}]
v_6.   154   [address of i]

Operator 1 initializes i, then operators 2–13 are the loop on i. Operator 2 moves a_i to a fixed cell of memory, and makes sure that operators 3–6 use that fixed cell; this programmer-supplied optimization reduces the number of addresses in instructions that have to be modified when i changes. Operators 3–5 set $x = |a_i|$, and operator 6 sets $y = f(a_i)$. (Notice the parentheses in operator 6; precedence was not recognized.) Operators 7–10 store the desired outputs in memory. Operators 11 and 12 decrease i and appropriately adjust the addresses of quantities that depend on i. Operators 13 and 14 control looping and stopping.

The algorithms used in ПП-2 are quite interesting from the standpoint of compiler history. For example, they avoided the recomputation of common subexpressions within a single formula, and they carefully optimized the use of working storage. They also produced efficient code for relational operators compounded from a series of elementary relations, so that, for example,

$$(p_1 \lor (p_2 \cdot p_3) \lor \overline{p_4}) \cdot p_5 \lor p_6$$

would be compiled as shown in Figure 3.

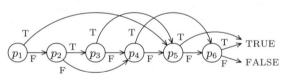

FIGURE 3. Optimization of Boolean expressions in an early Russian compiler.

Ershov's ПП language improved on ПП-2 in several respects, notably: (a) the individual operators did not need to be numbered, and they could be intermixed in the natural sequence; (b) no address modification needed to be specified, and there was a special notation for loops; (c) the storage for variables was allocated semiautomatically; (d) operator precedence could be used to reduce the number of parentheses within expressions. The TPK algorithm looks like this in ПП:

01   Massiv a (11 îâcheek)   [declares an array of 11 cells]
02 $a_0 = 0$ [address in array a]

03 $a_j = -1 \cdot j + 10$ [address in array a depending on j]
04 $j : j_{\text{nach}} = 0,\ j_{\text{kon}} = 11$ [information on loop indexes]
05 $0, 11, 10, 5, y, 400, 999, i$ [the remaining constants and variables]

06   (Ma, 080, 0, a_0); (Mb, 0, $0\bar{1}$, 0);

07 $\Big[\ \underset{j}{10 - j} \Rightarrow i;\ \sqrt{}\ \underset{0101}{\text{mod}}\ a_j + 5 \times a_j^3 \Rightarrow y;$

08 $R(y, 0102;\ \overset{0103}{\ulcorner}\ (400, \infty));$

09 $\underset{0101}{\llcorner}\ \text{Vyd}\ i, \Rightarrow 0;\ \text{Vyd}\ 999, \Rightarrow 0;\ \overset{0103}{\ulcorner}\ ;$

10 $\underset{0102}{\llcorner}\ \text{Vyd}\ i, \Rightarrow 0;\ \text{Vyd}\ y, \Rightarrow 0;\ \underset{0103}{\llcorner}\ ];$ stop.

After declarations on lines *01–05*, the program appears here on lines *06–10*. In ПП each loop was associated with a different index name, and the linear dependence of array variables on loop indices was specified as in line *03*; the notation a_j does not mean the jth element of a, it means an element of a that *depends* on j. The commands in line *06* are BESM machine language instructions that read 11 words into memory starting at a_0. Line *07* shows the beginning of the loop on j, which ends at the ']' on line *10*; all loop indices must step by $+1$. (The initial and final-plus-one values for the j loop are specified on line *04*.) Line *08* is a relational operator that means, "If y is in the interval $(400, \infty)$, that is, if $y > 400$, go to label 0101; otherwise go to 0102." Labels were given as hexadecimal numbers, and the notation $\underset{n}{\lfloor}$ stands for the program location of label n. The 'Vyd' instruction in lines *09* and *10* means convert to decimal, and '$\Rightarrow 0$' means print. Everything else should be self-explanatory.

The Russian computers had no alphabetic input or output, so the programs written in ПП-2 and ПП were converted into numeric codes. This was a rather tedious and intricate process, usually performed by two specialists who would compare their independent hand transliterations in order to prevent errors. As an example of this encoding process, here is how the program above would actually have been converted into BESM words in the form required by ПП. [Hexadecimal digits were written 0, 1, ..., 9, $\bar{0}$, $\bar{1}$, ..., $\bar{5}$. A 39-bit word in BESM could be represented either in instruction format,

$$bbh\ bqhh\ bqhh\ bqhh,$$

where b denotes a binary digit (0 or 1), q a quaternary digit (0, 1, 2, or 3), and h a hexadecimal digit; or in floating-binary numeric format,

$$\pm\ 2^k,\ hh\ hh\ hh\ hh,$$

where k is a decimal number between -32 and $+31$ inclusive. Both of these representations were used at various times in the encoding of a ПП program, as shown below.]

Location	Contents	Meaning
07	000 0000 0000 0000	no space needed for special subroutines
08	000 0000 0000 0013	last entry in array descriptor table
09	000 0000 0000 0015	first entry for constants and variables
$0\overline{0}$	000 0000 0000 001$\overline{2}$	last entry for constants and variables
$0\overline{1}$	000 0000 0000 002$\overline{5}$	base address for encoded program scheme
$0\overline{2}$	000 0000 0000 0042	last entry of encoded program
$0\overline{3}$	000 0000 0000 029$\overline{5}$	base address for "block γ"
$0\overline{4}$	000 0000 0000 02$\overline{1}$5	base address for "block α"
$0\overline{5}$	000 0000 0000 02$\overline{3}\overline{5}$	base address for "block β"
10	01$\overline{5}$ 0000 000$\overline{1}$ 0000	a = array of size 11
11	000 1001 0000 0000	coefficient of -1 for linear dependency
12	2^1, 00 00 00 00	$a_0 = 0$ relative to a
13	2^2, 14 00 00 0$\overline{0}$	$a_j = -1 \cdot j + 10$ relative to a
14	000 0015 0016 0000	j = loop index from 0 to 11
15	2^{-32}, 00 00 00 00	0
16	2^4, $\overline{1}$0 00 00 00	11
17	2^4, $\overline{0}$0 00 00 00	10
18	2^3, $\overline{0}$0 00 00 00	5
19	2^9, $\overline{2}$8 00 00 00	400
$1\overline{0}$	2^{10}, $\overline{5}$9 $\overline{2}$0 00 00	999
$1\overline{1}$	000 0000 0000 0000	i
$1\overline{2}$	000 0000 0000 0000	y
30	016 0080 0000 0012	$(\text{Ma}, 080, 0, a_0)$
31	017 0000 000$\overline{1}$ 0000	$(\text{Mb}, 0, 0\overline{1}, 0)$
32	018 0014 0000 0000	$[_j$
33	2^0, 17 04 14 08	$10 - j \Rightarrow$
34	2^0, 1$\overline{1}$ $\overline{5}$3 $\overline{5}$2 13	$i \sqrt{} \bmod a_j$
35	2^0, 03 18 09 13	$+ 5 \times a_j$
36	2^0, 0$\overline{2}$ 08 1$\overline{2}$ 00	$^3 \Rightarrow y$
37	018 0000 001$\overline{2}$ 0102	$\text{R}(y, 0102;$
38	008 0019 0000 0101	$\ulcorner$ (400, ∞))
39	018 0101 0000 0000	$\llcorner$
$3\overline{0}$	2^0, $\overline{5}$4 1$\overline{1}$ 07 00	Vyd i, $\Rightarrow 0$
$3\overline{1}$	2^0, $\overline{5}$4 1$\overline{0}$ 07 00	Vyd 999, $\Rightarrow 0$
$3\overline{2}$	01$\overline{1}$ 0000 0000 0103	$\ulcorner$
$3\overline{3}$	018 0102 0000 0000	$\llcorner$
$3\overline{4}$	2^0, $\overline{5}$4 1$\overline{1}$ 07 00	Vyd i, $\Rightarrow 0$

35	2^0, $\bar{5}4$ $1\bar{2}$ 07 00	Vyd y, $\Rightarrow 0$
40	018 0103 0000 0000	$\underset{0103}{\llcorner}$
41	$01\bar{5}$ $13\bar{5}5$ $13\bar{5}5$ $13\bar{5}5$	]
42	$01\bar{5}$ 0000 0000 0000	stop

The BESM had 1024 words of core memory, plus some high-speed read-only memory, and a magnetic drum holding 5 × 1024 words. The ПП compiler worked in three passes (formulas and relations, loops, final assembly) and it contained a total of 1200 instructions plus 150 constants. Ershov published detailed specifications of its structure and all its algorithms in [ER 58], a book that was extremely influential at the time — for example, a Chinese translation was published in Peking in 1959. The book shows that Ershov was aware of Rutishauser's work [page 9], but he gave no other references to non-Russian sources.

A Western Development

Computer professionals at the Boeing Airplane Company in Seattle, Washington, felt that "in this jet age, it is vital to shorten the time from the definition of a problem to its solution." So they introduced BACAIC, the Boeing Airplane Company Algebraic Interpretive Computing system for the IBM 701 computer.

BACAIC was an interesting language and compiler developed by Mandalay Grems and R. E. Porter, who began work on the system in the latter part of 1954; they presented it at the Western Joint Computer Conference held in San Francisco, in February 1956 [GP 56]. Although the 'I' in BACAIC stands for "interpretive," their system actually translated algebraic expressions into machine-language calls on subroutines, with due regard for parentheses and precedence, so we would now call it a compiler.

The BACAIC language was unusual in several respects, especially in its control structure, which assumed one-level iterations over the entire program; a program was considered to be a nearly straight-line computation to be applied to various "cases" of data. There were no subscripted variables. However, the TPK algorithm could be performed by inputting the data in reverse order using the following program:

1. $I - K1 * I$
2. X
3. WHN X GRT $K2$ USE 5
4. $K2 - X * 2$
5. SRT $2 + K3 . X$ PWR $K4$

6. WHN 5 GRT $K5$ USE 8
7. TRN 9
8. $K6 * 5$
9. TAB I 5

Here '*' is used for assignment, and '.' for multiplication; variables are given single-letter names (except K), and constants are denoted by $K1$ through $K99$. The program above is to be used with the following input data:

Case 1. $K1 = 1.0$ $K2 = 0.0$ $K3 = 5.0$ $K4 = 3.0$
$\qquad\qquad$ $K5 = 400.0$ $K6 = 999.0$ $I = 11.0$ $X = a_{10}$
Case 2. $X = a_9$
Case 3. $X = a_8$
$\qquad\quad \vdots$
Case 11. $X = a_0$

Data values for BACAIC are identified by name when input. All variables are zero initially, and values carry over from one case to the next unless changed. For example, expression 1 means '$I - 1 \to I$', so the initial value $I = 11$ needs to be input only in case 1.

Expressions 2–4 ensure that the value of expression 2 is the absolute value of X when we get to expression 5. (The '2' in expression 4 means *expression* 2, not the constant 2.) Expression 5 therefore has the value $f(X)$.

A typical way to use BACAIC was to print the values associated with all expressions 1, 2, ...; this was a good way to locate errors. Expression 7 in the program above is an unconditional jump; expression 9 says that the values of I and of expression 5 should be tabulated (printed).

The BACAIC system was easy to learn and to use, but the language was too restrictive for general-purpose computing. One novel feature was its "check-out mode," in which the user furnished hand-calculated data and the machine would print out only the discrepancies it found.

According to [BE 57], BACAIC became operational also on the IBM 650 computer, in August 1956.

Kompilers

Another independent development was taking place almost simultaneously at the University of California Radiation Laboratory in Livermore, California; this work has apparently never been published, except as an internal report [EK 55]. In 1954, A. Kenton Elsworth began to experiment with the translation of algebraic equations into IBM 701 machine language and called his program Kompiler 1; at that time he dealt only with individual formulas, without control statements or constants or input-output. Elsworth and his associates Robert Kuhn, Leona Schloss, and Kenneth Tiede went on to implement a working system named Kompiler 2 during the following year. The latter system was somewhat similar in flavor to ПП-2, except that it was based on flow diagrams instead of operator schemata. They characterized its status in the following way [EK 55, page 4]:

> In many ways Kompiler is an experimental model; it is therefore somewhat limited in applications. For example it is designed to handle only full-word data and is restricted to fixed-point arithmetic. At the same time every effort was made to design a workable and worthwhile routine: the compiled code should approach very closely the efficiency of a hand-tailored code; learning to use it should be relatively easy; compilation itself is very fast.

In order to compensate for the fixed-point arithmetic, special features were included to facilitate scaling. As we shall see, this is perhaps Kompiler 2's most noteworthy aspect.

To solve the TPK problem, let us first agree to scale the numbers by writing

$$A_i = 2^{-10}a_i, \qquad Y = 2^{-10}y, \qquad I = 2^{-35}i.$$

Furthermore we will need to use the scaled constants

$$V = 5 \cdot 2^{-3}, \quad F = 400 \cdot 2^{-10}, \quad N = 999 \cdot 2^{-10}, \quad W = 1 \cdot 2^{-35}.$$

The next step is to draw a special kind of flow diagram for the program, as shown in Figure 4.

The third step is to allocate data storage, for example as follows:

$$61 \equiv I, \quad 63 \equiv Y, \quad 65 \equiv V, \quad 67 \equiv F, \quad 69 \equiv N, \quad 71 \equiv W;$$
$$81 \equiv A_0, \quad 83 \equiv A_1, \quad \ldots, \quad 101 \equiv A_{10}.$$

(Addresses in the IBM 701 go by half-words, but variables in Kompiler 2 occupy full words. Address 61 denotes half-words 60 and 61 in the "second frame" of the memory.)

The final step is to transcribe the flow-diagram information into a fixed format designated for keypunching. The source input to Kompiler 2 has two parts: the "flow-diagram cards," one card per box in the flow diagram; and the "algebraic cards," one per complex equation. In our

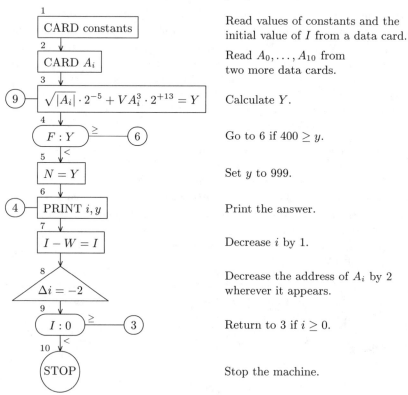

Read values of constants and the initial value of I from a data card.

Read $A_0, \ldots, A_{10}$ from two more data cards.

Calculate Y.

Go to 6 if $400 \geq y$.

Set y to 999.

Print the answer.

Decrease i by 1.

Decrease the address of A_i by 2 wherever it appears.

Return to 3 if $i \geq 0$.

Stop the machine.

FIGURE 4. This flow diagram for Kompiler input is to be transcribed into numeric format and punched onto cards.

case the flow-diagram cards are

```
1CARD      61   2       235   0     103 310     310 135      0  61
2CARD      81   2       310 310     310 310     310 310    310  95  14
3CALC     101   8        65         101   8      63
4TRPL      67  63   6
5PLUS      69       63
6PRNT      61  63    2    1  35  10
7MINS      71  61   61
8DECR       2
9TRPL      61   Z    3
10STOP
```

and there are three algebraic cards:

```
1*ΔCARD
2*ΔPRNT
3ΔSRTΔABSA.-05+VA3.+13=Y
```

Here is a free translation of the meaning of the flow diagram cards:

1. Read data cards into locations beginning with 61 in steps of 2. The words of data are to be converted using respective scale codes 235, 0, 103, ..., 0; stop reading cards after the beginning location has become 61, that is, immediately. [The scale code ddbb means to take the 10-digit data as a decimal fraction, multiply it by 10^{dd}, convert to binary, and divide by 2^{bb}. In our case the first input datum will be punched as 1000000000, and the scale code 235 means that this is regarded first as $(10.00000000)_{10}$ and eventually converted to $(.00\ldots01010)_2 = 10 \cdot 2^{-35}$, the initial value of I. The initial value of N, with its scale code 310, would therefore be punched 9990000000. Up to seven words of data are punched per data card.]

2. Read data cards into locations beginning with 81 in steps of 2. The words of data are to be converted using respective scale codes 310, 310, ..., 310; stop reading cards after the beginning location has become 95. The beginning location should advance by 14 between data cards (hence exactly two cards are to be read).

3. Calculate a formula using the variables in the respective locations 101 (which changes at step 8); 65; 101 (which changes at step 8); and 63.

4. If the contents of location 67 minus the contents of location 63 is nonnegative, go to step 6.

5. Store the contents of location 69 in location 63.

6. Print locations 61 through 63, with 2 words per line and 1 line per block. The respective scale factors are 35 and 10.

7. Subtract the contents of location 71 from the contents of location 61 and store the result in location 61.

8. Decrease all locations referring to step 8 by 2 (see step 3).

9. If location 61 contains a nonnegative value (Z stands for zero), go to step 3.

10. Stop the machine.

The first two algebraic cards in our example simply cause the library subroutines for card reading and line printing to be loaded with the object program. The third card is used to encode

$$\sqrt{|A_i|} \cdot 2^{-5} + VA_i^3 \cdot 2^{13} = Y.$$

The variable names on an algebraic card are actually nothing but dummy placeholders, since the storage locations must be specified on the corresponding CALC card. Thus, the third algebraic card could also have been punched as

3ΔSRTΔΔABSX.-05+XX3.+13=X

without any effect on the result.

Kompiler 2 was used for several important production programs at Livermore. By 1959 it had been replaced by Kompiler 3, a rather highly developed system for the IBM 704 that used three-line format analogous to the notation of MAC (although it apparently was designed independently).

A Declarative Language

During 1955 and 1956, E. K. Blum at the U.S. Naval Ordnance Laboratory developed a language of a completely different type. His language ADES (Automatic Digital Encoding System) was presented at the ACM national meetings in 1955 (of which no proceedings were published) and in 1956 [BL 56″], and at the ONR symposium in 1956 [BL 56′]. He described it as follows:

> The ADES language is essentially mathematical in structure. It is based on the theory of the recursive functions and the schemata for such functions, as given by Kleene [BL 56′, page 72].
>
> The ADES approach to automatic programming is believed to be entirely new. Mathematically, it has its foundations in the bedrock of the theory of recursive functions. The proposal to apply this theory to automatic programming was first made by C. C. Elgot, a former colleague of the author's. While at the Naval Ordnance Laboratory, Elgot did some research on a language for automatic programming. Some of his ideas were adapted to ADES [BL 56, page iii].

A full description of the language was given in a lengthy report [BL 56]. Several aspects of ADES are rather difficult to understand, and we will content ourselves with a brief glimpse into its structure by considering the following ADES program for TPK. The conventions of [BL 57′] are followed here since they are slightly simpler than the original proposals in [BL 56].

$$01 \quad a_0 11 : q_0 11,$$
$$02 \quad\quad f_{50} = + \sqrt{} \text{ abs } c_1 \cdots 5\, c_1\, c_1\, c_1,$$
$$03 \quad d_{12} b_1 = r_0,$$
$$04 \quad d_{22} b_2 = \leq b_3\, 400,\, b_3,\, 999,$$
$$05 \quad\quad b_3 = f_{50}\, a_0\, r_0,$$
$$06 \quad\quad r_0 = -\, 10\, q_0,$$
$$07 \quad \forall\, 0\, q_0\, 10\, b_0 = f_0\, b_1\, b_2,$$

Here is a rough translation: Line *01* is the so-called "computer table," meaning that input array a_0 has 11 positions, and that the "independent index symbol" q_0 takes 11 values. Line *02* defines the auxiliary function f_{50}, our $f(t)$; arithmetic expressions were defined in Łukasiewicz's parenthesis-free notation [LU 51, Chapter 4], now commonly known as "left Polish." Variable c_1 here denotes the first parameter of the function. (Incidentally, "right Polish" notation seems to have been first proposed shortly afterwards by C. L. Hamblin in Australia; see [HA 57].)

Line *03* states that the dependent variable b_1 is equal to the dependent index r_0; the 'd_{12}' here means that this quantity is to be output as component 1 of a pair. Line *04* similarly defines b_2, which is to be component 2. This line is a "branch equation" meaning 'if $b_3 \leq 400$ then b_3 else 999'. (Such branch equations are an embryonic form of the conditional expressions introduced later by McCarthy into LISP and ALGOL. Blum remarked that the equation '$\leq x\, a, f, g,$' could be replaced by $\varphi f + (1 - \varphi)g$, where φ is a function that takes the value 1 or 0 according as $x \leq a$ or $x > a$ [BL 56, page 16].)

> The function φ is a primitive recursive function, and could be incorporated into the library as one of the given functions of the system. Nevertheless, the branch equation is included in the language for practical reasons. Many mathematicians are accustomed to that terminology, and it leads to more efficient programs.

In spite of these remarks, Blum may well have intended that f or g not be evaluated or even defined when $\varphi = 0$ or 1, respectively.

Line *05* says that b_3 is the result of applying f_{50} to the r_0th element of a_0. Line *06* explains that r_0 is $10 - q_0$. Finally, line *07* is a so-called "phase equation" that specifies the overall program flow, by saying that b_1 and b_2 are to be evaluated for $q_0 = 0, 1, \ldots, 10$.

The ADES language is "declarative" in the sense that the programmer states relationships between variable quantities without explicitly specifying the order of evaluation. John McCarthy put it this way, in 1958 [ER 58', page 275]:

> Mathematical notation as it presently exists was developed to facilitate stating mathematical facts, i.e., making declarative sentences. A program gives a machine orders and hence is usually constructed out of imperative sentences. This suggests that it will be necessary to invent new notations for describing complicated procedures, and we will not merely be able to take over

intact the notations that mathematicians have used for making declarative sentences.

The transcript of a 1965 discussion of declarative versus imperative languages, with comments by P. Abrahams, P. Z. Ingerman, E. T. Irons, P. Naur, B. Raphael, R. V. Smith, C. Strachey, and J. W. Young, appears in *Communications of the ACM* **9** (1966), 155–156, 165–166.

Although ADES was based on recursive function theory, it did not really include recursive procedures in the sense of ALGOL 60; it dealt primarily with special types of recursive equations over the integers, and the emphasis was on studying the memory requirements for evaluating such recurrences.

An experimental version of ADES was implemented on the IBM 650 and described in [BL 57, BL 57']. Blum's translation scheme was what we now recognize as a recursive approach to the problem, but the recursion was not explicitly stated; he essentially moved things on and off various stacks during the course of the algorithm. This implementation points up the severe problems people had to face in those days: The ADES encoder consisted of 3500 instructions while the Type 650 calculator had room for only 2000, so it was necessary to insert the program card decks into the machine repeatedly, once for each equation! Because of further machine limitations, the program above would have been entered into the computer by punching the following information onto six cards:

```
A00   011   P02   Q00   011   P01   F50   E00   F02   F20
F06   C01   F04   F04   F04   005   C01   C01   C01   P01
D12   B01   E00   R00   P01   D22   B02   E00   F11   B03
400   P01   B03   P01   999   P01   B03   E00   F50   A00
R00   P01   R00   E00   F03   010   Q00   P01   P03   000
Q00   010   B00   E00   F00   B01   B02   P01    -     -
```

Here Pnn was a punctuation mark, Fnn a function code, etc. Actually the implemented version of ADES was a subset that did not allow auxiliary f-equations to be defined, so the definition of b_3 in line *05* would have been written out explicitly.

The IT

In September, 1955, four members of the Purdue University Computing Laboratory — Mark Koschman, Sylvia Orgel, Alan Perlis, and Joseph W. Smith — began a series of conferences to discuss methods of automatic coding. Joanne Chipps joined the group in March, 1956. A compiler, programmed to be used on the Datatron, was the goal and result [OR 58, page 1].

Purdue received one of the first Datatron computers, manufactured by Electrodata Corporation (see *Journal of the Association for Computing Machinery* **2** (1955), 122, and [PE 55]); this machine was known later as the Burroughs 205. By the summer of 1956, the Purdue group had completed an outline of the basic logic and language of its compiler, and they presented some of their ideas at the ACM national meeting [CK 56]. (This paper, incidentally, used both the words "compiler" and "statement" in the modern sense; a comparison of the ONR 1954 and 1956 symposium proceedings makes it clear that the word "compiler" had by now acquired its new meaning. Furthermore the contemporary FORTRAN manuals [IB 56, IB 57] also used the term "statement" where [IB 54] had said "formula." Terminology was crystallizing.)

At that time Perlis and Smith moved to the Carnegie Institute of Technology, taking copies of the flowcharts with them, and they adapted their language to the IBM 650 (a smaller machine) with the help of Harold Van Zoeren. The compiler was put into use in October 1956 (see [PS 57, page 102]), and it became known as IT, the Internal Translator.

> Compilation proceeds in two phases: 1) translation from an IT program into a symbolic program, PIT and 2) assembly from a PIT program into a specific machine coded program, SPIT [PS 57', page 1.23].

The intermediate "PIT" program was actually a program in SOAP language [PM 55], the source code for an excellent symbolic assembly program for the IBM 650. Perlis stated that the existence of SOAP was an important simplifying factor in their implementation of IT, which was completed about three months after its authors had learned the 650 machine language.

This software system was the first really *useful* compiler; IT and IT's derivatives were used frequently and successfully in hundreds of computer installations until the 650 became obsolete. (Indeed, R. B. Wise stated in October 1958 that "the IT language is about the closest thing we have today to the universal language among computers" [WA 58, page 131].) The previous systems we have discussed were important steps along the way, but none of them had the combination of powerful language and adequate implementation and documentation needed to make a significant impact in the use of machines. Furthermore, IT proved that useful compilers could be constructed for small computers without enormous investments of manpower.

Here is an IT program for TPK:

```
1:  READ
2:  3, I1, 10, −1, 0,
5:  Y1 ← "20E, AC(I1 + 1)"
          + (5 × (C(I1 + 1) ∗ 3))
6:  G3 IF 400.0 ≥ Y1
7:  Y1 ← 999
3:  TI1 TY1
10: H
```

Each statement has an identifying number, but the numbers need not be in order. The READ statement does not specify the names of variables being input, since such information appears on the data cards themselves. Floating-point variables are called Y1, Y2, ..., or C1, C2, ...; the example program assumes that the input data will specify eleven values for C1 through C11.

Statement number 2 designates an iteration of the following program through statement number 3 inclusive; variable I1 runs from 10 in steps of −1 down to 0. Statement 5 sets Y1 to $f(C_{I1+1})$; the notation "20E, x" is used for "language extension 20 applied to x," where extension 20 happens to be the floating-point square root subroutine. Notice the use of mixed integer and floating-point arithmetic in the second line of statement 5. The redundant parentheses emphasize that IT did not deal with operator precedence, although in this case the parentheses need not have been written since IT evaluated expressions from right to left.

The letter A is used to denote absolute value, and ∗ means exponentiation. Statement 6 goes to 3 if Y1 ≤ 400; and statement 3 outputs I1 and Y1. Statement 10 means "halt."

Since the IBM 650 did not have such a rich character set at the time, the program above would actually be punched onto cards in the following form — using K for comma, M for minus, Q for quotes, L and R for parentheses, etc.:

```
0001  READ                            F
0002  3K I1K 10K M1K 0K               F
0005  Y1 Z Q 20EK ACLI1S1R Q
0005         S L5 X LCLI1S1R P 3RR    F
0006  G3 IF 400J0 W Y1                F
0007  Y1 Z 999                        F
0003  TI1 TY1                         F
0010  H                               FF
```

The programmer also supplied a "header card," stating the limits on array subscripts actually used; in this case the header card would specify one I variable, one Y variable, 11 C variables, 10 statements. An array of statement locations was kept in the running program, since the language allowed programmers to 'go to' statement number n, where n was the value of any integer expression.

The Purdue compiler language discussed in [CK 56] was in some respects richer than this; it included the ability to type out alphabetic information and to define new extensions (functions) in source language. On the other hand, [CK 56] did not mention iteration statements or data input. Joanne Chipps and Sylvia Orgel completed the Datatron implementation in the summer of 1957; the language had lost the richer features in [CK 56], however, probably since they were unexpectedly difficult to implement. Our program would have looked like this in the Purdue compiler language [OR 58]:

input $i0$ $y0$ $c10$ $s10$ f		[maximum subscripts used]
1	e "800e" f	[read input]
2	s $i0 = 10$ f	[set $i_0 = 10$]
5	s $y0 = $ "200e, $aci0$" $+ (5 \times (ci0p3))$ f	
6	r $g8$, r $y0 \leq 400.0$ f	[go to 8 if $y_0 \leq 400.0$]
7	s $y0 = 999$ f	
8	o $i0$ f	[output i_0]
9	o $y0$ f	[output y_0]
4	s $i0 = i0 - 1$ f	
3	r $g5$, r $0 \leq i0$ f	[go to 5 if $i_0 \geq 0$]
10	h f	[halt]

Notice that subscripts now may start with 0, and that each statement begins with a letter identifying its type. There are enough differences between this language and IT to make mechanical translation nontrivial.

The Arrival of FORTRAN

During all this time the ongoing work on FORTRAN was widely publicized. Max Goldstein may have summed up the feelings of many people when he made the following remark in June 1956: "As far as automatic programming goes, we have given it some thought and in the scientific spirit we intend to try out FORTRAN when it is available. However ..." [GO 56, page 40].

The day was coming. October 1956 witnessed another "first" in the history of programming languages, namely, the first language description that was carefully written and beautifully typeset, neatly bound with a glossy cover. It began thus [IB 56]:

This manual supersedes all earlier information about the FOR-TRAN system. It describes the system which will be made available during late 1956, and is intended to permit planning and FORTRAN coding in advance of that time [page 1].

Object programs produced by FORTRAN will be nearly as efficient as those written by good programmers [page 2].

"Late 1956" was, of course, a euphemism for April 1957. Here is how Saul Rosen described FORTRAN's debut [RO 64, page 4]:

Like most of the early hardware and software systems, FOR-TRAN was late in delivery, and didn't really work when it was delivered. At first people thought it would never be done. Then when it was in field test with many bugs, and with some of the most important parts unfinished many thought it would never work. It gradually got to the point where a program in FOR-TRAN had a reasonable expectancy of compiling all the way through and maybe even of running.

In spite of these difficulties, FORTRAN I was clearly worth waiting for; it soon was accepted even more enthusiastically than its proponents had dreamed [BA 58, page 246]:

A survey in April of this year [1958] of twenty-six 704 installations indicates that over half of them use FORTRAN for more than half of their problems. Many use it for 80% or more of their work (particularly the newer installations) and almost all use it for some of their work. The latest records of the 704 users' organization, SHARE, show that there are some sixty installations equipped to use FORTRAN (representing 66 machines) and recent reports of usage indicate that more than half the machine instructions for these machines are being produced by FORTRAN.

On the other hand, not everyone had been converted. The second edition of programming's first textbook, by Wilkes, Wheeler, and Gill, was published in 1957, and the authors concluded their newly added chapter on "automatic programming" with the following cautionary remarks [WW 57, pages 136–137]:

The machine might accept formulas written in ordinary mathematical notation, and punched on a specially designed keyboard perforator. This would appear at first sight to be a very significant development, promising to reduce greatly the labor of programming. A number of schemes of formula recognition have been described or proposed, but on examination they are found to be of more limited utility than might have been hoped. ... The best that one could expect a general purpose formula-recognition routine to do, would be to accept a statement of the problem after it had been examined, and if necessary transformed, by a numerical analyst. ... Even in more favorable cases, experienced programmers will be able to obtain greater efficiency by using more conventional methods of programming.

An excellent paper by the authors of FORTRAN I, describing both the language and the organization of the compiler, was presented at the Western Joint Computer Conference in 1957 [BB 57]. The new techniques for global program flow analysis and optimization, due to Robert A. Nelson, Irving Ziller, Lois M. Haibt, and Sheldon Best, were particularly important. By expressing TPK in FORTRAN I we can see most of the changes to FORTRAN 0 that had been adopted:

```
C   THE TPK ALGORITHM, FORTRAN STYLE
    FUNF(T) = SQRTF(ABSF(T))+5.0*T**3
    DIMENSION A(11)
1   FORMAT(6F12.4)
    READ 1, A
    DO 10 J = 1, 11
    I = 11 - J
    Y = FUNF(A(I+1))
    IF (400.0-Y) 4, 8, 8
4   PRINT 5, I
5   FORMAT(I10, 10H TOO LARGE)
    GO TO 10
8   PRINT 9, I, Y
9   FORMAT(I10, F12.7)
10  CONTINUE
    STOP 52525
```

The chief innovations were

1) Provision for comments: No programming language designer had thought to do this before! (Assembly languages had comment cards, but programs in higher-level languages were generally felt to be self-explanatory.)

2) Arithmetic statement functions were introduced. These were not mentioned in [IB 56], but they appeared in [BB 57] and (in detail) in the Programmer's Primer [IB 57, pages 25 and 30–31].

3) Formats were provided for input and output. This feature, due to Roy Nutt, was a major innovation in programming languages; it probably had a significant effect in making FORTRAN popular, since input-output conversions were otherwise very awkward to express on the 704.

4) Lesser features not present in [IB 54] were the `CONTINUE` statement, and the ability to display a five-digit *octal* number when the machine halted at a `STOP` statement.

MATH-MATIC and FLOW-MATIC

Meanwhile, Grace Hopper's programming group at UNIVAC had also been busy. They had begun to develop an algebraic language in 1955, a project that was headed by Charles Katz, and the compiler was released to two installations for experimental tests in 1956 (see [BE 57, page 112]). The language was originally called AT-3; but it received the catchier name MATH-MATIC in April 1957, when its preliminary manual [AB 57] was released. The following program for TPK gives MATH-MATIC's flavor:

```
 (1)  READ-ITEM A(11) .
 (2)  VARY I 10(-1)0 SENTENCE 3 THRU 10 .
 (3)  J = I+1 .
 (4)  Y = SQR |A(J)| + 5*A(J)³ .
 (5)  IF Y > 400 JUMP TO SENTENCE 8 .
 (6)  PRINT-OUT I, Y .
 (7)  JUMP TO SENTENCE 10 .
 (8)  Z = 999 .
 (9)  PRINT-OUT I, Z .
(10)  IGNORE .
(11)  STOP .
```

The language was quite readable; notice the vertical bar and the superscript 3 in sentence (4), indicating an extended character set that could be used with some peripheral devices. But the MATH-MATIC programmers did *not* share the FORTRAN group's enthusiasm for efficient machine code; they translated MATH-MATIC source language into A-3 (an extension of A-2), and this produced extremely inefficient programs, especially when we consider the fact that arithmetic was all done by floating point subroutines. The UNIVAC computer was no match for an IBM 704 even when it was expertly programmed, so MATH-MATIC was of limited utility.

The other product of Grace Hopper's programming staff was far more influential and successful, since it broke important new ground. This was what she originally called the data processing compiler in January, 1955; it was soon to be known as 'B-0', later as the "Procedure Translator" [KM 57], and finally as FLOW-MATIC [HO 58, TA 60]. The FLOW-MATIC language used English words, somewhat as MATH-MATIC did but more so, and its operations concentrated on business applications. The following examples are typical of FLOW-MATIC operations:

```
(1) COMPARE PART-NUMBER (A) TO PART-NUMBER (B); IF
    GREATER GO TO OPERATION 13; IF EQUAL GO TO
    OPERATION 4; OTHERWISE GO TO OPERATION 2 .
(2) READ-ITEM B; IF END OF DATA GO TO OPERATION 10 .
```

The allowable English templates are shown in [SA 69, pages 317–322].

The first experimental B-0 compiler was operating in 1956 [HO 58, page 171], and it was released to UNIVAC customers in 1958 [SA 69, page 316]. FLOW-MATIC had a significant effect on the design of COBOL in 1959.

A Formula-Controlled Computer

At the international computing colloquium in Dresden, 1955, Klaus Samelson presented the rudiments of a particularly elegant approach to algebraic formula recognition [SA 55], improving on Böhm's technique. Samelson and his colleague F. L. Bauer developed this method during the ensuing years, and their subsequent paper describing it [SB 59] became well known.

One of the first things they did with their approach was to design a computer in which algebraic formulas *themselves* were the machine language. This computer design was submitted to the German patent office in the spring of 1957 [BS 57], and to the U.S. patent office (with the addition of wiring diagrams) a year later. Although the German patent was never granted, and the machines were never actually constructed, Bauer and Samelson eventually received U.S. Patent 3,047,228 for this work [BS 62].

Their patent describes four possible levels of language and machine. At the lowest level they introduced something like the language used on pocket calculators of the 1970s, allowing formulas that consist only of operators, parentheses, and numbers; their highest level included provision for a full-fledged programming language incorporating such features as variables with multiple subscripts, and decimal arithmetic with arbitrary precision.

The language of Bauer and Samelson's highest-level machine is of principal concern to us here. A program for TPK could be entered on its keyboard by typing the following:

$$
\begin{array}{lll}
01 & \diamond & 0000.00000000 \Rightarrow a{\downarrow}11{\uparrow} \\
02 & & 2.27 \Rightarrow a{\downarrow}1{\uparrow} \\
& \cdots & \\
12 & & 5.28764 \Rightarrow a{\downarrow}11{\uparrow} \\
13 & & 10 \Rightarrow i \\
14 & 44* & a{\downarrow}i{+}1{\uparrow} \Rightarrow t \\
15 & & \sqrt{\mathrm{B}t} + 5 \times t \times t \times t \Rightarrow y \\
16 & & i = \square\square \Rightarrow i \\
17 & & y > 400 \to 77* \\
18 & & y = \square\square\square.\square\square\square \Rightarrow y \\
19 & & \to 88* \\
20 & 77* & 999 = \square\square\square \Rightarrow y \\
21 & 88* & i - 1 \Rightarrow i \\
22 & & i > -1 \to 44*
\end{array}
$$

(This is the American version; the German version would be the same if all the decimal points were replaced by commas.)

The "$\diamond$" at the beginning of this program is optional; it means that the ensuing statements up to the next label (44*) will not enter the machine's "formula storage," they will simply be performed and forgotten. The remainder of line *01* specifies storage allocation; it says that a is an 11-element array whose entries will contain at most 12 digits.

Lines *02–12* enter the data into array a. The machine also included a paper-tape reader in addition to its keyboard input; and if the data were to be entered from paper tape, lines *02–12* could be replaced by the code

$$
\begin{array}{ll}
& 1 \Rightarrow i \\
33* & \bullet\bullet\bullet\bullet\bullet\bullet \Rightarrow a{\downarrow}i{\uparrow} \\
& i + 1 \Rightarrow i \\
& i < 12 \to 33*
\end{array}
$$

Actually this input convention was not specifically mentioned in the patent, but Bauer [BA 76′] recalls that such a format was intended.

The symbols $\downarrow$ and $\uparrow$ for subscripts would be entered on the keyboard but they would not actually appear on the printed page; instead, the printing mechanism was intended to shift up and down. The equal signs followed by square boxes on lines *16*, *18*, and *20* indicate output of a specified number of digits, showing the desired decimal point location. The rest of the program above should be self-explanatory, except perhaps for the B in line *15*, which denotes absolute value (*Betrag*).

Summary

We have now reached the end of our story, having covered essentially every high-level language whose design began before 1957. It is impossible to summarize all of the languages we have discussed by preparing a neat little chart; but everybody likes to see a neat little chart, so here is an attempt at a rough but perhaps meaningful comparison (see Table 1).

Table 1 shows the principal mathematically oriented languages we have discussed, together with their chief authors and approximate year of greatest research or development activity. The "arithmetic" column shows X for languages that deal with integers, F for languages that deal with floating-point numbers, and S for languages that deal with scaled numbers. The remaining columns of Table 1 are filled with highly subjective "ratings" of the languages and associated programming systems according to various criteria.

> Implementation: Was the language implemented on a real computer? If so, how efficient and/or easy was it to use?

> Readability: How easy is it to read programs in the language? (This aspect includes such things as the variety of symbols usable for variables, and the closeness to familiar notations.)

> Control structures: At how high a level are the control structures? Are the existing control structures sufficiently powerful? (By "high level" we mean a level of abstraction — something that the language has but the machine does not.)

> Data structures: At how high a level are the data structures? (For example, can variables be subscripted?)

> Machine independence: How much does a programmer need to keep in mind about the underlying machine?

> Impact: How many people are known to have been directly influenced by this work at the time?

Finally there is a column of "firsts," which states some new thing(s) that this particular language or system introduced.

The Sequel

What have we not seen, among all these languages? The most significant gaps are the lack of high-level *data structures* other than arrays (except in Zuse's unpublished language); the lack of high-level *control structures* other than iteration controlled by an index variable; and the lack of *recursion*. These three concepts, which now are considered absolutely fundamental in computer science, did not find their way into high-level languages until the 1960s. Our languages today probably have too many features, but the languages up to FORTRAN I had too few.

TABLE 1

Language	Principal author(s)	Year	Arithmetic	Implementation	Readability	Control structures	Data structures	Machine independence	Impact	First
Plankalkül	Zuse	1945	X, S, F	F	D	B	A	B	C	Programming language, hierarchic data
Flow diagrams	Goldstine & von Neumann	1946	X, S	F	A	D	C	B	A	Accepted programming methodology
Composition	Curry	1948	X	F	D	C	D	C	F	Code generation algorithm
Short Code	Mauchly	1950	F	C	C	F	F	B	D	High-level language implemented
Intermediate PL	Burks	1950	?	F	A	D	C	A	F	Common subexpression notation
Klammer-ausdrücke	Rutishauser	1951	F	F	B	F	C	B	B	Simple code generation, loop expansion
Formules	Böhm	1951	X	F	B	D	C	B	D	Compiler in own language
AUTOCODE	Glennie	1952	X	C	C	C	C	D	D	Useful compiler
A-2	Hopper	1953	F	C	D	F	F	C	B	Macroexpander
Whirlwind translator	Laning & Zierler	1953	F	B	A	D	C	A	B	Constants in formulas, manual for novices
AUTOCODE	Brooker	1954	X, F	A	B	D	C	A	C	Clean two-level storage
ПП-2	Kamynin & Liubimskii	1954	F	B	C	D	C	B	D	Code optimization
ПП	Ershov	1955	F	B	B	C	C	B	C	Book about a compiler
BACAIC	Grems & Porter	1955	F	A	A	D	F	A	D	Use on two machines
Kompiler 2	Elsworth & Kuhn	1955	S	C	C	D	C	C	F	Scaling aids
PACT I	Working Committee	1955	X, S	A	C	D	C	A	C	Cooperative effort
ADES	Blum	1956	X, F	D	D	B	C	A	F	Declarative language
IT	Perlis	1956	X, F	A	B	C	C	A	A	Successful compiler
FORTRAN I	Backus	1956	X, F	A	A	C	C	A	A	I/O formats, comments, global optimization
MATH-MATIC	Katz	1956	F	B	A	C	C	A	D	Heavy use of English
Patent 3,047,228	Bauer & Samelson	1957	F	D	B	D	C	B	C	Formula-controlled computer

At the time our story leaves off, explosive growth in language development was about to take place, since the successful compilers touched off a language boom. Programming languages had reached a stage when people began to write translators from IT to FORTRAN [GR 58] and from FORTRAN to IT; see [IB 57′] and [BO 58], which describe the FOR-TRANSIT compiler, developed by Robert W. Bemer, David A. Hemmes, Otto Alexander, Florence H. Pessin, and Leroy May. An excellent survey of the state of automatic programming at the time was prepared by R. W. Bemer [BE 57].

Perhaps the most significant development then in the wind was an international project attempting to define a "standard" algorithmic language. Just after an important meeting in Darmstadt, 1955, a group of European computer scientists began to plan a new language (see [LE 55]), under the auspices of the Gesellschaft für Angewandte Mathematik und Mechanik (GAMM, the Association for Applied Mathematics and Mechanics). They later invited American participation, and an ad hoc ACM committee chaired by Alan Perlis met several times beginning in January 1958. During the summer of that year, Zürich was the site of a meeting attended by representatives of the American and European committees: J. W. Backus, F. L. Bauer, H. Bottenbruch, C. Katz, A. J. Perlis, H. Rutishauser, K. Samelson, and J. H. Wegstein. (See [BB 58] for the language proposed by the European delegates.)

It seems fitting to bring our story to a close by stating the TPK algorithm in the "international algebraic language" (IAL, later called ALGOL 58) developed at that historic Zürich meeting [PS 58]:

```
procedure TPK (a[ ]) =: b[ ];
array (a[0:10], b[0:21]);
comment Given 11 input values a[0],...,a[10], this procedure
            produces 22 output values b[0],...,b[21], according
            to the classical TPK algorithm;
begin for i := 10(−1)0;
   begin   y := f(a[i]);
           f(t) := sqrt(abs(t)) + 5 × t↑3↓;
           if (y > 400); y := 999;
           b[20 − 2 × i] := i;
           b[21 − 2 × i] := y
   end;
   return;
   integer (i)
end TPK
```

The preparation of this paper was supported in part by National Science Foundation Grant MCS 72-03752 A03, by Office of Naval Research contract N00014-76-C-0330, and by IBM Corporation. The authors wish to thank the originators of the languages cited for their many helpful comments on early drafts of this paper.

References

[AB 57] R. Ash, E. Broadwin, V. Della Valle, C. Katz, M. Greene, A. Jenny, and L. Yu, *Preliminary Manual for MATH-MATIC and ARITH-MATIC systems (for Algebraic Translation and Compilation for UNIVAC I and II)* (Philadelphia, Pennsylvania: Remington Rand Univac, 1957), ii + 125 pages.

[AL 54] Charles W. Adams and J. H. Laning, Jr., "The M.I.T. systems of automatic coding: Comprehensive, Summer Session, and Algebraic," *Symposium on Automatic Programming for Digital Computers* (Washington: Office of Naval Research, 1954), 40–68. [Although Laning is listed as co-author, he did not write the paper or attend the conference; in fact, he states that he learned of his "coauthorship" only 10 or 15 years later!]

[BA 54] J. W. Backus, "The IBM 701 Speedcoding system," *Journal of the Association for Computing Machinery* **1** (1954), 4–6.

[BA 58] J. W. Backus, "Automatic programming: Properties and performance of FORTRAN systems I and II," in *Mechanisation of Thought Processes*, National Physical Laboratory Symposium 10 (London: Her Majesty's Stationery Office, 1959), 231–255.

[BA 59] J. W. Backus, "The syntax and semantics of the proposed International Algebraic Language of the Zürich ACM–GAMM conference," in *International Conference on Information Processing*, Proceedings (Paris: UNESCO, 1959), 125–131.

[BA 61] Philip Morrison and Emily Morrison (eds.), *Charles Babbage and his Calculating Engines* (New York: Dover, 1961), xxxviii + 400 pages.

[BA 76] John Backus, "Programming in America in the 1950s — Some personal impressions," in *A History of Computing in the Twentieth Century*, edited by N. Metropolis, J. Howlett, and Gian-Carlo Rota (New York: Academic Press, 1980), 125–135.

[BA 76'] F. L. Bauer, letter to D. E. Knuth (7 July 1976), 2 pages.

[BA 79] John Backus, "The history of FORTRAN I, II, and III," *Annals of the History of Computing* **1** (1979), 21–37. Extended in *History of Programming Languages*, edited by Richard L. Wexelblat (New York: Academic Press, 1981), 25–73.

[BB 57] J. W. Backus, R. J. Beeber, S. Best, R. Goldberg, L. M. Haibt, H. L. Herrick, R. A. Nelson, D. Sayre, P. B. Sheridan, H. Stern, I. Ziller, R. A. Hughes, and R. Nutt, "The FORTRAN automatic coding system," *Proceedings of the Western Joint Computer Conference* **11** (1957), 188–197.

[BB 58] F. L. Bauer, H. Bottenbruch, H. Rutishauser, and K. Samelson, "Proposal for a universal language for the description of computing processes," in *Computer Programming and Artificial Intelligence*, edited by John W. Carr III (Ann Arbor, Michigan: College of Engineering, University of Michigan, 1958), 353–373. [Translation of an original German draft dated 9 May 1958, in Zürich.]

[BC 54] Arthur W. Burks, Irving M. Copi, and Don W. Warren, *Languages for Analysis of Clerical Problems*, Informal Memorandum 5 (Ann Arbor, Michigan: Engineering Research Institute, University of Michigan, 1954), iii + 24 pages.

[BE 57] R. W. Bemer, "The status of automatic programming for scientific problems," *Computer Applications Symposium* **4** (Chicago, Illinois: Armour Research Foundation, 1957), 107–117.

[BG 53] J. M. Bennett and A. E. Glennie, "Programming for high-speed digital calculating machines," in *Faster Than Thought*, edited by B. V. Bowden (London: Pitman, 1953), 101–113.

[BH 54] John W. Backus and Harlan Herrick, "IBM 701 Speedcoding and other automatic-programming systems," *Symposium on Automatic Programming for Digital Computers* (Washington: Office of Naval Research, 1954), 106–113.

[BH 64] J. W. Backus and W. P. Heising, "FORTRAN," *IEEE Transactions on Electronic Computers* **EC-13** (1964), 382–385.

[BL 56] E. K. Blum, *Automatic Digital Encoding System. II (ADES II)*, NAVORD Report 4209, Aeroballistic Research Report 326 (Washington: U.S. Naval Ordnance Laboratory, 8 February 1956), v + 45 pages plus appendices.

[BL 56′] E. K. Blum, "Automatic Digital Encoding System, II," *Symposium on Advanced Programming Methods for Digital Computers*, ONR Symposium Report ACR-15 (Washington: Office of Naval Research, 1956), 71–76.

[BL 56″] E. K. Blum, "Automatic Digital Encoding System, II (ADES II)," *Proceedings of the ACM National Meeting* **11** (1956), paper 29, 4 pages.

[BL 57] E. K. Blum, *Automatic Digital Encoding System II (ADES II), Part 2: The Encoder*, NAVORD Report 4411 (Washington: U.S. Naval Ordnance Laboratory, 29 November 1956), 82 pages plus appendix.

[BL 57′] E. K. Blum and Shane Stern, *An ADES Encoder for the IBM 650 Calculator*, NAVORD Report 4412 (Washington: U.S. Naval Ordnance Laboratory, 19 December 1956), 15 pages.

[BO 52] Corrado Böhm, "Calculatrices digitales: Du déchiffrage de formules logico-mathématiques par la machine même dans la conception du programme [Digital computers: On the deciphering of logical-mathematical formulae by the machine itself during the conception of the program]," *Annali di Matematica Pura ed Applicata* (4) **37** (1954), 175–217.

[BO 52′] Corrado Böhm, "Macchina calcolatrice digitale a programma con programma preordinato fisso con tastiera algebrica ridotta atta a comporre formule mediante la combinazione dei singoli elementi simbolici [Programmable digital computer with a fixed preset program and with an algebraic keyboard able to compose formulae by means of the combination of single symbolic elements]," Domanda di brevetto per invenzione industriale [Patent application] No. 13567 di Verbale (Milan: 1 October 1952), 26 pages plus 2 tables.

[BO 54] Corrado Böhm, "Sulla programmazione mediante formule [On programming by means of formulas]," *Atti 4° Sessione Giornate della Scienza*, supplement to *La ricerca scientifica* (Rome: 1954), 1008–1014.

[BO 58] B. C. Borden, "FORTRANSIT, a universal automatic coding system," *Canadian Conference for Computing and Data Processing* (Toronto: University of Toronto Press, 1958), 349–359.

[BP 52] J. M. Bennett, D. G. Prinz, and M. L. Woods, "Interpretative sub-routines," *Proceedings of the ACM National Meeting* (Toronto: 1952), 81–87.

[BR 55] R. A. Brooker, "An attempt to simplify coding for the Manchester electronic computer," *British Journal of Applied Physics* **6** (1955), 307–311. [This paper was received in March 1954.]

[BR 56] R. A. Brooker, "The programming strategy used with the Manchester University Mark I computer," *Proceedings of the Institution of Electrical Engineers* **103**, Supplement, Part B, Convention on Digital Computer Techniques (London: 1956), 151–157.

[BR 58] R. A. Brooker, "The Autocode programs developed for the Manchester University computers," *The Computer Journal* **1** (1958), 15–21.

[BR 58'] R. A. Brooker, "Some technical features of the Manchester Mercury AUTOCODE programme," in *Mechanisation of Thought Processes*, National Physical Laboratory Symposium 10 (London: Her Majesty's Stationery Office, 1959), 201–229.

[BR 60] R. A. Brooker, "MERCURY Autocode: Principles of the program library," *Annual Review in Automatic Programming* **1** (1960), 93–110.

[BS 57] Friedrich Ludwig Bauer and Klaus Samelson, "Verfahren zur automatischen Verarbeitung von kodierten Daten und Rechenmaschine zur Ausübung des Verfahrens," *Auslegeschrift 1094019* (Deutsches Patentamt, 30 March 1957, published December 1960), 26 columns plus 6 figures.

[BS 62] Friedrich Ludwig Bauer and Klaus Samelson, "Automatic computing machines and method of operation," *U.S. Patent 3,047,228* (31 July 1962), 32 columns plus 17 figures.

[BU 50] Arthur W. Burks, "The logic of programming electronic digital computers," *Industrial Mathematics* **1** (1950), 36–52.

[BU 51] Arthur W. Burks, *An Intermediate Program Language as an Aid in Program Synthesis*, Report for Burroughs Adding Machine Company (Ann Arbor, Michigan: Engineering Research Institute, University of Michigan, 1951), ii + 15 pages.

[BW 53] R. A. Brooker and D. J. Wheeler, "Floating operations on the EDSAC," *Mathematical Tables and Other Aids to Computation* **7** (1953), 37–47.

[BW 72] F. L. Bauer and H. Wössner, "The 'Plankalkül' of Konrad Zuse: A forerunner of today's programming languages," *Communications of the ACM* **15** (1972), 678–685.

[CH 36] Alonzo Church, "An unsolvable problem of elementary number theory," *American Journal of Mathematics* **58** (1936), 345–363.

[CK 56] J. Chipps, M. Koschmann, S. Orgel, A. Perlis, and J. Smith, "A mathematical language compiler," *Proceedings of the ACM National Meeting* **11** (1956), paper 30, 4 pages.

[CL 61] R. F. Clippinger, "FACT — A business compiler: Description and comparison with COBOL and Commercial Translator," *Annual Review in Automatic Programming* **2** (1961), 231–292.

[CU 48] Haskell B. Curry, *On the Composition of Programs for Automatic Computing*, Memorandum 9806 (Silver Spring, Maryland: Naval Ordnance Laboratory, 1949), 52 pages. [Written in July 1948.]

[CU 50] H. B. Curry, *A Program Composition Technique as Applied to Inverse Interpolation*, Memorandum 10337 (Silver Spring, Maryland: Naval Ordnance Laboratory, 1950), 98 pages plus 3 figures.

[CU 50′] H. B. Curry, "The logic of program composition," *Applications Scientifiques de la Logique Mathématique: Actes de 2e Colloque International de Logique Mathématique, Paris, 25–30 Août 1952* (Paris: Gauthier–Villars, 1954), 97–102. [Paper written in March 1950.]

[EK 55] A. Kenton Elsworth, Robert Kuhn, Leona Schloss, and Kenneth Tiede, *Manual for KOMPILER 2*, Report UCRL-4585 (Livermore, California: University of California Radiation Laboratory, 7 November 1955), 66 pages.

[ER 58] A. P. Ershov, Программирующая Программа для Быстродействующей Электронной Счетной Машины = *Programmirui͡ushchai͡a Programma dli͡a Bystrodeĭstvui͡ushcheĭ Elektronnoĭ Schetnoĭ Mashiny* (Moscow: USSR Academy of Sciences, 1958), 116 pages. English translation, *Programming Programme for the BESM Computer*, translated by M. Nadler (London: Pergamon, 1959), v + 158 pages.

[ER 58′] A. P. Ershov, "The work of the Computing Centre of the Academy of Sciences of the USSR in the field of automatic programming," in *Mechanisation of Thought Processes*, National Physical Laboratory Symposium 10 (London: Her Majesty's Stationery Office, 1959), 257–278.

[FE 60] G. E. Felton, "Assembly, interpretive and conversion programs for PEGASUS," *Annual Review in Automatic Programming* **1** (1960), 32–57.

[GL 52] A. E. Glennie, "The automatic coding of an electronic computer," unpublished lecture notes (14 December 1952), 15 pages. [This lecture was delivered at Cambridge University in February 1953.]

[GL 52'] A. E. Glennie, *Automatic Coding*, unpublished manuscript (undated, probably 1952), 18 pages. [This appears to be a draft of a user's manual to be entitled "The Routine AUTO-CODE and Its Use."]

[GL 65] Alick E. Glennie, letter to D. E. Knuth (15 September 1965), 6 pages.

[GO 54] Saul Gorn, "Planning universal semi-automatic coding," *Symposium on Automatic Programming for Digital Computers* (Washington: Office of Naval Research, 1954), 74–83.

[GO 56] Max Goldstein, "Computing at Los Alamos, Group T-1," *Symposium on Advanced Programming Methods for Digital Computers*, ONR Symposium Report ACR-15 (Washington: Office of Naval Research, 1956), 39–43.

[GO 57] Saul Gorn, "Standardized programming methods and universal coding," *Journal of the Association for Computing Machinery* **4** (1957), 254–273.

[GO 72] Herman H. Goldstine, *The Computer from Pascal to von Neumann* (Princeton, New Jersey: Princeton University Press, 1972), xi + 378 pages.

[GP 56] Mandalay Grems and R. E. Porter, "A truly automatic computing system," *Proceedings of the Western Joint Computer Conference* **9** (1956), 10–21.

[GR 58] Robert M. Graham, "Translation between algebraic coding languages," *Proceedings of the ACM National Meeting* **13** (1958), paper 29, 2 pages.

[GV 47] Herman H. Goldstine and John von Neumann, *Planning and Coding of Problems for an Electronic Computing Instrument: Report on the Mathematical and Logical Aspects of an Electronic Computing Instrument* (Princeton, New Jersey: Institute for Advanced Study, 1947–1948), Volume 1, iv + 69 pages; Volume 2, iv + 68 pages; Volume 3, iii + 23 pages. Reprinted in von Neumann's *Collected Works* **5**, edited by A. H. Taub (Oxford: Pergamon, 1963), 80–235.

[HA 52] Staff of the Computation Laboratory [Howard H. Aiken and 55 others], "Description of a Magnetic Drum Calculator," *The*

Annals of the Computation Laboratory of Harvard University **25** (Cambridge, Massachusetts: Harvard University Press, 1952), xi + 318 pages.

[HA 57] C. L. Hamblin, "Computer languages," *The Australian Journal of Science* **20** (1957), 135–139.

[HM 53] Grace M. Hopper and John W. Mauchly, "Influence of programming techniques on the design of computers," *Proceedings of the Institute of Radio Engineers* **41** (1953), 1250–1254.

[HO 52] Grace Murray Hopper, "The education of a computer," *Proceedings of the ACM National Meeting* (Pittsburgh, Pennsylvania: 1952), 243–250.

[HO 53] Grace Murray Hopper, "The education of a computer," *Symposium on Industrial Applications of Automatic Computing Equipment* (Kansas City, Missouri: Midwest Research Institute, 1953), 139–144.

[HO 53'] Grace M. Hopper, "Compiling routines," *Computers and Automation* **2**, 4 (May 1953), 1–5.

[HO 55] G. M. Hopper, "Automatic coding for digital computers," *Computers and Automation* **4**, 9 (September 1955), 21–24.

[HO 56] Grace M. Hopper, "The interlude 1954–1956," *Symposium on Advanced Programming Methods for Digital Computers*, ONR Symposium Report ACR-15 (Washington: Office of Naval Research, 1956), 1–2.

[HO 57] Grace M. Hopper, "Automatic programming for business applications," *Computer Applications Symposium* **4** (Chicago, Illinois: Armour Research Foundation, 1957), 45–50.

[HO 58] Grace Murray Hopper, "Automatic programming: Present status and future trends," in *Mechanisation of Thought Processes*, National Physical Laboratory Symposium 10 (London: Her Majesty's Stationery Office, 1959), 155–200.

[HO 71] C. A. R. Hoare, "Proof of a program: FIND," *Communications of the ACM* **14** (1971), 39–45.

[IB 54] Programming Research Group, I.B.M. Applied Science Division, *Specifications for The IBM Mathematical FORmula TRANslating System, FORTRAN*, Preliminary report (New York: I.B.M. Corporation, 1954), i + 29 pages.

[IB 56] J. W. Backus, R. J. Beeber, S. Best, R. Goldberg, H. L. Herrick, R. A. Hughes, L. B. Mitchell, R. A. Nelson, R. Nutt,

D. Sayre, P. B. Sheridan, H. Stern, and I. Ziller, *Programmer's Reference Manual: The FORTRAN Automatic Coding System for the IBM 704 EDPM* (New York: Applied Science Division and Programming Research Department, I.B.M. Corporation, 15 October·1956), 51 pages.

[IB 57] International Business Machines Corporation, *Programmer's Primer for FORTRAN Automatic Coding System for the IBM 704* (New York: I.B.M. Corporation, 1957), iii + 64 pages.

[IB 57′] International Business Machines Corporation, Applied Programming Department, *FOR TRANSIT: Automatic Coding System for the IBM 650* (New York: I.B.M. Corporation, 1957). See also David A. Hemmes, "FORTRANSIT recollections," *Annals of the History of Computing* **8** (1986), 70–73.

[KA 57] Charles Katz, "Systems of debugging automatic coding," in *Automatic Coding*, Franklin Institute Monograph No. 3 (Lancaster, Pennsylvania: 1957), 17–27.

[KL 58] S. S. Kamynin, E. Z. Lîubimskiĭ, and M. R. Shura-Bura, "Об автоматизации программирования при помощи программирующей программы = Ob avtomatizatsii programmirovaniîa pri pomoshchi programmiruîûshcheĭ programmy," *Problemy Kibernetiki* **1** (1958), 135–171. English translation, "Automatic programming with a programming programme," *Problems of Cybernetics* **1** (1960), 149–191.

[KM 57] Henry Kinzler and Perry M. Moskowitz, "The procedure translator — A system of automatic programming," in *Automatic Coding*, Franklin Institute Monograph No. 3 (Lancaster, Pennsylvania: 1957), 39–55.

[KN 64] Donald E. Knuth, "Backus Normal Form vs. Backus Naur Form," *Communications of the ACM* **7** (1964), 735–736. [Reprinted as Chapter 2 of the present volume.]

[KN 68] Donald E. Knuth, *Fundamental Algorithms*, Volume 1 of *The Art of Computer Programming* (Reading, Massachusetts: Addison–Wesley, 1968), xxi + 634 pages.

[KN 69] Donald E. Knuth, *Seminumerical Algorithms*, Volume 2 of *The Art of Computer Programming* (Reading, Massachusetts: Addison–Wesley, 1969), xi + 624 pages.

[KN 72] Donald E. Knuth, "Ancient Babylonian algorithms," *Communications of the ACM* **15** (1972), 671–677; **19** (1976), 108.

[Reprinted as Chapter 11 of *Selected Papers on Computer Science*, CSLI Lecture Notes 59 (Stanford, California: Center for the Study of Language and Information, 1996), 185–203.]

[KO 58] L. N. Korolev, "Some methods of automatic coding for BESM and STRELA computers," in *Computer Programming and Artificial Intelligence*, edited by John W. Carr III (Ann Arbor, Michigan: College of Engineering, University of Michigan, 1958), 489–507.

[LA 65] J. H. Laning, letter to D. E. Knuth (13 January 1965), 1 page.

[LA 76] J. H. Laning, letter to D. E. Knuth (2 July 1976), 11 pages.

[LE 55] N. Joachim Lehmann, "Bemerkungen zur Automatisierung der Programmfertigung für Rechenautomaten (Zusammenfassung)," *Elektronische Rechenmaschinen und Informationsverarbeitung*, proceedings of a conference in October 1955 at Darmstadt (Nachrichtentechnische Gesellschaft, 1956), 143. English summary on page 224.

[LJ 58] A. A. Lîâpunov, "О логических схемах программ = O logicheskikh skhemakh programm," *Problemy Kibernetiki* 1 (1958), 46–74. English translation, "The logical structure [sic] of programs," *Problems of Cybernetics* 1 (1960), 48–81.

[LM 70] J. Halcombe Laning and James S. Miller, *The MAC Algebraic Language*, Report R-681 (Cambridge, Massachusetts: Instrumentation Laboratory, Massachusetts Institute of Technology, November 1970), 23 pages.

[LU 51] Jan Łukasiewicz, *Aristotle's Syllogistic from the Standpoint of Modern Formal Logic* (Oxford: Clarendon Press, 1951), xii + 141 pages.

[LZ 54] J. H. Laning Jr. and N. Zierler, *A Program for Translation of Mathematical Equations for Whirlwind I*, Engineering Memorandum E-364 (Cambridge, Massachusetts: Instrumentation Laboratory, Massachusetts Institute of Technology, January 1954), v + 21 pages.

[MG 53] E. N. Mutch and S. Gill, "Conversion routines," in *Automatic Digital Computation*, Proceedings of a symposium at the National Physical Laboratory on 25–28 March 1953 (London: Her Majesty's Stationery Office, 1954), 74–80.

[MO 54] Nora B. Moser, "Compiler method of automatic programming," *Symposium on Automatic Programming for Digital Computers* (Washington: Office of Naval Research, 1954), 15–21.

[NA 54] U.S. Navy Mathematical Computing Advisory Panel, *Symposium on Automatic Programming for Digital Computers* (Washington: Office of Naval Research, 1954), v + 152 pages.

[OR 58] Sylvia Orgel, *Purdue Compiler: General Description* (West Lafayette, Indiana: Purdue Research Foundation, 1958), iv+33 pages.

[PE 55] A. J. Perlis, "DATATRON," transcript of a lecture given 11 August 1955, in *Digital Computers and Data Processors*, edited by J. W. Carr III and N. R. Scott (Ann Arbor, Michigan: College of Engineering, University of Michigan, 1956), Section VII.20.1.

[PE 57] Richard M. Petersen, "Automatic coding at G.E.," in *Automatic Coding*, Franklin Institute Monograph No. 3 (Lancaster, Pennsylvania: 1957), 3–16.

[PM 55] Stanley Poley and Grace Mitchell, *Symbolic Optimum Assembly Programming (SOAP)*, 650 Programming Bulletin 1, Form 22-6285-1 (New York: IBM Corporation, November 1955), 4 pages.

[PR 55] Programming Research Section, Eckert Mauchly Division, Remington Rand, "Automatic programming: The A-2 Compiler System," *Computers and Automation* **4**, 9 (September 1955), 25–29; **4**, 10 (October 1955), 15–27.

[PS 57] A. J. Perlis and J. W. Smith, "A mathematical language compiler," in *Automatic Coding*, Franklin Institute Monograph No. 3 (Lancaster, Pennsylvania: 1957), 87–102.

[PS 57'] A. J. Perlis, J. W. Smith, and H. R. Van Zoeren, *Internal Translator (IT): A Compiler for the 650* (Pittsburgh, Pennsylvania: Computation Center, Carnegie Institute of Technology, March 1957), iv + 47 + 68 + 12 pages. Part I, Programmer's Guide; Part II, Program Analysis (the complete source code listing); Part III, Addenda; flow charts were promised on page 3.12, but they may never have been completed. Reprinted in *Applications of Logic to Advanced Digital Computer Programming* (Ann Arbor, Michigan: College of Engineering, University of Michigan, 1957); this report was also available from IBM Corporation as a 650 Library Program, File Number 2.1.001. [Autobiographical note: D. E. Knuth learned about system programming by reading the program listings of Part II in the summer of 1957; this experience changed his life.]

[PS 58] A. J. Perlis and K. Samelson, "Preliminary report, International Algebraic Language," *Communications of the ACM* **1**, 12 (December 1958), 8–22. Report on the Algorithmic Language ALGOL by the ACM Committee on Programming Languages and the GAMM Committee on Programming, *Numerische Mathematik* **1** (1959), 41–60. Reprinted in *Annual Review in Automatic Programming* **1** (1960), 268–290.

[RA 73] Brian Randell, *The Origins of Digital Computers: Selected Papers* (Berlin: Springer, 1973), xvi + 464 pages.

[RO 52] Nathaniel Rochester, "Symbolic programming," *IRE Transactions on Electronic Computers* **EC-2**, 1 (March 1953), 10–15.

[RO 64] Saul Rosen, "Programming systems and languages, a historical survey," *Proceedings of the Spring Joint Computer Conference* **25** (1964), 1–16.

[RR 53] Remington Rand, Inc., *The A-2 Compiler System Operations Manual* (15 November 1953), ii + 54 pages. (Prepared by Richard K. Ridgway and Margaret H. Harper under the direction of Grace M. Hopper.)

[RR 55] Remington Rand UNIVAC, *UNIVAC Short Code*, an unpublished collection of dittoed notes. Preface by A. B. Tonik (25 October 1955), 1 page; preface by J. R. Logan (undated but apparently from 1952), 1 page; Preliminary Exposition (1952?), 22 pages, where pages 20–22 appear to be a later replacement; Short Code Supplementary Information, Topic One, 7 pages; Addenda #1–4, 9 pages.

[RU 52] Heinz Rutishauser, *Automatische Rechenplanfertigung bei programmgesteuerten Rechenmaschinen [Automatic Machine-Code Generation on Program-Directed Computers]*, Mitteilungen aus dem Institut für Angewandte Mathematik an der ETH Zürich, No. 3 (Basel: Birkhäuser, 1952), ii + 45 pages.

[RU 55] Heinz Rutishauser, "Some programming techniques for the ERMETH," *Journal of the Association for Computing Machinery* **2** (1955), 1–4.

[RU 55'] H. Rutishauser, "Maßnahmen zur Vereinfachung des Programmierens (Bericht über die in fünfjähriger Programmierungsarbeit mit der Z4 gewonnenen Erfahrungen)," *Elektronische Rechenmaschinen und Informationsverarbeitung*, proceedings of a conference in October 1955 at Darmstadt (Nachrichten-technische Gesellschaft, 1956), 26–30. English summary on page 225.

[RU 61] H. Rutishauser, "Interference with an ALGOL procedure," *Annual Review in Automatic Programming* **2** (1961), 67–76.

[RU 63] H. Rutishauser, letter to D. E. Knuth (11 October 1963), 2 pages.

[SA 55] Klaus Samelson, "Probleme der Programmierungstechnik," in *Aktuelle Probleme der Rechentechnik*, edited by N. Joachim Lehmann, Bericht über das Internationale Mathematiker-Kolloquium, Dresden, 22–25 November 1955 (Berlin: Deutscher Verlag der Wissenschaften, 1957), 61–68.

[SA 69] Jean E. Sammet, *Programming Languages: History and Fundamentals* (Englewood Cliffs, New Jersey: Prentice–Hall, 1969), xxx + 785 pages.

[SB 59] K. Samelson and F. L. Bauer, "Sequentielle Formelübersetzung," *Elektronische Rechenanlagen* **1** (1959), 176–182; "Sequential formula translation," *Communications of the ACM* **3** (1960), 76–83, 351.

[SM 73] Leland Smith, "Editing and printing music by computer," *Journal of Music Theory* **17** (1973), 292–309.

[ST 52] C. S. Strachey, "Logical or non-mathematical programmes," *Proceedings of the ACM National Meeting* (Toronto: 1952), 46–49.

[TA 56] D. Tamari, review of [BO 52], *Zentralblatt für Mathematik und ihre Grenzgebiete* **57** (1956), 107–108.

[TA 60] Alan E. Taylor, "The FLOW-MATIC and MATH-MATIC automatic programming systems," *Annual Review in Automatic Programming* **1** (1960), 196–206.

[TH 55] Bruno Thüring, "Die UNIVAC A-2 Compiler Methode der automatischen Programmierung," *Elektronische Rechenmaschinen und Informationsverarbeitung*, proceedings of a conference in October 1955 at Darmstadt (Nachrichtentechnische Gesellschaft, 1956), 154–156. English summary on page 226.

[TU 36] A. M. Turing, "On computable numbers, with an application to the Entscheidungsproblem," *Proceedings of the London Mathematical Society* (2) **42** (1936), 230–265; **43** (1937), 544–546.

[WA 54] John Waite, "Editing generators," *Symposium on Automatic Programming for Digital Computers* (Washington: Office of Naval Research, 1954), 22–29.

[WA 58] F. Way III, "Current developments in computer programming techniques," *Computer Applications Symposium* **5** (Chicago, Illinois: Armour Research Foundation, 1958), 125–132.

[WH 50] D. J. Wheeler, "Programme organization and initial orders for the EDSAC," *Proceedings of the Royal Society* **A202** (1950), 573–589.

[WI 52] M. V. Wilkes, "Pure and applied programming," *Proceedings of the ACM National Meeting* (Toronto: 1952), 121–124.

[WI 53] M. V. Wilkes, "The use of a 'floating address' system for orders in an automatic digital computer," *Proceedings of the Cambridge Philosophical Society* **49** (1953), 84–89.

[WO 51] M. Woodger, "A comparison of one and three address codes," *Manchester University Computer, Inaugural Conference* (Manchester: 1951), 19–23.

[WR 71] W. A. Wulf, D. B. Russell, and A. N. Habermann, "BLISS, a language for systems programming," *Communications of the ACM* **14** (1971), 780–790.

[WW 51] Maurice V. Wilkes, David J. Wheeler, and Stanley Gill, *The Preparation of Programs for an Electronic Digital Computer: With special reference to the EDSAC and the use of a library of subroutines* (Cambridge, Massachusetts: Addison–Wesley, 1951), xi + 170 pages. Reprinted, with an introduction by Martin Campbell-Kelly, as Volume 1 in the Charles Babbage Institute Reprint Series for the History of Computing (Los Angeles: Tomash, 1982).

[WW 57] Maurice V. Wilkes, David J. Wheeler, and Stanley Gill, *The Preparation of Programs for an Electronic Digital Computer*, second edition (Reading, Massachusetts: Addison–Wesley, 1957), xii + 238 pages.

[ZU 44] K. Zuse, "Ansätze einer Theorie des allgemeinen Rechnens unter besonderer Berücksichtigung des Aussagenkalküls und dessen Anwendung auf Relaisschaltungen [Beginnings of a theory of calculation in general, considering in particular the propositional calculus and its application to relay circuits]," manuscript prepared in 1944. Chapter 1 has been published in *Berichte der Gesellschaft für Mathematik und Datenverarbeitung* **63** (1972), Part 1, 32 pages. English translation, **106** (1976), 7–20.

[ZU 45] K. Zuse, *Der Plankalkül*, manuscript prepared in 1945. Published in *Berichte der Gesellschaft für Mathematik und Datenverarbeitung* **63** (1972), Part 3, 285 pages. English translation of all but pages 176–196, **106** (1976), 42–244.

[ZU 48] K. Zuse, "Über den Allgemeinen [sic] Plankalkül als Mittel zur Formulierung schematisch-kombinativer Aufgaben," *Archiv der Mathematik* **1** (1949), 441–449.

[ZU 59] K. Zuse, "Über den Plankalkül," *Elektronische Rechenanlagen* **1** (1959), 68–71.

[ZU 72] Konrad Zuse, "Kommentar zum Plankalkül," *Berichte der Gesellschaft für Mathematik und Datenverarbeitung* **63** (1972), Part 2, 36 pages. English translation, **106** (1976), 21–41.

Addendum

Another language, PACT I, deserves to be part of the story as well, so it has been included in Table 1 above although it was unfortunately missed by the authors when we first compiled this history. The "Project for the Advancement of Coding Techniques" was a joint effort between programmers from many different installations of IBM 701 computers in Southern California, as they sought ways to make their programs more easily coded, debugged, and portable to future machines without introducing run-time inefficiency.

Their solution was to introduce a nearly machine-independent language with one step per card and automatic scaling of fixed-point arithmetic. For example, TPK would look like this:

Region	Step	Op	Clue	Factor	S_1	S_2	
F	1			X			[Take X]
F	2	ABS					[Compute the absolute value]
F	3	SQRT					[Compute the square root]
F	10			X			[Take X]
F	11	X					[Multiply by itself]
F	12	X		X			[Multiply by X]
F	13	X		5			[Multiply by 5]
F	20	+	R	3			[Add the result of step 3]
F	30	EQ		Y			[Store in Y]

TPK	0	READ					[Read all data cards]
TPK	2				11		[Take 11]
TPK	3	EQ			II		[Store in II]
TPK	4	SET		I	1		[Begin loop, with $I = 1$]
TPK	6	USE		J	II		[Begin nonloop, with $J = II$]
TPK	10			A	J		[Take A_J]
TPK	11	EQ			X		[Store in X]
TPK	12	DO			F		[Perform F]
TPK	15		N		Y		[Take the negative of Y]
TPK	16	+			400		[Add 400]
TPK	17	TP			25		[Transfer to step 25 if ≥ 0]
TPK	18				999		[Take 999]
TPK	19	EQ			Y		[Store in Y]
TPK	25	LIST					[Print II and Y]
TPK	26	ID			II		
TPK	27	ID			Y		
TPK	30				II		[Take II]
TPK	31	-			1		[Subtract 1]
TPK	32	EQ			II		[Store in II]
TPK	33	TEST			II	11	[$I \leftarrow I+1$, repeat loop if ≤ 11]
TPK	40	HALT					[Stop]

Variable	Q	D_1	D_2	
X	25			[X has 25 fraction bits]
Y	25			[Y has 25 fraction bits]
II	0			[II is an integer]
A	25	11		[$A_1, \ldots, A_{11}$ have 25 fraction bits]

Details can be found in a series of seven articles by some of the principal contributors: Wesley S. Melahn, "A description of a cooperative venture in the production of an automatic coding system," *Journal of the Association for Computing Machinery* **3** (1956), 266–271; Charles L. Baker, "The PACT I coding system for the IBM Type 701," *Journal of the Association for Computing Machinery* **3** (1956), 272–278; Owen R. Mock, "Logical organization of the PACT I compiler," *Journal of the Association for Computing Machinery* **3** (1956), 279–287; Robert C. Miller, Jr., and Bruce G. Oldfield, "Producing computer instructions for the PACT I compiler," *Journal of the Association for Computing Machinery* **3** (1956), 288–291; Gus Hempstead and Jules I. Schwartz, "PACT loop expansion," *Journal of the Association for Computing Machinery* **3** (1956), 292–298; J. I. Derr and R. C. Luke, "Semi-automatic allocation of data storage for PACT I," *Journal of the Association for Computing Machinery* **3** (1956), 299–308; I. D. Greenwald and H. G. Martin, "Conclusions after using the PACT I advanced coding technique," *Journal of the Association for Computing Machinery* **3** (1956), 309–313.

This project was accomplished through joint effort on the part of many companies where competition is extremely high and almost all discoveries and techniques are considered proprietary information. In the midst of this highly competitive industry, a group of far-sighted men in charge of computing groups realized a need for a better coding technique and established what is now known as the Project for the Advancement of Coding Techniques. The formation of the project was unique, and, we feel, the result of the project is also unique. And it is our sincere desire that the spirit of cooperation exemplified here will continue and possibly prove contagious.

One of the first fruits of this cooperation was the founding late in 1955 of SHARE, the first computer users' organization. See Paul Armer, "SHARE, a eulogy to cooperative effort," *Annals of the History of Computing* **2** (1980), 122–129, the transcript of a lecture given in 1956; Fred J. Gruenberger, "A short history of digital computing in Southern California," *Annals of the History of Computing* **2** (1980), 246–250.

An interesting article by Martin Campbell-Kelly, "Programming the EDSAC: Early programming activity at the University of Cambridge," *Annals of the History of Computing* **2** (1980), 7–36 [reprinted in *IEEE Annals of the History of Computing* **20**, 4 (October–December 1998), 46–67] reconstructs how the TPK algorithm might have been programmed on the EDSAC 1 in late 1949 or early 1950. David J. Wheeler has also explained how TPK would have appeared in 1958 on EDSAC 2, in an appendix to his paper "The EDSAC programming systems," *IEEE Annals of the History of Computing* **14**, 4 (1992), 34–40.

Chapter 2

Backus Normal Form versus Backus Naur Form

*[Originally published in Communications of the ACM **7** (1964), 735–736.]*

Dear Editor:

In recent years it has become customary to refer to syntax presented in the manner of the ALGOL 60 report as "Backus Normal Form." I am not sure where this terminology originated; personally I first recall reading it in a survey article by S. Gorn [2].

Several of us working in the field have never cared for the name Backus Normal Form because it isn't a "Normal Form" in the conventional sense. A normal form usually refers to some sort of special representation that is not necessarily a canonical form.

For example, any ALGOL-60-like syntax can readily be transformed so that all definitions except the definition of $\langle$empty$\rangle$ have one of the three forms

(i) $\langle A \rangle ::= \langle B \rangle \mid \langle C \rangle$, (ii) $\langle A \rangle ::= \langle B \rangle \langle C \rangle$, or (iii) $\langle A \rangle ::= a$.

A syntax in which all definitions are of this kind may be said to be in "Floyd Normal Form," since this point was first raised in a note by R. W. Floyd [1]. But I hasten to withdraw such a term from further use, since other people have doubtless used that simple fact independently in their own work, and the point is only incidental to the main considerations of Floyd's note.

Many people have objected to the term Backus Normal Form because it is just a new name for an old concept in linguistics: An equivalent type of syntax has been used under various other names (Chomsky type 2 grammar, simple phrase structure grammar, context free grammar, and so forth).

There is still a reason for distinguishing between the names, however, since linguists present the syntax in the form of productions while the Backus version has a quite different *form*. (It is a Form for a syntax,

95

not a Normal Form.) The five principal things that distinguish Backus's form from production form are:

i) Nonterminal symbols are distinguished from terminal letters by enclosing them in special brackets.

ii) All alternatives for a definition are grouped together. (That is, in a production system the three productions 'A → BC, A → d, A → C' would all be written separately, instead of combining them in the single rule '⟨A⟩ ::= ⟨B⟩⟨C⟩ | d | ⟨C⟩'.)

iii) The symbol ' ::= ' is used to separate left from right.

iv) The symbol '|' is used to separate alternatives.

v) Full names, indicating the meaning of the strings being defined, are used for nonterminal symbols.

Of these five items, (iii) is clearly irrelevant and the peculiar symbol ' ::= ' can be replaced by anything desired; ' → ' is perhaps better, to correspond more closely with productions.

But (i), (ii), (iv), and (v) are each important for the *explanatory power* of a syntax. It is quite difficult to fathom the significance of a language defined by productions, compared to the documentation afforded by a syntax that incorporates (i), (ii), (iv), and (v).

On the other hand, it is much easier to do *theoretical* manipulations by using production systems and systematically *avoiding* (i), (ii), (iv), and (v).

For these reasons, Backus's form deserves a special distinguishing name.

Actually, however, only (i) and (ii) were really used by John Backus when he proposed his notation; (iii), (iv), and (v) are due to Peter Naur, who incorporated these changes when drafting the ALGOL 60 report. Naur's additions, particularly (v), are quite important.

Furthermore, if it had not been for Naur's work in recognizing the potential of Backus's ideas and popularizing them with the ALGOL committee, Backus's work would have become virtually lost; and much of the knowledge we have today about languages and compilers would not have been acquired.

Therefore I propose that henceforth we always say "*Backus Naur Form*" instead of Backus Normal Form, when referring to such a syntax. This terminology has several advantages: (1) It gives the proper credit to both Backus and Naur. (2) It preserves the oft-used abbreviation "BNF". (3) It does not call a Form a Normal Form.

I have been saying Backus Naur Form for about two months now and am still quite pleased with it, so I think perhaps everyone else will enjoy this term also.

Donald E. Knuth
California Institute of Technology
Pasadena, California

References

[1] Robert W. Floyd, "Note on mathematical induction in phrase structure grammars," *Information and Control* **4** (1961), 353–358.

[2] Saul Gorn, "Specification languages for mechanical languages and their processors — a baker's dozen," *Communications of the ACM* **4** (1961), 532–542.

Addendum

The proposed change has been widely adopted — and with an en-dash, which makes it even better. For example, the standard reference manual for the Ada programming language [3, §1.1.4] says that Ada's context-free syntax "is described using a simple variant of Backus–Naur form." Michael Woodger has noted [5] that

> One of the key modifications made by Naur to Backus' notation was to choose the designations of the syntactic constituents, such as the "basic statement," to be exactly the same as those used in describing the semantics, without abbreviation. This is what makes the syntax readable, rather than just a useful mathematical notation, and is largely responsible for the success of "BNF" as we know it. Peter Naur was too modest to say this himself in the appendix to his paper [4].

[3] *Consolidated Ada Reference Manual: Language and Standard Libraries*, International Standard ISO/IEC 8652/1995(E) with Technical Corrigendum 1, edited by S. Tucker Taft, Robert A. Duff, Randall L. Brukardt, and Erhard Ploedereder (Berlin: Springer, 2001).

[4] Peter Naur, "The European side of the last phase of the development of ALGOL 60," in *History of Programming Languages*, edited by Richard L. Wexelblat (New York: Academic Press, 1981), 92–139, 147–170.

[5] Mike Woodger, "What does BNF stand for?" *Annals of the History of Computing* **12** (1990), 71–72.

Chapter 3

Teaching ALGOL 60

*[Originally published in ALGOL Bulletin **19** (Amsterdam: Mathematisch Centrum, January 1965), 4–6.]*

Dear Editor:

Many readers of the *ALGOL Bulletin* are directly or indirectly concerned with teaching the ALGOL 60 language. The following two exercises and/or test problems have proved to be especially instructive in the ALGOL classes that I have been teaching intermittently since the spring of 1961, so I feel they will be of interest.

Problem 1. Find all ways to write an unsigned number meaning "one," using at most five basic symbols. The ALGOL report defines unsigned numbers as follows:

⟨digit⟩ ::= 0 | 1 | 2 | 3 | 4 | 5 | 6 | 7 | 8 | 9

⟨unsigned integer⟩ ::= ⟨digit⟩ | ⟨unsigned integer⟩⟨digit⟩

⟨integer⟩ ::= ⟨unsigned integer⟩ | +⟨unsigned integer⟩
      | −⟨unsigned integer⟩

⟨decimal fraction⟩ ::= .⟨unsigned integer⟩

⟨exponent part⟩ ::= $_{10}$⟨integer⟩

⟨decimal number⟩ ::= ⟨unsigned integer⟩ | ⟨decimal fraction⟩
      | ⟨unsigned integer⟩⟨decimal fraction⟩

⟨unsigned number⟩ ::= ⟨decimal number⟩ | ⟨exponent part⟩
      | ⟨decimal number⟩⟨exponent part⟩

Examples: 1, 1.0, 001$_{10}$0, etc.; notice that '$_{10}$' is considered to be a single basic symbol. A prize will be given for any paper with 42 or more correct answers.

Problem 2. When I tried to run the following program, the compiler did not accept it. What errors have I made? [*Note:* The compiler reports that there are at least 20 bad mistakes, and it makes several other minor objections that are not clear-cut errors. You are only supposed to find errors that are specifically outlawed in the ALGOL 60 language.]

begin real I; $I := 5$;
   begin array $M[1{:}I]$;
      integer I, J, K;
      real X, Y, Z;
      Boolean P, Q, R;
      switch $S = L1$;
      real procedure $A(B, C)$;
         integer B;
         label C;
         value B;
         begin integer R;
            $X := (B \uparrow {-2}) \uparrow (-2)$;
            go to if P **then** $S[B]$ **else** $L2$;
        $L1$: $Y := P$;
          if $M(5) = X \div Y$ **then**
            for $B = 1$ **step** 0 **until** $A(B, C)$ **do**
            $L2$: **comment** now the fun **begins**;
               begin own array $N[$**if** $R = $ **true then** $2{:}10$ **else** $1{:}10]$;
               if $X \neq 0$ **then**
                  if $Y = 1$ **or** 2 **then go to** C
            end;
          return
         end procedure A;
      $X := I := 0$;
      if $X = 0$ **then**
         for $Q := $ **true, false do**
         $L3$: $Z = A(B)$ the 2nd parameter is: $(L3\,)$
      else
   end
end of program;

Remarks. Problem 1 can be used very early in a training course. It teaches not only the admissible forms of constants, but also gives important instruction on the use of syntax. Readers may convince themselves that there are precisely 41 correct solutions; exactly (11, 0, 9, 12, 6, and 3) of them have an exponent part of length (0, 1, 2, 3, 4, and 5), respectively. The solution most often missed is perhaps '$.01_{10}2$'.

Problem 2 is suitable for a final exam. This problem stresses the errors that are most commonly made, as well as a few subtle ones and a few obvious ones (to make the problem more interesting). The following errors are considered most important:

1. **array** M: No bound pairs may use variables not declared in an external block. The identifier I is declared in the present block, so its scope is clear.

2. **switch** S: '$=$' should be '$:=$'.

3. $L1$ is undeclared in the block where it has been used.

4. The **value** part should come before the specification part.

5. '$B \uparrow -2$' is not well formed according to ALGOL's syntax.

6. **else** $L2$: We aren't allowed to **go to** $L2$ from outside the **for** statement in which $L2$ is a statement label.

7. $Y := P$: Only Boolean variables can receive Boolean values.

8. '$M(5)$' should be '$M[5]$'.

9. $X \div Y$ is improper because X and Y are **real**.

10. '**for** $B =$ ' should be '**for** $B :=$ '.

11. **comment** must follow ';' or '**begin**'.

12. '**own array**' should be '**own real array**' or have some other type.

13. '2:10 **else** 1:10' should be, for example, '2 **else** 1 : 10'.

14. '**if** $Y = 1$ **or** 2' is COBOL, not ALGOL. The programmer presumably meant to say '**if** $Y = 1 \vee Y = 2$'.

15. '**then if**' is syntactically wrong, since no conditional statement may follow an **if** clause.

16. '**return**' is an undeclared procedure, or something left over from ALGOL 58.

17. $X := I := 0$: In a multiple assignment, variables must have the same type.

18. **for** $Q :=$ **true, false do**: Boolean expressions aren't allowed as elements of a **for** list.

19. $Z = :$ Again, '$=$' should be '$:=$'.

20. $A(B)$: B is not a declared identifier in this block.

21. 'the 2nd parameter' is illegal because 2 is not a letter; only letter strings are allowed within a parameter delimiter.

22. '**else**' should never complete '**then**' when a **for** statement intervenes.

23. A is a real procedure, but no assignment '$A :=$ value' appears.

24. The final semicolon does not belong there, according to the syntax for ⟨program⟩ and the comment conventions.

25. Many variables are used before any assignment of a value has been given.

26. '$R = $ **true**' is not well formed, since R has been redeclared to have integer type.

Problem 2 is also of possible interest for authors of compiler error-detection procedures.

Donald E. Knuth
Assistant Professor of Mathematics
California Institute of Technology
Pasadena, California, USA

Chapter 4

ALGOL 60 *Confidential*

*[Written with Jack N. Merner. Originally published in Communications of the ACM **4** (1961), 268–272.]*

> *I would question the ability of anybody who uses that feature.*
> —H. D. Huskey

> *Although permitted, . . . this will clearly not ordinarily be used.*
> —H. C. Thatcher, Jr.

The ALGOL 60 Report [5], when first encountered, seems to describe a very complex language that will be difficult to learn. Its "metalinguistic formulae" admirably serve the purpose of specifying a language precisely, but they are certainly not very readable for a beginner.

Experience has shown, however, that ALGOL is in fact easily approachable, once the report is explained, and that ALGOL programs are easy to write. The language is so general and powerful, it can handle an enormous class of problems. The parts of ALGOL that are present in other compiler languages are particularly simple: One quickly learns how to write assignment and **go to** and **for** statements, etc. Indeed, a lot of the unnecessary restrictions imposed by other languages have finally been lifted.

But ALGOL also allows many nonobvious things to be written, and herein lies a problem: ALGOL seems to have become too general. So many restrictions have been lifted that a lot of technical details crop up; many of its permissible constructions are hard to understand and to use correctly. In this paper some of the more obscure features of the language are considered and their usefulness is discussed. Remarks are based on the authors' interpretations of the ALGOL 60 Report.

1. Types

The expression $2 \uparrow X$, where X has been declared to be an integer variable, has either real or integer type depending on whether the value of X at running time is negative or not. This rule makes it unnecessarily difficult, on most machines,* for a compiler to decide whether to use a floating-point instruction or a fixed-point instruction, and it causes inefficient output. There seems to be no need for such generality.

2. Expressions

A procedure call within an expression might change the value of other components of the expression. For example, suppose that in $F(X, Y)$ the real procedure F stores $\cos(X)$ in Y, and that the value of the procedure is $\sin(X)$. Such a procedure is quite reasonable because people often wish to calculate both the sine and cosine of the same angle. But what then is the meaning of $F(X, Y) + Y$? Is it different from $Y + F(X, Y)$?

A strict interpretation of ALGOL would seem to require that such addition would be noncommutative, for "the sequence of operations is generally from left to right." In other words, the machine program for $F(X, Y) + Y$ would have the form

```
(CALL   F(X,Y))
FLOAT-ADD   Y
```

while the corresponding left-to-right program for $Y + F(X, Y)$ would be

```
LOAD        Y
STORE       TEMP
(CALL   F(X,Y))
FLOAT-ADD   TEMP
```

A question then arises on how to evaluate $Y + F(X, Y) \uparrow 2$. We are told to perform exponentiation before addition; so one might argue that Y should be changed before the addition. But, looking at this example together with the previous one, we see that a '+' operation is to be performed; so the left-to-right rule tells us to first evaluate its left operand Y, *then* evaluate its right operand $F(X, Y) \uparrow 2$, then perform the addition.

Furthermore, consider the Boolean expression

$$W = 0 \ \wedge \ F(X, Y) = 0$$

with respect to the same procedure F. If W is unequal to zero, must we evaluate $F(X, Y)$? We know that the value of the Boolean expression

---

* The Burroughs B5000 computer will handle integer and real values with the same operation code, but traditional machines do not.

will be false; but does Y get set to $\cos(X)$ or not? A strict interpretation of [5] would evaluate $F(X, Y)$ even when W is nonzero.

Of what value is this extra generality, when it actually causes machine implementations to be less efficient and the language to be more difficult to comprehend?

At the other extreme, there is a restriction in the formation of expressions that seems to be totally unnecessary. We are forbidden from writing $A \uparrow -2$, $X/-Y$, and so on, although such expressions are unambiguous and quite common in mathematical usage (and easy to translate into machine language).

3. Unfinished Expressions

Suppose $G(X, L)$ is a real procedure for which L is a label parameter. Can we write, for example, $Y := G(X, L)$ and then allow procedure G to 'go to L'? Although this case is not mentioned explicitly in the ALGOL Report, we believe it is not well-formed, since function designators are supposed to "define single numerical or logical values." If G exits to L, it does not define any value. Thus there seems to be no use for a designational expression as an actual parameter to a function-like procedure.

4. Labels

What good are numeric labels? In the designational expression

$$\textbf{if } Ab < c \textbf{ then } 17 \textbf{ clse } q[\textbf{if } w < 0 \textbf{ then } 2 \textbf{ else } n]$$

(which occurs at least twice in the ALGOL Report) one has to look closely to discover that 17 is a label, but 2 is not.

Programmers can get into trouble using numeric labels. Consider

$$\textbf{procedure } a(b); \quad \textbf{procedure } b; \ 2: \ b(2)$$

for example. In this procedure declaration, is 2 supposed to mean the label 2 or the number 2? As a matter of fact, the procedure parameter b might want 2 to be a label in some calls of a and a numeric value in other calls, perhaps *both* in others. Such behavior can be implemented in machine language, but is there a practical reason to do so?

It is gratifying to see that some machine implementations of ALGOL 60 (in particular Irons's PSYCO for the 1604, and Naur's DASK ALGOL [6] for the DASK computer) have ruled numeric labels out of the language. We move that they be completely abandoned.

5. The *go to* Problem

A recent article by Irons and Feurzeig [4] proposes a method to implement recursive procedures and blocks. A minor part of their overall
approach is the "Go To Interpreter," which is designed to handle a
go to leading out of a block. Closer analysis shows, however, that the
suggested Go To Interpreter must be modified to handle recursive procedures correctly.

Briefly, the method described by Irons and Feurzeig assumes that
the coding for any given block will be located sequentially in memory.
The beginning address '*blockbottom*' and ending address '*blocktop*' of the
innermost block currently being executed are kept in a last-in, first-out
list as the object program is running. When **go to** comes along, if the
address of the designational expression lies within the limits of the current interval from *blockbottom* to *blocktop*, the Go To Interpreter simply
jumps to that part of the program; otherwise it exits from the innermost block (doing the necessary things like releasing the array storage
declared there) and recycles, comparing the address against the newly
popped-up block limits.

As a simple example of where that method fails, consider:

> **procedure** $A(L)$; **label** L;
> **begin** $\cdots$; $A(K)$; $\cdots$;
> K: **go to** L; $\cdots$
> **end** A.

In this procedure the dots '$\cdots$' stand for statements by which we mean
to calculate something; and in case of trouble we want to exit to statement L. The procedure might call itself recursively, and in that case if
trouble occurs it wants to exit to K, which will then exit all the way
out to L. A little study will convince the reader that a procedure of this
kind would not be unnatural in practice. Yet if the Go To Interpreter
would try to go to K, it would not exit the procedure as it should; in
fact it would get into a tight loop.

The following solution to this **go to** problem should always work,
and it also has the advantage of not requiring the program to be stored
sequentially.

a) The value of a designational expression has three parts: a machine
address (to which we wish to jump eventually), the block number in
which this address is local, and the level of recursion to which this block
is currently nested (the number of times this block has been entered
minus the number of times it has been left).

b) The Go To Interpreter is given such a value. It compares the block number and recursion number with the topmost block number and its current recursion number; if they are equal, we simply jump, otherwise we exit from the block and start the process over, considering the new block in the same way.

6. "Undefined"

Peter Naur has recently pointed out [7] that the following sequence is undefined:

> **integer** I; $\cdots$
> **begin procedure** A; $I := I + 1$;
>   **begin real** I;
> A;
>   **end**;
> **end** A.

Here the procedure A uses a nonlocal variable I. There is nothing illegal about this; but then I is redeclared in another block, and A is called again. Perhaps the nonlocal variable I is now to be the redeclared I? No, it is undefined by virtue of the stipulation in ALGOL Report 4.7.6. We say that the call of A is "outside the scope of the outer I" although the word "outside" is probably misleading; it really is "inside a hole in the scope of the outer I."

Maybe it's good to leave such things undefined. But a programmer who writes such a procedure obviously wants A to maintain a global count of how often it has been invoked, and doesn't want the procedure to become undefined just because the name it has chosen for the counter happens to have been redeclared. Thus a more useful language would have defined the situation so that A always accesses the variable I in the scope of its declaration, not a different variable in the scope of its call.

Here is a more complicated example of something that is undefined in ALGOL 60. It is similar to the example we gave earlier for labels:

> **procedure** $A(L)$; **switch** L;
> **begin switch** $K := J$; $\cdots$;
> $A(K)$; $\cdots$;
> J: **go to** $L[1]$; $\cdots$
> **end** A.

Suppose we call A, then it calls itself recursively with K as the actual parameter, and we somehow get to statement J. At that point we want to go to $L[1]$, which is $K[1]$, which is J; but this J is *outside* the scope of the J that belonged to the switch parameter K, so the result is *undefined*, according to ALGOL Report 5.3.5. (See also paragraph 4.7.3.2. As we recursively call A we rename the local switch K to, say, K', as K is a parameter whose name conflicts with switch K. But J is not a parameter, so we do not change J to J' but we in fact go out of the scope of the outer J.)

A similar example seems to reveal an inconsistency in ALGOL 60. Consider:

> **switch** $S := J$;
> **procedure** $A(T)$; **switch** T;
> **begin** $\cdots$;
> J: **go to** $T[1]$; $\cdots$
> **end** A;
> $\cdots$
> J: $A(S)$;

We claim that this example is undefined according to the ALGOL Report, although nothing tricky has been used. For when we call $A(S)$, we can insert the identifier S into the procedure body without conflict; but we cannot legitimately call $S[1]$ outside the scope of the label J that appears in the declaration of S. This reasoning leads to a curious restriction: When using a procedure that has switches as parameters, you must make sure that none of the labels you can go to through those switches have the same identifier as a label that is local to the procedure body.

In paragraph 4.3.5 of the Report, a **go to** statement is not supposed to transfer control if the designational expression is a switch designator whose value is undefined. We sincerely hope that this "undefined" is different from the "undefined" of paragraph 5.3.5! Furthermore, just what does "undefined" mean in 4.3.5? Does it mean simply that the subscript expression is not between 1 and the number of items in the switch, or does it mean that *any* of the subscripts are out of bounds as we proceed to evaluate the designational expressions (possibly evaluating many more switches before we come to a label)? Or perhaps one of the subscript expressions is $0 \uparrow 0$ or some other undefined value?

The "**go to** an undefined switch designator" seems in any event an impossible thing to implement efficiently on a machine. The object program will have to make unnecessary tests to determine whether or not something is defined, and this effort seems wasted because the use of an undefined switch does not seem like a particularly powerful tool in the first place.

7. Own Variables and Arrays

Two major interpretations can be given to **own** quantities. Consider the following:

> **procedure** A; **begin own integer** I; $\cdots$ **end** A;
> $\cdots$; A; $\cdots$
> $\cdots$; A; $\cdots$

Are *two* **own** variables 'I' supposed to be kept, one for the first call of procedure A, the other for the second? If we are supposed to consider a procedure call as a replacement of the code for A into the program (see Report 4.7.3.3), apparently every call of A will have its own **own**.

Such behavior is the desired interpretation in several situations. For example, suppose A is a procedure that successively gives out permutations of the numbers 1 through 4 in a table, the first time outputting 1234, next 1243, next 1324, and so on. If the two calls of A are made from two *independent* parts of the program (say one part is a compiler and the other is an assembler and they work asynchronously with each other, each wanting to use A for a different purpose) we certainly would want the different calls of A to have separate **own** variables.

A second interpretation of **own** is that implicitly given by Ingerman [3] and Sattley [8], namely to have one **own** variable for the block, regardless of the number of places from which that block is called. Then those **own** quantities act as if they are nonlocal to the entire program. (Naur's letter [7], point 7, uses the phrase "local concept of ALGOL 60"; does he favor this second interpretation of **own**?)

The nonlocal **own** interpretation is desirable in a random-number-generating procedure R. An old problem given to students of the ILLIAC was to estimate π by picking points at random inside the unit square; the probability that such points would lie in the unit circle would then be about $\pi/4$. Assuming that R is a **real** procedure, which outputs a pseudo-random number between 0 and 1, the test for "inside the unit circle" would be:

$$R \uparrow 2 + R \uparrow 2 \leq 1$$

Clearly the local **own** interpretation would not be satisfactory here, for the value of R would then be the same at both points.

In general, if the calls on a procedure with **own** variables come from unrelated points of a program, the *local* interpretation will probably be preferred, but if the parts of the program are interrelated, the *nonlocal* interpretation is probably preferable.

Thatcher has pointed out in [9] that **own** quantities are virtually useless if they cannot be initialized somehow. But if we allow initialization they are very powerful indeed and easy to use. For example, the declaration

$$\textbf{own integer } I := 2$$

would mean that the **own** variable I would be set to 2 upon *first* entry to the block in which it is declared, but not changed upon subsequent reentries. The authors strongly favor the inclusion of such initialization schemes.

The *local* interpretation of **own** can become extremely complicated. First we are to distinguish between calls of a procedure from various places in the program. Then if the procedure is used recursively, we must distinguish also the various places it is called on various levels, building up a whole tree of **own** variables. The following example, constructed by Joseph Speroni, admirably illustrates what horrendous complications can occur when using a *local* interpretation of **own**. If that interpretation were taken, the following procedure would calculate the Fibonacci sequence:

```
integer procedure FIB;    begin own integer K := 1;
   integer procedure RIB;
   begin own integer L := 1;
      RIB := if L = 1 then 1 else RIB + FIB;
      L := L + 1
   end RIB;
   FIB := if K ≤ 2 then 1 else RIB + FIB;
   K := K + 1
end FIB.
```

Now the statement 'for $I := 1$ step 1 until 9 do $F[I] := FIB$' will set $F[1] = F[2] = 1$, $F[3] = 2$, $F[4] = 3$, $F[5] = 5$, $F[6] = 8$, $F[7] = 13$, $F[8] = 21$, $F[9] = 34$, causing a tree of **own** variables to be set up. For example, after $F[6]$ is set to 8 we will have the following **own** variables, with their current values:

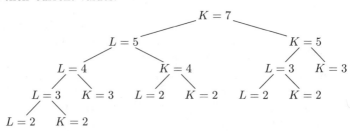

Needless to say, the authors prefer to take the *nonlocal* interpretation of **own** rather than this one.

8. The Specification Part

In a procedure heading, the programmer apparently *may* specify the nature of all the parameters, but does not *have* to. Presumably each specification is to provide some hints with which a compiler can produce more efficient code. In this connection we suggest that programmers be allowed to give the compiler even more information; for example, one could specify how many subscripts an array has, and the lower bound expressions for an array (if they are constant).

9. An Innerproduct Procedure

Here is a generalization of the *Innerproduct* procedure given in paragraph 5.4.2 of the ALGOL Report. We modestly call it *GPS*, for General Problem Solver:

> **real procedure** $GPS(I, N, Z, V)$; **real** I, N, Z, V;
> **begin for** $I := 1$ **step** 1 **until** N **do** $Z := V$; $GPS := 1$
> **end** GPS.

Is not that the most harmless looking procedure ever written? But wait a minute, look more closely: Those call-by-name parameters make a compiler work much harder than the programmer probably expects.

If we wish to calculate the inner product of the N-place vectors A and B, we simply write two statements

$$Z := 0; \quad I := GPS(I, N, Z, Z + A[I] \times B[I])$$

and Z is the answer.

But we can do much more than that. Suppose we want to multiply the array $A[1{:}m, 1{:}n]$ by $B[1{:}n, 1{:}p]$ and store the result in $C[1{:}m, 1{:}p]$. This can also be done using *GPS*, by writing

$$
\begin{aligned}
I := GPS(&I, 1.0, C[1, 1], 0.0) \\
&\times GPS\big(I, \\
&\quad (m{-}1) \times GPS\big(J, \\
&\qquad (p{-}1) \times GPS(K, n, C[I, J], \\
&\qquad\qquad C[I, J] + A[I, K] \times B[K, J]), \\
&\qquad C[I, J + 1], 0.0\big), \\
&\quad C[I + 1, 1], 0.0\big);
\end{aligned}
$$

does your ALGOL translator handle that statement correctly?

Problems that are quite unrelated to matrix multiplication can also be done with *GPS*. For example, the following little program will set P equal to the mth prime number:

$$I := GPS(I, \text{ if } I = 0 \text{ then } -1.0 \text{ else } I, P,$$
$$\quad \text{if } I = 1 \text{ then } 1.0$$
$$\quad \text{else if } GPS(A, I, Z,$$
$$\qquad\qquad \text{if } A = 1 \text{ then } 1.0$$
$$\qquad\qquad \text{else if } entier(A) \times (entier(I) \div entier(A))$$
$$\qquad\qquad\qquad = entier(I) \wedge A < I$$
$$\qquad\qquad \text{then } 0.0 \text{ else } Z) = Z$$
$$\quad\quad \text{then (if } P < m \text{ then } P + 1$$
$$\qquad\qquad \text{else } I \times GPS(A, 1.0, I, -1.0))$$
$$\quad \text{else } P)$$

In fact, using *GPS* we can actually compute any computable function (see [1]), using a single ALGOL assignment statement.

10. Miscellaneous Minor Quibbles

According to part 1 of the ALGOL 60 Report, a "compound statement which includes declarations is called a block." But that remark is in direct conflict with the syntax of section 4.1.1, because a compound statement does not include declarations.

If we believe further that an entire ALGOL program is a "compound statement" as the introduction tells us, programs must start off with *two* **begin**s! For example,

begin own integer i; $i := i + 1$ **end**

is not an ALGOL program, strictly speaking, but

begin begin own integer i; $i := i + 1$ **end end**

is. This example, incidentally, has suggested to Ingerman [2] that **own** variables declared in the outermost block should be saved from one run of the program to another. His interesting point seems worthy of consideration with respect to *all* of a program's uninitialized **own** variables, not only those declared in the outermost block.

Finally, we pose the following question: "Is it possible to label your entire ALGOL program by placing a label and colon before everything else? Can you **go to** this label?" Such a question would no doubt have amused medieval philosophers.

11. Conclusions

In some respects the ALGOL language seems to us to be more general than necessary. A certain amount of generality is essential to express algorithms, but extra things that are not needed have been put in. Those extras serve only to confuse people who are trying to learn the language, and they give more headaches to the people who are trying to write ALGOL translators. Multiplying matrices and computing primes as we did using the *GPS* procedure is just ALGOL for ALGOL's sake, not something to present as an algorithm. The ALGOL language should not be merely a challenge to compiler writers: "Can you implement me?" — it should be an efficient and useful tool for all who wish to program machines. The full generality of the ALGOL language as described above can actually be translated into machine language code that will give the proper results, but is this task really worth the effort?

In order to *fully* comprehend ALGOL, as it stands now, one must essentially be an "ALGOL specialist." And even those of us who do claim to be such specialists encounter new things we had not noticed before, week after week, as we re-read the ALGOL Report. Although it is an easy matter to learn the basic parts of ALGOL, the excess generality of the full language tends to reduce the number of people who can utilize it.

In order to take care of the more general cases that are used only infrequently, a compiler-translator program will tend to turn out much less efficient code than is necessary.

Some of the legal constructions are so subtle that ALGOL translators cannot be trusted to handle them correctly ... and need not be expected to.

We therefore wish to de-emphasize using such obscure features of ALGOL. Specifically, we believe ALGOL 60 would be better if at least the following aspects of its present definition were undefined:

1. The order in which components of an expression are evaluated.
2. Numeric labels.
3. Going to an undefined switch designator.
4. The "local" interpretation of **own** variables.

In short, let us all rather try to write ALGOL programs in the most easily understandable way. Then ALGOL becomes a very good language indeed, both for stating algorithms and for writing computer programs.

References

[1] Martin Davis, *Computability and Unsolvability* (New York: McGraw–Hill, 1958).

[2] Peter Zilahy Ingerman, Memorandum to ALGOL Working Group (6 March 1961); see *ALGOL Bulletin* **13** (Copenhagen: Regnecentralen, August 1961), 4.

[3] P. Z. Ingerman, "Dynamic declarations," *Communications of the ACM* **4** (1961), 59–60.

[4] E. T. Irons and W. Feurzeig, "Comments on the implementation of recursive procedures and blocks in ALGOL 60," *Communications of the ACM* **4** (1961), 65–69.

[5] Peter Naur, editor, "Report on the algorithmic language ALGOL 60," *Communications of the ACM* **3** (1960), 299–314.

[6] Peter Naur, *A Manual of the DASK ALGOL Language* (Copenhagen: Regnecentralen, November 1960).

[7] Peter Naur, "Answers to comments on ALGOL 60," *Communications of the ACM* **4**, 2 (February 1961), A16–A17.

[8] Kirk Sattley, "Allocation of storage for arrays in ALGOL 60," *Communications of the ACM* **4** (1961), 60–65.

[9] Henry C. Thatcher, Jr., Letter to ALGOL Maintenance Subcommittee (21 October 1960); see *ALGOL Bulletin* **13** (Copenhagen: Regnecentralen, August 1961), 2.

Chapter 5

SMALGOL-61

*[Presented by the Subcommittee on Common Languages for Small Computers of the Communications Committee, Joint Users Special Interest Group of the ACM. Written with G. A. Bachelor, J. R. H. Dempster, and J. Speroni (editors), E. L. Manderfield (chair), and subcommittee members R. H. Bernard, J. B. Callaghan, A. W. Carroll, E. C. Cronin, D. E. Hamilton, R. L. Hooper, R. R. Kenyon, J. W. Ritchie, A. Savitzky, L. J. Schaefer, Lee Schmidt, D. W. Scott, Jack Sherman, R. L. Stearman, and H. C. Thatcher. Originally published in Communications of the ACM **4** (1961), 499–502.]*

Prior to and during the 1961 Western Joint Computer Conference, several people in the Joint Users Groups had expressed interest in defining a "smalgol" language. This is to be an ALGOL language for use with compilers on relatively small size computers. A preliminary report resulted. At the ACM National Conference four months later, after considering several counter proposals, a final version was agreed upon by a subcommittee. The recommendations of the subcommittee for a standard subset of ALGOL 60 for use on small computers are presented here.

Why Have SMALGOL?

ALGOL 60 is an excellent language for expressing computer programs, but it is easy to see that the full repertoire of ALGOL 60 could not be implemented on a small-size computer. Are the users of small computers therefore supposed to forget about ALGOL?

It is hard to define the term "small computer" as used here; we are thinking of machines comparable to the ALWAC III-E, Burroughs 205, Honeywell 400, IBM 650, LGP 30, PB-250, RECOMP II, RPC 4000, UNIVAC 80, and so on.

Three things make compiler-writing harder on a small computer than on a large machine:

1) There is less memory space in which to write the compiler.

2) There are less powerful operation codes to use while writing the compiler.

3) It is harder to produce object programs. Since the operation codes are less powerful, efficient use should be made of high speed memory, drum storage allocation should minimize latency time, and so on.

It is actually harder for a large computer to compile programs for a small computer than for itself.

Some sort of ALGOL language is desirable for small machines, but the complete ALGOL 60 is impractical. We wish to have a standardized language that can be implemented on small computers.

Philosophy of SMALGOL

SMALGOL is not a "dialect" of ALGOL; it is a subset. Programs written for small computers using SMALGOL will be perfectly good ALGOL programs, and will be acceptable input to any ALGOL translator on a large machine (possibly subject to a different hardware representation). Given this requirement, decisions have to be made as to what portions of ALGOL 60 to omit from SMALGOL. Some of the decisions reached may seem arbitrary, but they are based on the following general principles:

Something is to be taken out when

1) it can be written in another way without much difficulty — it is just a "frill" and not a necessary part of the language;

2) it is of doubtful usefulness, although it is allowed in ALGOL 60;

3) it is not necessary in problems that are to run on small computers, although it would be useful in extremely complex problems (for example, playing chess);

4) it would be very inefficient on small machines.

Something is to be kept when

1) it is useful or notationally convenient;

2) it can be implemented on small machines.

The resulting language is still fairly close to ALGOL 60: Example 1 at the end of the ALGOL 60 Report [4], the *euler* procedure, is actually written in SMALGOL. In fact, almost all of the algorithms that have appeared in *Communications of the ACM* before May 1960 could be changed to use the SMALGOL language with only minor revisions. The only apparent exceptions are Algorithms 33 and 34, *Factorial* and *Gamma*, which use themselves recursively; and as a matter of fact, those two algorithms are very inefficient for an actual machine computation. Algorithm 31, on the other hand, shows how to calculate the Gamma function in a reasonable way [2], and it is written in SMALGOL except that the phrase '**value** X' must be added.

The language of SMALGOL is not beyond the range of compilers on small computers. The ALGOL 58 compiler for the Burroughs 205, a translator that handles nearly all of the ALGOL 58 language [1], shows what is possible. For these reasons we feel that the SMALGOL subset is neither too large nor too small.

Definition of SMALGOL

Here we will list all the things that are *deleted* from ALGOL 60 rather than things that are included in SMALGOL. The numbered sections refer to the corresponding parts of the ALGOL 60 Report [4].

Some of the changes mentioned below are really not changes in the reference language, but rather come under the category of hardware representation. They are specified here, however, in order to facilitate conversion of the reference language to a hardware representation and to facilitate interchange of programs between computer installations.

2. Basic Symbols

2.1 LETTERS

The alphabet is restricted either to all lowercase letters or to all uppercase letters; that is, there are only 26 letters in the SMALGOL alphabet.

2.2.1 DIGITS

No changes.

2.2.2 LOGICAL VALUES

No logical values will be allowed. (They are unnecessary, because Boolean variables have also been taken out of the language.)

2.3 DELIMITERS

a) Different hardware representations will use different characters here, and we recommend substituting words for some special symbols. The following are suggested for hardware representation:

* for $\times$	GEQ for $\geq$	= for :=
PWR for $\uparrow$	LSS for $<$	.. for :
DIV for $\div$	LEQ for $\leq$	TEN for $_{10}$
EQL for $=$	AND for $\wedge$	$\langle$space$\rangle$ for $\sqcup$
NEQ for $\neq$	OR for $\vee$	LSQ for '
GTR for $>$	NOT for $\neg$	RSQ for '

b) The basic symbols

$\equiv$	**Boolean**	**true**
$\supset$	**while**	**false**

are not used in SMALGOL.

c) Since the specification parts of procedure declarations must be filled in completely, it is possible to substitute the characters '(' and ')' for '[' and ']' without ambiguity. Programs for larger computers that translate the full ALGOL 60 language can be designed to accept parentheses for brackets in unambiguous cases.

d) Basic symbols such as **real**, **array**, and so on will be written as if they were identifiers. Blank spaces will have meaning since they will be delimiters between successive identifiers. Two or more blank spaces will be equivalent to a single blank space.

2.4 IDENTIFIERS

a) Identifiers should be five characters or less in length. However, if more characters are used, the first five characters must be different for different identifiers. In particular, no variable, array, or label names may begin with the following five characters:

ARCTA	BOOLE	FALSE	PROCE	UNTIL
ARRAY	COMME	INTEG	STRIN	VALUE
BEGIN	ENTIE	LABEL	SWITC	WHILE

b) The following words may not be used as identifiers:

ABS	ELSE	GEQ	LN	OR	SIGN	THEN
AND	END	GO	LSQ	OWN	SIN	TO
COS	EQL	GTR	LSS	PWR	SQRT	TRUE
DIV	EXP	IF	NEQ	REAL	STEP	
DO	FOR	LEQ	NOT	RSQ	TEN	

2.5 NUMBERS

No changes.

2.6 STRINGS

No changes.

2.7 SCOPES

No changes regarding the scopes of quantities have been made, but restrictions will be listed below forbidding the use of procedure names before they are declared.

2.8 VALUES AND TYPES
No changes.

3. Expressions

3.1 VARIABLES
No changes.

3.2 FUNCTION DESIGNATORS

a) No procedure other than a standard library function may be called unless it has been declared earlier in the program.

b) The standard procedures *abs* and *sign* may not be used as procedure parameters to other procedures; see 4.7(e) below.

3.3 ARITHMETIC EXPRESSIONS

The expression $a \uparrow b$ where a and b are type **integer** is allowed only when b is positive or zero.

3.4 BOOLEAN EXPRESSIONS

Variables cannot be of type **Boolean**. Programmers who wish to have Boolean variables can substitute integer variables, replacing the Boolean variable P by the relation $P = 1$ wherever it occurs in an expression; by replacing **false** by 0 and **true** by 1; and by rewriting the Boolean assignment statement $P := \langle$Boolean expression$\rangle$ as:

$$P := \textbf{if} \ \langle\text{Boolean expression}\rangle \ \textbf{then} \ 1 \ \textbf{else} \ 0$$

The operators $\supset$ and $\equiv$ are deleted. The relation $P \supset Q$ is equivalent to $\neg P \vee Q$; and $P \equiv Q$ is equivalent to $P \wedge Q \vee \neg P \wedge \neg Q$.

3.5 DESIGNATIONAL EXPRESSIONS

Unsigned integers may not be used as labels. This change causes no trouble for the programmer, who can replace the label n by the label Ln or something; and it makes life much easier for the compiler.

4. Statements

4.1 COMPOUND STATEMENTS AND BLOCKS
No changes.

4.2 ASSIGNMENT STATEMENTS

No Boolean assignment statements will be allowed. As mentioned previously, a truth value (0 or 1) may be assigned to an integer variable.

4.3 GO TO STATEMENTS

Going to an undefined switch designator is undefined.

4.4 DUMMY STATEMENTS
No changes.

4.5 CONDITIONAL STATEMENTS

No changes.

4.6 FOR STATEMENTS

a) The 'step' value must have one of the two forms '⟨primary⟩' or '−⟨primary⟩', where the primary must have a positive value while the program is running. The first form will be used when "stepping up," the second for "stepping down." This restriction allows a translator to produce more efficient coding for the for statement and removes little of the useful generality of ALGOL 60.

b) The 'for list' must be a single 'step-until' element. A great increase in efficiency of object programs is realized from this restriction, since a translator need not treat the statement within the scope of a for statement as a subroutine.

4.7 PROCEDURE STATEMENTS

a) Actual parameters may not be strings, except in procedures for input and output.

b) No procedure may be called before it is declared. Previously it was possible for two procedures declared within the same block heading to use each other. Removing such a feature guarantees that, when a procedure is called, a translator will know which of the parameters are called by value and which are called by name.

c) Recursive calls on procedures are not permitted. A *recursive call* is defined as one where the program has begun to set up parameters for a call on a certain procedure or has entered it, and then the procedure is entered again before it is exited. For example, if $F(G)$ is a procedure whose parameter G is a formal procedure, then $F(F)$ is a recursive call on F. On the other hand $sin(sin(X))$ is not a recursive call on sin since its parameter is called by value. The construction $F(X, F(Y, Z))$ would be a recursive call on procedure F, even if both of its parameters were called by value, since F is entered a second time while the parameters are being set up for the first call on F.

d) If a procedure P is an actual parameter to some procedure Q, all of the parameters of P must be called by value. This rule combined with (b) ensures that the translator will know which parameters of a given procedure call are called by name and which are called by value.

e) The two standard library procedures *abs* and *sign* may not be used as actual parameters to a procedure. This restriction is imposed because those functions will probably be coded as open subroutines on most computers. A programmer who wants to use them as actual parameters can do so by defining two new procedures as follows:

> **real procedure** *absf* (x); **value** x; **real** x;
> **begin** *absf* $:= abs(x)$ **end**

> **integer procedure** *signf* (x); **value** x; **real** x;
> **begin** *signf* $:= sign(x)$ **end**

and by using the names *absf*, *signf* as actual parameters.

f) The type of an actual parameter must agree with the type of the corresponding formal parameter. For example, '1' may not be substituted for a **real** parameter; '1.0' should be used.

5. Declarations

5.1 TYPE DECLARATIONS

a) No variables may be declared to have type **Boolean**.

b) Own variables are to be treated as being nonlocal to the entire program, except that they cannot be referred to from outside the block in which they are declared (see [3]).

5.2 ARRAY DECLARATIONS

The upper and lower bound expressions must be integer constants. The removal of "dynamic" arrays and recursive procedures from the language allows the compiler to assign all storage at compilation time. A large amount of storage is thus saved for the object program. If necessary, array sizes can be varied by re-compiling.

5.3 SWITCH DECLARATIONS

The elements of a switch list may only be labels. Thus

> **switch** $S := S1, S2, Q[m],$ **if** $V > -5$ **then** $S3$ **else** $S4$

is not allowed, but it can be rewritten as

> **switch** $S := S1, S2, S5, S6$;
> $S5$: **go to** $Q[m]$;
> $S6$: **go to if** $V > -5$ **then** $S3$ **else** $S4$

5.4 PROCEDURE DECLARATIONS

a) Procedures may not be of type **Boolean**.

b) No formal parameter may be of type **Boolean**.

c) If a procedure is to define a value, all of its parameters must be called by value. Such a procedure must not store quantities into nonlocal variables. This important rule allows a translator to evaluate expressions in any order [3]. Now each translator may take advantage of specific hardware for object programs.

d) The specification part must always contain an entry for each parameter. This rule is necessary so that a procedure call can be differentiated from an array variable within a procedure body, and for several other reasons.

e) No parameter specified as an array may be called by value. This rule is necessary because an object program cannot assign storage dynamically.

f) Procedure declarations must follow all type, switch, and array declarations of the block in which they occur. Because of this ordering, a translator can determine in a single pass what are the nonlocal parameters of the procedure, except for some labels.

g) The procedure identifier may occur inside the procedure body only as the left part of an assignment statement. Recursive calls on a procedure are *not* allowed.

References

[1] *The Burroughs Algebraic Compiler for the 205*, Publication No. 205-21003-D (Detroit, Michigan: Burroughs Corporation, October 1961), 30 pages. [The anonymous author of this user's manual was actually D. E. Knuth.]

[2] Robert M. Collinge, "Algorithm 31: Gamma function," *Communications of the ACM* **4** (1961), 105–106.

[3] Donald E. Knuth and Jack N. Merner, "ALGOL 60 *Confidential*," *Communications of the ACM* **4** (1961), 268–272. [Reprinted as Chapter 4 of the present volume.]

[4] Peter Naur, editor, "Report on the algorithmic language ALGOL 60," *Communications of the ACM* **3** (1960), 299–314.

Addendum

See also E. L. Manderfield, "A report on the status of SMALGOL," *Digest of Technical Papers, ACM 62 National Conference* (1962), 92–93; IFIP Working Group 2.1, "Report on SUBSET ALGOL 60 (IFIP)," *Communications of the ACM* **7** (1964), 626–628.

Chapter 6

Man or Boy?

*[Originally published in ALGOL Bulletin **17** (Amsterdam: Mathematisch Centrum, July 1964) 7; **19** (January 1965), 8–9.]*

Dear Editor:

Quite a few ALGOL 60 translators have been designed to handle recursion and nonlocal references properly, and I thought perhaps a little test program may be of value. Hence I've written the following simple routine, which may separate the "man-compilers" from the "boy-compilers":

> **begin real procedure** $A(k, x1, x2, x3, x4, x5)$;
>   **value** k; **integer** k;
>   **begin real procedure** B;
>   **begin** $k := k - 1$;
> $B := A := A(k, B, x1, x2, x3, x4)$
>   **end**;
>   **if** $k \leq 0$ **then** $A := x4 + x5$ **else** B
>   **end**;
> $outreal(A(10, 1, -1, -1, 1, 0))$
> **end**;

This program uses nothing known to be tricky or ambiguous. My question is: What should the answer be? Unfortunately, I don't have access to a "man-compiler" myself, and so I was forced to try hand calculations. My conjecture (probably wrong) is that the answer will be

$$73 - 119 - 177 + 102 = -121$$

I'd be very glad to know the right answer.

Dear Editor (six months later):

My previous letter (published under the title "Man or boy?") gave an ALGOL 60 program that made heavy use of ALGOL's ability to refer to nonlocal quantities in the presence of recursion, when many quantities of the same name (but different scope) are present. I have received answers of all types, but unfortunately none of them agreed with my original conjecture of -121. Therefore in order to save face, if possible, let me say that a slight error in my hand calculations caused the conjecture to be faulty. (I have an excuse: At the time I did the original work I had broken my right wrist, so the calculations were done left-handed!)

Since then my right hand has observed that the value of $A(k, x1, x2, x3, x4, x5)$ is equal to $c1 \times x1 + c2 \times x2 + c3 \times x3 + c4 \times x4 + c5 \times x5$, where the coefficients are given in the following table:

k	$c1(k)$	$c2(k)$	$c3(k)$	$c4(k)$	$c5(k)$
≤ 0	0	0	0	1	1
1	0	0	1	1	0
2	0	1	1	0	0
3	1	1	0	0	0
4	2	1	0	0	0
5	3	2	1	0	0
6	5	3	3	2	0
7	8	6	9	6	0
8	14	15	22	13	0
9	29	37	48	26	0
10	66	85	102	54	0

When $k \geq 5$, these values may be obtained by the relations

$$c1(k + 1) = c1(k) + c2(k)$$
$$c2(k + 1) = c2(k) + c3(k)$$
$$c3(k + 1) = c3(k) + c4(k + 1)$$
$$c4(k + 1) = c1(k) + c4(k) - 1$$
$$c5(k) = 0$$

With the help of such a table, the program can be used as a test on machines with smaller memories, by writing for example

$$outreal(0, A(8, 4, -5, 6, -7, 0))$$

in place of the call with $k = 10$.

Dr. Zonneveld's results [1] agree perfectly with these values.

I apologize for omitting a channel number in my previous use of '*outreal*'; I guess I just do not know enough about ALGOL input-output.

Donald E. Knuth
Assistant Professor of Mathematics
California Institute of Technology
Pasadena, California, USA

Reference

[1] J. A. Zonneveld, "Man compiler needs big brother machine," *AL-GOL Bulletin* **18** (Amsterdam: Mathematisch Centrum, September 1964), 9.

Addendum

The first ALGOL 60 compiler to be completed was written by E. W. Dijkstra and J. A. Zonneveld for the Electrologica X1 computer, a machine with only 12,000 27-bit words of memory. The man-or-boy test requires storage proportional to 2^k, so Zonneveld was able to run it only for $k \leq 9$ on the EL-X1; but he obtained the correct value -67 for $k = 10$ on a machine at Kiel with a bigger memory. Correct results were also reported subsequently by Alan Price and L. R. Hodges [using the Kidsgrove AL-GOL compiler for the English Electric KDF9]; by W. L. van der Poel [using the ZEBRA computer]; by Peter Naur [using GIER]; by F. R. A. Hopgood [using the I.C.L. Atlas]; and by people who wished to remain anonymous because their systems needed up to 80 minutes to obtain the answer. Details can be found in *ALGOL Bulletin* **19** (Amsterdam: Mathematisch Centrum, January 1965), 7–8; **20** (July 1965), 8.

C. H. Lindsey presented an ALGOL 68 version of the same program in *ALGOL Bulletin* **52** (Manchester: John Rylands Library, 1988), 27–28.

Chapter 7

A Proposal for Input-Output Conventions in ALGOL 60

[A report of the Subcommittee on ALGOL of the ACM Programming Languages Committee. Written with L. L. Bumgarner, D. E. Hamilton, P. Z. Ingerman, M. P. Lietzke, J. N. Merner, and D. T. Ross. Originally published in Communications of the ACM 7 (1964), 273–283.]

The ALGOL 60 language as first defined made no explicit reference to input and output processes. Such processes appeared to be quite dependent on the computer used; agreement on those matters was therefore difficult to obtain.

As time has passed, a great many ALGOL compilers have come into use, and each compiler has incorporated some input-output facilities. Experience has shown that such facilities can be introduced in a manner that is compatible and consistent with the ALGOL language, and that (more importantly) is almost completely machine-independent. But the existing implementations have taken many different approaches to the subject, and this diversity has hampered the interchange of programs between installations. The ACM ALGOL committee has carefully studied various proposals in an attempt to define a set of conventions for doing input and output that would be suitable for use on most computers. The present report constitutes the recommendations of that committee.

The input-output conventions described here do not involve extensions or changes to the ALGOL 60 language. Hence they can be incorporated into existing processors with a minimum of effort. The conventions take the form of a set of system procedures,[1] which are to be written in code for the various machines; this report discusses the function and use

---

[1] Throughout this report, names of system procedures are in *lowercase* letters; names of procedures used in illustrative examples are in *UPPERCASE*.

of those procedures. The material contained in the present proposal is intended to supplement the procedures *in real*, *out real*, *in symbol*, and *out symbol*, which have been defined by the international ALGOL committee;[2] the procedures described here could, with trivial exceptions, be expressed in terms of those four.

The first part of this report describes the methods by which formats are represented. Then calls on the input and output procedures themselves are discussed. The primary objective of the present report is to describe the proposal concisely and precisely, rather than to give a programmer's introduction to the input-output conventions. A simpler and more intuitive (but less exact) description should, of course, be written to serve as a teaching tool.

Many useful ideas were suggested by input-output conventions of the compilers listed in the references below. We are also grateful for the extremely helpful contributions of F. L. Bauer, M. Paul, H. Rutishauser, K. Samelson, G. Seegmüller, W. L. v. d. Poel, and other members of the European computing community, as well as A. Evans, Jr., R. W. Floyd, A. G. Grace, J. Green, G. E. Haynam, and W. C. Lynch of the USA.

A. Formats

In this section a certain type of string, which specifies the format of quantities to be input or output, is defined, and its meaning is explained.

A.1. NUMBER FORMATS (compare with ALGOL Report 2.5)

A.1.1. Syntax.

Basic components:

⟨replicator⟩ ::= ⟨unsigned integer⟩ | X
⟨insertion⟩ ::= B | ⟨replicator⟩ B | ⟨string⟩
⟨insertions⟩ ::= ⟨empty⟩ | ⟨insertions⟩ ⟨insertion⟩
⟨Z⟩ ::= Z | ⟨replicator⟩ Z | Z ⟨insertions⟩ C
          | ⟨replicator⟩ Z ⟨insertions⟩ C
⟨Z part⟩ ::= ⟨Z⟩ | ⟨Z part⟩ ⟨Z⟩ | ⟨Z part⟩ ⟨insertion⟩
⟨D⟩ ::= D | ⟨replicator⟩ D | D ⟨insertions⟩ C
          | ⟨replicator⟩ D ⟨insertions⟩ C
⟨D part⟩ ::= ⟨D⟩ | ⟨D part⟩ ⟨D⟩ | ⟨D part⟩ ⟨insertion⟩
⟨T part⟩ ::= ⟨empty⟩ | T ⟨insertions⟩
⟨sign part⟩ ::= ⟨empty⟩ | ⟨insertions⟩ + | ⟨insertions⟩ −
⟨integer part⟩ ::= ⟨Z part⟩ | ⟨D part⟩ | ⟨Z part⟩ ⟨D part⟩

---

[2] Defined at the meeting of IFIP/WG2.1 — ALGOL in Delft, September 1963.

Format structures:

⟨unsigned integer format⟩ ::= ⟨insertions⟩ ⟨integer part⟩
⟨decimal fraction format⟩ ::= . ⟨insertions⟩ ⟨D part⟩ ⟨T part⟩
      | V ⟨insertions⟩ ⟨D part⟩ ⟨T part⟩
⟨exponent part format⟩ ::= $_{10}$ ⟨sign part⟩ ⟨unsigned integer format⟩
⟨decimal number format⟩ ::= ⟨unsigned integer format⟩ ⟨T part⟩
      | ⟨insertions⟩ ⟨decimal fraction format⟩
      | ⟨unsigned integer format⟩ ⟨decimal fraction format⟩
⟨number format⟩ ::= ⟨sign part⟩ ⟨decimal number format⟩
      | ⟨decimal number format⟩ + ⟨insertions⟩
      | ⟨decimal number format⟩ − ⟨insertions⟩
      | ⟨sign part⟩ ⟨decimal number format⟩ ⟨exponent part format⟩

Note. This syntax could have been described more simply, but the rather awkward constructions here have been formulated so that no syntactic ambiguities will exist in the sense of formal language theory.

A.1.2. Examples. Examples of number formats appear in Figure 1.

A.1.3. Semantics. The syntax above defines the allowable strings that can comprise a "number format." We will first describe the interpretation to be taken during *output*.

A.1.3.1. Replicators. An unsigned integer n used as replicator means that the quantity is repeated n times; thus 3B is equivalent to BBB. The character X as replicator means a number of times that will be specified when the format is called (see Section B.3.1).

A.1.3.2. Insertions. The syntax has been set up so that strings, delimited by string quotes, may be inserted anywhere within a number format. The corresponding information in the strings (except for the outermost string quotes) will appear inserted in the same place with respect to the rest of the number. Similarly, the letter B may be inserted anywhere within a number format, and it stands for a blank space.

A.1.3.3. Sign, zero, and comma suppression. The portion of a number to the left of the decimal point consists of an optional sign, then a sequence of Z's and a sequence of D's, with possible C's following a Z or a D, plus possible insertion characters.

The convention on signs is the following: (a) if no sign is specified, the number is assumed to be positive, and the treatment of negative numbers is undefined; (b) if a plus sign is specified, the sign will appear as + or − on the external medium; and (c) if a minus sign is specified, the sign will appear if minus, and will be suppressed if plus.

Number format	Result from −13.296	Result from 1007.999
+ZZZCDDD.DD	-013.30	+1,008.00
+3ZC3D.2D	-013.30	+1,008.00
-3D2B3D.2DT	-000 013.29	001 007.99
5Z.5D−	13.29600-	1007.99900
−.5D$_{10}$+2D '...'	-.13296$_{10}$+02...	.10080$_{10}$+04...
+ZD$_{10}$2Z	-13	+10$_{10}$ 2
+D.DDBDDBDDB$_{10}$+DD	-1.32 96 00 $_{10}$+01	+1.00 79 99 $_{10}$+03
XB.XD$_{10}$−DDD	(depends on call)	(depends on call)
'integer⎵part' −ZZZDV	integer part -13,	integer part 1007,
',⎵fraction' B3D	fraction 296	fraction 999

FIGURE 1. Example number formats and outputs.

The letter Z stands for zero suppression, and the letter D stands for digit printing *without* zero suppression. Each Z and D stands for a single digit position; a zero digit specified by Z will be suppressed, that is, replaced by a blank space, when all digits to its left are zero. A digit specified by D will always be printed. Notice that the number zero printed with all Z's in the format will give rise to all blank spaces; that at least one D should usually be given somewhere in the format.

The letter C stands for a comma. A comma following a D will always be printed; a comma following a Z will be printed except when zero suppression takes place at that Z. Whenever zero or comma suppression takes place, the leading sign (if any) is printed in place of the rightmost character suppressed.

A.1.3.4. Decimal points. The position of the decimal point is indicated either by the character '.' or by the letter V. In the former case, the decimal point appears on the external medium; in the latter case, the decimal point is "implied"; that is, it takes up no space on the external medium. (The V feature is most commonly used to save time and space when preparing input data.) Only D's (no Z's) may appear to the right of the decimal point.

A.1.3.5. Truncation. On output, nonintegral numbers are usually rounded to fit the format specified. If the letter T is used, however, truncation takes place instead. Rounding and truncation of a number X to d decimal places are defined as follows:

$$\text{Rounding} \qquad 10^{-d}\, entier\,(10^{d}X + .5)$$
$$\text{Truncation} \qquad 10^{-d}\, sign\,(X)\, entier\,(10^{d}\, abs\,(X))$$

A.1.3.6. Exponent part. The number following a '$_{10}$' is treated exactly the same as the portion of a number to the left of a decimal point

(Section A.1.3.3), except that if no D's appear, and if the exponent is zero, the '$_{10}$' and the sign are suppressed.

A.1.3.7. Two types of numeric format. Number formats are of two principal kinds:

(a) Decimal number with no exponent. In this case, the number is aligned according to the decimal point in the format, and it is then truncated or rounded to the appropriate number of decimal places. The sign may precede or follow the number.

(b) Decimal number with exponent. In this case, a nonzero number is transformed into the format of the decimal number with its most significant digit nonzero; the exponent is adjusted accordingly. If the number is zero, both decimal part and exponent part are output as zero.

If in case (a) the number is too large to be output in the specified form, or if in case (b) the exponent is too large, an overflow error occurs. The action that takes place on overflow is undefined; it is recommended that the number of characters used in the output be the same as if no overflow had occurred, and that as much significant information as possible be output.

A.1.3.8. Input. A number input with a particular format specification should in general be the same as the number that would be output with the same format, except that less error checking is done. The rules are, more precisely:

(a) Leading zeros and commas may appear even though Z's are used in the format. Leading spaces may appear even if D's are used. In other words, no distinction between Z and D is made on input.

(b) Insertions take the same amount of space in the same positions, but the characters appearing there are ignored on input. In other words, an insertion specifies only the number of characters to ignore, when it appears in an input format.

(c) If the format specifies a sign at the left, the sign may appear in any Z, D, or C position as long as it is to the left of the number. A sign specified at the right must appear in place.

(d) The following things are checked: The positions of commas, decimal points, '$_{10}$', and the presence of digits in place of Z or D after the first significant digit. If an error is detected in the data, the result is undefined; it is recommended that the input procedure attempt to reread the data as if it were in standard format (Section A.5) and also to give some error indication compatible with the system being used. Such an error indication might be suppressed at the programmer's option if the data became meaningful when reread in standard format.

A.2. OTHER FORMATS

A.2.1. Syntax

⟨S⟩ ::= S | ⟨replicator⟩ S
⟨string format⟩ ::= ⟨insertions⟩ ⟨S⟩ | ⟨string format⟩ ⟨S⟩
    | ⟨string format⟩ ⟨insertion⟩
⟨A⟩ ::= A | ⟨replicator⟩ A
⟨alpha format⟩ ::= ⟨insertions⟩ ⟨A⟩ | ⟨alpha format⟩ ⟨A⟩
    | ⟨alpha format⟩ ⟨insertion⟩
⟨nonformat⟩ ::= I | R | L
⟨Boolean part⟩ ::= P | 5F | FFFFF | F
⟨Boolean format⟩ ::= ⟨insertions⟩ ⟨Boolean part⟩ ⟨insertions⟩
⟨title format⟩ ::= ⟨insertion⟩ | ⟨title format⟩ ⟨insertion⟩
⟨alignment mark⟩ ::= / | ↑ | ⟨replicator⟩ / | ⟨replicator⟩ ↑
⟨format item 1⟩ ::= ⟨number format⟩ | ⟨string format⟩
    | ⟨alpha format⟩ | ⟨nonformat⟩ | ⟨Boolean format⟩
    | ⟨title format⟩ | ⟨alignment mark⟩ ⟨format item 1⟩
⟨format item⟩ ::= ⟨format item 1⟩ | ⟨alignment mark⟩
    | ⟨format item⟩ ⟨alignment mark⟩

A.2.2. Examples

      ↑5Z.5D///
      3S'=' 6S4B
      AA'='
      ↑R
      P
      /'Execution.'↑

A.2.3. Semantics

A.2.3.1. String format. A string format is used for output of string quantities. Each of the S-positions in the format corresponds to a single character in the string that is output. If the string is longer than the number of S's, the leftmost characters are transferred; if the string is shorter, ⊔-symbols are effectively added at the right of the string.

The word "character" as used in this report refers to one unit of information on the external input or output medium; if ALGOL basic symbols are used in strings that do not have a single-character representation on the external medium being used, the result is undefined.

A.2.3.2. Alpha format. Each letter A means that one character is to be transmitted; this is the same as S-format, except that the ALGOL equivalent of the alphabetics is of type integer rather than a string. The translation between external and internal codes will vary from one machine to another, hence programmers should refrain from using this feature in a machine-dependent manner. Each implementor should specify the maximum number of characters that can be used for a single integer variable. The following operations are undefined for quantities that have been input using alpha format: arithmetic operations, relations except '$=$' and '$\neq$', and output using a different number of A's in the output format. If the integer is output using the same number of A's, the same string will be output as was input.

A programmer may work with such alphabetic quantities in a machine-independent manner by using the transfer function $equiv(S)$ where S is a string; the value of $equiv(S)$ is of type integer, and it is defined to have exactly the same value as if the string S had been input using alpha format. For example, one may write

if $X = equiv(\text{'ALPHA'})$ **then go to** *PROCESS ALPHA*

where the value of X has been input using the format AAAAA.

A.2.3.3. Nonformat. An I, R, or L is used to indicate that the value of a single variable of integer, real, or Boolean type, respectively, is to be input or output from or to an external medium, using the internal machine representation. If a value of type integer is output with R-format or if a value of type real is input with I-format, the appropriate transfer function is invoked. The precise behavior of this format, and particularly its interaction with other formats, is undefined in general.

A.2.3.4. Boolean format. The format P, F, 5F, or FFFFF must be used when Boolean quantities are input or output. The correspondence is defined as follows:

Internal to ALGOL	P	F	5F = FFFFF
true	1	T	TRUE␣
false	0	F	FALSE

On input, anything failing to be in the proper form is undefined.

A.2.3.5. Title format. All formats discussed so far have specified a correspondence between a single ALGOL real, integer, Boolean, or string quantity and a sequence of characters in the input or output. A title format item consists entirely of insertions and alignment marks; therefore it does not require a corresponding ALGOL quantity. On input, it merely causes skipping of the characters, and on output it causes emission of the insertion characters it contains.

A.2.3.6. Alignment marks. The characters '/' and '↑' in a format item indicate line and page control actions. The precise definition of these actions will be given later (see Section B.5); they have the following intuitive interpretation: (a) '/' means go to the next line, in a manner similar to the "carriage return" operation on a typewriter. (b) '↑' means do a /-operation and then skip to the top of the next page.

Two or more alignment marks indicate the number of times the operations are to be performed; for example, '//' on output means that the current line is completed and the next line is effectively set to all blanks. Alignment marks at the left of a format item cause actions to take place before the regular format operation, and if they are at the right they take place afterwards.

Note. On machines that do not have the character ↑ in their character set, some convenient character such as an asterisk should be substituted for ↑ in format strings.

A.3. FORMAT STRINGS

The format items mentioned above are combined into format strings according to the rules in this section.

A.3.1. Syntax

⟨format primary⟩ ::= ⟨format item⟩
    | ⟨replicator⟩ (⟨format secondary⟩)
    | (⟨format secondary⟩)
⟨format secondary⟩ ::= ⟨format primary⟩
    | ⟨format secondary⟩, ⟨format primary⟩
⟨format string⟩ ::= '⟨format secondary⟩' | ''

A.3.2. Examples

'4(15ZD), //'
'↑'
'.5D$_{10}$+D, X(2(20B.8D$_{10}$+D), 10S)'
"...This⊔is⊔a⊔peculiar⊔'format⊔string'"

A.3.3. Semantics. A format string is simply a list of format items, which are to be interpreted from left to right. The construction '⟨replicator⟩ (⟨format secondary⟩)' is simply an abbreviation for 'replicator' repetitions of the parenthesized quantity (see Section A.1.3.1). The construction '(⟨format secondary⟩)' is used to specify an infinite repetition of the parenthesized quantity.

All spaces within a format string are irrelevant, except those that are part of insertion substrings.

It is recommended that the ALGOL compiler check the syntax of strings that are known to be format strings (from their context), as the program is compiled. In most cases a compiler will also be able to translate format strings into an intermediate code designed for highly efficient input-output processing by the other procedures.

A.4. Summary of Format Codes

A	alphabetic character represented as an integer	X	dynamic replicator
		Z	zero-suppressed digit
B	blank space	+	print the sign
C	comma	−	print the sign if it is minus
D	digit	10	exponent part indicator
F	Boolean **TRUE** or **FALSE**	()	delimiters of replicated format secondaries
I	integer untranslated		
L	Boolean untranslated	,	format item separator
P	Boolean bit	/	line alignment mark
R	real untranslated	↑	page alignment mark
S	string character	' '	delimiters of an inserted string
T	truncation		
V	implied decimal point	.	decimal point

A.5. "Standard" Format

There is a format available *without* specification (see Section B.5), having the following characteristics:

(a) On input, any number written according to the ALGOL syntax for ⟨number⟩ is accepted with the conventional meaning. Such inputs are of *arbitrary* length, and they are delimited at the right by the following conventions: (i) A letter or character other than a decimal point, sign, digit, or '10' occurring to the right of a decimal point, sign, digit, or '10' is a delimiter. (ii) A sequence of k or more blank spaces serves as a delimiter as in (i); a sequence of fewer than k blank spaces is ignored. This number $k \geq 1$ is specified by the implementor (and the implementor may choose to let the programmer specify k on a control card of some sort). (iii) If the number contains a decimal point, sign, digit, or '10' on the line where the number begins, the right-hand margin of that line serves as a delimiter of the number. However, if the first line of a field contains no such characters, the number is determined by reading several lines until finding a delimiter of type (i) or (ii). In other words, a number is not usually split across more than one line, unless its first line contains nothing but spaces or characters that do not enter into the number itself. (See Section B.5 for further discussion of standard input format.)

(b) On output, a number is given in the form of a decimal number with an exponent. This decimal number has as many significant figures as the machine can represent; it is suitable for reading by the standard input format. Standard output format occupies a fixed number of characters on the output medium, specified by each ALGOL installation. Standard output format can also be used for the output of strings, and in this case the number of characters is equal to the length of the string.

B. Input and Output Procedures

B.1. GENERAL CHARACTERISTICS

The over-all approach to input and output that is provided by the procedures of this report will be introduced here by means of a few examples, and the precise definition of the procedures will be given later.

Consider first a typical case, in which we want to print a line containing the values of the integer variables M and N, each of which is nonnegative, with at most five digits; we also want to print the value of $X[N]$, in the form of a signed number with a single nonzero digit to the left of the decimal point, and with an exponent indicated; and finally we want to print the value of $cos(t)$, using a format with a fixed decimal point and no exponent. The following statement does the job.

$$output\,4(6, \text{'}2(BBBZZZD),3B,+D.DDDDDD_{10}+DDD,3B,$$
$$-Z.DDDDBDDDD/\text{'}, M, N, X[N], cos(t))$$

This example has the following significance: (a) The '4' in *output* 4 means that four values are being output. (b) The '6' means that output is to go to unit number 6. This is the *logical* unit number, namely, the programmer's number for that unit, and it does not necessarily mean *physical* unit number 6; Section B.1.1 discusses unit numbers in detail. (c) The next parameter, '2(BBB ... DDDD/', is a format string, which specifies the desired format for outputting the four values. (d) The last four parameters are the values to be printed. If $M = 500$, $N = 0$, $X[0] = 18061579$, and $t = 3.1415926536$, we obtain the line

⊔⊔⊔⊔⊔500⊔⊔⊔⊔⊔⊔⊔0⊔⊔⊔+1.806158$_{10}$+007⊔⊔⊔−1.0000⊔0000

as output (where '⊔' denotes a blank space).

The '/' used in this example format signifies the end of a line. If it had not been present, more numbers could have been placed on the same line in a future output statement. The programmer may build the contents of a line in several steps, as an algorithm proceeds, without automatically starting a new line each time output is called. For example, the statement above could also have been written

$output2(6, \text{'2(BBBZZZZD)'}, M, N)$;
$output1(6, \text{'3B,+D.DDDDDD}_{10}\text{+DDD,3B'}, X[N])$;
$output1(6, \text{'$-$Z.DDDDBDDDD'}, cos(t))$;
$output0(6, \text{'/'})$

with equivalent results.

This example outputs a line of 48 characters. If for some reason the output statements are used with a device incapable of printing 48 characters on a single line, the output would actually have been recorded on two or more lines, according to a rule that automatically avoids breaking a number between two consecutive lines wherever possible. (The exact rule appears in Section B.5.)

Now let us go to a slightly more complicated example: The real array $A[1{:}m, 1{:}n]$ is to be printed, starting on a new page. Assuming that each element should appear in the format 'BB$-$ZZZZ.DD', which uses ten characters per item, we can write the following program:

$output0(6, \text{'↑'})$;
for $i := 1$ **step** 1 **until** m **do**
   begin for $j := 1$ **step** 1 **until** n **do**
      $output1(6, \text{'BB$-$ZZZZ.DD'}, A[i, j])$;
    $output0(6, \text{'//'})$
   end.

If $10n$ characters will fit on one line, this little program will print m lines, double spaced, with n values per line; otherwise m groups of k lines separated by blank lines will be produced, where k lines are necessary for the printing of n values. For example, if $n = 10$ and if the printer has 120 character positions, m double-spaced lines are produced. If, however, a 72-character printer is being used, 7 values are printed on the first line, 3 on the next, the third is blank, then 7 more values are printed, and so on.

There is another way to achieve the same output and to obtain more control over the page format as well; the subject of page format will be discussed further in Section B.2. As a preview, let's consider the manner in which the output of an entire array can be done conveniently using a single output statement. The procedures $output0$, $output1$, ... that we've mentioned so far provide only for the common cases of output; they are essentially a special abbreviation for certain calls on a more general procedure called *out list*. This more general procedure could be used for the problem above in the following manner:

$$out\,list\,(6, LAYOUT, LIST\,);$$

here *LAYOUT* and *LIST* are the names of *procedures* that appear below. The first parameter of *out list* is the logical unit number, as described above. The second parameter is the name of a so-called "layout procedure"; general layout procedures are discussed in Section B.3. The third parameter of *out list* is the name of a so-called "list procedure"; general list procedures are discussed in Section B.4.

In general, a *layout procedure* specifies the format control of the input or output. For the case we are considering, we could write a simple layout procedure (named *LAYOUT*) as follows:

procedure *LAYOUT*; *format*1('↑, (X(BB−ZZZZ.DD), //)', *n*);

the '1' in *format*1 means that a format string containing one X is given. The format string is

$$↑, (X(BB-ZZZZ.DD), //)$$

and it means, "Skip to a new page, then repeat the format

$$X(BB-ZZZZ.DD), //$$

until the last value has been output." The latter format means, "Use format BB−ZZZZ.DD exactly X times, then finish a line and skip to a new line." Finally, *format*1 is a procedure that effectively inserts the value of *n* where the letter X appears in the format string.

A *list procedure* serves to specify a list of quantities. For the problem under consideration, we could write a simple list procedure (named *LIST*) as follows:

procedure *LIST* (*ITEM*);
    for $i := 1$ **step** 1 **until** m **do**
        for $j := 1$ **step** 1 **until** n **do** *ITEM* (*A*[*i*, *j*]);

here '*ITEM* (*A*[*i*, *j*])' means that *A*[*i*, *j*] is the next item of the list. The procedure *ITEM* is a formal parameter that might have been given a different name such as *PIECE* or *CHUNK*; list procedures are discussed in more detail in Section B.4.

The declarations of *LAYOUT* and *LIST* above, together with the procedure statement *out list* (6, *LAYOUT*, *LIST*), accomplish the desired output of the array *A*.

Input is done in a manner dual to output, in such a way that it is the exact inverse of the output process wherever possible. The procedures *in list* and *input* 0, *input* 1, *input* 2, ... correspond to *out list* and *output* 0, *output* 1, *output* 2, ...

Two other procedures, *get* and *put*, allow programmers to store intermediate data on external devices. For example, the statement *put* (100, *LIST*) causes the values specified in the list procedure named *LIST* to be recorded in the external medium that has the identification number 100. The subsequent statement *get* (100, *LIST*) will then restore those values. The external medium might be a disk file, a drum, a magnetic tape, etc.; the type of device and the format in which data is stored there are of no concern to the programmer.

B.1.1. Unit numbers. The first parameter of input and output procedures is the logical unit number, which is an integer that the programmer has chosen to identify some input or output device. The connection between logical unit numbers and the actual physical unit numbers is specified by the programmer *outside* of the ALGOL language, by means of "control cards" preceding or following a program, or in some other way provided by the ALGOL implementor. The situation that arises if the same physical unit is being used for two different logical numbers, or if the same physical unit is used both for input and for output, is undefined in general.

It is recommended that the internal computer memory (for example, the core memory) be available as an "input-output device," so that data can be edited efficiently by means of input and output statements.

B.2. Horizontal and Vertical Control

This section deals with the way in which a sequence of characters, described by the rules of formats in Section A, is mapped onto input and output devices. Mapping is done in a manner that is essentially independent of the device being used, in the sense that with these specifications the programmer can anticipate how the input or output data will appear on virtually any device. Some of the features of the following description will, of course, be more appropriately used on certain devices than on others.

We will begin by assuming that we are doing *output* to a *printer*. This situation is essentially the most difficult case to handle, and once it is understood we will be ready to discuss the manner in which other devices fit into the same general framework.

The page format is controlled by specifying the horizontal and the vertical layout. Horizontal layout is controlled in essentially the same manner as vertical layout, and this symmetry between the horizontal and vertical dimensions should be kept in mind for easier understanding of the concepts in this section.

Refer to Figure 2; the horizontal format is described in terms of three parameters (L, R, P), and the vertical format has corresponding parameters (L', R', P'). The parameters L, L' and R, R' indicate left and right margins, respectively; Figure 2 shows a case where $L = L' = 4$ and $R = R' = 12$. Only positions L through R of a horizontal line are used, and only lines L' through R' of the page are used; we require that $1 \leq L \leq R$ and $1 \leq L' \leq R'$. The parameter P is the number of characters per line, and P' is the number of lines per page. Although L, R, L', and R' are chosen by the programmer, the values of P and P' are characteristics of the device and they are usually out of the programmer's control. For those devices on which P and P' can vary — for example, some printers have two settings, one with which there are 66 lines per page, and another with which there are 88 — the values are specified to the system in some manner external to the ALGOL program, possibly on control cards. For certain devices, the values of P or P' might be essentially infinite.

Although Figure 2 shows a case where $P \geq R$ and $P' \geq R'$, it is quite possible that $P < R$ or $P' < R'$ (or both) might occur, since the values of P and P' are in general unknown to the programmer. In such cases, the algorithm described in Section B.5 is used to break up logical lines that are too wide to fit on a physical line, and to break up logical pages that are too large to fit a physical page. On the other hand, the conditions $L \leq P$ and $L' \leq P'$ are ensured by setting L or L' equal to 1 automatically if they happen to be greater than P or P', respectively.

Characters determined by the output values are put onto a horizontal line, and there are three conditions that cause a transfer to the next line: (a) normal line alignment, specified by a '/' in the format; (b) R-overflow, which occurs when a group of characters is to be transmitted that would pass position R; and (c) P-overflow, which occurs when a group of characters is to be transmitted that would not cause R-overflow but would pass position P. When any of these three things occurs, control is transferred to a procedure specified by the programmer in case special action is desired (for instance, a change of margins in case of overflow; see Section B.3.3).

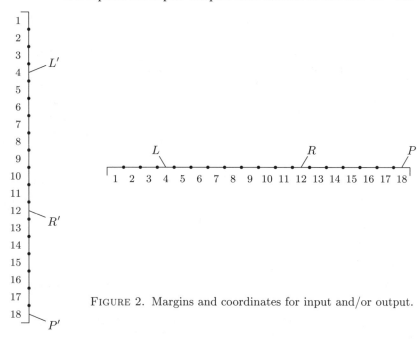

FIGURE 2. Margins and coordinates for input and/or output.

Similarly, there are three conditions that cause a transfer to the next page: (a') normal page alignment, specified by a '↑' in the format; (b') R'-overflow, which occurs when a group of characters is to be transmitted that would appear on line $R' + 1$; and (c') P'-overflow, which occurs when a group of characters is to be transmitted that would appear on line $P' + 1 < R' + 1$. The programmer may indicate special procedures to be executed at this time if desired; one could, for example, insert a page heading.

Further details concerning pages and lines will be given later. Now we will consider how devices other than printers can be thought of in terms of the same ideas.

A typewriter is, of course, very much like a printer and it requires no further comment.

Punched cards with, say, 80 columns, have $P = 80$ and $P' = \infty$. Vertical control would appear to have little meaning for punched cards, although the implementor might choose to interpret '↑' to mean the insertion of a coded or blank card.

With paper tape, we might again say that vertical control has little or no meaning; in this case, P could be the number of characters read or written at a time.

On magnetic tape capable of writing arbitrarily long blocks, we have $P = P' = \infty$. We might think of each page as being a "record," an amount of contiguous information on the tape that is read or written at once. The lines are subdivisions of a record, and R' lines form a record; R characters are in each line. In this way we can specify so-called "blocking of records." Other interpretations might be more appropriate for magnetic tapes at certain installations; for example, one tape format might correspond exactly to printer format for future offline listing.

These examples are given merely to indicate how the concepts described above for printers can be applied to other devices. Each implementor will decide what method is most appropriate for each particular device, and if choices are to be made the programmer can specify them by means of control cards. The manner in which such specification is done is of no concern in this report; our procedures are defined solely in terms of P and P'.

B.3. LAYOUT PROCEDURES

Whenever input or output is done, certain "standard" operations are assumed to take place, unless otherwise specified by the programmer. Therefore one of the parameters of the input or output procedure is a so-called "layout" procedure, which specifies all of the nonstandard operations desired. The specification is accomplished by using any or all of the six "descriptive procedures" *format*, *h end*, *v end*, *h lim*, *v lim*, *no data* described in this section.

The precise action of these procedures can be described in terms of the mythical concept of six "hidden variables," H1, H2, H3, H4, H5, H6. The effect of each descriptive procedure is to set one of the hidden variables to a certain value; and as a matter of fact, that may be regarded as the sum total of the effect of a descriptive procedure. The programmer normally has no other access to these hidden variables (see, however, Section B.7). The hidden variables have a scope that is local to *in list* and to *out list*.

B.3.1. Format procedures. The descriptive procedure call

$$format(string)$$

has the effect of setting hidden variable H1 to indicate the string parameter. This parameter may either be a string explicitly written, or a formal parameter; but in any event, the string it refers to must be a format string that satisfies the syntax of Section A.3, and it must have no 'X' replicators.

The procedure *format* is just one of a class of procedures that have the names *format*0, *format*1, *format*2, ...; the name *format* is equivalent to *format*0. In general, the procedure *format n* is used with format strings that have exactly n X-replicators, and the call is

$$format\ n(string, X_1, X_2, \ldots, X_n)$$

where each X_i is an integer parameter called by value. The effect is to replace each X of the format string by one of the X_i, with the correspondence defined from left to right. Each X_i must be nonnegative.

For example, the statements

$$format\ 2(\text{`XB.XD}_{10}+\text{DD'}, 5, 10)$$

and

$$format\ (\text{`5B.10D}_{10}+\text{DD'})$$

are equivalent.

B.3.2. Limits. The descriptive procedure call

$$h\,lim\,(L, R)$$

has the effect of setting hidden variable H2 to indicate the two parameters L and R. Similarly,

$$v\,lim\,(L', R')$$

sets H3 to indicate L' and R'. These parameters have the significance described in Section B.2. If $h\,lim$ and $v\,lim$ are not used, the default values are $L = L' = 1$ and $R = R' = \infty$.

B.3.3. End control. The descriptive procedure calls

$$h\,end\,(P_N, P_R, P_P) \qquad \text{and} \qquad v\,end\,(P_{N'}, P_{R'}, P_{P'})$$

have the effect of setting hidden variables H4 and H5, respectively, to indicate their parameters. The parameters P_N, P_R, P_P, $P_{N'}$, $P_{R'}$, $P_{P'}$ are names of procedures (ordinarily dummy statements, if $h\,end$ and $v\,end$ are not specified), which are activated in case of normal line alignment, R-overflow, P-overflow, normal page alignment, R'-overflow, and P'-overflow, respectively.

B.3.4. End of data. The descriptive procedure call

$$no\,data\,(L)$$

has the effect of setting hidden variable H6 to indicate the parameter L, where L is a label. End of data, as defined here, has meaning only on input, and it does not refer to any specific hardware features; it occurs when data is requested for input but no more data remains on the corresponding input medium. At this point, a transfer to the statement labeled L will occur. If the procedure *no data* is not used, transfer will occur to a "label" that has effectively been inserted just before the final **end** in the ALGOL program, thus terminating the program. (In such a case the implementor may elect to provide an appropriate error message.)

B.3.5. Examples. A layout procedure might look as follows:

procedure *LAYOUTX*;
begin *format*('/');
   if B **then begin** *format*1('XB', $Y + 10$);   *no data*($L32$) **end**;
   h lim(**if** B **then** 1 **else** 10, 30);
end.

Layout procedures never have formal parameters. This procedure, for example, refers to three global quantities, B, Y, and $L32$. Suppose $Y = 3$; then *LAYOUTX* accomplishes the following:

hidden variable	procedure	if B = **true**	if B = **false**
H1	*format*	'13B'	'/'
H2	*h lim*	$(1, 30)$	$(10, 30)$
H3	*v lim*	$(1, \infty)$	$(1, \infty)$
H4	*h end*	(, ,)	(, ,)
H5	*v end*	(, ,)	(, ,)
H6	*no data*	$L32$	end program

As a more useful example, we can take the procedure *LAYOUT* of Section B.1 and rewrite it so that the horizontal margins $(11, 110)$ are used on the page, except that if P-overflow or R-overflow occurs we wish to use the margins $(16, 105)$ for overflow lines.

procedure *LAYOUT*;
begin *h lim*(11, 110);   *h end*(K, L, L);
   *format*1('↑, (X(BB−ZZZZ.DD), //)', n);
end;
procedure K; *h lim*(11, 110);
procedure L; *h lim*(16, 105);

This specification causes the limits $(16, 105)$ to be set whenever overflow occurs, and each '/' in the format will reinstate the original margins by causing procedure K to be called. (Programmers who wish a more elaborate treatment of the overflow case, depending on the value of P, can use the procedures of Section B.6.)

B.4. LIST PROCEDURES

B.4.1. General characteristics. The concept of a list procedure is quite important to the input-output conventions described in this report, and it may also prove useful in other applications of ALGOL. It represents a specialized application of ALGOL's ability to use one procedure as a parameter of another.

The purpose of a list procedure is to describe a sequence of items that are to be transmitted for input or output. A procedure is written in which the name of each item, say V, is written as the argument of a parametric procedure, say $ITEM$, thus: $ITEM(V)$. When the list procedure is called by an input-output system procedure, another procedure (such as the internal system procedure $out\,item$) will be "substituted" for $ITEM$, V will be called by name, and the value of V will be transmitted for input or output. The standard sequencing of ALGOL statements in the body of the list procedure therefore determines the sequence of items in the list.

For example,

procedure $LIST(ITEM)$; **begin** $ITEM(A)$; $ITEM(B)$; $ITEM(C)$ **end**

says that the values of A, B, and C are to be transmitted. A more typical list procedure might be:

> **procedure** $PAIRS(ELT)$;
> **for** $i := 1$ **step** 1 **until** n **do**
>   **begin** $ELT(A[i])$; $ELT(B[i])$;
>   **end**.

This procedure says that the values of $A[1]$, $B[1]$, $A[2]$, $B[2]$, $\ldots$, $A[n]$, $B[n]$ are to be transmitted, in that order. Notice that no items are transmitted at all if $n \leq 0$.

The parameter of the "item" procedure (for example, the parameter of $ITEM$ or ELT in the list procedures just considered) is called by name. It may be an arithmetic expression, a Boolean expression, or a string, in accordance with the format that will be associated with the item. Any of the ordinary features of ALGOL may be used in a list procedure, so there is great flexibility.

Unlike layout procedures, which simply run through their statements and set up hidden variables H1 through H6, a list procedure is executed step by step with the input or output procedure, with control transferring back and forth. This effect is achieved by special system procedures such as *in item* and *out item*, which are "interlaced" with the list procedure as described in Sections B.4.2 and B.5. The list procedure is called by a system procedure with *in item* (or *out item*) as actual parameter, and the actual input or output takes place whenever that procedure is called within the list procedure. Through the interlacing, special format control can take place during the transmission process, including the important device-independent overflow procedures.

A list procedure may change the hidden variables by calling a descriptive procedure. Such behavior would be desirable if, for example, different formats are present in a file record, depending on the value of the first item that is input from the record.

B.4.2. Other applications. List procedures can actually be used in many ways in ALGOL besides their use with input or output routines; they are useful for manipulating linear lists of items of a quite general nature. To illustrate this fact, and to point out how the interlacing of control between list and driver procedures can be accomplished, here is an example of a procedure that calculates the sum of all elements in a list (assuming that all elements are of integer or real type):

> **procedure** $ADD(Y, Z)$;
> **begin procedure** $A(X)$; $Z := Z + X$;
> $Z := 0$; $Y(A)$
> **end**.

The call $ADD(PAIRS, SUM)$ will set the value of SUM to be the sum of all of the items in the list $PAIRS$ defined in Section B.4.1. The reader should study this example carefully to grasp the essential significance of list procedures. Notice that it uses ALGOL's ability to declare procedure A local to procedure ADD. Another simple list procedure — which has been left as an instructive exercise for the reader's edification — sets all elements of a list to zero.

B.5. INPUT AND OUTPUT CALLS

Now we are ready to consider in detail the procedures that cause data to be transmitted.

B.5.1. Output. An output process is initiated by the following call:

$$out\,list\,(unit, LAYOUT, LIST)$$

Here *unit* is an integer parameter called by value, denoting the number of an output device (see Section B.1.1). The parameter *LAYOUT* is the name of a layout procedure (Section B.3), and *LIST* is the name of a list procedure (Section B.4).

There is also another class of procedures, named *output*0, *output*1, *output*2, ..., used for output as follows:

$$output\ n(unit, format\ string, e_1, e_2, \ldots, e_n)$$

Each of these latter procedures can be defined in terms of *out list* as follows:

> **procedure** *output n(unit, format string, $e_1, e_2, \ldots, e_n$)*;
> **begin procedure** *A*; *format(format string)*;
>   **procedure** *B(P)*; **begin** *P(e_1)*; *P(e_2)*; ...; *P(e_n)* **end**;
>   *out list(unit, A, B)*
> **end**.

Thus we may assume henceforth that *out list* has been called.

Let the variables ρ and ρ' indicate the current position in the output for the unit under consideration; that is, lines 1, 2, ..., ρ' of the current page have been completed, as well as character positions 1, 2, ..., ρ of line $\rho' + 1$. At the beginning of the program, $\rho = \rho' = 0$. The symbols P and P' denote the line size and page size (see Section B.2). Output takes place according to the following algorithm:

Step 1. The hidden variables are set to standard values:
  H1 is set to the "standard" format ''.
  H2 is set so that $L = 1$ and $R = \infty$.
  H3 is set so that $L' = 1$ and $R' = \infty$.
  H4 is set so that P_N, P_R, P_P are all effectively equal to the *DUMMY* procedure defined as follows: **procedure** *DUMMY*; **begin end**.
  H5 is set so that $P_{N'}$, $P_{R'}$, $P_{P'}$ are all effectively equal to *DUMMY*.
  H6 is set to terminate the program in case the data ends. (This hidden variable actually has meaning only on input.)
Step 2. The layout procedure is called; it may change some of the variables H1, H2, H3, H4, H5, H6.
Step 3. The next format item of the format string is examined; if the format string has been exhausted, the "standard" format described in Section A.5 is used. (In particular, if the format string is '', standard format is used from the beginning.) Now if the next format item is a title format, requiring no data item, we proceed directly to step 4. Otherwise, the list procedure is activated. This activation

is done the first time by *calling* the list procedure, using as actual parameter a procedure named *out item*; it is done on all subsequent times by merely *returning* from the procedure *out item*, which will cause the list procedure to be continued from the latest *out item* call. (*Note:* The identifier *out item* has scope local to *out list*, so a programmer may not call *out item* directly.)

After the list procedure has been activated in this way, it will either terminate or will call the procedure *out item*. In the former case, the output process is completed; in the latter case, we continue at step 4.

Step 4. Take the next item from the format string. (*Notes:* If the list procedure was called in step 3, it may have called the descriptive procedure *format*, thereby changing from the format that was examined during step 3. In such a case, the new format is used here. But at this point the format item is effectively removed from the format string and copied elsewhere; the format string itself, possibly changed by further calls of *format*, will not be interrogated until the next occurrence of step 3. If the list procedure has substituted a title format for a nontitle format, the "item" it specifies will not be output, since a title format consists entirely of insertions and alignment marks.)

Set *toggle* to **false**. (This variable, local to *out list*, is used to control the breaking of entries between lines.) The alignment marks, if any, at the left of the format item, now cause process A (below) to be executed for each '/', and process B for each '↑'. If the format item consists entirely of alignment marks, then go immediately to step 3. Otherwise determine the size S of the format, namely the number of characters specified in the output medium; continue with step 5.

Step 5. Execute process C, to ensure proper page alignment.

Step 6. Line alignment: If $\rho < L - 1$, effectively insert blank spaces so that $\rho = L - 1$. Now if *toggle* = **true**, go to step 9; otherwise, test for line overflow as follows: If $\rho + S > R$, perform process D, then call P_R and go to step 8; otherwise, if $\rho + S > P$, perform process D, call P_P, and go to step 8.

Step 7. Evaluate the next output item and output it according to the rules given in Section A. (In the case of a title format, this is simply a transmission of the insertions without the evaluation of an output item.) Set the pointer ρ to $\rho + S$. Any alignment marks at the right of the format item now cause activation of process A for each '/' and of process B for each '↑'. Return to step 3.

Step 8. Set *toggle* to **true**. Prepare a formatted output item as in step 7, but do not record it on the output medium yet (recording will be done in step 9). Go to step 5. (It is necessary to re-examine page and line alignment, which may have been altered by the overflow procedure; hence we go to step 5 rather than proceeding immediately to step 9.)

Step 9. Transfer as many characters of the current output item as possible into positions $\rho + 1$, $\rho + 2$, ..., without exceeding position P or R. Adjust ρ appropriately. If the output of this item is still unfinished, execute process D again, call P_R (if $R \leq P$) or P_P (if $P < R$), and return to step 5. The entire item will eventually be output, and then we process alignment characters as in step 7, finally returning to step 3.

Process A. ('/' operation) Check page alignment with process C, then execute process D and call procedure P_N.

Process B. ('↑' operation) If $\rho > 0$, execute process A. Then execute process E and call procedure $P_{N'}$.

Process C. (Page alignment) If $\rho' < L' - 1$ and $\rho > 0$, execute process D, call procedure P_N, and repeat process C. Otherwise if $\rho' < L' - 1$ and $\rho = 0$, execute process D until $\rho' = L' - 1$. Otherwise if $\rho' + 1 > R'$, execute process E, call procedure $P_{R'}$, and repeat process C. Otherwise if $\rho' + 1 > P'$, execute process E, call procedure $P_{P'}$, and repeat process C.

Process D. Skip the output medium to the next line, set $\rho = 0$, and set $\rho' = \rho' + 1$.

Process E. Skip the output medium to the next page, and set $\rho' = 0$.

B.5.2. Input. An input process is initiated by the following call:

$$in\,list\,(unit, LAYOUT, LIST)$$

The parameters have the same significance as they did in the case of output, except that *unit* is in this case the number of an input device. There is a class of procedures *input n* that stand for a call with a particularly simple type of layout and list, just as discussed in Section B.5.1 for the case of output. In the case of input, the parameters of the "item" procedure within the list procedure must be variables.

The various steps that take place during the execution of *in list* are very much the same as those in the case of *out list*, with obvious changes. Instead of transferring characters of title format, the characters are ignored on input. If the data is improper, some standard error procedure is used (see Section A.1.3.8).

The only significant change occurs in the case of standard input format, in which the size variable S in the algorithm above cannot be determined in step 4. The tests $\rho + S > R$ and $\rho + S > P$ now become a test on whether positions $\rho + 1$, $\rho + 2$, ..., $\min(R, P)$ contain at least one number. If so, the first number is used, up to its delimiter; the R and P positions serve as delimiters here. If not, however, overflow occurs, and subsequent lines are searched until a number is found (possibly causing additional overflows). The right boundary $\min(R, P)$ will not count as a delimiter in the case of overflow. This rule has been made so that the process of input is dual to that of output: An input item is not split across more than one line unless it has overflowed twice.

Notice that programmers are able to determine the presence or absence of data on a card when using standard format, because of the way overflow is defined. For example, the following program will count the number n of data items on a single input card and will read them into $A[1]$, $A[2]$, ..., $A[n]$. (Assume that unit 5 is a card reader.)

> **procedure** *LAY*; *h end*(*EXIT*, *EXIT*, *EXIT*);
> **procedure** *LIST*(*ITEM*); *ITEM*(*A*[*n* + 1]);
> **procedure** *EXIT*; **go to** *L2*;
> $n := 0$;
> *L1*: *in list*(5, *LAY*, *LIST*);
> $n := n + 1$; **go to** *L1*;
> *L2*: **comment** mission accomplished;

B.5.3. Skipping. Two procedures are available that achieve an effect similar to that of the "tab" key on a typewriter:

$$h\,skip\,(position, OVERFLOW)$$

$$v\,skip\,(position, OVERFLOW)$$

Here *position* is an integer variable called by value, and *OVERFLOW* is the name of a procedure. These procedures are defined only if they are called within a list procedure during an *in list* or *out list* operation. For *h skip*, if $\rho < position$, set $\rho = position$; but if $\rho \geq position$, call the procedure *OVERFLOW*. For *v skip*, an analogous procedure is carried out: if $\rho' < position$, effectively execute process A of Section B.5.1 a total of $(position - \rho')$ times; but if $\rho' \geq position$, call the procedure *OVERFLOW*.

B.5.4. Intermediate data storage. The procedure call

$$put\,(n, LIST)$$

takes the values specified by *LIST* and stores them, together with the identification number n. Here n is an integer parameter called by value and *LIST* is the name of a list procedure (Section B.4). Anything previously stored with the same identification number is lost. The variables entering into the list do not lose their values.

The procedure call

$$get(n, LIST)$$

retrieves the set of values that has previously been *put* away with identification number n. As before, n is an integer parameter called by value and *LIST* is the name of a list procedure (Section B.4). The items in *LIST* must be variables. The stored values are retrieved in the same order as they were placed, and they must be compatible with the types of the elements specified by *LIST*; transfer functions may be invoked to convert from real to integer type or vice versa. If fewer items are in *LIST* than are associated with n, only the first are retrieved; if *LIST* contains more items, the situation is undefined. The values associated with n in the external storage are not changed by *get*.

B.6. CONTROL PROCEDURES

Programmers may use the procedure calls

$$in\,control(unit, x1, x2, x3, x4)$$
$$out\,control(unit, x1, x2, x3, x4)$$

to determine the values of normally "hidden" system parameters, in order to have finer control over input and output. Here *unit* is the number of an input or output device, and $x1$, $x2$, $x3$, $x4$ are variables. The action of these procedures is to set $x1$, $x2$, $x3$, $x4$ equal to the current values of ρ, P, ρ', P', respectively, corresponding to the device specified.

B.7. OTHER PROCEDURES

Other procedures that apply to specific input or output devices may be defined at certain installations — for example, *tape skip* and *rewind* for controlling magnetic tape. An installation may also define further descriptive procedures (thus introducing further hidden variables). For example, a procedure might be added to name a label to which control is transferred in case of an input error. Procedures for obtaining the current values of hidden variables might also be incorporated.

C. An Example

The following simple example prints the first 20 lines of Pascal's triangle in triangular form, beginning with

$$
\begin{array}{ccccccc}
 & & & 1 & & & \\
 & & 1 & & 1 & & \\
 & 1 & & 2 & & 1 & \\
1 & & 3 & & 3 & & 1
\end{array}
$$

These first 20 lines involve numbers that are at most five digits in magnitude. The output is to begin a new page, and it is to be double-spaced and preceded by the title 'PASCALS TRIANGLE'. We assume that unit number 3 is a line printer.

Two solutions of the problem are given, each of which uses slightly different portions of the input-output conventions.

```
begin integer N, K, printer;
   integer array A[0:19];
   procedure AK(ITEM);  ITEM(A[K]);
   procedure TRIANGLE;
   begin format('6Z');
      h lim(58 − 3 × N, 63 + 3 × N)
   end;
   printer := 3;
   output 0(printer, '↑'PASCALS␣TRIANGLE'//');
   for N := 0 step 1 until 19 do
      begin A[N] := 1;
         for K := N − 1 step −1 until 1 do
            A[K] := A[K − 1] + A[K];
         for K := 0 step 1 until N do
            out list(printer, TRIANGLE, AK);
         output 0(printer, '//')
      end
end


begin integer N, K, printer;
   integer array A[0:19];
   procedure LINES; format 2('XB, X(6Z), //', 57 − 3 × N, N + 1);
   procedure LIST(Q); for K := 0 step 1 until N do Q(A[K]);
   printer := 3;
   output 1(printer, '↑20S//', 'PASCALS␣TRIANGLE');
```

```
    for N := 0 step 1 until 19 do
        begin A[N] := 1;
            for K := N − 1 step −1 until 1 do
                A[K] := A[K − 1] + A[K];
            out list(printer, LINES, LIST)
        end
    end
```

D. Machine-Dependent Aspects

Since input-output processes must be machine-dependent to a certain extent, the portions of this proposal that are machine-dependent are summarized here.

1) The values of P and P' for the input and output devices.
2) The treatment of I, L, and R (unformatted) format.
3) The number of characters in standard output format.
4) The internal representation of alpha format.
5) The number of spaces, k, that serve to delimit standard input format values.

References

[1] *AED Compiler* (Cambridge, Massachusetts: Electronic Systems Laboratory, Massachusetts Institute of Technology).

[2] R. Baumann, editor, "ALGOL-Manual der ALCOR-Gruppe," *Elektronische Rechenanlagen* **3** (1961), 206–212, 259–264; **4** (1962), 71–85.

[3] F. G. Duncan, "Input and output for ALGOL 60 on KDF 9," *The Computer Journal* **5** (1963), 341–344.

[4] *Extended ALGOL Reference Manual for the Burroughs B-5000*, Report 5000-21012 (Detroit, Michigan: Burroughs Corporation, 1963).

[5] C. A. R. Hoare, "The Elliott ALGOL input/output system," *The Computer Journal* **5** (1963), 345–348.

[6] P. Z. Ingerman and J. N. Merner, "Revised revised ALGOL 60 report," unpublished.

[7] Peter Zilahy Ingerman, *A Syntax-Oriented Compiler* (Philadelphia: Moore School of Electrical Engineering, 1963). Later published as *A Syntax-Oriented Translator* (New York: Academic Press, 1966).

[8] D. D. McCracken, *Guide to ALGOL Programming* (New York: Wiley, 1962).

[9] Peter Naur, editor, "Revised report on the algorithmic language ALGOL 60," *Communications of the ACM* **6** (1963), 1–17.

[10] *Oak Ridge ALGOL Compiler for the Control Data 1604 Computer* (Oak Ridge, Tennessee: Oak Ridge National Laboratory).

[11] A. J. Perlis, "A format language," *Communications of the ACM* **7** (1964), 89–97.

[12] *SHARE ALGOL 60 translator manual*, No. 1426, 1577 (Hawthorne, New York: SHARE Distribution Agency).

Addendum

The procedures discussed in this report never became very popular, nor did many programmers come to appreciate the elegant features of list procedures. But on 17 July 1968, I was at least able to print Pascal's triangle using the procedures of section C with Control Data Corporation's ALGOL compiler for the 6600 computer ... and everything worked!

Corrections to the "Nine Steps" of section B.5 proved to be necessary, and they were incorporated into ISO Recommendation 1538, a document published by the International Organization for Standardization in 1972. That recommendation was, however, withdrawn a few years later.

Chapter 8

The Remaining Trouble Spots
in ALGOL 60

*This paper lists the ambiguities remaining in the language ALGOL 60
that have been noticed since the publication of the Revised Report in 1963.*

[Originally published in Communications of the ACM **10** *(1967),
611–618.]*

There is little doubt that the programming language ALGOL 60 has had
a great impact on many areas of computer science, and it seems fair to
state that this language has been more carefully studied than any other
programming language.

When ALGOL 60 was first published in 1960 [8], many new features
were introduced into programming languages, primarily with respect to
the generality of "procedures." It was quite difficult at first for anyone to
grasp the full significance of each of the linguistic features with respect to
other aspects of the language; therefore people would commonly discover
ALGOL 60 constructions they had never before realized were possible,
each time they reread the Report. Such constructions often provided
counterexamples to many of the usual techniques of compiler implementation, and in many cases it was possible to construct programs that
could be interpreted in more than one way.

The most notable feature of the first ALGOL 60 Report was the
new standard it set for language definition, based on an almost completely systematic use of syntactic rules that prescribed the structure of
programs. This innovation made it possible to know exactly what the
language ALGOL 60 was, to a much greater degree than had ever been
achieved previously.

Of course it was inevitable that a complex document such as the
ALGOL 60 Report (roughly 75 typewritten pages, prepared by an international committee) would contain some ambiguities and contradictions,

155

since it involves a very large number of highly interdependent elements. As time passed, and especially as ALGOL 60 translators were written, these problems were noticed by many people, and in 1962 a meeting of the international committee was called to help resolve the issues that had come up. The result was the Revised ALGOL 60 Report [10], which cleaned up most of the unclear points [14].

Now that several more years have gone by, it is reasonable to expect that ALGOL 60 is pretty well understood. A few points of ambiguity and contradiction still remain in the Revised ALGOL 60 Report, some of which were left unresolved at the 1962 meeting (primarily because of high feelings between people who had already implemented conflicting interpretations of ambiguous aspects), and some of which have come to light more recently.

In view of the widespread interest in ALGOL 60 it seems appropriate to have a list of all its remaining problem areas, or at least of those that are now known. This list will be useful as a guide to users of ALGOL 60, who may find it illuminating to explore some of the comparatively obscure parts of the language and who will want to know what ambiguous constructions should be avoided; and useful also to designers of other programming languages, who will want to avoid making similar mistakes in the future.

The following sections of this paper therefore enumerate the blemishes that remain. A preliminary list of all the known trouble spots was compiled by the author for use by the ALGOL 60 subcommittee of the ACM Programming Languages committee in November 1963; and after receiving extensive assistance from the committee members, the author prepared a revised document that appeared in *ALGOL Bulletin* **19**, AB19.3.7 (Amsterdam: Mathematisch Centrum, January 1965), 29–38. The present paper is, in turn, a fairly extensive modification of the *ALGOL Bulletin* article; it has been prepared at the request of several people who do not have ready access to that publication and who have pointed out the desirability of wider circulation.

The list below is actually more remarkable for its shortness than for its length. A complete critique that goes to the same level of detail would be almost out of the question for other languages comparable to ALGOL 60, since the list would probably be a full order of magnitude longer.

This paper is divided into two parts, one that lists *ambiguities* and another that lists *corrections*. The word "ambiguous" is itself quite ambiguous, and it is used here in the following sense: An aspect of ALGOL 60 is said to be ambiguous if, on the basis of the Revised ALGOL 60

Report, it is possible to write an ALGOL 60 program for which the feature in question can be interpreted in two ways, leading to different computations in the program; and if it is impossible to prove conclusively from the Revised Report that either of the conflicting interpretations is incorrect.

So-called "syntactic ambiguities" are not necessarily ambiguities of the language in the sense considered here, although the original AL-GOL 60 Report contained some syntactic ambiguities that did lead to discrepancies. (See [1] and [7] for a discussion of the former ambiguities; and see correction 7 below and the discussion at the end of Section 3 in [5] for comments on syntactic ambiguities remaining in the Revised Report.)

The distinction between an "ambiguity" in ALGOL 60 and a "correction" that is necessary to the Report is not clear cut. When the Report contains an error or contradictory statement, the error might lead to ambiguous interpretations; conversely, any ambiguity might be considered an error in the Report. The difference is mainly a matter of degree: The true meanings of points that merely need to be corrected are almost universally agreed upon by people who have studied the Report carefully, because of the overall spirit of the language, in spite of the fact that some of the rules are stated incorrectly.

Frequent references are made in the discussions below to the numbered sections of the Revised Report [10]. Readers are advised to have that document available for comparison if they wish to understand the full significance of the comments that follow.

People who have studied the ALGOL Report carefully have often been called "ALGOL theologians," because of an analogy between the Bible and the Revised Report — which is the ultimate source of wisdom about ALGOL 60. Using the same analogy, it is possible to view the following sections as a more or less objective discussion of the conflicting doctrines that have been based on those Scriptures.

Part 1. Ambiguities

Ambiguity 1: Side Effects

A "side effect" of a call on a function designator is conventionally regarded as a change to the state of some quantity that is not local to the function designator, or a change to an **own** variable. In other words, when a procedure is being called in the midst of some expression it has side effects if, in addition to computing a value, it does input or output or changes the value of some variable that is not internal to the procedure.

For example, let us consider the following program:

```
begin integer a;
    integer procedure f(x, y); value y, x; integer y, x;
        a := f := x + 1;
    integer procedure g(x); integer x;
        x := g := a + 2;
    a := 0;
    outreal(1, a + f(a, g(a))/g(a))
end.
```

Here both f and g have, as a side effect, the alteration of a nonlocal variable.

It is clear that the value output by this program depends heavily upon the order of computation. Many compilers find that more efficient object programs are obtained if the denominator of a complicated fraction is evaluated before the numerator. If we first compute $g(a)$, then $f(a, g(a))$, then $a + f(a, g(a))/g(a)$, and if the evaluation of the **value** parameters in $f(a, g(a))$ is done in the order a, $g(a)$, then we get the answer $3 + 3/2 = 9/2$. Other possible answers are $1/3$, $3/5$, $3/2$, $5/2$, $4/3$, $18/5$, $10/3$, $28/5$, $7/2$, and $15/2$.

The major point left unresolved in the Revised Report was the ambiguity about side effects: Are they allowed in ALGOL 60 programs, and if so what do the programs mean? If side effects are allowable, then the order of computation must be specified in the following places: evaluating the primaries of an expression; evaluating the subscripts of a variable; evaluating bound pairs in a block head; evaluating **value** parameters; and (perhaps) the step-until element of a for clause. Note, for example, that **value** parameters — which are to be evaluated just after entry to a procedure, according to Section 4.7.3.1 — might conceivably be evaluated in the order of their appearance in the parameter list or the order of their appearance in the value part.

An argument may actually be made for the opinion that side effects are implicitly outlawed by the fifth paragraph in Section 4.5.3.2 — or at least for the claim that any side effects occurring during the evaluation of the if clause of a conditional statement must be cancelled, as stipulated by that paragraph, if the expression happens to come out false! A similar situation occurs in Section 4.3.5, where side effects that may occur during the evaluation of a designational expression that is ultimately undefined must presumably be nullified. (On the other hand, the wording of those sections was probably an oversight, and the implication about side effects was almost certainly not intended.)

How close does the Report come to prescribing the order of computation? Section 3.3.5 says that "the sequence of operations within one expression is generally from left to right," but the context there refers to the order of carrying out arithmetic operations; and it does not say whether the value of the first term 'a' in the example above should be calculated before or after the second term '$f(a, g(a))/g(a)$' since no "operation" in the sense of the Report is actually involved. Section 4.2.3.1 says that subscript expressions occurring in the left part variables of an assignment statement are evaluated "in sequence from left to right." (So in the assignment statement

$$A[a + B[f(a)] + g(a)] := C[a] := 0$$

we are perhaps to evaluate '$a + B[f(a)] + g(a)$' first, then '$f(a)$' again, then 'a'?)

Footnote 4 of Section 1 says, "Whenever ... the outcome of a certain process is left undefined ... a program only fully defines a computational process if accompanying information specifies ... the course of action to be taken in all such cases as may occur during the execution of the computation." In Section 3.3.6 we read, "It is indeed understood that different hardware representations may evaluate arithmetic expressions differently." The latter remark was made with reference to arithmetic on **real** quantities (that is, floating-point arithmetic), but it is remarkable when viewed also from the standpoint of side effects! Footnote 4 says essentially that ALGOL 60 is not intended to be free of ambiguity, and much can be said for the desirability of incompletely specified formalisms; indeed, such incompleteness is the basis of the axiomatic method in mathematics and it is also the basis of many good jokes. But ambiguous side effects do not seem to be particularly advantageous. (For further remarks in this vein see Ambiguity 9.)

Ambiguous side effects catch many people unawares, because programmers usually know only the interpretations made by the ALGOL compiler that they use. Therefore the author has founded SPAASEPA, the Society for the Prevention of the Appearance of Ambiguous Side Effects in Published Algorithms. Members and/or donations are earnestly solicited.

It may be of value to digress for a moment here and to ask whether side effects are desirable or not, supposing that they could be defined unambiguously. Should ALGOL or comparable languages allow side effects? Do side effects serve any useful purpose, or are they just peculiar constructions for programmers who like to be tricky? Objections to side effects have often been voiced, and the most succinct formulation is perhaps that due to Samelson and Bauer in *ALGOL Bulletin* **12**, pages 7–8. The principal points raised are that (i) an explanation of the "use" of side effects tends to waste inordinate amounts of classroom time when explaining ALGOL, giving an erroneous impression of the spirit of the language; (ii) familiar identities such as $f(x)+x = x+f(x)$ are no longer valid, and this is an unnatural deviation from mathematical conventions; (iii) many "applications" of side effects are merely programming tricks making puzzles of programs; other uses can almost always be reprogrammed easily by changing a function designator to a procedure call statement. Essentially the same objections have been voiced with respect to the concept of parameters "called by name," which was the most radical new feature of ALGOL 60.

Another objection to side effects is that they may cause apparently needless computation. For example, consider

$$\textbf{if } g(a) = 2 \vee g(a) = 3 \textbf{ then } 1 \textbf{ else } 0$$

in connection with the procedure $g(x)$ above. According to the rules of the Revised Report it is necessary to evaluate $g(a)$ twice, thereby increasing a by 4, even if the first relation involving $g(a)$ is found to be true.

We might also mention the fact that ALGOL's call-by-name feature is deficient in the following respect: One cannot write an ALGOL 60 procedure '*increment*(x)' that increases the value of the variable x by unity. In particular, the procedure statement '*increment*$(A[i])$' should increase the current value of $A[i]$ by unity, when i is a function designator that may produce different values when it is invoked twice.

On the other hand, consider the following procedure:

```
real procedure SIGMA(i, l, u, x); value l, u;
    integer i, l, u; real x;
begin real s;
    s := 0;
    for i := l step 1 until u do s := s + x;
    SIGMA := s
end SIGMA.
```

This procedure computes $\sum_{i=l}^{u} x$ and has the additional side effect of changing variable i. It is quite natural to be able to write

$$SIGMA(i, 1, m, SIGMA(j, 1, n, A[i,j])) \qquad \text{for} \qquad \sum_{i=1}^{m}\sum_{j=1}^{n} A_{ij}$$

without adding special summation conventions to the language itself; this is a tame and unambiguous use of side effects, which also is the principal example that has been put forward to point out the usefulness of parameters called by name. (See [3] for further discussion.)

If we alter the *SIGMA* procedure by inserting '**integer** $i0$; $i0 := i$;' after '**real** s;' and '; $i := i0$' before '**end**', we would find that no side effect is introduced as a consequence of the total execution of the function $SIGMA(i, l, u, x)$, unless the actual parameter x does something tricky. So procedure *SIGMA* does not constitute an inherent use of side effects. In fact, a study of this particular case indicates that one might rather have some sort of facility for defining bound variables (like i and j), which have existence only during the evaluation of a function but which may appear within the arguments to that function.

We should remark also that the principal objection to allowing parameters called by name, even in natural situations like the example above, is that the machine language implementation of those constructions is necessarily much slower than we would expect a simple summation operation to be. The inner loop — namely, incrementation of i, testing against u, and adding x to s — involves a great deal of more or less irrelevant bookkeeping because i and x are called by name, even on machines like the Burroughs B5500 [2] whose hardware was specifically designed to facilitate such aspects of ALGOL. The use of "macro" definition facilities to extend languages, instead of relying solely on ALGOL-like procedures for this purpose, results in a more satisfactory running program.

Other situations for which function designators with side effects can be useful are not uncommon. Consider, for example, a procedure for input or for random number generation.

Side effects also arise naturally in connection with the manipulation of data structures, when a function changes the structure while it computes a value. For example, programmers often use a function '$pop(S)$' that deletes the top value from a "stack" S and returns the deleted value as its result. See also [6] for examples of Boolean function designators with side effects that are specifically intended for use in constructions like $p \lor q$, where q is *never* to be evaluated when p is true, and where p is to be evaluated first in any case.

The objection above that $x + f(x)$ should be equal to $f(x) + x$, because of age-old mathematical conventions, is not very strong; there are simple and natural rules for sequencing operations of an expression so that programmers know what they are doing when they are using side effects. The people who complain about '$x + f(x)$' are generally compiler writers who don't want to generate extra code to save x in temporary storage before computing $f(x)$, since the extra code is almost always unnecessary. Such inefficiency is the real reason for the objections to side effects. These same people would *not* like to see '$x = 0 \vee f(x) = 0$' be treated the same as '$f(x) = 0 \vee x = 0$' since the former relation can be used to suppress the computation of '$f(x) = 0$' when it is known that '$x = 0$'. In fact one naturally likes to write '$x = 0 \vee f(x) = 0$' in situations where $f(0)$ is undefined.

Ambiguity 2: Incomplete Functions

The question of exit from a function designator via a go to statement is another lively issue. This might be regarded as a special case of point 1, since such an exit is a "side effect," and indeed the discussion under point 1 does apply here. Some further considerations are relevant to this case, however.

Some people feel that aborted function calls provide an important feature because of "error exits." However, the same effect can be achieved by using a procedure call statement and adding an output parameter.

Two rather convincing arguments can be put forward to contend that incomplete functions are not really allowed by ALGOL, so the matter is not really an ambiguity at all.

(a) In Section 3.2.3 we read, "Function designators define single numerical or logical values." An incomplete function doesn't do that. Or, if it did, there would be mysterious, ambiguous consequences such as this:

```
begin real x, y;
   real procedure F;
   begin F := 1;
      go to L
   end;
   x := F + 1;  y := 1;  L:
end.
```

We question whether x is replaced by 2, and if so, whether y is replaced by 1 (thus incorporating simultaneity into the language?). After all, F rigorously defines the value 1 and "the value so assigned is used to continue the evaluation of the expression in which the function designator occurs." (See Section 5.4.4.)

(b) The discussion of the control of the program in Section 5.4.3.2 is based entirely on the values of the Boolean expressions, and the wording of that section implicitly excludes such a possibility. In many places the Report speaks of expressions as if they have a value, and no mention is ever made of expressions that are left unevaluated due to exits from function designators.

A further point about incomplete functions (though not really part of the ambiguity) concerns the implementation problems caused when such an exit occurs during the evaluation of the bound expressions while array declarations are being processed. Since the control words for a storage allocation scheme are not entirely set up at this time, such exits have uncovered bugs in more than one ALGOL compiler.

Ambiguity 3: Step–Until

The exact sequence occurring during the evaluation of the "step-until" element of a for clause has been the subject of much (rather heated) debate. The construction

$$\textbf{for } V := A \textbf{ step } B \textbf{ until } C \textbf{ do } S$$

(where V is a variable, A, B, C are expressions, and S is a procedure) can be replaced by a procedure call

$$for(V, A, B, C, S)$$

with a suitable procedure named 'for'. The debate centers, more or less, on which of the parameters V, A, B, C, S are to be thought of as called by value, and which are inherently called by name.

Conservative ALGOL theologians follow the sequence given in Section 4.6.4.2 very literally, so that if statement S is executed n times, the value of A is computed once, B is computed $2 \times n + 1$ times, C is computed $n + 1$ times and (if V is subscripted) the subscripts of V are evaluated $3 \times n + 2$ times. Liberal theologians take the expansion more figuratively, evaluating each of these things just once. There are many points of view between these two "extremist" positions. As a result, the following program will probably give at least four or five different output values when run on different present-day implementations of ALGOL:

```
begin array V, A, C[1:1]; integer k;
   integer procedure i; begin i := 1;  k := k + 1 end;
   k := 0;  A[1] := 1;  C[1] := 3;
   for V[i] := A[i] step A[i] until C[i] do;
   outreal(1, k)
end.
```

The liberal interpretation gives an output of 4, the conservative interpretation gives something like 23, and intermediate interpretations give intermediate values; for example, the compromise suggested in [12] gives the value 16.

The conservative argument is, "Read Section 4.6.4.2." The liberal arguments are: (a) "If Section 4.6.4.2 is to be taken literally, it gives a perfectly well defined value for the controlled variable upon exit. But Section 4.6.5 says that the value is undefined; therefore Section 4.6.4.2 is not meant to be taken literally." (b) "The repeated phase '*the* controlled variable' is always used in the singular, implying that the subscript(s) of the controlled variable need be evaluated only once during the entire for clause. Other interpretations make Section 4.6.5 meaningless."

Examination of published algorithms shows that in well over 99% of the uses of for statements, the value of the "step" B is $+1$, and in the vast majority of the exceptions the step is a constant. It is clear that programmers seldom feel the need to make use of any ambiguous cases. The liberal interpretation is clearly more efficient, and it deserves to be recommended for future programming languages. A programmer who really feels the need for some of the woollier uses of a for statement can be told to write the statements out by adding a tiny bit of program instead of using a for statement. Even though uses can be contrived for examples like

$$\textbf{for } x := .1 \textbf{ step } x \textbf{ until } 1000000$$

or

$$\textbf{for } y := 1 \textbf{ step } 1 \textbf{ until } y + 1$$

they are rewritten easily using the "while" element.

Ambiguity 4: Specifications

The wording of Section 5.4.5 can be interpreted as saying that parameters called by value must be specified only if the specification part is given at all! Furthermore, the Report doesn't state to what extent, *if any*, the actual parameters must agree with a given specification, and to what extent the specifications that do appear will affect the meaning of the program. For example, is the following program legitimate?

```
begin integer array A, B, C[0:10]; array D[0:10];
   procedure P(A, B, C); array A, B, C;
   begin integer i;
      for i := 0 step 1 until 10 do
         C[i] := A[i]/B[i]
   end P;
```

```
    integer i;
    for i := 0 step 1 until 10 do
        begin A[i] := 1; B[i] := 2
        end;
    P(A, B, C);  P(A, B, D)
end.
```

If so, the assignment statement inside the procedure will have to *round* the result or not, depending on the actual parameter used. Consider also the same procedure with the formal parameters specified to be **integer** arrays. For further discussion see [12].

Ambiguity 5: Repeated Parameters

Several published algorithms have a procedure heading like

$$\textbf{procedure } invert(A) \; order{:}(n) \; output{:}(A)$$

where two of the formal parameters have the same name. The Report does not specifically exclude this, and it does not say what interpretation is to be taken.

Ambiguity 6: Value Labels

It has never been clear whether or not a designational expression can be called by value, and if so, whether its value may be "undefined" as used in Section 4.3.5. Such constructions may or may not be allowed by the language of Section 4.7.3.1 (which talks about "assignment" of values to the formal parameters in a "fictitious block"). See also Section 4.7.5.4; if a designational expression could be called by value, a switch identifier with a single component could be also, in the same way as an array identifier can be called by value. The first paragraph of Section 2.8 is relevant here as well.

Ambiguity 7: Own

Variables declared **own** have so many interpretations that it would take too much space to repeat the arguments here. See [4] and [12] for discussions of the two principal interpretations, "dynamic" and "static," each of which can be useful. The additional complications of **own** arrays with dynamically varying subscript bounds, combined with recursion, adds further ambiguities. One apparently reasonable way to define the behavior in such cases appears in [9].

Ambiguity 8: Numeric Labels and "Quantities"

Most ALGOL compilers exclude implementation of numeric labels, primarily because a correct implementation requires an unsigned integer constant parameter to be denoted, in machine language, both as a number and a label. Consider, for example,

> **begin integer** x;
>   **procedure** $P1(q,r)$; **if** $q < 5$ **then go to** r;
>   **procedure** $P2(q,r)$; **if** $r < 5$ **then go to** q;
>   **procedure** $W(Z)$; **procedure** Z; $Z(2,2)$;
> $W(P1)$; $x := 0$; $W(P2)$;
>   2: *outreal*$(1,x)$
> **end**.

There is no ambiguity here in the sense we are considering, just a difficulty of implementation — in view of the double meaning of the parameter '2'.

The author has shown the following procedure declaration to several authoritative people, however, and a 50% split developed between those who said it was or was not valid ALGOL:

$$\text{\bf procedure } P(q); \text{ \bf if } q < 5 \text{ \bf then go to } q;$$

The idea of course is that we might later call $P(2)$, where 2 is a numeric label. Actually this sort of example seems to be specifically outlawed by Section 2.4.3 (because the identifier q cannot refer to two different quantities). But consider

> **procedure** $P(q)$; **if** $B(q)$ **then** $G(q)$;
> **procedure** $G(q)$; **go to** q;
> **Boolean procedure** $B(q)$; $B := q < 5$;

Are these declarations now valid?

Consider also

> **begin integer** I; **array** $A[0{:}0]$;
>   **procedure** $P1(X)$; **array** X; $X[0] := 0$;
>   **procedure** $P2(X)$; **integer** X; $X := 0$;
>   **procedure** $call(X,Y)$; $X(Y)$;
> $call(P1,A)$; $call(P2,I)$
> **end**.

The identifier Y is used to denote two different quantities (an array and a simple variable) that have the same scope, yet this program seems to be valid in spite of the wording of Section 2.4.3.

The latter procedure is believed to be admissible because the expansion of procedure bodies should be considered from a dynamic (not static) point of view. For example, consider

> **integer procedure** *factorial*(n); **integer** n;
> *factorial* := **if** $n > 0$ **then** $n \times factorial(n - 1)$ **else** 1;

In this procedure body the call of *factorial*($n - 1$) should not be expanded unless $n > 0$; otherwise the expansion will never terminate. From the dynamic viewpoint the identifier Y in *call*(X, Y) never does in fact denote two different quantities at the same time.

Another strong argument can be put forward that even our earlier example '**if** $q < 5$ **then go to** q' is allowable. Notice that Section 2.4.3 does *not* say that an identifier may denote a string; but in fact a formal parameter *may* denote a string. Therefore we conclude that Section 2.4.3 does not apply specifically to formal parameters. This interpretation is consistent with the entire spirit of the Report, which does not speak of formal parameters except where it tells how they are to be replaced by actual parameters. The syntax equations in particular reflect such a philosophy. Consider, for example,

> **procedure** $P(Q, S)$; **procedure** Q; **string** S; $Q(S)$;

there is no way to use the syntax of ALGOL to show that '$Q(S)$' is a procedure statement and at the same time to reflect the fact that S is a string. Clearly S is an ⟨identifier⟩, but to show that it is an ⟨actual parameter⟩ we must show that it is either an ⟨expression⟩, an ⟨array identifier⟩, a ⟨switch identifier⟩, or a ⟨procedure identifier⟩, and it really is not any of these. So the only way to account for $Q(S)$ as a procedure statement is to first replace Q and S by their actual parameters, in any invocation of P, and *then* to apply the syntax equations to the result.

Ambiguity 9: Real Arithmetic

The precision of arithmetic on **real** quantities has intentionally been left ambiguous (see Section 3.3.6). In an interesting discussion, van Wijngaarden [13] has presented arguments to show, among other things, that because of this ambiguity it is not necessarily true that the relation '3.14 = 3.14' is the same as '**true**' in all implementations of ALGOL. We have already mentioned that ambiguities as such are not necessarily undesirable; but ambiguities 1–8 are certainly of a different nature than this one, since it can be quite useful to describe fixed ALGOL programs with varying arithmetic substituted.

Thus a good language need not be unambiguous. But of course when intentionally ambiguous elements are introduced, it is far better to state specifically what the ambiguities are, not merely to leave them undefined, lest too many people think they are writing unambiguous programs when they are not.

Part 2. Corrections
Correction 1: Else Clauses

Section 3.3.3 states that the construction

$$\textbf{else } \langle \text{simple arithmetic expression} \rangle$$

is equivalent to the construction

$$\textbf{else if true then } \langle \text{simple arithmetic expression} \rangle$$

But the latter construction is erroneous, since it fails to meet the syntax: We cannot write '$A :=$ **if** B **then** C **else if true then** D'. The original incorrect sentence adds nothing to the Report and means little or nothing to non-LISP programmers.

Correction 2: Conditional Statement Sequence

In Section 4.5.3.2, the paragraph "If none ... dummy statement" should be deleted, or at least accompanied by a qualification that it applies only to the second form of a conditional statement. This well-known error and also Correction 10 below would have been fixed in the Revised Report except for the fact that those proposals were tied to other ones involving side effects. In the heated discussion that took place, the less controversial issues were overlooked.

The Revised Report changed the syntax of conditional statements, thereby making Section 4.5.3.2 even more erroneous. And the revised explanation is incorrect in yet another respect, since control of the program should not pass to the statement called '$S4$' when the conditional statement is a procedure body or is preceded by a for clause. Therefore Section 4.5.3.2 should be completely rewritten, perhaps as follows:

4.5.3.2. Conditional statement. According to the syntax, three forms of unlabeled conditional statements are possible. These may be illustrated as follows:

$$\textbf{if } B \textbf{ then } S_u$$
$$\textbf{if } B \textbf{ then } S_u \textbf{ else } S$$
$$\textbf{if } B \textbf{ then } S_{for}$$

Here B is a Boolean expression, S_u is an unconditional statement, S is a statement, and S_{for} is a for statement.

The execution of a conditional statement may be described as follows: The Boolean expression B is evaluated. If its value is **true**, the statement S_u or S_{for} following 'then' is executed. If its value is **false** and if the conditional statement has the second form, the statement S following 'else' is executed. (This statement S may of course be another conditional statement, which is to be interpreted according to the same rule.)

If a go to statement refers to a label within S_u or S_{for} the effect is the same as if the remainder of the conditional statement (namely 'if B then', and in the second case also 'else S') were not present.

Correction 3: For Example

The second example in Section 4.6.2 is not very good, since (precluding side effects) it nearly always gets into an unending loop. Therefore '$V1$' should be changed to 'k' in both places.

Correction 4: Function Values

Two sentences of Section 5.4.4 should say "... as a left part ..." rather than "... in a left part ..." since a function designator may appear in a subscript. A clarification, stating that the value is lost if a **real**, **integer**, or **Boolean** procedure is called in a procedure statement, might also be added here.

Change sentence 2, Section 4.2.3, to say "... a function designator of the same name ... ," to make an implied rule explicit. Or else, consider

> **real procedure** A; $A := B := 0$;
> **integer procedure** $B(k)$; **if** $k > 0$ **then** A **else** $B := 2$;

all of the present rules appear to be obeyed.

Correction 5: Expressions

In the second sentence of Section 3, insert "labels, switch designators," after "function designators." Then the constituents of expressions are described much more accurately.

Correction 6: Division By Zero

After the second sentence of 3.3.4.2, change 'The operator ...' to: 'The operation is undefined if the factor has the value zero. In other cases, the operator ...'. (The present wording of this section seems to imply that $1/0$ is defined somehow.)

Correction 7: String Syntax

The advent of syntax-oriented compilers, and the fact that the syntax of ALGOL is (in large measure) formally unambiguous, make it desirable to change the most flagrantly ambiguous syntax rule in the Report. Therefore the definition of open string in Section 2.6.1 should become

⟨open string⟩ ::= ⟨proper string⟩ | ⟨open string⟩⟨string⟩⟨proper string⟩

Correction 8: Library Procedures

Section 2.4.3 says, "[Identifiers] may be chosen freely (cf. however, Section 3.2.4, Standard Functions)." Section 3.2.4 says, "Certain identifiers should be reserved for the standard functions of analysis, which will be expressed as procedures." If the quotation from 2.4.3 is not self-contradictory it seems to be saying that an identifier like '*abs*' may not be used by a programmer. But this would be disastrous since the list of reserved identifiers is not defined. A programmer using the name '*gamma*' for a variable may find out next year that this identifier is reserved for the gamma function. It should be made clear that any identifier may be redeclared (although redeclaration can of course lead to some difficulties when a procedure is copied from the literature into the middle of a program).

Moreover, the fourth paragraph of Section 5 specifically disallows the use of any procedures assumed to exist without declaration, except function designators denoting "standard functions of analysis." Thus, procedures such as *inreal* for accomplishing input would have to be declared in any program that uses them! A suggested change (which most people would presumably say was no change from the original intention) would be to drop the sentence "Apart from labels ... must be declared" from the paragraph mentioned, and to add the following paragraph to Section 5:

"It is understood that certain identifiers may have meaning without explicit declaration, as if they were declared in a block external to the entire program (see Section 3.2.4). Such identifiers might include, for example, names of standard input and output procedures. Apart from labels, formal parameters of procedure declarations, and these standard identifiers, each identifier appearing in a program must be declared."

This paragraph makes available other types of identifiers if there is a need for them. For example, some implementations might provide an identifier denoting a real-time clock, or a label denoting a particular part of a control program, etc.

Correction 9: Programs

The syntax for ⟨program⟩ allows a program to be labeled but the remainder of the Report always talks about labels being local to some block. To rectify this, insert three words into Section 4.1.3:

"... a procedure body <u>or a program</u> must be considered ..."

This is in fact the way a compiler should probably do the implementation (see [11]).

Correction 10: Undefined Designational Expressions

The use of the word "undefined" in Section 4.3.5 is highly ambiguous, and under some interpretations it leads to undecidable questions that would make ALGOL 60 truly impossible to implement. Under what conditions is a switch designator "undefined"? For example, we could say it is undefined if its evaluation procedure makes use of real arithmetic, or if its evaluation procedure never terminates. By a suitable construction, the latter condition can be made equivalent to the problem of deciding whether or not a Turing Machine will ever stop.

The following procedure is an amusing (although unambiguous) example of the application of an undefined go to statement, which points out how difficult it can be for an optimizing ALGOL 60 translator to detect the fact that a procedure is being called recursively:

```
begin integer nn;
    switch A := B[1], B[2];
    switch B := A[G], A[2];
    integer procedure F(n, S); value n; integer n; switch S;
        begin nn := n; go to S[1]; F := nn end F;
    integer procedure G;
    begin integer n;
        n := nn;  G := 0;
        nn := if n ≤ 1 then n else F(n − 1, A) + F(n − 2, A)
    end G;
    outreal(1, F(20, A))
end.
```

The output of this program should be 6765 (the twentieth Fibonacci number).

Correction 11: Call By Name

Instead of "Some important particular cases of this general rule" at the end of Section 4.7.5, the Report should say, for example, "Some important particular cases of this general rule, and some additional restrictions." The restrictions of Subsection 4.7.5.2 are not always special cases of the general rule, as shown in the following amusing example:

> **begin procedure** $S(x)$; $x := 0$;
>   **real procedure** r; $S(r)$;
>   **real** x; $x := 1$;
> $S(\textbf{if } x = 1 \textbf{ then } r \textbf{ else } x)$; *outreal*$(1, x)$
> **end**.

This program seems to have a historical claim of being the last "surprise" noticed by ALGOL punsters; it contains two unexpected twists, the first of which was suggested independently by P. Ingerman and H. Bekić:

a) Procedure r uses $S(r)$ to set the value of r to zero.

b) The expansion of the procedure statement on the last line, according to the rules of "call by name," leads to a valid ALGOL program that has a completely different structure from the body of S:

$$\textbf{if } x = 1 \textbf{ then } r \textbf{ else } x := 0$$

Here an unconditional statement plus a conditional expression has become a conditional statement.

Fortunately both of these situations have been ruled out by Section 4.7.5.2.

Conclusion

For centuries, astronomers have given the name ALGOL to a star that is also called Medusa's head. The author has tried to indicate every known blemish in [10]; and he hopes that nobody will ever scrutinize any of his own writings as meticulously as he and others have examined the ALGOL Report.

The preparation of this paper has been supported in part by the National Science Foundation and in part by the Burroughs Corporation.

References

[1] Paul W. Abrahams, "A final solution to the dangling **else** of ALGOL 60 and related languages," *Communications of the ACM* **9** (1966), 679–682.

[2] *B5500 Information Processing Systems Reference Manual* (Pasadena, California: Burroughs Corporation, 1964).

[3] E. W. Dijkstra, "Defense of ALGOL 60," *Communications of the ACM* **4** (1961), 502–503.

[4] Donald E. Knuth and Jack N. Merner, "ALGOL 60 *Confidential*," *Communications of the ACM* **4** (1961), 268–272. [Reprinted as Chapter 4 of the present volume.]

[5] Donald E. Knuth, "On the translation of languages from left to right," *Information and Control* **8** (1965), 607–639. [Reprinted as Chapter 15 of the present volume.]

[6] B. M. Leavenworth, "FORTRAN IV as a syntax language," *Communications of the ACM* **7** (1964), 72–80.

[7] J. N. Merner, Discussion question, *Communications of the ACM* **7** (1964), 71.

[8] Peter Naur, editor, "Report on the algorithmic language ALGOL 60," *Communications of the ACM* **3** (1960), 299–314.

[9] Peter Naur, "Questionnaire," *ALGOL Bulletin* **14** (Copenhagen: Regnecentralen, 16 January 1962), 1–14. [Fifty-one interesting responses to this questionnaire are presented in *ALGOL Bulletin* **15** (16 June 1962), 3–51.]

[10] Peter Naur, editor, "Revised report on the algorithmic language ALGOL 60," *Communications of the ACM* **6** (1963), 1–17.

[11] B. Randell and L. J. Russell, *ALGOL 60 Implementation* (London: Academic Press, 1964).

[12] R. E. Utman, editor, "Suggestions on ALGOL 60 (Rome) issues," *Communications of the ACM* **6** (1963), 20–23.

[13] A. van Wijngaarden, "Switching and programming," in *Switching Theory in Space Technology*, edited by Howard Aiken and William F. Main (Stanford, California: Stanford University Press, 1963), 275–283.

[14] M. Woodger, editor, "Supplement to the ALGOL 60 report," *Communications of the ACM* **6** (1963), 18–20.

Addendum

For the final official word on these issues, see R. M. De Morgan, I. D. Hill, and B. A. Wichmann, "A supplement to the ALGOL 60 Revised Report," *The Computer Journal* **19** (1976), 276–287, 379; "Modified report on the algorithmic language ALGOL 60," *The Computer Journal* **19** (1976), 364–379.

Chapter 9

SOL — A Symbolic Language for General-Purpose Systems Simulation

*[Written with J. L. McNeley. Originally published in IEEE Transactions on Electronic Computers **EC-13** (1964), 401–408.]*

This paper illustrates the use of SOL, a general-purpose algorithmic language useful for describing and simulating complex systems. Such systems can be represented as a number of individual processes, which simultaneously enact programs that are similar to computer programs. (Some features of the SOL language are directly applicable to programming languages for parallel computers, as well as for simulation.) Once a system has been described in the language, the programs can be translated by the SOL compiler into an interpretive code, and the execution of this code produces statistical information about the model. A detailed example of a SOL model for a multiple online console system is exhibited, indicating the notational simplicity and intuitive nature of the language.

Simulation by computer is one of the most important tools available to scientists and engineers who are studying complex systems. The first computer programs of this type were especially designed to simulate some particular model; but afterwards the authors of several such programs abstracted the essential features of their work and developed *general-purpose* simulation programs. The most extensively used general-purpose programs of this type have apparently been the SIMSCRIPT compiler of Markowitz, Hausner, and Karr [1] and the GPSS (General-Purpose Systems Simulator) routines of Gordon [2]–[4].

Although SIMSCRIPT and GPSS are both general-purpose simulation programs, they are built around quite different concepts because of their independent evolution; hence they bear little resemblance to each other. SOL (Simulation-Oriented Language) is another general-purpose simulation routine, in which we have attempted to incorporate the best

175

features of the other languages. After a careful study of SIMSCRIPT and GPSS, and after having implemented a version of GPSS on another computer, we found that it would be possible to generalize the characteristics of both programs, while at the same time obtaining a language that is simpler and more convenient for the preparation of models. This simplification was achieved by extracting the essential characteristics of GPSS and recasting them into a symbolic language such as SIMSCRIPT.

There are, of course, a great many ways in which such a combination could be done, and we are not sure that the compromises we have chosen have been optimal. But a year of experience with the SOL language, after applying it to several problems of different kinds, indicates that SOL is quite a powerful and flexible way to describe systems for simulation. We also found that the increased generality available in SOL was actually simpler to implement into a computer program than the previous routines were.

A complex system can be represented as a number of individual processes, each of which follows a *program* very much like a computer program. For example, if we want to simulate traffic in a network of streets, we might have one program describing a typical automobile (or perhaps two programs, one that describes all of the women drivers and one that describes all of the men); another program might represent the action of traffic signals; and additional programs might be included to represent pedestrians, etc. Each program depends not only on quantities that are specified in advance, but also on *random* quantities that describe a probabilistic behavior; thus, we can specify the probability that a driver will turn left, the probability that he or she will switch lanes, the distribution of speeds, and so forth. Although each program represents only a single entity (such as a single automobile), there can be many entities each carrying out the same program, each at its own place in the program.

Because of these considerations, SOL is very much like a problem-oriented language such as ALGOL or FORTRAN. But there are three major points of difference between SOL and conventional compiler languages. SOL provides

1) mechanisms for parallel computation;

2) a convenient notation for random elements within arithmetic expressions;

3) automatic means of gathering statistics about the elements involved.

On the other hand, many of the features of problem-oriented languages do not appear in SOL, not because they are incompatible with it, but rather because they introduce more complication than seems to be of practical value for simulation.

After a program written in the SOL language has been punched onto cards, it is compiled by the SOL *compiler* into an interpretive pseudocode. The SOL *interpreter* is another machine program, which executes the pseudocode and produces the results. (The SOL system has been implemented for the B5000 computer, but at the present time it is being used only for research within the Burroughs Corporation, and it is not currently available for distribution.)

A self-contained, complete description of SOL appears in another paper [5]. The definition there is rather terse, since it is intended primarily as a reference description; we will introduce the language here by means of a detailed example, discussing the significance of each statement in an intuitive fashion.

Example: Communication with Remote Terminals

The following example has been chosen not only to illustrate most of the features of SOL, but also because it is a practical application in which SOL has been used to evaluate the design of an actual system of some complexity.

Consider the configuration shown in Figure 1. This diagram represents one of four similar groups of devices, which all share the computer shown at the right. The tu's are terminal units that may be thought of as inquiry stations or typewriters. There are three groups of terminals, with three in the first group ($tu[1]$, $tu[3]$, $tu[5]$), two in the second group ($tu[2]$, $tu[4]$) and only one in the third ($tu[6]$). These groups are located many miles from each other and from the central processor. People come in at the rate of about five or six per minute to use each terminal, and they wait in the appropriate queue until the terminal is free.

These people will send one of three kinds of messages.

Message	Frequency	Compute time	Number of Response Words
A	20 percent	250 msec	3
B	50 percent	300 msec	4
C	30 percent	400 msec	5

Each message type has a different frequency and requires a different amount of central processor time.

Communication between the terminals and the computer is handled by *site buffers* ($sb[1]$, $sb[2]$, $sb[3]$), one at each remote site, and by two *processor buffer units* ($pbu[1]$, $pbu[2]$), which receive the information and

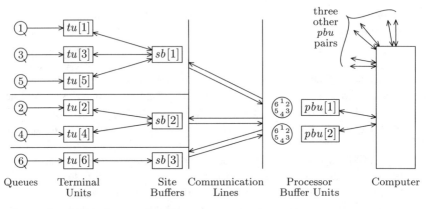

FIGURE 1. Multiple console online communication system.

transmit it to the computer. These processor buffers sequentially scan $tu[1]$, $tu[2]$, ..., $tu[6]$, $tu[1]$, ... until locating a terminal ready to transmit information; this scanning is done by sending control pulses to all lines, then receiving a "positive" response from the sb if the appropriate tu is ready. Then a message is transferred from the sb to the pbu and from there to the computer; after calculating the answer, the computer refills the pbu, and the appropriate number of words is sent back to the sb and is typed on the tu (one word at a time). Further details will be given as we discuss the program.

We will compose three programs:

1) A program that describes the action of each person who uses the remote terminals.

2) A program that describes the action of each of the two pbu's.

3) A program that simulates the action of the other six pbu's, which share the central computer with the configuration shown in Fig. 1.

Figure 2 shows these three programs together with the control information, as a complete SOL model.

The independent entities that enact the programs as the simulation proceeds are called *transactions*. (Much of the terminology used in SOL is taken from Gordon's simulator [2]–[4].) As simulation begins, there are only three transactions: one for each of the programs (1), (2), (3). Therefore, these programs describe not only the actions of the entities mentioned above, they also describe the creation and dissolution of new transactions.

Each transaction contains *local variables*, which have values that can be referred to only by that transaction. There are also *global variables*, and a few other types of global quantities, which can be referred to by all transactions. Thus, transactions can interact with each other by setting and testing global quantities. Only one "copy" of each global variable is present in the system, but there are in general many copies of each local variable (one for each transaction).

Program (1), which represents the people using the terminals, might begin as follows:

> **process** *users*;
> **begin integer** *q*, *start time*, *message type*;
>   **new transaction to** *start*; **new transaction to** *start*;
> *origin*: **new transaction to** *start*; **wait** $0:5000$;
>   **go to** *origin*;
> *start*:

The first line merely identifies a *process* (that is, a program) with the name *users*. The language resembles ALGOL, and we distinguish control words by putting them in bold-face type. The second line states that transactions for users have three local variables: *q*, *start time*, and *message type*.

The statement '**new transaction to** *start*' describes the creation of a new transaction whose local variables have the same values as the local variables of the parent transaction (in this case zero, since local variables are always zero at the beginning of a process); this new transaction begins executing the program at the statement labeled *start*.

The statement '**wait** $0:5000$' means that an amount of simulated time, chosen randomly from 0 to 5000, is to elapse before the next statement is executed. In general, the statement '**wait** E', where E is some expression, means that E units of time are to pass before executing the next statement. The expression $E_1:E_2$ always denotes a random integer chosen between E_1 and E_2; therefore '**wait** $0:5000$' has the meaning stated above. A unit of time in this case represents 1 millisecond in the simulated model.

The reader should now reread the opening statements of the *users* process above before proceeding further. The gist of that process is that three transactions will begin executing the program beginning at the statement called *start*, and thereafter a new transaction (that is, a new user entering the system) will be created at intervals of about 2.5 seconds. We have started the system with three user transactions so that it will not take very long to arrive at a more or less stable condition.

begin comment an online communication system;
    facility $tu[6]$, $sb[3]$, *line*, *computer*;
    store (10) *queue*[6];
    integer *tustate*[6], *sbnumber*[6], *tumessage*[6];
    table (2000 **step** 1000 **until** 15000) *table*[6];

    process *master control*;
    begin $sbnumber[1] \leftarrow 1$; $sbnumber[2] \leftarrow 2$; $sbnumber[3] \leftarrow 1$;
        $sbnumber[4] \leftarrow 2$; $sbnumber[5] \leftarrow 1$; $sbnumber[6] \leftarrow 3$;
        wait $60 \times 60 \times 1000$;   **stop**;
    end *master control*;

    process *users*;
    begin integer q, *start time*, *message type*;
        new transaction to *start*;   **new transaction to** *start*;
    origin: **new transaction to** *start*;   **wait** $0{:}5000$;   **go to** *origin*;
    start: $q \leftarrow 1{:}6$;   **enter** *queue*[q];
        message type $\leftarrow (1, 1, 2, 2, 2, 2, 2, 3, 3, 3)$;
        seize $tu[q]$;
        tumessage[q] $\leftarrow$ *message type*;
        wait $6000{:}8000$;
        start time $\leftarrow$ **time**;
        output "tu", q, "sends message", *message type*,
                "at time", **time**;
        tustate[q] $\leftarrow 1$;
        wait until *tustate*[q] $= 0$;
        release $tu[q]$;   **leave** *queue*[q];
        tabulate (**time** $-$ *start time*) **in** *table*[q];
        output "tu", q, "receives reply at time", **time**;
        cancel;
    end *users*;

    process *pbu*;
    begin integer $s, t, words$;
        new transaction to *scan*; $t \leftarrow 3$;
    scan: $t \leftarrow t + 1$; **if** $t > 6$ **then** $t \leftarrow 1$;   **wait** 1;
        $s \leftarrow sbnumber[t]$;

FIGURE 2. A complete SOL program

```
    seize line;
    wait 5;
    if sb[s] busy then (wait 80; release line; go to scan);
    seize sb[s];  wait 15;
    if tustate[t] ≠ 1 then
        (wait 65; release line; release sb[s]; go to scan);
    wait 225;
send: wait 170; if pr(0.02) then (wait 20; go to send);
    new transaction to computation;  wait 20;  release sb[s];
    release line; tustate[t] ← 2; cancel;
computation: seize computer;  words ← tumessage[t] + 2;
    wait (if words = 3 then 250
            else if words = 4 then 300 else 400);
    release computer;
output: wait 1; seize line; wait 5;
    if sb[s] busy then (wait 80; release line; go to output);
    seize sb[s];  wait 75;
receive: wait 80; if pr(0.01) then (wait 20; go to receive);
    release line;
    words ← words − 1;
    if words = 0 then new transaction to scan;
    wait 325;  release sb[s];  wait 170;
    if words > 0 then go to output;
    tustate[t] ← 0;  cancel;
end pbu;

process other pbus;
begin integer i;  i ← 6;
create: new transaction to compute;
    i ← i − 1;  if i > 0 then go to create;
    cancel;
compute: wait 3200:5000;  seize computer;
    wait (250, 250, 300, 300, 300, 300, 300, 400, 400, 400);
    release computer;  go to compute;
end other pbus;
end.
```

for the online communication system.

The program now proceeds as follows:

start: $q \leftarrow 1\!:\!6$; **enter** *queue*$[q]$;

The statement '$q \leftarrow 1\!:\!6$' means that local variable q is set to a random number between 1 and 6; thus the user is assigned to one of the six terminals. The '**enter**' statement refers to one of six global quantities *queue*$[1]$, ..., *queue*$[6]$. At the conclusion of the simulation, data will be reported giving the average number of people in each queue per unit of time, and also the maximum number.

message type $\leftarrow (1, 1, 2, 2, 2, 2, 2, 3, 3, 3)$;

The expression $(E_1, E_2, \ldots, E_n)$ denotes a random choice selected from among the n expressions. Therefore, the given statement means that the local variable *message type* receives the value 1 with probability 20 percent, 2 with probability 50 percent, and 3 with probability 30 percent; this represents the choice of message A, B, or C as stated earlier.

seize *tu*$[q]$;

This **seize** statement refers to one of the global quantities $tu[1]$, $tu[2]$, ..., $tu[6]$, which are classified as *facilities*. A facility is *seized* by one transaction, and then it cannot be seized by another transaction until it has been *released* by the former transaction. Therefore, if transaction X comes to a seize statement, where the corresponding facility is *busy* (that is, has been seized by transaction Y), transaction X stops executing its program until transaction Y releases the facility. If several transactions are waiting for the same event, they are processed in a first-come-first-served fashion. Thus, the statement '**seize** *tu*$[q]$' expresses an activity in which the user takes control of terminal number q, after possibly waiting in line for it to become available.

tumessage$[q] \leftarrow$ *message type*;

This statement says that the global variable *tumessage*$[q]$ is set to indicate the type of message. This global variable is used to communicate with the *pbu* process that is described below.

wait $6000\!:\!8000$;

This statement simulates an elapsed time of 6 to 8 seconds, needed by the user to type a request on the terminal unit.

start time $\leftarrow$ **time**;

We now set the local variable *start time* equal to '**time**', the current value of the simulated clock.

> **output** "tu", q, "sends message", *message type*,
> "at time", **time**;

This statement causes a line to be printed during the simulation, having the form

> tu 3 sends message 2 at time 12610.

The '"' symbols delimit strings inserted into the output.

> *tustate* [q] ← 1;

Another global variable, *tustate* [q], is now set to 1, indicating that the typed message is ready to send. This variable *tustate* [q] has three possible settings:

> *tustate* $= 0$ means that the *tu* is free.
> *tustate* $= 1$ means that the message has been typed.
> *tustate* $= 2$ means that the answer message may be typed.

The next statement

> **wait until** *tustate* [q] $= 0$;

means that the transaction is to stop at this point until *tustate* [q] has been set to zero (by some other transaction). This statement indicates that we are to wait until the answer message has been fully received. When that occurs, the transaction finishes its work as follows:

> **release** *tu*[q]; **leave** *queue*[q];
> **tabulate** (**time** − *start time*) **in** *table*[q];

A **release** statement releases a facility that has been seized, and a **leave** statement exits a queue that has been entered. A **tabulate** statement is used for statistical data; here *table*[q] is a global quantity that receives "observations" of tabulated amounts. At the end of simulation, this table will be printed out giving the mean, the standard deviation, and a histogram of the observations that it has received.

> **output** "tu", q, "receives reply at time", **time**;
> **cancel**;
> **end** *users*;

A line will be printed, showing when the reply has been received. The last statement, '**cancel**', causes the disappearance of the transaction, and the word '**end**' indicates the end of the program for this process.

Program (2), which runs concurrently with (1) and (3), describes the action of the *pbu*'s in a similar way:

> **process** *pbu*; **begin integer** *s, t, words*;
>   **new transaction to** *scan*; $t \leftarrow 3$;
> *scan*:

This program has three local variables, *s*, *t*, and *words*. At the beginning, two transactions (representing the two *pbu*'s) start at *scan*, one with its variable $t = 0$, the other with $t = 3$.

> $t \leftarrow t + 1$; **if** $t > 6$ **then** $t \leftarrow 1$; **wait** 1;

These statements represent the cyclic scanning process, which we assume takes 1 millisecond. The variable *t* represents the number of the *tu* that the *pbu* will be interrogating.

> $s \leftarrow sbnumber[t]$;

Here '*sbnumber*' is a table of constants, which is used to tell which *sb* corresponds to the *tu* being scanned.

> **seize** *line*;

We now seize the *line* facility, which represents the long-distance communication lines. (If the other *pbu* has seized *line* already, we must wait until the line has been released.)

> **wait** 5;
> **if** *sb*[*s*] **busy then** (**wait** 80; **release** *line*; **go to** *scan*);

We wait 5 msec for a control signal to propagate to the *sb* unit. Here *sb*[*s*] is a facility; if it is busy (that is, if it has been seized by the other *pbu*) we wait 80 msec more, receiving no signal back, so we release the line and return to scan the next *tu*.

> **seize** *sb*[*s*]; **wait** 15;
> **if** *tustate*[*t*] $\neq$ 1 **then**
>   (**wait** 65; **release** *line*; **release** *sb*[*s*]; **go to** *scan*);

If *sb*[*s*] received the control signal, it is brought under the control of this *pbu*. Fifteen milliseconds later, the number *t* has been transmitted across the line, and it takes 65 msec for the *sb* to determine if *tu*[*t*] is ready to transmit or not. If not, we release the *sb* and the line, and scan again.

> **wait** 225;
> *send*: **wait** 170; **if** $\mathbf{pr}(0.02)$ **then** (**wait** 20; **go to** *send*);

It takes 225 msec for the *sb* to get ready to transmit the message and to send a warning signal across the line to the *pbu*. Then 170 msec are required to send the input message. The construction '**if** $\mathbf{pr}(0.02)$' means

"2 percent of the time"; this statement indicates that, with probability
0.02, a parity error in the transmission is detected. In such a case we
send back a signal calling for retransmission of the message.

> **new transaction to** *computation*; **wait** 20; **release** *sb*[*s*];
> **release** *line*; *tustate*[*t*] ← 2; **cancel**;

At this point two parallel processes take place. As the *pbu* tries to
send the message to the computer, it also sends a "message received"
signal across the lines to the *sb*, and, 20 msec later, the *sb* and the
lines are released. The *tustate* is adjusted, and then this portion of the
transaction is canceled.

> *computation*: **seize** *computer*; *words* ← *tumessage*[*t*] + 2;
>   **wait** (**if** *words* = 3 **then** 250
>   **else if** *words* = 4 **then** 300 **else** 400);
>   **release** *computer*;

Here we send the message to the computer facility, possibly waiting for
it to become available. The local variable *words* is set to the number of
words output for the current message, and we also wait the appropriate
amount of computer time. At this point, the output message has been
created by the computer, and it has been sent back to the *pbu*. The
final job is to output this message, one word at a time:

> *output*: **wait** 1; **seize** *line*; **wait** 5;
>   **if** *sb*[*s*] **busy then** (**wait** 80; **release** *line*; **go to** *output*);

A control word is sent out to interrogate the *sb*, as in the case of input
above.

> **seize** *sb*[*s*]; **wait** 75;
> *receive*: **wait** 80; **if** **pr**(0.01) **then** (**wait** 20; **go to** *receive*);
>   **release** *line*;

We have output one word to the *sb*; there was a 1 percent probability
that a transmission error was detected.

> *words* ← *words* − 1;
> **if** *words* = 0 **then new transaction to** *scan*;
> **wait** 325; **release** *sb*[*s*]; **wait** 170;

After the last word has been transmitted, a parallel activity starts with
another scan. It takes 325 msec for the *sb* to send the word to the
terminal, and another 170 msec are required for the terminal to finish
its typing.

> **if** *words* > 0 **then go to** *output*;
> *tustate* [*t*] ← 0; **cancel**;
> **end** *pbu*;

Finally, when the output has all been typed, *tustate* is reset to zero (thus activating the *user* transaction) and this parallel branch of the program disappears.

Program (3) is used to describe the traffic that takes place at the computer, by creating six simulated *pbu*'s as follows:

> **process** *other pbus*;
> **begin integer** *i*; *i* ← 6;
> *create*: **new transaction to** *compute*;
>   *i* ← *i* − 1; **if** *i* > 0 **then go to** *create*;
>   **cancel**;
> *compute*: **wait** 3200:5000; **seize** *computer*;
>   **wait** (250, 250, 300, 300, 300, 300, 300, 400, 400, 400);
>   **release** *computer*; **go to** *compute*;
> **end** *other pbus*;

Our example program is now almost complete. We precede the three processes given above by the following code, which declares the global quantities. There is also a fourth process, which accomplishes the initialization and which stops the simulation after 1 hour of simulated time.

> **facility** *tu* [6], *sb* [3], *line*, *computer*;
> **store** (10) *queue* [6];
> **integer** *tustate* [6], *sbnumber* [6], *tumessage* [6];
> **table** (2000 **step** 1000 **until** 15000) *table* [6];
>
> **process** *master control*;
> **begin** *sbnumber* [1] ← 1; *sbnumber* [2] ← 2; *sbnumber* [3] ← 1;
>   *sbnumber* [4] ← 2; *sbnumber* [5] ← 1; *sbnumber* [6] ← 3;
>   **wait** 60 × 60 × 1000;
>   **stop**;
> **end** *master control*;

Figure 3 presents a sample of typical output obtained from the SOL program in Figure 2.

Remarks

We have purposely chosen a rather complex example to show how SOL can be used to solve an actual problem of practical importance, and to show in what a natural manner the system can be described in the language.

The present implementation of SOL is able to be rather efficient, in spite of the fact that it runs interpretively, because it keeps separate lists for transactions that are waiting for different reasons. Transactions waiting for time to pass are kept sorted in order by the required time. Those waiting for a condition such as 'wait until $A = 0$', for some global variable A, are kept in a list associated with A; this list is interrogated only when the value of A has been changed.

The ideas used in SOL for creating and canceling transactions have applications in the design of languages for highly parallel computers. Furthermore, SOL has proved to be especially advantageous for simulating computer systems, since "typical programs" — which we assume are to be run on the simulated computers — are easily coded in SOL's language.

Acknowledgment

The authors wish to express their appreciation to J. Merner for many helpful suggestions.

The research described here was supported by Burroughs Corporation.

References

[1] Harry M. Markowitz, Bernard Hausner, and Herbert W. Karr, *SIMSCRIPT — A Simulation Programming Language* (Englewood Cliffs, New Jersey: Prentice–Hall, 1963).

[2] Geoffrey Gordon, "A general purpose systems simulation program," *Proceedings of the Eastern Joint Computer Conference* **20** (1961), 87–104.

[3] G. Gordon, "A general purpose systems simulator," *IBM Systems Journal* **1** (1962), 18–32.

[4] *Reference Manual, General Purpose Systems Simulator II* (White Plains, New York: IBM Corporation, 1963).

[5] D. E. Knuth and J. L. McNeley, "A formal definition of SOL," *IEEE Transactions on Electronic Computers* **EC-13** (1964), 409–414. [Reprinted as Chapter 10 of the present volume.]

[6] Michael R. Lackner, "Toward a general simulation capability," *Proceedings of the Spring Joint Computer Conference* **21** (1962), 1–14.

```
TU  6     SENDS MESSAGE    1     AT TIME      6586
TU  4     SENDS MESSAGE    1     AT TIME      7152
TU  5     SENDS MESSAGE    2     AT TIME      7295
TU  6     RECEIVES REPLY         AT TIME      9973
TU  4     RECEIVES REPLY         AT TIME     10305
TU  5     RECEIVES REPLY         AT TIME     13353
TU  6     SENDS MESSAGE    3     AT TIME     16908
TU  2     SENDS MESSAGE    2     AT TIME     17476
TU  5     SENDS MESSAGE    1     AT TIME     19405
TU  6     RECEIVES REPLY         AT TIME     21166
TU  2     RECEIVES REPLY         AT TIME     21412
TU  3     SENDS MESSAGE    2     AT TIME     21646
TU  5     RECEIVES REPLY         AT TIME     24229
TU  1     SENDS MESSAGE    2     AT TIME     25424
TU  3     RECEIVES REPLY         AT TIME     27959
TU  4     SENDS MESSAGE    1     AT TIME     30442
TU  5     SENDS MESSAGE    2     AT TIME     31409
TU  1     RECEIVES REPLY         AT TIME     31609
TU  4     RECEIVES REPLY         AT TIME     33278
TU  3     SENDS MESSAGE    3     AT TIME     34067
```

...

CLOCK TIME AT END OF SIMULATION WAS   3600000

NUMBER OF TIMES LABELS WERE ENCOUNTERED

LABEL	COUNT	LABEL	COUNT	LABEL	COUNT
ORIGIN –	1455	START –	1457	SCAN –	17303
SEND –	1477	COMPUTATION –	1446	OUTPUT –	8021
RECEIVE –	5990	CREATE –	6	COMPUTE–	4764

NAME OF STORE	CAPACITY	MAXIMUM USED	AVERAGE OCCUPANCY	AVERAGE UTILIZATION
QUEUE[001]	10	10	2.5272	0.2527
QUEUE[002]	10	10	2.4255	0.2426
QUEUE[003]	10	10	2.3835	0.2384
QUEUE[004]	10	7	1.7696	0.1770
QUEUE[005]	10	8	2.1844	0.2184
QUEUE[006]	10	5	1.4971	0.1497

NAME OF FACILITY	FRACTION OF TIME IN USE
TU[001]	0.8318
TU[002]	0.8055
TU[003]	0.7887
TU[004]	0.8085
TU[005]	0.8302
TU[006]	0.7585
SB[001]	0.6051
SB[002]	0.4221
SB[003]	0.2120
LINE	0.8649
COMPUTER	0.5509

TABLE NAME IS TABLE[003]

NUMBER OF TABLE ENTRIES	235	SUM OF ALL ENTRY VALUES	1201076
MEAN OF TABLE	5110.9617	STANDARD DEVIATION	1441.51124

UPPER LIMIT	NUMBER	PERCENT	CUMULATIVE	MULTIPLE OF MEAN
2000	0	0.00	0.00	0.3913
3000	5	2.13	2.13	0.5870
4000	50	21.28	23.40	0.7826
5000	78	33.19	56.60	0.9783
6000	48	20.43	77.02	1.1739
7000	30	12.77	89.79	1.3696
8000	15	6.38	96.17	1.5653
9000	5	2.13	98.30	1.7609
10000	2	0.85	99.15	1.9566
11000	1	0.43	99.57	2.1522
12000	1	0.43	100.00	2.3479
13000	0	0.00	100.00	2.5436
14000	0	0.00	100.0C	2.7392
15000	0	0.00	100.00	2.9349

FIGURE 3.   Samples of the output obtained from one run of the simulated system.

Chapter 10

A Formal Definition of SOL

[Written with J. L. McNeley. Originally published in IEEE Transactions on Electronic Computers EC-13 (1964), 409–414.]

This paper presents a formal definition of SOL, a general-purpose algorithmic language useful for describing and simulating complex systems. SOL is described using meta-linguistic formulas as used in the definition of ALGOL 60. The principal differences between SOL and problem-oriented languages such as ALGOL or FORTRAN is that SOL includes capabilities for expressing parallel computation, convenient notations for embedding random quantities within arithmetic expressions, and automatic means for gathering statistics about the elements involved. SOL differs from other simulation languages such as SIMSCRIPT primarily in simplicity of use and in readability, since it is capable of describing models without including computer-oriented characteristics.

I. General Description

SOL is an algorithmic language used to construct models of general systems for simulation in a readable form. The model builder describes models in terms of processes whose number and detail are completely arbitrary and definable within the constraints of the language elements. A SOL model consists of a sequence of statements and declarations that have a character similar to the statements and declarations found in programming languages such as ALGOL.

The model is not built to be executed in a sequential fashion as ordinary programming languages require. Rather, its processes are written and executed as if all were running in parallel. Control between processes is maintained by the interaction of *global* entities, and by control and communication instructions within the different processes. At the initiation of the simulation all processes begin simultaneously.

191

Variables declared within a process are called *local* variables. Within a given process it is possible to have several actions going on at once; therefore, we may think of several objects on which the action takes place each in its own place in the process at any given time. These objects will be referred to as *transactions.* A set of local variables corresponding in number to those declared in the process is "carried with" each transaction of that process. Transactions situated within one process may not refer to the local variables of another process nor to the local variables of another transaction in the same process.

Global quantities are of three major types: global variables, facilities, and stores. *Global variables* can be referenced or changed by any transaction from any process in the system, and the variable possesses only one value at any given time.

A *facility* is a global element that can be controlled by only one transaction at a time. Associated with each request for the facility is a "control strength," and an interrupt will occur if a requesting transaction has a higher strength than the transaction controlling the facility. Interrupts may be nested to any depth. If the requesting transaction is not of greater strength than the controlling transaction, then the requesting transaction stops and waits for the facility until the controlling transaction releases its control. When a transaction is interrupted, it cannot advance to any other position in its program until it regains control of the facility.

Stores are space-shared rather than time-shared global elements, and they are assigned a specific storage capacity. As long as there is sufficient storage to accommodate the requesting transaction, the request for space is satisfied; otherwise the transaction waits until the space it is requesting becomes available. In this sense, a facility may be regarded as a store that has a capacity of one unit only, except for the fact that no interrupt capability is provided for stores.

Simulated time passes in discrete units indicated in "wait statements." The model builder requires the transactions to wait a proper number of time units at appropriate places in the processes, and these delays specify the time element. The interpretation of the physical significance of a unit of time is immaterial in the SOL language; if all time interval specifications are multiplied by a factor of ten, the model will still be simulated at the same speed.

Control within or between processes can also be introduced into a simulation by forcing a transaction to wait until a global variable or expression obtains a certain value, or until a space- or time-shared element attains a certain status.

Output statements that display the progress of the simulation may be inserted at will in the model. Special types of statistics are automatically available, such as the percentage of time that a facility is busy, the average and maximum number of elements in a store at a given moment, etc. Another type of global quantity, called a *table*, is introduced to record statistical information about desired data. The mean, the standard deviation, and a histogram are provided for all data recorded in a table.

Processes initiate parallelism within themselves by using a duplication operation. The transaction makes an exact copy of itself and sends the copy to a specified location in the process while the original continues in sequence. A transaction is taken out of the system when it executes a "cancel" statement.

Other operations available in SOL are similar to those of existing algorithmic languages, but those portions of the language are at the present time less powerful than the features available in a large scale programming language.

A detailed example of a complete SOL model appears in a companion paper [1], which readers may wish to consult before studying the formal language definition presented here.

II. Syntax and Semantics of SOL

We will define the syntax of SOL using meta-linguistic formulas as given in the definition of ALGOL 60 [2]. Certain things that have been defined carefully in ALGOL 60 will not be redefined here, but will merely be stated to have the same interpretation as given by ALGOL. We will use the abbreviation *⟨A⟩* to mean "a list of ⟨A⟩ items separated by commas"; that is,

$$*⟨A⟩* ::= ⟨A⟩ \mid *⟨A⟩*, ⟨A⟩$$

Explanatory comments may be written in the form

comment ⟨string without semicolons⟩ ;

as in ALGOL 60.

A. Identifiers and Constants

⟨letter⟩ ::= $a \mid b \mid c \mid d \mid \ldots \mid z$
⟨digit⟩ ::= $0 \mid 1 \mid 2 \mid 3 \mid \ldots \mid 9$
⟨number⟩ ::= ⟨constant⟩ | ⟨decimal constant⟩
⟨constant⟩ ::= ⟨digit⟩ | ⟨constant⟩⟨digit⟩
⟨decimal constant⟩ ::= ⟨constant⟩ . ⟨constant⟩
⟨identifier⟩ ::= ⟨letter⟩ | ⟨identifier⟩⟨letter⟩ | ⟨identifier⟩⟨digit⟩

Identifiers are used as the names of variables, statistical tables, stores, facilities, processes, procedures, and statements. The same identifier can be used for only *one* purpose in a program. Constants are used to represent integer numbers. Decimal constants represent real numbers. Identifiers must be declared before they are used elsewhere.

B. Declarations

⟨declared item⟩ ::= ⟨identifier⟩ | ⟨identifier⟩ [⟨constant⟩]
⟨variable declaration⟩ ::= **integer** *⟨declared item⟩*
    | **real** *⟨declared item⟩*
⟨facility declaration⟩ ::= **facility** *⟨declared item⟩*
⟨store declaration⟩ ::= **store** *(⟨constant⟩) ⟨declared item⟩*
⟨table declaration⟩ ::= **table** *(⟨number⟩ **step** ⟨number⟩
         until ⟨number⟩) ⟨declared item⟩*
⟨monitor declaration⟩ ::= **monitor** *⟨identifier⟩*

If the declared item is simply an identifier, a single item of that name is being declared. The other possibility, for example if the declared item is $a[10]$, means that 10 similar items called $a[1]$, $a[2]$, ..., $a[10]$ are being declared.

A variable declaration is used to specify names of variables — either local variables or global variables, depending on where the declaration appears. All variables are initially set to zero when declared. "Integer" variables differ from "real" variables in that when a value is assigned to them it is rounded to the nearest integer.

When a facility is declared, it is initially "not busy". At the end of the simulation run, statistics are reported giving the percentage of time that each facility was in use.

A store declaration specifies the capacity of each store, as a parenthesized constant preceding the declared item. Statistics are given at the end of the simulation run, reporting the average and the maximum number of items occupying the store (as a function of time). Stores are empty when first declared.

A table is used to gather detailed statistical information of any desired numerical quantity. Observations are tabulated during the run; afterwards the mean, the standard deviation, and the histogram distribution are output. The constants preceding the table name give the starting point for histogram intervals, the increment between intervals, and the highest histogram value.

A monitor declaration names items that already have been declared, with the understanding that those identifiers are to be "monitored."

This means that whenever a change in the state of the corresponding quantity is detected, a line will be printed giving the details. Monitoring is especially useful when checking out a model, and it can also be used to advantage for output during a regular simulation run.

C. Expressions and Relations

⟨name⟩ ::= ⟨identifier⟩ | ⟨identifier⟩ [⟨expression⟩]

By ⟨variable name⟩, ⟨facility name⟩, etc., in the following syntax, we will mean that the identifier in the name has appeared in a ⟨variable declaration⟩, ⟨facility declaration⟩, etc., respectively.

⟨primary⟩ ::= ⟨variable name⟩ | ⟨store name⟩
    | ⟨constant⟩ | ⟨decimal constant⟩ | **time**
    | (*⟨expression⟩*) | **abs** (⟨expression⟩)
    | **max** (*⟨expression⟩*) | **min** (*⟨expression⟩*)
    | **normal** (⟨expression⟩ , ⟨expression⟩)
    | **exponential** (⟨expression⟩) | **poisson** (⟨expression⟩)
    | **geometric** (⟨expression⟩) | **random**
⟨term⟩ ::= ⟨primary⟩ | ⟨term⟩ × ⟨primary⟩
    | ⟨term⟩ ÷ ⟨primary⟩ | ⟨term⟩ / ⟨primary⟩
    | ⟨term⟩ **mod** ⟨primary⟩
⟨sum⟩ ::= ⟨term⟩ | + ⟨term⟩ | − ⟨term⟩ | ⟨sum⟩ + ⟨term⟩
    | ⟨sum⟩ − ⟨term⟩
⟨unconditional expression⟩ ::= ⟨sum⟩ | ⟨sum⟩ : ⟨sum⟩
⟨expression⟩ ::= ⟨unconditional expression⟩
    | **if** ⟨relation⟩ **then** ⟨expression⟩ **else** ⟨expression⟩

The meaning of the arithmetical operations $+$, $-$, $\times$, $\div$, and **abs** is identical to their meaning in ALGOL 60.

The new elements here are 'a **mod** b', the remainder obtained upon dividing a by b, namely $a - b \times entier(a/b)$; also '**max**$(e_1, \ldots, e_n)$' and '**min**$(e_1, \ldots, e_n)$', which denote the maximum and minimum values, respectively, of n given expressions; and there are several notations for expressing random values with special distributions that occur frequently in applications: The expression '$(e_1, \ldots, e_n)$' indicates that a random selection is made from among the n expressions, with equal probability of choosing any particular e_j. A random number drawn from the normal distribution with mean μ and standard deviation σ is denoted by **normal**(μ, σ) and is a real (not necessarily integer) value. A number drawn from the exponential distribution with mean μ is denoted by **exponential**(μ), again of type real. On the other hand the Poisson distribution, signified by **poisson**(μ), yields only integer values; the probability that **poisson**$(\mu) = n$ is $e^{-\mu}\mu^n/n!$. The geometric distribution with mean μ, denoted by **geometric**(μ), also yields integer values, where the probability that **geometric**$(\mu) = n$ is $\mu^{-1}(1 - 1/\mu)^{n-1}$ for $n \geq 1$. The symbol **random** denotes a random real number between 0 and 1 having the uniform distribution. Finally, we have the notation $e_1 : e_2$, which denotes a random integer between the limits e_1 and e_2; more formally

$$e_1 : e_2 = \begin{cases} 0, & \text{if } e_1 > e_2; \\ (e_1, e_1 + 1, \ldots, e_2), & \text{if } e_1 \leq e_2. \end{cases}$$

The normal, exponential, Poisson, and geometric distributions are mathematically expressible in terms of **random** as follows:

normal$(\mu, \sigma) = \mu + \sigma\sqrt{-2\ln \mathbf{random}} \times \sin(2\pi\, \mathbf{random})$;

exponential$(\mu) = -\mu \ln \mathbf{random}$;

poisson$(\mu) = n \iff$

$$1 + \frac{\mu}{1!} + \cdots + \frac{\mu^{n-1}}{(n-1)!} \leq e^{\mu}\, \mathbf{random} < 1 + \frac{\mu}{1!} + \cdots + \frac{\mu^n}{n!};$$

geometric$(\mu) = 1 + \mathit{entier}(\ln \mathbf{random}/\ln(1 - 1/\mu))$.

(The Poisson distribution should not be used for values of μ greater than 10.)

As examples of how these distributions might be used, consider a population of customers coming independently to a market with an average of one customer every μ minutes. The distribution of waiting time between successive arrivals is **exponential**(μ). On the other hand, if μ customers come in per hour, on the average, the distribution of the actual number of customers arriving in a given hour is **poisson**(μ). If an experiment is performed repeatedly with a chance of success $1/\mu$ on each independent trial, the number of trials needed to obtain the first success is **geometric**(μ).

The special symbol 'time' indicates the current value of a simulated time clock. Initially, **time** is zero.

The value of a store name is its current number of occupants.

⟨relational operator⟩ ::= = | ≠ | < | ≤ | > | ≥

⟨relation primary⟩ ::= ⟨unconditional expression⟩
⟨relational operator⟩ ⟨unconditional expression⟩
| ⟨facility name⟩ **busy** | ⟨facility name⟩ **not busy**
| ⟨store name⟩ **full** | ⟨store name⟩ **not full**
| ⟨store name⟩ **empty** | ⟨store name⟩ **not empty**
| **pr** (⟨expression⟩) | (⟨relation⟩)
⟨relation⟩ ::= ⟨relation primary⟩
| ⟨relation primary⟩ ∨ ⟨relation primary⟩
| ⟨relation primary⟩ ∧ ⟨relation primary⟩
| ¬ ⟨relation primary⟩

A relation is either true or false. All relations shown in the syntax have obvious meanings except for the construction '**pr**(p)', which stands for a random condition that is true with probability p. (Here p must lie between 0 and 1.) Thus '**pr**(p)' is equivalent to the relation '**random** $< p$'; the relation **pr**(0.12) is true 12 percent of the time.

III. Statements

A. Processes
Any number of processes may be active simultaneously during a simulation run. We may think of several objects, each in its own place in the process at any given time; these objects are referred to as *transactions*. The purpose of the present section is to describe the various manipulations that transactions can perform.

⟨process description⟩ ::= **process** ⟨identifier⟩ ; ⟨statement⟩
| **process** ⟨identifier⟩ ; **begin**
⟨process declaration list⟩ ; ⟨statement list⟩ ⟨end⟩
⟨end⟩ ::= **end** | **end** ⟨identifier⟩
⟨process declaration⟩ ::= ⟨variable declaration⟩
| ⟨procedure declaration⟩ | ⟨monitor declaration⟩
⟨process declaration list⟩ ::= ⟨process declaration⟩
| ⟨process declaration list⟩ ; ⟨process declaration⟩

There are two kinds of variables, *global* variables (not declared in a process) and *local* variables (those that are declared in a process). All transactions can refer to the global variables, and a global variable has only one value at any given time. But a local variable is "carried with" each transaction within a given process; in general, each local variable has different values in different transactions. Transactions situated within one process cannot refer to the local variables of another process, nor can the local variables of one transaction within a process be examined directly by other transactions in that same process. Communication between processes is accomplished solely with the help of global quantities.

B. Labels

A statement may be named by any identifier as follows:

⟨statement⟩ ::= ⟨unlabeled statement⟩
| ⟨identifier⟩ : ⟨statement⟩

In the syntax below, ⟨label⟩ stands for the name of a statement.

C. Creation of Transactions

At the beginning of simulation, one transaction is present for every process described. Each of these initial transactions starts at time zero and is positioned at the beginning of the process. More transactions may be created by using "start statements."

⟨start statement⟩ ::= **new transaction to** ⟨label⟩

A start statement, when executed, creates a new transaction, whose local variables are the same in number and value as those of the transaction that created it. The new transaction begins to execute the program at ⟨label⟩, while the original transaction continues in sequence. New transactions are also created by input statements (see Section III-T).

D. Disappearance of Transactions

Transactions "die" when they execute a cancel statement.

⟨cancel statement⟩ ::= **cancel**

An implied cancel statement appears at the end of every process, so cancel statements need not always be explicitly written.

E. Replacement Statements

⟨replacement statement⟩ ::= ⟨variable name⟩ ← ⟨expression⟩

A replacement statement replaces the value of the variable by the value of the expression. The variable may be global or local. If it is an integer variable, the expression is rounded to an integer: The value x becomes $entier(x + 0.5)$.

F. Priority

Time is measured in discrete units, so it may happen by coincidence that two transactions want to do something at precisely the same time. They may be in conflict; for example, they may both want to seize a facility, or to change the value of the same global variable, or one may want to change it while the other is using its value. In such cases of conflict, the simulator actually does choose a specific order for execution; no two things actually happen at the same instant. It would be more exact to say that we deal with *infinitesimal* units of time between the discrete units.

The choice of order is fairly arbitrary, except when a difference of priority is specified. In that case, the transaction with *higher* priority will be acted on before a transaction with lower priority. Each transaction has a priority, which is initially zero; priority is changed by the statement '*priority* $\leftarrow$ ⟨expression⟩'.

The declaration '**integer** *priority*' is implied at the beginning of every process; that is, *priority* is treated as a local variable. The effect of priority is spelled out further in Section IV.

G. Wait Statements

⟨wait statement⟩ ::= **wait** ⟨expression⟩

In a wait statement, the expression is rounded to the nearest integer t; then '**time**' advances by $\max(0, t)$, as far as this transaction is concerned. All time delays in a simulated process are, in the last analysis, specified by using wait statements.

H. Wait-Until Statements

⟨wait-until statement⟩ ::= **wait until** ⟨relation⟩

A wait-until statement causes the transaction to freeze at the current point until the relation becomes true (because of action by other transactions). The relation must not involve expressions that involve a random value; for example, it is not legal to write '**wait until pr**$(1/2)$' or '**wait until** $a[1\!:\!4] = 0$'.

I. Enter Statements

⟨enter statement⟩ ::= **enter** ⟨store name⟩
| **enter** ⟨store name⟩ , ⟨expression⟩

The first form of an enter statement is an abbreviation for '**enter** ⟨store name⟩, 1'. The value of the expression, rounded to the nearest integer, gives the number of units requested of the store. The transaction will remain at this statement until that number of units is available and until all other transactions of greater or equal priority that have been waiting for storage space have been serviced. An enter statement has no effect if the expression is zero or negative.

J. Leave Statement

⟨leave statement⟩ ::= **leave** ⟨store name⟩
| **leave** ⟨store name⟩ , ⟨expression⟩

The first form of a leave statement is an abbreviation for '**leave** ⟨store name⟩, 1'. This statement causes the store to regain the number of units equivalent to the value of the (rounded) expression. Like an enter statement, it has no effect unless the expression is positive.

K. Seize Statements

⟨seize statement⟩ ::= **seize** ⟨facility name⟩
| **seize** ⟨facility name⟩ , ⟨expression⟩

The first form of a seize statement is equivalent to '**seize** ⟨facility name⟩, 0'. The effect of this statement is usually rather simple, but complications can sometimes arise. If the facility is not busy when a seize statement occurs, then it becomes busy at this point and remains busy until later released by this transaction. (If the current transaction creates another transaction by means of a start statement, the new transaction does not control the facility.)

The expression appearing after the comma represents the "control strength," which is normally zero. But allowance is made for one transaction to interrupt another. If the facility is busy when the seize statement occurs, let E_1 be the control strength with which the facility was seized and let E_2 be the control strength of this seize statement. If $E_2 \leq E_1$, the transaction waits until the facility is not busy. If $E_2 > E_1$, however, *interrupt* occurs. The transaction T_1 that had control of the facility is stopped wherever it was in its program, and the present transaction T_2 seizes the facility. When T_2 releases the facility, the following occurs:

1) If T_1 was executing a wait statement when interrupted, the time of wait is increased by the time that passed during the interrupt.

2) Several transactions may now be waiting to seize the facility. If any of them has a higher control strength than E_1, then T_1 is interrupted again. The transaction that interrupts is chosen by the normal rules for deciding who obtains control of a facility upon release, as described in the next section.

L. Release Statements

⟨release statement⟩ ::= **release** ⟨facility name⟩

A release statement is permitted only when the current transaction is actually controlling the facility because of a previous seizure. When the facility is released, several other transactions might be waiting because of seize statements. The one that gets control of the facility next is chosen by considering the following three quantities in order:

1) highest control strength,
2) highest *priority*,
3) first to request the facility.

M. Go To Statements

⟨go to statement⟩ ::= **go to** ⟨label⟩
| **go to** (*⟨label⟩*) , ⟨expression⟩

A go to statement is used to transfer to another point in the same process; otherwise statements are executed sequentially. In the second form, the expression is used to select which statement to transfer to; if there are n labels, the expression, when rounded to the nearest integer, must have a value between 0 and n. Zero means "continue in sequence," 1 means "go to the first statement mentioned," and so on.

N. Compound Statements
Several statements may be combined into one, as follows:

⟨statement list⟩ ::= ⟨statement⟩
| ⟨statement list⟩ ; ⟨statement⟩
⟨compound statement⟩ ::= **begin** ⟨statement list⟩ ⟨end⟩
| (⟨statement list⟩)

As in Section III-A, the word **end** can be followed by an optional identifier (which is ignored but useful as a comment).

O. Conditional Statements

⟨conditional statement⟩ ::= **if** ⟨relation⟩ **then**
⟨unconditional statement⟩
else ⟨statement⟩
| **if** ⟨relation⟩ **then** ⟨unconditional statement⟩

The meaning of a conditional statement is the same as in ALGOL. Testing of the relation does not increase the simulated time clock.

P. Tabulate Statements

⟨tabulate statement⟩ ::= **tabulate** ⟨expression⟩ **in** ⟨table name⟩

The value of the expression in a tabulate statement is recorded as a statistical observation in the table specified.

Q. Output Statements

⟨carriage control⟩ ::= ⟨empty⟩ | **page** | **line**
⟨string⟩ ::= ⟨any sequence of characters excluding '"'⟩
⟨output list item⟩ ::= " ⟨string⟩ " | **quote** | ⟨expression⟩
    | ⟨store name⟩ | ⟨table name⟩ | ⟨facility name⟩
⟨output statement⟩ ::= **output**
        ⟨carriage control⟩⟨output list item⟩

Output occurs for all items listed, in turn, after doing the appropriate carriage control positioning (going to a new page or a new line). The output for a string is the string itself; the output for **quote** is '"'. The output for an expression is the numeric value. For a store, table, or facility, appropriate statistical information is output. At the conclusion of an output statement, the final line is printed out and a new line begins.

R. Stop Statements

⟨stop statement⟩ ::= **stop**

A stop statement causes simulation to terminate immediately, and all transactions cease. The statistics for all stores, tables, and facilities are output as in the output statement, as well as the final time, the number of times each labeled statement was referenced, and the number of transactions that appeared in each process.

S. Procedures

⟨procedure declaration⟩ ::= **procedure** ⟨identifier⟩ ; ⟨statement⟩
⟨procedure statement⟩ ::= ⟨procedure name⟩

A procedure is simply a subroutine used to save coding. Parameters are not allowed, but their effect can be achieved by setting local variables in the transactions before calling the procedure. Both local procedures and global procedures are allowed (the latter are declared outside of a process). Global procedures cannot refer to local variables. A go to statement cannot lead out of a procedure body. Procedures can be used recursively.

T. Transaction Input-Output

⟨transaction read statement⟩ ::= **read** ⟨constant⟩ **to** ⟨label⟩
⟨transaction write statement⟩ ::= **write** ⟨constant⟩

The read statement inputs a set of values of local variables for a transaction belonging to the same process as the one executing the read statement; these values are used to create a new transaction, which begins executing the program at the statement mentioned. The write statement writes the current values of the local variables of the transaction onto the unit specified and does not cancel the present transaction. The ⟨constant⟩ in each case refers to a tape or card unit number. The same unit should not be used for both input and output in the same simulation run.

U. Summary of Statements

> ⟨unlabeled statement⟩ ::= ⟨unconditional statement⟩
> | ⟨conditional statement⟩
> ⟨unconditional statement⟩ ::= ⟨start statement⟩
> | ⟨cancel statement⟩
> | ⟨replacement statement⟩ | ⟨wait statement⟩
> | ⟨wait-until statement⟩ | ⟨enter statement⟩
> | ⟨leave statement⟩ | ⟨seize statement⟩
> | ⟨release statement⟩ | ⟨go to statement⟩
> | ⟨compound statement⟩ | ⟨output statement⟩
> | ⟨tabulate statement⟩ | ⟨stop statement⟩
> | ⟨transaction read statement⟩ | ⟨procedure statement⟩
> | ⟨transaction write statement⟩ | ⟨empty⟩

IV. The Model as a Whole

> ⟨model⟩ ::= **begin** ⟨global declaration list⟩ ; ⟨process list⟩ ; **end.**
> ⟨declaration⟩ ::= ⟨variable declaration⟩ | ⟨facility declaration⟩
> | ⟨store declaration⟩ | ⟨table declaration⟩
> | ⟨monitor declaration⟩ | ⟨procedure declaration⟩
> ⟨global declaration list⟩ ::= ⟨declaration⟩
> | ⟨global declaration list⟩ ; ⟨declaration⟩
> ⟨process list⟩ ::= ⟨process description⟩
> | ⟨process list⟩ ; ⟨process description⟩

Initially all variables are zero, all facilities are "not busy," all stores are "empty," the time is zero, one transaction appears for each process described, and the simulator is in the "choice state."

When the simulator is in "choice state," each transaction is either positioned at a wait statement, a wait-until statement, a seize or enter statement, or has just been created. (We can dispense with the latter case by assuming that a "wait 0" statement has been inserted just before the relevant position when a new transaction is created.) If no transactions can move at this time, the time is advanced to the earliest completion time for a wait statement. Now, from the set of transactions able to move, one is selected that has the highest *priority*; in case of ties, one that has been waiting the longest is selected. (If there is still a tie, an arbitrary choice is made.) The selected transaction is activated, and it continues to execute its statements until encountering a cancel or stop statement, a priority assignment statement, a wait statement, a wait-until statement with a false relation, or a seize or enter statement that cannot take place at the current time. The simulator examines all other transactions that are stopped because of a wait-until statement involving global quantities changed by the present transaction; if the corresponding relation is now true, those transactions become free to move. Then we have once again reached "choice state."

Notice that all release statements that are passed during the time the selected transaction was moving are processed immediately, in such a way that the facility becomes not busy only if no other transactions were interrupted or were waiting to seize it. If other transactions *are* in the latter category, the choice of successor and the transfer of control described in Section III-L take place immediately as the release statement is executed. Therefore, the statement '**wait until** *fac* **not busy**' may conceivably never be passed if other transactions are always ready to seize *fac*. Similar remarks apply to enter and leave statements.

Since this paper was written, a few additions have been made to the SOL language, including "synchronous" variables and some additional diagnostic capabilities.

The research described here was supported by Burroughs Corporation.

References

[1] D. E. Knuth and J. L. McNeley, "SOL — A symbolic language for general-purpose systems simulation," *IEEE Transactions on Electronic Computers* **EC-13** (1964), 401–408. [Reprinted as Chapter 9 of the present volume.]

[2] Peter Naur, editor, "Revised report on the algorithmic language ALGOL 60," *Communications of the ACM* **6** (1963), 1–17.

Addendum

I have always liked SOL for its simplicity and for its interesting "wait-until" statement. But when I learned in 1966 about the elegant and more general language SIMULA designed by Dahl and Nygaard, I realized that SIMULA was even more useful than SOL. [See Ole-Johan Dahl and Kristen Nygaard, "SIMULA — an ALGOL-based simulation language," *Communications of the ACM* **9** (1966), 671–678.]

Chapter 11

The Science of Programming Languages

[Gerard Salton, as editor of Communications of the ACM, asked me in 1966 to prepare a survey article that would describe some of the principal concepts, goals, and methods of a rapidly growing new field of study called "programming languages." I began to draft some ideas, but was unable to complete the project for reasons discussed in Chapter 19. After recently coming across my rough notes from this long-abandoned project, I came to the conclusion that some of those old thoughts might still be of interest to modern readers. Therefore I'm including here some fragments from that unfinished manuscript.]

Preface

The last ten years have witnessed the birth of a new field of study, the science of programming languages, which forms an important part of a larger body of knowledge that is becoming known as Computer Science. The purpose of this paper is to indicate the main streams of research in programming languages, to acquaint the reader with the methods and terminology commonly being used in the field, and to survey some of the principal achievements made so far.

In such a young (and economically profitable) discipline, there is bound to be a great deal of change taking place at any moment, so this paper naturally represents only one person's view of the situation at the current time. If someone else were to write about the same topic, or if I myself would be writing this paper a year earlier or later, the result would probably not have much in common with what is reported here.

Therefore it is rather presumptuous of me to play the role of spokesman for the entire field. I accepted the invitation to write this paper only because, in the course of my duties as editor of the Programming Languages section of the ACM *Communications* during 1966, it was necessary for me to spend considerable time meditating about the definition, aims, and achievements of the field. Other specialists in programming languages may not have had such strong incentives to study the problems from such a general viewpoint, so I hope that the results of my meditations may prove to be useful.

Part 1: Theory of Languages

1.1. Phrase Structure Languages   . . .
1.2. Automata as Acceptors   . . .
1.3. Regular Languages   . . .
1.4. Context-Free Languages   . . .
1.5. Context-Sensitive Languages   . . .
1.6. Unsolvable Problems   . . .
1.7. Unsolved Problems   . . .

Part 2: Design and Documentation

2.1. Backus–Naur Form   . . .

2.2. Example of a Bad Language

Let us attempt to examine now the principles of programming language design. Perhaps the best way to bring these ideas into focus is to start by studying how *not* to design programming languages, so that bad policies may be contrasted with good ones.

It is almost axiomatic that no programming language can ever be optimum. Hence every programming language has some features that can be made better. (Ad infinitum, possibly getting into a loop.) There also is ample data to support the hypothesis that no designer of programming languages will ever be pleased by all the features of a language that has been designed by somebody else.

Thus it is wise for an author to avoid criticizing the existing programming languages too harshly. I have opted instead to present a completely new language in this section, designed expressly to be as awful as possible — yet in instructive ways.

In other words, the next few subsections attempt to build up a "straw man," so that we can knock it down later. The remainder of this section may be regarded as an excerpt from the user's manual of the new language. (Any resemblance between the bad language described here and any other bad programming language, living or dead, is purely coincidental.)

BL\I   (Bad Language \ One)*

The purpose of BL\I is to provide facilities for manipulating strings of characters, primarily oriented towards the editing of text.

2.2.1. Variables. Variables in BL\I are designated by a sequence of up to five letters and/or numbers, starting with a letter. If the first letter in the variable's name is I, J, K, L, M, N, or X, the variable takes on integer values; otherwise the variable takes on strings as its values.

2.2.2. Constants. An integer constant is designated by a sequence of digits, in decimal notation. A string constant has the general form

$$n\,\mathrm{H}\,\underbrace{\mathrm{xx}\ \ldots\ \mathrm{x}}_{n\ \text{characters}}$$

where n is a decimal number.

2.2.3. Size of strings. Every string variable must have a maximum size given by a MAXSIZE statement, whose general form is

$$\text{MAXSIZE } n_1\, v_1\, ,\, n_2\, v_2\, ,\, \ldots\, ,\, n_k\, v_k$$

where the n_i are positive integers and the v_i are variable names.

2.2.4. Subscripted variables. String variables have "subscripts" if they appear in a DIMENSION statement, whose general form is

$$\text{DIMENSION } v_1(n_1),\ v_2(n_2),\ \ldots,\ v_k(n_k)$$

where the n_i are positive integers and the v_i are variable names. For example, the statement

$$\text{DIMENSION A(20), B(10)}$$

means that A and B are subscripted variables. All references to a subscripted variable V must have the form

$$\text{V}(exp)$$

where exp is an integer-valued expression whose value is between 1 and the declared size of V. For example, 'A(2*J-1)' and 'B(J)' can be used in connection with A and B as above, if J lies between 1 and 10.

Since integer variables cannot be subscripted, it follows that subscripts cannot appear within subscripts.

---

* This description of BL\I is itself meant to be a pretty bad description. So the reader should not be surprised to encounter ambiguous notations, typos, and muddled concepts. However, the example BL\I program at the end is intended to represent the work of a good programmer who has tried valiantly to use the language as well as possible after reading the manual.

2.2.5. Integer expressions. Algebraic formulas can be built up from the basic operations of addition, subtraction, and multiplication, using the general forms

$$exp + exp, \qquad exp - exp, \qquad exp * exp.$$

Multiplication takes precedence over addition and subtraction; for example, in the expression 'I+J*K-L' the value of J times K is computed first, then I is added and L is subtracted. Parentheses may be used to indicate other orders of computation, such as (I+J)*(K-L).

The construction

$$\text{NVALUE}(string)$$

converts a string to an integer value, which is the equivalent of the digits appearing in the string in decimal notation. For example,

$$\text{NVALUE}(3H1+2)$$

equals 12, because the non-digit + is ignored by **NVALUE**.

Similarly, the construction

$$\text{LENGTH}(string)$$

stands for the number of characters in the string.

2.2.6. String expressions. The constructions

$$n : string \qquad \text{and} \qquad string : n$$

denote the first n characters and the last n characters, respectively, of the string. Here n is an integer and *string* is a string expression. Similarly,

$$n \backslash string \qquad \text{and} \qquad string / n$$

denote the string minus its first or last n characters. For example,

$$2:3\backslash 8\text{HLANGUAGE}/2$$

equals 'GU'.

The concatenation of two string expressions is represented by the operator '.CONC.'. Also, the notation

$$\text{STRING}(exp, n)$$

creates a string of length n for the value of exp. For example,

$$\text{STRING}(J+1,2).\text{CONC}.1H-.\text{CONC}.\text{STRING}(J,2)$$

when J equals 25 is the string '26-25'.

2.2.7. SET statements. A variable V changes its value by means of a SET statement, whose general form is

SET *V* EQUALS *exp* .

Here *exp* is a string expression if *V* is a string variable, or an integer expression if *V* is an integer variable. If *V* occurs in the expression, the old value of *V* is used to compute the value of the expression. For example,

SET N EQUALS N+1.

increases the value of N by one, and

SET S EQUALS S/1

deletes the last character of S. The variable V may be subscripted.

Two special forms of the set statement are permitted for string variables:

SET *V* EQUALS *exp* , TYPE 1.
SET *V* EQUALS *exp* , TYPE 2.

These statements are abbreviations for

SET *V* EQUALS *V* .CONC. *exp* .
SET *V* EQUALS *exp* .CONC. *V* .

respectively, and they operate more efficiently.

2.2.8. GO TO statements. Statements in BL\I are punched into columns 7–72 of a computer input card, and numbers less than 32768 may be punched in columns 1–5 to identify particular statements. The construction

GOTO *n*

means that the program should take its next instruction from the statement numbered *n*.

2.2.9. Conditional statements. The general form

IF (*relation*) , *statement* .

may be used to perform the statement only if the relation is true. Relations are of two kinds: A numeric relation has the form

$$exp \left\{ \begin{array}{c} \text{.ET.} \\ \text{.NE.} \\ \text{.GT.} \\ \text{.GE.} \\ \text{.LT.} \\ \text{.LE.} \end{array} \right\} exp$$

where the abbreviations stand respectively for Equal To, Not Equal to, Greater Than, Greater or Equal, Less Than, Less or Equal. A string relation has the form

$$\textit{string} \left\{ \begin{array}{l} \texttt{.EQUALS.} \\ \texttt{.GREATER.} \\ \texttt{.LESS.} \end{array} \right\} \textit{string}$$

which stands for left-to-right comparison of the strings.

Due to the way strings are represented internally within the computer, certain string values are said to be "packed." Unless both strings of a string relation have length one (i.e., are a single character), they must both be packed. This condition may be determined as follows: A constant string and an input string are always packed. If s is packed, so are $n\!:\!s$, s/n, $s\,.\texttt{CONC}.\textit{string}$, and also $n\backslash s$ if n is a multiple of 5. The variable V in a SET statement receives a packed value only if the expression in that statement is packed.

2.2.10. DO statements. The general form

$$\begin{array}{ll} & \texttt{DO } n\texttt{, V} = c_1\texttt{, } c_2\texttt{, } c_3\texttt{;} \\ & \texttt{statement.} \\ & \quad\vdots \\ n & \texttt{statement.} \end{array}$$

where V is an integer variable and c_1, c_2, c_3 are integer constants or variables, and where n is the number of the final statement, is an abbreviation for

$$\begin{array}{ll} & \texttt{SET V EQUALS } c_1\texttt{.} \\ n' & \texttt{statement} \\ & \quad\vdots \\ n & \texttt{statement} \\ & \texttt{SET V EQUALS V+}c_2\texttt{.} \\ & \texttt{IF (V .LE. } c_3\texttt{), GO TO } n'\texttt{.} \end{array}$$

This construction allows "looping." Notice that the loop is always performed at least once.

2.2.11. Input/Output. The word 'SINPUT' stands for a string input of 80 characters, which is the contents of the next punched card from the input. For example, the statement

$$\texttt{SET V EQUALS SINPUT}$$

may be used to set the value of V to the contents of the next card of the input.

The output statement is

SET OUTPUT EQUALS *string*

where '*string*' stands for a packed string that is exactly 120 characters long.

2.2.12. The END statement. The final statement of each BL\I program is 'END.'

2.2.13. Example program.

The following program illustrates most of the features available in the language. Its function is to edit some input text, so that right and left margins are "justified"; i.e., so that extra spaces between words are added, if necessary, to make the margins appear straight. No hyphenation is attempted by the routine.

The program attempts to do a neat job by putting most spaces alternately at the left and right in succeeding lines, and by preferring to insert spaces after punctuation marks. For example, the present paragraph and the preceding paragraph of this description would be edited as follows, assuming a line width of 40 characters:

```
     The   following   program illustrates
most of the features   available   in   the
language.    Its function is to edit some
input   text,   so  that   right  and   left
margins are "justified";  i.e.,   so that
extra spaces between words are added, if
necessary,   to   make   the margins appear
straight. No hyphenation is attempted by
the routine.
     The   program   attempts to do a neat
job by putting most   spaces   alternately
at   the   left   and   right   in succeeding
lines,   and   by   preferring   to   insert
spaces   after   punctuation   marks.    For
example,   the present paragraph and   the
preceding   paragraph of this description
would be edited as follows,   assuming   a
line width of 40 characters:
```

The first three characters of the input give the desired line width. The symbol '¶' (following a space) indicates the end of a paragraph; a double '¶¶' indicates the end of the input text.

Lines labeled 'C' in the program are merely comments, which serve to explain the algorithm. They have no effect on the program itself.

```
C       EXAMPLE PROGRAM
C        TEXT EDITING WITH JUSTIFICATION OF MARGINS
        MAXSIZE 80 SORCE, 60 C, 180 TLINE, 100 WORD, 120 BUFFR
        DIMENSION C(4)
C       READ IN THE DESIRED LINE WIDTH:
        SET SORCE EQUALS SINPUT.
        SET NWDTH EQUALS NVALUE(3:SORCE).
        SET SORCE EQUALS 3\SORCE.
C       PREPARE TO START A NEW PARAGRAPH:
1       SET TLINE EQUALS OH.
        SET C(4) EQUALS 4H
        SET NSIZE EQUALS 4.
        SET M EQUALS 0.
C       PREPARE TO START A NEW LINE:
2       DO 3, J=1,1,3;
3       SET C(J) EQUALS OH.
        GOTO 20.
C        FIRST PASS: BUILD LINE AND COUNT SPACES.
10      IF (LENGTH(TLINE) .ET. 0), GOTO 13.
        IF (TLINE:1 .EQUALS. 1H.), GOTO 14.
        IF (TLINE:1 .EQUALS. 1H:), GOTO 14.
        IF (TLINE:1 .EQUALS. 1H?), GOTO 14.
        IF (TLINE:1 .EQUALS. 1H!), GOTO 14.
        IF (TLINE:1 .EQUALS. 1H,), GOTO 15.
        IF (TLINE:1 .EQUALS. 1H;), GOTO 15.
        IF (TLINE:1 .EQUALS. 1H"), GOTO 15.
        SET J EQUALS 1. GOTO 16.
13      SET J EQUALS 4. GOTO 16.
14      SET J EQUALS 3. GOTO 16.
15      SET J EQUALS 2. GOTO 16.
C       THE STRINGS C(1), C(2), C(3), AND C(4) REPRESENT
C          EXTRA SPACES AFTER WORDS, COMMAS, PERIODS, AND INDENTS.
16      SET C(J) EQUALS 1H,, TYPE 1.
        SET TLINE EQUALS 1H  .CONC. STRING(J,1) .CONC.
                WORD, TYPE 1.
        SET NSIZE EQUALS NSIZE + N + 1.
20      IF (LENGTH(SORCE).ET.0), SET SORCE EQUALS SINPUT.
        IF (1:SORCE .EQUALS. 1H ), GOTO 21.
```

```
         GOTO 22.
21       SET SORCE EQUALS 1\SORCE.
         GOTO 20.
22       IF (1:SORCE .EQUALS. 1H¶), GOTO 100.
         SET N EQUALS 0. SET WORD EQUALS 0H.
23       SET WORD EQUALS 1:SORCE, TYPE 1.
         SET N EQUALS N+1.
         SET SORCE EQUALS 1\SORCE.
         IF (LENGTH(SORCE).ET.0), SET SORCE EQUALS SINPUT.
         IF (1:SORCE .EQUALS. 1H ), GOTO 25.
24       GOTO 23.
25       IF (NSIZE+N .LT. NWDTH), GOTO 10.
C        AT THIS POINT, WORD HAS N CHARACTERS, ALL NONBLANK
C        TLINE HAS NSIZE CHARACTERS, NSIZE .LE. NWDTH
C        NOW DISTRIBUTE EXTRA SPACES TO FILL THE LINE:
         SET XS EQUALS NWDTH - NSIZE.
         IF (XS .ET. 0), GOTO 100.
         IF (LENGTH(C(1))+LENGTH(C(2))+LENGTH(C(3)).GE.1), GOTO 30.
C        OOPS, THERE'S ONLY ONE WORD, OR ONLY THE INDENTATION.
         SET C(3) EQUALS 1H,.  SET TLINE EQUALS 2H 3, TYPE 1.
30       DO 39, I=1,1,4;
         SET J EQUALS 5-I.
         IF (I.ET.1), SET J EQUALS 3.
         IF (M.NE.1), GOTO 35.
C        HANDLE EVEN-NUMBERED LINES:
         SET C(J) EQUALS 1H., TYPE 1.
31       IF (1:C(J) .EQUALS. 1H ), GOTO 32.
         IF (1:C(J) .EQUALS. 1H,), GOTO 33.
         SET C(J) EQUALS 1\C(J). GOTO 39.
32       SET C(J) EQUALS 1\C(J) .CONC. 1H . GOTO 31.
33       SET C(J) EQUALS 1\C(J) .CONC. 2H ,.
         SET XS EQUALS XS-1.  IF (XS.ET.0), GOTO 100.
         GOTO 31.
C        HANDLE ODD-NUMBERED LINES:
35       SET C(J) EQUALS 1H., TYPE 2.
36       IF (C(J):1 .EQUALS. 1H ), GOTO 37.
         IF (XS .ET. 0), GOTO 100.
         IF (C(J):1 .EQUALS. 1H,), GOTO 38.
         SET C(J) EQUALS C(J)/1. GOTO 39.
37       SET C(J) EQUALS 1H  .CONC. C(J)/1. GOTO 36.
38       SET C(J) EQUALS 2H , .CONC. C(J)/1.
         SET XS EQUALS XS-1. GOTO 36.
39       SET J EQUALS J.
         GOTO 30.
```

```
C          SECOND PASS: INSERT SPACES AND OUTPUT.
   100 IF (LENGTH(TLINE).ET.0), IF (1:SORCE.ET.1H¶), GOTO 32767.
       SET BUFFR EQUALS OH. SET KBUF EQUALS 120.
   101 IF (LENGTH(TLINE).ET.0), GOTO 110.
       SET BUFFR EQUALS 1:TLINE, TYPE 1.
       SET TLINE EQUALS 1\TLINE. SET KBUF EQUALS KBUF-1.
       IF (BUFFR:1 .EQUALS. 1H ), GOTO 102.
       GOTO 101.

   102 SET J EQUALS NVALUE(1:TLINE).
   103 IF (1:C(J) .EQUALS. 1H.), SET C(J) EQUALS 1\C(J).
       IF (1:C(J) .EQUALS. 1H,), GOTO 104.
       SET C(J) EQUALS 1\C(J).
       SET BUFFR EQUALS 1H , TYPE 1. SET KBUF EQUALS KBUF-1.
       GOTO 103.
   104 SET C(J) EQUALS 1\C(J).
       SET TLINE EQUALS 1\TLINE. GOTO 101.

   110 IF (KBUF .ET. 0), GOTO 120.
       DO 111, I=1,1,KBUF;
   111 SET BUFFR EQUALS 1H , TYPE 1.
   120 SET OUTPUT EQUALS BUFFR.

   121 SET M EQUALS 1-M.
       IF (1:SORCE .ET. 1H¶), GOTO 130.
       IF (N.GT.NWDTH), GOTO 125.
       SET TLINE EQUALS WORD.
       SET NSIZE EQUALS N. GOTO 2.
C    THE NEXT WORD IS TOO LONG, MUST CHOP IT UP.
   125 SET TLINE EQUALS OH.
       DO 126, I=1,1,NWDTH;
       SET TLINE EQUALS 1:WORD, TYPE 1.
       SET WORD EQUALS 1\WORD.
   126 SET N EQUALS N-1.
       GOTO 100.
   130 SET SORCE EQUALS 1\SORCE.
       GOTO 1.
32767 END.
```

2.3. Critique of the Language Definition

The description of BL\I in Section 2.2 leaves many questions un-
answered, so it is unsatisfactory as a user's manual. In this section
we will discuss some of its inadequacies — but we'll confine our criticism
to the way BL\I has been *described*, ignoring for the moment all of the
bad features that are rampant in the language itself.

The worst aspect of Section 2.2 is its vagueness about exactly what constitutes an "expression" and what constitutes a "statement." Expressions are said to be "built up," and "parentheses may be used" (at least in integer expressions), but those rules hardly tell us how to characterize an expression. Is 'I+(J*K)+L' an allowable expression? Or how about '((I)+J)'? Those parentheses do not indicate an order of computation different from the precedence rule, as required by the wording of 2.2.5. Furthermore, the meaning of an expression isn't clear even in the absence of parentheses, because we aren't told whether A-B+C is supposed to mean (A-B)+C or A-(B+C).

No precedence rules are given for the string operations, but the fact that '2:3\8HLANGUAGE/2' is 'GU' apparently gives precedence to '/2' over '2:'. A construction like '$m\backslash string/n$' turns out to be unambiguous, in the sense that both $(m\backslash string)/n$ and $m\backslash(string/n)$ yield the same result. But '$m:string:n$' and '$m:string/n$' and '$m\backslash string:n$' are definitely ambiguous without parentheses.

Sections 2.2.3 and 2.2.4 refer to "a MAXSIZE statement" and "a DIMENSION statement"; but are such things really like other "statements" of the language? For example, the manual as it stands does not say that MAXSIZE and DIMENSION specifications must precede the variables they mention, nor does it rule out programs that start like this:

```
MAXSIZE 80 S
SET S EQUALS SINPUT.
IF (S .GREATER. 3HBIG), MAXSIZE 160 S.
```

The manual should have made it clear that every BL\I program must begin with a MAXSIZE specification for all the string variables, unless there are no string variables. Every string variable must be named exactly once in this specification, and the term 'MAXSIZE' must never appear again. Similarly, if at least one string variable is subscripted, exactly one DIMENSION specification must follow the MAXSIZE spec, naming every such variable exactly once.

The vagueness about statements goes further: When Section 2.2.12 speaks of "the END statement," it doesn't disallow

```
IF (LENGTH(S) .ET. 0), END.
```

Its phrase "final statement" might be interpreted in a dynamic sense, meaning the last statement to be performed, or in a static sense, meaning the last statement that appears in the program text. (The actual rule is that the final line of a BL\I program must be 'END.' with an optional numeric label, and that 'END' must not appear anywhere else in the program except perhaps as the name of a variable.)

Can a BL\I program include something like the following?

```
1 IF (J .NE. 2), DO 2, I=1,1,1;
  SET K EQUALS K+1.
2 SET J EQUALS 2.
```

And if so, does K change if statement 1 is encountered with $J = 2$? (See the expanded, unabbreviated form of the DO statement in 2.2.10.)

In fact, the designer of BL\I did not intend for DO to be used in conjunction with IF, so Section 2.2.10 should not have called it a "statement." Further commentary is needed there as well, to clarify that nested DOs are perfectly legal:

```
DO 2, I=1,2,9;
DO 2, J=3,3,I;
2 SET S EQUALS STRING(J,1).CONC.STRING(I,1),
    TYPE 1.
```

(This construction appends 3133353767396999 to the string S; it is, however, probably too tricky to be part of a well-written manual, except as a puzzle for readers who think they are smart.)

Here is another nested construction that is perfectly legitimate, but not discussed explicitly although used in statement 100 of the example:

```
IF (I .GT. 2), IF (I .LT. 5), GOTO 8.
```

The user's manual is sloppy and inconsistent when it refers to constituents of a "general construction." For example, a variable name is sometimes called v (Sections 2.2.3 and 2.2.4), sometimes V (Sections 2.2.4, 2.2.7, 2.2.9, 2.2.10, 2.2.11), sometimes V (Sections 2.2.7, 2.2.10, 2.2.11). The lapse in 2.2.10 within the DO statement is especially bizarre, because V cannot be the name of an integer variable.

Incidentally, Section 2.2.1 forgets to mention that the letters in a variable's name must be uppercase. At present, this rule can be inferred only from the examples, especially in 2.2.13, where all variable names are uppercase — although the example makes it clear that lowercase letters and even weird characters like '¶' are allowed to appear in strings and string constants.

Each n in Sections 2.2.6 and 2.2.8 must be an integer *constant*, not an expression that can vary dynamically. The manual only hints at this, by using '*exp*' elsewhere in rules that do allow general expressions. An industrious reader will also find confirmation in the example of 2.2.13 — which presumably would have said

```
SET TLINE EQUALS NWDTH:WORD, TYPE 1.
SET WORD EQUALS NWDTH\WORD.
SET N EQUALS N-NWDTH.
```

if such operations were permitted. (See the block of statements between 125 and 126.)

Section 2.2.6 fails to define n:S, S:n, n\S, and S/n when n exceeds the length of S. (In such cases, we are in fact supposed to pretend that n is equal to LENGTH(S).) Moreover, the single example of STRING is woefully inadequate; much better would be

```
STRING(J+1,1) .CONC. 1H- .CONC. STRING(J,3)
```

which turns out to be '6- 25', not '2-025', when J is 25.

The period following a statement is mistakenly omitted in Sections 2.2.8 and 2.2.11; also in one of the examples of 2.2.7. Conversely, spurious periods appear where Section 2.2.9 says '*statement*.' and where Section 2.2.10 says 'statement.'; both should really be just '*statement*', because the closing period is part of a statement.

The commas and periods in the first displayed expressions of Section 2.2.5 might also be confusing. And a period is missing at the very end of 2.2.12.

The detailed example in 2.2.13 is our only clue to the fact that several statements can be punched on a single card, or that a single statement might be split among several lines of the program. It also indicates that labels need not start in column 1 or end in column 5; they can be punched anywhere in columns 1–5.

A reader might, however, infer incorrectly from the example that numeric labels must appear in ascending order throughout a program. That is untrue, although they must be distinct.

Finally, a careful reader will also have at least one more quibble: Section 2.2.8 refers to "GO TO statements," yet spells the term 'GOTO' without a space. Such a space does appear in 2.2.10, but never in 2.2.13. Is the 'GO TO' in Section 2.2.10 a typographic error? (Answer: Yes.)

2.4. Example of a Better Language

Evidently the task of writing a definitive user's manual for a programming language is more daunting than it might appear at first glance. In this section we will try again, by introducing an experimental language as an alternative to BL\I.

Most of the problems we encountered in Section 2.2 can be cured by using Backus–Naur form to define the language precisely. A well-planned BNF syntax is able to specify the meaning of each construction in parallel with its specification of the allowable forms. Therefore the following user's manual is written for people who have already had a tutorial about BNF.

STROL, the STRing Oriented Language

The purpose of STROL is to provide facilities for manipulating strings of characters, primarily oriented towards the editing of text.

STROL programs are built from simple units combined in simple ways, according the grammatical rules given below. We will start with the most primitive constructions and work our way up to complete programs.

2.4.1. Identifiers and declarations.

Syntax:

⟨digit⟩ ::= 0 | 1 | 2 | 3 | 4 | 5 | 6 | 7 | 8 | 9
⟨letter⟩ ::= a | b | c | d | e | f | g | h | i | j | k | l | m | n | o | p
  | q | r | s | t | u | v | w | x | y | z
⟨unsigned integer⟩ ::= ⟨digit⟩ | ⟨unsigned integer⟩⟨digit⟩
⟨identifier⟩ ::= ⟨letter⟩ | ⟨identifier⟩⟨letter⟩ | ⟨identifier⟩⟨digit⟩
⟨subscript bound⟩ ::= ⟨empty⟩ | [⟨unsigned integer⟩]
⟨integer variable declaration⟩ ::= **integer** ⟨identifier⟩⟨subscript bound⟩
  | ⟨integer variable declaration⟩, ⟨identifier⟩⟨subscript bound⟩
⟨string variable declaration⟩ ::= **string** ⟨identifier⟩⟨subscript bound⟩
  | ⟨string variable declaration⟩, ⟨identifier⟩⟨subscript bound⟩
⟨variable declaration⟩ ::= ⟨integer variable declaration⟩
  | ⟨string variable declaration⟩
⟨label declaration⟩ ::= ⟨identifier⟩:
⟨empty⟩ ::=

Examples:

integer $table\,[100], i, j, k, h2o$
string $source, vowels, s, page\,[32], x1[5], x2[5], fib$
$caltech$:

Semantics: An unsigned integer denotes a nonnegative number according to the usual decimal notation.

Identifiers have no inherent meaning. They are used to denote variables (quantities that possess changeable value) and/or labels (positions within a program).

Every identifier used in a STROL program must appear exactly once in a "declaration"; this declaration specifies the use of that identifier. Thus, an identifier that appears in a label declaration must not be used elsewhere to denote a variable, and vice versa. The syntax rules below use the category ⟨integer identifier⟩ or ⟨string identifier⟩ to stand for an identifier that appears in an integer or string variable declaration, respectively; similarly, a ⟨label⟩ appears in a label declaration.

Every variable identifier stands for an ordered array of values. The number of such values is specified by the subscript bound in the corresponding declaration. An empty subscript bound is equivalent to '[1]'; this is the most common case, in which the variable is simply an "array" consisting of a single value. The value is either an integer or a string-and-cursor, depending on the declaration. (Cursors are discussed in Section 2.4.3.)

In the first example given, '*table*' identifies an array of 100 integer values, which may be referred to as *table*[1], *table*[2], ..., *table*[100].

The subscript bound '[0]' is syntactically permissible, but pointless, because a variable declared with such a bound cannot be referred to anywhere outside of its declaration.

2.4.2. Integer expressions.

Syntax:*
⟨subscript⟩ ::= ⟨empty⟩ | [⟨integer expression⟩]
⟨integer variable⟩ ::= ⟨integer identifier⟩⟨subscript⟩
⟨integer primary⟩ ::= ⟨unsigned integer⟩ | ⟨integer variable⟩
     | (⟨integer expression⟩)
     | **length**(⟨string expression⟩) | **integer**(⟨string expression⟩)
     | **minint** | **maxint**
⟨integer term⟩ ::= ⟨integer primary⟩ | ⟨integer term⟩ × ⟨integer primary⟩
⟨sign⟩ ::= + | −
⟨integer expression⟩ ::= ⟨integer term⟩ | ⟨sign⟩⟨integer term⟩
     | ⟨integer expression⟩⟨sign⟩⟨integer term⟩

---

* Here and elsewhere the right-hand side of a syntax rule sometimes refers to a syntactic category that is defined later. Context-free languages cannot always be defined by grammars in which all rules refer to themselves or to previously defined categories [3]. A strictly sequential grammar is almost certainly impossible for ALGOL 60, and for similar languages like STROL, although no rigorous proof of impossibility is presently known.

Examples:

$table[n-3]$
$2 \times h2o[1]$
$(-2) \times (-h2o)$
$i + j \times k + \textbf{integer}(source + 3)$
$(i + j) \times (k + \textbf{integer}(source + 3))$

Semantics: An integer expression denotes an integer value that is computed from constants and/or the values of variables. The value of an integer expression must lie between **minint** and **maxint**, inclusive, where the quantities **minint** and **maxint** may differ from one implementation of STROL to another but they always satisfy

$$-\textbf{maxint} - 1 \le \textbf{minint} \le -\textbf{maxint}, \qquad \textbf{maxint} \ge 32767.$$

(For example, a binary computer with 16-bit two's complement arithmetic will have **minint** $= -32768$ and **maxint** $= 32767$.)

An integer variable is specified by its identifier and a subscript, where the subscript is either empty (implying the subscript '[1]') or it is an integer expression whose value is used to select the appropriate entry from the array corresponding to the identifier. The value of the subscript must be positive, and it must not exceed the declared subscript bound for that identifier.

If α is a string, **length**(α) denotes its length, namely the number of characters it contains. The construction **integer**(α) denotes the integer obtained by disregarding all characters of α that are not digits, and by regarding the remaining digits as a number in decimal notation. For example, **integer**("1+2") is 12. If α contains no digits, **integer**$(\alpha) = 0$.

The symbols $+$, $-$, and $\times$ stand for the ordinary operations of addition, subtraction, and multiplication; expressions like '$+a$' and '$-b$' are equivalent to '$0 + a$' and '$0 - b$', respectively. The syntax explains how larger expressions are constructed from subexpressions, with multiplication taking precedence over addition and subtraction, and with expressions such as '$a - b + c$' interpreted as '$(a - b) + c$'.

2.4.3. String expressions.

Syntax:

⟨string constant⟩ ::= ⟨empty⟩ | ⟨string constant⟩⟨nonquote character⟩
    | ⟨string constant⟩""
⟨string variable⟩ ::= ⟨string identifier⟩⟨subscript⟩
⟨length specification⟩ ::= ⟨empty⟩ | ⟨integer primary⟩
⟨partial string⟩ ::= ⟨string variable⟩⟨sign⟩⟨length specification⟩
    | ⟨string variable⟩⟨sign⟩⟨string primary⟩

⟨string primary⟩ ::= "⟨string constant⟩" | ⟨partial string⟩
       | (⟨string expression⟩) | [⟨partial string⟩]
       | **string**(⟨integer expression⟩) | **input**(⟨channel⟩)
⟨channel⟩ ::= ⟨integer expression⟩
⟨string expression⟩ ::= ⟨string primary⟩
       | ⟨string expression⟩ & ⟨string primary⟩

   Examples:

```
"This is a ""string"" of length 32."
```
source + 3
source − (−3)
[*source* + " "]
```
"S[" & string(n) & "]"
```
page + & *vowels* −

   Semantics: A string constant denotes a sequence of zero or more characters. The syntactic category ⟨nonquote character⟩ will not be defined further here; it represents all characters that can appear in strings manipulated by a STROL program on a particular computer, except for the quote mark ("). A quote mark is represented within a string constant by two adjacent quote marks; this convention prevents ambiguity, since a string constant is delimited by placing it within quotes.

   A string variable is a subscripted identifier, in a manner exactly analogous to integer variables (see Section 2.4.2). Each string variable in STROL actually denotes two things: a *string*, namely a sequence of zero or more characters, and a *cursor*, which is a position within that string or at either end. For example, the variable *vowels* might denote at some point the string-and-cursor represented schematically as

aei|ou

with the cursor between i and o. As a program proceeds, the individual cursors usually move or "stroll through" the strings, thereby helping to control the desired actions.

   A length specification denotes an integer distance measured from the cursor; and a partial string is a substring that begins or ends at the cursor, extending to the right or left. For example, *vowels* + 1 is "o" and *vowels* − 2 is "ei" in the situation depicted above. An empty length specification denotes ∞, meaning "all the way to the end of the string"; thus, *vowels*+ is "ou" and *vowels*− is "aei". The partial string *vowels* − n will be "aei" if n is any integer value greater than 2. Furthermore, *vowels* + m will be "aei" if m is any integer value *less* than −2, because a negative value reverses the sign.

A partial string can also be obtained from a string variable by expressing it in terms of some other string α that is to be matched. In such a case it means "the substring that extends from the cursor up to and including the first occurrence of α in the given direction, or the empty string if α does not occur in that direction." For example, if *fib* is the string-and-cursor combination

$$abaab\overset{\downarrow}{a}ba$$

then *fib* + "ba" is "aba" and *fib* − "ba" is "baab", while *fib* + "baa" is empty.

A string expression, however, simply denotes a string of characters, *without* any associated cursor; a cursor position is an attribute only of a string variable.

The special string primary [⟨partial string⟩] stands for the value of the partial string and also means that the partial string is *removed* or "chopped" from the value of the associated variable. Thus, in the example, above, [*vowels* − 1] stands for "i", and *vowels* becomes

$$ae\overset{\downarrow}{o}u$$

afterward. Chopping helps lead to efficient programs, because it often avoids the need to make duplicate copies of the same information: Parts of one string can be chopped out and given to another.

If n is an integer value, **string**(n) denotes the decimal representation of n. For example, **string**$(41) = $ "41", **string**$(-41) = $ "-41", and **string**$(0) = $ "0".

The string primary **input**(n) stands for the next string from input channel n. For example, channel 1 might denote the card reader, and **input**(1) would be a string of length 80 representing the next card of input data. If the channel has no more data, **input** produces the empty string.

The operation & between strings denotes concatenation (juxtaposition); for example, "a" & "b" = "ab".

Chopping and **input** cause "side effects" that can affect other parts of a string expression, so their behavior needs to be understood carefully if the programmer wants to concoct certain complex expressions. The main principle is that side effects at the left of an expression occur before side effects at the right, whenever there is a choice. Thus a partial string removed from the left part of a concatenation is chopped out before the right part of the concatenation is evaluated:

$$[vowels - 1] \,\&\, [vowels - 2]$$

in the example above would yield `"iae"` and *vowels* $=$ $\overset{\curlyvee}{}$ou, because [*vowels* $-$ 1] chops out the `"i"`. Similarly,

$$\textbf{input}(1) \ \& \ \textbf{input}(1)$$

concatenates the images of two cards, with the first card to the left of the second. The more complicated example

$$[\mathit{fib} - [\mathit{fib} - 1]]$$

yields `"baa"` and changes *fib* to a$\overset{\curlyvee}{}$aba, because the innermost chop has the effect of reducing the overall expression to [*fib* $-$ `"b"`] with *fib* $=$ abaa$\overset{\curlyvee}{}$aba; the innermost chop must be done first.

Integer expressions can have side effects too, because they can involve strings in situations like

$$\textbf{length}([\mathit{vowels} - \text{"e"}]) - \textbf{length}([\mathit{vowels} - \text{"e"}]).$$

In such cases the left operands are always evaluated first. But programmers who use such things should ask themselves if they really want to be so tricky.

2.4.4. Conditions.

Syntax:

⟨relational operator⟩ ::= $=$ | $\neq$ | $<$ | $>$ | $\leq$ | $\geq$
⟨relation⟩ ::= ⟨string expression⟩⟨relational operator⟩⟨string expression⟩
    | ⟨integer expression⟩⟨relational operator⟩⟨integer expression⟩
⟨condition primary⟩ ::= ⟨relation⟩ | (⟨condition⟩)
⟨condition secondary⟩ ::= ⟨condition primary⟩
    | ⟨condition secondary⟩ **and** ⟨condition primary⟩
⟨condition⟩ ::= ⟨condition secondary⟩
    | ⟨condition⟩ **or** ⟨condition secondary⟩

Examples:

$k > 0$
$\mathit{page}[3] \leq \mathit{page}[4]$
$\mathit{source} + \text{" "} = \text{""}$
$s + 1 \geq \text{"a"}$ **and** $s + 1 \leq \text{"z"}$ **or** $s + 1 \geq \text{"A"}$ **and** $s + 1 \leq \text{"Z"}$
$k > 0$ **and** ($s+ \ \neq \ \text{""}$ **or** $s- \ \neq \ \text{""}$)

Semantics: A condition is either true or false, based on the values of the expressions it contains.

A relation compares two integers or two strings. String comparison is done lexicographically, as in a dictionary: If α, β, and γ are strings and if x and y are characters with $x < y$, then $\alpha < \alpha x\beta$ and $\alpha x\beta < \alpha y\gamma$.

If C_1 and C_2 are conditions, then 'C_1 **and** C_2' is true if and only if both C_1 and C_2 are true; 'C_1 **or** C_2' is false if and only if both C_1 and C_2 are false. The syntax specifies that **and** takes precedence over **or**.

If the evaluation of a condition involves side effects, they occur from left to right. For example, if *vowels* is aeiou then '[*vowels* $- 1] \leq$ [*vowels* $- 1$]' is false, because "i" $\geq$ "e". (See Section 2.4.3.)

2.4.5. Actions.

Syntax:

⟨action⟩ ::= ⟨integer command⟩ | ⟨string command⟩
        | ⟨output command⟩ | ⟨routine⟩ | ⟨empty⟩
⟨integer command⟩ ::= ⟨integer expression⟩ → ⟨integer variable⟩
⟨string command⟩ ::= ⟨string expression⟩ → ⟨string variable⟩⟨sign⟩
        | **pass** ⟨partial string⟩
        | **delete** ⟨partial string⟩
        | **erase** ⟨string variable⟩
⟨output command⟩ ::= ⟨string expression⟩ → **output**(⟨channel⟩)

Examples:

$k + 2 \to k$
"y" $\to$ *vowels* $-$
$[s + 1] \to s-$
pass $s + 1$
$s+ \to s+$
delete *source* $+1$
erase $x2[table[k]]$
$[title +]$ & $[page[j]-] \to$ **output**(2)

Semantics: An integer command assigns a specified value to a specified variable. For example, '$k + 2 \to k$' increases the value of k by two.

The first form of a string command inserts a specified string at the left or right of a string variable's cursor. The **pass** command moves the cursor past a given partial string. For example, if *vowels* is aeiou,

'"y" → *vowels*+'   changes *vowels* to   aeiyou;
'"y" → *vowels*−'   changes *vowels* to   aeiyou;
'**pass** *vowels* − 2'   changes *vowels* to   aeiou.

Notice that the commands '$[s+1] \to s-$' and '**pass** $s+1$' have exactly the same effect, because the former chops off the character at the right of the cursor (if any) and reinserts it at the left. Notice also that 'pass $s-$' rewinds the cursor all the way to the left of string s. The command '$s+ \rightarrow s+$' doubles the string at the right of s's cursor.

A **delete** command removes a partial string and makes it vanish. An **erase** command makes a variable string empty. Thus '**erase** s' is equivalent to '**delete** $s-$, **delete** $s+$' and also to '**pass** $s-$, **delete** $s+$'.

An **output** command sends a given string to a specified output channel. For example, **output**(2) might be a line printer and **output**(0) might be the user's control console where messages are received.

An ⟨action⟩ may also be a ⟨routine⟩ (meaning, "perform the routine," see Section 2.4.6); or it may be ⟨empty⟩ (meaning, "do nothing").

2.4.6. Sequences, steps, and routines.

Syntax:

⟨control transfer⟩ ::= **to** ⟨label⟩ | **exit**
⟨sequence⟩ ::= ⟨action⟩ | ⟨control transfer⟩ | ⟨action⟩ , ⟨sequence⟩
    | **if** ⟨condition⟩ **then** ⟨sequence⟩
⟨step⟩ ::= ⟨sequence⟩ | **if** ⟨condition⟩ **then** ⟨sequence⟩ ; **else** ⟨step⟩
⟨routine tail⟩ ::= **end** | **repeat**
    | ⟨label declaration⟩ ⟨routine tail⟩ | ⟨step⟩ ; ⟨routine tail⟩
⟨routine⟩ ::= **begin** ⟨routine tail⟩

Examples:

to *caltech*

$j \rightarrow i$, $k \rightarrow j$, $i \rightarrow k$

pass $s-$,   **if** $s+ > s-$ **then** $1 \rightarrow k$,   **exit**

if $k > 5$ **then** $i \rightarrow j$, $0 \rightarrow i$;
else if $k = 0$ **then** "ooops" $\rightarrow$ **output**(0);
else $k + 1 \rightarrow k$, **erase** $c[k]$

if $s- \neq$ "" **then**
  begin if $t+ =$ "T" **then to** *caltech*;   **else to** *stanford*;
  end;
else "!" $\rightarrow s-$, **exit**

begin if *length*$(s+) > 60$ **then exit**;
  double: $s+ \rightarrow s+$; *again*: **repeat**

Semantics: The flow of control passes from one action to another according to a few simple yet versatile rules, by which actions are combined into increasingly larger program units called sequences, steps, and routines.

If L is a label, the phrase 'to L' means that control should pass to the step labeled 'L:' or to the end-of-routine labeled 'L:'. The operation 'exit' terminates the activity of the current routine, namely of the smallest ⟨routine⟩ or ⟨program⟩ that contains this 'exit'.

A *sequence* is essentially a list of actions separated by commas, possibly conditional on certain relations, and possibly ending with a transfer of control. If A is an action, C is a condition, and S is a sequence, the sequence 'A, S' means to perform A and then to perform S; the sequence 'if C then S' means to evaluate C and then to perform S only if C turns out to be true. Thus in an extended sequence like

$$A_1, \ A_2, \ \textbf{if} \ C_1 \ \textbf{then} \ A_3, \ \textbf{if} \ C_2 \ \textbf{then if} \ C_3 \ \textbf{then} \ A_4, \ B$$

where the A's are simple actions (not routines), the C's are conditions, and B is either an action or a control transfer, the meaning is to perform A_1, then to perform A_2, then to evaluate C_1, then to do nothing further if C_1 is found to be false, otherwise to perform A_3, then to evaluate C_2 and (if that is true) to evaluate C_3 and (if that is also true) to perform A_4 and then B. This sequence will send control to another part of the program only if B is a control transfer and conditions C_1, C_2, C_3 are all found to be true. The same explanation holds also if any of the A's are routines, except that a routine might send control elsewhere with a 'to'.

A *step* is essentially a choice between one or more sequences. For example, a three-way choice has the form

$$\textbf{if} \ C_1 \ \textbf{then} \ S_1; \ \textbf{else if} \ C_2 \ \textbf{then} \ S_2; \ \textbf{else} \ S_3$$

and it means, "Evaluate condition C_1; if it is true, perform sequence S_1; otherwise evaluate C_2, and if it is true, perform S_2; otherwise perform S_3."

A *routine* is essentially a list of steps separated by semicolons, starting with 'begin' and ending with either 'end' or 'repeat'. The steps and/or the final end or repeat may also be labeled with one or more identifiers. The routine

$$\textbf{begin} \ T_1; \ T_2; \ T_3; \ \textbf{end}$$

means, "Perform T_1; then if control has not been transferred, perform T_2; then if control has still not been transferred, perform T_3." The routine

$$\textbf{begin} \ T_1; \ T_2; \ T_3; \ \textbf{repeat}$$

has the same meaning, except that if control reaches the end of T_3, step T_1 is performed again. Thus the second case has the same behavior as

$$\textbf{begin}\ \ L{:}\ T_1;\ \ T_2;\ \ T_3;\ \ \textbf{to}\ L;\ \ \textbf{end}$$

if L is an identifier not used elsewhere.

The techniques of Section 1.4 can be used to prove that the decomposition of a routine into sequences and steps is unambiguous. Therefore the flow of control in any STROL program is uniquely defined.

2.4.7. Programs.

Syntax:

$\langle$program tail$\rangle ::= \langle$routine tail$\rangle$
$\quad\quad | \langle$variable declaration$\rangle\langle$program tail$\rangle$
$\langle$program$\rangle ::= \textbf{begin}\ \langle$program tail$\rangle$

Example:

```
begin integer l, n;
   string fib, rib, lhs;
   "S[1] = b" → output(4);
   2 → n,  "b" → rib+,  "a" → fib+;
   begin "S[" & string(n) & "] = " → lhs+;
      begin length(lhs+) → l;
         if l + length(fib+) ≤ 80 then
            [lhs+] & fib+ → output(4),  exit;
         [lhs+] & fib+(79−l) & "-" → output(4);
         " " → lhs+,  pass fib+(79−l);
      repeat;
      if n = 20 then exit;
      pass fib+, [rib+] → fib+,  fib− → rib+;
      pass fib−,  n + 1 → n;
   repeat;
end
```

Semantics: A *program* is essentially a routine in which the steps are preceded by declarations of the variables to be used. Integer variables are initially zero when a program begins, and string variables are initially empty. The steps of a program are performed until control reaches the final **end**, or until an **exit** occurs that is not part of any routine except the program itself. (A program that ends with **repeat** can terminate only with an **exit**.)

The example program above shows how STROL can compute the "Fibonacci strings" beginning with

$$S[1] = b$$
$$S[2] = a$$
$$S[3] = ab$$
$$S[4] = aba$$
$$S[5] = abaab$$

and ending with $S[20]$, where $S[n] = S[n-1] \,\&\, S[n-2]$ for $n > 2$. The output is sent to channel 4 in units of at most 80 characters each. (Long strings need to be broken up because $S[20]$ is 6765 characters long.)

Special conventions are used when a STROL program is punched on cards otherwise prepared for computer input, in order to adapt it to the computer's character set. Words that appear in boldface type in the rules above, namely

and	**end**	**input**	**minint**	**repeat**
begin	**erase**	**integer**	**or**	**string**
delete	**exit**	**length**	**output**	**then**
else	**if**	**maxint**	**pass**	**to**

are treated like ordinary identifiers; therefore they are called "reserved words" and they must not be used as the identifiers of variables or labels. No distinction is made between uppercase letters and lowercase letters except within string constants.

Special symbols are encoded as follows if they do not appear in the machine's repertoire of characters:

As written above	As punched or typed
$\times$	*
$\neq$	<>
$\leq$	<=
$\geq$	>=
$\rightarrow$	=>
[	(/
]	/)

Blank spaces may not appear in the midst of an identifier or unsigned integer or within a two-character code like '<>'. Two adjacent words or identifiers must be separated by at least one blank space. Otherwise blanks have no significance in a STROL program — except, of course, within string constants, where they denote themselves. An identifier, unsigned integer, or string constant must not be split into parts across more than one line or card. (Long string constants can be fabricated from shorter ones by concatenation.)

Thus the example program above could be expressed in a typical computer's character set as follows:

```
begin integer l,n;
  string fib,rib,lhs;
  "S[1] = b" => output(4);
  2=>n, "b"=>rib+, "a"=>fib+;
  begin "S["&string(n)&"] = " => lhs+;
    begin length(lhs+) => l;
      if l+length(fib+)<=80 then
        [lhs+]&fib+ => output(4), exit;
      [lhs+] & fib+(79-1) & "-" => output(4);
      " "=>lhs+, pass fib+(79-1);
    repeat;
    if n=20 then exit;
    pass fib+, [rib+]=>fib+, fib-=>rib+;
    pass fib-, n+1=>n;
  repeat;
end
```

Explanatory comments can be included in a program by placing them at the right end of any line or card, preceded by a character such as '!' that does not ordinarily belong in a STROL program outside of string constants.

A more elaborate example, which solves the text-justification problem of Section 2.2.13, is shown in Figure 1 on the next two pages. Vertical dots have been added at the left so that each **begin** can readily be paired up with its matching **end** or **repeat**.

2.5. Principles of Language Design

A programming language generally tries to fulfill a number of objectives, which are often contradictory and cannot all be achieved simultaneously. The present section tries to list all of the most salient characteristics of a good language, so that the conflicting aims are spelled out explicitly. Such a checklist can provide a useful set of guidelines for people who are designing a new language, allowing them to pinpoint more easily the objectives that they consider to be of primary importance. Each of the characteristics listed below is already present in the back of a designer's mind, but decisions are made more easily when the criteria have all been listed together.

The following list is based on a brief memo composed by the author in 1963 [4]. After each general principle is stated, comments in brackets

```
begin           ! An example program: Justification of text to a given width
  string source;                   ! the input characters not yet absorbed
  integer width;                        ! the width of each justified line
  string line;                 ! the current line-so-far, with space codes
  integer size;                    ! the width of the current line-so-far
  string word;              ! the next word to contribute to the paragraph
  integer odd;                         ! the parity of the current line
  string buffer;                         ! the final assembled line
  integer i, j;                       ! indexes for the distribution loop
  integer excess;             ! the number of additional spaces needed
  string c[4];                ! control tables for extra spaces of four kinds:
                              ! after a word, comma, period, or indentation
  input(1) → source+, integer([source+3]) → width;
  if width > 120 then
     "width reduced from " & string(width) & " to 120" → output(3),
     120 → width;                     ! avoid widths that are too large
  else if width < 4 then
     "width increased from " & string(width) & " to 4" → output(3),
     4 → width;                       ! avoid widths that are too small
  begin 1 → odd,                           ! begin a new paragraph
    erase c[4], "      " → c[4]−, 4 → size;     ! set up the indentation
    begin                                    ! begin a new line
      begin                          ! try to add the next word
        begin if source+ = "" then input(1) → source+;
          if source+1 ≠ "  " then exit;
          delete source+1;                   ! pass over blanks in input
        repeat;
        if source+1 = "¶" then to ready; ! last line of paragraph is easy
        begin if source+" " ≠ "" then exit;   ! scan to the next blank
          pass source+, input(1) → source+;
          pass source−;
        repeat;
        [source+" "] → word−, delete word−1;  ! detach the next word
        if size + length(word−) ≥ width then exit;   ! is the line full?
        if line− = "" then 4 → j;            ! classify the previous blank
        else if line−1 = "." or line−1 = ":" or line−1 = "?"
              or line−1 = "!" then 3 → j;            ! end of sentence
        else if line−1 = "," or line−1 = ";"
              or line−1 = """" then 2 → j;           ! end of clause
        else 1 → j;                          ! ordinary word space
        "," → c[j]+, size + 1 + length(word−) → size,
        " " & string(j) & [word−] → line−;   ! append the new word
      repeat;
      width − size → excess, if excess = 0 then to ready;
      if c[1]− = "" and c[2]− = "" and c[3]− = "" then to ready;
```

```
      4 → i;                              ! prepare to distribute extra spaces
    begin if i = 4 then 3 → j; else i → j;   ! favor the spaces of case 3
      if odd = 0 then pass c[j]+,        ! distribute spaces right to left
        begin if c[j]-"," = "" then exit;
          pass c[j]-",", " " → c[j]+;
          excess - 1 → excess, if excess = 0 then to ready;
        repeat;
      else pass c[j]-,                  ! distribute spaces left to right
        begin if c[j]+"," = "" then exit;
          " " → c[j]-, pass c[j]+",";
          excess - 1 → excess, if excess = 0 then to ready;
        repeat;
      if i > 1 then i - 1 → i; else 4 → i;      ! cycle through the cases
    repeat;
  ready: if line- = "" and word- = "" then to done;
    pass c[1]-, pass c[2]-, pass c[3]-, pass c[4]-, pass line-;
    begin if line+" " = "" then [line+] → buffer-, exit;
      [line+" "] → buffer-, integer([line+1]) → j;
      [c[j]+","] → buffer-, delete buffer-1;          ! insert the spaces
    repeat;
    [buffer-] → output(2);                  ! output the completed line
    if word- = "" then exit;                ! did the paragraph end?
    begin 1 - odd → odd;                      ! no; carry on
      if length(word-) ≤ width then exit;
      pass word-, [word+width] → output(2), pass word+;
    repeat;                          ! break up an extralong word
    length(word-) → size, [word-] → line-;
  repeat;                          ! now we're ready for another line
  delete source+1;                    ! delete the paragraph mark
repeat;                          ! now we're ready for another paragraph
done:                          ! terminate when given an empty paragraph
end
```

FIGURE 1. The text-justification program of Section 2.2.13, à la STROL.

attempt to illustrate the point in question by discussing relevant aspects of BL\I and/or STROL.

Before setting out to design a language, one should of course have a good grasp of the language's purpose, including the class of problems that it is supposed to handle and the set of people who are going to use it.

2.5.1. Generality. The language must be able to express all conceivable sequences of operations that the user may wish to have for the specified class of problems.

[BL\I has only one kind of output statement, so it provides no way to report error messages to the user of the program in 2.2.13 when the specified line width is too large or too small.]

2.5.2. Conciseness; elegance. The language should be able to represent programs in a brief, compact manner rather than in an awkward, lengthy, redundant fashion. The operations that are used most frequently should have the most concise notation.

[Wordy locutions like 'SET SORCE EQUALS 1\SORCE' do not measure up to '**delete** *source*+1'; and STROL's "chop" operation also makes programs substantially shorter. Furthermore, STROL supports pattern matching in strings, a common task that can be tedious to code directly.

The DO statement of BL\I often forces a programmer to make a special check for the case that the loop should not be performed — for example, 'DO m, I = 1,1,n' when $n = 0$. And BL\I does not allow the controlled variable to decrease.

STROL's conventions for loops via **begin** ... **repeat** and **exit** capture many common idioms of programming and make most labels unnecessary. However, a simple loop that is to be performed for $i = 1, 2,$ ..., n is more easily expressed in BL\I.]

2.5.3. Consistency; unity. Similar operations should have similar notations. The same set of conventions should apply throughout the entire language. If some features are present and other features have the same "spirit," the other features should be present too.

[BL\I fails spectacularly here, having all the earmarks of a hodgepodge designed by committee. String constants have a peculiar form unlike anything else in the language; some operations are expressed by symbols but others have weird names like .CONC.; the comparison of strings uses operators that differ from those allowed for comparison of integers; some statements end with a period, others with a semicolon, others with no punctuation; the MAXSIZE and DIMENSION statements have quite different syntax. Notations such as $n : S$ are allowed when n is a constant but not when n is a variable, although variables would fit the spirit of that notation quite nicely.]

2.5.4. Simplicity. The rules of the language should be few in number. The language should be easy to learn and easy to teach.

[Many aspects of BL\I criticized elsewhere make it harder to learn, and the rules for "packed strings" in Section 2.2.9 are virtually incomprehensible. In order to deal with an unpacked string, one must first pack it by saying something like 'SET S EQUALS OH .CONC. S.'; the compiler could surely do that automatically when needed.

STROL's operations are quite straightforward except when chopping causes side effects. The rules covering such weird cases can make STROL seem much more complicated than it really is, so they should be deemphasized.]

2.5.5. Familiarity. The language should make use of existing notations that are already in wide use, unless the existing notations are inadequate. There is no need to change established conventions merely for the sake of change. Conversely, if the language adopts a widely used notation, it should retain the existing meaning, lest the user become confused.

[Standard notations for string manipulation have not yet materialized, so the field is still ripe for experimentation in this particular area of programming. BL\I's notations $n{:}S$, $S{:}n$, $n\backslash S$, and S/n are reasonably attractive, and STROL's notations for substrings near a cursor seem natural too. Only time will tell if either convention acquires a substantial following.

The abbreviations '.NE.', '.LT.', '.LE.', '.GT.', and '.GE.' that BL\I uses for integer comparisons agree with those found in FORTRAN; but '.ET.' doesn't match FORTRAN's '.EQ.'. This deviation is needlessly confusing.]

2.5.6. Intuitivity. The language should complement human thought processes; in other words, a person writing programs in the language should be able to think in the language. The ideas expressed in a program should be written in essentially the order and the form in which people might think about the algorithm as they are developing it. Any internal translation necessary on their part should be minimized.

[A BL\I user must choose names of variables so that integers start with I, J, K, L, M, N, or X, while strings start with other letters. Furthermore the names cannot have six or more letters. These conventions led to unnatural names like NWDTH, NSIZE, XS, and TLINE in Section 2.2.13 (corresponding to *width*, *size*, *excess*, and *line* in Figure 1).

BL\I programs have a "flat" structure in which one must use GOTO statements to jump around. Thus larger and larger programs become harder to keep in one's head. The sequences, steps, and routines of STROL are much better attuned to clarity of thought.

BL\I's special assignment statements called 'TYPE 1' and 'TYPE 2' are completely unintuitive (see Section 2.2.7). Why should a programmer have to keep arbitrary type numbers in mind, instead of having a mnemonic convention?

BL\I requires each string to have a predefined maximum size, while STROL places no restriction on individual string length.

The cursors of STROL are interesting, but possibly confusing because each string has one and only one cursor. A programmer might forget whether a cursor is at the left end or the right end or in the middle, because different string variables might use different strategies.]

2.5.7. Readability. Programs written in the language should be readily interpretable by a human reader. The syntax and semantics should not be so involved that a great deal of concentration is required to determine the meaning of the program's constructs.

[BL\I tries to gain readability by using verbose English-like statements. But it abuses the language: 'SET J EQUALS K+1' seems to be telling us about a certain set named J. A construction like 'LET J EQUAL K+1' would be more palatable; and COBOL's 'ADD 1 TO K GIVING J' is clearer yet. But the people who need to read string-manipulation programs probably prefer algebra to English.

The nested structure of STROL programs is logically sound, and it can be represented by indentation, but it too becomes unwieldy when a program becomes large. The dots in Figure 1 help, but a way to divide a large program into modules would be much better.]

2.5.8. Unambiguity. Every statement of the language should have a clear-cut, unique meaning.

[In this respect STROL seems to be quite admirable. But many dangers lurk in the dark corners of BL\I, as discussed in Section 2.3.]

2.5.9. Translatability. If the language is intended to be input to a computer, the task of mechanically recognizing the syntax of programs should not be extremely difficult or time-consuming.

[Neither BL\I nor STROL is hard to parse, although BL\I is rather more difficult because of its inconsistencies at all levels. Indeed, the worst aspect of BL\I is perhaps the fact that one could actually write a clumsy compiler for it, and people could actually use BL\I to write legacy programs that would have to be maintained for many years on many machines.]

2.5.10. Efficiency. If the language is meant to be translated mechanically into another language, it should allow programmers to take advantage of efficient constructions in the target language.

[BL\I is oriented toward manipulation of strings that are packed into consecutive computer words with five characters per word. A careful compiler and a smart runtime system could produce a fairly efficient running program from the example in Section 2.2.13; but that program was written by an unusually competent programmer. Several features of BL\I encourage the specification of algorithms that repeatedly recopy strings in very inefficient ways.

STROL is oriented toward string manipulation via linked lists. Then strings can share a common memory pool and substrings can be readily reconnected in different ways; but list processing has overhead costs too.]

2.5.11. Machine independence. Wherever possible, the language should not be tied to characteristics of a particular machine, if it is to be a common language for use by people with widely varying computers.

[The rule-of-5 in Section 2.2.9 is ghastly from this standpoint, and so is the fixed size of each OUTPUT string in 2.2.11.]

2.5.12. Adaptability. The language should be flexible enough so that users may readily change it for particular applications if desired.

[Both BL\I and STROL lack the ability to use or add to a library of subroutines, which are the main ways in which a language's primitive capabilities are generally extended.]

2.5.13. Best treatment for common cases. All of the considerations above can be tempered by saying that the language should have such a characteristic primarily when that characteristic applies to the most commonly occurring situations. Situations that arise only rarely need not be handled well, as long as programs can be written and translated for such situations in some (perhaps crude) manner.

[Considerable experience is required before common cases can be identified in the realm of string manipulation programs. In general, language designers need to spend a great deal of time *using* the languages that they develop.]

2.5.14. Appeal. People from a certain group are supposed to "like" the language when they first see it. If all of the preceding conditions are satisfied, any reasonable person will surely be happy with the result, but at any rate the key people must be kept in mind as a language is being designed.

[BL\I and STROL are of course quite atypical, because they both were designed expressly for readers of this article — not for real programmers faced with real string-manipulation tasks, but rather for people who want to improve their understanding of design tradeoffs.]

2.5.15. Identity. Finally, and perhaps most important of all, a good language should have an appropriate name that aptly characterizes its personality and mystique.

[In this respect both BL\I and STROL seem to be reasonably well endowed.]

References

[1] Charles Babbage, "On the influence of signs in mathematical reasoning," *Transactions of the Cambridge Philosophical Society* **2** (1827), 325–377.

[2] Daniel G. Bobrow and Joseph Weizenbaum, "List processing and the extension of language facility by embedding," *IEEE Transactions on Electronic Computers* **EC-13** (1964), 395–400.

[3] Seymour Ginsburg and H. Gordon Rice, "Two families of languages related to ALGOL," *Journal of the Association for Computing Machinery* **9** (1962), 350–371.

[4] D. Knuth, "Fourteen goals for a programming language," privately circulated (Pasadena, California: Mathematics Department, California Institute of Technology, July 1963), 3 pages.

Addendum

An uproariously bad language named INTERCAL, which features among other things the 'PLEASE DO' and 'PLEASE DON'T' statements, was designed by Donald R. Woods and James M. Lyon in the early morning hours of 26 May 1972. Several Internet sites are now devoted to it.

An interesting alternative to the string-and-cursor approach of STROL, featuring one large string but many different cursors, has been proposed by M. Rem, "On the programming of elastic stores," *Information Processing Letters* **3** (1975), 184–187.

Chapter 12

Programming Languages for Automata

*[Written with Richard H. Bigelow. Originally published in Journal of the Association for Computing Machinery **14** (1967), 615–635.]*

The techniques of automatic programming are useful for constructive proofs in automata theory. We present a formal definition of an elementary programming language for a stack automaton, and discuss how it may readily be adapted to other classes of automata. Then we apply the programming language to automata theory, by using it to prove that a stack automaton is able to accept certain non-context-sensitive languages.

Research connected with automata is generally aimed at proving two different kinds of theorems:

a) that a certain class of automata is able to do a certain job; or

b) that a certain class of automata is unable to do a certain job.

By "automata" we mean any of the three dozen or so types of abstract machines like Turing machines, finite state machines, pushdown automata, etc., that have been studied rather intensively in recent years. Such devices usually include a finite set of states and one or more tapes for internal storage, and they have a set of instructions of the form "if in state q_i and scanning symbols $(S_{j_1}, \ldots, S_{j_n})$ on the tapes, then go into state q_k and manipulate the storage tapes in manner x." The allowable instructions x are usually restricted so that only certain very primitive operations are performed by an automaton at each step.

Every restriction on the allowable instructions tends to make proofs of type (b) easier, because we can more easily prove that something is impossible if the number of possible things can be conveniently limited. But such limitations make proofs of type (a) correspondingly more complicated, because type (a) proofs generally require the writing of *programs* for the class of automata in question. Programs to do complicated things with only very primitive basic operations can involve a great amount of detail and complexity. The main point of this article is to show that "software" techniques, which have been developed for programming "real" computers, are equally useful for constructing automata programs.

Curiously most of the current papers on automata theory have not advanced past the "machine language" programming stage. Authors have been reluctant to simplify their constructions except by using classical mathematical notations, which are comparatively cumbersome for this purpose. Symbolic programs are considerably easier to write and to read, and they are less likely to contain careless errors; so it is surprising that such methods have not already spread from computer programming to automata programming. A first step in this direction has been taken in the input language for the Turing machine simulator described in [1]. The authors hope that the ideas expressed below, which make it possible to give a motivated formal description of an automaton in a brief space, will help to develop automata theory, because improvements in notation are often the primary reason for subsequent mathematical advances.

This paper has two main parts. First we define a programming language and show that any program in this language corresponds in a precise way to a set of automata instructions. The language is designed for use with *stack automata* as defined by Ginsburg, Greibach, and Harrison [3]. A stack automaton is a rather complicated type of machine, as automata go, so our language will work also with simpler classes of automata if it is modified in obvious ways. (*Note:* A stack automaton is much more general than a simple "pushdown automaton" as defined in [2]; readers should not be misled by the similar-sounding names.) The second part of this paper illustrates the advantages of such a programming language approach, as we resolve the principal conjecture stated in [3]: We show that *stack automata are able to accept certain languages that are not context-sensitive.* The proof of this theorem by conventional methods would have been almost hopeless, because it would have been quite difficult to define the construction in the first place, and then to present a convincing proof in a form that anyone besides the authors could have understood.

1. A Programming Language

1.1 Stack Automata

First let us review the definition of stack automata as given in [3]. A stack automaton M is an abstract machine consisting of a finite set K of *states*;

a finite set of characters called the *input alphabet Σ'*;

a finite set of characters called the *stack alphabet Γ*, disjoint from Σ';

the *input delimiters* $\rlap{/}{c}$ and $\$$, two characters not in Σ' or Γ;

the *stack bottom* Z_0, a specially designated element of Γ;

the *initial state* q_0, a designated element of K;

the set of *final states* F, where $F \subseteq K$;

the *instructions* δ, a function defined on $\Sigma \times K \times \Gamma$, where $\Sigma = \Sigma' \cup \{\rlap{/}{c}, \$\}$, having values as explained below.

The machine has two tapes: the *input tape*, which holds strings of characters of the form

$$a_0 a_1 a_2 \ldots a_n \quad (n \geq 1, \quad a_0 = \rlap{/}{c}, \quad a_n = \$, \quad a_i \text{ in } \Sigma' \text{ for } 0 < i < n); \quad (1)$$

and the *stack*, which holds strings of characters of the form

$$A_0 A_1 \ldots A_m \quad (m \geq 0, \quad A_0 = Z_0, \quad A_j \text{ in } \Gamma \text{ for } j > 0). \quad (2)$$

When M is in operation, it is always in a *configuration* denoted by

$$(q, a_0 \ldots a_{i-1} \upharpoonright a_i \ldots a_n, \; A_0 \ldots A_j \upharpoonright A_{j+1} \ldots A_m). \quad (3)$$

The configuration shows the current state q (an element of K), the input tape, the stack, and two pointers that indicate the positions currently being scanned on the tapes. In (3) we assume that $0 \leq i \leq n+1$ and $-1 \leq j \leq m$; the symbols a_i and A_j are currently under scan.

An instruction $\delta(a_i, q, A_j)$ tells what configuration will follow (3), provided $i \neq n+1$ and $j \neq -1$. Each instruction has one of two forms:

a) *Pointer manipulation.* In the first case

$$\delta(a_i, q, A_j) = (d, q', e) \quad (4)$$

where q' is in K; the quantities d and e are integers -1, 0, or 1. The machine goes into state q', the input pointer moves from a_i to a_{i+d}, and the stack pointer moves from A_j to A_{j+e}. The machine stops before the operation if $i + d = -1$ or if $j + e = m+1$; the machine stops after the operation if $i+d = n+1$ or if $j + e = -1$. Otherwise M continues to a new instruction based on the resulting configuration.

b) *Stack alteration.* In the second case

$$\delta(a_i, q, A_j) = (d, q', \alpha) \tag{5}$$

where q' is in K; $d = -1, 0$, or 1; and α is a string on Γ. The machine goes into state q', the input pointer moves from a_i to a_{i+d}, and the symbol A_m at the "top" of the stack is replaced by the string α. The machine stops before the operation if $i + d = -1$ or if $j \neq m$: Therefore this operation is allowed only if the stack pointer is at the extreme right. If α contains $k \geq 0$ characters, this operation changes both j and m to $m + k - 1$. The machine stops after the operation if $i + d = n + 1$ or if $m = k = 0$; otherwise it continues as usual.

The operations can be summarized informally by saying that the machine can read its stack and its input tape, and can move in both directions on either tape. It can write and erase only at the "top" of its stack (actually at the right end, in our notation).

We write $c \vdash^* c'$ if the machine goes from configuration c to configuration c' in zero or more steps. If α is a string on Σ' we say that α is *accepted* by M (equivalently, α is in $L(M)$) if and only if

$$(q_0, \lceil \not{c} \alpha \$, Z_0 \uparrow) \quad \vdash^* \quad (q', \not{c} \alpha \$ \lceil, \beta \uparrow \gamma) \tag{6}$$

for some final state q' and some strings β, γ. If the machine starts in configuration $(q_0, \lceil \not{c} \alpha \$, Z_0 \uparrow)$ and stops in some configuration not having the form in (6), or if it never stops, α is not accepted by M. Proofs are given in [3] that we can effectively decide whether or not α is accepted by M, given α and M, and that if L_c is any context-sensitive language there is a stack automaton M such that $L(M) = L_c$.

1.2 An Example Program

It is hard to learn the characteristics of a programming language by reading a formal definition of that language, until several examples have been studied. Therefore we present in this section an informal discussion of a "typical" program for a stack automaton, before giving a complete definition of the language.

Figure 1 displays a program that accepts the strings

$$L_0 = \{a_1 a_2 \ldots a_n c^{2n} d^{2n} a_n \ldots a_2 a_1 \mid n \geq 1\},$$

where each a_j is either a or b. The information enclosed within angle brackets '⟨' and '⟩' in Figure 1 is explanatory material; such comments do not explicitly affect the meaning of the program in any way.

⟨01⟩   **begin class** $ab = a, b$; **class** $AB = A, B$;
⟨02⟩   **input alphabet is** ab, c, d;
⟨03⟩   **stack alphabet is** Z, C, AB;
⟨04⟩   **input delimiters are** *start*, *stop*;
⟨05⟩   **stack bottom is** Z;
⟨06⟩   **procedure** *check*(x, y);
⟨07⟩   **begin** ⟨if the stack contains n AB's, check that
⟨08⟩   the input contains $2n$ x's followed by y⟩ **L**,
⟨09⟩   *shift*: $[x.AB \Rightarrow$ **rL**; $\Rightarrow$ **go to** *exit*],
⟨10⟩ $[x \Rightarrow$ **r**], **go to** *shift*,
⟨11⟩   *exit*: $[y.Z \Rightarrow$ **R**, $[AB \Rightarrow$ **R**, **repeat**; $C \Rightarrow]]$
⟨12⟩   **end** *check*;
⟨13⟩   ⟨the program begins here⟩
⟨14⟩   ⟨shift past the first character on the input tape⟩ $[start \Rightarrow$ **r**],
⟨15⟩   ⟨now copy a's and b's into the stack⟩
⟨16⟩ $[a \Rightarrow$ **r**'A', **repeat**; $b \Rightarrow$ **r**'B', **repeat**; $c \Rightarrow$ 'C'],
⟨17⟩   ⟨now look for $2n$ c's and $2n$ d's⟩
⟨18⟩   *check*(c, d), *check*(d, ab),
⟨19⟩   ⟨now see if the last part of the input mirrors the first part⟩
⟨20⟩ $[a.A \Rightarrow$ **r**Λ, **repeat**; $b.B \Rightarrow$ **r**Λ, **repeat**;
⟨21⟩ $stop.Z \Rightarrow$ **accept**; $C \Rightarrow \Lambda$, **repeat**]
⟨22⟩   **end**.

FIGURE 1. A program that accepts the language L_0.

Line 01 defines the "class" ab as the two letters a and b, and similarly defines $AB = \{A, B\}$. Thus, the input alphabet Σ' defined in line 02 is $\{a, b, c, d\}$; the stack alphabet Γ is $\{Z, C, A, B\}$ by line 03. Line 04 says that the delimiting characters ¢ and $ will be represented in this program by the identifying words *start* and *stop*, respectively; in our language, any word may be used to stand for a single character or class in the tape alphabets, although one-letter words (like a, b, c, d, Z, C, A, and B above) are usually used for this purpose. According to line 05, the symbol Z will be at the bottom of the stack.

Lines 06–12 constitute the declaration of a "procedure" (often called a "macro" or an "open subroutine"), which will be explained later. The program itself begins at line 13, following the procedure declaration.

Suppose we want to verify that the string *abccccdddba* is in L_0; then the machine starts out in the configuration

$$(\lceil start\ a\ b\ c\ c\ c\ c\ d\ d\ d\ d\ b\ a\ stop,\ Z\rceil),\qquad(7)$$

and it is ready to execute the instructions starting with line 13. We have omitted the state q from the configuration (7), since we conceptually substitute "current position in the program" for "state."

The instruction '[*start* $\Rightarrow$ **r**]' on line 14 means, literally, "If the input character scanned is '*start*', move the input pointer right; otherwise, reject the input string." The notation **r** stands for right motion of the input pointer, and ℓ (which does not appear in this program) stands for left motion. Motion of the stack pointer is denoted by **R** and **L**, as in lines 08, 09, and 11. Since the character '*start*' always is first in the input string, the net effect of line 14 is simply to change (7) to

$$(start \upharpoonright a \, b \, c \, c \, c \, c \, d \, d \, d \, d \, b \, a \, stop, \, Z \!\uparrow) \tag{8}$$

and we get to line 15.

The first part of the program's strategy for recognizing the language L_0 is to copy the leading a's and b's of the input into the stack, and line 16 accomplishes this. The code in line 16 means, literally, "If scanning a, move the input pointer right and push A onto the top of the stack, then repeat this step; if scanning b, similarly move right, push B, and repeat; if scanning c, push C and go on to the next instruction; otherwise do not accept the string." These steps of the program lead from (8) to

$$(start \, a \, b \upharpoonright c \, c \, c \, c \, d \, d \, d \, d \, b \, a \, stop, \, Z \, A \, B \, C \!\uparrow). \tag{9}$$

Notice that we are still scanning the first c of the input, since the program says simply 'C', not **r**'C'.

Line 18 refers us to the check procedure, with 'c' substituted for 'x' and 'd' substituted for 'y', in the program of lines 07–11. A procedure is merely a shorthand notation that allows us to avoid writing common parts of the program several times. Just writing '$check(c,d)$' is effectively like writing

⟨07a⟩	⟨if the stack contains n AB's, check that
⟨08a⟩	the input contains $2n$ c's followed by d⟩ **L**,
⟨09a⟩	*shift*: [$c.AB \Rightarrow$ **rL**; $\Rightarrow$ **go to** *exit*],
⟨10a⟩	[$c \Rightarrow$ **r**], **go to** *shift*,
⟨11a⟩	*exit*: [$d.Z \Rightarrow$ **R**, [$AB \Rightarrow$ **R**, **repeat**; $C \Rightarrow$]]

instead. Here line 08a simply moves the stack pointer left one. Line 09a checks if we are scanning c in the input *and* A or B in the stack (note that AB is the class $\{A, B\}$). If so, we do the action **rL** (that is, input pointer right, stack pointer left), and go to the next part of the program; otherwise we go to the part of the program labeled '*exit*'. Line 10a scans past another c and returns to line 09a. When $2n$ c's have been scanned, we get to line 11a, which ensures that we are now scanning a d and also the Z; then the stack pointer is systematically moved back to the top again, by the instructions $[AB \Rightarrow \mathbf{R}, \mathbf{repeat}; \quad C \Rightarrow]$ of line 11a. The net effect of $check(c, d)$ is therefore to change (9) to

$$(start \; a \; b \; c \; c \; c \; c \upharpoonright d \; d \; d \; d \; b \; a \; stop, \; Z \; A \; B \; C\!\uparrow),$$

and then '$check(d, ab)$' in line 18 similarly takes us to the configuration

$$(start \; a \; b \; c \; c \; c \; c \; d \; d \; d \; d \upharpoonright b \; a \; stop, \; Z \; A \; B \; C\!\uparrow). \qquad (10)$$

Notice that the '$check$' procedure will reject malformed input strings in the appropriate cases. Different invocations of $check$ implicitly introduce different names for the internal program steps labeled '$shift$' and '$exit$'.

The instructions of lines 20 and 21 introduce two new language features: 'Λ', which means that the top symbol of the stack is to be erased; and '$\mathbf{accept}$', which means that the input string is to be accepted. The machine goes from (10) to

$$(start \; a \; b \; c \; c \; c \; c \; d \; d \; d \; d \; b \; a \; stop \upharpoonright, \; Z \uparrow)$$

and accepts the string $abccccddddba$. But any string that causes line 22 to be reached is rejected. The automaton described here clearly accepts precisely the strings of L_0.

The program in Figure 1 is not the simplest way to define a stack automaton accepting L_0. For example, we need not erase the stack in lines 20–21; merely moving to the left would do. Also, lines 07–11 may be replaced by

$$[x.AB \Rightarrow \mathbf{rL}, \; [x \Rightarrow r], \; \mathbf{repeat};$$
$$y.Z \Rightarrow \mathbf{R}, \; [AB \Rightarrow \mathbf{R}, \; \mathbf{repeat}; \quad C \Rightarrow]] \qquad (11)$$

thereby avoiding the need for explicit labels $shift$ and $next$. The comparatively clumsy method of Figure 1 was chosen in order to illustrate more features of the language.

1.3 Syntax and Semantics of the Programming Language

The example program in Figure 1 shows the general appearance of our programs for stack automata. In this section we will define the syntax of the programming language in Backus–Naur form (see [6]), and we also will discuss the way in which any program in this language corresponds to a precisely defined stack automaton.

1.3.1. Identifiers.

⟨letter or digit⟩ → a | b | c | ⋯ | z | A | B | C | ⋯ | Z
       | 0 | 1 | 2 | ⋯ | 9
⟨identifier⟩ → ⟨letter or digit⟩ | ⟨identifier⟩ ⟨letter or digit⟩
⟨symbol identifier⟩ → ⟨identifier⟩
⟨class identifier⟩ → ⟨identifier⟩
⟨label identifier⟩ → ⟨identifier⟩
⟨procedure identifier⟩ → ⟨identifier⟩
⟨formal parameter⟩ → ⟨identifier⟩

Identifiers are used to name symbols (that is, characters of Σ or Γ), classes (that is, sets) of symbols, labels (places in the program), procedures (subroutines), and formal parameters of procedures (bound variables). Each identifier must have one and only one use in a single program. The last five syntax rules above are intended to reflect the unique use of the particular identifier concerned; an identifier's type can always be determined by the context in which it first appears.

1.3.2. Class declarations.

⟨class⟩ → ⟨symbol identifier⟩ | ⟨class identifier⟩
⟨class list⟩ → ⟨class⟩ | ⟨class list⟩, ⟨class⟩
⟨class declaration⟩ → **class** ⟨class identifier⟩ = ⟨class list⟩
⟨input class⟩ → ⟨class⟩
⟨stack class⟩ → ⟨class⟩
⟨stack symbol⟩ → ⟨symbol identifier⟩
⟨alphabet declarations⟩ → **input alphabet is** ⟨class list⟩;
       stack alphabet is ⟨class list⟩;
       input delimiters are ⟨symbol identifier⟩, ⟨symbol identifier⟩;
       stack bottom is ⟨stack symbol⟩;

Class declarations associate a single name with the set of symbols specified at the right of the '=' sign. For example, the declarations

$$\text{\textbf{class } } ALPHA = A,\ B;$$
$$\text{\textbf{class } } BETA = ALPHA,\ C,\ D2;$$

define $ALPHA$ as the name of the set $\{A, B\}$ and $BETA$ as the name of $\{A, B, C, D2\}$, unless any of A, B, C, or $D2$ have previously been declared as classes themselves. Symbols represent the individual characters in the tape alphabets. The declaration of a class must precede all other uses of that class identifier; for example, the declaration of $BETA$

in the example just given must not be placed before the declaration of *ALPHA*, since it involves *ALPHA*.

The alphabet declarations define the relevant parts of a stack automaton by means of an obvious notation. These specifications must obey the rules for stack automata; that is, the input alphabet and stack alphabet must be disjoint, etc. The syntactic category ⟨stack class⟩ in the rules below denotes a class that consists entirely of symbols in the stack alphabet, and ⟨input class⟩ refers to sets of characters from the input alphabet or delimiters.

1.3.3. Statements.

⟨statement⟩ → ⟨basic action⟩ | ⟨conditional statement⟩
　　　 | ⟨jump statement⟩ | ⟨procedure statement⟩
　　　 | ⟨accept statement⟩ | ⟨label identifier⟩: ⟨statement⟩
⟨statement list⟩ → ⟨statement⟩ | ⟨statement list⟩, ⟨statement⟩

Each statement stands for one or more program steps, and has a well-defined "start state" q and "next state" q' according to rules given later. A label standing in front of a statement stands for its start state, which can be used for cross references in the program. A list of statements separated by commas stands for a sequence of statements that are to be performed one after the other.

1.3.3.1. Basic actions.

⟨basic action⟩ → ⟨input shift⟩ ⟨stack shift⟩
⟨input shift⟩ → **r** | **ℓ** | ⟨empty⟩
⟨stack shift⟩ → **R** | **L** | ⟨empty⟩ | ⟨stack write⟩
⟨stack write⟩ → Λ | '⟨string⟩' | Λ'⟨string⟩'
⟨string⟩ → ⟨stack symbol⟩ | ⟨string⟩.⟨stack symbol⟩
⟨empty⟩ →

Basic actions correspond to the operations performed by the automaton: There is a one-one correspondence between basic actions and the components d, e, α of instructions $\delta(a, q, A) = (d, q', e)$ or (d, q', α), according to the following table (where ϵ denotes the empty string):

⟨input shift⟩	d	⟨stack shift⟩	e	⟨stack write⟩	α	
r	+1	**R**	+1	Λ	ϵ	
ℓ	−1	**L**	−1	'σ'	$A\sigma$	(12)
⟨empty⟩	0	⟨empty⟩	0	Λ'σ'	σ	

Note that Λ stands for the action of erasing the top stack symbol.

For example, the action $\mathbf{r}'B.C'$ means, "Move the input pointer to the right, and push the symbols B and C onto the top of the stack." The action $\Lambda'Z'$ means, "Replace the top symbol of the stack by the symbol Z." An empty action means, "Do nothing at all" (see Figure 1, line 11).

1.3.3.2. Conditional statements.

⟨conditional statement⟩ → [⟨segments⟩]
⟨segments⟩ → ⟨segment⟩ | ⟨segments⟩; ⟨segment⟩
⟨segment⟩ → ⟨scan condition⟩ ⇒ ⟨statement list⟩
⟨scan condition⟩ → ⟨input class⟩.⟨stack class⟩
   | ⟨input class⟩ | ⟨stack class⟩ | ⟨empty⟩

A scan condition denotes a set u of input symbols and a set U of stack symbols according to the following rules:

⟨scan condition⟩	denotes	
$u.U$	u and U	
u	u and Γ	(13)
U	Σ and U	
⟨empty⟩	Σ and Γ	

A conditional statement has the general form

$$[c_1 \Rightarrow L_1 ; \quad c_2 \Rightarrow L_2 ; \quad \ldots ; \quad c_n \Rightarrow L_n], \quad n \geq 1$$

where the c's are scan conditions and the L's are lists of statements. The essential meaning is, "If scanning c_1, then do the statements L_1; otherwise if scanning c_2, then do L_2; ...; otherwise if scanning c_n, then do L_n; otherwise go into the error state q_∞." A precise interpretation will be given later.

1.3.3.3. Jump statements.

⟨jump statement⟩ → **go to** ⟨label identifier⟩ | **repeat**

The first form of jump statement means, "Go to the start state of the statement labeled by the given name."

The second form of jump statement may be used only within a conditional statement: It jumps to the start state of that conditional statement. (If conditional statements are nested, as in (11), the *smallest* containing conditional statement is used.)

For example, assume that b and c are input symbols. Then

$$[b \Rightarrow \mathbf{r}, \ \mathbf{repeat}; \quad c \Rightarrow 'C']$$

means, "Scan to the right in the input string past all b's until coming to the first non-b; if it is a c, push C onto the top of the stack, otherwise go to the error state."

1.3.3.4. Procedure statements.

⟨procedure statement⟩ → ⟨procedure identifier⟩ ⟨arguments⟩
⟨arguments⟩ → ⟨empty⟩ | (⟨argument list⟩)
⟨argument list⟩ → ⟨argument⟩ | ⟨argument list⟩, ⟨argument⟩
⟨argument⟩ → ⟨comma-free nested text⟩
⟨comma-free nested text⟩ → ⟨comma-free text⟩
     | ⟨comma-free text⟩ (⟨nested text⟩) ⟨comma-free nested text⟩
     | ⟨comma-free text⟩ [⟨nested text⟩] ⟨comma-free nested text⟩
⟨nested text⟩ → ⟨text⟩ | ⟨text⟩ (⟨nested text⟩) ⟨nested text⟩
     | ⟨text⟩ [⟨nested text⟩] ⟨nested text⟩
⟨text⟩ → ⟨empty⟩ | ⟨character⟩⟨text⟩ | ,⟨text⟩
⟨comma-free text⟩ → ⟨empty⟩ | ⟨character⟩⟨comma-free text⟩
⟨character⟩ → ⟨letter or digit⟩ | : | . | ; | **r** | **ℓ** | **R** | **L**
     | ⇒ | **go to** | **repeat** | **accept** | Λ | '⟨string⟩'
⟨procedure declaration⟩ →
       procedure ⟨procedure identifier⟩ ⟨parameters⟩;
         begin ⟨nested text⟩ **end** ⟨procedure identifier⟩
⟨parameters⟩ → ⟨empty⟩ | (⟨parameter list⟩)
⟨parameter list⟩ → ⟨formal parameter⟩
     | ⟨parameter list⟩, ⟨formal paramcter⟩

A procedure statement is an abbreviation for the partial program consisting of all the statements in the corresponding procedure declaration copied in place of the given statement, with all formal parameters replaced by the specified arguments. The number of arguments must equal the number of formal parameters.

According to the syntax, any text whatsoever may be used as an argument, provided only that parentheses and brackets are properly nested, and that no commas appear except enclosed in parentheses or brackets. Furthermore, any nested text may appear as the "procedure body" between the words **begin** and **end**. However, the following additional rules are understood:

1) All appearances of formal parameters within the procedure body must be preceded and followed by characters that are neither letters nor digits. (This rule ensures that each appearance of a formal parameter is unambiguous.)

2) After a copy of the procedure body is made, with formal parameters replaced by arguments, the resulting text must be a syntactically correct ⟨statement list⟩.

After the copying process, the names of all labels attached to statements within the procedure declaration are systematically changed to new identifiers, so that there is no conflict in case the procedure is used several times. (See, for example, Figure 1, where the labels in $check(c, d)$ are distinct from those of $check(d, ab)$.)

A procedure statement must not appear until after the corresponding procedure declaration. Therefore the copying process will always terminate in a finite number of steps, even when one procedure uses another.

1.3.3.5. Accept statements.

⟨accept statement⟩ → **accept**

The "accept" statement means that the input string is to be accepted by the automaton.

1.3.4. Programs.

⟨program⟩ → **begin** ⟨class declarations⟩ ⟨alphabet declarations⟩
　　　　　⟨procedure declarations⟩ ⟨statement list⟩ **end**.
⟨class declarations⟩ → ⟨empty⟩
　　　　　| ⟨class declarations⟩ ⟨class declaration⟩;
⟨procedure declarations⟩ → ⟨empty⟩
　　　　　| ⟨procedure declarations⟩ ⟨procedure declaration⟩;

The text in Figure 1, with comments deleted, illustrates most of the features of a program.

1.3.5. The translation process. The instructions of the stack automaton corresponding to a program are defined to be

$$\delta(a, q_f, A) = (1, q_f, 0), \quad \delta(a, q_\infty, A) = (1, q_\infty, 0), \quad \text{for all } a \in \Sigma, A \in \Gamma,$$

plus the result of $trans(L, q_0, q_\infty)$, where L is the main statement list of the program (namely the statement list that appears in the syntax for ⟨program⟩), after all procedure statements have been effectively removed; here q_0 is the initial state, and q_f is the unique final state.

If L is the list $S_1, S_2, \ldots, S_n$ where the S's are statements, then $trans(L, q, q')$ is the set of instructions

$$trans(S_1, q, q^1) \cup trans(S_2, q^1, q^2) \cup \cdots \cup trans(S_n, q^{n-1}, q')$$

where q^1, q^2, ..., q^{n-1} are new states (namely, states that appear nowhere else in the translation).

It remains to define the set of instructions $trans(S, q, q')$ for statements S. Here q is the "start state" and q' is the "next state" of S. There are four cases:

i) S is a ⟨basic action⟩. Then $\delta(a, q, A) = (d, q', e)$ or (d, q', α), as defined in (12), for all a in Σ and A in Γ.

ii) S is a conditional statement of the form

$$[u_1.U_1 \Rightarrow L_1; \quad u_2.U_2 \Rightarrow L_2; \quad \ldots; \quad u_n.U_n \Rightarrow L_n],$$

where the scan conditions $u_j.U_j$ represent sets of characters as defined in (13). In this case we let $u_{n+1} = \Sigma$, $U_{n+1} = \Gamma$, and define

$$\delta(a, q, A) = (0, q^j, 0)$$

if (a, A) is in (u_j, U_j) but not in $(u_{j-1}, U_{j-1}) \cup \cdots \cup (u_1, U_1)$, for $1 \le j \le n+1$. Here q^1, q^2, ..., q^n are new states, and $q^{n+1} = q_\infty$. We also add the instructions of $trans(L_j, q^j, q')$ for $1 \le j \le n$.

iii) S is a jump statement. Then $\delta(a, q, A) = (0, q'', 0)$ for all a in Σ and A in Γ, where q'' is the state jumped to.

iv) S is an accept statement. Then $\delta(a, q, A) = (0, q_f, 0)$ for all a in Σ and A in Γ.

Figure 2 shows the machine that results when this process is applied to the program of Figure 1. If X and Y are sets, the notation $\delta(X, q, Y) = z$ is an abbreviation for the rules $\delta(x, q, y) = z$ for all x in X and y in Y; similarly $\delta(\Sigma, q_6, \Gamma) = (+1, q_9, \Gamma A)$ stands for all the rules $\delta(x, q_6, y) = (+1, q_9, yA)$ as x and y range over the elements of Σ and Γ, respectively.

1.4 Remarks

We could have defined a programming language that looks more like ALGOL; for example, we could have said that a programmer should write

> **if** $input[i] = \text{`c'} \wedge (stack[j] = \text{`}A\text{'} \vee stack[j] = \text{`}B\text{'})$
> **then begin** $i := i + 1$; $j := j - 1$ **end**
> **else go to** *exit*

instead of the briefer code

> $[c.AB \Rightarrow \mathbf{rL}; \quad \Rightarrow \mathbf{go\ to}\ exit]$

in the present language. This briefer code may look more cryptic to the uninitiated reader, but the authors believe that the brevity is a

$\Sigma' = \{a, b, c, d\}$, $\rlap{/}c = start$, $\$ = stop$, $\Gamma = \{A, B, C, Z\}$, $Z_0 = Z$,

$K = \{q_0, q_1, \ldots, q_{41}, q_\infty\}$, initial state q_0, final states $\{q_f\}$.

$\qquad \delta(\Sigma, q_f, \Gamma) = (1, q_f, 0)$, $\delta(\Sigma, q_\infty, \Gamma) = (1, q_\infty, 0)$;

$\langle 14 \rangle$ $\delta(start, q_0, \Gamma) = (0, q_5, 0)$, $\delta(\Sigma \setminus \{start\}, q_0, \Gamma) = (0, q_\infty, 0)$,

$\qquad \delta(\Sigma, q_5, \Gamma) = (+1, q_1, 0)$,

$\langle 16 \rangle$ $\delta(a, q_1, \Gamma) = (0, q_6, 0)$, $\delta(b, q_1, \Gamma) = (0, q_7, 0)$, $\delta(c, q_1, \Gamma) = (0, q_8, 0)$,

$\qquad \delta(\Sigma \setminus \{a, b, c\}, q_1, \Gamma) = (0, q_\infty, 0)$,

$\qquad \delta(\Sigma, q_6, \Gamma) = (+1, q_9, \Gamma A)$, $\delta(\Sigma, q_9, \Gamma) = (0, q_1, 0)$,

$\qquad \delta(\Sigma, q_7, \Gamma) = (+1, q_{10}, \Gamma B)$, $\delta(\Sigma, q_{10}, \Gamma) = (0, q_1, 0)$,

$\qquad \delta(\Sigma, q_8, \Gamma) = (0, q_2, \Gamma C)$,

$\langle 08 \rangle$ $\delta(\Sigma, q_2, \Gamma) = (0, q_{11}, -1)$,

$\langle 09 \rangle$ $\delta(c, q_{11}, \{A, B\}) = (0, q_{15}, 0)$, $\delta(c, q_{11}, \{C, Z\}) = \delta(\Sigma \setminus \{c\}, q_{11}, \Gamma) = (0, q_{16}, 0)$,

$\qquad \delta(\Sigma, q_{15}, \Gamma) = (+1, q_{12}, -1)$,

$\qquad \delta(\Sigma, q_{16}, \Gamma) = (0, q_{14}, 0)$,

$\langle 10 \rangle$ $\delta(c, q_{12}, \Gamma) = (0, q_{17}, 0)$, $\delta(\Sigma \setminus \{c\}, q_{12}, \Gamma) = (0, q_\infty, 0)$,

$\qquad \delta(\Sigma, q_{17}, \Gamma) = (+1, q_{13}, 0)$,

$\qquad \delta(\Sigma, q_{13}, \Gamma) = (0, q_{11}, 0)$,

$\langle 11 \rangle$ $\delta(d, q_{14}, Z) = (0, q_{18}, 0)$, $\delta(\Sigma \setminus \{d\}, q_{14}, \Gamma) = \delta(\Sigma, q_{14}, \Gamma \setminus \{Z\}) = (0, q_\infty, 0)$,

$\qquad \delta(\Sigma, q_{18}, \Gamma) = (0, q_{19}, +1)$,

$\qquad \delta(\Sigma, q_{19}, \{A, B\}) = (0, q_{20}, 0)$, $\delta(\Sigma, q_{19}, C) = (0, q_{21}, 0)$, $\delta(\Sigma, q_{19}, Z) = (0, q_\infty, 0)$,

$\qquad \delta(\Sigma, q_{20}, \Gamma) = (0, q_{22}, +1)$,

$\qquad \delta(\Sigma, q_{22}, \Gamma) = (0, q_{19}, 0)$,

$\qquad \delta(\Sigma, q_{21}, \Gamma) = (0, q_3, 0)$,

$\langle 08 \rangle$ $\delta(\Sigma, q_3, \Gamma) = (0, q_{23}, -1)$,

$\langle 09 \rangle$ $\delta(d, q_{23}, \{A, B\}) = (0, q_{27}, 0)$, $\delta(d, q_{23}, \{C, Z\}) = \delta(\Sigma \setminus \{d\}, q_{23}, \Gamma) = (0, q_{28}, 0)$,

$\qquad \delta(\Sigma, q_{27}, \Gamma) = (+1, q_{24}, -1)$,

$\qquad \delta(\Sigma, q_{28}, \Gamma) = (0, q_{26}, 0)$,

$\langle 10 \rangle$ $\delta(d, q_{24}, \Gamma) = (0, q_{29}, 0)$, $\delta(\Sigma \setminus \{d\}, q_{24}, \Gamma) = (0, q_\infty, 0)$,

$\qquad \delta(\Sigma, q_{29}, \Gamma) = (+1, q_{25}, 0)$,

$\qquad \delta(\Sigma, q_{25}, \Gamma) = (0, q_{23}, 0)$,

$\langle 11 \rangle$ $\delta(\{a, b\}, q_{26}, Z) = (0, q_{30}, 0)$, $\delta(\Sigma \setminus \{a, b\}, q_{26}, \Gamma) = \delta(\Sigma, q_{26}, \Gamma \setminus \{Z\}) = (0, q_\infty, 0)$,

$\qquad \delta(\Sigma, q_{30}, \Gamma) = (0, q_{31}, +1)$,

$\qquad \delta(\Sigma, q_{31}, \{A, B\}) = (0, q_{32}, 0)$, $\delta(\Sigma, q_{31}, C) = (0, q_{33}, 0)$, $\delta(\Sigma, q_{31}, Z) = (0, q_\infty, 0)$,

$\qquad \delta(\Sigma, q_{32}, \Gamma) = (0, q_{34}, +1)$,

$\qquad \delta(\Sigma, q_{34}, \Gamma) = (0, q_{31}, 0)$,

$\qquad \delta(\Sigma, q_{33}, \Gamma) = (0, q_4, 0)$,

$\langle 20 \rangle$ $\delta(a, q_4, A) = (0, q_{35}, 0)$, $\delta(b, q_4, B) = (0, q_{36}, 0)$, $\delta(stop, q_4, Z) = (0, q_{37}, 0)$,

$\qquad \delta(\Sigma, q_4, C) = (0, q_{38}, 0)$,

$\qquad \delta(a, q_4, \{B, Z\}) = \delta(b, q_4, \{A, Z\}) = \delta(stop, q_4, \{A, B, C\}) =$

$\qquad\qquad \delta(\{start, c, d\}, q_4, \{A, B, Z\}) = (0, q_\infty, 0)$,

$\qquad \delta(\Sigma, q_{35}, \Gamma) = (+1, q_{39}, \epsilon)$, $\delta(\Sigma, q_{39}, \Gamma) = (0, q_4, 0)$,

$\qquad \delta(\Sigma, q_{36}, \Gamma) = (+1, q_{40}, \epsilon)$, $\delta(\Sigma, q_{40}, \Gamma) = (0, q_4, 0)$,

$\qquad \delta(\Sigma, q_{37}, \Gamma) = (0, q_f, 0)$,

$\qquad \delta(\Sigma, q_{38}, \Gamma) = (0, q_{41}, \epsilon)$, $\delta(\Sigma, q_{41}, \Gamma) = (0, q_4, 0)$.

FIGURE 2. The stack automaton defined by Figure 1.

significant advantage to anyone who has learned the few simple rules of the language. Furthermore, coding in this brief notation is found to be quite natural.

The best test of any programming language or notation is the "user test," that is, whether people find it convenient for use. We now urge the reader to sit down and test our language: Write a program that accepts the set of strings

$$\{\alpha\alpha \mid \alpha \text{ is a string of } a\text{'s and } b\text{'s}\} = \epsilon, aa, bb, aaaa, abab, baba, \ldots.$$

For comparison, it may prove useful to try the same problem first using the customary technique of specifying the function $\delta(a, q, A)$ for all cases in classical mathematical notation. A solution to this problem may be found in Appendix 1.

Experience indicates that the most common error made by a person using this programming language is the failure to specify all the left and right shifting desired on the tapes; however, shiftless programmers soon overcome this tendency after they have written a few programs.

The language defined here can easily be adapted to other automata if we make obvious changes in the definitions of ⟨alphabet declarations⟩, ⟨basic action⟩, and ⟨scan condition⟩, and if the construction

$$(L_1) \text{ or } (L_2) \text{ or } \cdots \text{ or } (L_t)$$

is allowed as a statement for nondeterministic automata, meaning that any one of the statement lists L_j may now be performed.

Furthermore, it would not be difficult to add the concept of *variables* to programming languages of the kind we are considering. For example, one could add a declaration

variable $x_1, x_2, \ldots, x_n$;

here $x_1, x_2, \ldots, x_n$ are identifiers that can be used later in an assignment statement of the form '$x_j \leftarrow \omega$', where ω belongs to a given finite set Ω. Relations like '$x_i = x_j$' or '$x_i = \omega$' could be allowed in conditional statements, and other extensions in this vein also suggest themselves. The translation process would now be defined in terms of states $(q, \omega_1, \omega_2, \ldots, \omega_n)$, where q denotes a position in the program as in the language defined above and where $\omega_1, \omega_2, \ldots, \omega_n$ represent the "current values" of $x_1, x_2, \ldots, x_n$. The introduction of variables in this way leads to a still more powerful programming language for many applications.

2. Theoretical Applications

2.1 Linear-Bounded Automata

It is well known that the set of "context-sensitive" languages is precisely the set of languages that can be accepted by the class of abstract machines known as linear-bounded automata [5]. Such devices have one tape on which they can read and write; the tape has a fixed length, determined by the size of the input string. A linear-bounded automaton may be "nondeterministic"; that is, it may have more than one instruction applicable at a given time. Each of the alternative instructions leads to a possible "computation" carried out by the machine.

More formally, a linear-bounded automaton M consists of

a finite set K of *states*;

a finite set of characters called the *alphabet* Σ';

the *input delimiters* $\cent$ and $\$$, two characters not in Σ';

the *initial state* q_0, a designated element of K;

the set of *final states* F, where $F \subseteq K$;

the *instructions* δ, a function defined on $K \times \Sigma$, where $\Sigma = \Sigma' \cup \{\cent, \$\}$, as explained below.

A *configuration* of M has the form

$$(q, a_0 \ldots a_{j-1} \upharpoonright a_j \ldots a_n) \tag{14}$$

where $n \geq 1$, $a_0 = \cent$, $a_n = \$$, a_i is in Σ' for $0 < i < n$, and $0 \leq j \leq n+1$. We say that M is in state q, scanning a_j. If $j \neq n + 1$, the instructions $\delta(q, a_j)$ apply to configuration (14).

Each instruction $\delta(q, a)$ is a finite ordered set of zero or more "actions," which may take any of three different forms:

(q', a'): Replace symbol a by a', go to state q'. Here a' belongs to Σ.

$(q', -)$: Move the pointer left one position, go to state q'.

$(q', +)$: Move the pointer right one position, go to state q'.

The actions allowed in $\delta(q, a)$ are restricted when $a = \cent$ or $\$$; then the action (q', a') is allowed only if $a' = a$. Furthermore, the action $(q', -)$ is not allowed when $a = \cent$.

We write $c \xrightarrow{k} c'$ if c and c' are configurations such that M goes from c to c' by applying the kth action applicable to c. A string α on the alphabet Σ' is accepted by M (that is, α is in $L(M)$, the *language defined by* M) if and only if there are integers $k_1, \ldots, k_n$ and configurations c_0, $c_1, \ldots, c_n$ such that

$$(q_0, \lceil \text{¢}\alpha\$) = c_0 \xrightarrow{k_1} c_1 \xrightarrow{k_2} \cdots \xrightarrow{k_n} c_n = (q, \text{¢}\beta\$\rceil)$$

for some $n \geq 1$, some final state q, and some string β.

This rule defines the language accepted by a linear-bounded automaton. Ginsburg, Greibach, and Harrison have proved [3] that any such language is also accepted by a suitably defined stack automaton. We wish to show that the converse does not hold: Stack automata can accept some languages that *cannot* be accepted by any linear-bounded automaton.

If M is a linear-bounded automaton, and if α is a string on its input alphabet, we say that M *loops* on α if there exist integers $k_1, \ldots, k_n$ and configurations $c_0, c_1, \ldots, c_n$ such that

$$(q_0, \lceil \text{¢}\alpha\$) = c_0 \xrightarrow{k_1} c_1 \xrightarrow{k_2} \cdots \xrightarrow{k_n} c_n \tag{15}$$

for arbitrarily large n. If M does not loop on α it follows that there are only finitely many $k_1, \ldots, k_n, c_1, \ldots, c_n$ satisfying (15) for any given c_0.

The following result is well known [3][5]:

Lemma 1. *If M is a linear-bounded automaton, there exists a linear-bounded automaton $\overline{M}$ such that $L(M) = L(\overline{M})$, and $\overline{M}$ does not loop on any input string.* □

2.2 A Language That Is Not Context-Sensitive

Any string on the seven-character alphabet

$$[\, q \; s : + - \,] \tag{16}$$

defines a linear-bounded automaton $A(\alpha)$ under the following conventions:

The *state set* K is $\{q_1, q_2, \ldots, q_n\}$, where n is the largest integer such that q^n is a substring of α, or $n = 1$ if α contains no q.

The *alphabet* Σ' is $\{s_3, s_4, \ldots, s_m\}$, where m is the largest integer such that s^m is a substring of α. If $m \leq 2$, Σ' is empty.

The *input delimiters* are $\text{¢} = s_1$ and $\$ = s_2$.

The *initial state* is q_1.

The set of *final states* is

$$F = \{q_f \mid \alpha \text{ contains the substring } [q^f], \text{ and } f \geq 1\}.$$

The *instructions* are defined by the following table for $i, j, r, t \geq 1$:

$\delta(q_i, s_j)$ contains	if and only if α contains the substring	and also
(q_r, s_t)	$[q^i s^j{:}q^r s^t]$	$j \geq 3 \text{ or } j = t$
$(q_r, -)$	$[q^i s^j{:}q^r -]$	$j \geq 2$
$(q_r, +)$	$[q^i s^j{:}q^r +]$	

If $\delta(q_i, s_j)$ contains several actions, they are ordered by the relative order of the substrings within α.

Example: If $\alpha = [[qss{:}qqq+][qs{:}q+][qqq]-qqqq[qs{:}qqs]$, then $A(\alpha)$ is the automaton with

$$K = \{q_1, q_2, q_3, q_4\}, \quad \Sigma' = \emptyset, \quad \mathcent = s_1, \quad \$ = s_2, \quad q_0 = q_1, \quad F = \{q_3\},$$

and

$$\delta(q_1, s_2) = \{(q_3, +)\}; \quad \delta(q_1, s_1) = \{(q_1, +), (q_2, s_1)\}.$$

We see that $L(A(\alpha)) = \{\epsilon\}$.

If M is any linear-bounded automaton whose input alphabet includes the seven characters of (16), we may rename its states and inputs so that (i) $K = \{q_1, q_2, \ldots, q_n\}$ for some n; (ii) $\Sigma' = \{s_3, s_4, \ldots, s_m\}$ for some m; (iii) $q_0 = q_1$; and (iv) the following correspondence is valid:

$$\begin{array}{ccccccccc} \mathcent & \$ & [& q & s & : & + &] & - \\ s_1 & s_2 & s_3 & s_4 & s_5 & s_6 & s_7 & s_8 & s_9 \end{array} \qquad (17)$$

Let $R(M)$ be one such automaton obtained by renaming the states and inputs of M. Under this renaming it is clear that $R(M) = A(\alpha)$ for some string α; let $\sigma(M)$ be one such string α. If α is any string on the alphabet (16), let $R(\alpha)$ be the corresponding string under the renaming (17). Then $R(M)$ accepts $R(\alpha)$ if and only if M accepts α.

Theorem 1. *The following language L_s is not accepted by any linear-bounded automaton:*

$$L_s = \{\alpha \mid \alpha \text{ is a string on the alphabet (16), } A(\alpha) \text{ does not} $$
$$\text{loop on } R(\alpha), \text{ and } A(\alpha) \text{ does not accept } R(\alpha)\}.$$

Proof. If L_s were accepted by some M, then L_s would also be accepted by some $\overline{M}$ as in Lemma 1. Then we consider the string $\alpha = \sigma(\overline{M})$. We know that $A(\sigma(\overline{M})) = R(\overline{M})$ does not loop on any string, so it certainly does not loop when it is presented with the string $R(\sigma(\overline{M}))$. Therefore $\sigma(\overline{M})$ is in L_s if and only if $R(\overline{M})$ does *not* accept $R(\sigma(\overline{M}))$, that is, if and only if $\overline{M}$ does not accept $\sigma(\overline{M})$. Hence L_s cannot be the language accepted by $\overline{M}$.   □

2.3 The Main Construction

Theorem 2. *The language L_s of Theorem 1 is accepted by a stack automaton.*

Proof. We present below a program that defines such a stack automaton, using the notation of Section 1. The program is given in several parts. The idea is, of course, to take a string on the alphabet (16) and to simulate the behavior of $A(\alpha)$ on $R(\alpha)$.

2.3.1. The alphabets. First come some basic definitions:

> **begin class** $SPM = S$, $PLUS$, $MINUS$;
> **class** $COMRD = COMMA$, RD;
> **input alphabet is** q, s, lb, rb, $colon$, $plus$, $minus$;
> **stack alphabet is** Z, Q, S, LD, RD, A, PTR,
> $COMMA$, B, T, $PLUS$, $MINUS$;
> **input delimiters are** $start$, $stop$;
> **stack bottom is** Z;

Let α denote the input string given to our stack automaton; α is a string on alphabet (16). The symbols lb and rb in the following program signify "left bracket" and "right bracket"; LD, RD, and PTR signify "left delimiter," "right delimiter," and "pointer." The symbol T will almost always be at the very top of the stack, although we will speak of the top of the stack as if T were absent. The configuration

$$(q_r, s_{i_0}\, s_{i_1} \ldots s_{i_{j-1}} \upharpoonright s_{i_j} \ldots s_{i_n})$$

of $A(\alpha)$ will be represented on our stack by the sequence

$$LD\ S^{i_0}\ COMMA\ S^{i_1}\ COMMA\ \ldots\ COMMA\ S^{i_{j-1}}\ COMMA$$
$$PTR\ S^{i_j}\ COMMA\ \ldots\ COMMA\ S^{i_n}\ RD\ Q^r S^{i_j} \qquad (18)$$

where S^i denotes i S's in a row. It is evident that all possible configurations have

$$r, i_0, i_1, \ldots, i_n \leq \text{length}(\alpha) = n - 1 \qquad (19)$$

and this observation is crucial in the construction that follows. Notice that $i_0 = 1$ and $i_n = 2$.

2.3.2.   Elementary procedures. The following procedures do simple actions that are required rather often in the program.

procedure *search*(*x*, *dir*);
    begin ⟨This procedure searches in a given direction, **r**, **ℓ**, **R**, or **L**,
        until sensing the character *x*⟩
    [*x* ⇒; ⇒ *dir*, **repeat**]
    end *search*;
procedure *pass*(*x*, *dir*);
    begin ⟨This procedure searches in a given direction, **r**, **ℓ**, **R**, or **L**,
        until sensing a character *other* than *x*⟩
    [*x* ⇒ *dir*, **repeat**; ⇒]
    end *pass*;
procedure *presence*(*x*, *fail*);
    begin ⟨If not scanning *x*, go to the '*fail*' label⟩
    [*x* ⇒; ⇒ **go to** *fail*]
    end *presence*;
procedure *absence*(*x*, *fail*);
    begin ⟨If scanning *x*, go to the '*fail*' label⟩
    [*x* ⇒ **go to** *fail*; ⇒]
    end *absence*;
procedure *compare*(*X*, *x*, *fail*);
    begin ⟨Compare the string of *X*'s just to the right in the stack
        with the string of *x*'s just to the right in the input,
        and go to '*fail*' if they have unequal length; if successful,
        pointers are positioned at the right of the strings compared⟩
    [*X* ⇒ *presence*(*x*, *fail*), **rR**, **repeat**; *x* ⇒ **go to** *fail*; ⇒]
    end *compare*;
procedure *dup*(*x*, *X*);
    begin ⟨Place as many *X*'s at the top of the stack as there are
        x's just to the right in the input, and advance the input pointer⟩
    search(*T*, **R**), [*x* ⇒ **r**Λ'*X*.*T*', **repeat**; ⇒]
    end *dup*;
procedure *copy*(*Y*, *X*);
    begin ⟨Place as many *X*'s at the top of the stack as there are
        Y's just to the right in the position now scanned in the stack,
        provided that the number of *Y*'s does not exceed the length of
        the input string, plus 1; also reset the input pointer to the left⟩
    search(*start*, **ℓ**), [*Y* ⇒ **rR**, **repeat**; ⇒ *search*(*T*, **R**)],
    [*start* ⇒; ⇒ **ℓ**Λ'*X*.*T*', **repeat**]
    end *copy*;

These procedures build up the capabilities of our stack automaton. The programming in each case is completely straightforward, except possibly in the last procedure '*copy*'. The last procedure demonstrates that our stack automaton is able to copy a homogeneous string whose length is at most length(α) + 1 from within its stack. The procedure will fail if presented with any longer strings; but we will verify later that our stack automaton never needs longer strings, because of (19).

2.3.3. Phase 1: Initialization. The first step in the simulation is to put the initial configuration $(q_1, \lceil \cdot \cent R(\alpha)\$)$ on the stack, following the conventions of (17) and (18):

procedure *phase* 1;
    begin r'*LD.PTR.S.COMMA*',
trans: [*lb* $\Rightarrow$ '*S.S.S*';   *q* $\Rightarrow$ '*S.S.S.S*';   *s* $\Rightarrow$ '*S.S.S.S.S*';
        colon $\Rightarrow$ '*S.S.S.S.S.S*';   *plus* $\Rightarrow$ '*S.S.S.S.S.S.S*';
        rb $\Rightarrow$ '*S.S.S.S.S.S.S.S*';   *minus* $\Rightarrow$ '*S.S.S.S.S.S.S.S.S*';
        stop $\Rightarrow$ '*S.S.RD.Q.S.A.T*', **go to** *out*],
      r'*COMMA*', **go to** *trans*,
out:
    end *phase* 1;

Notice that the configuration is followed on the stack by A, and the symbol T is placed at the top of the stack.

2.3.4. Phase 2: Searching for an instruction. Given that the top of the stack has the form $Q^i S^j A^k$, we want to find the kth valid rule of the form $[q^i s^j : \ldots]$, if one exists. If so, the top of the stack is changed to

$$Q^i S^j A^k Q^r S^t, \quad Q^i S^j A^k Q^r PLUS, \quad \text{or} \quad Q^i S^j A^k Q^r MINUS \qquad (20)$$

for the respective rules $[q^i s^j : q^r s^t]$, $[q^i s^j : q^r +]$, or $[q^i s^j : q^r -]$. Phase 2 takes place in several stages:

procedure *nextrule*(*fail*);
    begin ⟨Find the next valid applicable rule to the right
        of the input pointer, or go to '*fail*'⟩
findQ: *search*(*RD*, **L**), **R**,
    [*lb* $\Rightarrow$ **r**;   *stop* $\Rightarrow$ **go to** *fail*; $\Rightarrow$ **r**, **repeat**],
    compare(*Q*, *q*, *findQ*),   *compare*(*S*, *s*, *findQ*),
    presence(*colon*, *findQ*), **r**, *presence*(*q*, *findQ*), *pass*(*q*, **r**),
    ⟨A substring '[$q^i s^j$:q^r' has just been found in the input;
        the stack pointer is scanning A, just right of S^j;
        now we want to see if the remainder of the rule is valid⟩
    [*s* $\Rightarrow$ **L**, **L**, *presence*(*S*, *eqtest*), **L**, *presence*(*S*, *eqtest*), *pass*(*s*, **r**);
        minus $\Rightarrow$ **rL**, **L**, *presence*(*S*, *findQ*);
        plus $\Rightarrow$ **r**; $\Rightarrow$ **go to** *findQ*],
    go to *rbtest*,
eqtest: **R**, *compare*(*S*, *s*, *findQ*),
rbtest: *presence*(*rb*, *findQ*)
    end *nextrule*; ⟨The input pointer now scans the *rb* of a suitable rule⟩

procedure *kthrule(fail)*;
   begin ⟨Find the *k*th valid applicable rule in the input, or go to '*fail*';
       assume that the top of stack contains $Q^i S^j A^k$, where
       k doesn't exceed the length of the input string plus 1⟩
     search$(T, \mathbf{R})$, *search*$(S, \mathbf{L})$, $\mathbf{R}$,
     copy(A, B), ⟨top of stack is now $Q^i S^j A^k B^k$, and we're scanning *start*⟩
loop: *nextrule(fail)*,
     search$(T, \mathbf{R})$, Λ, Λ'T'', $\mathbf{L}$, ⟨erase one B⟩
     $[B \Rightarrow$ **go to** *loop*; $\Rightarrow$ *search*$(colon, \boldsymbol{\ell})]$
   end *kthrule*; ⟨The input pointer now sees the colon of the *k*th valid rule⟩

procedure *phase2(fail)*;
   begin *kthrule(fail)*, $\mathbf{r}$,
     ⟨Having found the *k*th rule, we will now copy it to the top of the stack⟩
     dup(q, Q), *dup*(s, S), *dup*$(plus, PLUS)$, *dup*$(minus, MINUS)$
end *phase2*;

2.3.5. Phase 3: Simulating an instruction. The purpose of the third phase is to simulate one computational step of $A(\alpha)$. Assume that $\Phi A^k \beta$ appears at the top of the stack, where Φ is the representation of a configuration as in (18), and where β is either $Q^r S^t$, $Q^r PLUS$, or $Q^r MINUS$, denoting the instruction to be performed (see (20)). Phase 3 adds the new configuration Φ' obtained from Φ by applying β, so that we have essentially

$$\Phi \xrightarrow{\;k\;} \Phi'$$

and the top of the stack becomes $\Phi A^k \beta \Phi' A$. If the simulated machine stops after this instruction, we go to '*off*'.

   The main activity in this phase is to copy most of Φ, because Φ' is equal to Φ except in the vicinity of the pointer. The first procedure below shows how such copying can be done.

procedure *stackcopy(pointer, done)*;
   begin ⟨If the top of the stack has the form

$$\Phi A^k \beta\; LD\; \sigma_0\; COMMA\; \sigma_1\; \ldots\; COMMA\; \sigma_{m-1}\; COMMA\; \sigma_m \qquad (21)$$

     where the σ's are strings not involving *LD* or *COMMA*
     and where Φ and β are as described above, this procedure pushes
     $S^{im}\, COMMA$ onto the top of the stack, unless $m = j$ or $m = n + 1$;
     we go to '*done*' if $m = n + 1$ in (18), that is, if (21) has
     one *COMMA* too many; we go to '*pointer*' if $m = j$ in (18),
     that is, if the *PTR* is located at the *m*th part of Φ⟩
   search$(start, \boldsymbol{\ell})$, *search*$(T, \mathbf{R})$,
   ⟨First "count" the number *m* of times that *COMMA* occurs⟩

$[COMMA \Rightarrow [stop \Rightarrow \textbf{go to } done; \quad \Rightarrow \textbf{rL}], \textbf{repeat};$
$\quad LD \Rightarrow \textbf{L}; \quad \Rightarrow \textbf{L}, \textbf{repeat}],$
⟨Now we want to find the corresponding part of Φ⟩
$search(LD, \textbf{L}), \textbf{R},$
$[start \Rightarrow; \quad \Rightarrow search(COMMA, \textbf{R}), \ell\textbf{R}, \textbf{repeat}],$
$absence(PTR, pointer), copy(S, S), \Lambda`COMMA.T"$
$\quad \textbf{end } stackcopy;$

$\textbf{procedure } action;$
$\quad \textbf{begin } \langle$Assume that the top of the stack has the form (21),
$\qquad$ where $m = j$ in (18), and that the stack pointer
$\qquad$ now scans the first character of β following Q^r;
$\qquad$ this procedure adjusts the stack according to the action $\beta \rangle$
$\qquad [S \Rightarrow search(T, \textbf{R}), \Lambda`PTR.T", search(Q, \textbf{L}), \textbf{R}, \textbf{go to } write;$
$\qquad PLUS \Rightarrow \textbf{go to } right; MINUS \Rightarrow \textbf{go to } left],$
$right: search(PTR, \textbf{L}), \textbf{R}, copy(S, S), \Lambda`COMMA.PTR.T", \textbf{go to } exit,$
$\quad left: search(T, \textbf{R}), search(start, \ell),$
$\qquad \Lambda, \Lambda, \langle$remove T and $COMMA \rangle$
$\qquad [S \Rightarrow \textbf{r}\Lambda, \textbf{repeat}; \quad \Rightarrow `PTR', [start \Rightarrow; \quad \Rightarrow \ell`S', \textbf{repeat}]],$
$\qquad `COMMA.T", search(LD, \textbf{L}), search(PTR, \textbf{L}), \textbf{R},$
$write: copy(S, S), \Lambda`COMMA.T",$
$\quad exit:$
$\quad \textbf{end } action;$

$\textbf{procedure } phase3(off);$
$\quad \textbf{begin } \langle$Perform one computation step of the simulated
$\qquad$ linear-bounded automaton, and go to off if the autom-
$\qquad$ aton has just moved past the right end of its input⟩
$\qquad \Lambda`LD.T",$
$more: stackcopy(act, quit), \textbf{go to } more,$
$\quad act: search(A, \textbf{R}), search(SPM, \textbf{R}), action, \textbf{go to } more,$
$quit: search(T, \textbf{R}), \Lambda,$
$\qquad \langle$The top of stack now is $COMMA$ or $COMMA$ $PTR \rangle,$
$\qquad [PTR \Rightarrow `T', \textbf{go to } off; \quad COMMA \Rightarrow \Lambda`RD.T"],$
$\qquad \langle$The remaining job is to fill in the new state and symbol scanned⟩
$\qquad search(A, \textbf{L}), \textbf{R}, copy(Q, Q),$
$\qquad search(PTR, \textbf{L}), \textbf{R}, copy(S, S), \Lambda`A.T"$
$\quad \textbf{end } phase3;$

$\textbf{procedure } checkfinal(fail);$
$\quad \textbf{begin } \langle$Check if the simulated machine has q_f as a final state,
$\qquad$ where Q^f is the current state of the simulated machine;
$\qquad$ if not, go to $fail \rangle$
$\qquad search(start, \ell), search(T, \textbf{R}),$
$try: [lb \Rightarrow \textbf{r}; \quad stop \Rightarrow \textbf{go to } fail; \quad \Rightarrow \textbf{r}, \textbf{repeat}],$
$\qquad search(A, \textbf{L}), \textbf{R}, compare(Q, q, try), presence(rb, try)$
$\quad \textbf{end } checkfinal;$

2.3.6. The entire program. Finally we must fit all the pieces together. The nondeterministic nature of the simulated machine can be handled by applying the ordinary backtrack method [4]. Either the linear-bounded automaton loops on $R(\alpha)$, in which case our simulator also loops and does not accept the string, or else we run through all of its computations

$$c_0 \xrightarrow{k_1} c_1 \xrightarrow{k_2} \cdots \xrightarrow{k_n} c_n$$

in lexicographic order (with corresponding configurations

$$\Phi_0 \ldots A^{k_1} \ldots \Phi_1 \ldots A^{k_2} \ldots A^{k_n} \ldots \Phi_n$$

on the stack as we do the simulation) until the simulated machine accepts the string (when we reject it) or until all computations have been exhausted (when we accept it).

Here now is the body of the program, making use of the procedures given above:

> *phase* 1,
>
> *mainloop*: *phase* 2(*nomore*),   *phase* 3(*movedoff*),
>
> **go to** *mainloop*,
>
> *nomore*: ⟨All computations leading from the configuration Φ at the top of the stack have now been tried; so we erase it from the stack and add another A to the counter preceding Φ⟩
>
> *search*(T,**R**),
>
> [$LD \Rightarrow \Lambda$; $\Rightarrow \Lambda$, **repeat**],
>
> [$A \Rightarrow$ '$A.T$', **go to** *mainloop*; $Z \Rightarrow$ **accept**; $\Rightarrow \Lambda$, **repeat**],
>
> *movedoff*: *checkfinal*(*nomore*)
>
> **end**.

It is not difficult to verify that the program given above preserves all the inductive assumptions and does all of the actions specified in the comments that are interspersed within it. We should mention the one nontrivial part of the proof, namely that the '*copy*' procedure is never used to copy a string whose length exceeds n, where $n - 1$ is the length of the input α. The statement $copy(S, S)$ is used to copy a string S^t only if S^t is in the stack, which implies that either s^t is a substring of α or $t \le 9$ and S^t represents the character s_t in $R(\alpha)$. The latter case leads to $copy(S, S)$ only if α contains at least one valid instruction as a substring; and the shortest such α are $[qs{:}qs]$ and $[qs{:}q{+}]$, of length 7. We can always copy S^t, for $t \le 9$, if α has length 8 or more. Hence $copy(S, S)$ could fail only if α is one of the two strings of length 7 just given. But those strings contain no minus signs, so S^9 will never need to be copied. The statement $copy(Q, Q)$ is used to copy Q^t only when $t = 1$ or q^t is a substring of α. The statement $copy(A, B)$ is used to copy A^k only when α contains at least $k - 1$ valid instructions. Hence all uses of $copy$ are properly constrained.

This completes the proof of Theorem 2.   □

Comparable proofs using old notations would clearly have taken considerably more space and would have been much harder to read. The authors have recently learned that J. D. Ullman and John Hopcroft have informally described a stack automaton somewhat similar to the one above, with the addition of a counter in each configuration that makes it possible to detect if the simulated machine loops. Therefore the *complement* of the language L_s is also accepted by a stack automaton.

To guard against minor errors in the program above and in the other programs of this paper, a stack automaton simulator was written for the 7094 computer, capable of simulating the behavior of automata defined by the programming language of Section 1.3. Further details of the simulator can be found in *Journal of the Association for Computing Machinery* **14** (1967), 632–635.

Appendix 1. A Program to Accept $\{\alpha\alpha\}$

begin class $ab = a, b$; **class** $AB = A, B$;
   input alphabet is ab; **stack alphabet is** AB, C, Z;
   input delimiters are $start, stop$; **stack bottom is** Z;
   $[start \Rightarrow \mathbf{r}]$,
   $[a \Rightarrow \mathbf{r}`A\text{'}, \mathbf{repeat};\quad b \Rightarrow \mathbf{r}`B\text{'}, \mathbf{repeat};\quad stop \Rightarrow \ell`C\text{'}]$,
   $[ab \Rightarrow \ell\mathbf{L}, [ab \Rightarrow \ell], \mathbf{repeat};\quad start \Rightarrow \mathbf{r}]$,
   $[a.A \Rightarrow \mathbf{rR}, \mathbf{repeat};\quad b.B \Rightarrow \mathbf{rR}, \mathbf{repeat};\quad C \Rightarrow \mathbf{accept}]$
end.

The research reported in this paper was supported in part by the National Science Foundation and the Carnegie Corporation.

References

[1] M. W. Curtis, "A Turing machine simulator," *Journal of the Association for Computing Machinery* **12** (1965), 1–13.

[2] Seymour Ginsburg and Sheila A. Greibach, "Deterministic context free languages," *Information and Control* **9** (1966), 620–648.

[3] Seymour Ginsburg, Sheila A. Greibach, and Michael A. Harrison, "Stack automata and compiling," *Journal of the Association for Computing Machinery* **14** (1967), 172–201.

[4] Solomon W. Golomb and Leonard D. Baumert, "Backtrack programming," *Journal of the Association for Computing Machinery* **12** (1965), 516–524.

[5] S.-Y. Kuroda, "Classes of languages and linear bounded automata," *Information and Control* **7** (1964), 202–223.

[6] Peter Naur, editor, "Report on the algorithmic language ALGOL 60," *Communications of the ACM* **3** (1960), 299–314.

Addendum

Considerably stronger forms of Theorems 1 and 2 were found by J. E. Hopcroft and J. D. Ullman ["Nonerasing stack automata," *Journal of Computer and System Sciences* **1** (1967), 166–186], who proved that if a stack automaton is forbidden to erase, it is precisely equivalent in power to a Turing machine whose working tape holds at most $O(n \log n)$ characters, where n is the length of the input string. In particular, non-context-sensitive languages can be accepted even by programs that do not use Λ in any ⟨stack write⟩ actions.

The exact computational power of unrestricted stack automata was subsequently determined by Stephen A. Cook ["Characterizations of pushdown machines in terms of time-bounded computers," *Journal of the Association for Computing Machinery* **18** (1971), 4–18], who proved that they are equivalent to Turing machines that halt within $n^{O(n)}$ steps. J. D. Ullman ["Halting stack automata," *Journal of the Association for Computing Machinery* **16** (1969), 550–563] had previously shown that the languages accepted by stack automata are closed under complementation.

Chapter 13

A Characterization of Parenthesis
Languages

[Originally published in Information and Control **11** *(1967), 269–289.]*

A parenthesis language is a context-free language possessing a grammar in which each application of a production introduces a unique pair of parentheses, delimiting the scope of that production. Parenthesis languages are nontrivial since only one kind of parenthesis is used. In this paper it is shown that algorithms exist to determine if a context-free language is a parenthesis language, or if it is equal to the language defined by a given parenthesis grammar. A possible merit of these results lies in the fact that parenthesis languages are the most general class of languages for which such problems are now known to be solvable; in fact, other problems that are very similar to the one solved here are known to be recursively unsolvable.

1. Introduction

Robert McNaughton [3] has defined a special type of context-free grammar called a *parenthesis grammar* and he has shown that it is possible to determine if two parenthesis grammars generate the same language. He also has raised the question whether or not it is possible to decide if a given context-free language is a parenthesis language. An affirmative answer to his question is given below, in connection with some techniques for manipulating context-free grammars that may be of independent interest. A new proof of McNaughton's theorem is also given.

Let us define a *context-free grammar* $\mathcal{G}$ as a quadruple $(\Sigma, V, \mathcal{S}, \mathcal{P})$, where the "vocabulary" V is a finite set of letters; the "terminal alphabet" Σ is a subset of V; the "start set" $\mathcal{S}$ is a finite subset of V^* (where V^* as usual denotes the set of all strings on V); and the "production set" $\mathcal{P}$ is a finite set of relations of the form $A \rightarrow \theta$, where A is in the set of "nonterminal symbols" $N = V \setminus \Sigma$, and where θ is in V^*. For any strings α, ω in V^* we write $\alpha A \omega \rightarrow \alpha \theta \omega$, if $A \rightarrow \theta$ is a production in $\mathcal{P}$. The transitive completion of this relation is denoted $\rightarrow^+$, so that $\varphi \rightarrow^+ \psi$ means there exist strings $\varphi_0, \varphi_1, \ldots, \varphi_n$ such that $\varphi = \varphi_0$, $\varphi_j \rightarrow \varphi_{j+1}$ for $0 \leq j < n$, and $\varphi_n = \psi$, where $n \geq 1$. The same relation with $n \geq 0$ is denoted by $\rightarrow^*$, so that $\varphi \rightarrow^* \psi$ if and only if $\varphi \rightarrow^+ \psi$ or $\varphi = \psi$. The *language* $L(\mathcal{G})$ defined by grammar $\mathcal{G}$ is the set

$$\{\theta \text{ in } \Sigma^* \mid \sigma \rightarrow^* \theta \text{ for some } \sigma \text{ in } \mathcal{S}\}. \tag{1}$$

Two grammars $\mathcal{G}$, $\mathcal{G}'$ are called *equivalent* if $L(\mathcal{G}) = L(\mathcal{G}')$.

For the purposes of this paper we will always assume that the terminal alphabet Σ contains two distinguished characters (and). We write $T = \Sigma \setminus \{(,)\}$ to stand for the other letters of the terminal alphabet, and $U = V \setminus \{(,)\}$ to stand for the other letters of the vocabulary.

The context-free grammar $\mathcal{G}$ is a *parenthesis grammar* if $\mathcal{S}$ is a subset of U^*, that is, the strings of $\mathcal{S}$ contain no parenthesis symbols, and if all productions have the form

$$A \rightarrow (\theta)$$

where θ is in U^*. A set of strings $L \subseteq \Sigma^*$ is called a *parenthesis language* if $L = L(\mathcal{G})$ for some parenthesis grammar $\mathcal{G}$.

This definition is not identical to the one given by McNaughton, but it is easy to verify that L is a parenthesis language in our sense if and only if (L) is a parenthesis language in McNaughton's sense. Our definition has the slight advantage that parenthesis languages become closed under concatenation.

Our goal is to find a method to take an arbitrary context-free grammar $\mathcal{G}$ and to determine whether or not there is an equivalent parenthesis grammar $\mathcal{G}'$. Throughout the constructions below we will assume that no *useless* nonterminal symbols are present in the grammars we deal with. A nonterminal symbol A is called useless if it has no influence on $L(\mathcal{G})$, that is, unless there exist σ in $\mathcal{S}$ and α, θ, ω in Σ^* such that $\sigma \rightarrow^* \alpha A \omega \rightarrow^* \alpha \theta \omega$. Well-known methods exist to recognize and remove all useless nonterminals from a grammar.

In the discussion below we generally let uppercase letters A, B, $\ldots$ stand for nonterminals; lowercase letters a, b, $\ldots$ stand for elements of T; lowercase letters x, y, $\ldots$ stand for elements of V; and lowercase Greek letters stand for strings. The symbol ϵ denotes the empty string. The statement "α is an initial substring of θ" means that there exists a string ω such that $\alpha \omega = \theta$. The notation $|\theta|$ stands for the length of θ; thus $|\epsilon| = 0$ and $|\theta x| = |\theta| + 1$.

2. Parenthesis Structure

For any θ in Σ^* we define its "content" $c(\theta)$ and "deficiency" $d(\theta)$ as follows:

$$c(x) = \begin{cases} +1, & \text{if } x = (; \\ 0, & \text{if } x \in T; \\ -1, & \text{if } x =); \end{cases} \qquad d(x) = \begin{cases} 0, & \text{if } x = (; \\ 0, & \text{if } x \in T; \\ 1, & \text{if } x =); \end{cases} \qquad (2)$$

$c(\epsilon) = d(\epsilon) = 0$, $c(\theta x) = c(\theta) + c(x)$, $d(\theta x) = \max\big(d(\theta), d(x) - c(\theta)\big)$. It follows that for all θ and φ we have

$$c(\theta\varphi) = c(\theta) + c(\varphi); \quad d(\theta\varphi) = \max\big(d(\theta), d(\varphi) - c(\theta)\big). \qquad (3)$$

The value $c(\theta)$ is clearly the excess of left parentheses over right parentheses in θ, and $d(\theta)$ is the greatest deficiency of left parentheses from right parentheses in any initial substring of θ. We say that θ is *balanced* if $c(\theta) = d(\theta) = 0$.

The left and right parentheses in the string $\alpha(\theta)\omega$ are said to *match* if θ is balanced. The left parenthesis in the string $\alpha(\theta$ is said to be *free* if $d(\theta) = 0$. The right parenthesis in the string $\theta)\omega$ is said to be *free* if $d(\theta) = -c(\theta)$. It follows that every parenthesis in a string is either free or has a unique mate; that is, all non-free parentheses can be classified into matching pairs in a unique way. This matching process corresponds to the familiar rules for parenthesis grouping, and we see that balanced strings are precisely those strings whose parentheses all have mates in the conventional sense. Moreover we have the general situation given in the following lemma:

Lemma 1. *Any string φ on Σ can be written uniquely in the form*

$$\varphi = \varphi_0)\varphi_1) \dots)\varphi_p(\varphi_{p+1}(\dots(\varphi_q, \qquad (4)$$

where $0 \le p \le q$ and each φ_j is balanced. Moreover, the p right parentheses and the $q - p$ left parentheses indicated in (4) are precisely the free parentheses of φ, and

$$p = d(\varphi), \qquad q - p = c(\varphi) + d(\varphi). \qquad (5)$$

Proof. Although this lemma is intuitively clear it may be worthwhile to consider a formal proof. Let us use induction on $|\varphi|$.

Case 1, φ is balanced. Then all parentheses within φ have mates and there are no free parentheses. For example, if φ has the form $\alpha(\theta$

it follows that $c(\alpha) \geq 0$ and $c(\theta) = c(\varphi) - c(\alpha) - 1 < 0$; hence the left parenthesis is not free and θ contains a shortest initial substring θ' for which $c(\theta') < 0$. Clearly θ' has the form $\theta'')$ where θ'' is balanced. A dual argument shows that each right parenthesis within φ has a mate. Hence in any representation such as (4) the parentheses shown are precisely the free parentheses when $\varphi_0, \ldots, \varphi_q$ are balanced; and this fact proves that there is at most one such representation for any string φ. When φ is balanced the only possibility is $\varphi = \varphi_0$.

Case 2, $c(\varphi) > 0$ and $d(\varphi) = 0$. Let φ_0 be the longest initial substring of φ for which $c(\varphi) = 0$; then clearly φ has the form $\varphi_0(\varphi'$ where φ_0 is balanced, $c(\varphi') = c(\varphi) - 1$, and $d(\varphi') = 0$. By induction the lemma holds for φ', so it holds also for φ.

Case 3, $d(\varphi) > 0$. Let ψ be the shortest initial substring of φ for which $c(\psi) < 0$. Then ψ has the form $\varphi_0)$ where φ_0 is balanced; and $\varphi = \varphi_0)\varphi'$ where $c(\varphi') = c(\varphi) + 1$, $d(\varphi') = d(\varphi) - 1$. By induction the lemma holds for φ. $\square$

Together with the concept of matching parentheses we have a relation of *associate* symbols: The symbols x and y in the string $\alpha\, x\, \theta\, y\, \omega$ are called "associates" if θy is balanced. The relation of being associates breaks any string into equivalence classes; for example in the string $ab(_1c(_2d)_3(_4e)_5f)_6g$ the sets of associates are

$$\{a, b,)_6, g\}, \quad \{(_1, c,)_3,)_5, f\}, \quad \{(_2, d\}, \quad \{(_4, e)\}.$$

Here subscripts have been used to distinguish between different instances of parentheses.

Lemma 2. *If φ is a nonempty string with $c(\varphi) = 0$, the string φ^n contains a set of at least n associate symbols.*

Proof. By Lemma 1, we can write φ as $\varphi'\varphi''$ where φ' is nonempty, $c(\varphi') = -d(\varphi)$, $c(\varphi'') = d(\varphi)$, and $\varphi''\varphi'$ is balanced. Now $\varphi^n = \varphi'(\varphi''\varphi')^{n-1}\varphi''$, and the final characters of each φ' in this formula are associates. $\square$

A language $L \subseteq \Sigma^*$ is said to be *balanced* if every string in L is balanced. It is said to have *bounded associates* if there exists a constant m_0 such that, if θ is in L and if x is a symbol of θ, then x has at most m_0 associates in θ.

Lemma 3. *Let $\mathcal{G} = (\Sigma, V, \mathcal{S}, \mathcal{P})$ be a parenthesis grammar. Then $L(\mathcal{G})$ is balanced and has bounded associates.*

Proof. Extend the definitions above from Σ to V by defining $c(A) = d(A) = 0$ for A in N. Suppose $\varphi \to \psi$ where φ is balanced and no symbol of φ has more than m associates. Then $\varphi = \alpha A \omega$ and $\psi = \alpha(\theta)\omega$ where θ is in U^*. It follows that ψ is balanced. Moreover, two symbols of ψ are associates if and only if they are associates in φ, or if one is) and the other is associated with A in φ, or if they are both part of (θ. Hence no symbol of ψ has more than $\max(m, |\theta| + 1)$ associates.

Consider now the relation $\sigma \to^* \theta$ for σ in S. By induction on the length of the derivation, namely the number of $\to$ steps implied by $\to^*$, we see that θ is balanced and its symbols have at most

$$m_0 = 1 + \max\{|\theta| \mid \theta \in S \text{ or there is a production } A \to (\theta) \text{ in } \mathcal{P}\}$$

associates.   □

We shall eventually show that the converse of Lemma 3 is also true: Any context-free language that is balanced and has bounded associates must be a parenthesis language. First let us investigate balanced languages more closely.

Lemma 4. *Let $\mathcal{G} = (\Sigma, V, S, \mathcal{P})$ be a context-free grammar for which $L(\mathcal{G})$ is balanced. For each nonterminal A there exist numbers $c(A)$ and $d(A)$ that can be found effectively from $\mathcal{G}$, such that if $A \to^* \theta \in \Sigma^*$ then $c(\theta) = c(A)$ and $d(\theta) \leq d(A)$.*

Proof. By our standard assumption, A is not useless, so we can find σ in S and α, φ, ω in Σ^* such that $\sigma \to^* \alpha A \omega \to^* \alpha \varphi \omega$. Let $c(A) = c(\varphi)$ and $d(A) = c(\alpha)$. Then if $A \to^* \theta$ we have $\sigma \to^* \alpha \theta \omega$; so

$$c(\alpha) + c(\theta) + c(\omega) = c(\alpha \theta \omega) = 0 = c(\alpha \varphi \omega) = c(\alpha) + c(\varphi) + c(\omega),$$

and $c(\theta) = c(A)$. Also

$$d(\alpha \theta \omega) = \max\big(d(\alpha), \; d(\theta) - c(\alpha), \; d(\omega) - c(\alpha \theta)\big)$$

by (3); hence $d(\theta) - c(\alpha) \leq d(\alpha \theta \omega) = 0$ and $d(\theta) \leq d(A)$.   □

Theorem 1. *If $\mathcal{G} = (\Sigma, V, S, \mathcal{P})$ is a context-free grammar, there is an effective algorithm that determines whether or not $L(\mathcal{G})$ is balanced.*

Proof. Use the construction in the proof of the preceding lemma to define $c(A)$ and $d(A)$ for each nonterminal A. For each of the finitely many functions d_1 such that $0 \leq d_1(A) \leq d(A)$ when $A \in N$ and $d_1(x) = d(x)$ when $x \in \Sigma$, attempt to verify the following facts:

  i) $c(\sigma) = d_1(\sigma) = 0$ for all $\sigma \in S$.

  ii) $c(A) = c(\theta)$ for all productions $A \to \theta$.

  iii) $d_1(A) \geq d_1(\theta)$ for all productions $A \to \theta$.

In condition (iii), the value of $d_1(\theta)$ is calculated using formula (3); this is legitimate because one can easily prove that (3) defines $c(\theta)$ and $d(\theta)$ uniquely for all strings θ, whenever $c(x)$ and $d(x)$ are defined for one-letter strings x, if we also have $c(\epsilon) = d(\epsilon) = 0$ and $d(x) \geq 0$. Notice that $d(\theta)$ is always nonnegative.

If there is some choice of d_1 for which all three conditions hold, we can prove that $L(\mathcal{G})$ is balanced, by showing inductively that $c(\varphi) = d_1(\varphi) = 0$ whenever $\sigma \to^* \varphi$ and $\sigma \in \mathcal{S}$. This statement holds by (i) when $\varphi \in \mathcal{S}$; and if $\sigma \to^* \alpha A\omega \to \alpha\theta\omega$ where $c(\alpha A\omega) = d_1(\alpha A\omega) = 0$, we have $c(\alpha\theta\omega) = c(\alpha A\omega)$ by (ii), and $0 \leq d_1(\alpha\theta\omega) \leq d_1(\alpha A\omega) = 0$ by (iii).

Conversely, if $L(\mathcal{G})$ is balanced there will exist such a choice of d_1, namely $d_1(A) = \max\{\, d(\varphi) \mid A \to^* \varphi \in \Sigma^* \,\}$. This d_1 satisfies $d_1(\theta) = \max\{\, d(\varphi) \mid \theta \to^* \varphi \in \Sigma^* \,\}$ for all $\theta \in V^*$, by (ii) and formula (3). Consequently condition (iii) must hold, since there exists $\theta' \in \Sigma^*$ for which $\theta \to^* \theta'$ and $d_1(\theta) = d_1(\theta')$. And if $\sigma \to^* \alpha A\omega \to^* \alpha\varphi\omega$ for $\sigma \in \mathcal{S}$ and $\alpha\varphi\omega \in \Sigma^*$, we have $0 = d_1(\alpha A\omega) \geq d_1(A) - c(\alpha)$; therefore $d_1(A) \leq d(A)$. $\square$

The result of Lemma 4 can be refined further. Let us say that a grammar is *completely qualified* if, for each $A \in N$, there are numbers $c(A)$ and $d(A)$ such that we have $c(\theta) = c(A)$ and $d(\theta) = d(A)$ whenever $A \to^* \theta \in \Sigma^*$.

Lemma 5. *Let* $\mathcal{G} = (\Sigma, V, \mathcal{S}, \mathcal{P})$ *be a context-free grammar for which* $L(\mathcal{G})$ *is balanced. It is possible to construct a completely qualified grammar* $\mathcal{G}' = (\Sigma, V', \mathcal{S}', \mathcal{P}')$ *that is equivalent to* $\mathcal{G}$.

Proof. Let $c(A)$ and $d(A)$ be defined for all A as in Lemma 4. Let

$$V' = \Sigma \cup \{\, [A, j] \mid 0 \leq j \leq d(A),\ A \in N \,\}.$$

Define $\tau(A) = \{\, [A, j] \mid 0 \leq j \leq d(A) \,\}$, and $\tau(x) = \{x\}$ for $x \in \Sigma$. Extend τ to V^* by defining

$$\tau(x_1 x_2 \ldots x_n) = \{\, y_1 y_2 \ldots y_n \mid y_k \in \tau(x_k),\ 1 \leq k \leq n \,\} \subseteq V'^*.$$

Also define $c([A, j]) = c(A)$, $d([A, j]) = j$. Then Eq. (3) can be used to define $c(\theta)$ and $d(\theta)$ for all $\theta \in V'^*$. The grammar $\mathcal{G}'$ is now defined as follows:

$$\mathcal{S}' = \bigcup \{\, \tau(\sigma) \mid \sigma \in \mathcal{S} \,\},$$
$$\mathcal{P}' = \{\, [A, j] \to \varphi \mid d(\varphi) = j,\ \varphi \in \tau(\theta),\ A \to \theta \in \mathcal{P} \,\}.$$

It is obvious that $L(\mathcal{G}') \subseteq L(\mathcal{G})$, since any derivation in $\mathcal{G}'$ can be "mapped into" a derivation in $\mathcal{G}$ by replacing $[A, j]$ by A. And it is easy to show, by induction on the length of derivation, that if $\theta \rightarrow^* \varphi \in \Sigma^*$ in $\mathcal{G}$ there is some θ' in $\tau(\theta)$ for which $\theta' \rightarrow^* \varphi$ in $\mathcal{G}'$. Hence $L(\mathcal{G}) \subseteq L(\mathcal{G}')$. Furthermore any terminal string descended from $[A, j]$ in $\mathcal{G}'$ has deficiency j, so it is clear that $\mathcal{G}'$ is completely qualified. □

At this point it is tempting to conjecture that every balanced context-free language possesses a *balanced grammar*, namely, a completely qualified grammar such that $c(A) = d(A) = 0$ for all $A \in N$. However, the following counterexample dashes any such hopes:

Theorem 2. *The balanced language* $L_0 = \{a^n (b^n) \mid n \geq 0\}$ *cannot be defined by a balanced grammar.*

Proof. Suppose $\mathcal{G} = (\Sigma, V, \mathcal{S}, \mathcal{P})$ is a balanced grammar with $L(\mathcal{G}) = L_0$. Every nonterminal A belongs to one of two disjoint classes:

1. $A \rightarrow^* \theta \in \Sigma^*$ implies that θ contains precisely one occurrence of each of (and).
2. $A \rightarrow^* \theta \in \Sigma^*$ implies that θ contains no occurrences of parentheses.

This dichotomy follows from the facts that $c(\theta)$ must equal 0 and that each string of L_0 has just one pair of parentheses. Add a new nonterminal symbol S and add the productions $S \rightarrow \sigma$ for all $\sigma \in \mathcal{S}$; then replace $\mathcal{S}$ by $\{S\}$. The symbol S is of class 1, so we see that there must be a production where we switch to class 2, that is, a production of the form

$$A \rightarrow \alpha(\theta)\omega,$$

where A is of class 1 and all nonterminals in $\alpha\theta\omega$ are of class 2, and where $\theta \rightarrow^* b^n$ for infinitely many n. This clearly is a contradiction. □

3. The Main Construction

The example in Theorem 2 shows how difficult it is in general to obtain a balanced grammar for a balanced language. But if we add another hypothesis, such a transformation can always be carried out, as shown in Theorem 3 below.

Before considering the general construction of transformations, let us consider first the elementary operations that are involved. It is obvious that the following well-known transformations to a grammar do not change the language defined by that grammar:

Transformation 1. *Add a new nonterminal symbol X to the vocabulary; change a production $A \to \alpha\beta\gamma$ to the production $A \to \alpha X\gamma$, for some A, α, β, γ; and add the production $X \to \beta$.*

Transformation 2. *Let A be a nonterminal symbol and let $\rho(A) = \{\theta \mid A \to \theta \in \mathcal{P}\}$. Define $\rho(x) = \{x\}$ for all $x \in V \setminus \{A\}$, and*

$$\rho(x_1 \ldots x_n) = \{y_1 \ldots y_n \mid y_k \in \rho(x_k), \ 1 \le k \le n\}.$$

Then change $\mathcal{S}$ to $\rho(\mathcal{S}) = \{\sigma' \mid \sigma' \in \rho(\sigma), \text{ for some } \sigma \in \mathcal{S}\}$, and change $\mathcal{P}$ to $\mathcal{P}' = \{B \to \theta' \mid \theta' \in \rho(\theta), \text{ for some } \theta \text{ such that } B \to \theta \in \mathcal{P}\}$.

In essence, Transformation 1 adds one step to a derivation each time the production $A \to \alpha\beta\gamma$ is applied. Transformation 2 takes a shortcut by removing derivation steps when A is involved. Notice that if the nonterminal symbol A does not appear on the right-hand side of any production $A \to \theta$ then Transformation 2 makes A become "useless"; we will make use of this fact to remove A from the grammar.

Theorem 3. *Let $\mathcal{G} = (\Sigma, V, \mathcal{S}, \mathcal{P})$ be a context-free grammar for which $L(\mathcal{G})$ is balanced and has bounded associates. Then it is possible to construct an equivalent balanced grammar effectively from $\mathcal{G}$.*

Proof. We may assume from Lemma 5 that $\mathcal{G}$ is completely qualified. We may also assume that $\mathcal{G}$ is not "circular," namely that the relation $A \to^+ A$ does not hold for any nonterminal A; there are well-known methods for removing circularity, basically by defining $A \equiv B$ if $A \to^+ B \to^+ A$ and by replacing each equivalence class by a single symbol.

Consider now a typical production

$$A \to x_1 x_2 \ldots x_n \tag{6}$$

in a completely qualified grammar. We may form a "parenthesis image" of the string $x_1 x_2 \ldots x_n$ by replacing each symbol x_j by a sequence of $d(x_j)$ right parentheses followed by $c(x_j) + d(x_j)$ left parentheses; the result is a set of parentheses that has $d(A)$ free right parentheses and $c(A) + d(A)$ free left parentheses. (See Lemma 1; note that $c(x_j) + d(x_j)$ cannot be negative, since each x_j represents at least one string of Σ^*.)

For example, the c and d functions might have the following values:

x	$c(x)$	$d(x)$
A	-1	4
B	-1	2
C	2	3
$($	1	0
$)$	-1	1
a, b	0	0

If we have the production

$$A \;\to\;) \; b \; B \; (\; a \; C \; A \; B \; b \qquad\qquad (7)$$

its parenthesis image is

$$))))(((\to) \;\;))(\;\; (\;\;)))(((((\;\;)))(((\;\;))($$

and there are 4 free right parentheses and 3 free left parentheses on both sides of the image. We may now abstract (7), so that only the positions of free parentheses are shown, as follows:

$$[A)1][A)2][A)3][A)4][A(1][A(2][A(3]$$
$$\to)[B)1][B)2][C)3][C(1][A(1][B(1]. \qquad (8)$$

Here $[A)1]$ denotes the first free right parenthesis of A, $[A)2]$ is the second, etc. Thus, the second free left parenthesis of any terminal string derived from the right-hand side of (7) must be the first free left parenthesis of the string derived from the leftmost B.

Now for any completely qualified grammar $\mathcal{G}$, consider the directed graph $\mathcal{D}$ defined in the following way. The vertices of $\mathcal{D}$ are all the symbols $[A)u]$ and $[A(v]$ where A is a nonterminal and $1 \leq u \leq d(A)$, $1 \leq v \leq c(A) + d(A)$. For each production (6) we include at most $c(A) + 2d(A)$ directed arcs in $\mathcal{D}$, one for each free parenthesis that does not correspond to an actual parenthesis in the parenthesis image of the right side. From production (7), for example, we would include arcs from $[A)2]$ to $[B)1]$, $[A)3]$ to $[B)2]$, $[A)4]$ to $[C)3]$, $\ldots$, $[A(3]$ to $[B(1]$. (Compare with (8); no arc is drawn from $[A)1]$ since it corresponds to a real right parenthesis on the right of (8).)

The important property of $\mathcal{D}$ is that it contains no *oriented cycles* (no paths from a vertex to itself) when $\mathcal{G}$ is not circular and when $L(\mathcal{G})$ has bounded associates. To prove this property, suppose there is a path in $\mathcal{D}$ from $[A)u]$ to $[A)u]$ for some A and u. By the definition of $\mathcal{D}$ this assumption is equivalent to saying that there are strings α and ω in Σ^* for which $A \to^+ \alpha A \omega$, where the uth free right parenthesis in the parenthesis image of $\alpha A \omega$ is the uth free right parenthesis coming from the A. It follows that $c(\alpha) = 0$, since by Lemma 1 the uth free right parenthesis in any string φ is preceded by a string φ' with $c(\varphi') = 1 - u$. We also have $c(A) = c(\alpha) + c(A) + c(\omega)$, hence $c(\omega) = 0$. Now by assumption $\mathcal{G}$ is not circular, so α and ω are not both empty. Also $A \to^+ \alpha^n A \omega^n$ for all $n > 0$, and since A is not useless there are strings

α', θ, ω' such that $\alpha'\alpha^n \theta \omega^n \omega'$ is in $L(\mathcal{G})$ for all $n > 0$. By Lemma 2 this contradicts the assumption that $L(\mathcal{G})$ has bounded associates. A dual argument shows that there is no path in $\mathcal{D}$ from $[A(v]$ to $[A(v]$ for any A and v.

The directed graph $\mathcal{D}$ is empty (that is, has no vertices) if and only if $\mathcal{G}$ is a balanced grammar. Therefore the rest of the proof consists of showing, when $\mathcal{D}$ is not empty, that an equivalent grammar can be constructed whose corresponding graph is empty.

If $\mathcal{D}$ is not empty, the absence of cycles implies that there must be at least one "sink" vertex, that is, a vertex from which no arcs lead outward. Let $[A)u]$ be such a vertex; a dual argument will apply to a vertex $[A(v]$. By the definition of $\mathcal{D}$, the set of all productions whose left-hand side is A can be written in the form

$$
\begin{aligned}
A &\to \xi_1)\eta_1 \\
A &\to \xi_2)\eta_2 \\
&\;\;\vdots \\
A &\to \xi_n)\eta_n
\end{aligned}
\tag{9}
$$

where we have

$$
d(\xi_j) = -c(\xi_j) = u - 1, \quad c(\eta_j) = c(A) + u, \quad d(\eta_j) = d(A) - u, \tag{10}
$$

for $1 \leq j \leq n$.

We can apply Transformation 1 to form a new grammar $\mathcal{G}'$ equivalent to $\mathcal{G}$, replacing (9) by the productions

$$
A \to X_j)Y_j, \quad X_j \to \xi_j, \quad Y_j \to \eta_j \tag{11}
$$

for $1 \leq j \leq n$, where the X_j and Y_j are new nonterminal symbols. By (10), $\mathcal{G}'$ is a completely qualified grammar. Now form another equivalent grammar $\mathcal{G}''$ by applying Transformation 2 to the nonterminal A, and deleting A. Then $\mathcal{G}''$ is a completely qualified grammar equivalent to $\mathcal{G}$.

This construction $\mathcal{G} \to \mathcal{G}' \to \mathcal{G}''$ has a corresponding effect on the directed graphs $\mathcal{D} \to \mathcal{D}' \to \mathcal{D}''$. In order to study $\mathcal{D}'$ and $\mathcal{D}''$ it is convenient to introduce the following equivalence relation on the vertices of $\mathcal{D} \cup \mathcal{D}''$: For $1 \leq j \leq n$, let $[A)k] \equiv [X_j)k]$ for $1 \leq k < u$; $[A)u + k] \equiv [Y_j)k]$ for $1 \leq k \leq d(A) - u$; $[A(k] \equiv [Y_j(k]$ for $1 \leq k \leq c(A) + d(A)$. This definition can be completed to a definition of equivalence between the vertices of all digraphs derived later from $\mathcal{D}''$. It is now easy to see that the directed graph $\mathcal{D}''$ is like $\mathcal{D}$ with the following changes: (1) The vertices $[X_j)k]$, $[Y_j)k]$, $[Y_j(k]$ just mentioned are added. (2) The arcs that came from a vertex $[A)k]$ or $[A(k]$ in $\mathcal{D}$ now are shifted so that they emanate from an equivalent vertex in $\mathcal{D}''$. (3) The arcs of $\mathcal{D}$ that were directed into a vertex $[A)k]$, for $k \neq u$, or into a vertex $[A(k]$, now become n arcs directed into the n new equivalent vertices. (4) The arcs of $\mathcal{D}$ that were directed into $[A)u]$ are deleted. (5) The vertices $[A)k]$ and $[A(k]$ are deleted.

The transition from $\mathcal{G}$ to $\mathcal{G}''$ not only tends to increase the size of the grammar $\mathcal{G}$, it can also increase the number of arcs and vertices in $\mathcal{D}$. Therefore it is perhaps hard to believe that this process can be iterated until $\mathcal{D}$ loses all its vertices and arcs. But that is exactly what will happen, if the transformations are applied systematically. For let us consider the equivalence relation between vertices just defined, and let $\mathcal{D}_0$ be the directed graph whose vertices are equivalence classes of vertices of $\mathcal{D}$, and whose arcs go from class V to class V' if and only if there is at least one arc in $\mathcal{D}$ from a vertex of class V to a vertex of class V'. Then $\mathcal{D}_0''$ is equal to $\mathcal{D}_0$, except that when the class containing $[A)u]$ had only one element in $\mathcal{D}$, this class and the arcs leading to it are not present in $\mathcal{D}_0''$. If the class containing $[A)u]$ has more than one element, we can repeat the construction on vertices of this class until it disappears from $\mathcal{D}_0$. (Note that $[A)u]$ is never equivalent to $[A)k]$ for $k \neq u$, so the construction must decrease the size of the equivalence class we are currently working on.) Therefore it is possible to use induction on the number of vertices in $\mathcal{D}_0$, and the process ultimately terminates with a balanced grammar. □

The construction in the proof of Theorem 3 is rather involved, so it may be of interest to work a nontrivial example here. Consider the grammar $\mathcal{G}$ with $\Sigma = \{(,), a, b, c, d, e\}$, $V = \Sigma \cup \{A, B\}$, $\mathcal{S} = \{B)\}$, and productions

$$A \to Ba, \quad A \to (bB), \quad A \to (c(,$$
$$B \to (dA))((), \quad B \to (B)))(Ae).$$

Then $c(A) = c(B) = 2$ and $d(A) = d(B) = 0$. The directed graph $\mathcal{D}$ is

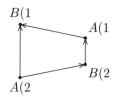

We wish to obtain an equivalent balanced grammar. First we eliminate the only sink vertex, $[B(1)]$:

$$S = \{B_{11}(B_{12})), \; B_{21}(B_{22}))\}$$
$$P = \{A \to B_{11}(B_{12}a,$$
$$A \to B_{21}(B_{22}a,$$
$$A \to (bB_{11}(B_{12}),$$
$$A \to (bB_{21}(B_{22}),$$
$$A \to (c(,$$
$$B_{11} \to \epsilon,$$
$$B_{12} \to dA))((),$$
$$B_{21} \to (B_{11}(B_{12}))),$$
$$B_{21} \to (B_{21}(B_{22}))),$$
$$B_{22} \to Ae)\}.$$

The construction can be simplified if we use Transformation 2 to remove all new nonterminals X_j, Y_j in (11) for which ξ_j or η_j respectively are merely balanced strings on Σ; we might as well use this simplification routinely, thereby reducing the size of the grammar. Thus, in the present example we may omit B_{11}:

$$S = \{(B_{12})), \; B_{21}(B_{22}))\}$$
$$P = \{A \to (B_{12}a,$$
$$A \to B_{21}(B_{22}a,$$
$$A \to (b(B_{12}),$$
$$A \to (bB_{21}(B_{22}),$$
$$A \to (c(,$$
$$B_{12} \to dA))((),$$
$$B_{21} \to ((B_{12}))),$$
$$B_{21} \to (B_{21}(B_{22}))),$$
$$B_{22} \to Ae)\}.$$

The next step is to remove $[A(1)]$, which has become a new sink:

$$S = \{(B_{12})), \; B_{21}(B_{22}))\}$$
$$P = \{A_{12} \to B_{12}a, \quad A_{21} \to B_{21}, \quad A_{22} \to B_{22}a, \quad A_{32} \to b(B_{12}),$$
$$A_{42} \to bB_{21}(B_{22}), \quad A_{52} \to c(,$$
$$B_{12} \to d(A_{12}))((), \quad B_{12} \to dA_{21}(A_{22}))((), \quad B_{12} \to d(A_{32}))((),$$
$$B_{12} \to d(A_{42}))((), \quad B_{12} \to d(A_{52}))((),$$
$$B_{21} \to ((B_{12}))), \quad B_{21} \to (B_{21}(B_{22}))),$$
$$B_{22} \to (A_{12}e), \quad B_{22} \to A_{21}(A_{22}e), \quad B_{22} \to (A_{32}e),$$
$$B_{22} \to (A_{42}e), \quad B_{22} \to (A_{52}e)\}.$$

Continuing, we remove the vertices equivalent to $[B(2)$, namely $[B_{12}(1]$ and $[B_{22}(1]$:

$$\mathcal{S} = \{(B_{1211}(())), \ (B_{1221}(())), \ (B_{1231}(())), \ (B_{1241}(())), \ (B_{1251}(())),$$
$$B_{21}((B_{2212})), \ B_{21}(B_{2221}(B_{2222})), \ B_{21}((B_{2232})), \ B_{21}((B_{2242})),$$
$$B_{21}((B_{2252}))\}$$

$$\mathcal{P} = \{A_{12} \to B_{1211}(()a, \quad A_{12} \to B_{1221}(()a, \quad A_{12} \to B_{1231}(()a,$$
$$A_{12} \to B_{1241}(()a, \quad A_{12} \to B_{1251}(()a,$$
$$A_{21} \to B_{21},$$
$$A_{22} \to (B_{2212}a, \quad A_{22} \to B_{2221}(B_{2222}a, \quad A_{22} \to (B_{2232}a,$$
$$A_{22} \to (B_{2242}a, \quad A_{22} \to (B_{2252}a,$$
$$A_{32} \to b(B_{1211}(())), \quad A_{32} \to b(B_{1221}(())), \quad A_{32} \to b(B_{1231}(())),$$
$$A_{32} \to b(B_{1241}(())), \quad A_{32} \to b(B_{1251}(())),$$
$$A_{42} \to bB_{21}((B_{2212})), \quad A_{42} \to bB_{21}(B_{2221}(B_{2222})),$$
$$A_{42} \to bB_{21}((B_{2232})), \quad A_{42} \to bB_{21}((B_{2242})),$$
$$A_{42} \to bB_{21}((B_{2252})),$$
$$A_{52} \to c(,$$
$$B_{1211} \to d(A_{12})), \quad B_{1221} \to dA_{21}(A_{22})),$$
$$B_{1231} \to d(A_{32})), \quad B_{1241} \to d(A_{42})), \quad B_{1251} \to d(A_{52})),$$
$$B_{21} \to ((B_{1211}(()))), \quad B_{21} \to ((B_{1221}(())))),$$
$$B_{21} \to ((B_{1231}(()))), \quad B_{21} \to ((B_{1241}(())))),$$
$$B_{21} \to ((B_{1251}(()))),$$
$$B_{21} \to (B_{21}((B_{2212}))), \quad B_{21} \to (B_{21}(B_{2221}(B_{2222}))),$$
$$B_{21} \to (B_{21}((B_{2232}))), \quad B_{21} \to (B_{21}((B_{2242}))),$$
$$B_{21} \to (B_{21}((B_{2252}))),$$
$$B_{2212} \to A_{12}e), \quad B_{2221} \to A_{21}, \quad B_{2222} \to A_{22}e),$$
$$B_{2232} \to A_{32}e), \quad B_{2242} \to A_{42}e), \quad B_{2252} \to A_{52}e) \}.$$

It is clear that the vertices equivalent to $[A(2)$, namely $[A_{12}(1]$, $[A_{22}(1]$, $[A_{32}(1]$, $[A_{42}(1]$, and $[A_{52}(1]$, may now be removed in the same fashion, and we will obtain a long, balanced grammar whose nonterminals are $\{A_{1211}, A_{1221}, A_{1231}, A_{1241}, A_{1251}, A_{21}, A_{2212}, A_{2221}, A_{2222}, A_{2232}, A_{2242}, A_{2252}, A_{3212}, A_{3222}, A_{3232}, A_{3242}, A_{3252}, A_{4211}, A_{4212}, A_{4221}, A_{4222}, A_{4231}, A_{4232}, A_{4241}, A_{4242}, A_{4251}, A_{4252}, B_{1211}, B_{1221}, B_{1231}, B_{1241}, B_{1251}, B_{21}, B_{2212}, B_{2221}, B_{2222}, B_{2232}, B_{2242}, B_{2252}\}$. And we will see shortly that $L(\mathcal{G})$ is in fact a parenthesis language.

4. The Main Theorem

The construction in the previous section allows us to work with balanced grammars. But there obviously are grammars (for example, those with no parentheses at all) that are balanced but do not correspond to a language with bounded associates.

   The next result is the final link in the chain needed to characterize parenthesis languages:

Lemma 6. *Let $\mathcal{G} = (\Sigma, V, \mathcal{S}, \mathcal{P})$ be a balanced grammar for which $L(\mathcal{G})$ is balanced and has bounded associates. Then it is possible to construct a parenthesis grammar $\mathcal{G}'$ effectively from $\mathcal{G}$, where $L(\mathcal{G}') = L(\mathcal{G})$.*

Proof. As in the proof of Theorem 3, we may assume that $\mathcal{G}$ is not circular. Let us also add a new nonterminal symbol S, new productions $S \to \sigma$ for all $\sigma \in \mathcal{S}$, and change $\mathcal{S}$ to $\{S\}$. The resulting equivalent grammar $\mathcal{G}_1$ is balanced since $L(\mathcal{G})$ and $\mathcal{G}$ are balanced.

   Now we can modify $\mathcal{G}_1$ by successively applying Transformation 1 of the previous section, until we obtain a grammar $\mathcal{G}_2$ in which the right-hand sides of all productions have one of the forms

$$\theta \quad \text{or} \quad (\theta)$$

where $\theta \in U^*$; that is, θ is a string with no parentheses. For example, the production

$$A \to a((Bc)d(e)f)$$

can be replaced by the set

$$A \to aX$$
$$X \to (YdZf)$$
$$Y \to (Bc)$$
$$Z \to (e)$$

where X, Y, and Z are new nonterminals.

   Now in $\mathcal{G}_2$ let us define the relation $A \prec B$ for nonterminals A and B if there exists a production $A \to \alpha B \omega$ such that α and ω are in U^*. This relation generates a transitive completion relation $A \prec^+ B$ as before.

   It is impossible to have $A \prec^+ A$ for any nonterminal A; for this would imply $A \to^+ \alpha A \omega$ for some balanced strings $\alpha, \omega \in \Sigma^*$. Since $\mathcal{G}$ is not circular we would have $\alpha \omega \neq \epsilon$; and (as in the proof of Theorem 3) $L(\mathcal{G})$ would not have bounded associates.

Therefore the relation $\prec^+$ is a partial ordering, and it is possible to arrange the nonterminals of $\mathcal{G}_2$ into a sequence $A_1, A_2, \ldots, A_n$ such that

$$A_j \prec^+ A_k \text{ implies } j < k.$$

Let us add new nonterminals $X_1, X_2, \ldots, X_n$ to $\mathcal{G}_2$, add the productions $A_j \to X_j$ for $1 \le j \le n$, and replace every production of the form $A_j \to (\theta)$ by the production $X_j \to (\theta)$. Finally let us remove the nonterminals $A_1, \ldots, A_n$ as follows: Assume that all A_k have been removed for $k > j$, and apply Transformation 2 of the previous section to A_j; this removes A_j. If this process is performed for $j = n, \ldots,$ 2, 1, we clearly obtain a parenthesis grammar, since all productions not involving parentheses have been removed and no new ones have been created. □

As an example of the construction in Lemma 6, consider the grammar $\mathcal{G}$ with $\Sigma = \{(,), a, b, c\}$, $V = \Sigma \cup \{A, B\}$, $\mathcal{S} = \{A(B), c\}$, and

$$\mathcal{P} = \{ A \to aBB, \quad A \to (A), \quad B \to \epsilon, \quad B \to (B)(Ab) \}.$$

The grammar $\mathcal{G}_1$ is $(\Sigma, V_1, \mathcal{S}_1, \mathcal{P}_1)$ where $V_1 = V \cup \{S\}$, $\mathcal{S}_1 = \{S\}$, $\mathcal{P}_1 = \mathcal{P} \cup \{S \to A(B), S \to c\}$. The grammar $\mathcal{G}_2$ is $(\Sigma, V_1 \cup \{C, D\}, \{S\}, \mathcal{P}_2)$ where

$$\mathcal{P}_2 = \{A \to aBB, \ A \to (A), \ B \to \epsilon, \ B \to CD,$$
$$C \to (B), \ D \to (Ab), \ S \to AC, \ S \to c\}.$$

We have $S \prec A \prec B \prec C$ and $B \prec D$. Adding new nonterminals X_A, X_B, X_C, X_D, and X_S, these productions are changed to

$$\{A \to X_A, \quad A \to aBB, \quad X_A \to (A),$$
$$B \to X_B, \quad B \to \epsilon, \quad B \to CD,$$
$$C \to X_C, \quad X_C \to (B),$$
$$D \to X_D, \quad X_D \to (Ab),$$
$$S \to X_S, \quad S \to AC, \quad S \to c\}.$$

Eliminating D, C, and then B, and noting that X_B and X_S are useless, we get

$$\{A \to X_A, \quad A \to a, \quad A \to aX_C X_D, \quad A \to aX_C X_D X_C X_D,$$
$$X_A \to (A),$$
$$X_C \to (), \quad X_C \to (X_C X_D),$$
$$X_D \to (Ab),$$
$$S \to AX_C, \quad S \to c\}.$$

Finally we eliminate A and then S, to obtain the parenthesis grammar $\mathcal{G}' = (\Sigma, V', \mathcal{S}', \mathcal{P}')$ where $V' = \Sigma \cup \{X_A, X_C, X_D\}$, $\mathcal{S}' = \{X_A X_C, a X_C,$ $a X_C X_D X_C, a X_C X_D X_C X_D X_C, c\}$, and

$$\mathcal{P}' = \{X_A \to (X_A), \quad X_A \to (a), \quad X_A \to (a X_C X_D),$$
$$X_A \to (a X_C X_D X_C X_D),$$
$$X_C \to (), \quad X_C \to (X_C X_D),$$
$$X_D \to (X_A b), \quad X_D \to (ab),$$
$$X_D \to (a X_C X_D b), \quad X_D \to (a X_C X_D X_C X_D b)\}.$$

Theorem 4. *A context-free language is a parenthesis language if and only if it is balanced and has bounded associates. If $\mathcal{G} = (\Sigma, V, \mathcal{S}, \mathcal{P})$ is a context-free grammar, there is an effective algorithm that determines whether or not $L(\mathcal{G})$ is a parenthesis language; and if $L(\mathcal{G})$ is a parenthesis language, a parenthesis grammar $\mathcal{G}' = (\Sigma, V', \mathcal{S}', \mathcal{P}')$ can be effectively constructed from $\mathcal{G}$.*

Proof. If $\mathcal{G}$ is a parenthesis grammar, $L(\mathcal{G})$ is balanced and has bounded associates by Lemma 3. Conversely if $\mathcal{G}$ is any grammar such that $L(\mathcal{G})$ is balanced and has bounded associates, we can apply Theorem 3 and then Lemma 6 to construct an equivalent parenthesis grammar.

To solve the stated decision problem, we can first decide if $L(\mathcal{G})$ is balanced, using the method of Theorem 1. If it is balanced, we can continue by finding a completely qualified grammar as in Lemma 5. Now the construction in the proof of Theorem 3 can be carried out, unless the directed graph $\mathcal{D}$ defined there has oriented cycles; $\mathcal{D}$ can be constructed effectively and examined for cycles. If we get through the construction in Theorem 3, we still cannot be sure that $L(\mathcal{G})$ has bounded associates, but the construction in the proof of Lemma 6 can be carried out unless the relation $A \prec^+ B$ is not a partial ordering; the latter condition is also equivalent to the existence of an oriented cycle in an appropriate directed graph (namely a directed graph with arcs from A to B if $A \prec B$). Hence we have an algorithm that either constructs the desired grammar $\mathcal{G}'$ or establishes the impossibility of such a construction. ☐

Corollary. *If $\mathcal{G} = (\Sigma, V, \mathcal{S}, \mathcal{P})$ is any context-free grammar and if $\mathcal{G}' = (\Sigma', V', \mathcal{S}', \mathcal{P}')$ is a parenthesis grammar, there is an effective algorithm to decide if $L(\mathcal{G}) = L(\mathcal{G}')$.*

Proof. First decide if $L(\mathcal{G})$ is a parenthesis language; and if it is, find a parenthesis grammar $\mathcal{G}''$ equivalent to $\mathcal{G}$. Then use the procedure of McNaughton [3], or the procedure described in the next section, to decide if $L(\mathcal{G}'') = L(\mathcal{G}')$. ☐

Theorem 4 and its corollary can be extended to grammars in which several kinds of parentheses are used — for example, both parentheses and brackets — as in Ginsburg and Harrison [2], where considerably more restrictive conditions are imposed. Each type of parenthesis pair can be replaced by two symbols $(a$ and $a)$, where a identifies the kind of parenthesis being used. It follows that we can solve the three open problems stated by Ginsburg and Harrison [2, page 20] by considering all possible choices for the parenthesis pairs, using rather simple arguments; details are omitted.

The corollary to Theorem 4 cannot be extended to the case that $\mathcal{G}'$ is a balanced grammar, since even the superficially simple problem of deciding whether $L(\mathcal{G}) = T^*$ is well-known to be recursively unsolvable (see Bar-Hillel, Perles, and Shamir [1]). It follows also that we cannot extend the corollary to "one-sided" parenthesis grammars, since we cannot decide if $L(\mathcal{G})$ equals

$$L\big((\{(,a,b\},\quad \{(,a,b,S\},\quad \{S\},\quad \{S \to \epsilon,\ S \to (aS,\ S \to (bS\,\}\big).$$

5. Boolean Properties of Parenthesis Languages

Now let us study the relationships satisfied by parenthesis languages with respect to set operations. It is obvious from the definition that the set of parenthesis languages is closed under union and concatenation; for if we are given parenthesis grammars $\mathcal{G}_1 = (\Sigma, V_1, \mathcal{S}_1, \mathcal{P}_1)$ and $\mathcal{G}_2 = (\Sigma, V_2, \mathcal{S}_2, \mathcal{P}_2)$, where we may assume that $V_1 \setminus \Sigma$ and $V_2 \setminus \Sigma$ are disjoint, then the grammars $\mathcal{G}_3 = (\Sigma, V_1 \cup V_2, \mathcal{S}_1 \cup \mathcal{S}_2, \mathcal{P}_1 \cup \mathcal{P}_2)$ and $\mathcal{G}_4 = (\Sigma, V_1 \cup V_2, \mathcal{S}_1 \mathcal{S}_2, \mathcal{P}_1 \cup \mathcal{P}_2)$ generate $L(\mathcal{G}_1) \cup L(\mathcal{G}_2)$ and $L(\mathcal{G}_1)L(\mathcal{G}_2)$, respectively. Much more is true:

Theorem 5. *The set of parenthesis languages is closed under relative complementation. (In other words, if L_1 and L_2 are parenthesis languages, so is $L_1 \setminus L_2$.)*

Proof. Let $\mathcal{G}_1 = (\Sigma, V_1, \mathcal{S}_1, \mathcal{P}_1)$ and $\mathcal{G}_2 = (\Sigma, V_2, \mathcal{S}_2, \mathcal{P}_2)$ be parenthesis grammars, and assume that the nonterminal alphabets $N_1 = V_1 \setminus \Sigma$ and $N_2 = V_2 \setminus \Sigma$ are disjoint. Let V be Σ plus the set of all pairs $[A, \mathcal{B}]$ where A is in N_1 and $\mathcal{B}$ is a subset of N_2. For any pair of strings θ_1 and θ_2 over $(V_1 \cup V_2 \cup V)^*$, let

$$\theta_1 \sim \theta_2$$

mean that θ_1 and θ_2 are of the same length and agree at all terminals, namely that we can write $\theta_1 = x_1 x_2 \ldots x_n$ and $\theta_2 = y_1 y_2 \ldots y_n$, where $x_j = y_j$ whenever either x_j or y_j is in Σ.

Now define the set $\alpha \doteq \beta$ for strings $\alpha \in V^*$ and $\beta \in V_2^*$ as follows, when $\alpha = x_1 \ldots x_n$ and $\beta = y_1 \ldots y_m$:

$$\alpha \doteq \beta = \begin{cases} \{ x_1 \ldots x_{k-1} [A, \mathcal{B} \cup \{y_k\}] x_{k+1} \ldots x_n \\ \qquad \mid 1 \leq k \leq n \text{ and } x_k = [A, \mathcal{B}] \}, & \text{if } \alpha \sim \beta; \\ \{\alpha\}, & \text{if } \alpha \not\sim \beta . \end{cases}$$

This "difference" operation may be extended to sets as follows:

$$\{\alpha_1, \ldots, \alpha_m\} \doteq \emptyset = \{\alpha_1, \ldots, \alpha_m\};$$
$$\{\alpha_1, \ldots, \alpha_m\} \doteq \beta = \bigcup_{j=1}^{m} (\alpha_j \doteq \beta);$$
$$\{\alpha_1, \ldots, \alpha_m\} \doteq \{\beta_1, \ldots, \beta_n\} =$$
$$\qquad (\{\alpha_1, \ldots, \alpha_m\} \doteq \{\beta_1, \ldots, \beta_{n-1}\}) \doteq \beta_n, \qquad n \geq 1.$$

It is not difficult to verify that $(\alpha \doteq \beta) \doteq \gamma = (\alpha \doteq \gamma) \doteq \beta$, so the definition of $\{\alpha_1, \ldots, \alpha_m\} \doteq \{\beta_1, \ldots, \beta_n\}$ does not depend on the order of the α's or the β's. Furthermore we have $\{\alpha_1, \ldots, \alpha_m\} \doteq \{\beta_1, \ldots, \beta_n\} = \bigcup_{j=1}^{m} (\alpha_j \doteq \{\beta_1, \ldots, \beta_n\})$.

Let us now proceed to construct a grammar $\mathcal{G}$ for $L(\mathcal{G}_1) \setminus L(\mathcal{G}_2)$. We define $\tau(a) = a$ for $a \in \Sigma$, $\tau(A) = [A, \emptyset]$ for $A \in N_1$, and $\tau(x_1 x_2 \ldots x_n) = \tau(x_1)\tau(x_2) \ldots \tau(x_n)$ for $x_1 x_2 \ldots x_n$ in V_1^*. This mapping embeds V_1^* into V^*. Now $\mathcal{G} = (\Sigma, V, \mathcal{S}, \mathcal{P})$ where

$$\mathcal{S} = \tau(\mathcal{S}_1) \doteq \mathcal{S}_2;$$
$$\mathcal{P} = \{[A, \mathcal{B}] \to \theta \mid \theta \in \tau(\rho(A)) \doteq \rho(\mathcal{B})\},$$

where $\rho(A) = \{\theta \mid A \to \theta\}$ and $\rho(\mathcal{B}) = \{\theta \mid B \to \theta \text{ for some } B \in \mathcal{B}\}$.

Let $\to_1$, $\to_2$, and $\to$ denote respectively the production relations in $\mathcal{G}_1$, $\mathcal{G}_2$, and $\mathcal{G}$. In order to show that $L(\mathcal{G}) = L(\mathcal{G}_1) \setminus L(\mathcal{G}_2)$, we will prove that for every terminal string $\theta \in \Sigma^*$, we have

$$[A, \mathcal{B}] \to^* \theta \text{ if and only if } A \to_1^* \theta \text{ and } B \not\to_2^* \theta \text{ for all } B \in \mathcal{B}.$$

This fact is almost obvious, yet it is almost impossible to explain in a few words; it is hoped that the reader will see (after the long explanation that follows) why it is obvious.

First assume that $[A, \mathcal{B}] \to^* \theta$. By replacing all pairs $[A', \mathcal{B}']$ by A' in this derivation we obtain a derivation $A \to_1^* \theta$ in $\mathcal{G}_1$. Let this derivation be $A \to_1 \varphi \to_1^* \theta$. Now since we have a parenthesis grammar, the string φ has the form $(\alpha_0 A_1 \alpha_1 A_2 \ldots \alpha_{k-1} A_k \alpha_k)$ where

$k \geq 0$ and $\alpha_0\alpha_1\ldots\alpha_k \in T^*$ and $A_1A_2\ldots A_k \in N_1^*$; furthermore $\theta = (\alpha_0\theta_1\alpha_1\theta_2\ldots\alpha_{k-1}\theta_k\alpha_k)$ where $A_j \to_1^* \theta_j$ for $1 \leq j \leq k$. Assume that there is some $B \in \mathcal{B}$ such that $B \to_2^* \theta$; then by the same reasoning $B \to_2 \chi = (\alpha_0 B_1\alpha_1 B_2\ldots\alpha_{k-1}B_k\alpha_k)$ and $B_j \to_2^* \theta_j$ for $1 \leq j \leq k$. Similarly $[A,\mathcal{B}] \to \psi = (\alpha_0[A_1,\mathcal{B}_1]\ldots[A_k,\mathcal{B}_k]\alpha_k)$ and $[A_j,\mathcal{B}_j] \to^* \theta_j$ for $1 \leq j \leq k$. In particular $\varphi \sim \chi \sim \psi$, and by the construction of $\mathcal{G}$ we know that $\chi \in \rho(\mathcal{B})$ and $\psi \in \tau(\rho(A)) \dot{-} \rho(\mathcal{B}) = \bigcup\{\tau(\sigma) \dot{-} \rho(\mathcal{B}) \mid \sigma \in \rho(A)\}$. Since $A_1,\ldots,A_k$ appear as the first components of the nonterminal symbols of ψ, and since the $\dot{-}$ operation does not affect those components, we must have $\psi \in \tau(\varphi) \dot{-} \rho(\mathcal{B})$. Hence by the definition of $\tau(\varphi) \dot{-} \rho(\mathcal{B})$ we must have $B_j \in \mathcal{B}_j$ for some j. But by induction on the length of derivation, $[A_j,\mathcal{B}_j] \to^* \theta_j$ implies $B_j \nleftrightarrow_2^* \theta_j$, and this is a contradiction.

Conversely assume that $A \to_1^* \theta$ and that $B \nleftrightarrow_2^* \theta$ for all $B \in \mathcal{B}$. Then as above there is some $\varphi \in \rho(A)$ having the form $(\alpha_0 A_1\ldots A_k\alpha_k)$, where $A_j \to_1^* \theta_j$ and $\theta = (\alpha_0\theta_1\ldots\theta_k\alpha_k)$. Let $\rho(\mathcal{B}) = \{\chi_1,\chi_2,\ldots,\chi_r\}$ and consider the sets $\mathcal{T}_q = \tau(\varphi) \dot{-} \{\chi_1,\ldots,\chi_q\}$ for $0 \leq q \leq r$. It suffices to show by induction on q that there is some element $\psi \in \mathcal{T}_q$ such that $\psi \to^* \theta$, for then we have $[A,\mathcal{B}] \to \psi \to^* \theta$ for some ψ in $\mathcal{T}_r$. The condition is obvious when $q = 0$ because $\mathcal{G}_1$ is actually embedded in $\mathcal{G}$; that is, $\sigma \to_1^* \sigma'$ certainly implies $\tau(\sigma) \to^* \tau(\sigma')$. When $q > 0$, suppose $\chi_q \nsim \varphi$; then $\mathcal{T}_q = \mathcal{T}_{q-1}$. If $\chi_q \sim \varphi$ then we know by hypothesis that $\chi_q = (\alpha_0 B_1\ldots B_k\alpha_k)$ where $B_j \nleftrightarrow_2^* \theta_j$ for some j. Take $\psi \in \mathcal{T}_{q-1}$ such that $\psi \to^* \theta$; then if $\psi = (\alpha_0[A_1,\mathcal{B}_1]\ldots[A_k,\mathcal{B}_k]\alpha_k)$, the element ψ' obtained from ψ by replacing $\mathcal{B}_j$ by $(\mathcal{B}_j \cup \{B_j\})$ is in $\mathcal{T}_q$. By induction on the length of derivation, $[A_j,\mathcal{B}_j \cup \{B_j\}] \to^* \theta_j$ so $\psi' \to^* \theta$.

To complete the proof that $L(\mathcal{G}) = L(\mathcal{G}_1) \setminus L(\mathcal{G}_2)$, note that the arguments just stated amount to a proof that $\alpha \to \theta \in \Sigma^*$ for some α in $\tau(\{\sigma_1,\ldots,\sigma_m\}) \dot{-} \{\rho_1,\ldots,\rho_n\}$ if and only if there is some $t \leq m$ such that $\sigma_t \to_1^* \theta$, yet $\rho_s \nleftrightarrow_2^* \theta$ for $1 \leq s \leq n$. Therefore the construction of $\mathcal{S}$ leads to precisely the strings of $L(\mathcal{G}_1) \setminus L(\mathcal{G}_2)$. $\quad\square$

As an example of this construction, let $\Sigma = \{(,)\} \cup T$ where

$$T = \{a,b,c,d\}, \quad V_1 = \Sigma \cup \{X,Y\}, \quad V_2 = \Sigma \cup \{A,B\},$$
$$\mathcal{S}_1 = \{aXY,a\},$$
$$\mathcal{S}_2 = \{aAB,aBB,b\},$$
$$\mathcal{P}_1 = \{X \to (YaX), \; X \to (b),$$
$$\qquad Y \to (XcX), \; Y \to (d)\},$$
$$\mathcal{P}_2 = \{A \to (BaA), \; A \to (b),$$
$$\qquad B \to (AcB), \; B \to (BcA), \; B \to (b), \; B \to (d)\}.$$

Using the notation $[X]$ to stand for $[X, \emptyset]$ and $[X; B_1, \ldots, B_n]$ to stand for $[X, \{B_1, \ldots, B_n\}]$, we have the following grammar $\mathcal{G}$ for the relative complement $L(\mathcal{G}_1) \setminus L(\mathcal{G}_2)$:

$$V = \Sigma \cup \{[X], [X; A], [X; B], [X; A, B], [Y], [Y; B]\},$$
$$S = \{a[X; A, B][Y], \ a[X; A][Y; B], \ a[X; B][Y; B], \ a[X][Y; B], \ a\},$$
$$\mathcal{P} = \{[X] \rightarrow ([Y]a[X]), \ [X] \rightarrow (b),$$
$$[X; A] \rightarrow ([Y; B]a[X]), \ [X; A] \rightarrow ([Y]a[X; A]),$$
$$[X; B] \rightarrow ([Y]a[X]),$$
$$[X; A, B] \rightarrow ([Y; B]a[X]), \ [X; A, B] \rightarrow ([Y]a[X; A]),$$
$$[Y] \rightarrow ([X]c[X]), \ [Y] \rightarrow (d),$$
$$[Y; B] \rightarrow ([X; A]c[X]), \ [Y; B] \rightarrow ([X]c[X; B]),$$
$$[Y; B] \rightarrow ([X; B]c[X]), \ [Y; B] \rightarrow ([X]c[X; A])\}.$$

The nonterminal symbols $[Y; A]$ and $[Y; A, B]$ are useless so they have been omitted.

Corollary 1. *The set of parenthesis languages is closed under intersection.*

Proof. $L_1 \cap L_2 = L_1 \cup L_2 \setminus \left(((L_1 \cup L_2) \setminus L_1) \cup ((L_1 \cup L_2) \setminus L_2)\right)$. Alternatively it is possible to construct $L_1 \cap L_2$ in a natural way: If $x_1 \ldots x_n \sim y_1 \ldots y_n$, define the string $x_1 \ldots x_n \cap y_1 \ldots y_n$ to be $(x_1 \cap y_1) \ldots (x_n \cap y_n)$ where $a \cap a = a$ for $a \in \Sigma$; $A \cap B = [A, B]$ for $A \in V_1$ and $B \in V_2$. The details are straightforward. □

Corollary 2. *If $\mathcal{G}_1$ and $\mathcal{G}_2$ are parenthesis grammars, there is an algorithm to decide if $L(\mathcal{G}_1) = L(\mathcal{G}_2)$.*

Proof. The construction in the proof of Theorem 5 yields grammars for $L(\mathcal{G}_1) \setminus L(\mathcal{G}_2)$ and $L(\mathcal{G}_2) \setminus L(\mathcal{G}_1)$, and it is easy to test if those languages are empty. (For typical languages, however, the construction of McNaughton [3] may lead to a simpler way to test this special condition.) □

Corollary 3. *The complement of a parenthesis language is a context-free language.*

Proof. By Theorem 4, every parenthesis language over Σ is contained in some language $P_n(\Sigma)$ given by the grammar $\mathcal{G} = (\Sigma, V, S_n, \mathcal{P}_n)$, where

$$V = \Sigma \cup \{A\},$$
$$S_n = \{\sigma \mid \sigma \in (T \cup \{A\})^* \text{ and } |\sigma| \leq n\},$$
$$\mathcal{P}_n = \{A \rightarrow (\theta) \mid \theta \in S_n\}.$$

This grammar defines the set of all parenthesized formulas over Σ with associates bounded by n. If $L \subseteq P_n(\Sigma)$, then $\Sigma^* \setminus L = (\Sigma^* \setminus P_n(\Sigma)) \cup (P_n(\Sigma) \setminus L)$, hence by Theorem 5 it suffices to show that $\Sigma^* \setminus P_n(\Sigma)$ is context-free. A grammar for the latter is readily constructed; for example:

$$(\Sigma, \quad \Sigma \cup \{A, B, C, X, Z\}, \quad \{A\}X, \ X(A, \ B\}, \quad \mathcal{P})$$

where $\mathcal{P}$ consists of the productions

$$A \to Y, \quad A \to Y(A)A,$$
$$B \to C^{n+1}A, \quad B \to A(B)A,$$
$$C \to Z, \quad C \to Y(A)A,$$
$$X \to \epsilon, \quad X \to aX \quad \text{for all } a \in \Sigma,$$
$$Y \to \epsilon, \quad Y \to aY \quad \text{for all } a \in T,$$
$$Z \to aY \quad \text{for all } a \in T.$$

Here $L(A) = \{$balanced strings$\}$, $L(B) = \{$balanced strings with more than n associates$\}$, $L(C) = L(A) \setminus \{\epsilon\}$, $L(X) = \Sigma^*$, $L(Y) = T^*$, and $L(Z) = T^+$. $\quad \Box$

Corollary 4. *If $\mathcal{G}_1$ is a context-free grammar and $\mathcal{G}_2$ is a parenthesis grammar, there is an algorithm to decide whether or not $L(\mathcal{G}_1) \subseteq L(\mathcal{G}_2)$.*

Proof. If $L(\mathcal{G}_1) \subseteq L(\mathcal{G}_2)$ then $L(\mathcal{G}_1)$ is balanced and has bounded associates, so $L(\mathcal{G}_1)$ must be a parenthesis language. Therefore we may test whether $L(\mathcal{G}_1)$ is a parenthesis language, and then whether $L(\mathcal{G}_1) \setminus L(\mathcal{G}_2)$ is empty. $\quad \Box$

The related problem, whether $L(\mathcal{G}_2) \subseteq L(\mathcal{G}_1)$, is *unsolvable* in general, as shown by the following construction. Let $\alpha_1, \ldots, \alpha_n, \beta_1, \ldots, \beta_n$ be nonempty strings on the alphabet $\{a, b\}$. Let L_0 be the language over the alphabet $\{(,), a, b, c_1, \ldots, c_n\}$ derivable from S via the productions

$$S \to S),$$
$$\left. \begin{array}{l} S \to (x_{j1}(x_{j2} \ldots (x_{jk_j} S c_j, \\ S \to (x_{j1}(x_{j2} \ldots (x_{jk_j} c_j, \end{array} \right\} \text{ if } \alpha_j = x_{j1} \ldots x_{jk_j}, \ 1 \leq j \leq n.$$

Let L_2 be the parenthesis language over the same alphabet derivable from S in the grammar

$$\left. \begin{array}{l} S \to (x_{j1}(x_{j2} \ldots (x_{jl_j} S c_j)^{l_j}, \\ S \to (x_{j1}(x_{j2} \ldots (x_{jl_j} c_j)^{l_j}, \end{array} \right\} \text{ if } \beta_j = x_{j1} \ldots x_{jl_j}, \ 1 \leq j \leq n.$$

Clearly the Post correspondence problem for $\alpha_1, \ldots, \alpha_n, \beta_1, \ldots, \beta_n$ has a solution if and only if $L_0 \cap L_2 \neq \emptyset$. It is also easy to verify that L_1, the complement of L_0, is context-free. Therefore the Post correspondence problem has a solution if and only if $L_2 \nsubseteq L_1$. □

Acknowledgment

The author wishes to express deep appreciation to the referee of this paper, for careful reading of the manuscript and for many helpful suggestions about the style of presentation.

The preparation of this paper was supported in part by the National Science Foundation under grant GP-3909.

References

[1] Y. Bar-Hillel, M. Perles, and E. Shamir, "On formal properties of simple phrase structure grammars," *Zeitschrift für Phonetik, Sprachwissenschaft und Kommunikationsforschung* **14** (1961), 143–172.

[2] Seymour Ginsburg and Michael A. Harrison, "Bracketed context-free languages," *Journal of Computer and System Sciences* **1** (1967), 1–23.

[3] Robert McNaughton, "Parenthesis grammars," *Journal of the Association for Computing Machinery* **14** (1967), 490–500.

Addendum

For more recent results, see Jean Berstel and Luc Boasson, "XML grammars," *Lecture Notes in Computer Science* **1893** (2000), 182–191.

Chapter 14

Top-Down Syntax Analysis

[Originally presented as a series of lectures at the NATO International Summer School on Computer Programming in Lyngby, Denmark, during August 1967, and published in Acta Informatica 1 (1971), 79–110.]

The theory and practice of classical "top-down" parsing methods are presented in a tutorial manner.

1. Introduction

Since the earliest days when automatic syntax analysis by computer was first attempted, many people (for example, Glennie [10], Brooker, Morris, and Rohl [3][4][19], Barnett and Futrelle [2], Conway [7], Cheatham and Sattley [6], Schorre [22], and Banerji [1]) have used a method that has become known as "top-down" analysis. The idea is still popular, and it is being used in many current compilers.

The discussion in these lectures will deal only with the *syntactic* properties of the top-down method of analysis, not with the manner in which the syntactic structure is ultimately used to obtain semantic information about the strings being analyzed. Semantic information is, of course, the real reason why syntactic analysis is done in the first place; and top-down analysis is popular chiefly because it lends itself so conveniently to semantic extensions. But we will accept this fact on faith, and concentrate only on the syntactic aspects. Further details can be found in the references cited above.

We shall be concerned principally with methods that apply to languages defined by unambiguous context-free grammars, which occur frequently in programming languages and in the input data formats for data-processing systems. The purpose of these lectures is to point out some interconnections between theory and practice, and to analyze the situations in which simple top-down syntax-oriented methods can be guaranteed to work.

Section 2 introduces an abstract computer-like device called the Parsing Machine, which resembles the interpretive routines often used for top-down syntax analysis. Section 3 shows how BNF grammars define programs for this machine in a natural way. Section 4 examines the problem of proving such programs correct.

Section 5 is an exposition of the basic theory of context-free grammars. Section 6 shows how to decide simple properties of grammars, and Section 7 gives graph-theoretical constructions that are useful for grammatical analysis. These results are applied in Section 8 to characterize all grammars for which a "no-backup" Parsing Machine program is valid.

Section 9 contrasts top-down and bottom-up analysis from a theoretical point of view, and Section 10 gives formal definitions of LR(k) and LL(k) grammars. Section 11 shows that the LL(1) languages are precisely those readable without backup by the machine of Section 2. Final observations and research problems are stated in Section 12.

2. The Parsing Machine (PM)

The Parsing Machine is an abstract machine that is designed to analyze strings over a given alphabet. It scans an "input string" one character at a time, from left to right, according to a program. A Parsing Machine program is made up of a family of procedures that call each other recursively; the program itself is one of those procedures. Each procedure attempts to find an occurrence of a particular syntactic type in the input, and it returns with the value "true" or "false" depending on whether it has been successful or not.

Let the input string be $s_1 s_2 \ldots s_n$, and let s_h be the "current" character being scanned by the machine.

All instructions have three fields: an "opcode" (operation code) field, and two addresses, AT and AF. Procedures are written using two types of instructions, corresponding to two different forms of the opcode.

First Type: The opcode is a letter of the alphabet, such as a.

Second Type: The opcode is the location of a procedure enclosed within square brackets, such as $[A]$.

The effects of these instructions are as follows.

Type 1: **if** $s_h = a$
then move past a (that is, set $h := h + 1$) and **go to** AT
else go to AF.

Type 2: Call on the procedure that starts in location A (recursively);
if it returns with the value true **then go to** AT
else if it returns with the value false **then go to** AF.

Each AT or AF field can contain either the location of an instruction, or one of the two special symbols T or F. If it contains T, the procedure returns with the value true. If it contains F, the procedure returns with the value false, and h is *reset* to the value it had when the procedure was called. (Thus the current value of h must be saved together with the return address, whenever a procedure is called by an opcode of Type 2.)

An example program for the Parsing Machine should help to make these definitions clear. Consider the following grammar for a simple language that bears some resemblance to "Boolean expressions," defined by means of classical Backus–Naur (BNF) notation:

⟨Boolean expression⟩ ::= ⟨relation⟩ | (⟨Boolean expression⟩)

⟨relation⟩ ::= ⟨expression⟩ = ⟨expression⟩

⟨expression⟩ ::= a | b | (⟨expression⟩ + ⟨expression⟩)

An equivalent but shorter notation is more convenient for developing the necessary theory; we shall write the grammar as

$$B \rightarrow R \mid (B)$$
$$R \rightarrow E = E \qquad\qquad (2.1)$$
$$E \rightarrow a \mid b \mid (E + E)$$

instead. Furthermore, we will add the additional grammatical rule

$$S \rightarrow B \dashv \qquad\qquad (2.2)$$

in order to make it clear that our overall goal is to parse a Boolean expression. Here '$\dashv$' is a special right delimiter that appears only at the right end of the string being analyzed. Thus S represents an acceptable input string, namely a Boolean expression followed by the end-of-input symbol.

Figure 1 illustrates a Parsing Machine program that corresponds directly to this example grammar (2.1)–(2.2). There are four procedures, B, R, E, and S, one for each nonterminal symbol of the grammar. Procedure B looks for a Boolean expression starting at the current place in the input, procedure R looks for a relation, and so on.

In this example as in all those that will follow later, PM instructions are written in an ad hoc assembly language, using symbolic addresses

location	opcode	AT	AF
B	$[R]$	T	
	(		F
	$[B]$		F
	)	T	F
R	$[E]$		F
	$=$		F
	$[E]$	T	F
E	a	T	
	b	T	
	(		F
	$[E]$		F
	$+$		F
	$[E]$		F
	)	T	F
S	$[B]$		ERROR
	$\dashv$	OK	ERROR

FIGURE 1. A Parsing Machine program that corresponds to (2.1) and (2.2).

and labels. A blank address refers to the location of the instruction that appears on the line immediately following the blank address.

Procedure S is special because it represents an entire input string. Figure 1 has been set up so that, if we start at location S, the machine will go to 'OK' if the entire string being analyzed is a B followed by $\dashv$, otherwise it will go to 'ERROR'.

If we set this PM program to work on the input string

$$(\ a = (\ b + a \ ) \ ) \dashv \ = \ s_1 s_2 \dots s_{10}$$

starting at location S, the sequence of actions begins as follows. (Initially $h = 1$; that is, the first character s_1 is being scanned when we start.)

Call B $(h = 1)$
   Call R $(h = 1)$
      Call E $(h = 1)$
         Look for a: no
         Look for b: no
         Look for (: yes, set $h := 2$

Call E $(h = 2)$
    Look for a: yes, set $h := 3$
    Return, true
  Look for $+$: no
  Return, false; set $h := 1$
Return, false; set $h := 1$
Look for (: yes, set $h := 2$
Call B $(h = 2)$
  Call R $(h = 2)$

and so on. Ultimately the program will go to the location 'OK' and the history of procedure calls with true returns will correspond to the following diagram ("parsing") of the input:

$$
\begin{array}{c}
S \\
B \\
B \\
R \\
E \qquad E \\
\qquad E \quad E \\
(\quad a \;=\; (\; b \;+\; a \;)\;)\;\dashv
\end{array}
\tag{2.3}
$$

This diagram may be thought of as being constructed from the top to bottom by the Parsing Machine program: The left portion of each bracket in the diagram is constructed when calling a procedure, and the right portion is completed when returning from that procedure.

    A study of this program should convince the reader that if $s_1 \ldots s_n$ is *any* sequence of the letters $\{a, b, (, +,), =, \dashv\}$, with only s_n equal to $\dashv$, the PM program goes to OK when $s_1 \ldots s_n$ is of the form $B\dashv$, and its history of true returns corresponds to a parse diagram; otherwise the PM program goes to ERROR. But this assertion requires proof! There are some grammars for which the corresponding PM program will *not* work correctly, as we shall see. Therefore we want to examine the general question, "For what grammars will the corresponding PM program work?"

3. PM Programming

To analyze the general question just asked, we must state carefully what we mean by the "corresponding PM program."

First assume that, as in the example above, all BNF rules have been written in the *standard form*

$$X \to Y_1 \mid Y_2 \mid \ldots \mid Y_m \mid Z_1 Z_2 \ldots Z_n \qquad (3.1)$$

where $m \geq 0$, $n \geq 0$, $m+n > 0$, and the Y's and Z's are either terminal characters (that is, letters of the alphabet) or nonterminal symbols (that is, syntactic types). The right-hand side of (3.1) has $m+1$ alternatives; in particular, it reduces to the simple form

$$X \to Z_1 Z_2 \ldots Z_n$$

when $m = 0$. If $n = 0$ the string $Z_1 Z_2 \ldots Z_n$ is to be regarded as the *empty* string. The PM program corresponding to a rule in standard form consists of the following $m + n$ instructions:

location	opcode	AT	AF	
X	$[Y_1]$	T		
	$[Y_2]$	T		
	$\vdots$	$\vdots$		
	$[Y_m]$	T	$*$	(3.2)
	$[Z_1]$		F	
	$\vdots$		$\vdots$	
	$[Z_{n-1}]$		F	
	$[Z_n]$	T	F	

Brackets around Y_j or Z_j in these opcodes should be removed when Y_j or Z_j is a terminal symbol. The address denoted by '$*$' is to be replaced by 'T' if $n = 0$, otherwise it should be left blank.

The specification (3.2) has to be modified in the trivial case when both $m = 0$ and $n = 0$; then the rule is $X \to \epsilon$, where ϵ denotes the empty string, and the procedure X should always return true without advancing h. The latter effect can be achieved by the PM program

X	$[Q]$	T	T
Q	a	F	F

where a is any terminal letter. Such anomalies are unimportant to the theory, and they disappear when semantic operations are added to the Parsing Machine's repertoire.

When a BNF rule is not in standard form, suppose that it has the form

$$X \to \alpha_1 \mid \ldots \mid \alpha_m \mid Z_1 Z_2 \ldots Z_n \qquad (3.3)$$

where $\alpha_1, \ldots, \alpha_m$ represent strings of terminal or nonterminal symbols. Then we can change it into standard form by introducing new nonterminal symbols $Y_1, \ldots, Y_m$, adding the rules

$$Y_1 \to \alpha_1$$
$$\vdots$$
$$Y_m \to \alpha_m$$

and replacing (3.3) by (3.1). For example, if our BNF grammar has a rule

$$X \to AB \mid CD$$

we change it to two rules

$$X \to Y \mid CD$$
$$Y \to AB$$

that are obviously equivalent. This change allows the PM to back up if it has found an A that is not followed by B; then it can try the other alternative CD.

It is important to observe that the order in which the PM rules are listed can drastically affect the behavior of the machine. For example, if we have the rule

$$X \to a \mid ab \tag{3.4}$$

the corresponding PM program will never recognize the string ab as X, since it will return true once it finds the first a. This rule might therefore be rewritten

$$X \to ab \mid a$$

and transformed into standard form.

A better idea, perhaps, is to avoid making the machine back up, by "factoring" the revised rule into

$$X \to aB$$
$$B \to b \mid \epsilon \tag{3.5}$$

instead.

Further problems can still arise, however, if another rule such as

$$Y \to Xbb \tag{3.6}$$

is also present in the grammar. Then it becomes impossible for the PM to know whether X should be a or ab, without looking ahead to see how many b's follow. This uncertainty can lead to serious difficulties, which we will consider later; fortunately we don't need to worry about such pathological problems in most languages of practical interest.

The principle of "factoring," illustrated in (3.5), can be quite important for simplifying and speeding up PM programs. It is convenient to rewrite (3.5) as

$$X \to a \, [\![\, b \mid \epsilon \,]\!]$$

making use of "meta-brackets" $[\![$ and $]\!]$ to group alternatives together, so that it is unnecessary to give a special name (like B in (3.5)) to the new syntactic type.

Consider now the rule

$$X \to a \mid b c k \mid b d k \mid b e f i k \mid b e g h i k \mid b e f j k \mid b e g h j k$$

which can be expressed as

$$X \to a \mid b \, [\![\, c \mid d \mid e \, [\![\, f \mid g h \,]\!] \, [\![\, i \mid j \,]\!] \,]\!] \, k \qquad (3.7)$$

in factored form. The introduction of factors in this case does not require procedure calls; only branching is necessary, since the following PM program can be written for X:

X	a	T	
	b		F
	c	X_1	
	d	X_1	
	e		F
	f	X_2	
	g		F
	h	X_2	F
X_2	i	X_1	
	j	X_1	F
X_1	k	T	F

It can be shown that simplifications of this kind can always be made if we redefine standard form (3.1) so that any of the Z's may be factored quantities, which themselves are in standard form. Rule (3.7) is an example of this more general kind of standard form.

Another simplification can be made when we have the "closure" operator A^*, meaning "zero or more occurrences of A in a row," that is, either ϵ or A or AA or AAA, etc. The corresponding syntactic rule is

$$A^* \to AA^* \mid \epsilon$$

which, by our previous conventions, must be expanded into the following rather long PM program, where Y corresponds to AA^*:

location	opcode	AT	AF
A^*	$[Y]$	T	T
Y	$[A]$		F
	$[A^*]$	T	F

A much faster code can be written, which obviously is equivalent except that it saves a great many subroutine calls:

$$A^* \qquad [A] \qquad A^* \qquad T \qquad\qquad (3.8)$$

We can extend the definition of standard form, (3.1), further, so that each Z is allowed to be also of the form W^* where W is a single symbol (terminal or nonterminal).

The two simplifications just discussed, namely factoring and closure, are instances of a general programming rule called "elimination of tail recursion," which allows us to replace a procedure call by a **go to** when that call is the last act of another procedure.

As an example, consider the ALGOL 60 definition of an unsigned number:

$$
\begin{aligned}
D &\to 0 \mid 1 \mid 2 \mid 3 \mid 4 \mid 5 \mid 6 \mid 7 \mid 8 \mid 9 \\
U &\to D\,U' \\
U' &\to U \mid \epsilon \\
P &\to .\,U \\
P' &\to P \mid \epsilon \\
S' &\to + \mid - \mid \epsilon \\
E &\to {}_{10}\,S'\,U \\
E' &\to E \mid \epsilon \\
M &\to P \mid U\,P' \\
N &\to E \mid M\,E'
\end{aligned}
\qquad\qquad (3.9)
$$

Here N is ALGOL's ⟨unsigned number⟩, E is ⟨exponent part⟩, P is ⟨fraction part⟩, and so on. A slight change has been made to the definition of U, ⟨unsigned integer⟩, since ALGOL's definition $U \to UD \mid D$ would get the PM into a loop. Such looping is called "left recursion," and it is the bane of top-down analysis; left recursion is analyzed further below.

Grammar (3.9) can be factored into the following extended standard form:

$$D \to 0 \mid 1 \mid 2 \mid 3 \mid 4 \mid 5 \mid 6 \mid 7 \mid 8 \mid 9$$
$$U \to DD^*$$
$$P \to . \, U \tag{3.10}$$
$$E \to {}_{10}[\![\, + \mid - \mid \epsilon \,]\!] \, U$$
$$N \to E \mid [\![\, P \mid U [\![\, P \mid \epsilon \,]\!] \,]\!] \, [\![\, E \mid \epsilon \,]\!]$$

The corresponding PM program is

location	opcode	AT	AF
D	0	T	
	1	T	
	2	T	
	3	T	
	4	T	
	5	T	
	6	T	
	7	T	
	8	T	
	9	T	F
U	$[D]$	U'	F
U'	$[D]$	U'	T
P	.	U	F
E	${}_{10}$		F
	$+$	U	
	$-$	U	U
N	$[E]$	T	
	$[P]$	N'	
	$[U]$		F
	$[P]$	N'	N'
N'	$[E]$	T	T

and it runs much more efficiently than the PM program corresponding to (3.9). Incidentally, this code has also simplified the two instructions

P	.		F
	$[U]$	T	F

to an equivalent (but faster) one-line form.

Exercise 3.1.* For which set of strings on the alphabet $\{a, b, c\}$ does the following PM program go to 'OK', starting at S?

location	opcode	AT	AF
A	a		T
	$[A]$		F
	b	T	F
B	$[A]$		T
	c	F	T
C	b		T
	$[C]$		F
	c	T	F
S	$[B]$	ERROR	
D	a	D	
	$[C]$		ERROR
	$\dashv$	OK	ERROR

4. The Partial Backup Problem

Examples (3.4) and (3.6) show that the Parsing Machine's limited backup capability makes it unsuitable for BNF grammars in general. But the example of Boolean expressions in Section 2 shows that the PM can handle a reasonably wide range of grammars of practical interest, and we now return to the question posed at the end of that section: "For which BNF grammars, supplemented by the inclusion of a right delimiter $\dashv$ symbol as in (2.2), then converted into standard form (3.1) by the technique of (3.3) and converted into PM programs by the schematic definition of (3.2), does the corresponding PM program accept precisely the strings belonging to the language defined by the grammar?" (In other words, when does the machine go to OK if the string is in the language and to ERROR if the string is not?)

Unfortunately this problem is *unsolvable* in general:

Theorem. *No effective algorithm is able to decide, from a given grammar, whether or not the corresponding PM program will always work.*

Proof. Let $\alpha_1, \ldots, \alpha_m, \beta_1, \ldots, \beta_m$ be strings of a's and b's; and let $z_1, \ldots, z_m, a, b, x$ be the terminal letters of a given alphabet. Consider

---

* Answers to the exercises appear in the appendix below.

the following rules:

$$A \to z_1\alpha_1 \mid \ldots \mid z_m\alpha_m \mid z_1A\alpha_1 \mid \ldots \mid z_mA\alpha_m$$
$$B \to z_1\beta_1 \mid \ldots \mid z_m\beta_m \mid z_1B\beta_1 \mid \ldots \mid z_mB\beta_m$$
$$C \to Ax$$
$$D \to Bxx \tag{4.1}$$
$$E \to C \mid D$$
$$S \to E\dashv$$

Here A represents the strings

$$L(A) = \{z_{i_n} \ldots z_{i_2} z_{i_1} \alpha_{i_1} \alpha_{i_2} \ldots \alpha_{i_n}\}$$

for $n = 1, 2, 3, \ldots$; and B similarly represents

$$L(B) = \{z_{i_n} \ldots z_{i_2} z_{i_1} \beta_{i_1} \beta_{i_2} \ldots \beta_{i_n}\}.$$

The whole language S is $Ax\dashv$ together with $Bxx\dashv$.

Consider a string α belonging to A; the PM will recognize that αx belongs to E.

Consider α not belonging to A but belonging to B; the PM will recognize that αxx belongs to E.

Consider α belonging to both A and B; αxx will not be recognized as belonging to E, although it does.

Therefore the partial backup method will work for this language if and only if $L(A) \cap L(B)$ is empty. And that happens if and only if there do not exist indices $i_1, \ldots, i_n$, $n > 0$, such that $\alpha_{i_1} \ldots \alpha_{i_n} = \beta_{i_1} \ldots \beta_{i_n}$.

But this is "Post's Correspondence Problem" [18], for which it is well known that no effective algorithm can decide if such indices exist. If we could solve the partial backup problem for all languages defined by BNF, we could solve Post's problem, but that is impossible. This completes the proof. □

Although the partial backup problem is unsolvable in general, we can of course solve it in special cases. The most important special case of the partial backup problem is the "No backup problem," which we will solve below.

A method of top-down analysis that includes "full backup" has been described elegantly by Floyd [9]; his method works on all BNF grammars that are not left recursive. We will not discuss Floyd's general method here, however, since most cases of practical interest for programming languages can be handled with little or no backing up.

5. Context-Free Grammars

Let us now look closely at the basic definition of context-free grammars, together with some notations associated with the mathematical theory of languages, in a somewhat more careful manner than we have been doing so far. We are going to solve a special case of an unsolvable problem, so it is worthwhile to prepare ourselves for the task.

An alphabet X is a set of distinguishable symbols, and X^* denotes the set of all strings on X, that is, all sequences $x_1 \ldots x_n$ for $n \geq 0$, where each x_j is in X. It is convenient to denote strings of symbols by lowercase Greek letters α, β, $\ldots$; as we have already observed, the empty (or "null") string is denoted by ϵ. The *length* of a string α, written $|\alpha|$, is the number of symbols it contains. When α and β are strings, their concatenation $\alpha\beta$ is the string obtained by writing the symbols of β in order after the symbols of α. It follows from these definitions, for example, that

$$|\epsilon| = 0, \qquad |\alpha\beta| = |\alpha| + |\beta|.$$

A set of strings is usually denoted by a capital letter, such as A or B. The concatenation of two sets of strings is defined by the rule

$$AB = \{\alpha\beta \mid \alpha \in A \text{ and } \beta \in B\}. \tag{5.1}$$

Notice that

$$A\{\epsilon\} = \{\epsilon\}A = A$$

and

$$A\emptyset = \emptyset A = \emptyset.$$

(The symbol $\emptyset$ denotes the empty set.)

We now define "powers" of a set of strings:

$$A^n = \text{ if } n = 0 \text{ then } \{\epsilon\} \text{ else } AA^{n-1}. \tag{5.2}$$

Two further operations of importance are the *closure* A^* and the *positive closure* A^+ of a set of strings:

$$A^* = \lim_{n \to \infty} \left(A^0 \cup A^1 \cup \cdots \cup A^n\right) = \bigcup_{n \geq 0} A^n \tag{5.3}$$

$$A^+ = \bigcup_{n \geq 1} A^n \tag{5.4}$$

Thus, for example,

$$A^+ = AA^* = A^*A, \qquad A^* = \{\epsilon\} \cup A^+.$$

A *context-free grammar* $\mathcal{G}$ has four parts:

i) A *terminal alphabet* T, whose elements are denoted here by lowercase letters a, b, c, ... and occasionally also by special symbols such as parentheses and plus signs.

ii) A *nonterminal alphabet* N, whose elements are denoted here by uppercase letters $A, B, C, \ldots$.

iii) An *initial symbol* S, which is a nonterminal symbol that represents the "sentences" of the language defined by $\mathcal{G}$.

iv) A set of *productions* $\mathcal{P}$, which is the most important part of the grammar $\mathcal{G}$. A production is a relation denoted by

$$A \to \theta \tag{5.5}$$

(read, "A directly produces θ"), where $A \in N$ and $\theta \in (N \cup T)^*$; that is, A is a nonterminal symbol and θ is a string of terminals and/or nonterminals.

Each set of productions $\mathcal{P}$ defines a relation on the strings $(N \cup T)^*$; we say that

$$\alpha A \omega \to \alpha \theta \omega \tag{5.6}$$

(with respect to $\mathcal{P}$) if $A \to \theta$ is a production of $\mathcal{P}$. In other words, we say that $\varphi \to \psi$ if and only if there are strings α, ω, A, and θ such that $\varphi = \alpha A \omega$, $\psi = \alpha \theta \omega$, and $A \to \theta$ is in $\mathcal{P}$. The production is called "context-free" because it applies regardless of the context α and ω surrounding A.

The relation $\varphi \to \psi$ between strings, defined in (5.6), can be extended as follows: We write

$$\varphi \to^* \psi \tag{5.7}$$

if $\varphi = \psi$, or if $\varphi \to \psi$, or if there is another string χ such that $\varphi \to \chi \to \psi$, or if there are two strings ξ and χ such that $\varphi \to \xi \to \chi \to \psi$, ..., or in general if

$$\varphi = \varphi_0, \qquad \varphi_j \to \varphi_{j+1} \quad \text{for} \quad 0 \le j < n, \quad \text{and} \quad \varphi_n = \psi \tag{5.8}$$

for some $n \ge 0$ and some strings $\varphi_0, \varphi_1, \ldots, \varphi_n$. Relation (5.7) may be read, "φ produces or equals ψ." Similarly we write

$$\varphi \to^+ \psi \tag{5.9}$$

if (5.8) holds for some $n \ge 1$ and some strings $\varphi_0, \ldots, \varphi_n$. Relation (5.9) may be read, "φ produces ψ"; it excludes the case $n = 0$, which in (5.8) is the trivial case that $\varphi = \psi$. Notice the analogy between (5.7)–(5.9) and (5.3)–(5.4).

In general if r denotes any relation between members of any set, we obtain the *reflexive transitive closure* r^* and the *transitive closure* r^+ of r as new relations that are often of interest, by using definitions (5.7)–(5.9) and replacing '$\rightarrow$' by r.

Now we are ready to define the significance of a context-free grammar $\mathcal{G} = (T, N, S, \mathcal{P})$. The *language* $L(\mathcal{G})$ defined by $\mathcal{G}$ is the set

$$L(\mathcal{G}) = \{\tau \in T^* \mid S \rightarrow^+ \tau\}, \tag{5.10}$$

that is, the set of all terminal strings produced by the initial symbol.

If θ is any string of terminals and/or nonterminals, we also write

$$L(\theta) = \{\tau \in T^* \mid \theta \rightarrow^* \tau\} \tag{5.11}$$

with respect to an understood context-free grammar $\mathcal{G}$.

We say that

$$A \rightarrow \theta_1 \mid \theta_2 \mid \ldots \mid \theta_n \tag{5.12}$$

is a *rule* of the grammar $\mathcal{G}$ if and only if

$$\{A \rightarrow \theta_1, \; A \rightarrow \theta_2, \; \ldots, \; A \rightarrow \theta_n\}$$

is the set of all productions of $\mathcal{G}$ whose left-hand side is A.

The reader should be able to see the connection between context-free grammars, as defined here, and BNF syntax specifications as in the ALGOL Report [17]. The only difference is in the notational conventions.

As an example of a context-free grammar, consider the following rules

$$E \rightarrow L \, [\![+L]\!]^*$$
$$L \rightarrow PP^*$$
$$P \rightarrow a \mid b \mid (E)$$

written in terms of the factoring and closure conventions of the previous section. From now on we will eliminate those conventions, in order to simplify the theory without decreasing our power of expression. The grammar above can be rewritten

$$\begin{aligned} &E \rightarrow LL' \\ &L' \rightarrow +LL' \mid \epsilon \\ &L \rightarrow PP' \\ &P' \rightarrow PP' \mid \epsilon \\ &P \rightarrow a \mid b \mid (E) \\ &S \rightarrow E\dashv \end{aligned} \tag{5.13}$$

if we also include a rule for S according to the conventions of our Parsing Machine.

The set of productions (5.13) may be said to define a context-free grammar $\mathcal{G}$ whose six terminal symbols are

$$a, \ b, \ +, \ (, \ ), \ \dashv$$

and whose six nonterminal symbols are

$$E, \ L', \ L, \ P', \ P, \ S.$$

The initial symbol is S. The grammar has six *rules* and ten *productions*. (Notice the distinction between a rule and a production, as in (5.12).) The language defined by $\mathcal{G}$ resembles simple arithmetic expressions on the variables a and b; for example, the string

$$a \ (\ b + a \ b \ ) \ \dashv$$

is a typical element of $L(\mathcal{G})$.

6. The Null String Problem

One of the first things we can do with a context-free grammar is determine which of its nonterminal symbols can produce the null string. That is, we can answer the question "Does $A \rightarrow^+ \epsilon$?" for each A.

A simple marking algorithm applies to this problem. We can imagine all nonterminal symbols to be either "marked" or "unmarked," where initially all are unmarked. Now we repeatedly do the following operation: Find a production in $\mathcal{P}$ whose left-hand side is unmarked, and whose right-hand string contains nothing but marked symbols. (In particular, ϵ is such a right-hand string. Terminal symbols are regarded as unmarked.) If no such productions exist, the algorithm terminates; otherwise, mark the nonterminal symbol on the left of the production that was found, and repeat the process.

At the conclusion of this algorithm, a nonterminal A can produce ϵ if and only if it is marked. For it is clear that every marked nonterminal produces ϵ. Conversely, if $A \rightarrow^+ \epsilon$ in n steps, then if $n = 1$, A must be marked; and if $n > 1$, we have some θ such that $A \rightarrow \theta \rightarrow^+ \epsilon$. Here each symbol in θ must produce ϵ in fewer than n steps, so by induction on n each symbol in θ is marked; hence A is marked.

Essentially the same algorithm can be used to determine whether or not $L(A)$ is empty, that is, whether A produces any terminal strings or not. We use the same procedure, except that all terminal symbols are regarded as if they were marked.

7. Directed Graphs

A *directed graph* is defined by a set of *vertices* and a set of ordered pairs of vertices called *arcs*. Each arc may be thought of as an arrow drawn from one vertex to another vertex (or to the same vertex). An *oriented path* in a directed graph from vertex V to vertex W is a sequence of vertices $V_0, \ldots, V_n$, such that $n \geq 1$, $V = V_0$, there is an arc from V_j to V_{j+1} for $0 \leq j < n$, and $V_n = W$. Efficient algorithms are known [23] by which we can readily determine whether or not there is an oriented path from V to W, given any two vertices V and W of a finite directed graph.

Given any context-free grammar $\mathcal{G}$, we can draw its *dependency graph*. Here the vertices are the terminal and nonterminal symbols, and an arc goes from A to x if x appears on the right-hand side of a production whose left-hand side is A. For example, the grammar of (5.13) has

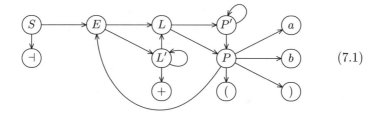

(7.1)

as its dependency graph.

There is an obvious correspondence between directed graphs and binary relations on objects of an abstract set S: Given any relation r, we can consider the directed graph whose vertices are the elements of S and whose arcs go from V to W if and only if $V r W$. Conversely each directed graph defines a relation on its vertices. There is a path from V to W if and only if $V r^+ W$, in the notation of Section 5.

In the case of context-free grammars, let us write

$$X d Y \quad (\text{“}X \text{ directly depends on } Y\text{”})$$

if and only if there is an arc from X to Y in the dependency graph; that is, if and only if there is a production rule $X \to \varphi Y \psi$ in the grammar, for some strings φ and ψ.

Now $X d^+ Y$ (“X depends on Y”) is easily seen to be equivalent to the statement that

$$X \to^+ \alpha Y \omega$$

for some strings α and ω. If $X d^+ X$, we say X is *recursive* (it depends on itself). This means there is an oriented cycle in the dependency graph. In (7.1), we see that all nonterminals are recursive except S.

A nonterminal symbol A of $\mathcal{G}$ is called *useless* if either $L(A) = \emptyset$ (that is, no terminal strings can be derived from A), or if S does not depend on A (that is, the strings derivable from A have no effect on $L(\mathcal{G})$). The discussion above shows that we can easily determine all of the useless nonterminal symbols. These symbols (and all productions involving them) can be removed from the grammar with no effect on the language, provided that S itself is not useless.

In addition to the dependency graph, we can also define the *right dependency graph*, which is a subgraph of the dependency graph of a grammar. In this case we draw an arc from X to Y if and only if there is a production of the form

$$X \to \alpha Y X_1 \dots X_n$$

where $n \geq 0$, and where each of $X_1, \dots, X_n$ can produce the null string. For the grammar (5.13), we have the right dependency graph

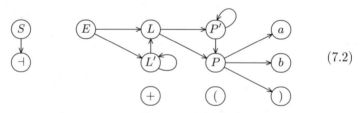

$$(7.2)$$

Interchanging left and right in these definitions gives the *left dependency graph*

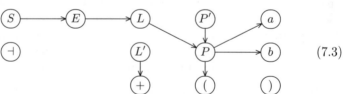

$$(7.3)$$

Let us write $X l Y$ ("X directly left-depends on Y") if there is an arc from X to Y in the left dependency graph. Then $X l^+ Y$ ("X left-depends on Y") is seen to be equivalent to saying that

$$X \to^+ Y \alpha$$

for some string α. We say that X is *left recursive* if $X l^+ X$. Similarly, we can define $X r Y$, $X r^+ Y$, etc., from the right dependency graph. In grammar (5.13), we see from (7.3) that no nonterminals are left recursive; but graph (7.2) shows that L' and P' are right recursive.

The dependency graphs can be used to determine several quantities of interest to us. If A is a nonterminal symbol, let first(A) denote the set of all terminal symbols that can be the initial character of a string in $L(A)$. It is clear from the discussion above that

$$\text{first}(A) = \{a \in T \mid A\,l^+\,a\},$$

so we can read off the first characters of any nonterminal by inspecting (7.3). Similarly, last(A) can be obtained from a consideration of the right dependency graph.

Finally, we want to define the set

$$\text{follow}(A) = \{a \in T \mid S \to^* \theta A a \varphi \text{ for some strings } \theta \text{ and } \varphi\}.$$

It is not difficult to see that, when there are no useless nonterminals, this definition is equivalent to saying that follow(A) is the set of all terminal a such that there is a production of the form

$$W \to \alpha X B_1 \ldots B_n Y \omega \tag{7.4}$$

where $n \geq 0$, B_1 through B_n can produce the null string, Y is either terminal or nonterminal, $X\,r^*\,A$, and $Y\,l^*\,a$. This observation makes it possible to compute the sets follow(A) for each A without difficulty.

(The reason (7.4) can be assumed is that there must be a production in the derivation of $S \to^* \theta A a \varphi$ that "combines" A and a.)

For the example grammar (5.13), we have

A	first(A)	last(A)	follow(A)
S	$\{a, b, (\}$	$\{\dashv\}$	$\emptyset$
E	$\{a, b, (\}$	$\{a, b,)\}$	$\{), \dashv\}$
L	$\{a, b, (\}$	$\{a, b,)\}$	$\{+,), \dashv\}$
P	$\{a, b, (\}$	$\{a, b,)\}$	$\{+, a, b, (,), \dashv\}$
L'	$\{+\}$	$\{a, b,)\}$	$\{), \dashv\}$
P'	$\{a, b, (\}$	$\{a, b,)\}$	$\{+,), \dashv\}$

8. The No-Backup Case

In Section 4 we showed that it was, in general, difficult—in fact impossible—to decide whether the Parsing Machine program for a given context-free grammar $\mathcal{G}$ will properly parse all strings belonging to the language defined by $\mathcal{G}$. The tools developed in Sections 5, 6, and 7 now give us enough ammunition to attack the most important special case of the partial backup problem, namely when the Parsing Machine never has to back up at all; that is, when h never is decreased.

The no-backup restriction has two practical consequences: First, we can be sure that the total time required for syntactic analysis is bounded by a constant times the length of the input string. Second, a computer program for parsing may read the input one character at a time without bothering to save the characters previously read.

In the general PM program (3.2) that corresponds to a standard-form grammar, the input pointer h can back up only when a false exit occurs after Z_2, Z_3, ..., or Z_n. This fact suggests that we redefine (3.2) as follows:

location	opcode	AT	AF	
X	$[Y_1]$	T		
	$[Y_2]$	T		
	$\vdots$	$\vdots$		
	$[Y_m]$	T	$*$	(8.1)
	$[Z_1]$		F	
	$[Z_2]$		ERROR	
	$\vdots$		$\vdots$	
	$[Z_{n-1}]$		ERROR	
	$[Z_n]$	T	ERROR	

We can now take any context-free grammar $\mathcal{G}$ with rules grouped as in (3.3); these rules can be transformed into standard form (3.1) and the corresponding "no-backup" program (8.1) can be constructed. The auxiliary rule introducing '⊣' can also be added as before.

We want the Parsing Machine to behave as follows, when it starts at location S, scanning $s_1 s_2 \ldots s_n$ where only s_n is the '⊣' symbol: If $s_1 \ldots s_n$ is not in $L(\mathcal{G})$, the program should go to ERROR. If $s_1 \ldots s_n$ *is* in $L(\mathcal{G})$, and if we have any diagram such as (2.3) that corresponds to a derivation $S \rightarrow^* s_1 \ldots s_n$, then the actions of the PM should correspond precisely to that diagram (in the obvious manner).

If the no-backup PM program satisfies the conditions of the preceding paragraph, we shall say "The no-backup method works for $\mathcal{G}$." Note that this condition implies in particular that $\mathcal{G}$ is *unambiguous*, that is, that no two different diagrams can be given for any string of $L(\mathcal{G})$. For if there are two diagrams, the PM program is supposed to correspond to both of them, and this clearly cannot happen since the PM executes only one set of actions. Unambiguous grammars are of principal interest for programming languages.

Given a grammar $\mathcal{G}$, we now wish to answer the question, "Does the no-backup method work for $\mathcal{G}$?" In order to study this problem, we first will replace a grammar with rules of the form (3.1) by another grammar whose rules have a more simple form, where the new grammar generates the same language with only a slightly different structure.

A standard-form rule $X \to Y_1 \mid \ldots \mid Y_m \mid Z_1 Z_2 \ldots Z_n$ with $m \geq 1$ can always be changed into two rules

$$X \to Y_1 \mid X'$$
$$X' \to Y_2 \mid \ldots \mid Y_m \mid Z_1 Z_2 \ldots Z_n$$

where X' is a new nonterminal symbol, without changing the essential behavior of the no-backup method; the change just introduces redundant procedure calls. We can therefore suppose that all rules have one of two forms:

$$X \to Z_1 \ldots Z_n$$
$$X \to Y \mid Z$$

Furthermore, if $n > 1$ in the first form, we can replace that rule by

$$X \to Z_1 X'$$
$$X' \to Z_2 \ldots Z_n$$

and again the no-backup method is unaffected. After repeated use of these transformations we are left with just four types of rules, namely

$$X \to Y \mid Z$$
$$X \to YZ$$
$$X \to Y$$
$$X \to \epsilon$$

If Y or Z is a terminal symbol (for example, $X \to a \mid Z$), then we can introduce a new rule of the form $X' \to a$ and change the Y or Z to the X' (for example, $X \to X' \mid Z$).

All rules now have one of five forms:

Type 1.	$X \to Y \mid Z$
Type 2.	$X \to YZ$
Type 3.	$X \to Y$
Type 4.	$X \to a$
Type 5.	$X \to \epsilon$

Here Y and Z are nonterminal symbols, and a is terminal. Moreover, we may assume that no "useless" nonterminals are present. Let us say that a grammar satisfying these conditions is *simple*.

8.1. Necessary conditions. We are now going to study four necessary conditions on grammars of the simple form we have just defined. These conditions must all be satisfied if the no-backup method works. Later we will prove that these four conditions are also sufficient, thereby solving the no-backup problem.

First Condition. *No nonterminal is left recursive.*

If X were left recursive, it would be necessary for procedure X to call itself without advancing the input, when the machine is mimicking a derivation of $S \to^* \alpha X \omega \to^+ \alpha X \theta \omega \to^+ \tau$, where τ is terminal. (Such strings τ, α, ω, and θ exist because X is assumed to be left recursive but not useless.) But then the PM would loop endlessly.   □

Lemma. *Whenever a grammar has no left recursive nonterminal symbols, the nonterminals X_1, X_2, ..., X_t can be ordered in such a way that*

$$X_p \, l^+ \, X_q \quad \text{only if} \quad q < p.$$

(In our example (5.13), L', P, P', L, E, S is such an ordering.)

Proof. This is a general result about the vertices of any finite directed graph that contains no oriented cycles. If there is no left recursion, the left dependency graph has no oriented cycles. The vertices of such a graph can always be ordered V_1, V_2, ..., V_t in such a way that there is a path from V_p to V_q only if $q < p$. (This is the problem of "topological sorting," which is analyzed more thoroughly in [13, Section 2.2.3].)

The reason is that we can always find a vertex from which no arcs emanate; otherwise we could find an oriented cycle. Such a vertex may be placed first in the ordering and removed from the graph, and this operation may be repeated until all vertices have been removed. The lemma has therefore been proved.   □

Let us now restate the five types of rules under this ordering assumption:

Type 1.	$X_p \to X_q \mid X_r$	$q < p$ and $r < p$.
Type 2.	$X_p \to X_q X_r$	$q < p$; and if $X_q \to^+ \epsilon$, also $r < p$.
Type 3.	$X_p \to X_q$	$q < p$.
Type 4.	$X_p \to a$	
Type 5.	$X_p \to \epsilon$	

Another condition must also be satisfied if the no-backup method is going to work, as illustrated in the following grammar.

$$X \to Y \mid Z$$
$$Y \to Y_1 Y_2$$
$$Z \to Z_1 Z_2$$
$$Z_1 \to a$$
$$Z_2 \to b$$
$$Y_1 \to a$$
$$Y_2 \to c$$

Here $L(X) = \{ab, ac\}$, and the Parsing Machine cannot parse ab as X without backing up. In general we can see that the following condition must be true:

Second Condition. *In every rule of Type 1,*

$$\text{first}(X_q) \cap \text{first}(X_r) = \emptyset.$$

To prove that this condition is necessary, suppose that there is a terminal symbol a in both $\text{first}(X_q)$ and $\text{first}(X_r)$. Thus $X_q \to^+ a\theta$ and $X_r \to^+ a\varphi$ for some terminal strings θ and φ. Now if the Parsing Machine can parse $a\theta$ as X_q and then as X_p, it cannot parse $a\varphi$ as X_r and then as X_p, since the X_p procedure calls X_q first; that call must advance past the letter a.   □

Another case in which the no-backup method has difficulty is reflected in the following grammatical rules:

$$W \to XY$$
$$X \to Y \mid Z$$
$$Z \to \epsilon$$
$$Y \to a$$

Now $L(W) = \{aa, a\}$, and the Parsing Machine cannot parse the string 'a' without backing up. Thus, we find a further condition, analogous to the second.

Third Condition. *In every rule of Type 1 where X_r can produce the null string,*

$$\text{first}(X_q) \cap \text{follow}(X_p) = \emptyset.   □$$

Here finally is another grammar that satisfies all three of the conditions discussed so far, yet it still causes the no-backup method to fail:

$$X \to Y \mid Z$$
$$Y \to WT$$
$$W \to V \mid U$$
$$T \to a$$
$$Z \to b$$
$$V \to c$$
$$U \to \epsilon$$

In this case $L(X) = \{ca, a, b\}$, and the Parsing Machine will not accept the string 'b'. Procedure U cannot ever return false, so procedure W cannot return false, and neither can Y. Therefore the procedure for X will never call Z in any circumstances! This example suggests adding yet another constraint.

Fourth Condition. *In every rule of Type 1, X_q must not be "non-false"; in other words it should not correspond to a procedure that will never return false.*   □

We see that a nonterminal X_p is *nonfalse* if and only if its rule is

       a) of Type 1 and X_q or X_r is nonfalse;
or b) of Type 2 and X_q is nonfalse;
or c) of Type 3 and X_q is nonfalse;
or d) of Type 5 ($X_p \to \epsilon$).

Therefore we can easily check Condition 4, by sequentially determining which of X_1, X_2, ..., X_t are nonfalse (in that order).

8.2. Solution to the no-backup problem.

Theorem. *If Conditions 1, 2, 3, and 4 hold in a simple grammar $\mathcal{G}$, then the no-backup method works.*

(In fact, it is possible to prove that Condition 1 follows from Conditions 2, 3, and 4, so that Condition 1 is redundant.)

The proof uses two lemmas. Let $s_1 \ldots s_n$ be the input string, and let s_h be the current symbol in the input string. We may assume by Condition 1 that the nonterminal symbols have been put into an appropriate order $X_1, X_2, \ldots$ as specified in Section 8.1.

Lemma 1. *Under the assumptions of the theorem, if X_p is not nonfalse and if $s_h \notin \mathrm{first}(X_p)$, then the Parsing Machine instruction $[X_p]\ L_1\ L_2$ will transfer to L_2.*

Proof. The proof is by induction on p, with respect to the ordering of nonterminals that we have defined.

Assume that the lemma is true for $X_1, \ldots, X_{p-1}$. (In particular, when $p = 1$ we are not assuming anything; proofs by induction are often convenient to state in this way, without singling out the case $p = 1$.)

First case:

$$X_p \to X_q \mid X_r, \qquad q < p \text{ and } r < p.$$

Since X_p is not nonfalse, X_q and X_r cannot be nonfalse, by the definition of that property. Also since $s_h \notin \text{first}(X_p)$, we have $s_h \notin \text{first}(X_q)$ and $s_h \notin \text{first}(X_r)$. Now the PM program for procedure X_p is

location	opcode	AT	AF	
X_p	$[X_q]$	T		(8.2)
	$[X_r]$	T	F	

Therefore by induction the machine will go to F.

Second case:

$$X_p \to X_q X_r, \qquad q < p.$$

Since X_p is not nonfalse, neither is X_q. And since $s_h \notin \text{first}(X_p)$, obviously $s_h \notin \text{first}(X_q)$. Now the PM program for X_p is

X_p	$[X_q]$		F	
	$[X_r]$	T	ERROR	(8.3)

so, by induction, procedure X_p will go to F.

Third case:

$$X_p \to X_q, \qquad q < p.$$

This case is obvious.

Fourth case:

$$X_p \to a.$$

The PM program is

X_p	a	T	F	(8.4)

and since $s_h \neq a$ this case is also obvious.

Fifth case:

$$X_p \to \epsilon.$$

This situation cannot occur since X_p is not nonfalse.   □

Lemma 2. *Under the assumptions of the theorem, let $X_p \to^* s_h \ldots s_{k-1}$ where $h \leq k$. (If $h = k$, this means that $X_p \to^* \epsilon$.) Assume also that $s_k \in \text{follow}(X_p)$. Then the Parsing Machine instruction $[X_p]\ L_1\ L_2$ will transfer to L_1 with h increased to k. Furthermore the actions of the machine during this time will correspond to the derivation of $X_p \to^* s_h \ldots s_{k-1}$.*

Proof.   The proof is by induction on $k - h = m$; and, for fixed m, on p. Thus, we assume that the lemma is true for all p and m' when $m' < m$, and for all $p' < p$ when m is given.

First case:

$$X_p \to X_q \mid X_r, \qquad q < p \text{ and } r < p.$$

The program for procedure X_p is (8.2).

Subcase 1a:

$$X_q \to^* s_h \ldots s_{k-1}.$$

By induction the lemma is true for X_q, thus it is also true for X_p.

Subcase 1b:

$$X_r \to^* s_h \ldots s_{k-1}.$$

If $h = k$ (null string), then by Condition 3 $s_h = s_k \in \text{follow}(X_p)$, so $s_h \notin \text{first}(X_q)$. On the other hand if $h > k$, we have $s_h \notin \text{first}(X_q)$ by Condition 2. Furthermore X_q is not nonfalse, by Condition 4.

Thus by Lemma 1, procedure X_p will call $[X_r]$; and since $r < p$, the lemma holds by induction.

Second case:

$$X_p \to X_q X_r, \qquad \text{where} \qquad \begin{matrix} X_q \to^* s_h \ldots s_{j-1} \\ X_r \to^* s_j \ldots s_{k-1}, \end{matrix}$$

for some j; $h \leq j \leq k$.

The PM program is (8.3). If $h < j$ the lemma is true for X_q and X_r (by induction, since $k - j$ is less than $k - h$ and q is less than p). If $h = j$, then X_q can produce the null string, so $r < p$; again the procedure X_p will go to T by induction.

Third case:

$$X_p \to X_q, \qquad q < p.$$

The lemma is valid for X_q, so it holds for X_p.

Fourth case:

$$X_p \to a.$$

We must have $s_h = a$ and $k = h + 1$. The PM program (8.4) clearly goes to T and advances h.

Fifth case:

$$X_p \to \epsilon.$$

Here h must equal k; the PM program for X_p always goes to T without changing h.

This completes the proof of Lemma 2.   □

Now the theorem can be proved as follows. If $s_1 \ldots s_n$ is in $L(\mathcal{G})$, the machine goes to 'OK', and its actions correspond to a given derivation, by applying Lemma 2 to the program for S.

If $s_1 \ldots s_n$ is not in $L(\mathcal{G})$, the machine cannot go to 'OK'; for each time the machine goes to 'OK' its actions obviously correspond to a derivation in the grammar. This derivation must be of the entire string, since only $s_n = \dashv$.

The remaining possibility is that $s_1 \ldots s_n$ is not in $L(\mathcal{G})$ but the PM program never terminates. This is impossible, since the grammar is not left recursive; we can prove by induction on $n - h$ and (for fixed h) on p that no call of $[X_p]$ can result in an infinite loop. The latter proof is straightforward as in Lemmas 1 and 2; but it is not completely trivial, since the PM can go rather slowly as in the grammar

$$
\begin{aligned}
X_1 &\to \epsilon \\
X_2 &\to X_1 X_1 \\
X_3 &\to X_2 X_2 \\
X_4 &\to X_3 X_3 \\
X_5 &\to a \\
X_6 &\to X_4 X_5
\end{aligned}
$$

when parsing 'a' as X_6.   □

8.3.   Summary. The four conditions of Section 8.1, derived for the special case of simple grammars, can now be translated back to the general situation in which all rules have the standard form

$$X \to Y_1 \mid \ldots \mid Y_m \mid Z_1 \ldots Z_n \tag{8.5}$$

From the theorem of Section 8.2 and the simplification procedure that we discussed earlier, we conclude that the following four conditions are necessary and sufficient for the validity of the no-backup method, provided that there are no useless nonterminal symbols:

1. No nonterminal symbol is left recursive.
2. The sets first(Y_1), ..., first(Y_m), first($Z_1 \ldots Z_n$) are mutually disjoint; that is, they have no letters in common.

3. If $Z_1 \ldots Z_n \rightarrow^* \epsilon$ then first(Y_j) contains no letters in common with follow(X), for $1 \leq j \leq m$.

4. $Y_1, \ldots, Y_m$ are not nonfalse.

A nonterminal symbol X corresponding to the rule (8.5) is defined to be *nonfalse* if and only if either

> a) Y_j is nonfalse, for some j with $1 \leq j \leq m$;
> or b) $n = 0$;
> or c) $n > 0$ and Z_1 is nonfalse.

As remarked earlier, Condition 1 is redundant since it can be deduced from the other three.

It is possible to design a rather efficient program to check all four conditions: First do a "topological sort" of the nonterminal symbols, based on the left dependency graph; at the same time, determine the sets first(X) and check Conditions 2 and 4, for each X as it is emitted by the topological sorting algorithm. Then compute follow(X) for each X and test Condition 3.

Exercise 8.1. Does the no-backup method work on the grammar (5.13)? Prove your answer, by testing the four conditions above.

9. An Overview of Top-Down and Bottom-Up Analysis

In addition to the relation $\rightarrow$ that we defined in connection with a context-free grammar $\mathcal{G}$ in Section 5, we can also define the restricted relation

$$\alpha A \omega \overset{\text{L}}{\rightarrow} \alpha \theta \omega \qquad (9.1)$$

if $A \rightarrow \theta$ is a production and if $\alpha \in T^*$; in such a case A is the leftmost nonterminal in $\alpha A \omega$. Similarly we define

$$\alpha A \omega \overset{\text{R}}{\rightarrow} \alpha \theta \omega \qquad (9.2)$$

if $\omega \in T^*$. These relations can be extended as before to $\overset{\text{L}}{\rightarrow}{}^*, \overset{\text{L}}{\rightarrow}{}^+, \overset{\text{R}}{\rightarrow}{}^*$, and $\overset{\text{R}}{\rightarrow}{}^+$; the relation

$$\varphi \overset{\text{L}}{\rightarrow}{}^+ \psi$$

may be read, "φ left-produces ψ."

There are in general many sequences of strings $\sigma_1, \sigma_2, \ldots, \sigma_m$ such that the sequence

$$S \rightarrow \sigma_1 \rightarrow \cdots \rightarrow \sigma_m \rightarrow \tau$$

is a derivation of any particular terminal string τ in a context-free language; whenever σ_j contains at least two nonterminal symbols, we have a choice as to which nonterminal to replace first. The importance of the $\overset{L}{\to}$ and $\overset{R}{\to}$ relations is that, for every diagram such as (2.3), there is exactly one corresponding $\overset{L}{\to}$ derivation, and exactly one corresponding $\overset{R}{\to}$ derivation. For example, using the parse diagram (2.3) and the grammar (2.1)–(2.2), we have

$$
\begin{aligned}
S \;&\overset{L}{\to}\; B\dashv \;\overset{L}{\to}\; (B)\dashv \;\overset{L}{\to}\; (R)\dashv \\
&\overset{L}{\to}\; (E = E)\dashv \;\overset{L}{\to}\; (a = E)\dashv \\
&\overset{L}{\to}\; (a = (E + E))\dashv \\
&\overset{L}{\to}\; (a = (b + E))\dashv \\
&\overset{L}{\to}\; (a = (b + a))\dashv
\end{aligned}
\tag{9.3}
$$

and

$$
\begin{aligned}
S \;&\overset{R}{\to}\; B\dashv \;\overset{R}{\to}\; (B)\dashv \;\overset{R}{\to}\; (R)\dashv \\
&\overset{R}{\to}\; (E = E)\dashv \;\overset{R}{\to}\; (E = (E + E))\dashv \\
&\overset{R}{\to}\; (E = (E + a))\dashv \\
&\overset{R}{\to}\; (E = (b + a))\dashv \\
&\overset{R}{\to}\; (a = (b + a))\dashv
\end{aligned}
\tag{9.4}
$$

as the corresponding left and right derivations. A context-free grammar $\mathcal{G}$ is *unambiguous* if each string in $L(\mathcal{G})$ has exactly one left derivation (or equivalently, exactly one right derivation).

The general problem of syntactic analysis is to start with a string τ of terminal symbols, for example, $(a = (b + a))\dashv$, and to find (when possible) a sequence of productions such that $S \to^* \tau$.

The *bottom-up method* (proceeding from left to right) attacks this problem by first "reducing" the string $(a = (b + a))\dashv$ to

$$(E = (b + a))\dashv$$

then reducing this to

$$(E = (E + a))\dashv$$

and then

$$(E = (E + E))\dashv$$

and

$$(E = E)\dashv$$

and so on. (A *reduction* is the opposite of a production.) The leftmost possible reduction is applied at each step. This process continues until we either reduce everything to S or show that such a reduction would be impossible. Notice that the sequence of intermediate steps is exactly the reverse of the right production sequence (9.4). In general, *bottom-up analysis (from left to right) proceeds by right reductions*, that is, by reversing the right production sequence.

The *top-down method* (proceeding from left to right) attacks the problem somewhat differently. It starts with S, and attempts to reach the given terminal string τ by a sequence of left productions, as in (9.3). At each step we must decide which production to apply to the leftmost nonterminal symbol. In general, *top-down analysis (from left to right) proceeds by left productions*.

Similarly we can describe top-down and bottom-up methods that go from right to left, by interchanging the roles of left and right in the discussion above. (Some extended methods, which are more symmetrical between left and right, are currently being explored by several people.)

Various "backup" procedures can be given for reconsidering some alternatives of the derivation sequence that prove later to be incorrect. Principal interest, however, centers on the cases where the syntactic analysis proceeds *without* backing up: Then each step of the derivation sequence is known to be the only possible step. Such procedures are usually called *deterministic* analysis methods.

In a previous paper [12], the author has described the general conditions under which strings of a grammar can be analyzed deterministically, bottom-up, from left to right, looking k characters ahead of where the next reduction step will be made. Such grammars are called LR(k) grammars. The analogous property for top-down analysis, first suggested by Lewis and Stearns [16], will be called here the 'LL(k)' property; it means that a top-down analysis is to be performed from left to right, looking k characters ahead of the terminal symbols that have already been matched. Formal definitions of these concepts appear in the next section. For the present, let us quickly review the significance of four algorithms that a context-free grammar may support:

> LL(k) : scanning from the left, using left productions;
> LR(k) : scanning from the left, using right reductions;
> RL(k) : scanning from the right, using left reductions;
> RR(k) : scanning from the right, using right productions.

(In each case, k represents the number of symbols of "lookahead," used to decide what production or reduction to perform next. A "right reduction" is the opposite of a "right production" (9.2).) The cases LL(k) and RR(k) correspond to top-down analysis.

10. Definitions of LL(k) and LR(k)

Let us now introduce some useful notations. If k is a nonnegative integer and α is a string, we define

$$k : \alpha = \begin{cases} \text{the first } k \text{ characters of } \alpha, & \text{if } |\alpha| \geq k; \\ \alpha & \text{if } |\alpha| < k; \end{cases} \qquad (10.1)$$

$$\alpha : k = \begin{cases} \text{the last } k \text{ characters of } \alpha, & \text{if } |\alpha| \geq k; \\ \alpha & \text{if } |\alpha| < k. \end{cases} \qquad (10.2)$$

Furthermore if A is a set of strings, we write

$$k : A = \{k : \alpha \mid \alpha \in A\}, \qquad (10.3)$$

$$A : k = \{\alpha : k \mid \alpha \in A\}. \qquad (10.4)$$

Notice that $k : \beta = k : \gamma$ implies $k : (\alpha\beta) = k : (\alpha\gamma)$, for all strings α, β, and γ. Also

$$\text{first}(A) \;=\; (1 : L(A)) \cap T \;=\; (1 : L(A)) \setminus \{\epsilon\}.$$

The informal discussion of Section 9 can now be formulated precisely in terms of this notation.

Definition. *A context-free grammar is* LR(k) *if the following condition holds for all* α_1, α_1', α_2, *and* α_2' *in* $(N \cup T)^*$, *for all* α_3 *and* α_3' *in* T^*, *and for all* A *and* A' *in* N:

$$S \xrightarrow{\text{R}}{}^* \alpha_1 A \alpha_3 \xrightarrow{\text{R}} \alpha_1 \alpha_2 \alpha_3$$

and

$$S \xrightarrow{\text{R}}{}^* \alpha_1' A' \alpha_3' \xrightarrow{\text{R}} \alpha_1' \alpha_2' \alpha_3'$$

and

$$(|\alpha_1 \alpha_2| + k) : \alpha_1 \alpha_2 \alpha_3 \;=\; (|\alpha_1 \alpha_2| + k) : \alpha_1' \alpha_2' \alpha_3'$$

implies that

$$\alpha_1 = \alpha_1', \quad A = A', \quad \text{and} \quad \alpha_2 = \alpha_2'.$$

Definition. *A context-free grammar is* LL(k) *if the following condition holds for all* α_1, α_4, *and* α_4' *in* T^*, *and for all* α_2, α_3, *and* α_2' *in* $(N \cup T)^*$:

$$S \overset{L}{\to}{}^* \alpha_1 A \alpha_3 \overset{L}{\to} \alpha_1 \alpha_2 \alpha_3 \overset{L}{\to}{}^* \alpha_1 \alpha_4$$

and

$$S \overset{L}{\to}{}^* \alpha_1 A \alpha_3 \overset{L}{\to} \alpha_1 \alpha_2' \alpha_3 \overset{L}{\to}{}^* \alpha_1 \alpha_4'$$

and

$$k : \alpha_4 \; = \; k : \alpha_4'$$

implies that

$$\alpha_2 \; = \; \alpha_2'.$$

Let us now define a generalization of the "follow" function that allows us to derive further information about the LL(k) property: If $\beta \in T^*$ and $A \in N$, and if k is a nonnegative integer, let

$$F_k(A, \beta) = k : \{\theta \mid \theta \in T^* \text{ and } S \to^* \beta A \theta\}. \tag{10.5}$$

Thus in our earlier notation,

$$\text{follow}(A) = \bigcup_{\beta \in T^*} F_1(A, \beta)$$

if $A \neq S$ and if we regard $\dashv$ as an element of T.

Theorem (Lewis and Stearns). *If* $A \to \alpha_1$ *and* $A \to \alpha_2$ *are two distinct productions of an* LL(k) *grammar, and if* β *is in* T^*, *then*

$$\big(k : (L(\alpha_1)\theta_1)\big) \cap \big(k : (L(\alpha_2)\theta_2)\big) = \emptyset \tag{10.6}$$

for all θ_1 *and* θ_2 *in* $F_k(A, \beta)$.

(In fact this condition can be proved equivalent to the LL(k) property; see [16]. The condition leads to a fairly simple algorithm to test whether a context-free grammar is LL(k) for a given k.)

Proof. Suppose there are strings $\omega, \theta_1, \theta_2$, such that

$$\begin{aligned}
\omega &\in k : (L(\alpha_1)\theta_1); \\
\omega &\in k : (L(\alpha_2)\theta_2); \\
\theta_1, \theta_2 &\in F_k(A, \beta).
\end{aligned}$$

We will show that this implies $\alpha_1 = \alpha_2$, which contradicts the hypothesis that $A \to \alpha_1$ and $A \to \alpha_2$ are distinct production rules.

The proof is mostly a matter of translating between notations. By hypothesis there are θ_1' and θ_2' in T^* such that

$$S \to^* \beta A \theta_1', \quad S \to^* \beta A \theta_2', \quad k : \theta_1' = \theta_1, \quad k : \theta_2' = \theta_2.$$

Hence by considering the corresponding left derivations, there are strings γ_1 and γ_2 in $(N \cup T)^*$ such that

$$S \overset{L}{\to}{}^* \beta A \gamma_1, \quad S \overset{L}{\to}{}^* \beta A \gamma_2, \quad \gamma_1 \to^* \theta_1', \quad \gamma_2 \to^* \theta_2'.$$

There are also τ_1 and τ_2 in $L(\alpha_1)$ and $L(\alpha_2)$, respectively, such that

$$k : \tau_1 \theta_1' = k : \tau_1 \theta_1 = \omega = k : \tau_2 \theta_2 = k : \tau_2 \theta_2'.$$

Therefore we may assume that $\gamma_1 \to^* \gamma_2$ (see exercise 10.2).

Now we have

$$S \overset{L}{\to}{}^* \beta A \gamma_1 \overset{L}{\to} \beta \alpha_1 \gamma_1 \overset{L}{\to}{}^* \beta \tau_1 \gamma_1 \overset{L}{\to}{}^* \beta \tau_1 \theta_1'$$
$$S \overset{L}{\to}{}^* \beta A \gamma_1 \overset{L}{\to} \beta \alpha_2 \gamma_1 \overset{L}{\to}{}^* \beta \tau_2 \gamma_1 \overset{L}{\to}{}^* \beta \tau_2 \gamma_2 \overset{L}{\to}{}^* \beta \tau_2 \theta_2'$$

so $\alpha_1 = \alpha_2$ by the definition of LL(k).   □

Exercise 10.1. Show that an LL(k) grammar with no useless nonterminals has no left-recursive nonterminals.

Exercise 10.2. Show that every LL(k) grammar satisfies the following condition: For all α_1, α_3, α_3' in T^* and all α_2, α_2' in $(N \cup T)^*$, if

$$S \overset{L}{\to}{}^* \alpha_1 A \alpha_2 \overset{L}{\to}{}^* \alpha_1 \alpha_3$$

and

$$S \overset{L}{\to}{}^* \alpha_1 A \alpha_2' \overset{L}{\to}{}^* \alpha_1 \alpha_3'$$

and

$$k : \alpha_3 = k : \alpha_3'$$

then $\alpha_2 \to^* \alpha_2'$ or $\alpha_2' \to^* \alpha_2$.

Exercise 10.3. Under the hypotheses of the previous exercise, can we conclude, in fact, that $\alpha_2 = \alpha_2'$?

11. LL(1) Grammars

The special case $k = 1$ in the preceding discussion of LL(k) seems to be quite a bit simpler than the case of higher values of k, and it is directly related to our previous discussion of the "no-backup method," so we shall now study it in detail.

Suppose $\mathcal{G}$ is a grammar with no useless nonterminals; let us test the condition of the last theorem in the case $k = 1$. Let A be a nonterminal symbol whose rule is

$$A \to \alpha_1 \mid \alpha_2 \mid \ldots \mid \alpha_m, \qquad m \geq 1. \tag{11.1}$$

If $p \neq q$, and if $a \in \text{first}(\alpha_p)$, $b \in \text{first}(\alpha_q)$, condition (10.6) says that $a \neq b$. Furthermore we cannot have both $\alpha_p \to^* \epsilon$ and $\alpha_q \to^* \epsilon$, since (10.6) would be violated if we take $\theta_1 = \theta_2$. And if $\alpha_p \to^* \epsilon$ and $b \in \text{first}(\alpha_q)$, condition (10.6) says that $b \notin F_1(A, \beta)$ for any β, that is, $b \notin \text{follow}(A)$.

Thus we have three conditions that are necessary for each rule (11.1) of an LL(1) grammar:

1. $\text{first}(\alpha_1)$, ..., $\text{first}(\alpha_m)$ are mutually disjoint, that is, they contain no common elements.

2. At most one of α_1, ..., α_m can produce a null string.

3. If $\alpha_p \to^* \epsilon$, then $\text{first}(\alpha_q)$ has no elements in common with $\text{follow}(A)$, for $1 \leq q \leq m$, $q \neq p$.

(*Note:* Conditions 1 and 2 can be combined by saying that

$$(1 : L(\alpha_p)) \cap (1 : L(\alpha_q)) = \emptyset \quad \text{when } p \neq q.$$

Furthermore, D. B. Johnson and R. Sethi have pointed out in a letter to the author that the third condition can be stated more elegantly: If $A \to^* \epsilon$ then $\text{first}(A) \cap \text{follow}(A) = \emptyset$.)

Now these three conditions are obviously *sufficient* to show that $\mathcal{G}$ is LL(1): For if we are to replace A by one of α_1, ..., α_m, the choice of which α_j to use is uniquely determined by examining the first character of the terminal string that ultimately is to be produced by A.

Grammars satisfying the no-backup condition stated at the end of Section 8 also satisfy the three conditions above, so they are LL(1) grammars. But a grammar such as

$$\begin{aligned}
B &\to Ab \mid Cd \\
A &\to aA \mid \epsilon \\
C &\to cC \mid \epsilon \\
S &\to B\dashv
\end{aligned} \tag{11.2}$$

does not satisfy the non-backup condition, although it is LL(1). Both A and C are nonfalse, so the Parsing Machine will not be able to work with this grammar, regardless of whether we write

$$B \to Ab \mid Cd \text{ or } B \to Cd \mid Ab$$

before converting to standard form.

Any LL(1) grammar can, however, be changed into a fairly simple standard form, which can be treated by the Parsing Machine.

If a set of strings can be defined by an LL(k) *grammar*, let us call it an LL(k) *language*.

Theorem. *Any* LL(1) *language has a grammar in which all rules have one of the two forms*

$$\text{Type 1.} \quad A \to a_1\alpha_1 \mid \ldots \mid a_m\alpha_m$$
$$\text{Type 2.} \quad A \to a_1\alpha_1 \mid \ldots \mid a_m\alpha_m \mid \epsilon$$

Here $a_1, \ldots, a_m$ *are distinct terminal characters; and in rules of Type 2, no* a_j *is in* follow(A).

(Conversely, such a grammar is obviously LL(1), and it obviously also satisfies the conditions of the no-backup method. So the LL(1) languages are precisely those analyzable by some no-backup PM program.)

Proof. Given a grammar $\mathcal{G}$ satisfying conditions 1, 2, 3 above and with no useless nonterminals, we can prove (see for example exercise 10.1) that $\mathcal{G}$ has no left-recursive nonterminals. Thus we can order the nonterminal symbols $A_1, A_2, \ldots, A_t$ where $A_p \, l^+ A_q$ only if $q < p$.

It follows that the rule for A_1 must be of either Type 1 or Type 2 as in the theorem.

Suppose that the rules for nonterminals A_q have the form of Type 1 or Type 2 for all $q < p$. Suppose further that, if

$$A_q \to a_{q1}\alpha_{q1} \mid \ldots \mid a_{qm_q}\alpha_{qm_q} \mid \epsilon \qquad (11.3)$$

is a rule of Type 2, where $q < p$, we also have added the additional rule

$$A'_q \to a_{q1}\alpha_{q1} \mid \ldots \mid a_{qm_q}\alpha_{qm_q} \qquad (11.4)$$

to the grammar, where A'_q is a new nonterminal symbol. We will show how to change the rule of A_p so that it has the form of either Type 1 or Type 2.

Let the rule for A_p be

$$A_p \to \alpha_1 \mid \alpha_2 \mid \ldots \mid \alpha_n.$$

If α_j begins with a nonterminal symbol, so that α_j has the form $A_q\beta$, we must have $q < p$. If the rule for A_q is of Type 2, replace α_j by two alternatives $A_q'\beta \mid \beta$, where A_q' is given by (11.4). This leaves us with an LL(1) grammar: For

$$\mathrm{first}(A_q) \cap \mathrm{first}(\beta) \subseteq \mathrm{first}(A_q') \cap \mathrm{follow}(A_q) = \emptyset;$$

and $\mathrm{first}(A_q') \cup \mathrm{first}(\beta) = \mathrm{first}(\alpha_j)$ has no letters in common with the set $\mathrm{first}(\alpha_i)$ for $i \neq j$. Furthermore if $\beta \to^* \epsilon$, we must verify that $\mathrm{first}(A_q')$ has no letters in common with $\mathrm{follow}(A_p)$, and this condition holds because $\mathrm{follow}(A_p) \subseteq \mathrm{follow}(A_q)$ when $\beta \to^* \epsilon$.

By repeating this process, we may assume that A_p has a rule

$$A_p \to \alpha_1 \mid \alpha_2 \mid \ldots \mid \alpha_n$$

where none of the α_j begins with a nonterminal whose rule is of Type 2. Now if α_j begins with a nonterminal A_q, we may write $\alpha_j = A_q\beta$, where $q < p$. We may replace the alternative α_j by

$$a_{q1}\alpha_{q1}\beta \mid \ldots \mid a_{qm_q}\alpha_{qm_q}\beta$$

where the rule for A_q is

$$A_q \to a_{q1}\alpha_{q1} \mid \ldots \mid a_{qm_q}\alpha_{qm_q}$$

and we still clearly have an LL(1) grammar. Thus the rule for A_p can ultimately be reduced to either Type 1 or Type 2, and the proof is complete. (The auxiliary rules (11.4) are not needed after the construction has terminated.) $\square$

As an example, the grammar (11.2) above would be changed to

$$
\begin{aligned}
A &\to aA \mid \epsilon \\
C &\to cC \mid \epsilon \\
B &\to aAb \mid b \mid cCd \mid d \\
S &\to aAb\dashv \mid b\dashv \mid cCd\dashv \mid d\dashv
\end{aligned}
\tag{11.5}
$$

(and symbol B has become useless). Grammars in which all rules are of Type 1 are obviously LL(1). They have been called "s-grammars" by Korenjak and Hopcroft [14], who proved (among other things) that the *equivalence problem* is solvable for s-languages. In other words, if $\mathcal{G}_1$ and $\mathcal{G}_2$ are s-grammars, we can decide if $L(\mathcal{G}_1) = L(\mathcal{G}_2)$.

The grammar (11.5) can be transformed into an s-grammar for the same language if we introduce new nonterminal symbols $[Ab]$ and $[Cd]$ standing respectively for $L(Ab)$ and $L(Cd)$. The s-grammar is

$$[Ab] \to a[Ab] \mid b$$
$$[Cd] \to c[Cd] \mid d$$
$$S \to a[Ab]{\dashv} \mid b{\dashv} \mid c[Cd]{\dashv} \mid d{\dashv}$$

While preparing these lectures, the author found that many other LL(1) grammars are amenable to similar transformations; so it seemed reasonable to make the conjecture that, whenever L is an LL(1) language, then $L{\dashv}$ is an s-language. If this conjecture were true, it would provide a solution to the equivalence problem for LL(1) languages.

One grammar that seemed to provide a counterexample to this conjecture was the following:

$$P \to +PP \mid xA$$
$$A \to aA \mid \epsilon \tag{11.6}$$
$$S \to P{\dashv}$$

These productions define Polish prefix notation, with the binary operator $+$ and the variables x, xa, xaa, ... The author made several fruitless attempts to find an s-grammar for this language, before finally hitting on the following trick: We can write $P = P'A$, where P' represents those strings of P not ending in a; and we can therefore give the following s-grammar for the strings defined by (11.6):

$$P' \to +P'[AP'] \mid x$$
$$[AP'] \to a[AP'] \mid +P'[AP'] \mid x$$
$$S \to P'[A{\dashv}]$$
$$[A{\dashv}] \to a[A{\dashv}] \mid {\dashv}$$

This example gave added weight to the conjecture.

However, R. Kürki-Suonio found a simple counterexample [15], which shows that ϵ cannot in general be removed from an LL(1) grammar followed by $\dashv$. Thus, *the null string plays an important role in top-down analysis.*

Exercise 11.1. (suggested by Karel Čulik II). Show that the following grammar is LL(2). Is there an LL(1) grammar for the same language?

$$S \to a\,a\,S\,b\,b \mid a \mid \epsilon$$

12. Concluding Remarks

It is natural to inquire which is better, top-down or bottom-up analysis? A complete answer to this question may never be found, but some comments can be made.

First, every LL(k) grammar is an LR(k) grammar. (This fact can be proved using a rather involved but intuitively clear argument. A careful and clear proof would make a suitable master's thesis and would be an instructive project.)

On the other hand, the "Boolean expression" grammar (2.1) is LR(0) but not LL(k) for any k: The string $((((((((((a = b))))))))))$ needs to be parsed quite differently from the string

$$((((((((((a + b) + b) + b) + b) + b) + b) + b) + b) + b) + b) = b$$

which begins with the same 12 symbols. One can in fact show that the strings derivable from B do not even form an LL(k) *language*; that is, there is no equivalent LL(k) grammar. Thus, bottom-up analysis can deterministically parse a larger family of languages than top-down analysis can.

On the other hand when we are fortunate enough to have an LL(1) grammar, we have more flexibility in applying semantic rules, since we know what production is being used *before* we actually process its components. This foreknowledge can be extremely important in practice. The bottom-up procedure only discovers what is present after it has scanned the text. A theoretical model that nicely demonstrates this advantage of top-down analysis has been discussed at length by Lewis and Stearns [16].

A simple model for bottom-up analysis, which might be considered the bottom-up analog of the *no-backup* Parsing Machine, is the technique of "simple precedence grammars" developed by Wirth and Weber [24]. The bottom-up analog of the *partial backup* method is the original method of Irons [11], which has not yet been given a theoretical treatment.

In conclusion, here are some research problems that are (perhaps) listed in increasing order of difficulty:

1. Is every LL(k) language, $k \geq 1$, an LL(1) language? (The corresponding statement is true for LR(k) and LR(1) languages.)

2. Is the equivalence problem solvable for LL(1) languages? (The work of Korenjak and Hopcroft [14] makes this likely.)

3. Can the method of Irons [11] be analyzed theoretically in a fashion analogous to the partial backup method discussed above?

4. What class of languages can the Parsing Machine accept? (See Exercise 3.1.)

5. Is the equivalence problem decidable for LR(1) languages? (This question seems to be the most important unsolved problem at the present time. We would also like to answer it efficiently in very special cases, for example with respect to Wirth's precedence grammars [24]).

Postscript, added May 1971. Research problems 1 and 2 have now been resolved. R. Kürki-Suonio proved that the LL$(k + 1)$ grammar

$$S \rightarrow aSA \mid \epsilon$$
$$A \rightarrow a^k bS \mid c$$

defines a non-LL(k) language [15]. D. J. Rosenkrantz and R. E. Stearns showed that the equivalence problem for LL(k) grammars is solvable [21]. Both of these papers establish a number of other important facts about LL(k) grammars and languages.

Substantial progress has also been made on the theory related to research problem 3. The author (and others) believed in 1967 that Irons's original algorithm was "bottom up" as stated above, but it has subsequently become clear that the true bottom-up methods are those of Cocke, Younger, Kasami, et al. (see [8]). The method of Irons is neither top-down nor bottom-up, and it has become known as "left-corner parsing"; the corresponding grammars, called LC(k), have been studied by Rosenkrantz and Lewis [20], who showed that all LC(k) languages are LL(k) languages and conversely.

Appendix. Answers to the Exercises

Exercise 3.1. $\{a^n b^n c^n \mid n = 1, 2, 3, \ldots\}$. Hence the PM can accept languages that are not context-free.

Exercise 8.1. Condition 1 has been verified in the text. Condition 2 needs only to be verified for the rule $P \rightarrow a \mid b \mid (E)$, where the sets first$(a) = \{a\}$, first$(b) = \{b\}$, first$((E)) = \{(\}$ are obviously disjoint. (In the other rules, $m = 0$ or $n = 0$.) Condition 3 is true because follow$(L') = \{), \dashv\}$ has no letters in common with first$(+LL') = \{+\}$; and follow$(P') = \{), +, \dashv\}$ has no letters in common with first$(PP') = \{a, b, (\}$. Finally, the nonfalse nonterminals are L' and P', so Condition 4 holds.

Exercise 10.1. If $A \rightarrow^+ A$ the grammar is ambiguous and therefore not LL(k). If $A \rightarrow^+ A\alpha$ and $A \rightarrow^+ \beta$, where α and β are in T^* and $\alpha \neq \epsilon$, then $A \rightarrow^+ \beta\alpha^n$ for arbitrarily large n. So examining the first k characters of $\beta \alpha^n$ will not tell us how many times to do the left production sequence corresponding to $A \to^+ A\alpha$.

Exercise 10.2. Consider the initial steps of the derivation; if

$$S \xrightarrow{L}^* \beta_1 B \beta_3 \xrightarrow{L} \beta_1 \beta_2 \beta_3 \xrightarrow{L}^* \alpha_1 A \alpha_2$$
$$S \xrightarrow{L}^* \beta_1 B \beta_3 \xrightarrow{L} \beta_1 \beta_2' \beta_3 \xrightarrow{L}^* \alpha_1 A \alpha_2'$$

then $\alpha_1 = \beta_1 \gamma$ for some γ in T^*. Since $k : \gamma \alpha_3 = k : \gamma \alpha_3'$, the definition of LL($k$) implies that $\beta_2 = \beta_2'$. Thus if $S \xrightarrow{L}^* \alpha_1 A \alpha_2$ in m steps and if $S \xrightarrow{L}^* \alpha_1 A \alpha_2'$ in $n \geq m$ steps, the first m steps must be identical. It follows that $\alpha_1 A \alpha_2 \xrightarrow{L}^* \alpha_1 A \alpha_2'$ in $n - m$ steps.

If $m = n$, we are done. Otherwise the previous exercise tells us that A is not left recursive; hence $A \to^* \epsilon$ and we must have

$$\alpha_3 \xrightarrow{L}^* A \alpha_3' \to^* \alpha_3'.$$

Exercise 10.3. (Solution by Gérard Terrine.) No. Consider the LL(0) grammar

$$S \to a S A \mid \epsilon$$
$$A \to \epsilon$$

where $\alpha_1 = aa$, $\alpha_2 = A$, $\alpha_2' = \epsilon$, $\alpha_3 = \alpha_3' = \epsilon$.

Exercise 11.1. The strings are $\{a^n b^{2\lfloor n/2 \rfloor} \mid n \geq 0\}$. By looking two characters ahead, we apply $S \to aaSbb$ if there are two a's, $S \to a$ if one a but not two, $S \to \epsilon$ otherwise.

An equivalent LL(1) grammar is

$$S \to a T \mid \epsilon$$
$$T \to a U b \mid \epsilon$$
$$U \to a T b \mid b$$

Acknowledgments

The author wishes to thank V. Tixier and R. Guedj for their assistance in preparing the first draft of these lecture notes.

The publication of this paper was supported in part by IBM Corporation.

References

[1] Ranan B. Banerji, "Some studies in syntax-directed parsing," in *Computation in Linguistics*, edited by Paul L. Garvin (Bloomington, Indiana: Indiana University Press, 1966), 76–123.

[2] M. P. Barnett and R. P. Futrelle, "Syntactic analysis by digital computer," *Communications of the ACM* **5** (1962), 515–526.

[3] R. A. Brooker and D. Morris, "A description of MERCURY autocode in terms of a phrase structure language," *Annual Review in Automatic Programming* **2** (1961), 29–65.

[4] R. A. Brooker, D. Morris, and J. S. Rohl, "Trees and routines," *The Computer Journal* **5** (1962), 33–47.

[5] R. A. Brooker, "Top-to-bottom parsing rehabilitated?" *Communications of the ACM* **10** (1967), 223–224.

[6] T. E. Cheatham, Jr., and Kirk Sattley, "Syntax-directed compiling," *Proceedings of the Spring Joint Computer Conference* **25** (1964), 31–57.

[7] Melvin E. Conway, "Design of a separable transition-diagram compiler," *Communications of the ACM* **6** (1963), 396–408.

[8] Jay Earley, "An efficient context-free parsing algorithm," *Communications of the ACM* **13** (1970), 94–102.

[9] Robert W. Floyd, "The syntax of programming languages — A survey," *IEEE Transactions on Electronic Computers* **EC-13** (1964), 346–353.

[10] A. E. Glennie, "On the syntax machine and the construction of a universal compiler," Technical Report Number 2 (Pittsburgh, Pennsylvania: Computation Center, Carnegie Institute of Technology, July 1960).

[11] Edgar T. Irons, "A syntax directed compiler for ALGOL 60," *Communications of the ACM* **4** (1961), 51–55.

[12] Donald E. Knuth, "On the translation of languages from left to right," *Information and Control* **8** (1965), 607–639. [Reprinted as Chapter 15 of the present volume.]

[13] Donald E. Knuth, *Fundamental Algorithms*, Volume 1 of *The Art of Computer Programming* (Reading, Massachusetts: Addison–Wesley, 1968).

[14] A. J. Korenjak and J. E. Hopcroft, "Simple deterministic languages," *IEEE Symposium on Switching and Automata Theory* **7** (1966), 36–46.

[15] R. Kürki-Suonio, "Notes on top-down languages," *BIT* **9** (1969), 225–238.

[16] P. M. Lewis II and R. E. Stearns, "Syntax-directed transduction," *Journal of the Association for Computing Machinery* **15** (1968), 465–488.

[17] Peter Naur, editor, "Revised report on the algorithmic language ALGOL 60, *Communications of the ACM* **6** (1963), 1–17.

[18] Emil L. Post, "Recursive unsolvability of a problem of Thue," *Journal of Symbolic Logic* **12** (1947), 1–11.

[19] Saul Rosen, "A compiler-building system developed by Brooker and Morris," *Communications of the ACM* **7** (1964), 403–414.

[20] D. J. Rosenkrantz and P. M. Lewis II, "Deterministic left corner parsing," *IEEE Symposium on Switching and Automata Theory* **11** (1970), 139–152.

[21] D. J. Rosenkrantz and R. E. Stearns, "Properties of deterministic top-down grammars," *Information and Control* **17** (1970), 226–256.

[22] D. V. Schorre, "META II: A syntax-oriented compiler writing language," *Proceedings of the ACM National Conference* **19** (1964), D 1.3.1–D 1.3.11.

[23] Stephen Warshall, "A theorem on Boolean matrices," *Journal of the Association for Computing Machinery* **9** (1962), 11–12.

[24] Niklaus Wirth and Helmut Weber, "Euler: A generalization of ALGOL, and its formal definition," *Communications of the ACM* **9** (1966), 13–23, 25, 89–99, 878.

Addendum

For many years, research problem 5 reigned supreme as perhaps the most famous and tantalizing of all unsolved questions in the theory of languages. It was finally resolved in 1997 by Géraud Sénizergues, who showed that equivalence is indeed decidable. His original proof was quite complex, but simplifications have been found more recently: See Géraud Sénizergues, "L(A) = L(B)? A simplified decidability proof," *Theoretical Computer Science* **281** (2002), 555–608; Colin Stirling, "Deciding DPDA equivalence is primitive recursive," *Lecture Notes in Computer Science* **2380** (2002), 821–832.

Research problem 4 remains mysterious. Perhaps it does not have an elegant answer.

Chapter 15

On the Translation of Languages from Left to Right

*[Originally published in Information and Control **8** (1965), 607–639.]*

There has been much recent interest in languages whose grammar is sufficiently simple that an efficient left-to-right parsing algorithm can be produced mechanically from the grammar. In this paper, we define LR(k) *grammars, which are perhaps the most general systems of this type; such grammars provide the basis for understanding all of the special tricks that have been used in the construction of parsing algorithms for languages with simple structure, such as algebraic languages. We give algorithms for deciding if a given grammar satisfies the* LR(k) *condition, for given k, and also give methods by which recognizers for* LR(k) *grammars can be constructed. The problem of deciding whether or not a grammar is* LR(k) *for some k is shown to be undecidable. The paper concludes by establishing various connections between* LR(k) *grammars and deterministic languages. In particular, the* LR(k) *condition is shown to be a natural analog, for grammars, of the deterministic condition for languages.*

1. Introduction and Definitions

The word "language" will be used here to denote a set of character strings that has variously been called a *context free language*, a *(simple) phrase structure language*, a *constituent-structure language*, a *definable set*, a *BNF language*, a *Chomsky type 2 (or type 4) language*, a *push-down automaton language*, etc. Such languages have aroused wide interest because they serve as approximate models for natural languages and computer programming languages, among others. In this paper we single out an important class of languages that will be called *translatable from left to right*; this term means that if we read the characters of a string from left to right, and look a given finite number of characters ahead, we are able to parse the given string without ever backing up to reconsider a previous decision. Such languages are particularly important in the case of computer programming, since the left-to-right condition means that a parsing algorithm requires an execution time at worst proportional to the length of the string being parsed. Moreover, such an algorithm can be constructed mechanically from the grammar.

Special-purpose methods for translating computer languages — for example, the well-known precedence algorithm, see Floyd [4] — are based on the fact that the languages being considered have a simple left-to-right structure. By considering the entire family of languages that are translatable from left to right, we are able to study all of these special techniques in their most general framework, and to find for a given language and grammar the "best possible" way to translate it from left to right. The study of such languages is also of possible interest to those who are investigating human parsing behavior, perhaps helping to explain the fact that certain English sentences are unintelligible to a listener.

Let us now consider precise definitions of the concepts discussed informally above. The well-known properties of *characters* and *strings* of characters will be assumed. We are given two disjoint sets of characters, the "nonterminals" N and the "terminals" T; we will use uppercase letters A, B, C, ... to stand for nonterminals, and lowercase letters a, b, c, ... to stand for terminals, while the letters X, Y, Z will be used to denote either nonterminals or terminals. The letter S denotes the "principal nonterminal," which has special significance as explained below. Strings of characters will be denoted by lowercase Greek letters α, β, γ, ..., and the *empty string* will be represented by ϵ. The notation α^n denotes n-fold concatenation of string α with itself; thus $\alpha^0 = \epsilon$, and $\alpha^n = \alpha\alpha^{n-1}$ when $n > 0$.

A *production* is a relation $A \to \theta$ where A is in N and θ is a string on $N \cup T$; a *grammar* $\mathcal{G}$ is a set of productions. We write $\varphi \to \psi$ (with respect to $\mathcal{G}$, a grammar that is usually understood from the context) if there exist strings α, θ, ω, and A such that $\varphi = \alpha A \omega$, $\psi = \alpha\theta\omega$, and $A \to \theta$ is a production in $\mathcal{G}$. The transitive completion of this relation is of principal importance: $\alpha \Rightarrow \beta$ means that there exist strings α_0, α_1, ..., α_n (with $n > 0$) for which $\alpha = \alpha_0 \to \alpha_1 \to \cdots \to \alpha_n = \beta$. It is not necessarily true that $\alpha \Rightarrow \alpha$, because we require that $n > 0$; we will write $\alpha \Rightarrow\!\!\!\!\Rightarrow \beta$ to mean that $\alpha = \beta$ or $\alpha \Rightarrow \beta$. A grammar is said to be *circular* if $\alpha \Rightarrow \alpha$ for some α. (Some of this notation is more complicated than we would need for the purposes of the present paper, but it has been introduced in this way in order to be compatible with that used in related papers.)

The *language defined by* $\mathcal{G}$ is

$$\{\alpha \mid S \Rightarrow \alpha \text{ and } \alpha \text{ is a string over } T\}, \tag{1}$$

namely the set of all terminal strings derivable from the principal nonterminal S by using the productions of $\mathcal{G}$ as substitution rules. A *sentential form* is any string α for which $S \Rightarrow \alpha$. For example, the grammar

$$S \to AD, \; A \to aC, \; B \to bcd, \; C \to BE, \; D \to \epsilon, \; E \to e \tag{2}$$

defines the language consisting of the single string '*abcde*', and one of its sentential forms is '*aBE*'.

Any sentential form in a grammar may be given at least one representation as the leaves of a *derivation tree* or "parse diagram." For example, there is but one derivation tree for the string *abcde* in the grammar (2), namely

$$\tag{3}$$

(The root of the derivation tree is S, and the branches correspond in an obvious manner to applications of productions.) A grammar is said to be *unambiguous* if every sentential form has a unique derivation tree. The grammar (2) is clearly unambiguous, even though there are several different *sequences* of derivations possible; for example,

$$S \to AD \to aCD \to aBED \to abcdED \to abcdeD \to abcde \tag{4}$$

and

$$S \to AD \to A \to aC \to aBE \to aBe \to abcde \tag{5}$$

are two of the possibilities. In order to avoid the unimportant difference between sequences of derivations corresponding to the same tree, we can stipulate a particular order, such as insisting that we always substitute for the leftmost nonterminal (as done in (4)) or the rightmost one (as in (5)).

In practice, however, we must start with the terminal string *abcde* and try to reconstruct the derivation leading back to S, and that changes our outlook somewhat. Let us define the *handle* of a tree to be the leftmost set of adjacent leaves forming a complete branch; in (3) the handle is *bcd*. In other words, if X_1, X_2, ..., X_t are the respective leaves of the tree (where each X_i is a nonterminal or terminal character or ϵ), we look for the smallest n such that the tree has the form

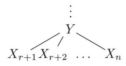

for some r and Y. (Here r might be equal to n, if the relevant production is $Y \to \epsilon$.) If we consider going from *abcde* backwards to reach S, we can imagine starting with tree (3), and "pruning off" its handle; then prune off the handle ('*e*') of the resulting tree, and so on until only the root S is left. This process of pruning the handle at each step corresponds exactly to derivation (5) in reverse. The reader may easily verify, in fact, that "handle pruning" always produces, in reverse, the derivation obtained by replacing the *rightmost* nonterminal character at each step, and this formulation may be regarded as an alternative way to define the concept of handle. During the pruning process, all leaves to the right of the handle are terminals, if we begin with all terminal leaves.

We are interested in algorithms for parsing, and thus we want to be able to recognize the handle when only the leaves of the tree are given. Let us number the productions of the grammar 1, 2, ..., s in some arbitrary fashion. Suppose $\alpha = X_1 \ldots X_n \ldots X_t$ is a sentential form, and suppose that there is a derivation tree in which the handle is $X_{r+1} \ldots X_n$, obtained by application of the pth production. (Here $0 \leq r \leq n \leq t$ and $1 \leq p \leq s$.) We will say that (n, p) is a *handle* of α.

A grammar is said to be *translatable from left to right with bound k* (briefly, an "LR(k) grammar") under the following circumstances. Let $k \geq 0$, and let '$\dashv$' be a new character not in $N \cup T$. A k-sentential form is a sentential form followed by k '$\dashv$' characters. Let

$$\alpha = X_1 X_2 \ldots X_m X_{m+1} \ldots X_{m+k} Y_1 \ldots Y_u$$
$$\text{and } \beta = X_1 X_2 \ldots X_m X_{m+1} \ldots X_{m+k} Z_1 \ldots Z_v$$

be k-sentential forms in which $u \geq 0$ and $v \geq 0$, and in which none of X_{m+1}, ..., X_{m+k}, Y_1, ..., Y_u, Z_1, ..., Z_v is a nonterminal character. If (m, p) is a handle of α and (n, q) is a handle of β, where $m \leq n$, we require that $m = n$ and $p = q$. In other words, a grammar is LR(k) if and only if any handle is always uniquely determined by the string to its left and the k terminal characters to its right.

This definition is more readily understandable if we take a particular value of k, say $k = 1$. Suppose we are constructing a derivation sequence such as (5) in reverse, and the current string (followed by the delimiter $\dashv$ for convenience) has the form $X_1 \ldots X_n X_{n+1} \alpha \dashv$, where the tail end '$X_{n+1} \alpha \dashv$' represents part of the string we have not yet examined; but all possible reductions have been made at the left of the string so that the right boundary of the handle must be at some position $\geq n$. We want to know, by looking at the next character X_{n+1}, if there is in fact a handle whose right boundary is at position n. If so, we want this handle to correspond to a unique production, so that we can reduce the string and repeat the process; if not, we know that we can move to the right and read a new character of the string to be translated. This process will work if and only if the following condition, called LR(1), always holds in the grammar: If $X_1 X_2 \ldots X_n X_{n+1} \omega_0$ is any sentential form followed by '$\dashv$' for which all characters of $X_{n+1} \omega_0$ are terminals or '$\dashv$', and if this string has a handle (n, p) ending at position n, then *all* 1-sentential forms $X_1 X_2 \ldots X_n X_{n+1} \omega$ with $X_{n+1} \omega$ as above must have the same handle (n, p). The definition has been phrased carefully to account for the possibility that the handle is the empty string, which if inserted between X_n and X_{n+1} is regarded as having right boundary n.

It should now be clear that our definition of an LR(k) grammar coincides with the intuitive notion of translation from left to right, looking k characters ahead. Assume that at some stage of translation we have made all possible reductions to the left of X_n; by looking at the next k characters $X_{n+1} \ldots X_{n+k}$, we want to know if a reduction on $X_{r+1} \ldots X_n$ is to be made, *regardless* of what appears to the right of X_{n+k}. In an LR(k) grammar we are able to decide without hesitation whether or not such a reduction should be made. If a reduction is called for, we perform it and repeat the process; if none should be made, we move one character to the right.

An LR(k) grammar is clearly unambiguous, since the definition implies that every derivation tree must have the same handle, and by induction there is only one possible tree. It is interesting to point out furthermore that nearly every grammar for which a proof of unambiguity has been published to date is either an LR(k) grammar, or (dually) is a right-to-left translatable grammar, or is some grammar that is translated using "both ends toward the middle." Thus, the LR(k) condition may be regarded as the most powerful general test for nonambiguity that is now available.

When k is given, we will show in Section 2 that it is possible to decide if a grammar is LR(k) or not. The essential reason underlying this result is that the possible configurations of a tree above its handle can be represented by a regular (finite automaton) language.

Several related ideas have appeared in previous literature. Lynch [9] considered special cases of LR(1) grammars, which he showed are unambiguous. Paul [11] gave a general method to construct left-to-right parsers for certain very simple LR(1) languages. Floyd [5] and Irons [8] independently developed the notion of *bounded context* grammars, which have the property that one knows whether or not to reduce any sentential form $\alpha\theta\omega$ using the production $A \to \theta$ by examining only a finite number of characters immediately to the left and right of θ. Eickel [3] later developed an algorithm that would construct a certain form of push-down parsing program from a bounded context grammar, and Earley [2] independently developed a somewhat similar method that was applicable to a rather large number of LR(1) languages but had several important omissions. Floyd [5] also introduced the more general notion of a *bounded right context* grammar; in our terminology, this is an LR(k) grammar in which one knows whether or not $X_{r+1} \ldots X_n$ is the handle by examining only a given *finite* number of characters immediately to the left of X_{r+1}, as well as knowing $X_{n+1} \ldots X_{n+k}$. At that time it seemed plausible that a bounded right context grammar was the natural way to formalize the intuitive notion of a grammar by which one could translate from left to right without backing up or looking ahead by more than a given distance; but subsequent study showed that Earley's construction provided a parsing method for some grammars that were *not* of bounded right context, although intuitively they should have been. These considerations led to the definition of an LR(k) grammar given above, in which the *entire* string to the left of X_{r+1} is known.

It is natural to ask if we can in fact always parse the strings corresponding to an LR(k) grammar by going from left to right. Infinitely many strings $X_1 \ldots X_{n+k}$ might face us when we are supposed to make a parsing decision, so we might need infinite wisdom to be able to make the decision correctly; the definition of LR(k) merely says that a correct decision *exists* for each of these infinitely many strings. But we will see in Section 2 that only a finite number of essential possibilities really arise.

To illustrate these notions, let us look at a few simple examples. Consider the following two grammars:

$$S \to aAc, \quad A \to bAb, \quad A \to b; \tag{6}$$

$$S \to aAc, \quad A \to Abb, \quad A \to b. \tag{7}$$

They both are unambiguous and define the same language, $\{ab^{2n+1}c\}$. Grammar (6) is not LR(k) for any k, for if we are given the partial string

ab^m there is no information by which we can replace any b by A; parsing must wait until the 'c' has been read. On the other hand grammar (7) is LR(0), in fact it is a bounded context language; the sentential forms are $\{aAb^{2n}c\}$ and $\{ab^{2n+1}c\}$, and to parse we must reduce a substring ab to aA, a substring Abb to A, and a substring aAc to S. This example shows that LR(k) is definitely a property of the *grammar*, not of the *language* alone. The distinction between grammar and language is extremely important when semantics is being considered as well as syntax.

The grammar

$$S \to aAd, \ S \to bAB, \ A \to cA, \ A \to c, \ B \to d \qquad (8)$$

has the sentential forms $\{ac^nAd\} \cup \{ac^{n+1}d\} \cup \{bc^nAB\} \cup \{bc^nAd\} \cup \{bc^{n+1}B\} \cup \{bc^{n+1}d\}$. In the string $bc^{n+1}d$, d must be replaced by B, while in the string $ac^{n+1}d$, this replacement must not be made; so the decision depends on an unbounded number of characters to the left of d, and the grammar is not of bounded context (nor is it translatable from right to left). On the other hand this grammar is clearly LR(1), and in fact it is of bounded right context since the handle is immediately known by considering the character to its right and two characters to its left; when the character d is considered the sentential form will have been reduced to either aAd or bAd.

The grammar

$$S \to aA, \ S \to bB, \ A \to cA, \ A \to d, \ B \to cB, \ B \to d \qquad (9)$$

is not of bounded right context, since the handle in both ac^nd and bc^nd is 'd'; yet this grammar is certainly LR(0). A more interesting example is

$$S \to aAc, \ S \to b, \ A \to aSc, \ A \to b. \qquad (10)$$

Here the terminal strings are $\{a^nbc^n\}$, and the b must be reduced to S or A according as n is even or odd. This is another LR(0) grammar that fails to be of bounded right context.

In Section 3 we will give further examples and will discuss the relevance of these concepts to the grammar for ALGOL 60. Section 4 contains a proof that the existence of a nonnegative integer k, such that a given grammar is LR(k), is recursively undecidable.

Ginsburg and Greibach [7] have recently defined the notion of a *deterministic language*; we will show in Section 5 that such languages are precisely those for which *there exists* an LR(k) grammar, and thereby we obtain a number of interesting consequences.

2. Analysis of LR(k) Grammars

Given a grammar $\mathcal{G}$ and an integer $k \geq 0$, we will now give two ways to test whether $\mathcal{G}$ is LR(k) or not. We may assume as usual that $\mathcal{G}$ does not contain useless productions, namely that, for any A in N, there are terminal strings α, β, γ such that $S \Rightarrow \alpha A \gamma \Rightarrow \alpha \beta \gamma$.

The first method of testing is to construct another grammar $\mathcal{F}$ that reflects all possible configurations of a handle and k characters to its right. The nonterminal symbols of $\mathcal{F}$ will be $[A; \alpha]$, where α is a k-letter string on $T \cup \{\dashv\}$; and also $[p]$, where p is the number of a production in $\mathcal{G}$. The terminal symbols of $\mathcal{F}$ will be $N \cup T \cup \{\dashv\}$.

For convenience we define $H_k(\sigma)$ to be the set of all k-letter strings β over $T \cup \{\dashv\}$ such that $\sigma \dashv^k \Rightarrow \beta \gamma$ with respect to $\mathcal{G}$ for some γ; this is the set of all possible initial strings of length k derivable from $\sigma \dashv^k$.

Let the pth production of $\mathcal{G}$ be

$$A_p \to X_{p1} \ldots X_{pn_p}, \quad \text{for } 1 \leq p \leq s, \tag{11}$$

where $n_p \geq 0$. We construct all productions of the form

$$[A_p; \alpha] \to X_{p1} \ldots X_{p(j-1)} [X_{pj}; \beta] \tag{12}$$

where $1 \leq j \leq n_p$, X_{pj} is nonterminal, and α, β are k-letter strings over $T \cup \{\dashv\}$ with β in $H_k(X_{p(j+1)} \ldots X_{pn_p} \alpha)$. Add also the productions

$$[A_p; \alpha] \to X_{p1} \ldots X_{pn_p} \alpha [p] \tag{13}$$

for $1 \leq p \leq s$ and all α.

It is now easy to see that with respect to $\mathcal{F}$, we have

$$[S; \dashv^k] \Rightarrow X_1 \ldots X_n X_{n+1} \ldots X_{n+k} [p]$$

if and only if there exists a k-sentential form

$$X_1 \ldots X_n X_{n+1} \ldots X_{n+k} Y_1 \ldots Y_u$$

with handle (n, p) and with $X_{n+1} \ldots Y_u$ all terminals or $\dashv$. Therefore by definition, $\mathcal{G}$ will be LR(k) if and only if $\mathcal{F}$ satisfies the following property:

$$[S; \dashv^k] \Rightarrow \theta[p] \text{ and } [S; \dashv^k] \Rightarrow \theta \varphi[q] \text{ implies } \varphi = \epsilon \text{ and } p = q. \tag{14}$$

But $\mathcal{F}$ is a *regular* grammar, and well-known methods exist for testing condition (14) in regular grammars. (Basically one first transforms

$\mathcal{F}$ so that all of its productions have the form $Q_i \to aQ_j$, and then if $Q_0 = [S; \dashv^k]$ one can systematically prepare a list of all pairs (i, j) such that there exists a string α for which $Q_0 \Rightarrow \alpha Q_i$ and $Q_0 \Rightarrow \alpha Q_j$.)

When $k = 2$, the grammar $\mathcal{F}$ corresponding to (2) is

$$[S; \dashv\dashv] \to [A; \dashv\dashv], \quad [S; \dashv\dashv] \to A[D; \dashv\dashv], \quad [S; \dashv\dashv] \to AD\dashv\dashv[1],$$
$$[A; \dashv\dashv] \to a[C; \dashv\dashv], \quad [A; \dashv\dashv] \to aC\dashv\dashv[2],$$
$$[C; \dashv\dashv] \to [B; e\dashv], \quad [C; \dashv\dashv] \to B[E; \dashv\dashv], \quad [C; \dashv\dashv] \to BE\dashv\dashv[4],$$
$$[B; e\dashv] \to bcde\dashv[3],$$
$$[D; \dashv\dashv] \to \dashv\dashv[5],$$
$$[E; \dashv\dashv] \to e\dashv\dashv[6]. \tag{15}$$

It is, of course, unnecessary to list productions that cannot be reached from $[S; \dashv\dashv]$. Condition (14) is immediate. Notice also that there is an intimate connection between (15) and the tree (3).

Our second method for testing the LR(k) condition is related to the first, but it is perhaps more natural and at the same time it gives a method for parsing the grammar $\mathcal{G}$ when $\mathcal{G}$ is indeed LR(k). The parsing method is complicated by the appearance of ϵ in the grammar, when it becomes necessary to be very careful about whether to insert a nonterminal symbol that corresponds to the production $A \to \epsilon$. To treat this condition properly we will define $H'_k(\sigma)$ to be the same as $H_k(\sigma)$ except that we omit all derivations that contain a step of the form

$$A\omega \to \omega,$$

that is, when a nonterminal as the *initial character* is replaced by ϵ. This means we are avoiding derivation trees whose handle is an empty string at the extreme left. For example, in the grammar

$$S \to BC, \ B \to Ce, \ B \to \epsilon, \ C \to D, \ C \to Dc, \ D \to \epsilon, \ D \to d$$

we would have

$$H_3(S) = \{\dashv\dashv\dashv, \ c\dashv\dashv, \ ce\dashv, \ cec, \ ced, \ d\dashv\dashv, \ dc\dashv, dce,$$
$$de\dashv, \ dec, \ ded, \ e\dashv\dashv, \ ec\dashv, \ ed\dashv, \ edc\}$$
$$H'_3(S) = \{dce, \ de\dashv, \ dec, \ ded\}.$$

As before we assume that the productions of $\mathcal{G}$ are written in the form (11). We will also change $\mathcal{G}$ by introducing a new nonterminal S_0 and adding a "zeroth" production

$$S_0 \to S\dashv^k \tag{16}$$

with S_0 replacing S as the principal nonterminal. The sentential forms are now identical to the k-sentential forms as defined above, and this fact will prove to be quite convenient.

Our construction is based on the notion of a "state," which will be denoted by $[p, j; \alpha]$; here p is the number of a production, j is an index in the range $0 \leq j \leq n_p$, and α is a k-letter string of terminals. Intuitively, we will be in state $[p, j; \alpha]$ if the partial parse so far has the form $\beta X_{p1} \ldots X_{pj}$ for some string β and if $\mathcal{G}$ contains at least one sentential form beginning with $\beta A_p \alpha$; that is, state $[p, j; \alpha]$ means that we have found j of the characters needed to complete the pth production, and α is a string that may legitimately follow the entire production if production p is completed.

At any time during translation we will be in a *set* S of states. There are of course only a finite number of possible sets of states, although it may be an enormous number. Hopefully the total number of state sets that can actually arise during translation will not be too large. For each of the possible sets of states we will give a rule that explains what parsing step to perform and what new set of states to enter.

During the translation process we maintain a *stack*, denoted by

$$S_0 X_1 S_1 X_2 S_2 \ldots X_n S_n \mid Y_1 \ldots Y_k \omega. \tag{17}$$

The portion to the left of the vertical line consists alternately of state sets and characters; this represents the portion of a string that has already been translated (with the possible exception of the handle) together with the state sets S_i we were in just after considering $X_1 \ldots X_i$. To the right of the vertical line appear the k terminal characters $Y_1 \ldots Y_k$ that may be used to govern the translation decision, followed by a string ω that has not yet been examined.

Initially we are in the state set S_0 that consists of the single state $[0, 0; \dashv^k]$; the stack to the left of the vertical line in (17) contains only S_0, and the string to be parsed (followed by $\dashv^k$) appears at the right. Inductively at a given stage of translation, we assume that the stack contents are given by (17) and that we are in state set $S = S_n$.

Step 1. Compute the "closure" S' of S, which is defined recursively as the smallest set satisfying the following equation:

$$S' = S \cup \{[q, 0; \beta] \mid \text{there exists } [p, j; \alpha] \text{ in } S' \text{ such that}$$
$$j < n_p, \ X_{p(j+1)} = A_q, \text{ and } \beta \in H_k(X_{p(j+2)} \ldots X_{pn_p} \alpha)\}. \tag{18}$$

(We thus have added to S all productions that we might begin to work on, in addition to those we are already working on.)

Step 2. Compute the following sets of k-letter strings:

$$Z = \{\beta \mid \text{there exists } [p, j; \alpha] \text{ in } \mathcal{S}' \text{ such that}$$
$$j < n_p \text{ and } \beta \in H'_k(X_{p(j+1)} \ldots X_{pn_p}\alpha)\} \qquad (19)$$
$$Z_p = \{\alpha \mid [p, n_p; \alpha] \in \mathcal{S}'\}, \quad \text{for } 0 \leq p \leq s. \qquad (20)$$

Here Z represents all terminal strings $Y_1 \ldots Y_k$ for which the handle does *not* appear on the stack, and Z_p represents all for which the pth production should be used to reduce the stack. Therefore, $Z, Z_0, \ldots, Z_s$ *must all be disjoint sets*, or the grammar is not LR(k). These formulas and remarks are meaningful even when $k = 0$.

Assuming that the Z's are disjoint, $Y_1 \ldots Y_k$ must lie in one of them, or else an error has occurred. If $Y_1 \ldots Y_k$ lies in Z, we shift the entire stack left:

$$\mathcal{S}_0 X_1 \mathcal{S}_1 \ldots \mathcal{S}_n Y_1 \mid Y_2 \ldots Y_k \omega$$

and rename its contents by letting $X_{n+1} = Y_1$, $Y_1 = Y_2$, ...:

$$\mathcal{S}_0 X_1 \mathcal{S}_1 \ldots \mathcal{S}_n X_{n+1} \mid Y_1 \ldots Y_k \omega'$$

where ω' is obtained by removing the first character (the new Y_k) from ω; then we go on to Step 3. On the other hand if $Y_1 \ldots Y_k$ lies in Z_p, let $r = n - n_p$; the stack now contains $X_{r+1} \ldots X_n$, equaling the right-hand side of production p. Replace the stack contents (17) by

$$\mathcal{S}_0 X_1 \mathcal{S}_1 \ldots X_r \mathcal{S}_r A_p \mid Y_1 \ldots Y_k \omega \qquad (21)$$

and let $n = r$, $\mathcal{S} = \mathcal{S}_r$, $X_{n+1} = A_p$. (Notice that obvious notational conventions have been used here to deal with empty strings; we have $0 \leq r \leq n$. If $n_p = 0$, that is, if the right-hand side of production p is empty, we have just *increased* the stack size by going from (17) to (21); otherwise the stack has gotten smaller.)

Step 3. The stack now has the form

$$\mathcal{S}_0 X_1 \mathcal{S}_1 \ldots X_n \mathcal{S}_n X_{n+1} \mid Y_1 \ldots Y_k \omega. \qquad (22)$$

Compute $\mathcal{S}'_n$ by Eq. (18) and then compute the new set $\mathcal{S}_{n+1}$ as follows:

$$\mathcal{S}_{n+1} = \{[p, j+1; \alpha] \mid [p, j; \alpha] \in \mathcal{S}'_n \text{ and } X_{n+1} = X_{p(j+1)}\}. \qquad (23)$$

This is the state set into which we now advance; we insert $\mathcal{S}_{n+1}$ into the stack (22) just to the left of the vertical line and return to Step 1, with $\mathcal{S} = \mathcal{S}_{n+1}$ and with n increased by one. However, if $\mathcal{S}$ now equals $\{[0, 1; \dashv^k]\}$ and $Y_1 \ldots Y_k = \dashv^k$, the parsing is complete.

Our parsing method is now complete. In order to take care of the most general case, the method is necessarily complicated, because all of the relevant information must be preserved. But the structure of the general method sheds light on the important special cases that arise when the LR(k) grammar is of a simpler type.

We will not give a formal proof that this parsing method works, since the reader may easily verify that each step preserves the assertions we have made about the state sets and the stack. The construction of all possible state sets that can arise will terminate, since there are finitely many of them. The grammar will be LR(k) unless the Z sets of Eqs. (19) and (20) fail to be disjoint for some reachable state set. The parsing method just described will terminate, since any string in the language has a finite derivation, and since every execution of Step 2 either finds a step in the derivation or reduces the length of string not yet examined.

3. Examples

Now let us give three examples of applications to some nontrivial languages. Consider first the grammar

$$S \to \epsilon, \ S \to aAbS, \ S \to bBaS,$$

$$A \to \epsilon, \ A \to aAbA, \ B \to \epsilon, \ B \to bBaB, \qquad (24)$$

which defines the set of all strings on $\{a, b\}$ having exactly the same total number of a's and b's; the productions of (24) probably represent the briefest possible unambiguous grammar for this language. We will prove that (24) is unambiguous by showing that it is LR(1), using the first construction in Section 2. The grammar $\mathcal{F}$ is

$$[S; \dashv] \to \dashv[1],$$
$$[S; \dashv] \to a[A; b], \ [S; \dashv] \to aAb[S; \dashv], \ [S; \dashv] \to aAbS\dashv[2],$$
$$[S; \dashv] \to b[B; a], \ [S; \dashv] \to bBa[S; \dashv], \ [S; \dashv] \to bBaS\dashv[3],$$
$$[A; b] \to b[4],$$
$$[A; b] \to a[A; b], \ [A; b] \to aAb[A; b], \ [A; b] \to aAbAb[5],$$
$$[B; a] \to a[6],$$
$$[B; a] \to b[B; a], \ [B; a] \to bBa[B; a], \ [B; a] \to bBaBa[7].$$

The strings entering into condition (14) are therefore

$$\{aAb, bBa\}^*\dashv[1], \ \{aAb, bBa\}^*aAbS\dashv[2], \ \{aAb, bBa\}^*bBaS\dashv[3],$$
$$\{aAb, bBa\}^*a\{a, aAb\}^*b[4], \ \{aAb, bBa\}^*a\{a, aAb\}^*aAbAb[5],$$
$$\{aAb, bBa\}^*b\{b, bBa\}^*a[6], \ \{aAb, bBa\}^*b\{b, bBa\}^*bBaBa[7].$$

Here $\{\alpha, \beta\}^*$ denotes the set of all strings that can be formed by concatenation of α and β; clearly condition (14) is met.

Our second example is rather different. Consider first the set of all strings obtainable by *fully parenthesizing* algebraic expressions involving the letter a and the binary operation $+$:

$$S \to a, \quad S \to (S + S) \tag{25}$$

where in this grammar '(', '+', and ')' denote terminals. Given any such string we will perform the following acts of sabotage:

i) All plus signs will be erased.

ii) All parentheses appearing at the extreme left or extreme right will be erased.

iii) *Both* left and right parentheses will be replaced by the letter b.

Question: After all these changes, is it still possible to recreate the original string? The answer is, surprisingly, yes. Indeed, this question is equivalent to being able to parse any terminal string of the following grammar unambiguously:

Production Number	Production
0	$S \to B\dashv$
1	$B \to a$
2	$B \to LR$
3	$L \to a$
4	$L \to LAb$
5	$R \to a$
6	$R \to bAR$
7	$A \to a$
8	$A \to bAAb$

$$(26)$$

Here B, L, R, A denote the sets of strings formed from (25) with alterations (i) and (iii) performed, and with parentheses removed from *both* ends, the *left* end, the *right* end, or *neither* end, respectively. The shortest strings derivable from B are

$$\{a, \; aa, \; aaba, \; abaa, \; aababa, \; aabbaa, \; ababaa, \; abaabba, \; abbaaba, \; \ldots\}.$$

It is not immediately obvious that grammar (26) is unambiguous, nor is it immediately clear how one could design an efficient parsing algorithm for it. The second construction of Section 2 shows however that (26) is an LR(1) grammar, and it also gives us a parsing method. Table 1 shows the details, using an abbreviated notation.

TABLE 1. Parsing method for grammar (26).

State set $\mathcal{S}$	Additional states in $\mathcal{S}'$	In Step 2 if Y_1 is	then	In Step 3 if X_{n+1} is	then go to
00⊣	10⊣ 20⊣ 30ab 40ab	a	shift	B	01⊣
				a	11⊣ 31ab
				L	21⊣ 41ab
01⊣		⊣	stop		
11⊣ 31ab		⊣	reduce 1		
		a, b	reduce 3		
21⊣ 41ab	50⊣ 60⊣ 70b 80b	a, b	shift	R	22⊣
				A	42ab
				a	51⊣ 71b
				b	61⊣ 81b
22⊣		⊣	reduce 2		
42ab		b	shift	b	43ab
51⊣ 71ab		⊣	reduce 5		
		a, b	reduce 7		
61⊣ 81ab	70ab 80ab	a, b	shift	A	62⊣ 82ab
				a	71ab
				b	81ab
43ab		a, b	reduce 4		
62⊣ 82ab	50⊣ 60⊣ 70b 80b	a, b	shift	R	63⊣
				A	83ab
				a	51⊣ 71b
				b	61⊣ 81b
63⊣		⊣	reduce 6		
83ab		b	shift	b	84ab
84ab		a, b	reduce 8		

In Table 1, the symbol 21⊣ stands for the state $[2, 1; \dashv]$, and 41ab stands for the two states $[4, 1; a]$ and $[4, 1; b]$. "Shift" means "perform the shift left operation" mentioned in Step 2; "reduce p" means "perform the transformation (21) with production p." The first lines of Table 1 are formed as follows: Given the initial state $\mathcal{S} = \{00\dashv\}$, we must form $\mathcal{S}'$ according to Eq. (18). Since $X_{01} = B$ and $X_{02} = \dashv$ we must include 10⊣ and 20⊣ in $\mathcal{S}'$. Since $X_{21} = L$ and $X_{22} = R$ we must include 30ab and 40ab in $\mathcal{S}'$ (a and b being the possible initial characters of $R\dashv$). Since $X_{41} = L$ and $X_{42} = A$ we must, similarly, include 30ab and 40ab in $\mathcal{S}'$; but these have already been included, hence $\mathcal{S}'$ is completely determined. Now $Z = \{a\}$ in this case, so the only possibility in Step 2 is to have $Y_1 = a$ and shift. Step 3 is more interesting: If we ever get to Step 3 with $\mathcal{S}_n = \{00\dashv\}$ (possibly later, just after a reduction (21) has been performed), there are three possibilities for X_{n+1}. They are determined by the seven states in $\mathcal{S}'$, and the right-hand column is an application of Eq. (23).

An important shortcut has been taken in Table 1. Although the state set '51⊣ 71b' is one of the possibilities in the right-hand column, we have no entry for that set in the leftmost column; the reason is that

$51\dashv 71b$ is *contained in* $51\dashv 71ab$. *A procedure for a given state set must be valid for any of its subsets.* (This shortcut leads to less error detection in Step 2, but we will soon justify that.) We can often take the union of several state sets whose parsing actions do not conflict, thereby considerably shortening the parsing algorithm generated by the construction of Section 2.

When only one possibility occurs in Step 2 there is no need to test the validity of $Y_1 \ldots Y_k$; for example, in Table 1 line 1 there is no need to make sure that $Y_1 = a$. One need do no error detection until an attempt is made to shift $Y_1 = \dashv$ left of the vertical line. At that point the stack will contain '$\mathcal{S}_0 S \mathcal{S}_1 \mid \dashv^k$' if and only if the input string was well-formed. For we know that a well-formed string will be parsed, and that (by definition!) a malformed string cannot possibly be reduced to '$S\dashv^k$' by applying the productions in reverse. Thus, any or all error detection may be saved until the end, provided of course that we do verify in Step 2 that $X_{r+1}\ldots X_n$ matches the right-hand side of production p before applying a reduction. (When $k = 0$, a final delimiter $\dashv$ must be appended at the right in order to do this delayed error check.)

One can hardly think about parsing without considering the traditional example of arithmetic expressions. Therefore our third example is the following typical grammar:

Production Number	Production	
0	$S \to E\dashv$	
1	$E \to -T$	
2	$E \to T$	
3	$E \to E - T$	(27)
4	$T \to P$	
5	$T \to T * P$	
6	$P \to a$	
7	$P \to (E)$	

This grammar has the terminal alphabet $\{a, -, *, (\ , \ ), \dashv\}$, and its nonterminal symbols $\{S, E, T, P\}$ correspond respectively to algebraic sentences, expressions, terms, and primaries. For example, the string '$a - a * (-a * a - a)\dashv$' belongs to the language. Table 2 shows how our construction would produce a parsing method. On the line following rule 9, the notation '4, 5, 6' appearing in the 'X_{n+1}' column means that rules 4, 5, and 6 apply to this state set also. Such "factoring" of rules is another way to simplify the parsing routine produced by our construction, and the reader will undoubtedly see other ways to simplify Table 2.

TABLE 2. Parsing method for grammar (27).

State set S	Additional states in S'	Y_1	Step 2 action	Rule number	X_{n+1}	Step 3 destination
00⊣ 71⊣)−*	10⊣)− 20⊣)− 30⊣)− 40⊣)−* 50⊣)−* 60⊣)−* 70⊣)−*	−(a	shift	1 2 3 4 5 6	E − T P a (	01⊣ 72⊣)−* 31⊣)− 11⊣)− 21⊣)− 51⊣)−* 41⊣)−* 61⊣)−* 71⊣)−*
01⊣ 72⊣)−* 31⊣)−		⊣)−	stop shift	7 8	) −	73⊣)−* 32⊣)−
11⊣)−	40⊣)−* 50⊣)−* 60⊣)−* 70⊣)−*			9	T 4, 5, 6	12⊣)− 51⊣)−*
21⊣)− 51⊣)−*		* ⊣)−	shift reduce 2	10	*	52⊣)−*
32⊣)−	40⊣)−* 50⊣)−* 60⊣)−* 70⊣)−*			11	T 4, 5, 6	33⊣)− 51⊣)−*
12⊣)− 51⊣)−*		* ⊣)−	shift reduce 1	12	*	52⊣)−*
52⊣)−*	60⊣)− 70⊣)−*	(a	shift	13	P 5, 6	53⊣)−*
33⊣)− 51⊣)−*		* ⊣)−	shift reduce 3	14	*	52⊣)−*
$pn_p X$		X	reduce p			

By means of our construction it is possible to determine exactly what information about the string being parsed is known at any given time. This detailed knowledge makes it possible to study how much of the information is not really essential (that is, how much is redundant), thereby determining the "best possible" parsing method for a grammar, in some sense. The two simplifications already mentioned — delayed error checking and taking the union of state sets that are compatible — are simplifications of this kind, and more study is needed to analyze this problem further.

In many cases it will not be necessary to store the state sets S_i in the stack, since the states S_r that are used in the latter part of Step 2 can often be determined by examining a few of the X's at the top of the stack. Indeed, this will always be true if we have a bounded right context grammar, as defined in Section 1. Both grammars (26) and (27) are of bounded context.

From Table 1 we can see how to recover the necessary state set information without storing it in the stack. We need only consider those state sets with at least one nonterminal character in the 'X_{n+1}' column; otherwise the state set is never used by the parser. Thus it is immediately clear from Table 1 that $\{00\dashv\}$ is always at the bottom of the stack, $\{21\dashv, 41ab\}$ is always to the right of L, $\{61\dashv, 81ab\}$ is always to the right of b, and $\{62\dashv, 82ab\}$ is always to the right of A.

Grammar (27) is related to the definition of arithmetic expressions in the ALGOL 60 language, and it is natural to ask whether ALGOL 60 is an LR(k) language. The answer is a little difficult because the definition of this language (see Naur [10]) is not done completely in terms of productions; there are "comment conventions" and occasional informal explanations. The grammar as it stands cannot be LR(k) because it has a number of syntactic ambiguities; for example, one of its productions

$$\langle \text{open string} \rangle \rightarrow \langle \text{open string} \rangle \, \langle \text{open string} \rangle$$

is always ambiguous. Another type of ambiguity arises in the parsing of ⟨identifier⟩ as ⟨actual parameter⟩. There are eight ways to do this:

⟨actual parameter⟩ → ⟨array identifier⟩ → ⟨identifier⟩

⟨actual parameter⟩ → ⟨switch identifier⟩ → ⟨identifier⟩

⟨actual parameter⟩ → ⟨procedure identifier⟩ → ⟨identifier⟩

⟨actual parameter⟩ → ⟨expression⟩

$\qquad\qquad$ → ⟨designational expression⟩ ⇒ ⟨identifier⟩

⟨actual parameter⟩ → ⟨expression⟩
→ ⟨Boolean expression⟩
⇒ ⟨variable⟩ ⇒ ⟨identifier⟩

⟨actual parameter⟩ → ⟨expression⟩
→ ⟨Boolean expression⟩
⇒ ⟨function designator⟩ ⇒ ⟨identifier⟩

⟨actual parameter⟩ → ⟨expression⟩
→ ⟨arithmetic expression⟩
⇒ ⟨variable⟩ ⇒ ⟨identifier⟩

⟨actual parameter⟩ → ⟨expression⟩
→ ⟨arithmetic expression⟩
⇒ ⟨function designator⟩ ⇒ ⟨identifier⟩

These syntactic ambiguities reflect bona fide *semantic* ambiguities, if the identifier in question is a formal parameter to a procedure, for it is then impossible to determine what sort of identifier will be the actual argument in the absence of specifications. At the time the ALGOL 60 report was written, of course, the whole question of syntactic ambiguity was just emerging, and the authors of that document naturally made little attempt to avoid such occurrences. In fact, the differentiation between array identifiers, switch identifiers, and so forth in this example was done intentionally, to provide explanation along with the syntax (referring to identifiers that have been declared in a certain way). In view of this, a *ninth* alternative

⟨actual parameter⟩ → ⟨string⟩ → ⟨formal parameter⟩ → ⟨identifier⟩

might also have been included in the ALGOL 60 syntax (since Section 4.7.5.1 specifically allows a formal parameter whose actual parameter is a string to be used as an actual parameter, and this event is not reflected in any of the eight possibilities above). The omission of this ninth alternative is significant, because it indicates the philosophy of the ALGOL 60 report towards procedure parameters: Formal parameters are to be replaced conceptually by the actual parameters *before* rules of syntax are employed.

At any rate, when parsing is considered it is desirable to have an unambiguous syntax, and it seems clear that with little trouble one could redefine the syntax of ALGOL 60 so that we would have an LR(1) grammar for the same language.

By the "ALGOL 60 language" we mean the set of strings meeting the *syntax* for ALGOL 60, not necessarily satisfying any semantical restrictions. For example,

$$\textbf{begin array } x[100000:0]; \;\; y := z/0 \textbf{ end}$$

may be regarded as a string belonging to the ALGOL 60 language.

It is interesting to speculate, however, that there might be no way to define ALGOL 60 with an RL(k) grammar (where by RL(k) we mean "translatable from right to left," defined dually to LR(k)). Several features of ALGOL 60 make it most suited to a left-to-right reading; for example, going from right to left, we find that the basic symbol **comment** radically affects the parsing of the characters to its right. A similar language, for which some LR(k) grammars but no RL(k) grammars exist, is considered in Section 5 of this paper; but we also will give an example there to support the hypothesis that ALGOL 60 *could* be RL(k).

4. An Unsolvable Problem

In 1947, Post [12] introduced a famous *correspondence problem* that has been used to prove the undecidability of numerous linguistic questions. We will define here a similar unsolvable problem, and apply it to the study of LR(k) grammars.

THE PARTIAL CORRESPONDENCE PROBLEM. *Let* (α_1, β_1), (α_2, β_2), ..., (α_n, β_n) *be ordered pairs of nonempty strings. Do there exist, for all* $p > 0$, *ordered p-tuples of integers* $(i_1, i_2, \ldots, i_p)$ *such that the first p characters of the string* $\alpha_{i_1}\alpha_{i_2}\ldots\alpha_{i_p}$ *are respectively equal to the first p characters of* $\beta_{i_1}\beta_{i_2}\ldots\beta_{i_p}$?

The ordinary correspondence problem asks for the existence of a $p > 0$ for which the entire strings $\alpha_{i_1}\ldots\alpha_{i_p}$ and $\beta_{i_1}\ldots\beta_{i_p}$ are equal. A solution to the ordinary correspondence problem implies an affirmative answer to the partial correspondence problem, but the general solvability of either problem is not directly related to the solvability of the other. There are relations between the partial correspondence problem and the Tag problem (see Cocke and Minsky [1]) but no apparent simple connection. We can, however, prove that the partial correspondence problem is recursively unsolvable, using methods analogous to those devised by Floyd [6] for dealing with the ordinary correspondence problem and using the determinacy of Turing machines.

Proof. Let us use the definition and notation for Turing machines as given by Post [12]; we will construct a partial correspondence problem for any Turing machine and any initial configuration. The characters used in our partial correspondence problem will be

$$\vdash q_i \bar{q}_i S_j \bar{S}_j h \bar{h}, \quad \text{for } 1 \leq i \leq r \text{ and } 0 \leq j \leq m$$

when the Turing machine has r states $q_1, \ldots, q_r$ and $m + 1$ symbols $S_0, S_1, \ldots, S_m$ (including the "blank" symbol S_0). If the initial configuration is

$$S_{j_1} S_{j_2} \ldots S_{j_{k-1}} q_{i_1} S_{j_k} \ldots S_{j_l}$$

the pair of strings

$$(\vdash, \vdash h S_{j_1} \ldots S_{j_{k-1}} q_{i_1} S_{j_k} \ldots S_{j_l} h) \tag{28}$$

will enter into our partial correspondence problem. We also add the pairs

$$(\bar{h}, h), \quad (h, \bar{h}), \quad (S_j, \bar{S}_j), \quad (\bar{S}_j, S_j), \quad (\bar{q}_i, q_i), \tag{29}$$

for $1 \leq i \leq r$ and $0 \leq j \leq m$. Finally, we give pairs determined by the quadruples of the Turing machine:

Form of quadruple	Corresponding pairs, $0 \leq t \leq m$:	
$q_i S_j L q_l$	$(h q_i S_j, \bar{h} \bar{q}_l \bar{S}_0 \bar{S}_j),$	$(S_t q_i S_j, \bar{q}_l \bar{S}_t \bar{S}_j)$
$q_i S_j R q_l$	$(q_i S_j h, \bar{S}_j \bar{q}_l \bar{S}_0 \bar{h}),$	$(q_i S_j S_t, \bar{S}_j \bar{q}_l \bar{S}_t)$ (30)
$q_i S_j S_k q_l$	$(q_i S_j, \bar{q}_l \bar{S}_k)$	

Now it is easy to see that these corresponding pairs will simulate the behavior of the Turing machine. Since the pair (28) is the only pair having the same initial character in both strings, and since the pairs in (30) are the only ones involving an unbarred q_i in the left-hand string, the only possible strings that can be initial substrings of both $\alpha_{i_1} \alpha_{i_2} \ldots$ and $\beta_{i_1} \beta_{i_2} \ldots$ are initial substrings of

$$\vdash \sigma_0 \bar{\sigma}_1 \sigma_1 \bar{\sigma}_2 \sigma_2 \bar{\sigma}_3 \sigma_3 \ldots , \tag{31}$$

where σ_0, σ_1, σ_2, σ_3, ... represent the successive stages of the Turing machine's tape (with h's placed at either end, and where $\bar{\sigma}$ is an obvious notation signifying the "barring" of each letter of σ). For these pairs, therefore, *the partial correspondence problem has an affirmative answer if and only if the Turing machine never halts.* And the problem of telling if a Turing machine will ever halt is, of course, well known to be recursively unsolvable.   □

We will apply this result to LR(k) grammars as follows:

Theorem. *The problem of deciding, for a given grammar $\mathcal{G}$, whether or not there exists a $k \geq 0$ such that $\mathcal{G}$ is LR(k), is recursively unsolvable.*

This theorem stands in contrast to the results of Section 2, where we showed the problem to be solvable when k is also given. To prove the theorem we will reduce the partial correspondence problem to the LR(k) problem for a particular class of grammars.

Proof. Let $(\alpha_1, \beta_1), \ldots, (\alpha_n, \beta_n)$ be pairs of strings entering into the partial correspondence problem, and let

$$\{X_1, X_2, \ldots, X_n, +\}$$

be $n + 1$ characters distinct from those appearing among the α's and β's. Let $\mathcal{G}$ be the following grammar:

$$S \to A, \; S \to B, \; A \to X_i + \alpha_i, \; B \to X_i + \beta_i,$$
$$A \to X_i A \alpha_i, \; B \to X_i B \beta_i, \quad \text{for } 1 \leq i \leq n. \qquad (32)$$

The sentential forms are

$$\{X_{i_m} \ldots X_{i_1} A \alpha_{i_1} \ldots \alpha_{i_m}\} \cup \{X_{i_m} \ldots X_{i_1} B \beta_{i_1} \ldots \beta_{i_m}\}$$
$$\cup \{X_{i_m} \ldots X_{i_1} + \alpha_{i_1} \ldots \alpha_{i_m}\} \cup \{X_{i_m} \ldots X_{i_1} + \beta_{i_1} \ldots \beta_{i_m}\}.$$

We will show that $\mathcal{G}$ is LR(k) for some k if and only if the partial correspondence problem has a negative answer. If the answer is affirmative, for every p we have two sentential forms $X_{i_p} \ldots X_{i_1} + \alpha_{i_1} \ldots \alpha_{i_p}$, $X_{i_p} \ldots X_{i_1} + \beta_{i_1} \ldots \beta_{i_p}$ in which the first p characters following '+' agree. The handle must include the '+' sign, but the $p - q$ characters following the handle do not tell us whether the production $A \to X_{i_1} + \alpha_{i_1}$ or $B \to X_{i_1} + \beta_{i_1}$ is to be applied, if q is the maximum length of the strings $\{\alpha_1, \ldots, \alpha_n, \beta_1, \ldots, \beta_n\}$. Hence the grammar is not LR($p - q$). On the other hand, if the answer to the partial correspondence problem is negative, there is a p for which, knowing $(i_1, \ldots, i_{\min(p,m)})$ and the first p characters of $\alpha_{i_1} \alpha_{i_2} \ldots \alpha_{i_m} \dashv^p$ or $\beta_{i_1} \beta_{i_2} \ldots \beta_{i_m} \dashv^p$, we can distinguish between a string of α's and a string of β's; therefore $\mathcal{G}$ is in fact a bounded context grammar. □

We have proved slightly more, answering a question posed by Floyd [5, page 66]:

Corollary. *The problems of deciding whether a given grammar* (i) *has bounded context, or* (ii) *has bounded right context, are recursively unsolvable.* □

These theorems can be sharpened in the usual ways to show that we could assume that the grammar $\mathcal{G}$ is unambiguous, linear, has at most two terminals, and has either a bounded number of productions or a bounded length of string in a production, yet the problems remain unsolvable.

5. Connections with Deterministic Languages

Ginsburg and Greibach [7] have recently defined a *deterministic language* as one that is accepted by a so-called *deterministic push-down automaton* (DPDA). The latter is a device with a finite number of states q_0, q_1, q_2, ..., q_r, which manipulates strings of characters in two alphabets T and N according to production rules of the following two types:

$$Aq_i \to \theta q_j \tag{33}$$

$$Aq_i a \to \theta q_j \tag{34}$$

Here A and a are single characters in N and T, respectively, and θ is any string over N. When A is the special character $\vdash$ we require θ to be a nonempty string whose initial character is $\vdash$. For each pair Aq_i, where A is in N and $0 \le i \le r$, we stipulate that there is either a unique rule of type (33) and none of type (34), or there are no rules of type (33) and at most one of type (34) for each a in T. Some of the states are designated as "final states," and the terminal string α is *accepted* by the DPDA if and only if $\vdash q_0 \alpha \Longrightarrow \vdash \omega q_i$ for some final state q_i and some string ω. Here the relation '$\Longrightarrow$' is generated from '$\to$' as in Section 1.

Theorem. *If $\mathcal{G}$ is an* LR(k) *grammar, and if $\mathcal{G}$ defines the language L, there is a DPDA that accepts the language $L \dashv^k$.*

Proof. The second construction of Section 2 is in fact closely related to a DPDA. The grammar $\mathcal{G}$, augmented by production (16), defines the language $L \dashv^k$. To construct such a DPDA we will take as our states, q_i, all possible k-letter terminal strings $[Y_1 \dots Y_k]$, and there will also be various auxiliary states. The terminal alphabet for the DPDA will be $T \cup \{\dashv\}$ and the nonterminal alphabet will be $N \cup T \cup \{\vdash\}$ together with all possible state sets $\mathcal{S}$. We want our DPDA to arrive at the configuration

$$\vdash \mathcal{S}_0 X_1 \mathcal{S}_1 \dots X_n \mathcal{S}_n [Y_1 \dots Y_k] \omega \tag{35}$$

if and only if the stack in the parsing algorithm of Section 2 contains '$\mathcal{S}_0 X_1 \mathcal{S}_1 \ldots X_n \mathcal{S}_n \mid Y_1 \ldots Y_k \omega$' at a corresponding stage of the calculation.

Clearly we can construct productions of the form (34) that essentially read the first k characters of a given input string $Y_1 \ldots Y_k \omega$ and get us to the initial configuration $\vdash \{[0, 0; \dashv^k]\}[Y_1 \ldots Y_k]\omega$. Now assume that the DPDA has arrived at the configuration (35); we can compute the sets Z and Z_p as in Step 2 of the parsing algorithm. If $Y_1 \ldots Y_k$ is in Z, we create instructions of the form (34),

$$\mathcal{S}_n[Y_1 \ldots Y_k]a \rightarrow \mathcal{S}_n Y_1 \mathcal{S}_{n+1}[Y_2 \ldots Y_k a], \tag{36}$$

where $\mathcal{S}_{n+1}$ is determined by $X_{n+1} = Y_1$ in (23) (or $X_{n+1} = a$ if $k = 0$). If $Y_1 \ldots Y_k$ is in Z_p, we let $q^{(0)}, q^{(1)}, \ldots, q^{(2n_p)}$ be new auxiliary states and write

$$\mathcal{S}_n[Y_1 \ldots Y_k] \rightarrow \mathcal{S}_n q^{(0)};$$
$$\mathcal{S}q^{(2t)} \rightarrow q^{(2t+1)}, \quad X_{p(n_p - t)}q^{(2t+1)} \rightarrow q^{(2t+2)}, \quad \text{for } 0 \le t < n_p; \tag{37}$$
$$\mathcal{S}q^{(2n_p)} \rightarrow \mathcal{S}A_p\mathcal{S}_{n+1}[Y_1 \ldots Y_k];$$

the productions leading from $\mathcal{S}q^{(2t)}$ are defined for all state sets $\mathcal{S}$, and in the last productions we determine $\mathcal{S}_{n+1}$ from $\mathcal{S}$ by using (23) with $\mathcal{S}_n = \mathcal{S}$ and $X_{n+1} = A_p$. We make one exception to this rule; namely, if $Y_1 \ldots Y_k = \dashv^k$ and $\mathcal{S} = \{[0, 0; \dashv^k]\}$ we change the last instruction to

$$\mathcal{S}q^{(2n_p)} \rightarrow q_f$$

where q_f is the unique final state of our DPDA.

The rules (36) and (37), for all possible combinations of $\mathcal{S}_n$ and $[Y_1 \ldots Y_k]$, plus the few initial and final ones, give us a DPDA that exactly mimics the procedure of the parsing algorithm in Section 2.   □

Corollary. *If $\mathcal{G}$ is an LR(k) grammar and if $\mathcal{G}$ defines the language L, there is a DPDA that accepts the language L.*

Proof. The corollary follows because Ginsburg and Greibach [7] have proved, among several other interesting theorems, that if L_0 is deterministic and R is regular, then the language $\{\alpha \mid \alpha\beta \text{ in } L_0 \text{ for some } \beta \text{ in } R\}$ is deterministic. We may take $L_0 = L\dashv^k$ and $R = \{\dashv^k\}$.   □

We now prove a converse result.

Theorem. *If L is a deterministic language, there is an* LR(1) *grammar that defines* L.

Proof. To prove this theorem, we want to take an arbitrary DPDA with its instructions of the forms (33) and (34), and construct a corresponding grammar. First it will be convenient to simplify the problem a little, so we will restrict the instructions of our DPDA to just three types,

$$
\begin{array}{rl}
\text{i)} & Aq_ia \to Aq_j \\
\text{ii)} & Aq_i \to q_j \\
\text{iii)} & Aq_i \to ABq_j
\end{array}
\tag{38}
$$

where A and B are nonterminals and a is terminal. This restriction involves no loss of generality, since a rule (34) can be replaced by $Aq_ia \to Aq$, $Aq \to \theta q_j$ for some new state q, and we are left with type (i) and rules of the form (33). The rule $Aq_i \to \theta q_j$ is of type (ii) if θ is empty; otherwise we have $\theta = A_1 A_2 \dots A_t$ for some $t \geq 1$. If $A_1 \neq A$ we have $A \neq \vdash$, so we can replace (33) by new rules

$$
Aq_i \to q, \quad Bq \to BA_1q' \text{ for all nonterminals } B, \quad A_1q' \to \theta q_j
$$

where q and q' are new states. Thus we may assume that $A = A_1$; and the rule (33) may be replaced by a sequence of $t - 1$ rules of type (iii), introducing $t - 2$ new states, whenever $t > 1$. Finally if $t = 1$, the rule $Aq_i \to Aq_j$ may be replaced by

$$
Aq_i \to AAq, \quad Aq \to q_j
$$

where q is a new state, thereby reducing all rules to the forms in (38).

For any pair Aq_i, we still have the deterministic property that if more than one rule appears with Aq_i on the left, all such rules are of type (i), and there is at most one such rule for any particular terminal character a.

A further simplification about *final states* is desirable as well. If q_f and q'_f are final states (possibly identical), we want to avoid the situation

$$
\alpha q_f \Rightarrow \beta q'_f
\tag{39}
$$

since this would imply that an input string could be "accepted twice" by the DPDA. To exclude this possibility, we double the number of states in the DPDA, using two states q_i and $\bar{q}_i$ for each original state q_i. The instructions (38) are then replaced by

$$
\begin{array}{rl}
\text{i)} & Aq_ia \to Aq_j, \quad A\bar{q}_ia \to Aq_j; \\
\text{ii)} & Aq_i \to q_j^{(i)}, \quad A\bar{q}_i \to \bar{q}_j; \\
\text{iii)} & Aq_i \to ABq_j^{(i)}, \quad A\bar{q}_i \to AB\bar{q}_j;
\end{array}
$$

here $q_j^{(i)}$ is $\bar{q}_j$ if q_i is final, otherwise $q_j^{(i)}$ is q_j. One easily verifies that (39) cannot occur, and that the new DPDA accepts the same set of strings as the old. We get into a state $\bar{q}_j$ if the current string has been accepted; then we do not accept the string again, but return to an unbarred state when the next rule of type (i) is used.

Once the DPDA has been modified to meet these assumptions, let it have the states $q_0, \ldots, q_r$; we are ready to construct a grammar for the language it accepts. We begin by defining the "transition languages" L_{iAt} for $0 \le i, t \le r$ and for all nonterminals A of the DPDA:

$$L_{iAt} = \{\alpha \mid Aq_i\alpha \overset{\prime}{\Rightarrow} Aq \to q_t \text{ for some } q\} \tag{40}$$

where no step in the derivation represented by '$\overset{\prime}{\Rightarrow}$' affects the A appearing at the left.

Construct the following productions for all rules (38) of the DPDA:

	Rule	Productions for $\mathcal{G}$	
i)	$Aq_ia \to Aq_j$	$L_{iAt} \to aL_{jAt}$ for $0 \le t \le r$	
ii)	$Aq_i \to q_j$	$L_{iAj} \to \epsilon$	(41)
iii)	$Aq_i \to ABq_j$	$L_{iAt} \to L_{jBs}L_{sAt}$ for $0 \le s, t \le r$	

An easy induction based on the length of the derivation '$\overset{\prime}{\Rightarrow}$' or the length of the derivation in $\mathcal{G}$ establishes the equality of the sets of strings defined in (40) and the sets of strings derivable from L_{iAt} using the productions (41).

Another set of languages is also important:

$$L_{iA} = \{\alpha \mid Aq_i\alpha \overset{\prime}{\Rightarrow} A\omega q_f,$$
$$\text{for some string } \omega \text{ and some final state } q_f\}. \tag{42}$$

We construct the following further productions:

	Rule	Productions for $\mathcal{G}$	
i)	$Aq_ia \to Aq_j$	$L_{iA} \to aL_{jA}$	
ii)	$Aq_i \to q_j$	(none)	(43)
iii)	$Aq_i \to ABq_j$	$L_{iA} \to L_{jB}$, $L_{iA} \to L_{jBs}L_{sA}$ for $0 \le s \le r$	
	q_i is final	$L_{iA} \to \epsilon$ for all A	

Again, induction establishes the equivalence of (42) and (43). We conclude that *the language derivable from $L_{0\vdash}$ using $\mathcal{G}$ is precisely the language L of the theorem*, by the definition of a DPDA.

Now remove all useless productions from $\mathcal{G}$, that is, all productions that can never appear in a derivation of a terminal string starting from $L_{0\vdash}$. We claim that the resulting grammar $\mathcal{G}$ is LR(1). This result could be proved using either of the constructions in Section 2, where the state sets have a rather simple form, but for purposes of exposition we will give here a more intuitive explanation that illustrates the connection between the operation of the DPDA and the parsing process.

Given any string $\alpha\dashv$ where α is accepted by the DPDA, we will consider the step-by-step behavior of the DPDA as it processes α. At the same time we will be building a partial derivation tree, which reflects all of the information known at a given stage of the parse. The branch nodes of this partial tree will contain symbols $[i, A, *]$, which mean that, in the only possible parsing of the string, the position of $[i, A, *]$ must be occupied by either L_{iA0} or L_{iA1} or $\cdots$ or L_{iAr} or L_{iA}. We will be "at" some node $[i, A, *]$ of the tree, meaning that this particular node above the handle is of interest, and also that the DPDA's current configuration will contain the substring Aq_i.

All of this can be clarified by considering an example, so we will consider the following more-or-less "random" DPDA:

Rules of DPDA	Productions of $\mathcal{G}$ (useless ones deleted)
$\vdash q_0 a \to \vdash q_1$	$L_{0\vdash} \to aL_{1\vdash}$
$\vdash q_1 \to \vdash Aq_2$	$L_{1\vdash} \to L_{2A}$, $L_{1\vdash} \to L_{2A5}L_{5\vdash}$
$Aq_2 a \to Aq_1$	$L_{2A2} \to aL_{1A2}$, $L_{2A5} \to aL_{1A5}$,
	$L_{2A6} \to aL_{1A6}$, $L_{2A} \to aL_{1A}$
$Aq_1 \to AAq_2$	$L_{1A} \to L_{2A}$, $L_{1A} \to L_{2A2}L_{2A}$,
	$L_{1A2} \to L_{2A2}L_{2A2}$, $L_{1A5} \to L_{2A2}L_{2A5}$,
	$L_{1A6} \to L_{2A2}L_{2A6}$, $L_{1A2} \to L_{2A6}L_{6A2}$ (44)
$Aq_2 b \to Aq_3$	$L_{2A5} \to bL_{3A5}$, $L_{2A} \to bL_{3A}$
$Aq_2 c \to Aq_4$	$L_{2A6} \to cL_{4A6}$
$Aq_3 \to q_5$	$L_{3A5} \to \epsilon$
$Aq_4 \to q_6$	$L_{4A6} \to \epsilon$
$Aq_6 \to q_2$	$L_{6A2} \to \epsilon$
$\vdash q_5 c \to \vdash q_1$	$L_{5\vdash} \to cL_{1\vdash}$
q_1 final	$L_{1A} \to \epsilon$, $L_{1\vdash} \to \epsilon$
q_3 final	$L_{3A} \to \epsilon$

Consider the action of the DPDA when given the string $aaacb\dashv$. The first few steps that it takes are

$$\vdash q_0 aaacb\dashv \to \vdash q_1 aacb\dashv \to \vdash Aq_2 aacb\dashv \to \vdash Aq_1 acb\dashv \to \vdash AAq_2 acb\dashv$$
$$\to \vdash AAq_1 cb\dashv \to \vdash AAAq_2 cb\dashv \to \vdash AAAq_4 b\dashv.$$

Corresponding to these seven transitions we will build the following partial tree, one node at a time:

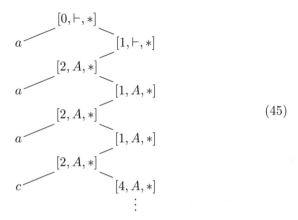

$$(45)$$

We are now "at" node $[4, A, *]$, signified by the three dots below it. At this point the DPDA uses the rule $Aq_4 \rightarrow q_6$ and we transform the bottom five levels of tree (45) to

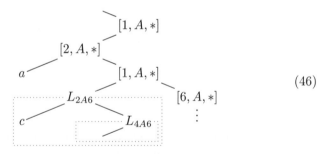

$$(46)$$

(Thus, two handles are recognized and then removed from the tree.) Then the DPDA uses the rule $Aq_6 \rightarrow q_2$ and (46) becomes

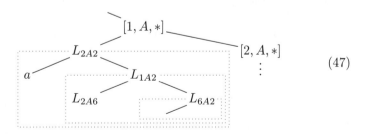

$$(47)$$

by reducing three more handles. When the rule $Aq_2b \rightarrow Aq_3$ is applied next, the tree becomes

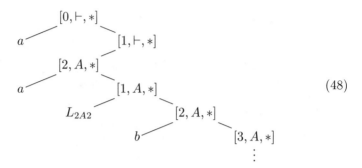

$$(48)$$

Now q_3 is a final state and the next character is '$\dashv$', so we complete the parsing; (48) becomes

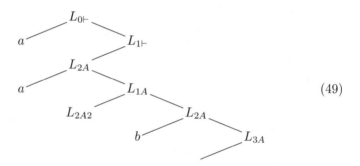

$$(49)$$

Having worked the example, we can consider the general case. Suppose the DPDA is in the configuration $\dots CAq_ia\dots$, and suppose we are at node $[i, A, *]$ of the tree. If q_i is a final state and $a = $ '$\dashv$', by condition (39) we must now complete the parsing, so we proceed to replace each $[i, A, *]$ in the tree by L_{iA} until the root is reached (as in going from (48) to (49)). If q_i is not final or $a \neq$ '$\dashv$', there are three cases depending on the pair Aq_i:

i) The DPDA contains a rule of the form $Aq_ia \rightarrow Aq_j$. Then the only possible parse must occur by changing

from $\begin{array}{c} [i, A, *] \\ \vdots \end{array}$ to $\begin{array}{c} [i, A, *] \\ a \diagup \quad \diagdown \\ [j, A, *] \\ \vdots \end{array}$

as we did in changing (47) to (48).

ii) The DPDA contains a rule of the form $Aq_i \rightarrow q_j$. Then our tree must be changed from

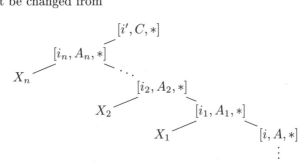

(where $n \geq 0$) to

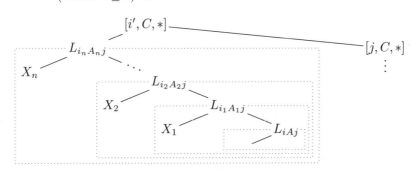

as we did in changing from (45) to (46) and (46) to (47).

iii) The DPDA contains a rule of the form $Aq_i \rightarrow ABq_j$. Then the only possible parse must occur by changing

$$\text{from} \quad [i, A, *] \quad \text{to} \quad [i, A, *]$$
$$\vdots \qquad\qquad\qquad [j, B, *]$$
$$\vdots$$

as we did for transitions 2, 4, and 6 while building tree (45).

Cases (i), (ii), (iii) are mutually exclusive by the definition of DPDA, and the arguments are justified by the fact that our partial tree represents all possible productions of the grammar that could conceivably work. Notice that in the parsing we actually have almost an LR(0) grammar, since it was necessary to look at the character following the handle only when q_i was a final state, to see if the next character is '⊣' or not. □

As a consequence of our two theorems, we conclude that a language can be generated by an LR(k) grammar if and only if it is deterministic, if and only if it can be generated by an LR(1) grammar.

The theorem cannot be improved to 'LR(0) grammar', since the simple language $\{\epsilon, a\}$ obviously has no LR(0) grammar. However, if L is any deterministic language, we can show that the language $L\dashv$ can always be given an LR(0) grammar; to find such a grammar we simply take the LR(1) grammar of the second theorem and reapply the first theorem to get another DPDA for $L\dashv$. This DPDA has only one final state q_f, which leads to no further states, so the construction of the second theorem applied to this new grammar will be LR(0). Any deterministic language in which no accepted string is a proper initial substring of any other will likewise have an LR(0) grammar.

Our last theorem shows that the property of being "deterministic" is essentially asymmetric, because there are languages that are translatable from right to left but not deterministic.

Theorem. *The following productions constitute an* RL(0) *grammar for which the corresponding language is not deterministic:*

$$S \to Ac, \ S \to B, \ A \to aAbb, \ A \to abb, \ B \to aBb, \ B \to ab. \quad (50)$$

Proof. The terminal strings of this language are either $a^n b^{2n} c$ or $a^n b^n$, where $n > 0$. The grammar is clearly RL(0). On the other hand suppose we could find an LR(k) grammar for the same language. (The problem is, of course, the appearance of 'c' at the extreme right.) If we consider the derivations of the infinitely many strings $a^n b^n$ we must find one in which a *recursive* nonterminal appears; thus, there will be a nonterminal C and strings α, φ, μ, ψ, ω such that $S \Rightarrow \alpha C \omega \Rightarrow \alpha \varphi C \psi \omega \Rightarrow \alpha \varphi \mu \psi \omega = a^n b^n$ for some n. Now $\alpha \varphi^t \mu \psi^t \omega$ must be in the language for all $t \geq 0$, and $\varphi \psi$ is not empty since the grammar is unambiguous. We see therefore that $\varphi = a^p$, $\psi = b^p$ for some $p > 0$. This implies that C cannot appear in the derivation of any of the strings $a^n b^{2n} c$. For arbitrarily large t, the language contains strings $\alpha \varphi^{t+1} \mu \psi^{t+1} \omega = a^{n+pt} b^{n+pt}$ in which, by nonambiguity, the handle must be at least $p(t+1)$ characters from the right and must lead to a sentential form $\alpha \varphi^{t+1} C \psi^{t+1} \omega$ with $p(t+1)$ characters to the right of the handle; yet the language also contains the strings $a^{n+pt} b^{2(n+pt)} c$ which must *not* have the same handle, so the grammar cannot be LR(k). By the preceding theorem the language is not deterministic in the left-to-right sense.   □

When this paper was being prepared, the author attempted to show that the language $\{a^n b^n\} d \cup \{a, b\}^* c$ cannot be given an LR(k) grammar.

This conjecture seemed plausible at first, but further study showed that the following grammar actually does work:

$$S \to A, \; S \to bC, \; S \to Bd, \; S \to BbC, \; S \to c,$$
$$A \to Bc, \; A \to BaC, \; A \to aA,$$
$$B \to ab, \; B \to aBb,$$
$$C \to c, \; C \to aC, \; C \to bC. \tag{51}$$

In fact, (51) is an LR(0) grammar.

Indeed, we can note that a DPDA is able to recognize the complement of the strings it accepts, so that if L is a deterministic language not involving the character 'c', the language

$$L \cup \{\alpha c \mid \alpha \text{ is any string on the terminal symbols of } L\}$$

is actually deterministic, contrary to expectations. This example weakens the argument that '**comment**' in ALGOL 60 might make it a non-RL language.

6. Remarks and Open Questions

The concept of LR(k) grammars sheds much light on the translation problem for phrase structure languages, and it suggests several interesting areas for further investigation.

Of principal interest, perhaps, is the study of grammatical transformations that preserve the LR(k) condition. Many transformations are well known (for example, the removal of ϵ from a grammar; elimination of left recursion; reducing to a "normal form" in which all productions are of type $A \to BC$ or $A \to a$; the operation of transduction that converts a grammar for some language L to a grammar for a translation of L; and many special cases of the latter). Which of these grammatical modifications take LR(k) grammars into LR(k) grammars? Similar questions apply to bounded context and bounded right context grammars.

Another important area of research is to develop algorithms that accept LR(k) grammars, or special classes of them, and to produce efficient parsing programs mechanically. In Section 3 we indicated three ways to simplify the general parsing schemes produced by our construction, and many more techniques certainly exist. A table such as Table 2 shows essentially all of the information available during the parsing, and much of it can be recognized as repetitive or redundant.

There also are implications for automata theory. We have shown that a deterministic push-down automaton accepts precisely those languages that can be given an LR(k) grammar. This result can be strengthened to show that in fact such languages can always be given a *bounded right context* grammar: We simply modify the construction of (41) and (43) by changing

$$L_{iAt} \to \alpha \qquad \text{to} \qquad L_{iAt} \to M_{iA}\alpha$$
$$L_{iA} \to \alpha \qquad \text{to} \qquad L_{iA} \to M_{iA}\alpha$$

and adding the productions $M_{iA} \to \epsilon$ for all i and all A. This change has the effect of keeping the necessary information in the sentential form that has been parsed.

The question is, however: What type of automaton is capable of accepting precisely those languages for which a *bounded context* grammar can be given? The bounded context condition is symmetric with respect to left and right, and we have shown that the deterministic property is not; for example, the mirror reflection of language (50) is a deterministic language that cannot be defined by a bounded context grammar.

The speed of parsing is another area of interest. Although LR(k) grammars can be parsed efficiently with an execution time essentially proportional to the length of the input string, there are more general grammars that can be parsed at a linear rate of speed. Such parsing may involve, for example, backing up a bounded number of times, or scanning back and forth from left to right and right to left in combination, etc. Are there particular grammars for which no conceivable parsing method will be able to find one parse of each string in the language with running time at worst linearly proportional to the length of string? Or are there general parsing methods for which a linear parsing time can be guaranteed for all grammars? (In these questions, a parsing method means a process of constructing a derivation sequence from a terminal string by scanning a bounded number of characters at a time.)

Finally, we might mention another generalization of LR(k) to be explored. The "second handle" of a tree may be regarded as the leftmost complete branch of terminals lying to the right of the handle, and similarly we can consider the rth handle. A parsing process that always reduces one of the first t handles leads to what might be called an LR(k, t) grammar. (In our case, $t = 1$.) The grammar

$$S \to ACc, \ S \to BCd, \ A \to a, \ B \to a, \ C \to Cb, \ C \to b \qquad (52)$$

is not LR($k, 1$) for any k, since 'a' is the handle in both $ab^n c$ and $ab^n d$; but it is LR(0, 2). The following reduction rules serve to parse (52):

$$ab \to aC, \ Cb \to C, \ aCc \to ACc, \ aCd \to BCd, \ ACc \to S, \ BCc \to S.$$

One might choose to call this left-to-right translation, although we must back up a finite amount.

References

[1] John Cocke and Marvin Minsky, "Universality of Tag systems with $P = 2$," *Journal of the Association for Computing Machinery* **11** (1964), 15–20.

[2] J. Earley, "Generating Productions from BNF (preliminary report)" (Pittsburgh, Pennsylvania: Carnegie Institute of Technology, 1964).

[3] Jürgen Eickel, *Generation of Parsing Algorithms for Chomsky 2-type Languages*, Bericht #6401 (Munich: Mathematisches Institut, Technische Hochschule München, 1964), 24 pages.

[4] Robert W. Floyd, "Syntactic analysis and operator precedence," *Journal of the Association for Computing Machinery* **10** (1963), 316–333.

[5] Robert W. Floyd, "Bounded context syntactic analysis," *Communications of the ACM* **7** (1964), 62–66.

[6] Robert W. Floyd, *New Proofs of Old Theorems in Logic and Formal Linguistics* (Wakefield, Massachusetts: Computer Associates, 1964). [A revised version was issued in November 1966 as a report of the Carnegie Institute of Technology Computer Science Department.]

[7] Seymour Ginsburg and Sheila Greibach, "Deterministic context-free languages," *Information and Control* **9** (1966), 620–648.

[8] E. T. Irons, " 'Structural connections' in formal languages," *Communications of the ACM* **7** (1964), 67–72.

[9] William Charles Lynch, *Ambiguities in BNF Languages* (Ph.D. thesis, University of Wisconsin, 1963).

[10] Peter Naur, editor, "Revised report on the algorithmic language ALGOL 60," *Communications of the ACM* **6** (1963), 1–17.

[11] M. Paul, "A general processor for certain formal languages," *Symbolic Languages in Data Processing* (New York: Gordon and Breach, 1962), 65–74.

[12] Emil L. Post, "Recursive unsolvability of a problem of Thue," *Journal of Symbolic Logic* **12** (1947), 1–11.

Addendum

Many papers have significantly developed the theory of LR(k) parsing, notably the discovery of an important special case now called "LALR" (lookahead left-to-right) that significantly reduces the size of associated tables. See the Ph.D. thesis of Franklin Lewis DeRemer, "Practical translators for LR(k) languages," Project MAC Report MAC TR-65 (Cambridge, Massachusetts: Massachusetts Institute of Technology, 1969), and his paper "Simple $LR(k)$ grammars," *Communications of the ACM* **14** (1971), 453–460.

Subsequent research has been admirably summarized by A. V. Aho and S. C. Johnson, "LR parsing," *Computing Surveys* **6** (1974), 99–124. Johnson's `yacc` system, which stands for "yet another compiler-compiler," has been a successful component of UNIX ever since those days.

Chapter 16

Context-Free Multilanguages

[Originally published in Theoretical Studies in Computer Science, edited by Jeffrey D. Ullman, a festschrift for Seymour Ginsburg (Academic Press, 1992), 1–13.]

Inspired by ideas of Chomsky, Bar-Hillel, Ginsburg, and their coworkers, I spent the summer of 1964 drafting Chapter 11 of a book that I had been asked to write. The main purpose of that book, tentatively entitled *The Art of Computer Programming*, was to explain how to write compilers; compilation was to be the subject of the twelfth and final chapter. Chapter 10 was called "Parsing," and Chapter 11 was "The theory of languages." I wrote the drafts of those chapters in the order 11, 10, 12, because Chapter 11 was the most fun to do.

Terminology and notation for formal linguistics were in a great state of flux in the early 60s, so it was natural for me to experiment with new ways to define the notion of what was then being called a "Chomsky type 2" or "ALGOL-like" or "definable" or "phrase structure" or "context-free" language. As I wrote Chapter 11, I made two changes to the definitions that had been appearing in the literature. The first change was comparatively trivial, although it simplified the statements and proofs of quite a few theorems: I replaced the "starting symbol" S by a "starting set" of strings from which the language was derived. The second change was more substantial: I decided to keep track of the multiplicity of strings in the language, so that a string would appear several times if there were several ways to parse it. This second change was natural from a programmer's viewpoint, because transformations on context-free grammars had proved to be most interesting in practice when they yielded isomorphisms between parse trees.

I never discussed those ideas in journal articles at the time, because I thought my book would soon be ready for publication. (I published an article about LR(k) grammars [4] only because it was an idea that occurred to me after finishing the draft of Chapter 10; the whole concept of LR(k) was well beyond the scope of my book, as envisioned in 1964.) My paper on parenthesis grammars [5] did make use of starting sets, but in my other relevant papers [4, 6, 8] I stuck with the more conventional use of a starting symbol S. I hinted at the importance of multiplicity in the answer to exercise 4.6.3–19 of *The Art of Computer Programming* (written in 1967, published in 1969 [7]): "The terminal strings of a noncircular context-free grammar form a multiset that is a set if and only if the grammar is unambiguous." But as the years went by and computer science continued its explosive growth, I found it more and more difficult to complete final drafts of the early chapters, and the date for the publication of Chapter 11 kept advancing faster than the clock was ticking.

Some of the early literature of context-free grammars referred to "strong equivalence," which meant that the multiplicities 0, 1, and ≥ 2 were preserved; if $\mathcal{G}_1$ was strongly equivalent to $\mathcal{G}_2$, then $\mathcal{G}_1$ was ambiguous if and only if $\mathcal{G}_2$ was ambiguous. But this concept did not become prominent enough to deserve mention in the standard textbook on the subject [1].

The occasion of Seymour Ginsburg's 64th birthday has reminded me that the simple ideas I played with in '64 ought to be aired before too many more years go by. Therefore I would like to sketch here the basic principles that I plan to expound in Chapter 11 of *The Art of Computer Programming* when it is finally completed and published — currently scheduled for the year 2008. My treatment will be largely informal, but I trust that interested readers will see easily how to make everything rigorous. If these ideas have any merit they may lead some readers to discover new results that will cause further delays in the publication of Chapter 11. That is a risk I'm willing to take.

Multisets

A *multiset* is like a set, but its elements can appear more than once. An element can in fact appear infinitely often, in an infinite multiset. The multiset containing 3 a's and 2 b's can be written in various ways, such as $\{a, a, a, b, b\}$, $\{a, a, b, a, b\}$, or $\{3 \cdot a, 2 \cdot b\}$. If A is a multiset of objects and if x is an object, $[x]A$ denotes the number of times x occurs in A; this quantity is either a nonnegative integer or ∞. We have $A \subseteq B$ when $[x]A \leq [x]B$ for all x; thus $A = B$ if and only if $A \subseteq B$ and $B \subseteq A$. A multiset is a *set* if no element occurs more than once, that is, if $[x]A \leq 1$ for all x. If A and B are multisets, we define $A \cap$, $A \cup B$,

$A \cap B$, $A \uplus B$, and $A \cap B$ by the rules

$$[x]\, A^\cap = \min(1, [x]\, A)\,;$$
$$[x]\, (A \cup B) = \max([x]\, A,\, [x]\, B)\,;$$
$$[x]\, (A \cap B) = \min([x]\, A,\, [x]\, B)\,;$$
$$[x]\, (A \uplus B) = ([x]\, A) + ([x]\, B)\,;$$
$$[x]\, (A \cap B) = ([x]\, A) \cdot ([x]\, B)\,.$$

(We assume here that ∞ plus anything is ∞ and that 0 times anything is 0.) Two multisets A and B are *similar*, written $A \asymp B$, if $A^\cap = B^\cap$; this means that they would agree as sets, if multiplicities were ignored. Notice that $A \cup B \asymp A \uplus B$ and $A \cap B \asymp A \cap B$. All four binary operations are associative and commutative. Several distributive laws also hold; for example,

$$(A \cap B) \cap C = (A \cap C) \cap (B \cap C)\,.$$

Multiplicities are taken into account when multisets appear as index sets (or rather as "index multisets"). For example, if $A = \{2, 2, 3, 5, 5, 5\}$, we have

$$\{\, x - 1 \mid x \in A \,\} = \{1, 1, 2, 4, 4, 4\}\,;$$

$$\sum_{x \in A} (x - 1) = \sum \{\, x - 1 \mid x \in A \,\} = 16\,;$$

$$\biguplus_{x \in A} B_x = B_2 \uplus B_2 \uplus B_3 \uplus B_5 \uplus B_5 \uplus B_5\,.$$

If $P(n)$ is the multiset of prime factors of n, we have the basic identity $\prod \{\, p \mid p \in P(n) \,\} = n$ for all positive integers n.

If A and B are multisets, we also write

$$A + B = \{\, a + b \mid a \in A,\ b \in B \,\}\,,$$
$$AB = \{\, ab \mid a \in A,\ b \in B \,\}\,;$$

therefore if A has m elements and B has n elements, both multisets $A + B$ and AB have mn elements. Notice that

$$[x]\, (A + B) = \sum_{a \in A} [x - a]\, B = \sum_{b \in B} [x - b]\, A$$

$$= \sum_{a \in A} \sum_{b \in B} [x = a + b]$$

where $[x = a+b]$ denotes 1 if $x = a+b$ and 0 otherwise. Similar formulas hold for $[x](AB)$.

It is convenient to let Ab stand for the multiset

$$Ab = \{ ab \mid a \in A \} = A\{b\};$$

similarly, aB stands for $\{a\}B$. This means, for example, that $2A$ is not the same as $A + A$; a special notation, perhaps $n * A$, is needed for the multiset

$$\overbrace{A + \cdots + A}^{n \text{ times}} = \{ a_1 + \cdots + a_n \mid a_j \in A \text{ for } 1 \leq j \leq n \}.$$

Similarly we need notations to distinguish the multiset

$$AA = \{ aa' \mid a, a' \in A \}$$

from the quite different multiset

$$\{ a^2 \mid a \in A \} = \{ aa \mid a \in A \}.$$

The product

$$\overbrace{A \ldots A}^{n \text{ times}} = \{ a_1 \ldots a_n \mid a_j \in A \text{ for } 1 \leq j \leq n \}$$

is traditionally written A^n, and I propose writing

$$A \uparrow n = \{ a^n \mid a \in A \} = \{ a \uparrow n \mid a \in A \}$$

on the rarer occasions when we need to deal with multisets of nth powers.

Multilanguages

A *multilanguage* is like a language, but its elements can appear more than once. Thus, if we regard a language as a set of strings, a multilanguage is a multiset of strings.

An *alphabet* is a finite set of distinguishable characters. If Σ is an alphabet, Σ^* denotes the set of all strings over Σ. Strings are generally represented by lowercase Greek letters; the empty string is called ϵ. If A is any multilanguage, we write

$$A^0 = \{\epsilon\},$$

$$A^* = A^0 \uplus A^1 \uplus A^2 \uplus \cdots = \biguplus_{n \geq 0} A^n;$$

this will be a language (that is, a set) if and only if the string equation $\alpha_1 \ldots \alpha_m = \alpha'_1 \ldots \alpha'_{m'}$ for strings $\alpha_1, \ldots, \alpha_m, \alpha'_1, \ldots, \alpha'_{m'} \in A$ implies that $m = m'$ and that $\alpha_k = \alpha'_k$ for $1 \leq k \leq m$. If $\epsilon \notin A$, every element of A^* has finite multiplicity; otherwise every element of A^* has infinite multiplicity.

A *context-free grammar* $\mathcal{G}$ has four component parts $(T, N, S, \mathcal{P})$: T is an alphabet of *terminals*; N is an alphabet of *nonterminals*, disjoint from T; S is a finite multiset of *starting strings* over the alphabet $V = T \cup N$; and $\mathcal{P}$ is a finite multiset of *productions*, where each production has the form

$$A \to \theta, \quad \text{for some } A \in N \text{ and } \theta \in V^*.$$

We usually use lowercase letters to represent elements of T, uppercase letters to represent elements of N. The starting strings and the right-hand sides of all productions are called the *basic strings* of $\mathcal{G}$. The multiset $\{\, \theta \mid A \to \theta \in \mathcal{P} \,\}$ is denoted by $\mathcal{P}(A)$; thus we can regard $\mathcal{P}$ as a mapping from N to multisets of strings over V.

The productions are extended to relations between strings in the usual way. Namely, if $A \to \theta$ is in $\mathcal{P}$, we say that $\alpha A \omega$ produces $\alpha \theta \omega$ for all strings α and ω in V^*; in symbols, $\alpha A \omega \to \alpha \theta \omega$. We also write $\sigma \to^n \tau$ if σ produces τ in n steps; this means that there are strings $\sigma_0, \sigma_1, \ldots, \sigma_n$ in V^* such that $\sigma_0 = \sigma$, $\sigma_{j-1} \to \sigma_j$ for $1 \leq j \leq n$, and $\sigma_n = \tau$. Furthermore we write $\sigma \to^* \tau$ if $\sigma \to^n \tau$ for some $n \geq 0$, and $\sigma \to^+ \tau$ if $\sigma \to^n \tau$ for some $n \geq 1$.

A *parse Π* for $\mathcal{G}$ is an ordered forest in which every node is labeled with a symbol of V; every internal (non-leaf) node is also labeled with a production of $\mathcal{P}$. An internal node whose production label is $A \to v_1 \ldots v_l$ must be labeled with the symbol A, and it must have exactly l children labeled $v_1, \ldots, v_l$, respectively. If the labels of the root nodes form the string σ and the labels of the leaf nodes form the string τ, and if there are n internal nodes, we say that Π parses τ as σ in n steps. There is an n-step parse of τ as σ if and only if $\sigma \to^n \tau$.

In many applications, we are interested in the number of parses; so we let $L(\sigma)$ be the multiset of all strings $\tau \in T^*$ such that $\sigma \to^* \tau$, with each τ occurring exactly as often as there are parses of τ as σ. This defines a multilanguage $L(\sigma)$ for each $\sigma \in V^*$.

It is not difficult to see that the multilanguages $L(\sigma)$ are characterized by the following multiset equations:

$$L(\tau) = \{\tau\}, \quad \text{for all } \tau \in T^*;$$
$$L(A) = \biguplus \{\, L(\theta) \mid \theta \in \mathcal{P}(A) \,\}, \quad \text{for all } A \in N;$$
$$L(\sigma \sigma') = L(\sigma) L(\sigma'), \quad \text{for all } \sigma, \sigma' \in V^*.$$

According to the conventions outlined above, the stated formula for $L(A)$ takes account of multiplicities, if any productions $A \to \theta$ are repeated in $\mathcal{P}$. Parse trees that use different copies of the same production are considered different; we can, for example, assign a unique number to each production, and use that number as the production label on internal nodes of the parse.

Notice that the multiplicity of τ in $L(\sigma)$ is the number of parses of τ as σ, not the number of derivations $\sigma = \sigma_0 \to \cdots \to \sigma_n = \tau$. For example, if $\mathcal{P}$ contains just two productions $\{A \to a, B \to b\}$, then $L(AB) = \{ab\}$ corresponds to the unique parse

$$
\begin{array}{cc}
A & B \\
| & | \\
a & b
\end{array}
$$

although there are two derivations $AB \to Ab \to ab$ and $AB \to aB \to ab$.

The multilanguages $L(\sigma)$ depend only on the alphabets $T \cup N$ and the productions $\mathcal{P}$. The *multilanguage defined by* $\mathcal{G}$, denoted by $L(\mathcal{G})$, is the multiset of strings parsable from the starting strings S, counting multiplicity:

$$
L(\mathcal{G}) = \biguplus \{ L(\sigma) \mid \sigma \in S \}.
$$

Transformations

Programmers are especially interested in the way $L(\mathcal{G})$ changes when $\mathcal{G}$ is modified. For example, we often want to simplify grammars or put them into standard forms without changing the strings of $L(\mathcal{G})$ or their multiplicities.

A nonterminal symbol A is *useless* if it never occurs in any parses of strings in $L(\mathcal{G})$. This happens if and only if either $L(A) = \emptyset$ or there are no strings $\sigma \in S$, $\alpha \in V^*$, and $\omega \in V^*$ such that $\sigma \to^* \alpha A \omega$. We can remove all productions of $\mathcal{P}$ and all strings of S that contain useless nonterminals, without changing $L(\mathcal{G})$. A grammar is said to be *reduced* if every element of N is useful.

Several basic transformations can be applied to any grammar without affecting the multilanguage $L(\mathcal{G})$. One of these transformations is called *abbreviation*: Let X be a new symbol $\notin V$ and let θ be any string of V^*. Add X to N and add the production $X \to \theta$ to $\mathcal{P}$. Then we can replace θ by X wherever θ occurs as a substring of a basic string, except in the production $X \to \theta$ itself, without changing $L(\mathcal{G})$; this follows from the fact that $L(X) = L(\theta)$. By repeated use of abbreviations we can obtain an equivalent grammar whose basic strings all have length 2 or less. The total length of all basic strings in the new grammar is less than twice the total length of all basic strings in the original.

Another simple transformation, sort of an inverse to abbreviation, is called *expansion*. It replaces any basic string of the form $\alpha X\omega$ by the multiset of all strings $\alpha\theta\omega$ where $X \to \theta$. If $\alpha X\omega$ is the right-hand side of some production $A \to \alpha X\omega$, this means that the production is replaced in $\mathcal{P}$ by the multiset of productions $\{ A \to \alpha\theta\omega \mid \theta \in \mathcal{P}(X) \}$; we are essentially replacing the element $\alpha X\omega$ of $\mathcal{P}(A)$ by the multiset $\{ \alpha\theta\omega \mid \theta \in \mathcal{P}(X) \}$. Again, $L(\mathcal{G})$ is not affected.

Expansion can cause some productions and/or starting strings to be repeated. If we had defined context-free grammars differently, taking S and $\mathcal{P}$ to be sets instead of multisets, we would not be able to apply the expansion process in general without losing track of some parses.

A third basic transformation, called *elimination*, deletes a given production $A \to \theta$ from $\mathcal{P}$ and replaces every remaining basic string σ by $D(\sigma)$, where $D(\sigma)$ is a multiset defined recursively as follows:

$$D(A) = \{A, \theta\} \,;$$
$$D(\sigma) = \{\sigma\} \,, \text{ if } \sigma \text{ does not include } A \,;$$
$$D(\sigma\sigma') = D(\sigma)D(\sigma') \,.$$

If σ has n occurrences of A, these equations imply that $D(\sigma)$ has 2^n elements. Elimination preserves $L(\mathcal{G})$ because it simply removes all uses of the production $A \to \theta$ from parse trees.

We can use elimination to make the grammar "ϵ-free," that is, to remove all productions whose right-hand side is empty. Complications arise, however, when a grammar is also "circular"; this means that it contains a nonterminal A such that $A \to^+ A$. The grammars of most practical interest are noncircular, but we need to deal with circularity if we want to have a complete theory. It is easy to see that strings of infinite multiplicity occur in the multilanguage $L(\mathcal{G})$ of a reduced grammar $\mathcal{G}$ if and only if $\mathcal{G}$ is circular.

One way to deal with the problem of circularity is to modify the grammar so that all the circularity is localized. Let $N = N_c \cup N_n$, where the nonterminals of N_c are circular and those of N_n are not. We will construct a new grammar $\mathcal{G}' = (T, N', S' \cup S'', \mathcal{P}')$ with $L(\mathcal{G}') = L(\mathcal{G})$, for which all strings of the multilanguage $L(S') = \biguplus \{ L(\sigma) \mid \sigma \in S' \}$ have infinite multiplicity and all strings of $L(S'') = \biguplus \{ L(\sigma) \mid \sigma \in S'' \}$ have finite multiplicity. The nonterminals of $\mathcal{G}'$ are $N' = N_c \cup N_n \cup N_n' \cup N_n''$, where $N_n' = \{ A' \mid A \in N_n \}$ and $N_n'' = \{ A'' \mid A \in N_n \}$ are new nonterminal alphabets in one-to-one correspondence with N_n. The new grammar will be defined in such a way that $L(A) = L(A') \uplus L(A'')$, where $L(A')$ contains only strings of infinite multiplicity and $L(A'')$ contains only strings of finite multiplicity. For each $\sigma \in S$ we include the members of σ' in S' and σ'' in S'', where σ' and σ'' are multisets of strings defined as follows: If σ includes a nonterminal in N_c, then $\sigma' = \{\sigma\}$ and $\sigma'' = \emptyset$. Otherwise suppose $\sigma = \alpha_0 A_1 \alpha_1 \ldots A_n \alpha_n$, where each $\alpha_k \in T^*$ and each $A_k \in N_n$; then

$$\sigma' = \{ \alpha_0 A_1'' \alpha_1 \ldots A_{k-1}'' \alpha_{k-1} A_k' \alpha_k A_{k+1} \ldots A_n \alpha_n \mid 1 \leq k \leq n \},$$

$$\sigma'' = \{ \alpha_0 A_1'' \alpha_1 \ldots A_n'' \alpha_n \}.$$

(Intuitively, the leftmost use of a circular nonterminal in a derivation from σ' will occur in the descendants of A_k'. No circular nonterminals will appear in derivations from σ''.) The productions $\mathcal{P}'$ are obtained from $\mathcal{P}$ by letting

$$\mathcal{P}'(A') = \biguplus \{ \sigma' \mid \sigma \in \mathcal{P}(A) \},$$

$$\mathcal{P}'(A'') = \biguplus \{ \sigma'' \mid \sigma \in \mathcal{P}(A) \}.$$

This completes the construction of $\mathcal{G}'$.

We can also add a new nonterminal symbol Z, and two new productions

$$Z \to Z,$$

$$Z \to \epsilon.$$

The resulting grammar $\mathcal{G}''$ with starting strings $ZS' \uplus S''$ again has $L(\mathcal{G}'') = L(\mathcal{G})$, but now all strings with infinite multiplicity are derived from ZS'. This implies that we can remove circularity from all nonterminals except Z, without changing any multiplicities; then Z will be the only source of infinite multiplicity.

The details are slightly tricky but not really complicated. Let us remove accumulated primes from our notation, and work with a grammar $\mathcal{G} = (T, N, S, \mathcal{P})$ having the properties just assumed for $\mathcal{G}''$. We want $\mathcal{G}$ to have only Z as a circular nonterminal. The first step is to remove instances of co-circularity: If $\mathcal{G}$ contains two nonterminals A and B such that $A \to^+ B$ and $B \to^+ A$, we can replace all occurrences of B by A and delete B from N. This leaves $L(\mathcal{G})$ unaffected, because every string of $L(\mathcal{G})$ that has at least one parse involving B has infinitely many parses both before and after the change is made. Therefore we can assume that $\mathcal{G}$ is a grammar in which the relations $A \to^+ B$ and $B \to^+ A$ imply $A = B$.

Now we can topologically sort the nonterminals into order A_0, A_1, $\ldots$, A_m so that $A_i \to^+ A_j$ only if $i \leq j$; let $A_0 = Z$ be the special, circular nonterminal introduced above. The grammar will be in *Chomsky normal form* if all productions except those for Z have one of the two forms

$$A \to BC \quad \text{or} \quad A \to a$$

where $A, B, C \in N$ and $a \in T$. Assume that this condition holds for all productions whose left-hand side is A_l, for some l strictly greater than a given index $k > 0$; we will show how to make it hold also for $l = k$, without changing $L(\mathcal{G})$.

Abbreviations will reduce any productions on the right-hand side to length 2 or less. Moreover, if $A_k \to v_1 v_2$ for $v_1 \in T$, we can introduce a new abbreviation $A_k \to X v_2$, $X \to v_1$; a similar abbreviation applies if $v_2 \in T$. Therefore systematic use of abbreviation will put all productions with A_k on the left into Chomsky normal form, except those of the forms $A_k \to A_l$ or $A_k \to \epsilon$. By assumption, we can have $A_k \to A_l$ only if $l \geq k$. If $l > k$, the production $A_k \to A_l$ can be eliminated by expansion; it is replaced by $A_k \to \theta$ for all $\theta \in \mathcal{P}(A_l)$, and these productions all have the required form. If $l = k$, the production $A_k \to A_l$ is redundant and can be dropped; this does not affect $L(\mathcal{G})$, since every string whose derivation uses A_k has infinite multiplicity because it is derived from ZS'. Finally, a production of the form $A_k \to \epsilon$ can be removed by elimination as explained above. This does not lengthen the right-hand side of any production. But it might add new productions of the form $A_k \to A_l$ (which are handled as before) or of the form $A_j \to \epsilon$. The latter can occur only if there was a production $A_j \to A_k^n$ for some $n \geq 1$; hence $A_j \to^+ A_k$ and we must have $j \leq k$. If $j = k$, the new production $A_k \to \epsilon$ can simply be dropped, because its presence merely gives additional parses to strings whose multiplicity is already infinite.

This construction puts $\mathcal{G}$ into Chomsky normal form, except for the special productions $Z \to Z$ and $Z \to \epsilon$, without changing the multilanguage $L(\mathcal{G})$. If we want to proceed further, we could delete the production $Z \to Z$; this gives a grammar $\mathcal{G}'$ with $L(\mathcal{G}') \asymp L(\mathcal{G})$ and no circularity. And we can then eliminate $Z \to \epsilon$, obtaining a grammar $\mathcal{G}''$ in Chomsky normal form with $L(\mathcal{G}'') = L(\mathcal{G}')$. If $\mathcal{G}$ itself was originally noncircular, the special nonterminal Z was always useless so it need not have been introduced; our construction produces Chomsky normal form directly in such cases.

The construction in the preceding paragraphs can be illustrated by the following example grammar with terminal alphabet $\{a\}$, nonterminal alphabet $\{A, B, C\}$, starting set $\{A\}$, and productions

$$A \to AAa,\ A \to B,\ A \to \epsilon,\ B \to CC,\ C \to BB,\ C \to \epsilon.$$

The nonterminals are $N_n = \{A\}$ and $N_c = \{B, C\}$. So we add nonterminals $N_n' = \{A'\}$ and $N_n'' = \{A''\}$, change the starting strings to

$$S' = \{A'\}, \qquad S'' = \{A''\},$$

and add the productions

$$A' \to A'Aa,\ A' \to A''A'a,\ A' \to B;$$
$$A'' \to A''A''a,\ A'' \to \epsilon.$$

Now we introduce Z, replace C by B, and make the abbreviations $X \to AY$, $X' \to A'Y$, $X'' \to A''Y$, $Y \to a$. The current grammar has terminal alphabet $\{a\}$, nonterminal alphabet $\{Z, A, A', A'', B, X, X', X'', Y\}$ in topological order, starting strings $\{ZA', A''\}$, and productions

$$Z \to \{Z, \epsilon\},$$
$$A \to \{AX, B, \epsilon\},$$
$$A' \to \{A'X, A''X', B\},$$
$$A'' \to \{A''X'', \epsilon\},$$
$$B \to \{BB, BB, \epsilon\},$$

plus those for X, X', X'', Y already stated. Eliminating the production $B \to \epsilon$ yields new productions $A \to \epsilon$, $A' \to \epsilon$; eliminating $A'' \to \epsilon$ yields a new starting string ϵ and new productions $A' \to X'$, $A'' \to X''$, $X'' \to a$. We eventually reach a near-Chomsky-normal grammar with starting strings $\{Z, ZA', ZA'', A'', \epsilon\}$ and productions

$$Z \to \{Z, \epsilon\},$$
$$A \to \{AX, AY, AY, BB, BB, a, a, a, a\},$$
$$A' \to \{AY, A'X, A'Y, A''X', BB, BB, a, a, a\},$$
$$A'' \to \{A''X'', A''Y, a\},$$
$$B \to \{BB, BB\},$$
$$X \to \{AY, a, a\},$$
$$X' \to \{A'Y, a\},$$
$$X'' \to \{A''Y, a\},$$
$$Y \to \{a\}.$$

Once a grammar is in Chomsky normal form, we can go further and eliminate left recursion. A nonterminal symbol X is called *left recursive* if $X \to^+ X\omega$ for some $\omega \in V^*$. The following transformation makes X non-left-recursive without introducing any additional left-recursive nonterminals: Introduce new nonterminals $N' = \{ A' \mid A \in N \}$, and new productions

$$\{ B' \to CA' \mid A \to BC \in \mathcal{P} \},$$
$$\{ X \to aA' \mid A \to a \in \mathcal{P} \},$$
$$X' \to \epsilon,$$

and delete all the original productions of $\mathcal{P}(X)$. It is not difficult to prove that $L(\mathcal{G}') = L(\mathcal{G})$ for the new grammar $\mathcal{G}'$, because there is a one-to-one correspondence between parse trees for the two grammars. The basic idea is to consider all "maximal left paths" of nodes labeled $A_1, \ldots, A_r$, corresponding to the productions

$$A_1 \to A_2 B_1 \to A_3 B_2 B_1 \to \cdots$$
$$\to A_r B_{r-1} B_{r-2} \ldots B_1 \to a B_{r-1} B_{r-2} \ldots B_1$$

in $\mathcal{G}$, where A_1 labels either the root or the right subtree of A_1's parent in a parse for $\mathcal{G}$. If X occurs as at least one of the nonterminals $\{A_1, \ldots, A_r\}$, say $A_j = X$ but $A_i \neq X$ for $i < j$, the corresponding productions of $\mathcal{G}'$ change the left path into a right path after branch j:

$$A_1 \to \cdots \to A_j B_{j-1} \ldots B_1 \to a A'_r B_{j-1} \ldots B_1$$
$$\to a B_{r-1} A'_{r-1} B_{j-1} \ldots B_1$$
$$\to \cdots \to a B_{r-1} \ldots B_j A'_j B_{j-1} \ldots B_1$$
$$\to a B_{r-1} \ldots B_j B_{j-1} \ldots B_1 .$$

The subtrees for $B_1, \ldots, B_{r-1}$ undergo the same reversible transformation.

Once left recursion is removed, it is a simple matter to put the grammar into *Greibach normal form* [3], in which all productions can be written

$$A \to a A_1 \ldots A_k , \qquad k \geq 0 ,$$

for $a \in T$ and $A, A_1, \ldots, A_k \in N$. First we order the nonterminals $X_1, \ldots, X_n$ so that $X_i \to X_j X_k$ only when $i < j$; then we expand all such productions, for decreasing values of i.

Transduction

A general class of transformations that change one context-free language into another was discovered by Ginsburg and Rose [2], and the same ideas carry over to multilanguages. My notes from 1964 use the word "juxtamorphism" for a slightly more general class of mappings; I don't remember whether I coined that term at the time or found it in the literature. At any rate, I'll try it here again and see if it proves to be acceptable.

If F is a mapping from strings over T to multilanguages over T', we can conveniently write α^F instead of $F(\alpha)$ for the image of α under F. A family of such mappings $F_1, \ldots, F_r$ is said to define a *juxtamorphism* if, for all j and for all nonempty strings α and β, the multilanguage $(\alpha\beta)^{F_j}$ can be expressed as a finite multiset union of multilanguages each having "bilinear form"

$$\alpha^{F_k}\beta^{F_l} \quad \text{or} \quad \beta^{F_k}\alpha^{F_l}.$$

The juxtamorphism family is called *context-free* if a^{F_j} and ϵ^{F_j} are context-free multilanguages for all $a \in T$ and all j.

For example, many mappings satisfy this condition with $r = 1$. The reflection mapping, which takes every string $\alpha = a_1 \ldots a_m$ into $\alpha^R = a_m \ldots a_1$, obviously satisfies $(\alpha\beta)^R = \beta^R\alpha^R$. The composition mapping, which takes $\alpha = a_1 \ldots a_m$ into $\alpha^L = L(a_1) \ldots L(a_m)$ for any given multilanguages $L(a)$ defined for each $a \in T$, is a simple juxtamorphism that satisfies $(\alpha\beta)^L = \alpha^L\beta^L$.

The prefix mapping, which takes the string $\alpha = a_1 \ldots a_m$ into $\alpha^P = \{\epsilon, a_1, a_1a_2, \ldots, a_1 \ldots a_m\}$, is a member of a juxtamorphism family with $r = 3$, because it satisfies

$$(\alpha\beta)^P = \alpha^P\beta^E \uplus \alpha^I\beta^P,$$
$$(\alpha\beta)^I = \alpha^I\beta^I,$$
$$(\alpha\beta)^E = \alpha^E\beta^E,$$

where I is the identity and $\alpha^E = \epsilon$ for all α.

Any finite-state transduction, which maps $\alpha = a_1 \ldots a_m$ into

$$\alpha^{q_0} = \{\, f(q_0, a_1)f(q_1, a_2) \ldots f(q_{m-1}, a_m)f(q_m, \epsilon) \mid q_j \in g(q_{j-1}, a_j)\,\}$$

is a special case of a juxtamorphism. Here $q_0, \ldots, q_m$ are members of a finite set of states Q, and g is a next-state function from $Q \times T$ into subsets of Q; the mapping f takes each member of $Q \times (T \cup \{\epsilon\})$ into a context-free multilanguage. The juxtamorphism can be defined as follows: Given $q, q' \in Q$, let $\alpha^{qq'}$ be

$$\{\, f(q_0, a_1) \ldots f(q_{m-1}, a_m) \mid q_0 = q \text{ and } q_j \in g(q_{j-1}, q_j) \text{ and } q_m = q' \,\}.$$

Then we have

$$(\alpha\beta)^{qq'} = \biguplus_{q'' \in Q} \alpha^{qq''} \beta^{q''q'} \,;$$

$$(\alpha\beta)^q = \biguplus_{q' \in Q} \alpha^{qq'} \beta^{q'} \,.$$

The following extension of the construction by Ginsburg and Rose yields a context-free grammar $\mathcal{G}_j$ for $L(\mathcal{G})^{F_j}$, given any juxtamorphism family $F_1, \ldots, F_r$. The grammar $\mathcal{G}$ can be assumed in Chomsky normal form, except for a special nonterminal Z as mentioned above. The given context-free multilanguages a^{F_j} and ϵ^{F_j} have terminal alphabet T', disjoint nonterminal alphabets $N^{(a, F_j)}$ and $N^{(\epsilon, F_j)}$, starting strings $S^{(a, F_j)}$ and $S^{(\epsilon, F_j)}$, productions $\mathcal{P}^{(a, F_j)}$ and $\mathcal{P}^{(\epsilon, F_j)}$. Each grammar $\mathcal{G}_j$ has all these, plus nonterminal symbols A^{F_j} for all j and for all nonterminal A in $\mathcal{G}$. Each production $A \to a$ in $\mathcal{G}$ leads to productions $A^{F_j} \to \{\, \sigma \mid \sigma \in S^{(a, F_j)} \,\}$ for all j. Each production $A \to BC$ in $\mathcal{G}$ leads to the productions for each A^{F_j} based on its juxtamorphism representation. For example, in the case of the prefix mapping above we would have the productions

$$A^P \to B^P C^E \,, \quad A^P \to B^I C^P \,, \quad A^I \to B^I C^I \,, \quad A^E \to B^E C^E \,.$$

The starting strings for $\mathcal{G}_j$ are obtained from those of $\mathcal{G}$ in a similar way. Further details are left to the reader.

In particular, one special case of finite-state transduction maps each string α into $\{k \cdot \alpha\}$ if α is accepted in exactly k ways by a finite-state automaton. (Let $f(q, a) = a$, and let $f(q, \epsilon) = \{\epsilon\}$ or $\emptyset$ according as q is an accepting state or not.) The construction above shows that if L_1 is a context-free multilanguage and L_2 is a regular multilanguage, the multilanguage $L_1 \cap L_2$ is context-free.

Quantitative Considerations

Since multisets carry more information than the underlying sets, we can expect that more computation will be needed in order to keep track of everything. From a worst-case standpoint, this is bad news. For example, consider the comparatively innocuous productions

$$A_0 \to \epsilon, \quad A_0 \to \epsilon,$$
$$A_1 \to A_0 A_0, \quad A_2 \to A_1 A_1, \quad \ldots, \quad A_n \to A_{n-1} A_{n-1},$$

with starting string $\{A_n\}$. This grammar is almost in Chomsky normal form, except for the elimination of ϵ. But ϵ-removal is rather horrible: There are 2^{2^k} ways to derive ϵ from A_k. Hence we will have to replace the multiset of starting strings by $\{2^{2^n} \cdot \epsilon\}$.

Let us add further productions $A_k \to a_k$ to the grammar above, for $0 \le k \le n$, and then reduce to Chomsky normal form by "simply" removing the two productions $A_0 \to \epsilon$. The normal-form productions will be

$$A_k \to \left\{ 2^{2^k - 2^j + k - j} \cdot A_{j-1} A_{j-1} \mid 1 \le j \le k \right\}$$
$$\uplus \left\{ 2^{2^k - 2^j + k - j} \cdot a_j \mid 0 \le j \le k \right\}.$$

Evidently if we wish to implement the algorithms for normal forms, we should represent multisets of strings by counting multiplicities in binary rather than unary; even so, the results might blow up exponentially.

Fortunately this is not a serious problem in practice, since most artificial languages have unambiguous or nearly unambiguous grammars; multiplicities of reasonable grammars tend to be low. And we can at least prove that the general situation cannot get much worse than the behavior of the example above: Consider a noncircular grammar with n nonterminals and with m productions each having one of the four forms $A \to BC$, $A \to B$, $A \to a$, $A \to \epsilon$. Then the process of conversion to Chomsky normal form does not increase the set of distinct right-hand sides $\{BC\}$ or $\{a\}$; hence the total number of distinct productions will be at most $O(mn)$. The multiplicities of productions will be bounded by the number of ways to attach labels $\{1, \ldots, m\}$ to the nodes of the complete binary tree with 2^{n-1} leaves, namely $m^{2^n - 1}$.

Conclusions

String coefficients that correspond to the exact number of parses are important in applications of context-free grammars, so it is desirable to keep track of such multiplicities as the theory is developed. This concept is familiar when context-free multilanguages are considered as algebraic power series in noncommuting variables, except in cases where the coefficients are infinite. But the intuition that comes from manipulations on trees, grammars, and automata nicely complements the purely algebraic approaches to this theory. It's a beautiful theory that deserves to be remembered by computer scientists of the future, even though it is no longer a principal focus of contemporary research.

Let me close by stating a small puzzle. Context-free multilanguages are obviously closed under ⊎. But they are not closed under ∪, because for example the language

$$\{\, a^i b^j c^i d^k \mid i, j, k \geq 1 \,\} \cup \{\, a^i b^j c^k d^j \mid i, j, k \geq 1 \,\}$$

is inherently ambiguous [9]. Is it true that $L_1 \cup L_2$ is a context-free multilanguage whenever L_1 is context-free and L_2 is regular?

References

[1] Seymour Ginsburg, *The Mathematical Theory of Context-Free Languages* (New York: McGraw–Hill, 1966).

[2] Seymour Ginsburg and G. F. Rose, "Operations which preserve definability in languages," *Journal of the Association for Computing Machinery* **10** (1963), 175–195.

[3] Sheila A. Greibach, "A new normal-form theorem for context-free phrase structure grammars," *Journal of the Association for Computing Machinery* **12** (1965), 42–52.

[4] Donald E. Knuth, "On the translation of languages from left to right," *Information and Control* **8** (1965), 607–639. [Reprinted as Chapter 15 of the present volume.]

[5] Donald E. Knuth, "A characterization of parenthesis languages," *Information and Control* **11** (1967), 269–289. [Reprinted as Chapter 13 of the present volume.]

[6] Donald E. Knuth, "Semantics of context-free languages," *Mathematical Systems Theory* **2** (1968), 127–145; errata, *Mathematical Systems Theory* **5** (1971), 95–96. [Reprinted as Chapter 17 of the present volume.]

[7] Donald E. Knuth, *Seminumerical Algorithms*, Volume 2 of *The Art of Computer Programming* (Reading, Massachusetts: Addison–Wesley, 1969).

[8] Donald E. Knuth, "Top-down syntax analysis," *Acta Informatica* **1** (1971), 79–110. [Reprinted as Chapter 14 of the present volume.]

[9] Rohit J. Parikh, "On context-free languages," *Journal of the Association for Computing Machinery* **13** (1966), 570–581.

Chapter 17

Semantics of Context-Free Languages

*[Originally published in Mathematical Systems Theory **2** (1968), 127–145; **5** (1971), 95–96.]*

"Meaning" may be assigned to a string in a context-free language by defining "attributes" of the symbols in a derivation tree for that string. The attributes can be defined by functions associated with each production in the grammar. This paper examines the implications of this process when some of the attributes are "synthesized," that is, defined solely in terms of attributes of the descendants of the corresponding nonterminal symbol, while other attributes are "inherited," that is, defined in terms of attributes of the ancestors of the nonterminal symbol. An algorithm is given that detects when such semantic rules could possibly lead to circular definition of some attributes. An example is given of a simple programming language defined with both inherited and synthesized attributes, and the method of definition is compared to other techniques for formal specification of semantics that have appeared in the literature.

A simple technique for specifying the "meaning" of languages that are defined by context-free grammars is introduced in Section 1 of this paper, and its basic mathematical properties are investigated in Sections 2 and 3. An example that indicates how the technique can be applied to the formal definition of programming languages is described in Section 4; finally, Section 5 contains a somewhat biased comparison of the present method to other known techniques for semantic definition. The discussion in this paper is oriented primarily towards programming languages, but the same methods appear to be relevant also in the study of natural languages.

1. Introduction

Let us suppose that we want to give a precise definition of binary notation for numbers. There are many ways to do the job, but in the present section we want to consider a general manner of definition by which the meaning of more complicated notations could be formulated in essentially the same way. One such approach to the semantics of binary notation is to base a definition on the following context-free grammar:

$$B \to 0$$
$$B \to 1$$
$$L \to B$$
$$L \to LB$$
$$N \to L$$
$$N \to L \cdot L$$

(1.1)

(Here the terminal symbols are 0, 1, and $\cdot$; the nonterminal symbols are B, L, and N, standing respectively for bit, list of bits, and number; and a binary number is intended to be any string of terminal symbols that can be obtained from N by application of the productions above.) This grammar says in effect that a binary number is a sequence of one or more 0s and 1s, optionally followed by a radix point and another sequence of one or more 0s and 1s. Furthermore, the grammar assigns a certain *tree structure* to each binary number; for example, the string 1101·01 receives the following structure:

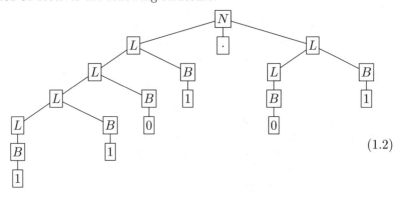

(1.2)

It is natural to define the meaning of binary notation (1.1) in a step-by-step manner corresponding to the syntactic structure; the meaning of the notation as a whole is built up from meanings of each part. This can be done by assigning *attributes* to the nonterminal symbols, as follows:

Each bit B has a "value" $v(B)$, which is an integer.

Each list of bits L has a "length" $l(L)$, which is an integer.

Each list of bits L has a "value" $v(L)$, which is an integer.

Each number N has a "value" $v(N)$, which is a rational number.

(Notice that each L has two attributes; in general we might want to ascribe any desired number of attributes to each nonterminal symbol.)

The grammar (1.1) may now be augmented so that semantic rules are given for each rule of the syntax:

$$
\begin{aligned}
B &\to 0 & v(B) &= 0 \\
B &\to 1 & v(B) &= 1 \\
L &\to B & v(L) &= v(B),\ \ l(L) = 1 \\
L_1 &\to L_2 B & v(L_1) &= 2v(L_2) + v(B),\ \ l(L_1) = l(L_2) + 1 \\
N &\to L & v(N) &= v(L) \\
N &\to L_1 \cdot L_2 & v(N) &= v(L_1) + v(L_2)/2^{l(L_2)}
\end{aligned}
\tag{1.3}
$$

(Subscripts have been used in the fourth and sixth rules, to distinguish between occurrences of like nonterminals.) Here the semantic rules define all of the attributes of a nonterminal in terms of the attributes of its immediate descendants, so the values are ultimately defined for each attribute. The semantic rules are phrased in terms of notations that are assumed to be already understood. Notice for example that the symbol '0' in the semantic rule '$v(B) = 0$' is to be interpreted quite differently from the symbol '0' in the production '$B \to 0$'; the former denotes a mathematical concept, the integer zero, while the latter denotes a written character that has a certain oval shape. In a sense it is just coincidence that the two symbols look the same.

The structure (1.2) may be augmented by showing the attributes at each level:

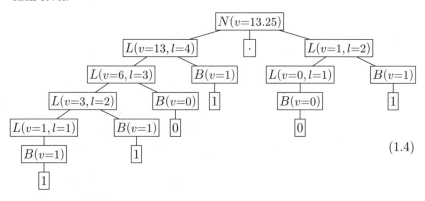

$$(1.4)$$

Thus '1101·01' means 13.25 (in decimal notation).

This manner of defining semantics for context-free languages is essentially well known, since it has already been used by several authors.

But there is an important way to extend the method, and it is such an extension that will be of primary interest to us.

Suppose for example that we want to define the semantics of binary notation in a way that corresponds more closely to the manner in which we usually think of the notation. The leading '1' in '1101·01' really denotes 8, although according to (1.4) it is ascribed the value 1. Perhaps therefore it would be better to define the semantics by letting positional characteristics play more of a role. We could have the following attributes:

Each B has a "value" $v(B)$, which is a rational number.

Each B has a "scale" $s(B)$, which is an integer.

Each L has a "value" $v(L)$, which is a rational number.

Each L has a "length" $l(L)$, which is an integer.

Each L has a "scale" $s(L)$, which is an integer.

Each N has a "value" $v(N)$, which is a rational number.

And we could define them in the following way:

Syntactic rules	*Semantic rules*	
$B \to 0$	$v(B) = 0$	
$B \to 1$	$v(B) = 2^{s(B)}$	
$L \to B$	$v(L) = v(B), \ s(B) = s(L), \ l(L) = 1$	
$L_1 \to L_2 B$	$v(L_1) = v(L_2) + v(B), \ s(B) = s(L_1),$	(1.5)
	$s(L_2) = s(L_1) + 1, \ l(L_1) = l(L_2) + 1$	
$N \to L$	$v(N) = v(L), \ s(L) = 0$	
$N \to L_1 \cdot L_2$	$v(N) = v(L_1) + v(L_2), \ s(L_1) = 0,$	
	$s(L_2) = -l(L_2)$	

(Here the semantic rules are listed using the convention that the right-hand side of each equation is the definition of the left-hand side; thus, '$s(B) = s(L)$' means that $s(L)$ is to be evaluated first, then $s(B)$ is defined to have this same value.)

The important feature of grammar (1.5) is that some of the attributes are defined for nonterminals that appear on the *right* side of the corresponding production, while in (1.3) all attributes were defined when the nonterminal appeared on the left. In other words we are using both *synthesized attributes* (which are based on the attributes of the *descendants* of the nonterminal symbol) and *inherited attributes* (which are based on attributes of the *ancestors*). Synthesized attributes are evaluated from the bottom up in the tree structure, while inherited attributes are evaluated from the top down. Grammar (1.5) contains not only the synthesized attributes $v(B)$, $v(L)$, $l(L)$, $v(N)$, but also the inherited attributes $s(B)$ and $s(L)$, so the evaluation involves going in both directions. The evaluated structure corresponding to the string 1101·01 is

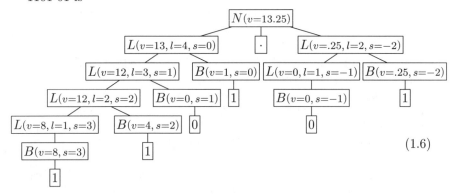

$$(1.6)$$

Here it can be noted that the "length" attributes of the L's to the right of the radix point must be evaluated from the bottom up, before the "scale" attributes can be evaluated (from the top down) and finally the "value" attributes (from the bottom up).

Grammar (1.5) is probably not the best possible way to define binary notation, but it does seem to correspond better to our intuition than grammar (1.3). (A grammar that agrees more exactly with our conventional understanding of binary notation could be based on a different set of productions, in which '$N \to L \cdot L$' is replaced by three rules

$$N \to L \cdot R$$
$$R \to B \qquad\qquad (1.7)$$
$$R \to BR$$

that assign a more appropriate structure to the string of bits at the right of the radix point. Then the "length" attribute, which is not really relevant, would be unnecessary.)

Our interest in grammar (1.5) is not that it is an ideal definition of binary notation, but rather that it shows an interaction between inherited and synthesized attributes. There is not always an obvious way to be sure that semantic rules such as those in (1.5) do not amount to a circular definition, because the attributes are not evaluated in a single direction; an algorithm that tests for circularity appears in Section 3 below.

The importance of inherited attributes is that they arise naturally in practice, and that they are "dual" to synthesized attributes in a straightforward manner. Although binary notation can be formulated using nothing but synthesized attributes, there are many languages for which such a restriction leads to a very awkward and unnatural definition of semantics. Situations that involve a mixture of inherited and synthesized attributes are essentially the same as the cases that have been most difficult to handle in previous formulations of semantic rules.

2. Formal Properties

Let us now put the ideas of synthesized and inherited attributes into a more precise and more general setting.

Suppose we have a context-free grammar $\mathcal{G} = (V, N, S, \mathcal{P})$, where V is the (finite) vocabulary of terminal and nonterminal symbols; $N \subseteq V$ is the set of nonterminal symbols; $S \in N$ is the "start symbol," which appears on the right-hand side of no production rule; and $\mathcal{P}$ is the set of production rules.

Semantic rules are added to $\mathcal{G}$ in the following manner: To each symbol $X \in V$ we associate a finite set $A(X)$ of attributes; $A(X)$ is partitioned into two disjoint sets, the *synthesized attributes* $A_0(X)$ and the *inherited attributes* $A_1(X)$. We require $A_1(S)$ to be empty (that is, the start symbol S has no inherited attributes); similarly we require $A_0(X)$ to be empty if X is a terminal symbol. Each attribute α in $A(X)$ has a (possibly infinite) set of possible values V_α, from which one value will be selected (by means of the semantic rules) for each appearance of X in a derivation tree.

Let $\mathcal{P}$ consist of m productions, and let the pth production be

$$X_{p0} \to X_{p1} X_{p2} \ldots X_{pn_p}, \tag{2.1}$$

where $n_p \geq 0$, $X_{p0} \in N$, and $X_{pj} \in V$ for $1 \leq j \leq n_p$. The semantic rules are functions $f_{pj\alpha}$ defined for all $1 \leq p \leq m$, $0 \leq j \leq n_p$, and $\alpha \in A_0(X_{pj})$ if $j = 0$, $\alpha \in A_1(X_{pj})$ if $j > 0$. Every such function is a mapping of $V_{\alpha_1} \times V_{\alpha_2} \times \cdots \times V_{\alpha_t}$ into V_α, for some $t = t(p, j, \alpha) \geq 0$, where each $\alpha_i = \alpha_i(p, j, \alpha)$ is an attribute of some X_{pk_i}, for $0 \leq k_i = k_i(p, j, \alpha) \leq n_p$, $1 \leq i \leq t$. In other words, each semantic rule maps values of certain attributes of $X_{p0}, X_{p1}, \ldots, X_{pn_p}$ onto the value of some attribute of X_{pj}.

For example, (1.5) is the grammar

$$\mathcal{G} = (\{0, 1, \cdot, B, L, N\}, \{B, L, N\}, N,$$
$$\{B \to 0,\ B \to 1,\ L \to B,\ L \to LB,\ N \to L,\ N \to L{\cdot}L\}).$$

The attributes are $A_0(B) = \{v\}$, $A_1(B) = \{s\}$, $A_0(L) = \{v, l\}$, $A_1(L) = \{s\}$, $A_0(N) = \{v\}$, $A_1(N) = \emptyset$, and $A_0(x) = A_1(x) = \emptyset$ for $x \in \{0, 1, \cdot\}$. The attribute value sets are $V_v = \{\text{rational numbers}\}$, $V_s = V_l = \{\text{integers}\}$. A typical production rule is the fourth production $X_{40} \to X_{41} X_{42}$, where $n_4 = 2$, $X_{40} = X_{41} = L$, $X_{42} = B$. A typical semantic rule corresponding to this production is f_{40v}, which defines $v(X_{40})$ in terms of other attributes; in this case f_{40v} maps $V_v \times V_v$ into V_v and it is the mapping $f_{40v}(x, y) = x + y$. (This is the rule '$v(L_1) = v(L_2) + v(B)$' of (1.5); in terms of the rather cumbersome but totally logical notation of the preceding paragraph we have $t(4, 0, v) = 2$, $\alpha_1(4, 0, v) = \alpha_2(4, 0, v) = v$, $k_1(4, 0, v) = 1$, $k_2(4, 0, v) = 2$.)

The semantic rules may be used to assign a "meaning" to strings of the context-free language, in the following way. For any derivation of a terminal string t from S by a sequence of productions, construct the derivation tree as usual: The root of this tree is S, and each node is labeled either with a terminal symbol, or with a nonterminal symbol X_{p0} corresponding to an application of the pth production, for some p; in the latter case the node has n_p immediate descendants,

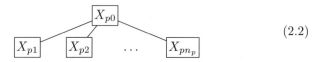

$$(2.2)$$

(see (1.2)). Now let X be the label of a node of the tree and let $\alpha \in A(X)$ be an attribute of X. If $\alpha \in A_0(X)$ then $X = X_{p0}$ for some p, while if $\alpha \in A_1(X)$ then $X = X_{pj}$ for some j and p, where $1 \le j \le n_p$; and in either case the tree in the neighborhood of this node has the form (2.2). The attribute α is defined to have the value v at this node if, in the corresponding semantic rule

$$f_{pj\alpha} : V_{\alpha_1} \times \cdots \times V_{\alpha_t} \to V_\alpha \tag{2.3}$$

all of the attributes $\alpha_1, \ldots, \alpha_t$ have previously been defined to have the respective values $v_1, \ldots, v_t$ at the respective nodes labeled X_{pk_1}, $\ldots, X_{pk_t}$, and if $v = f_{pj\alpha}(v_1, \ldots, v_t)$. This process of attribute definition is to be applied throughout the tree until no more attribute values can be defined, and then the defined attributes at the root of the tree constitute the "meaning" corresponding to the derivation tree (see (1.6)).

It is natural to stipulate that the semantic rules should be formulated in such a way that all attributes can always be defined at all nodes, in any conceivable derivation tree. Let us say that the semantic rules are *well defined* if this condition holds. Infinitely many derivation trees are possible in general, so it is important to be able to decide if a given grammar has well defined semantic rules or not. An algorithm for testing this condition is presented in Section 3.

Let us note that the method of semantic definition discussed here is as powerful as any conceivable method could be, in the sense that the value of any attribute of any node of a derivation tree may depend in any desired way on the entire tree. For example, suppose we ascribe two inherited attributes l ("location") and t ("tree") to each symbol except S in a context-free grammar, and one synthesized attribute s ("subtree") to each nonterminal symbol. Here l ranges over finite sequences of positive integers $\{a_1.a_2.\ \ldots\ .a_k\}$ that specify the location of tree nodes in a familiar "Dewey decimal" notation (see [8, Section 2.3]); t and s consist of sets of ordered pairs (l, X), where l is a node location and X is a symbol of the grammar denoting the label of the node at location l. The semantic rules, for each production (2.1), are

$$l(X_{pj}) = \begin{cases} l(X_{p0}).j, & \text{if } 1 \le j \le n_p \text{ and } X_{p0} \ne S; \\ j, & \text{if } 1 \le j \le n_p \text{ and } X_{p0} = S; \end{cases}$$

$$t(X_{pj}) = \begin{cases} t(X_{p0}), & \text{if } 1 \le j \le n_p \text{ and } X_{p0} \ne S; \\ s(X_{p0}), & \text{if } 1 \le j \le n_p \text{ and } X_{p0} = S; \end{cases} \tag{2.4}$$

$$s(X_{p0}) = \left\{ \big(l(X_{pj}), X_{pj}\big) \mid 1 \le j \le n_p \right\} \cup \bigcup_{j=1}^{n_p} \{ s(X_{pj}) \mid X_{pj} \in N \}.$$

Thus, for example, in the tree (1.2) we have

$$\begin{aligned}
s(N) = \{ &(1, L),\ (2, \cdot),\ (3, L),\ (1.1, L),\ (1.2, B),\ (3.1, L),\ (3.2, B), \\
&(1.1.1, L),\ (1.1.2, B),\ (1.2.1, 1),\ (3.1.1, B),\ (3.2.1, 1), \\
&(1.1.1.1, L),\ (1.1.1.2, B),\ (1.1.2.1, 0),\ (3.1.1.1, 0), \\
&(1.1.1.1.1, B),\ (1.1.1.2.1, 1),\ (1.1.1.1.1.1, 1) \}.
\end{aligned}$$

This set clearly contains all the information of the entire derivation tree. The semantic rules (2.4) define the attribute t on all nodes (except the root) to be the set representing the entire derivation tree, while l is the location of that node. It is therefore evident that any conceivable function of the derivation tree can be an attribute of any node, since such a function is $f(t, l)$ for some f.

Similarly we can show that synthesized attributes alone are sufficient to define the meaning associated with any derivation tree, since the synthesized attribute w defined by the rule

$$w(X_{p0}) = \{p\} \cup \bigcup_{\substack{1 \leq j \leq n_p \\ X_{pj} \in N}} \{j.\alpha \mid \alpha \in w(X_{pj})\}, \tag{2.5}$$

evaluated at the root, specifies the entire tree. Any semantic rules definable by the method of this section can be considered to be a function of
this attribute w; consequently the method is inherently no more powerful than a method that uses no inherited attributes. But this statement
is quite misleading, since semantic rules that do not use inherited attributes are often considerably more complicated (and more difficult
to understand and to manipulate) than semantic rules that allow both
kinds of attributes. The ability to let the whole tree influence the attributes of each node of the tree often leads to rules of semantics that
are much simpler, rules that correspond to the way in which we actually
understand the meanings involved.

3. Testing for Circularity

Now let us consider an algorithm that determines whether or not a collection of semantic rules, as described in the previous section, is well
defined; in other words, we want to know when the semantic rules will
always lead to definitions of all attributes at all nodes of all derivation
trees. We may assume that the grammar contains no "useless" productions, namely, that each production of $\mathcal{P}$ appears in the derivation of at
least one terminal string.

Let $\mathcal{T}$ be any derivation tree obtainable in the grammar, having
only terminal symbols as labels of its terminal nodes, but allowed to
have any symbol of V (not only the start symbol S) as the label of the
root. Then we can define a directed graph $D(\mathcal{T})$ corresponding to $\mathcal{T}$ by
taking the ordered pairs (X, α) as vertices, where X is a node of $\mathcal{T}$ and
α is an attribute of the symbol that is the label of node X. The arcs of
$D(\mathcal{T})$ go from (X_1, α_1) to (X_2, α_2) if and only if the semantic rule for
the value of attribute α_2 depends directly on the value of attribute α_1.
In other words, the vertices of $D(\mathcal{T})$ are the attribute values that must
be determined; the arcs specify the dependency relations, which imply
that certain attribute values must be computed before others.

It is clear that the semantic rules are well defined if and only if no
directed graph $D(\mathcal{T})$ contains an oriented cycle. For if there are no oriented cycles, there is a well-known procedure that assigns values to each
attribute (see [8, Algorithm 2.2.3T]). And if there is an oriented cycle in

some $D(\mathcal{T})$, the fact that the grammar contains no useless productions implies that there is an oriented cycle in some $D(\mathcal{T})$ in which the root of $\mathcal{T}$ has the label S; this $\mathcal{T}$ is a derivation tree of the language for which it is impossible to evaluate all of the attributes. Therefore the problem, "Are the semantic rules well-defined?" reduces to the problem, "Do the directed graphs $D(\mathcal{T})$ contain any oriented cycles?"

For example, if $\mathcal{T}$ is the tree (1.2) and if the semantic rules are given by (1.5), then $D(\mathcal{T})$ is the directed graph

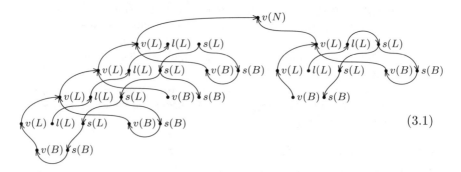

$$(3.1)$$

This directed graph accounts for the order in which the attributes of (1.6) need to be computed.

Each directed graph $D(\mathcal{T})$ may be regarded as the superposition of smaller directed graphs D_p, corresponding to each of the productions $X_{p0} \rightarrow X_{p1} \ldots X_{pn_p}$ of the grammar for $1 \leq p \leq m$. In the notation of Section 2, the directed graph D_p has vertices (X_{pj}, α), for $0 \leq j \leq n_p$ and $\alpha \in A(X_{pj})$; its arcs run from (X_{pk_i}, α_i) to (X_{pj}, α) for $0 \leq j \leq n_p$, where $k_i = k_i(p, j, \alpha)$ and $\alpha_i = \alpha_i(p, j, \alpha)$ for $1 \leq i \leq t(p, j, \alpha)$, and $\alpha \in A_0(X_{pj})$ if $j = 0$, $\alpha \in A_1(X_{pj})$ if $j > 0$. In other words, D_p reflects the local dependencies of all the semantic rules associated with the pth production. For example, the six productions of grammar (1.5) correspond to six directed graphs, namely

D_1: $\bullet v(B) \bullet s(B)$

D_2: $v(B) \, s(B)$

D_3: $v(L) \bullet l(L) \, s(L)$
$\qquad v(B) \, s(B)$

D_4:

D_5:

D_6:

$$(3.2)$$

The directed graph (3.1) is obtained by "pasting together" various sub-graphs having these forms.

In general if T has a terminal symbol as the label of the root, $D(T)$ has no arcs; if the root of T is labeled with a nonterminal symbol, T has the form

$$(3.3)$$

for some p, where T_j is a derivation tree with X_{pj} as the label of the root, for $1 \le j \le n_p$. In the former case we will say T is a derivation tree of type 0, and in the latter case we will say T is a *derivation tree of type p*; according to the definition, $D(T)$ is obtained in this case from D_p, $D(T_1)$, ..., $D(T_{n_p})$ by identifying the vertices for attributes of X_{pj} with the corresponding vertices for the attributes of the root of T_j in $D(T_j)$, for $1 \le j \le n_p$.

In order to test whether $D(T)$ contains oriented cycles, one further concept is useful. Let p be the number of a production, and for $1 \le j \le n_p$ suppose G_j is any directed graph whose vertices are a subset of $A(X_{pj})$, the attributes of X_{pj}; then let

$$D_p[G_1, \ldots, G_{n_p}] \qquad (3.4)$$

be the directed graph obtained from D_p by adding an arc from (X_{pj}, α) to (X_{pj}, α') whenever there is an arc from α to α' in G_j. For example, if we have

$$G_1 = \overset{v\ \ l\ \ s}{\smile}, \quad G_2 = \overset{v\ \ s}{\smile}$$

and if D_4 is the directed graph appearing in (3.2), then $D_4[G_1, G_2]$ is

The following algorithm may now be used:* "For $1 \leq p \leq m$ let D'_p be the directed graph with vertices $A(X_{p0})$, and with an arc from α to α' if and only if there is an oriented path from (X_{p0}, α) to (X_{p0}, α') in D_p. Let D'_0 be the empty directed graph having no vertices. Now add further arcs to $D'_1, \ldots, D'_m$ by the following procedure until no more arcs can be added: Choose an integer p, with $1 \leq p \leq m$, and for $1 \leq j \leq n_p$ let $q(j) = 0$ if X_{pj} is terminal, or choose an integer $q(j)$ such that X_{pj} is the left-hand side of the $q(j)$th production; that is, $X_{q(j)0} = X_{pj}$. Then if there is an oriented path from (X_{p0}, α) to (X_{p0}, α') in the directed graph

$$D_p[D'_{q(1)}, \ldots, D'_{q(n_p)}],\tag{3.5}$$

there should be an arc from α to α' in D'_p." It is clear that this process must ultimately terminate with no more arcs added, because only finitely many arcs are possible in all.

In the case of grammar (1.5), this algorithm begins with

$$D'_1 = \overset{v}{\bullet}\ \overset{s}{\bullet} \qquad D'_2 = \overset{v}{\smile}\overset{s}{\smile} \qquad D'_3 = \overset{v}{\bullet}\ \overset{l}{\bullet}\ \overset{s}{\bullet}$$

$$D'_4 = \overset{v}{\bullet}\ \overset{l}{\bullet}\ \overset{s}{\bullet} \qquad D'_5 = \overset{v}{\bullet} \qquad D'_6 = \overset{v}{\bullet}$$

and adds arcs until finally we have

$$D'_1 = \overset{v}{\bullet}\ \overset{s}{\bullet} \qquad D'_2 = \overset{v}{\smile}\overset{s}{\smile} \qquad D'_3 = \overset{v}{\smile}\overset{l}{\bullet}\overset{s}{\smile}$$

$$D'_4 = \overset{v}{\smile}\overset{l}{\bullet}\overset{s}{\smile} \qquad D'_5 = \overset{v}{\bullet} \qquad D'_6 = \overset{v}{\bullet}$$

After the algorithm terminates, we can prove that *there is an oriented path from (X, α) to (X, α') in some $D(\mathcal{T})$, where $\mathcal{T}$ is a derivation tree of type p with root X, if and only if there is an arc from α to α' in D'_p.* For the construction does not add any arc from α to α' unless such a $D(\mathcal{T})$ exists; the algorithm could readily be extended so that it would in fact print out an appropriate derivation tree $\mathcal{T}$ for each arc in $D'_1, \ldots, D'_m$. Conversely, suppose $\mathcal{T}$ is a derivation tree with root X, for which $D(\mathcal{T})$ contains an oriented path from (X, α) to (X, α'); we can prove by induction on the number of nodes of $\mathcal{T}$ that there is an arc from α to α' in D'_p, where $\mathcal{T}$ is of type p: Since $D(\mathcal{T})$ contains at least one arc, $\mathcal{T}$ must be of the form (3.3), and $D(\mathcal{T})$ is "pasted together" from D_p and $D(\mathcal{T}_1), \ldots, D(\mathcal{T}_{n_p})$. By induction and the fact that no arcs run from $D(\mathcal{T}_j)$ to $D(\mathcal{T}_{j'})$ for $j \neq j'$, any arcs of the assumed path that appear in $D(\mathcal{T}_1), \ldots, D(\mathcal{T}_{n_p})$ may be replaced by appropriate arcs

---

* The circularity problem is actually more difficult than the author realized in 1968, and the algorithm presented on this page is incorrect. See the errata below for a correct procedure.

in $D_p[D'_{q(1)}, \ldots, D'_{q(n_p)}]$, where $\mathcal{T}_j$ is of type $q(j)$ for $1 \leq j \leq n_p$; and we have an oriented path from (X_{p0}, α) to (X_{p0}, α') in this directed graph, hence there is an arc from α to α' in D'_p.

The algorithm now affords a solution to the problem we have posed:

Theorem. *Semantic rules added to a grammar as described in Section 2 are well defined for all derivation trees in the language if and only if none of the directed graphs* (3.5), *for any admissible choice of* p, $q(1)$, $\ldots$, $q(n_p)$ *as specified in the algorithm above, contains an oriented cycle.*

Proof. If (3.5) contains an oriented cycle, the remarks just made prove that some $D(\mathcal{T})$ contains an oriented cycle. Conversely, if $\mathcal{T}$ is a tree with the fewest possible nodes such that $D(\mathcal{T})$ contains an oriented cycle, then $\mathcal{T}$ must be of the form (3.3), and $D(\mathcal{T})$ is "pasted together" from D_p and $D(\mathcal{T}_1), \ldots, D(\mathcal{T}_{n_p})$. By the minimality of $\mathcal{T}$, the oriented cycle involves at least one arc of D_p. Therefore we may argue as above that any arcs of the cycle lying within $D(\mathcal{T}_1), \ldots, D(\mathcal{T}_{n_p})$ may be replaced by arcs of (3.5). $\square$

4. A Simple Programming Language

Now let us consider an example of how these techniques of semantic definition can be applied to programming languages. For simplicity we will study the formal definition of a little language that describes Turing machine programs.

A Turing machine (in the classical sense) processes an infinite tape, which may be thought of as divided into squares; the machine can read or write characters from a finite alphabet on the tape in the square that is currently being scanned, and it can move the scanning position to the left or right. The following program, for example, adds unity to an integer expressed in binary notation and prints a radix point at the right of this number, assuming that the square just to the right of the input number is to be scanned at the beginning and end of the program:

> **tape alphabet is** *blank, one, zero, point*;
> **print** '*point*';
> **go to** *carry*;
>
>   *test*: **if the tape symbol is** '*one*' **then**
>   {**print** '*zero*'; *carry*: **move left one square**; **go to** *test*};
>   **print** '*one*';
>   *realign*: **move right one square**;   (4.1)
>   **if the tape symbol is** '*zero*' **then go to** *realign*.

(It is hoped that readers will find this programming language sufficiently self-explanatory that they understand it before any formal definition of the language is given, although of course immediate understanding is not necessary. Program (4.1) is not intended as an example
of good programming, rather as an illustration of various features of the
simple language considered in this section.)

Since every programming language must have a name, let us call the
language Turingol. Any well-formed Turingol program defines a program
for a Turing machine. Such a program consists of

a set Q of "states";

a set Σ of "symbols";

an "initial state" $q_0 \in Q$;

a "final state" $q_\infty \in Q$;

and a "transition function" δ that maps the set $(Q \setminus \{q_\infty\}) \times \Sigma$ into
$\Sigma \times \{-1, 0, +1\} \times Q$. If $\delta(q, s) = (s', k, q')$ we say informally that, if
the machine is in state q and scanning symbol s, it will print symbol s',
move k spaces to the right (meaning one space to the left if $k = -1$),
and go into state q'.

More formally, a Turing machine program defines a computation on
any "initial tape contents," that is, on any doubly infinite sequence

$$\ldots, \ a_{-3}, \ a_{-2}, \ a_{-1}, \ a_0, \ a_1, \ a_2, \ a_3, \ \ldots \tag{4.2}$$

of elements of Σ, as follows: At any moment of the computation there is
a "current state" $q \in Q$ and an integer-valued "tape position" p; initially
$q = q_0$ and $p = 0$. If $q \neq q_\infty$, and if $\delta(q, a_p) = (s', k, q')$, the computation
proceeds by replacing the value of a_p by s', then by changing p to $p + k$
and q to q'. If $q = q_\infty$ the computation terminates. (The computation
might never terminate; for program (4.1) this will happen if and only if
$a_j = \text{'one'}$ for all $j < 0$.)

Now that we have a precise definition of Turing machine programs,
we wish to define the Turing machine program corresponding to any
given Turingol program — and at the same time to define the syntax of
Turingol. For this purpose it is convenient to introduce a few abbreviation conventions.

(1) The semantic rule '**include** x **in** B' associated with a production
will mean that x is to be a member of set B, where B is an attribute of
the start symbol S of the grammar. The value of B will be the set of all
x for which such a semantic rule has appeared, corresponding to each

appearance of the production in the derivation tree. (This convention may be regarded as an abbreviation for the semantic rule

$$B(X_{p0}) = \bigcup_{j=1}^{n_p} B(X_{pj}) \cup \{x \mid \text{`\textbf{include} } x \text{ \textbf{in} } B\text{' is associated} \atop \text{with the } p\text{th production}\} \quad (4.3)$$

added to each production, with a set B added as a synthesized attribute of each nonterminal symbol, and with $B(X)$ equal to the empty set for each terminal symbol X. These rules clearly make $B(S)$ the desired set.)

(2) The semantic rule '**define** $f(x) = y$' associated with a production will mean that y is to be the value of the function f evaluated at x, where f is an attribute of the start symbol S of the grammar. If two rules occur defining $f(x)$ for the *same* value of x, an error has arisen; any derivation tree that allows this condition to occur will be said to be *malformed*. Furthermore, f may be used as a function in any other semantic rules, with the proviso that $f(x)$ may appear only when f has been defined at x; any derivation tree that calls for an undefined value of $f(x)$ is *malformed*. (This type of rule is important, for example, to ensure that there is agreement between the declaration and use of identifiers. In the example below this convention implies that programs are malformed if the same identifier is used twice as a label, or if a **go to** statement specifies an identifier that is not a statement label. The rule may essentially be thought of as '**include** (x, y) **in** f', as in (1), if f is regarded as a set of ordered pairs; additional checks for malformedness are also included. We may regard "well-formed or malformed" as an attribute of S; appropriate semantic rules analogous to (4.3), which completely specify this '**define** $f(x) = y$' convention and propagate it throughout the tree, are readily constructed and left to the reader.)

(3) The function '**newsymbol**' appearing in any semantic rule will have, as its value, an abstract element that differs from the abstract elements produced by any other evaluations of **newsymbol**. (This convention can readily be expressed in terms of other semantic rules, for example by making use of the l attribute of (2.3), because that attribute has a different value at each node of a tree. The function **newsymbol** serves as a convenient source of "raw material" for constructing sets.)

We have observed that conventions (1), (2), (3) can be replaced by other constructions of semantic rules that do not use these conventions; so they are not "primitives" for semantics. But they are of fairly wide utility, since they correspond to concepts that are often needed, so they may be regarded as fundamental aspects of the techniques for semantic definition presented in this paper. The effect of using these conventions is to reduce the number of attributes that are explicitly mentioned, and to avoid unnecessarily long rules.

Now it is a simple matter to present a formal definition of the syntax and semantics of Turingol.

Nonterminal symbols: P (program), S (statement), L (list of statements), I (identifier), O (orientation), A (alphabetic character), D (declaration).

Terminal symbols: $a\ b\ c\ d\ e\ f\ g\ h\ i\ j\ k\ l\ m\ n\ o\ p\ q\ r\ s\ t\ u\ v\ w\ x\ y\ z\ .\ ,\ :\ ;$
' ' { } **tape alphabet is print go to if the symbol then move left right one square**

Start symbol: P

Attributes: See Table 1.

Productions and semantics: See Table 2.

TABLE 1. Attributes for Turingol semantics.

Name	Type of Value	Purpose
Q	set	states of the program
Σ	set	symbols of the program
δ	function from $(Q \setminus \{q_\infty\}) \times \Sigma$ into $\Sigma \times \{-1, 0, +1\} \times Q$	transition function
label	function from strings of letters into elements of Q	state table for statement labels
symbol	function from strings of letters into elements of Σ	symbol table for tape symbols
text	string of letters	identifier
d	± 1	direction
q_0	element of Q	initial state
q_∞	element of Q	final state
start	element of Q	state at the beginning of a statement or list of statements
follow	element of Q	state that immediately follows a statement or list of statements

The first attributes in Table 1, namely Q, Σ, δ, 'label', and 'symbol', belong to the start symbol P according to our conventions (1), (2), and (3). The attributes 'text', 'd', q_0, q_∞, and 'follow' are synthesized, while 'start' is inherited. The reader should study Table 2 at this point before proceeding.

One of the main points of interest in Table 2 is that two states correspond to each statement S: start(S) is the state corresponding to the

TABLE 2. Productions and semantic rules for Turingol.

Description	Number	Syntactic Rule	Example	Semantic Rules
Letters	1.1	$A \to a$	a	$\text{text}(A) = a.$
		.... (similarly for all letters)		
	1.26	$A \to z$	z	$\text{text}(A) = z.$
Identifiers	2.1	$I \to A$	m	$\text{text}(I) = \text{text}(A).$
	2.2	$I \to IA$	$marilyn$	$\text{text}(I) = \text{text}(I)\text{text}(A).$
Declarations	3.1	$D \to$ **tape alphabet is** I	**tape alphabet is** $marilyn$	**define** $\text{symbol}(\text{text}(I)) =$ **newsymbol**; **include** $\text{symbol}(\text{text}(I))$ **in** Σ.
	3.2	$D \to D, I$	**tape alphabet is** $marilyn$, $jayne$, $birgitte$	**define** $\text{symbol}(\text{text}(I)) =$ **newsymbol**; **include** $\text{symbol}(\text{text}(I))$ **in** Σ.
Print statement	4.1	$S \to$ **print** 'I'	**print** '$jayne$'	**define** $\delta(\text{start}(S), s) = \big(\text{symbol}(\text{text}(I)), 0,$ $\text{follow}(S)\big)$ for all $s \in \Sigma$; $\text{follow}(S) =$ **newsymbol**; **include** $\text{follow}(S)$ **in** Q.
Move statement	4.2	$S \to$ **move** O **one square**	**move left one square**	**define** $\delta(\text{start}(S), s) = \big(s, \text{d}(O),$ $\text{follow}(S)\big)$ for all $s \in \Sigma$; $\text{follow}(S) =$ **newsymbol**; **include** $\text{follow}(S)$ **in** Q.
Orientation	4.2.1	$O \to$ **left**	**left**	$\text{d}(O) = -1.$
	4.2.2	$O \to$ **right**	**right**	$\text{d}(O) = +1.$
Go statement	4.3	$S \to$ **go to** I	**go to** $boston$	**define** $\delta(\text{start}(S), s) = \big(s, 0,$ $\text{label}(\text{text}(I))\big)$ for all $s \in \Sigma$; $\text{follow}(S) =$ **newsymbol**; **include** $\text{follow}(S)$ **in** Q.
Null statement	4.4	$S \to$		$\text{follow}(S) = \text{start}(S).$
Conditional statement	5.1	$S_1 \to$ **if the tape symbol is** 'I' **then** S_2	**if the tape symbol is** '$marilyn$' **then print** '$jayne$'	**define** $\delta(\text{start}(S_1), s) = \big(s, 0,$ $\text{follow}(S_2)\big)$ for all $s \in$ $\Sigma \setminus \text{symbol}(\text{text}(I))$; **define** $\delta(\text{start}(S_1), s) =$ $\big(s, 0, \text{start}(S_2)\big)$ for $s = \text{symbol}(\text{text}(I))$; $\text{start}(S_2) =$ **newsymbol**; $\text{follow}(S_1) = \text{follow}(S_2)$; **include** $\text{start}(S_2)$ **in** Q.
Labeled statement	5.2	$S_1 \to I{:}\ S_2$	$boston{:}$ **move left one square**	**define** $\text{label}(\text{text}(I)) =$ $\text{start}(S_1)$; $\text{start}(S_2) = \text{start}(S_1)$; $\text{follow}(S_1) = \text{follow}(S_2)$.
Compound statement	5.3	$S \to \{L\}$	$\{$**print** '$jayne$';; **go to** $boston\}$	$\text{start}(L) = \text{start}(S)$; $\text{follow}(S) = \text{follow}(L)$.
List of statements	6.1	$L \to S$	**print** '$jayne$'	$\text{start}(S) = \text{start}(L)$; $\text{follow}(L) = \text{follow}(S)$.
	6.2	$L_1 \to L_2; S$	**print** '$jayne$';; **go to** $boston$	$\text{start}(L_2) = \text{start}(L_1)$; $\text{start}(S) = \text{follow}(L_2)$; $\text{follow}(L_1) = \text{follow}(S)$.
Program	7	$P \to D; L.$	**tape alphabet is** $marilyn$ $jayne$, $birgitte$; **print** '$jayne$'.	$q_0(P) =$ **newsymbol**; **include** $q_0(P)$ **in** Q; $\text{start}(L) = q_0(P)$; $q_\infty(P) = \text{follow}(L)$.

first instruction of the statement (if any), and it is an inherited attribute of S; follow(S) is the state that "follows" the statement, the state that is normally reached after the statement is executed. In the case of a "go statement," however, the program does not transfer to follow(S), since the action of the statement is to change control to another place; follow(S) may be said to follow statement S "statically" or "textually," not "dynamically" during a run of the program.

Although follow(S) is a synthesized attribute in Table 2, we could have formulated similar semantic rules in which follow(S) is inherited, but a less efficient program would be obtained for null statements (see Rule 4.4). Similarly, both start(S) and follow(S) could have been synthesized attributes, but at the expense of additional instructions in the Turing machine program for statement lists (Rule 6.2).

This example would be somewhat simpler if we had used a less standard definition of Turing machine instructions. The definition we have used requires reading, printing, and shifting in each instruction, and it also makes the Turing machine into a kind of "one-plus-one-address computer" in which each instruction specifies the location (state) of the next instruction.

The method of defining semantic rules in this example, with an inherited 'start(S)' and a synthesized 'follow(S)' attribute, lends itself readily also to computers or automata in which the $(n+1)$st instruction is normally performed after the nth. Then (follow(S) $-$ start(S)) would be the number of instructions "compiled" for statement S.

This definition of Turingol seems to approach the desirable goal of stating almost exactly the same things that would appear in an informal programmer's manual explaining the language, except that the description is completely formal and unambiguous. In other words, this definition perhaps corresponds to the way in which we actually understand the language in our minds. The definition 4.1 of a print statement, for example, might be freely rendered in English as follows:

"A statement may have the form

print 'I'

where I is an identifier. Whenever such a statement is executed, the tape symbol on the currently scanned square will be replaced by the symbol denoted by I, regardless of what symbol was being scanned; afterwards the program will continue with a new instruction, which is defined (by other rules) to be the instruction following this statement."

5. Discussion

The idea of defining semantics by associating synthesized attributes with each nonterminal symbol, and by associating semantic rules with each production, is due to Irons [6, 7]. Originally each nonterminal symbol was given exactly one attribute, its "translation." This idea was applied by Irons and later authors, notably McClure [14], to the design of "syntax-directed compilers" that translate programming languages into machine instructions.

As we have observed in Section 2, synthesized attributes alone are sufficient (in principle) to define any function of a derivation tree. But the inclusion of inherited attributes as well as synthesized attributes, as described in this paper, leads to important simplifications in practice. The definition of Turingol, for example, shows that the agreement between declaration and use of symbols, and the association of labels to statements, may easily be treated. "Block structure" is another common aspect of programming languages whose definition is greatly facilitated by the use of inherited attributes. In general, inherited attributes are useful when part of the meaning of some construction is determined by the context in which that construction appears. The method of Section 2 shows that both inherited and synthesized attributes can be given a rigorous formal underpinning, and Section 3 shows that it is possible to rule out problems of circularity (which are potential sources of difficulty when inherited and synthesized attributes are both present simultaneously).

The principal contributions to formal semantic definition of programming languages, at least those known to the author at the time of writing, are de Bakker's definition of ALGOL 60 by means of a growing Markovian algorithm [1]; Landin's definition of ALGOL 60 by means of the λ-calculus [9, 10, 11] (see also Böhm [2, 3]); McCarthy's definition of Micro-ALGOL by means of recursive functions applied to the program and to "state vectors" [12] (see also McCarthy and Painter [13]); Wirth and Weber's definition of Euler, by means of semantic rules applied as a program is parsed [16]; and the IBM Vienna Laboratory's definition of PL/I [15], based on the work of McCarthy and Landin and on abstract machines defined by Elgot [4, 5].

The most striking difference between the previous methods and the definition of Turingol in Table 2 is that the other definitions are processes that are defined on programs as a whole in a rather intricate manner; it may be said that a person must understand an entire compiler for the language before understanding the definition of the language. This difficulty is most pronounced in the work of de Bakker, who defines a machine having approximately 800 instructions, analogous to Markov algorithms but somewhat more complicated; at each stage of this machine's computations we are to execute the last applicable instruction, so we cannot verify that instruction number 100 will be performed until we can prove to ourselves that the 700 subsequent instructions are inapplicable; furthermore, additional instructions are placed on the list dynamically by the actions of the machine. It is clearly very difficult for a reader to understand the workings of such a machine, or to give formal proofs of its important properties. By contrast, the definition of Turingol in Table 2 defines each construction of the language only in terms of its "immediate environment," minimizing to a large extent the interconnections between the definitions of different parts of the language. The definitions of compound statements and go statements, etc., do not influence the definition of print statements in a substantial way; for example, any of Rules 4.1, 4.2, 4.3, 4.4, 5.1, 5.3 could be deleted and we would obtain a valid definition of another language. This localization and partitioning of the semantic rules tends to make the definition easier to understand and more concise.

Although the other authors cited above do not make use of such an intricately interwoven definition as de Bakker's, the relatively complex interdependence is still present. For example, consider the formal definition of Euler given by Wirth and Weber [16, pages 94–98]; this is a concise definition of a very sophisticated language, and so it is certainly one of the most successful formal definitions ever devised. Yet even though Wirth and Weber tested their definition by means of extensive computer simulation, it is quite probable that their language contains some features that would surprise its authors. For example, the following Euler program is syntactically and semantically well-formed, although the label L is never followed by a colon:

$\perp$ **begin label** L; **new** A; $A \leftarrow 0$;
    if false then go to L **else** L;
    out 1; L; $A \leftarrow A + 1$; **out** 2;
    if false then go to L **else**
    if $A < 2$ **then go to** L **else out** 3; L **end** $\perp$

The output of this program is 1, 2, 2, 3! Oversights such as this are not unexpected when an algorithmic definition of a language is constructed; they are less likely to occur when the methods of Section 4 are employed.

It appears to be reasonable to assert that none of the previous schemes for formal definition of semantics could produce a definition of Turingol that is as brief or as easy to comprehend as the definition given above; and (although the details have not of course been worked out) it also appears that ALGOL 60, Euler, Micro-ALGOL, and PL/I can be defined using the methods of Section 4 in a manner that has advantages over the definitions previously given. But of course the author cannot judge these things impartially, and considerably more experience is needed before such claims can be substantiated.

Notice that semantic rules as given in this paper do not depend on any particular form of syntactic analysis. In fact, they need not even be tied down to specific forms of the syntax: All that the semantic rules depend on is the name of the nonterminal symbol on the left of a production and the names of the nonterminals on the right. Particular punctuation marks, and the order in which the nonterminals appear on the right-hand side of any production, are immaterial as far as the semantic rules are concerned. Thus, the method of semantics considered here blends well with McCarthy's idea [12, 13] of "abstract syntax."

When a syntax is ambiguous, in the sense that some strings of the language have more than one derivation tree, the semantic rules give us one "meaning" for each derivation tree. For example, suppose the rules

$$L_1 \to BL_2 \qquad v(L_1) = 2^{l(L_2)}v(B) + v(L_2), \qquad l(L_1) = l(L_2) + 1$$

are added to grammar (1.3) for binary numbers. Then the grammar becomes syntactically ambiguous; but it still is semantically unambiguous, because the attribute $v(N)$ has the same value over all derivation trees. On the other hand, if we were to change production 5.2 of Turingol from $S \to I : S$ to $S \to S : I$, the grammar would become syntactically and semantically ambiguous.

References

[1] J. W. de Bakker, *Formal Definition of Programming Languages, With an Application to the Definition of ALGOL 60*, Mathematisch Centrum Tracts **16** (Amsterdam: Mathematisch Centrum, 1967).

[2] C. Böhm, "The CUCH as a formal and description language," in *Formal Language Description Languages for Computer Programming*, edited by T. B. Steel, Jr. (Amsterdam: North-Holland, 1966), 179–197.

[3] Corrado Böhm and Wolf Gross, "Introduction to the CUCH," in *Automata Theory*, edited by E. R. Caianiello (New York: Academic Press, 1966), 35–65.

[4] C. C. Elgot, "Machine species and their computation languages," in *Formal Language Description Languages for Computer Programming*, edited by T. B. Steel, Jr. (Amsterdam: North-Holland, 1966), 160–179.

[5] Calvin C. Elgot and Abraham Robinson, "Random-access stored-program machines, an approach to programming languages," *Journal of the Association for Computing Machinery* **11** (1964), 365–399.

[6] Edgar T. Irons, "A syntax directed compiler for ALGOL 60," *Communications of the ACM* **4** (1961), 51–55.

[7] E. T. Irons, "Towards more versatile mechanical translators," *Proceedings of Symposia in Applied Mathematics* **15** (Providence, Rhode Island: American Mathematical Society, 1963), 41–50.

[8] Donald E. Knuth, *Fundamental Algorithms*, Volume 1 of *The Art of Computer Programming* (Reading, Massachusetts: Addison–Wesley, 1968).

[9] P. J. Landin, "The mechanical evaluation of expressions," *The Computer Journal* **6** (1964), 308–320.

[10] P. J. Landin, "A formal description of ALGOL 60," in *Formal Language Description Languages for Computer Programming*, edited by T. B. Steel, Jr. (Amsterdam: North-Holland, 1966), 266–294.

[11] P. J. Landin, "A correspondence between ALGOL 60 and Church's lambda-notation," *Communications of the ACM* **8** (1965), 89–101, 158–165.

[12] John McCarthy, "A formal definition of a subset of ALGOL," in *Formal Language Description Languages for Computer Programming*, edited by T. B. Steel, Jr. (Amsterdam: North-Holland, 1966), 1–12.

[13] John McCarthy and James Painter, "Correctness of a compiler for arithmetic expressions," *Proceedings of Symposia in Applied Mathematics* **19** (Providence, Rhode Island: American Mathematical Society, 1967), 33–41.

[14] Robert M. McClure, "TMG — A syntax directed compiler," *Proceedings of the ACM National Conference* **20** (1965), 262–274.

[15] PL/I Definition Group of the Vienna Laboratory, *Formal Definition of PL/I*, IBM Technical Report TR 25.071 (Vienna: 1966).

[16] Niklaus Wirth and Helmut Weber, "Euler: A generalization of ALGOL, and its formal definition," *Communications of the ACM* **9** (1966), 13–23, 25, 89–99, 878.

Errata

The argument presented in Section 3, as justification of the algorithm stated there, is fallacious. For example, we might have productions $S \to A$ and $S \to B$, where A links $\alpha_1(S)$ to $\alpha_2(S)$ and B links $\alpha_2(S)$ to $\alpha_3(S)$ but no single tree links $\alpha_1(S)$ to $\alpha_3(S)$. Therefore the algorithm might reject grammars that are not actually circular. A more careful circularity test should be substituted, before a set of semantic rules is judged to be ill-defined.

The following algorithm may be used: For each X in V let $S(X)$ be a set of directed graphs on the vertices $A(X)$. Initially $S(X)$ is empty for all $X \in N$; and $S(X)$ is the single directed graph with vertices $A(X)$ and no arcs, for all $X \notin N$. Now we add further directed graphs to the sets $S(X)$ by the following procedure until no more graphs can be added: Choose an integer p, with $1 \leq p \leq m$, and for $1 \leq j \leq n_p$ choose a directed graph D'_j in $S(X_{pj})$. Then include in $S(X_{p0})$ the directed graph whose vertices are $A(X_{p0})$ and whose arcs run from α to α' if and only if there is an oriented path from (X_{p0}, α) to (X_{p0}, α') in the directed graph

$$D_p[D'_1, \ldots, D'_{n_p}]. \tag{3.5}$$

It is clear that this process must ultimately terminate with no more directed graphs created, since only finitely many directed graphs are possible in all.

In the case of grammar (1.5), this algorithm constructs the sets

$$S(N) = \{\overset{v}{\bullet}\}, \quad S(L) = \{\overset{v\ \ l\ \ s}{\bullet\ \bullet\ \bullet}, \overset{v\ \ l\ \ s}{\bullet\ \bullet\ \bullet}\},$$

$$S(B) = \{\overset{v\ \ s}{\bullet\ \bullet}, \overset{v\ \ s}{\bullet\ \bullet}\}, \quad S(0) = S(1) = S(\cdot) = \{\ \}.$$

If $\mathcal{T}$ is a derivation tree with root X, let $D'(\mathcal{T})$ be the directed graph with vertices $A(X)$ whose arcs run from α to α' if and only if there is an oriented path from (X, α) to (X, α') in $D(\mathcal{T})$. After the algorithm terminates, we can show for all $X \in V$ that $S(X)$ *is the set of all* $D'(\mathcal{T})$, *where* $\mathcal{T}$ *is a derivation tree with root* X. For the construction does not add any directed graph to $S(X)$ unless it is such a $D'(\mathcal{T})$; the algorithm could readily be extended so that it would in fact print out an appropriate derivation tree $\mathcal{T}$ for each graph in $S(X)$. Conversely if $\mathcal{T}$ is any derivation tree, we can prove by induction on the number of nodes of $\mathcal{T}$ that $D'(\mathcal{T})$ is in the relevant $S(X)$. Otherwise $\mathcal{T}$ must have the form (3.3), and $D(\mathcal{T})$ is "pasted together" from D_p and $D(\mathcal{T}_1)$, $\ldots, D(\mathcal{T}_{n_p})$. By induction and the fact that no arcs run from $D(\mathcal{T}_j)$ to

$D(\mathcal{T}_{j'})$ for $j \neq j'$, any arcs of the assumed path that appear in $D(\mathcal{T}_1)$, $\ldots$, $D(\mathcal{T}_{n_p})$ may be replaced by appropriate arcs in $D_p[D'_1, \ldots, D'_{n_p}]$, where D'_j is a member of $S(X_{pj})$ for $1 \leq j \leq n_p$. This directed graph is therefore in $S(X_{p0})$, and it is equal to $D'(\mathcal{T})$.

The algorithm above now affords a solution to the problem posed in this section:

Theorem. *Semantic rules added to a grammar as described in Section 2 are well defined for all derivation trees in the language if and only if none of the directed graphs* (3.5), *for any choice of p and $D'_1 \in S(X_{p1})$, $\ldots$, $D'_{n_p} \in S(X_{pn_p})$, contains an oriented cycle.*

[With this restatement of the theorem, the original proof as given in Section 3 becomes valid.]

Addendum

Chapter 19 discusses the background to this paper and some of its sequels. In particular, it explains that the idea of inherited attributes was first suggested to the author by Peter Wegner, and gives further information about the roots of this work.

Some attribute grammars have turned out to be useful even in the presence of circularity, for example in studies of VLSI design; therefore additional algorithms have been developed. For an excellent discussion of these issues, see Michael Rodeh and Mooly Sagiv, "Finding circular attributes in attribute grammars," *Journal of the ACM* **46** (1999), 556–575.

Chapter 18

Examples of Formal Semantics

*[Originally published in Symposium on Semantics of Algorithmic Languages, edited by E. Engeler, Lecture Notes in Mathematics **188** (Berlin: Springer, 1971), 212–235.]*

A technique of formal definition, based on relations between "attributes" associated with nonterminal symbols in a context-free grammar, is illustrated by several applications to simple, yet typical, problems. First we define the basic properties of lambda expressions, involving substitution and renaming of bound variables. Then a simple programming language is defined using several different points of view. The emphasis is on "declarative" rather than "imperative" or "algorithmic" forms of definition.

Perhaps the most natural way to define the "meaning" of strings in a context-free language is to define *attributes* for each of the nonterminal symbols that arise when the strings are parsed according to the grammatical rules. The attributes of each nonterminal symbol correspond to the meaning of the phrase produced from that symbol. This point of view is expressed in some detail in [3], where two kinds of attributes are discussed, "inherited" and "synthesized." Inherited attributes are, roughly speaking, the aspects of meaning that come from the context of a phrase, while synthesized attributes are the aspects that are built up from within the phrase. There can be considerable interplay between inherited and synthesized attributes; the essential idea is that the meaning of an entire string is built up from the parse of that string, using only local rules that relate the attributes belonging to each production step.

For each production in the context-free grammar, we specify "semantic rules" that define (i) all of the synthesized attributes of the nonterminal symbol on the left hand side of the production, and (ii) all of the inherited attributes of the nonterminal symbols on the right hand side of the production. The initial nonterminal symbol, at the root of the parse tree, has no inherited attributes. Potentially circular definitions can be detected using an algorithm formulated in [3].

The purpose of this paper is to develop the ideas a little further and to present some additional examples of the "inherited attribute–synthesized attribute" approach to formal semantics. The first example defines the class of lambda expressions that have a reduced equivalent, in terms of a "canonical" reduced form. The second example defines the simple programming language Turingol; this language was defined in [3], in terms of conventional Turing machine quintuples, while the definition in the present paper is intended to come closer to the fundamental issues of what computation really is, and to correspond more closely to problems that arise in the definition of large-scale contemporary programming languages.

The formal definitions in this paper are probably not the best possible ways to define semantics, but they seem to be a step in the right direction. It is hoped that the reader who has time to study these examples will be stimulated to develop the ideas further.

1. Lambda Expressions

Our first example of a formal definition concerns lambda expressions as discussed by Wegner [4], restricting the set of variables to the forms x, x', x'', x''', etc. Informally, the lambda expressions we consider are either (i) variables standing alone; or (ii) strings of the form $\lambda V E$, where V is a variable (called a "bound variable") and E is a lambda expression; or (iii) strings of the form $(E_1 E_2)$, where E_1 and E_2 are lambda expressions. If E_1 has form (ii), $(E_1 E_2)$ denotes functional application; that is, we may substitute E_2 for all "free" occurrences of V in E, making suitable changes to bound variables within E so that free variables of E_2 do not become bound. For example, $\lambda x(x'x)$ is a lambda expression in which x' is free but x is bound; it has the same meaning as $\lambda x''(x'x'')$ by renaming the bound variable, but $\lambda x'(x'x')$ has a different meaning. The lambda expression $(\lambda x' \lambda x(x'x)x)$ has the same meaning as $(\lambda x' \lambda x''(x'x'')x)$, by renaming a bound variable; and this has the same meaning as $\lambda x''(xx'')$, by substituting x for x'.

A lambda expression that contains no subexpressions of the form $(\lambda V E E_2)$ is called *reduced*. Some lambda expressions cannot be converted into an equivalent reduced form; the shortest example is

$$(\lambda x(xx)\lambda x(xx)),$$

which goes into itself under substitution. We say that a lambda expression is *reducible* if it is equivalent to some reduced lambda expression.

Our goal is to give a formal definition of the class of all reducible lambda expressions; this definition must make precise the notions of "free variables," "bound variables," "renaming," "substitution," etc. Fortunately, it is possible to create such a definition in a fairly natural way, using inherited and synthesized attributes.

Let E be a lambda expression. If E is reducible, our formal definition will define the meaning of E to be a string of characters that is a reduced lambda expression equivalent to E. The definition has the attractive property that two reducible lambda expressions are equivalent if and only if their meanings are exactly identical, character for character. (A proof of this assertion is beyond the scope of this paper, but can be based on the Church–Rosser theorem; see [1].) The definition is iterative, in that the meaning of E might turn out to be the meaning of another lambda expression E_1; if E is irreducible, the process will never terminate, so we will obtain no meaning for E, but if E is reducible, the process will terminate in a finite number of steps. (Again the proof is beyond the scope of this paper, but uses well-known properties of lambda expressions.) The problem of deciding whether or not a given lambda expression has a reduced form is recursively unsolvable, as is the problem of deciding whether or not a given lambda expression is equivalent to the reduced form x; therefore an iterative procedure such as the one described below is probably the best we can do.

Our formal definition involves some more or less standard notation. Let $\mathbf{N}$ be the set of nonnegative integers; $2^{\mathbf{N}}$ is the set of all subsets of $\mathbf{N}$. A *string* is a sequence of zero or more of the characters

$$x \qquad \lambda \qquad) \qquad ' \qquad ($$

and we let ϵ denote the empty string. A function f is a set of ordered pairs $\{(x, f(x))\}$ whose first components are distinct; we define $\mathrm{domain}(f) = \{x \mid (x, f(x)) \in f\}$. We write $\emptyset$ for the empty set or empty function; and

$$f \uplus g = \{(x, g(x)) \mid x \in \mathrm{domain}(g)\}$$
$$\cup \{(x, f(x)) \mid x \in \mathrm{domain}(f) \setminus \mathrm{domain}(g)\}$$

denotes the function f "overridden" by the function g. If f is a function taking some subset of $\mathbf{N}$ into $2^{\mathbf{N}}$, and if $S \subseteq \mathbf{N}$, we write

$$\text{image of } S \text{ under } f = \bigcup \{f(x) \mid x \in S \cap \mathrm{domain}(f)\}$$
$$\cup \{x \mid x \in S \setminus \mathrm{domain}(f)\}.$$

For example, if $S = \{2, 3, 4\}$ and $f = \{(2, \{1, 4, 5\}), (4, \{5, 6\})\}$, then image of S under $f = \{1, 3, 4, 5, 6\}$.

If n is a nonnegative integer, 'var(n)' denotes the string consisting of the letter x followed by n prime (') characters; thus, var(2) $= x''$. The number of prime characters is called the *index* of the variable.

Now we are ready for the formal definition itself, which may be presented in a tabular format for convenience.

Terminal symbols: x λ)   '   (

Nonterminal symbols: S E V

Start symbol: S

Inherited attributes: See Table 1.

Synthesized attributes: See Table 2.

Productions and semantics: See Table 3.

TABLE 1. Inherited attributes for lambda expressions.

Name	Type of Value	Significance
bound(E)	subset of $\mathbf{N}$	indices of variables whose meaning is bound by the context of E
subst(E)	function from bound(E) into the set of all strings	replacement text for substitutions
substf(E)	function from bound(E) into $2^{\mathbf{N}}$	indices of free variables present in subst(E)
arg(E)	string	text (if any) used as argument in functional application
argf(E)	subset of $\mathbf{N}$	indices of free variables present in arg(E)

TABLE 2. Synthesized attributes for lambda expressions.

Name	Type of Value	Significance
meaning(S)	string	reduced text of lambda expression (if it exists)
text(E)	string	string equivalent to E (includes substitutions and reductions)
free(E)	subset of $\mathbf{N}$	indices of free variables present in E (before substitutions and reductions)
function(E)	*true* or *false*	is E explicitly a function?
reduced(E)	*true* or *false*	is E reduced?
index(V)	nonnegative integer	number of prime (') characters in the representation of V

TABLE 3. Productions and semantic rules for lambda expressions.

Description	Number	Production	Example	Semantic Rules
Statement	1	$S \to E$	$(\lambda x(xx)$ $\lambda x'(x'x))$	$\text{meaning}(S) = \textbf{if } \text{reduced}(E) \textbf{ then}$ $\text{text}(E) \textbf{ else } \text{meaning}(\text{text}(E));$ $\text{bound}(E) = \text{subst}(E) =$ $\text{substf}(E) = \text{argf}(E) = \emptyset;$ $\text{arg}(E) = \epsilon.$
Variable	2.1	$V \to x$	x	$\text{index}(V) = 0.$
	2.2	$V_1 \to V_2'$	x'	$\text{index}(V_1) = \text{index}(V_2) + 1.$
Expression	3.1	$E \to V$	x'	$\text{function}(E) = \textit{false};$ $\text{free}(E) = \{\text{index}(V)\};$ $\text{reduced}(E) = \textit{true};$ $\text{text}(E) = \textbf{if } \text{index}(V) \in \text{bound}(E)$ $\textbf{then } \text{subst}(E)(\text{index}(V))$ $\textbf{else } \text{var}(\text{index}(V)).$
	3.2	$E_1 \to$ $\lambda V E_2$	$\lambda x'(x'x)$	$\text{function}(E_1) = \textit{true};$ $\text{free}(E_1) = \text{free}(E_2) \setminus \{\text{index}(V)\};$ $\text{reduced}(E_1) = \text{reduced}(E_2);$ $\textbf{if } \text{arg}(E_1) = \epsilon \textbf{ then}$ $\quad m = \min\{k \in \mathbf{N} \mid k \notin \text{image of}$ $\quad \text{free}(E_1) \text{ under substf}(E_1)\},$ $\quad s = \text{var}(m),\ t = \{m\}$ $\quad \textbf{else } s = \text{arg}(E_1),\ t = \text{argf}(E_1);$ $\text{text}(E_1) = \textbf{if } \text{arg}(E_1) = \epsilon \textbf{ then}$ $\quad \text{`}\lambda\text{' } s\ \text{text}(E_2) \textbf{ else } \text{text}(E_2);$ $\text{bound}(E_2) = \text{bound}(E_1) \cup$ $\quad \{\text{index}(V)\};$ $\text{subst}(E_2) = \text{subst}(E_1) \uplus$ $\quad \{(\text{index}(V), s)\};$ $\text{substf}(E_2) = \text{substf}(E_1) \uplus$ $\quad \{(\text{index}(V), t)\};$ $\text{arg}(E_2) = \epsilon;\ \text{argf}(E_2) = \emptyset.$
	3.3	$E_1 \to$ $(E_2 E_3)$	$(x'x)$	$\text{function}(E_1) = \textit{false};$ $\text{free}(E_1) = \text{free}(E_2) \cup \text{free}(E_3);$ $\text{reduced}(E_1) = \textbf{if } \text{function}(E_2)$ $\quad \textbf{then } \textit{false}$ $\quad \textbf{else } \text{reduced}(E_2) \wedge \text{reduced}(E_3);$ $\text{text}(E_1) = \textbf{if } \text{function}(E_2)$ $\quad \textbf{then } \text{text}(E_2)$ $\quad \textbf{else } \text{`(' } \text{text}(E_2)\,\text{text}(E_3)\text{ `)';}$ $\text{bound}(E_2) = \text{bound}(E_3) =$ $\quad \text{bound}(E_1);$ $\text{subst}(E_2) = \text{subst}(E_3) =$ $\quad \text{subst}(E_1);$ $\text{substf}(E_2) = \text{substf}(E_3) =$ $\quad \text{substf}(E_1);$ $\text{arg}(E_2) = \text{text}(E_3);$ $\text{argf}(E_2) = \text{image of } \text{free}(E_3)$ $\quad \text{under substf}(E_3);$ $\text{arg}(E_3) = \epsilon;\ \text{argf}(E_3) = \emptyset.$

Several local variables are used for brevity in the semantic rules 3.2: The nonnegative integer m stands for an index chosen as the new name of a bound variable; the string s is a replacement text; and the set $t \in 2^{\mathbf{N}}$ stands for the indices of free variables in s.

In rule 1, 'meaning(text(E))' stands for meaning(S) in the derivation tree that arises when text(E) is parsed.

As an example of this formal definition, consider finding the "meaning" of $(\lambda x' \lambda x (x' x) x)$. We have the following parse tree, giving integer subscripts to the nonterminal symbols:

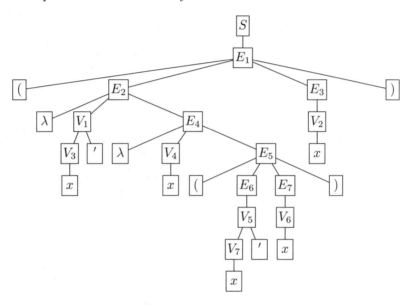

The semantic rules define attributes by moving up and down the tree. We clearly have index(V_2) = index(V_3) = index(V_4) = index(V_6) = index(V_7) = 0 and index(V_1) = index(V_5) = 1. The expression attributes are more interesting:

Node	bound	subst	substf	arg	argf	function	free	reduced	text
E_1	$\emptyset$	$\emptyset$	$\emptyset$	ϵ	$\emptyset$	*false*	$\{0\}$	*false*	$\lambda x'(xx')$
E_2	$\emptyset$	$\emptyset$	$\emptyset$	x	$\{0\}$	*true*	$\emptyset$	*true*	$\lambda x'(xx')$
E_3	$\emptyset$	$\emptyset$	$\emptyset$	ϵ	$\emptyset$	*false*	$\{0\}$	*true*	x
E_4	$\{1\}$	$\{(1,x)\}$	$\{(1,\{0\})\}$	ϵ	$\emptyset$	*true*	$\{1\}$	*true*	$\lambda x'(xx')$
E_5	$\{0,1\}$	F	G	ϵ	$\emptyset$	*false*	$\{0,1\}$	*true*	(xx')
E_6	$\{0,1\}$	F	G	x'	$\{1\}$	*false*	$\{1\}$	*true*	x
E_7	$\{0,1\}$	F	G	ϵ	$\emptyset$	*false*	$\{0\}$	*true*	x'

Here $F = \{(0, x'), (1, x)\}$ and $G = \{(0, \{1\}), (1, \{0\})\}$. It follows that meaning(S) = meaning($\lambda x'(xx')$), and we must therefore parse $\lambda x'(xx')$. A similar but much simpler derivation shows that meaning($\lambda x'(xx')$) = $\lambda x'(xx')$.

Some of the semantic rules can be eliminated by making the syntax more complicated. For example, the class of reduced lambda expressions is defined by

$$S \to \lambda V S \mid N$$
$$N \to (NS) \mid V$$
$$V \to x \mid V'$$

and the class of nonreduced lambda expressions can be defined similarly. But it seems unwise in general to play such games with the syntax. In fact, as semantic rules become better understood, we will probably go the other way and simplify syntax at the expense of semantics.

The syntactic and semantic rules above show that inherited and synthesized attributes can interact to provide a natural solution to a rather complicated problem. But they define lambda expressions in terms of lambda expressions, so it may be argued that they do not come to grips with the problem of what lambda expressions really mean. Another alternative is discussed in Section 4.

2. Turingol

A simple little language that describes Turing machine programs was introduced in [3], where a semantic definition based on quintuples was given. The following example program gives the flavor of the "Turingol" language; it is a program designed to add unity to the binary integer that appears just left of the initially scanned square:

> **tape alphabet is** *blank*, *one*, *zero*, *point*;
> **print** '*point*';
> **go to** *carry*;
>
> *test*: **if the tape symbol is** '*one*' **then**
>   {**print** '*zero*'; *carry*: **move left one square**; **go to** *test*};
>   **print** '*one*';
> *realign*: **move right one square**;
>   **if the tape symbol is** '*zero*' **then go to** *realign*.

Let us try to construct a formal definition of Turingol that goes directly into the essential nature of computation itself, instead of assuming the knowledge of an artificial representation of Turing machines based on quintuples. The mapping from Turingol to quintuples in [3] is nontrivial and worthy of attention, but it deals with only part of the problem. Therefore we shall now consider some approaches to the "total" problem of a Turingol definition.

One way to define Turingol, which we shall criticize later, is to introduce an intermediate language called TL/I; we can define Turingol in terms of TL/I, and then we can define TL/I in terms of "conceptual computation." TL/I is a machine-like language, consisting essentially of sequential instructions whose operation codes are **print**, **move**, **if**, **jump**, and **stop**. The example TL/I program in Table 5 below is almost self-explanatory, so we shall turn immediately to the formal definition of Turingol.

It is convenient to let the symbol ν denote any positive integer, and to let the symbol σ stand for any string of alphabetic letters. These quantities could be syntactically defined, and we could make use of their attributes value(ν) and text(σ); but for simplicity we shall ignore such elementary operations, and we will identify numbers and letter strings with their representations. (In other words, we are assuming the existence of a "lexical scanning" mechanism, which must exist in some primitive form anyway to recognize the terminal symbols. We could in the same way have dispensed with index(V) in the lambda-expression example above.)

The definition below involves "global" quantities, which may be regarded as attributes of the start symbol at the root of the parse tree, although their values are accessible at any node. All actions on global quantities can be reduced to a sequence of semantic rules relating appropriate local attributes, as explained in [3], but it is simpler and more natural to abbreviate such rules using global quantities.

Global quantities may be global variables, global sets, or global counters. If ξ is a global variable and a is an expression, the notation

$$\textbf{define} \ \ \xi \equiv a$$

stands for a *definition* of ξ. A string of the language is "semantically erroneous" if its parse tree causes any global variable ξ to be defined more than once, or if any undefined global variable is used in an expression.

If Σ is a global set, the notation

$$a \in \Sigma$$

denotes *inclusion* of the value of expression a in the set Σ.

If κ is a global counter, the notation

$$\kappa + a$$

denotes *augmentation* of the value of κ by the value of the integer expression a.

Global sets start out empty, and global counters start out zero. When they appear in expressions, their value denotes the accumulated result of all inclusion or augmentation operations specified in the entire parse tree. (Notice that two or more inclusion and augmentation operations can be done in any order.)

Here, then, is a formal definition of Turingol in terms of TL/I:

Terminal symbols: σ . , : ; } { ' ' **tape alphabet is print move left right one square go to if the symbol then**

Nonterminal symbols: P S L D O

Start symbol: P

Inherited attributes:

Name	Type of Value	Significance
init(S), init(L)	positive integer	address of the beginning of this statement or list

Synthesized attributes:

Name	Type of Value	Significance
fin(S), fin(L)	positive integer	address following this statement or list
index(D)	positive integer	number of symbols in declaration
d(O)	**left** or **right**	a direction

Global variables:

Name	Type of Value	Significance
label(σ), for all σ	positive integer	address associated with the identifier σ
symbol(σ), for all σ	positive integer	symbol number associated with the identifier σ

Global counters:

Name	Type of Value	Significance
nsym	nonnegative integer	size of tape alphabet

Global sets:

Name	Type of Value	Significance
objprog	set of strings	a TL/I program

Productions and semantics: See Table 4.

TABLE 4. Productions and semantic rules for Turingol → TL/I translation.

Description	Number	Production	Example	Semantic Rules
Declarations	1.1	$D \to$ **tape alphabet is** σ	**tape alphabet is** *helen*	index$(D) = 1$; nsym $+ 1$; **define** symbol$(\sigma) \equiv 1$.
	1.2	$D_1 \to D_2, \sigma$	**tape alphabet is** *helen*, *phyllis*, *pat*	index$(D_1) =$ index$(D_2) + 1$; nsym $+ 1$; **define** symbol$(\sigma) \equiv$ index(D_1).
Print statement	2.1	$S \to$ **print** 'σ'	**print** '*pat*'	(init(S): **print**, symbol$(\sigma)) \in$ objprog; fin$(S) =$ init$(S) + 1$.
Move statement	2.2	$S \to$ **move** O **one square**	**move left one square**	(init(S): **move**, d$(O)) \in$ objprog; fin$(S) =$ init$(S) + 1$.
Orientation	2.2.1	$O \to$ **left**	**left**	d$(O) =$ **left**.
	2.2.2	$O \to$ **right**	**right**	d$(O) =$ **right**.
Go statement	2.3	$S \to$ **go to** σ	**go to** *pieces*	(init(S) : **jump**, label$(\sigma)) \in$ objprog; fin$(S) =$ init$(S) + 1$.
Null statement	2.4	$S \to$		fin$(S) =$ init(S).
Conditional statement	3.1	$S_1 \to$ **if the tape symbol is** 'σ' **then** S_2	**if the tape symbol is** '*helen*' **then print** '*pat*'	(init(S): **if**, symbol(σ), fin$(S_2)) \in$ objprog; init$(S_2) =$ init$(S_1) + 1$; fin$(S_1) =$ fin(S_2).
Labeled statement	3.2	$S_1 \to \sigma: S_2$	*pieces*: **move left one square**	**define** label$(\sigma) \equiv$ init(S_1); init$(S_2) =$ init(S_1); fin$(S_1) =$ fin(S_2).
Compound statement	3.3	$S \to \{L\}$	{**print** '*pat*'; **go to** *pieces*}	init$(L) =$ init(S); fin$(S) =$ fin(L).
List of statements	4.1	$L \to S$	**print** '*pat*'	init$(S) =$ init(L); fin$(L) =$ fin(S).
	4.2	$L_1 \to L_2; S$	**print** '*pat*'; **go to** *pieces*	init$(L_2) =$ init(L_1); init$(S) =$ fin(L_2); fin$(L_1) =$ fin(S).
Program	5	$P \to D; L.$	**tape alphabet is** *helen*, *phyllis*, *pat*; **print** '*pat*'.	init$(L) = 1$; (fin(L) : **stop**) $\in$ objprog.

Example: When Table 4 is applied to the Turingol program for binary incrementation given earlier, the global quantities become

$$\text{symbol}(blank) = 1 \qquad \text{nsym} = 4$$
$$\text{symbol}(one) = 2 \qquad \text{label}(carry) = 5$$
$$\text{symbol}(zero) = 3 \qquad \text{label}(test) = 3$$
$$\text{symbol}(point) = 4 \qquad \text{label}(realign) = 8,$$

and 'objprog' is the (unordered) set of 11 strings in Table 5. This set of strings is a TL/I program.

TABLE 5. A TL/I program generated by Table 4.

(1: **print**, 4)	(4: **print**, 3)	(7: **print**, 2)	(10: **jump**, 8)
(2: **jump**, 5)	(5: **move**, **left**)	(8: **move**, **right**)	(11: **stop**)
(3: **if**, 2, 7)	(6: **jump**, 3)	(9: **if**, 3, 11)	

Now we can present a formal definition of TL/I. For this purpose, it is handy to extend context-free syntax slightly, allowing the production

$$A \to \text{set of } B$$

where A and B are nonterminal symbols. This means that A can be an unordered *set* of quantities having the form B (instead of being a *string*, which is ordered).

A TL/I program acts on a doubly infinite *tape*, which is divided into squares and contains positive integers in each square. There is a *pointer*, which designates a square on the tape. Our first attempt at a formal definition of TL/I will be based on these concepts together with an English language description of the operations to be done, as follows.

Nonterminal symbols: $P\ S\ C$

Terminal symbols: ν) (, : **if print jump move left right stop**

Start symbol: P

Inherited attribute: loc(C), a positive integer denoting the position of command C within the program.

Synthesized attribute: meaning(C), a description in English of operations to be performed.

Global variable: action(ν), a description in English of the operations that begin at step ν of the program.

Productions and semantics: See Table 6.

The reader should study Table 6 at this point before proceeding.

— * — — * — — * — — * —

The semantic rules in Table 6 seem clear enough at first, but further study reveals some more or less undesirable features, if not outright errors. We will see, however, that the deficiencies can be overcome in several interesting ways.

TABLE 6. Productions and semantic rules for TL/I → English translation.

Description	Number	Production	Example	Semantic Rules
Program	1	$P \to$ set of S	{(1: **print**, 3), (2: **stop**)}	meaning(P) = "perform action(1)".
Statement	2	$S \to (\nu\colon C)$	(2: **stop**)	**define** action(ν) $\equiv$ meaning(C); loc(C) = ν.
Command	3.1	$C \to$ **if**, ν_1, ν_2	**if**, 2, 7	meaning(C) = "if the tape square pointed to contains ν_1, then perform action(loc(C)+1); otherwise perform action(ν_2)".
	3.2.1	$C \to$ **move, left**	**move, left**	meaning(C) = "move the tape pointer one square left, then perform action(loc(C)+1)".
	3.2.2	$C \to$ **move, right**	**move, right**	meaning(C) = "move the tape pointer one square right, then perform action(loc(C)+1)".
	3.3	$C \to$ **print**, ν	**print**, 3	meaning(C) = "erase the number on the square pointed to, replace it by ν, and then perform action(loc(C)+1)".
	3.4	$C \to$ **jump**, ν	**jump**, 5	meaning(C) = "perform action(ν)".
	3.5	$C \to$ **stop**	**stop**	meaning(C) = "stop".

The main problem with Table 6 is that, if we take the definition literally as it stands, most TL/I programs will have "infinite" meanings; that is, meaning(P) will never be defined in a finite number of steps, and we need to consider a limiting process. Thus, the meaning of our binary addition example comes out to be

> "perform "erase the number on the square pointed to, replace it by 4, and then perform "perform "move the tape pointer one square left, then perform "perform "if the tape square pointed to contains 2, then perform "erase the symbol ..."; otherwise

perform "erase the number on the square pointed to, replace it by 2, and then perform "move the tape point one square right, then ... """"""""""

Being infinite, this doesn't really constitute an English sentence, nor does it read too well! It is essentially an infinite branching structure:

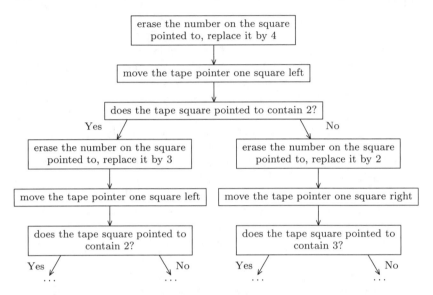

Instead of this infinite branching structure, we can take another point of view: Rather than expanding the "action" parts of the meanings, we can consider the set of defined actions to be a *table* that constitutes the meaning. Our example program then means "perform action(1)", where

action(1) = "erase the number on the square pointed to, replace it by 4, and then perform action(2)";

action(2) = "perform action(5)";

action(3) = "if the tape square pointed to contains 2, then perform action(4); otherwise perform action(7)";

$$\vdots$$

action(11) = "stop".

We can now imagine a two-armed robot who performs the process specified by a TL/I program, given a doubly infinite tape and a table of defined actions as above. With one hand, the robot points to the action that it is currently doing, while the other hand points to a place on the tape (and holds a pencil and an eraser). This is the "ambidextrous robot" model of computation.

At this point we ought to step back and contemplate the two-level definition of Turingol that appears above. Was it really necessary to introduce something like TL/I, or should we have gone directly to, say, the infinite branching structure or to the ambidextrous-robot model? A glance at the definitions shows that, indeed, we could have done things in one step. The introduction of TL/I provides a convenient shorthand, or a conceptual level slightly higher than the base, in which to think about Turing machines; yet it is really so close to our ultimate models of computation that it could have been avoided. For more sophisticated languages than Turingol, however, intermediate levels of semantics would become increasingly more important and helpful.

But are our "ultimate" models of computation correct? Some people believe that the users of a programming language should not really understand their programs in terms of a TL/I-like list of rules, or in terms of a branching structure or flowchart; they should really think of it in terms very close to the source language itself. The ambidextrous robot of our model should perhaps be interpreting the source language directly. Such a viewpoint is defensible; but on the other hand it seems to be asking for too much built-in sophistication on the part of the users, who have been able to acquire such sophistication only after gaining quite a bit of experience with high-level languages. Grade school children can understand simple machine languages, but they are not ready for ALGOL.

Perhaps that is the reason why many computer science educators are reporting that introductory courses in programming are usually more successful if the students are first taught a simple machine-like language before they learn algebraic languages. Students need to understand the underlying principles of computation — what computers do — before they see "problem-oriented languages." Therefore it is likely that the models discussed above are *not* too primitive. Furthermore, as a practical reality, people who program well in some current language (FORTRAN, COBOL, ALGOL, PL/I, SNOBOL, ...) should certainly be able to think of their programs in some terms related to the actual machine representation, so that they have a feeling for what the different constructions really "cost."

If our models aren't too primitive, are they too sophisticated? For example, positive integers should perhaps be defined in terms of Peano's postulates, etc.; maybe all the concepts should be formalized further in terms of set theory or category theory. Such an approach would take things from a domain that children can understand into a more formal area that is able to support mechanical proof procedures. In this paper, our concern is with finding a natural conceptual basis for definitions; the basis must correspond to the way we actually think about computation, otherwise the related formalisms are not likely to be fruitful. Suitable formalisms will correspond to the natural conceptual basis rather closely, so we need not choose a more primitive formalism.

3. Software Automation: A Digression

Definition of programming language semantics by means of synthesized and inherited attributes is intended to correspond closely to the way people understand the language being defined. The problem of producing compilers for that language is *not* a main goal, for we can understand the meaning of a language without having to understand how to write a compiler for it. Similarly, the success of context-free grammars as a model for syntax is based on its natural intuitive appeal, since the syntactic tree structures form a first approximation to the semantic structures; context-free grammars do not owe their success to the fact that they support efficient parsing algorithms.

A grammar is "declarative" rather than "imperative." It expresses the essential relationships between things without implying that these relationships have been deduced using any particular algorithm. In general, we want to avoid any preoccupation with bits, advancing pointers, building and unbuilding lists, when such things have little or nothing to do with the intrinsic meaning of the language we are defining.

On the other hand, once a "natural" mode of definition has been found, the next step should be to make practical use of it in the automation of software production. It is a happy circumstance when an intuitive description of a system can be transformed almost automatically into a practical working model based on that system. Much work remains to be done on the question of whether formal definitions such as those of this paper can be converted automatically to decent software programs; the following example may prove to be useful as a test case for such techniques.

Consider the problem of writing an assembler for TL/I, converting a TL/I program into a sequence of bits suitable for interpretation by a microprogrammed computer. To make the problem interesting, we shall assume that we want to compress the length of the code, letting the number of bits that represent addresses and symbols be tunable parameters. The following "formal semantics" specifies this transformation precisely, in a problem-oriented fashion.

Let Memory(n, k) stand for the sequence of k consecutive bit positions

$$\text{Memory}(n) \ \text{Memory}(n+1) \ \ldots \ \text{Memory}(n+k-1),$$

and let Binary(n, k) stand for the sequence of k bits that represent the number $n \bmod 2^k$ in binary notation. Let length(a) denote the length of string a. An optimizing TL/I assembler can now be defined as follows:

Nonterminal symbols: $P \ S \ C$

Terminal symbols: ν) (, : **if print jump move left right stop**

Start symbol: P

Synthesized attributes:
 code(C), a string of bits that represents the command C;
 length(C), the number of bits in code(C).

Global variables:
 Memory(ν), a bit that represents part of the encoded program;
 loc(ν), a positive integer that represents the first bit location of an instruction;
 a, a nonnegative integer that represents the size of address specifications;
 b, a nonnegative integer that represents the size of symbol specifications.

Global counts:
 addrs, the number of address fields in the program;
 bits, the number of bits in non-address fields of the program;
 msym, the number of the largest symbol used; this variable is computed via the operation 'msym max x', which is analogous to the operation 'count + x' used for ordinary global counters.

Productions and semantics: See Table 7.

Notice that the rules in Table 7 specify a three-pass process in a compact, "declarative" manner: First we count the addrs, then we can compute a and the loc's, then we can fill in the addresses.

4. Information Structures

The definitions above have adhered to old-fashioned conventions by which information is represented in terms of integers, functions, sets, etc. But Computer Science might be better off if we were to adopt some slightly different models and to develop their formalisms further. A wide variety of applications (see, for example, [2, Chapter 2]) suggests that it is useful to represent the information in the real world, and its

TABLE 7. Productions and semantic rules for a TL/I → microcode assembler.

Number	Production	Semantic Rules
1	$P \to$ set of S	**define** $\mathrm{loc}(1) \equiv 1$; **define** $a \equiv \min\{k \in \mathbf{N} \mid \mathrm{bits} + (k-1) \cdot \mathrm{addrs} \leq 2^k\}$; **define** $b \equiv \min\{k \in \mathbf{N} \mid \mathrm{msym} \leq 2^k\}$.
2	$S \to (\nu\colon C)$	**define** $\mathrm{Memory}(\mathrm{loc}(\nu), \mathrm{length}(C)) \equiv \mathrm{code}(C)$; **define** $\mathrm{loc}(\nu+1) \equiv \mathrm{loc}(\nu) + \mathrm{length}(C)$.
3.1	$C \to$ **if**, ν_1, ν_2	$\mathrm{code}(C) = 00\ \mathrm{Binary}(\nu_1 - 1, b)\ \mathrm{Binary}(\mathrm{loc}(\nu_2), a)$; bits $+ (2{+}b)$; addrs $+ 1$; msym max ν_1; $\mathrm{length}(C) = 2 + b + a$.
3.2.1	$C \to$ **move, left**	$\mathrm{code}(C) = 010$; bits $+ 3$; $\mathrm{length}(C) = 3$.
3.2.2	$C \to$ **move, right**	$\mathrm{code}(C) = 011$; bits $+ 3$; $\mathrm{length}(C) = 3$.
3.3	$C \to$ **print**, ν	$\mathrm{code}(C) = 10\ \mathrm{Binary}(\nu - 1, b)$; bits $+ (2{+}b)$; msym max ν; $\mathrm{length}(C) = 2 + b$.
3.4	$C \to$ **jump**, ν	$\mathrm{code}(C) = 11\ \mathrm{Binary}(\mathrm{loc}(\nu), a)$; bits $+ 2$; addrs $+ 1$; $\mathrm{length}(C) = 2 + a$.
3.5	$C \to$ **stop**	$\mathrm{code}(C) = 11\ \mathrm{Binary}(0, a)$; bits $+ 2$; addrs $+ 1$; $\mathrm{length}(C) = 2 + a$.

structural interrelationships, by means of things called "nodes." Each node consists of several "fields," which contain values. The values may be integers, or strings, or sets, etc., but (more importantly) the values may also be *references* (that is, pointers or links) to other nodes.

The idea of references can be and has been formalized in various ways in terms of classical concepts, but recent experience suggests the usefulness of regarding references themselves as primitives. This approach often frees us from making arbitrary but conceptually irrelevant choices when we are representing information. For example, index sets are often used in mathematics when other conventions would be better; and integers were used in our definition of lambda expressions and Turingol above, although we really wanted only unique labels and a notion of order.

Let us, therefore, consider making semantic definitions in terms of the proper data structures. A study of the Turingol-to-TL/I example indicates that we could replace the set of location-instruction pairs in TL/I by a string of nodes (that is, an ordered sequence of nodes). Each node corresponds to an instruction; **jump** and **if** nodes contain references to other nodes. We can concatenate strings of nodes just like strings of letters; so, for example, we can do away with the inherited attribute 'init(S)'. Rule 4.2, '$L_1 \to L_2; S$', now corresponds to the almost trivial semantics 'meaning(L_1) = meaning(L_2) meaning(S)'. In this way, we obtain a more appealing (and simpler) formal definition, because all attributes are synthesized except for those that are implicitly present in global quantities. This idea of node strings containing pointers between the nodes, instead of absolute addresses that have to be determined by strict sequence rules, has been very successful in some studies recently conducted by the author on an experimental compiler-generating language.

Instead of making a complete listing of Turingol's semantics from the string-of-nodes point of view, let us raise our sights a bit higher and consider the slightly more complicated problem of translating Turingol into a "self-explanatory flowchart." We may regard the meaning of a Turingol program as a set of nodes whose structure is that of a flowchart, easily readable by any ambidextrous robot who wants to perform the algorithm. We use the notation

$$\mathbf{new}\,(\xi_1 = \eta_1;\ \xi_2 = \eta_2;\ \ldots;\ \xi_m = \eta_m)$$

to denote the creation of a new node with m fields; the field named ξ_j contains the value η_j, for $1 \leq j \leq m$. The value of $\mathbf{new}\,(\ldots)$ is a reference to this node. It is interesting to compare the Turingol definition below with the definition above, since the inherited-versus-synthesized roles of "init" and "fin" are now reversed(!).

Terminal symbols: σ . , : ; } { ' ' **tape alphabet is print move left right one square go to if the symbol then**

Nonterminal symbols: $P\ S\ L\ D\ O$

Start symbol: P

Inherited attributes:
  fin(S) or fin(L), a reference to the node that follows a statement or list.

Synthesized attributes:
  init(S) or init(L), a reference to the node that begins a statement or list;
  index(D), a positive integer, the number of symbols in a declaration;
  d(O), left or right, a direction.

Global variables:
  label(σ), for all σ, a reference to the node that corresponds to the label identifier σ;
  symbol(σ), for all σ, a positive integer, the symbol number associated with the identifier σ.

Fields of nodes: The COMMAND field contains strings of words and numbers explaining what to do when reaching this node; the YES, NO, and NEXT fields contain references to other nodes.

Productions and semantics: See Table 8. All nodes generated by the **new** operation constitute the "meaning" of a Turingol program.

The definition in Table 8 will, for example, produce the following flowchart from the binary addition example:

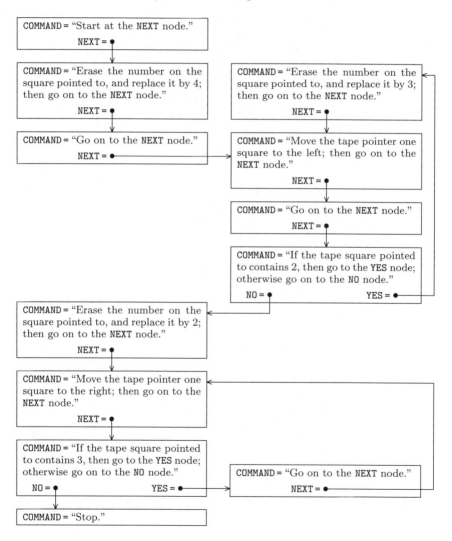

TABLE 8. Productions and semantic rules to define Turingol in terms of nodes.

Number	Production	Semantic Rules
1.1	$D \to$ **tape alphabet is** σ	index(D) = 1; **define** symbol(σ) $\equiv$ 1.
1.2	$D_1 \to D_2, \sigma$	index(D_1) = index(D_2) + 1; **define** symbol(σ) $\equiv$ index(D_1).
2.1	$S \to$ **print** 'σ'	init(S) = **new**(COMMAND = "Erase the number on the square pointed to, and replace it by symbol(σ); then go on to the NEXT node."; NEXT = fin(S)).
2.2	$S \to$ **move** O **one square**	init(S) = **new**(COMMAND = "Move the tape pointer one square to the d(O); then go on to the NEXT node."; NEXT = fin(S)).
2.2.1	$O \to$ **left**	d(O) = left.
2.2.2	$O \to$ **right**	d(O) = right.
2.3	$S \to$ **go to** σ	init(S) = **new**(COMMAND = "Go on to the NEXT node."; NEXT = label(σ)).
2.4	$S \to$	init(S) = **new**(COMMAND = "Go on to the NEXT node."; NEXT = fin(S)).
3.1	$S_1 \to$ **if the tape symbol is** 'σ' **then** S_2	init(S_1) = **new**(COMMAND = "If the tape square pointed to contains symbol(σ), then go on to the YES node; otherwise go on to the NO node."; YES = init(S_2); NO = fin(S_1); fin(S_2) = fin(S_1).
3.2	$S_1 \to \sigma: S_2$	init(S_1) = init(S_2); fin(S_2) = fin(S_1); **define** label(σ) $\equiv$ init(S_1).
3.3	$S \to \{L\}$	init(S) = init(L); fin(L) = fin(S).
4.1	$L \to S$	init(L) = init(S); fin(S) = fin(L).
4.2	$L_1 \to L_2; S$	init(L_1) = init(L_2); fin(L_2) = init(S); fin(S) = fin(L_1).
5	$P \to D; L.$	**new**(COMMAND = "Start at the NEXT node."; NEXT = init(L)); fin(L) = **new**(COMMAND = "Stop.").

As before, symbol(*blank*) $\equiv$ 1, symbol(*one*) $\equiv$ 2, symbol(*zero*) $\equiv$ 3, and symbol(*point*) $\equiv$ 4. (The flowchart contains three 'go on' nodes that seem redundant. Cases such as '*loop*: **go to** *loop*' show that such nodes cannot be eliminated entirely.)

We could also go back and reconsider lambda expressions from the standpoint of appropriate information structures. It would be an easy exercise to define the semantics so that, for example, the lambda expression $(\lambda x' \lambda x(x'x)x)$ is mapped into the nodes of Figure 1. Thus, bound variables become "formal parameter" nodes, which refer back to the appropriate function definition in which the variable is bound. Such a structure gives the essential content of the lambda notation, except for the definition of functional application, which can now be formalized in various ways in terms of the node structures.

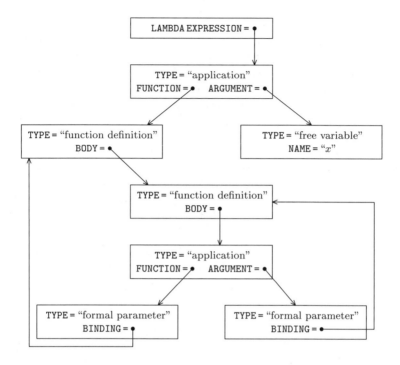

FIGURE 1. The meaning of $(\lambda x' \lambda x (x' x) x)$.

5. Summary

We have discussed several examples in which rather complicated functions have been defined on context-free languages. In each case it was possible to give a definition that is concise, in the sense that hardly anything is defined that isn't "necessary"; and at the same time the definitions seem to be intuitive, in the sense that they mirror the structure by which we "understand" the function. These definitions are based on assigning attributes to the nonterminal symbols of a context-free grammar, and relating the attributes that correspond to each production.

We have also discussed some of the choices for a semantic basis of programming languages. If we are interested in information-theoretic properties of algorithms, we may prefer an infinite branching structure as a computational model; if we are interested in representations of algorithms that are analogous to real live computer programs, we may prefer an "ambidextrous robot" (essentially an automaton) model; if we are interested in the underlying structure, we may prefer a flowchart model. Other models are also possible. Whatever the model, formal definition via attributes seems to be helpful.

At the present time these ideas are being used and extended by Wayne Wilner to construct a formal definition of a major programming language, SIMULA 67. The complexity of this language (over 300 productions in the syntax) makes the semantics slightly less transparent than the examples in this paper; but, in fact, the definition turns out to be simpler than anticipated.

Perhaps the main direction for future work that is suggested by the examples of this paper is to devise a suitable "context-free grammar" for arbitrary node structures instead of just strings. Attribute definition on such grammars may lead to a very natural declarative language for problem solving in terms of relevant structures.

Acknowledgment

I wish to thank Clement L. McGowan III for several stimulating discussions, especially for pointing out errors in my original attempts to define the semantics of lambda expressions.

The research reported here was supported in part by the Advanced Research Projects Agency of the Office of the Secretary of Defense (SD 183), and in part by IBM Corporation.

References

[1] Alonzo Church and J. B. Rosser, "Some properties of conversion," *Transactions of the American Mathematical Society* **39** (1936), 472–482.

[2] Donald E. Knuth, *Fundamental Algorithms*, Volume 1 of *The Art of Computer Programming* (Reading, Massachusetts: Addison–Wesley, 1968).

[3] Donald E. Knuth, "Semantics of context-free languages," *Mathematical Systems Theory* **2** (1968), 127–145. [Reprinted with corrections as Chapter 17 of the present volume.]

[4] Peter Wegner, *Programming Languages, Information Structures, and Machine Organization* (New York: McGraw–Hill, 1968).

Chapter 19

The Genesis of Attribute Grammars

*[Keynote address at the International Conference on Attribute Grammars and their Applications, Paris, France, September 1990. Originally published in Lecture Notes in Computer Science **461** (1990), 1–12.]*

I have always been fascinated by the origin of ideas, so I am pleased that the organizers of this conference have asked me to open the proceedings by taking a look back at how the subject began. In other words, I'm glad that my job is to give this conference a "history attribute."

Attribute grammars were born in the exhilarating days of the mid-60s when a great many fundamental principles of computer science were beginning to be understood. An enormous number of ideas were floating in the air, waiting to be captured in just the right combinations that would prove to be powerful sources of future energy.

The human mind is notoriously bad at reconstructing past experiences, so I have tried to make my story as accurate as possible by digging up as many scraps of authentic information from the early days as I could find. People say that nostalgia isn't what it used to be, but I hope that the participants of this conference will be able to share some of the pleasure I have experienced while preparing this retrospective study.

Much of my story takes place in 1967, by which time a great many sophisticated computer programs had been written all over the world. Computing machines had come a long way since their invention in the 30s and 40s; for example, the recently announced Burroughs B6500 was aptly called a "third generation" system [35], and J. P. Eckert was noting a trend toward parallelism in new computer designs [37]. Yet many problems without easy solutions made people well aware that the vast potential of computers was only beginning to be tapped, and that a great many important issues were not at all well understood.

One of the puzzling questions under extensive investigation at the time was the problem of programming language semantics: How should

423

we define the meaning of statements in algorithmic languages? Dozens of experts had gathered in Vienna in 1964 for a conference on formal language description, and the prevailing mood at that conference is well summarized by the remarks of T. B. Steel, Jr.: "Improvements in programming language description methods are imperative. ... I don't fully know myself how to describe the semantics of a language. I daresay nobody does or we wouldn't be here" [31]. Steel edited the proceedings of that meeting, which include lively transcriptions of discussions among the participants [30]. None of the presented papers had much connection with what we now call attribute grammars, although some hints could be found in the explorations of Čulík [4]. Preprints of a strongly related paper by L. Petrone were also distributed in Vienna (see [28]). At the closing session, Fraser Duncan remarked, "We have not actually got all or perhaps any of the ultimate answers. But we have a lot of ideas of where to look and where not to look" [6].

All of the known methods for defining the meaning of computer programs were based on rather intricate algorithms having roughly the same degree of complexity as compilers, or worse. This was in stark contrast to Chomsky's simple and elegant method of syntax definition via context-free grammars. As Dr. Caracciolo said, "How simple to realize [semantic correctness] if you write a procedure. The problem is, however, to find a metalanguage for doing that in a declarative way, not in an operational way" [3].

There was one bright light on the horizon, a notable exception to the perceived difficulty of semantic definition: Comparatively simple languages such as arithmetic expressions could be understood by a mechanism proposed in 1960 by Ned Irons [9; see also 10, 11]. If we know the meaning of α and the meaning of β, then we know the meanings of such things as $\alpha + \beta$, $\alpha - \beta$, $\alpha \times \beta$, α/β, and (α). Thus the meaning of an arbitrarily large expression can be synthesized in a straightforward way by recursively building up the meanings of its subexpressions.

Simple subexpressions like 'x' still remained problematical, because of their context-dependent meaning. For example the ALGOL 60 program

> **begin real** x; $x := x$ **end**

was implicitly supposed to be parsed by treating the final appearance of x as an ⟨arithmetic expression⟩, while the analogous x in

> **begin Boolean** x; $x := x$ **end**

was to be parsed as a ⟨Boolean expression⟩. The official syntax in [27] allowed several distinct parses for both programs, but only one of them was considered to be semantically valid. Furthermore, a program such as

begin real x; $x := y$ **end**

could also be parsed in several ways, from a syntactic standpoint; but none of those parse trees was legal from a semantic standpoint, because the undeclared variable y was neither an ⟨arithmetic expression⟩ nor a ⟨Boolean expression⟩. Therefore Irons developed his syntax-directed approach by including mechanisms to reject certain parse trees based on declarations that the parser had found earlier [12].

The prevailing view (see [8]) was that strings of tokens like '**begin real** x; $x := y$ **end**' were not members of the language ALGOL 60, because such strings had no semantically valid parse tree.

In retrospect, we can see why this approach had evolved; syntax was much better understood than semantics, so syntax acquired additional responsibilities. People found it convenient to incorporate semantical information, about such things as types, into syntactic categories.

My own private opinion was different; I regarded ALGOL 60 as a context-free language defined solely by ordinary productions. To me the "meaning" of a program like

begin real x; $x := y$ **end**

was clearly defined: "Improper assignment of an undeclared variable named y to the real variable named x." But I had no good ideas about how to define such meanings in a simple and systematic way that would generalize nicely.

Besides, I was far too busy with another project; I couldn't think about doing anything new. In the summer of 1962 I had begun to write a book called *The Art of Computer Programming* [14], and I had finished the hand-written draft (some 2500 pages) in June of 1965. By October of that year I had typed the first of its 12 chapters, and at the rate I was going it seemed almost certain that I would be finished typing the entire manuscript by the summer of 1968.

And indeed, I would have finished by then if Computer Science had only cooperated and stood still; and if I hadn't tried to maintain a complete coverage of new ideas as they were developing. I failed to anticipate the fact that the field would grow explosively, that thousands of brilliant people would continually be inventing ever deeper and more important ideas, faster than I could type.

I did realize, of course, that a lot was going on; therefore I agreed to be on the editorial boards of both *Journal of the ACM* and *Communications of the ACM*. In fact, I plunged into those jobs with enthusiasm, because editorial work gave me a chance to learn the new ideas as they were being born. I wrote numerous lengthy critiques of articles that were submitted, trying to improve the quality of the publications as best I could; during the first nine months of 1966 I refereed 21 papers, and I'm sure that the hours I devoted to that work were well spent. My "territory" at the time was called Programming Languages [36]. In March, 1966, I wrote a letter to *Communications of the ACM* editor Gerry Salton making it plain that I was enjoying myself. I said: "The job of being editor in a subject area that is rather new and not too clearly defined is very educational since I am forced to do a lot of reflection on goals and motives which I would never otherwise have done." Thus I had plenty of opportunity to think about thorny issues such as semantics that were much discussed at the time.

Still, I made absolutely no attempt to solve those problems myself. I was plenty busy completing old tasks and keeping up with what other people were doing. When I was on campus at Caltech I had classes to teach and a backlog of editorial work to process; when I came home at the end of the day, there was plenty of typing and revising to do on *The Art of Computer Programming*. At the beginning of 1967 I was beginning to type Chapter 4, which by then was scheduled to appear as the second half of Volume 2 in a projected seven-volume series; the galley proofs of Volume 1 were due to begin arriving in March. Moreover, I was the proud father of a 17-month-old son and a 19-day-old daughter. Research was the farthest thing from my mind.

But I was an ACM Lecturer that year [38], and I spent the middle of February visiting nine campuses and giving sixteen lectures. During that trip I had some fateful encounters; and presto! Attribute Grammars were born.

My first stop was Cornell, and I spent the first weekend staying at Peter Wegner's home in Ithaca, New York. Many details of those two days (4–5 February 1967) still remain fresh in my mind. For example, I went with Peter to a synagogue on Saturday, and he went with me to a church on Sunday. We hiked outside the city in a beautiful river valley that contained many frozen waterfalls. But mostly we talked Computer Science.

Peter asked me what I thought about formal semantics, and I said I liked Irons's idea of synthesizing an overall meaning from submeanings. I also said that I liked the way other people had combined Irons's approach with a top-down or "recursive-descent" parser; Irons had used a more complex parsing scheme. In particular, I was impressed by the metacompiler of Val Schorre [29] and by the more powerful (though less elegant) "transmogrifier" of Bob McClure [26]. I told Peter about my draft manuscript for Chapter 12 of *The Art of Computer Programming*, which included an example system of a similar kind, called TROL ("Translation-Oriented Language"). Programs in TROL were, in essence, collections of recursive subroutines corresponding to the definitions of nonterminal symbols, in a given language whose compiler was being described. Every such nonterminal could have a variety of attributes of types integer, Boolean, string, or link (that is, reference); the values of those attributes would be synthesized as parsing proceeded. Context-dependent aspects of semantics were handled in the traditional brute-force way by maintaining global data structures, including symbol tables that allowed the dynamic insertion and deletion of ⟨identifier, value⟩ pairs as parsing proceeded. I had prepared two examples of TROL programs for the book, one for a procedural language called 3.5-TRAN and another for TROL itself. (The first of these was a compiler that translated 3.5-TRAN source programs into MIX code; the second compiled TROL source programs into TROLL, an internal representation of TROL code used by a special interpretive routine.)

I probably also told Peter about a significant paper by Lewis and Stearns that I had recently been handling for *Journal of the ACM*. That paper [24] extended the automata-based theory of languages from syntax to semantics, under the assumption that semantics was defined by repeated combination of synthesized string-valued attributes.

Thus, in general, my answer to Peter's question was that the best way I knew to define semantics was to use attributes whose values could be defined on a parse tree from bottom to top. And I said that, unfortunately, we also needed to include some complicated ad hoc methods, in order to get context-dependent information into the tree.

So Peter asked, "Why can't attributes be defined from the top down as well as from the bottom up?"

A shocking idea! Of course I instinctively replied that it was impossible to go both bottom-up and top-down. But after some discussion I realized that his suggestion wasn't so preposterous after all, if circular definitions could somehow be avoided. (The title of my present paper should really be, "The Revelation of Attribute Grammars.")

Well, we didn't pursue the matter, because we had many other things to talk about. But in retrospect, it is clear that a large share of the credit for inventing attribute grammars should be attributed to

Peter Wegner, because he was the one who first suggested the concept of inherited attributes. (I've often been kicking myself for failing to acknowledge his important contribution when I wrote my first papers on the subject.)

I kept thinking about the combination of inherited and synthesized attributes at odd moments as my trip continued, but I never had a chance to write anything down on paper. A few days later — I think it was on Wednesday, 15 February — I found myself at Stanford University, in a conference room with half a dozen or so graduate students of Computer Science. This was a "meet the students" session scheduled after my regular lecture. And one of the students (probably Sue Graham) asked me what I thought was the best way to define the semantics of programming languages. Wow! This was a chance to try out the thoughts I'd been formulating, after Peter had planted that idea in my mind. And there was a blackboard at hand, with plenty of chalk. So I marched up to the board and started to write down a definition of a language very much like what later became Turingol [15, 18]. I have no idea if what I said made any sense to the students, since I must have had to go back and erase a lot of things before getting them right; and I doubt that anybody took notes that day. But I do recall that the first time I ever constructed a nontrivial attribute grammar was during that online meeting with students.

Soon I was back home in Southern California, and of course there was no time to write down any of these thoughts. I did, however, take a few minutes to mail a copy of my *curriculum vitæ* to George Forsythe, the chairman of Stanford's department, since I had enjoyed my visit there most of all. (I also wrote a letter to Bob Floyd, who was then at Carnegie–Mellon University, saying that I was seriously considering a move to Stanford, or perhaps Cornell; I was hoping that he felt the same way, so that we could be together.)

The next chapter in the story of attribute grammars took place in France, of all places. My recollections here are somewhat hazy, because I haven't been able to find any of the related correspondence. But I know that I came to France in May, a week before going to the Simulation Languages conference in Norway [2]. Maurice Nivat had invited me to speak at the Institute Blaise Pascal, and someone (probably Louis Bolliet) had arranged for me to spend two days in Grenoble. On one of those two days — I think it was Friday, 19 May — I was once again asked my opinion about semantics, and I made an informal presentation of a definition for Turingol to about a dozen people. That was the second time I had had occasion to write down an attribute grammar.

On the following day I went to Zandvoort, Holland, where a meeting of the IFIP ALGOL working group was being held. About 50 people were sitting around a large round table, making decisions about ALGOL X (which had previously been called ALGOL 66 and which eventually became ALGOL 68); as you know, this language was an extensive development of ALGOL 60, based on Aad van Wijngaarden's method of semantic definition via recursive interpretation of texts [33]. My main impression of that meeting was that Chris Strachey's prediction from 1964 was unfortunately being fulfilled: He had said, "In anything like a complicated language ..., the process of defining a compiler for it is extremely elaborate. The details of the special compiler written by the committee are bound to be confined to the people who wrote it, and they will be the only people who understand it" [32].

Back home in California, I once again was completely preoccupied by editorial work and by fatherhood; there was no question of looking any further into semantics and such. I was getting into some very difficult parts of Volume 2 that I decided were necessary additions to my first draft. (For example, I had gone to a conference in April [1], where I had learned about Berlekamp's amazing new method for factoring polynomials modulo 2.) Still, I returned a batch of galley proofs to Addison–Wesley on the 5th of June saying, "I had a very nice rest on this trip to Europe and I am ready to dive into work this summer."

But those months of June and July, 1967, were destined to be the most traumatic of my entire life. While I was working out the answer to a new exercise for my book (exercise 4.5.2–18), I suddenly had to make an unscheduled trip to the hospital. The ensuing dark days are best summarized by quoting from a letter that I sent to my publishers at the end of July:

> ... my "iron stomach" sprung a leak. I was forced to go five weeks without doing any work (all I could do was eat Jello, plain, and read Agatha Christie stories). After this I began to feel fine again, probably since I have always liked Agatha Christie. So then like a fool I began to work once more at a strenuous pace, and in two more days I was down again. It is clear that I have been trying to do more concentrated work than my body will stand, so I will have to systematically decrease my work load. In the immediate future (say the next month) I should relax except for about five hours a day when I can concentrate on my writing, etc.; after this I should be knit together enough to work say nine or ten hours a day, but never go back to the 14-hour schedule I had been keeping.

On 11 September, 1967, I reluctantly resigned from my position on the *ACM Journal* editorial board.

Meanwhile, other responsibilities were still in place. I had agreed to give a week's lectures at a NATO Summer School near Copenhagen in August, and my plan was to come a week early so that I would have time to figure out what to say. Well, I arrived in Denmark on the 6th of August as planned, only to learn that Klaus Wirth had become seriously ill and was forced to cancel his lectures; therefore I was asked to take his place. I agreed to begin on Wednesday afternoon, although that gave me only 2.5 days to prepare. My announced title was "Top-Down Syntax Analysis," and I was hoping that I would be able to prove some useful new theorems in time to present them in the lectures. In order to keep my stomach calm, I decided to work outdoors, sitting under some stately pine trees in the woods near the campus at Lyngby. Thank goodness, my luck held; the concepts of $LL(k)$ took shape as I had hoped they would, during those 2.5 days in the Danish woods. I lectured all day Thursday and Friday without serious side effects, stomachwise; but a bug in the theory surfaced on Friday afternoon, just as I was finishing. I fixed everything on Saturday morning, and finally began to enjoy the sights of Denmark. (Notes from those lectures were eventually published in [19].)

You might think that I now had a week free to think about semantics, but that was not the case. I was on my way to another conference at Oxford, where I was scheduled to speak about another topic entirely. I had stumbled across this other idea (which has become known as the "Knuth–Bendix algorithm") while teaching an undergraduate class in 1966. Peter Bendix, a student in the class, had implemented the method, and we had carried out numerous experiments; so the research was all done and I merely had to write up the paper [16]. That was how I spent my "free" week in Denmark.

I remember talking to John McCarthy about sensory overload during my visit to Stanford in February. I said I was in a dilemma because I was sitting on two ideas I thought were going to be important (namely, the Knuth–Bendix algorithm and the definition of attribute grammars), but I couldn't investigate either one carefully because I had to devote all my spare time to *The Art of Computer Programming*. I asked his advice: Should I publish them in embryonic form (and let other people have the fun of developing them), or should I hold back awhile until I had time to study them thoroughly, then present more mature concepts? John said I should wait until I had time to work everything out personally, otherwise there was a danger that the ideas would be misunderstood and distorted. I guess I didn't follow his advice very well, but I did at least take time to explain the ideas as well as I could when I did publish them. And I've been lucky that both ideas seem to have inspired many other people to do things that I could never have accomplished.

Although attribute grammars remained at the back of my mind for several months, my next chance to think seriously about them didn't come until I was away from home again — this time at a SIAM conference in Santa Barbara, California, at the end of November. Although the conference record lists me as one of the participants [39], the truth is that I spent almost the whole time sitting on the beach outside the conference hotel writing a paper about "semantics of context-free languages" [15]. That paper explained everything I knew (or thought I knew) about attribute grammars. I spent the first day working on a test for circularity; after rejecting three obviously false starts, I thought I had found a correct algorithm, and I didn't try too hard to find fault with it.

So that's the story of my paper [15], which was effectively written in Ithaca, Stanford, Grenoble, and Santa Barbara. (The published paper [15] says "Received 15 November 1967"; that must be a misprint for December.) I've presented this background information in some detail because it suggests that research institutes may not be the best places to do research. Perhaps new ideas emerge most often from hectic, disorganized activity, when a great many sources of stimulation are present at once — when numerous deadlines need to be met, and when other miscellaneous activities like child-rearing are also mixed into the agenda. (On the other hand I'm quite content to be leading a much more orderly life nowadays. One attack of ulcers is enough for me.)

I moved to Stanford and began teaching there in the fall of 1969. Now I was officially a computer scientist instead of a mathematician. Several Stanford students asked me to give them further examples of attribute grammars, and in February 1970 I received a letter from Erwin Engeler requesting the same thing. In April and May, I taught a graduate course about compilers based on my notes for Volume 7 of *The Art of Computer Programming*; it was the one and only time in my life that I have ever taught such a course. My class notes give no indication that I lectured at all about attribute grammars; there was very little time, less than nine weeks altogether, because classes were often disrupted by political crises in those exciting days. I did, however, devote a number of lectures to the TROL language, which was the basis of the main homework assignments. (Two of the students submitted an interesting term paper containing a critique of TROL and a suggested successor called STROL. Their names? Ron Rivest and Bob Tarjan.)

My work pattern in 1970 was somewhat different from the frenetic pace of 1967. At home, I continued to type away at *The Art of Computer Programming*; I was then finishing up the treatment of Shellsort, in Section 5.2.1 of Volume 3. But I would go to sleep when I got tired. At school, I was now expected to do some original work, in addition to classroom teaching, in order to please my research sponsors. Thus, I was no longer confining my research activities to odd moments when I was away from home (although it is true that paper [17] was written on another California beach).

It was hard for me to do anything creative in my office, with the phone ringing and people dropping in all the time; so I found a few quiet hideaways on the Stanford campus. In particular, I spent three or four pleasant days sitting under an oak tree near Lake Lagunita, writing the requested chapter for Engeler's book [18]. Sitting under this tree in springtime was an ideal way to get into the right mood to write about an intermediate language TL/I for Turing machines, and to come up with the philosophical discussions in that paper. (I had previously corresponded with Clem McGowan of Cornell about the semantics of lambda expressions, hence that part of [18] could be gleaned from older notes.) Incidentally, Stanfordians will appreciate the fact that baby caterpillars kept falling on me as I was sitting under the oak tree.

A tree that was the source of many attributes. (Reenactment in 1990 of a scene from 1970, when this area was still undeveloped. A student residence, now visible behind the tree, was built here about 1980.)

It is clear from reading [18] that I was still unaware of the serious error in the circularity test of [15] when I wrote the new paper. Indeed, I returned the galley proofs of [18] to the printer on 28 July; then on 6 August, I received a letter from Stein Krogdahl in Norway, containing an elegantly presented counterexample to my circularity algorithm. (His letter had come by surface mail, taking six weeks to reach me, otherwise I could have alluded to the problem in [18].) I soon found a way to patch up the difficulty, but the worst-case running time of the new algorithm was now exponential instead of polynomial. I immediately sent an errata notice [20] to the publishers of my original article, including also a correction to equation (2.4); Jiří Kopřiva had written to me in 1968, pointing out an oversight in that formula.

Alas, it is impossible to get everything right, even when (or especially when?) we are writing about how to make careful definitions.

Sometime during 1970 — I cannot recall whether it was in the winter, spring, or fall — John McCarthy challenged me to a public debate about how semantics ought to be defined.* (John did this for fun; he loves to debate things. See, for instance, [25].) Unfortunately, I saved no notes of what happened during our friendly hour-long confrontation; but I do recall that our main point of disagreement concerned inherited attributes, which John thought were unnecessary. His recommended alternative was, in essence, to associate parameters with the nonterminal symbols of a grammar; these parameters could bring contextual information down to the leaves of the tree. For example, instead of a nonterminal symbol E for expressions, we could have $E(s)$, where s was an appropriate symbol table for declared identifiers allowed within the expressions. I had never given much thought to such an approach, so I had no counterexamples handy to show why inherited attributes would be more powerful and/or more natural than a parameter mechanism. I don't think either of us "won" the debate; but I do remember promising myself afterward never to engage in such a thing again, because I have never enjoyed verbal argumentation.

My own work on attribute grammars had to become dormant soon afterward, because there were too many other things to do. (My chief

---

* While preparing this paper, I tried to discover the date of our debate by looking at John's computer files from that era. Thanks to the modern-day wizardry of Martin Frost and Joe Weening, it is still possible to reconstruct many of his electronic files from 1969 and 1970; but all we could find relevant to attribute grammars was an entry within a file called `TOREAD`, last updated 26 October 1970, in which my paper [18] was listed sixth from the top.

activity during the summer of 1970, besides the ongoing work on Volume 3 of *The Art of Computer Programming*, was an empirical study of FORTRAN programs [21] carried out with the help of a dozen students and other volunteers.) I gave a talk that November to the participants in a Research Workshop in Grammar and Semantics of Natural Languages that Pat Suppes had organized at Stanford. I'm not sure exactly what I said, nor have I any evidence that my talk made a great impression on anybody in the audience, but my views at the time can be faithfully summarized by the following abstract, which I sent to the participants in September:

> My motivation for this work was entirely directed to semantics of computer programming languages, but there is reason to believe that the approach is useful for natural languages as well.
>
> The enclosed pages introduce the idea, which is essentially very simple. For natural languages the "synthesized attributes" would be things like number, gender, denotation, etc., while the "inherited attributes" would be things like the meaning of prepositions based on context. This approach to semantics also seems to make it possible to simplify the syntax of a language in a fairly natural way.

During my first years at Stanford I supervised two students whose Ph.D. theses explored the large-scale application of attribute grammars [7, 34]. But I soon discovered that I could no longer participate adequately in widely different parts of Computer Science all at once, so I began to concentrate on mathematical analysis of algorithms [22].

Of course it's been a treat for me to see how attribute grammars have grown in popularity during the past 20 years. When I first learned about the astonishing results of Jazayeri, Ogden, and Rounds [13] — that circularity can always be tested in A^n steps and that every correct algorithm needs to perform at least $B^{n/\log n}$ steps on infinitely many examples — it blew my mind. This made circularity testing one of the first "natural" problems to have provably exponential complexity. Never would I have dared to conjecture such a remarkable theorem. Then I learned that even my incorrect circularity algorithm was turning out to be useful, because it provides a test for "strongly noncircular" grammars (see [5, page 18]).

In 1977 I began to work on a language for computer typesetting called TEX, and you might ask why I didn't use an attribute grammar to define the semantics of TEX. Good question. The truth is, I haven't been able to figure out *any* good way to define TEX precisely, except by exhibiting its lengthy implementation in Pascal [23]. I think that the program for TEX is as readable as any program of its size, yet a computer program is surely an unsatisfying way to define semantics. Still, it's the best I have been able to do. Moreover, I don't know any way to define any other language for general-purpose typesetting that would have an easily defined semantics, without making it a lot less useful than TEX. The same remarks apply also to METAFONT. "Macros" are the main difficulty: As far as I know, macros are indispensable but inherently tricky to define. And when we also add a capability to change the interpretation of input characters, dynamically, we get into a realm for which clean formalisms seem impossible.

During the ten years I was working intensively on TEX, I occasionally ran into people who said that they were interested in attribute grammars. But when I saw the book *Attribute Grammars* by Deransart, Jourdan, and Lorho [5], I was astonished. I could hardly believe the fact that its bibliography cited about 600 relevant papers. Wow; surely I would never have predicted such dramatic growth.

I'm delighted, above all, to see that people not only use attribute grammars, and prove deep results about them, they have fun doing so. I looked at about dozen of the papers cited in [5], and in each case I noticed the authors' evident enthusiasm for the work they were doing. Nothing could make me happier.

My own contribution obviously amounts to only a minuscule portion of the many things that have been discovered. Attribute grammars would not have become so widespread so quickly if the concept had not been quite a natural one. Therefore somebody would surely have invented attribute grammars even if Ned Irons, Peter Wegner, and I had never existed. Yet as a writer I'm extremely pleased to have written a few papers that people have found inspiring.

The preparation of this paper was supported in part by the National Science Foundation under grant CCR–8610181.

Bibliography

[1] R. C. Bose and T. A. Dowling, editors, *Combinatorial Mathematics and Its Applications*, Proceedings of a conference held at Chapel Hill, North Carolina, 10–14 April 1967; *University of North Carolina Monograph Series in Probability and Statistics* **4** (1969).

[2] J. N. Buxton (editor), *Simulation Programming Languages*, Proceedings of an IFIP Working Conference held at Oslo, Norway, 22–26 May 1967 (Amsterdam: North-Holland, 1968).

[3] A. Caracciolo di Forino, "On the concept of formal linguistic systems," in [30], 37–51.

[4] Karel Čulík, "Well-translatable grammars and Algol-like languages," in [30], 76–85.

[5] Pierre Deransart, Martin Jourdan, and Bernard Lorho, "Attribute Grammars," *Lecture Notes in Computer Science* **323** (1988), ix + 232 pages.

[6] F. G. Duncan, "Our ultimate metalanguage: An after dinner talk," in [30], 295–299.

[7] Isu Fang, *FOLDS, a Declarative Formal Language Definition System*, report STAN-CS-72-329 (Ph.D. thesis, Stanford University, 1972).

[8] Robert W. Floyd, "On the nonexistence of a phrase structure grammar for ALGOL 60," *Communications of the ACM* **5** (1962), 483–484.

[9] Edgar T. Irons, "A syntax directed compiler for ALGOL 60," *Communications of the ACM* **4** (1961), 51–55.

[10] Edgar T. Irons, "The structure and use of the syntax-directed compiler," *Annual Review in Automatic Programming* **3** (1962), 207–227.

[11] Edgar T. Irons, "Towards more versatile mechanical translators," *Proceedings of Symposia in Applied Mathematics* **15** (Providence, Rhode Island: American Mathematical Society, 1963), 41–50.

[12] E. T. Irons, " 'Structural connections' in formal languages," *Communications of the ACM* **7** (1964), 67–72.

[13] Mehdi Jazayeri, William F. Ogden, and William C. Rounds, "The intrinsically exponential complexity of the circularity problem for attribute grammars," *Communications of the ACM* **18** (1975), 697–706.

[14] Donald E. Knuth, *The Art of Computer Programming* (Reading, Massachusetts: Addison–Wesley). Volume 1, 1968; Volume 2, 1969; Volume 3, 1973; Volume 4, in progress.

[15] Donald E. Knuth, "Semantics of context-free languages," *Mathematical Systems Theory* **2** (1968), 127–145. [Reprinted as Chapter 17 of the present volume.]

[16] Donald E. Knuth and Peter B. Bendix, "Simple word problems in universal algebras," in *Computational Problems in Abstract Algebra*, edited by John Leech, Proceedings of a conference held at

Oxford, England, 29 August–2 September 1967 (Oxford: Pergamon Press, 1970), 263–297.

[17] Donald E. Knuth, "The analysis of algorithms," *Actes du Congrès International des Mathématiciens 1970*, **3** (Paris: Gauthier-Villars, 1971), 269–274. [Reprinted as Chapter 3 of *Selected Papers on Analysis of Algorithms*, CSLI Lecture Notes 102 (Stanford, California: Center for the Study of Language and Information, 2000), 27–34.]

[18] Donald E. Knuth, "Examples of formal semantics," in *Symposium on Semantics of Algorithmic Languages*, edited by E. Engeler, *Lecture Notes in Mathematics* **188** (1971), 212–235. [Reprinted as Chapter 18 of the present volume.]

[19] Donald E. Knuth, "Top-down syntax analysis," *Acta Informatica* **1** (1971), 79–110. [Reprinted as Chapter 14 of the present volume.]

[20] Donald E. Knuth, "Semantics of context-free languages: Correction," *Mathematical Systems Theory* **5** (1971), 95–96. [Reprinted in Chapter 17 of the present volume.]

[21] Donald E. Knuth, "An empirical study of FORTRAN programs," *Software — Practice & Experience* **1** (1971), 105–133. [Reprinted as Chapter 24 of the present volume.]

[22] Donald E. Knuth, "Mathematical analysis of algorithms," *Information Processing 71*, Proceedings of IFIP Congress 71 (Amsterdam: North-Holland, 1972), 19–27. [Reprinted as Chapter 1 of *Selected Papers on Analysis of Algorithms*, CSLI Lecture Notes 102 (Stanford, California: Center for the Study of Language and Information, 2000), 1–18.]

[23] Donald E. Knuth, *TEX: The Program* (Reading, Massachusetts: Addison–Wesley, 1986), xv + 594 pages.

[24] P. M. Lewis II and R. E. Stearns, "Syntax-directed transduction," *Journal of the Association for Computing Machinery* **15** (1968), 465–488.

[25] John McCarthy, in "General discussion," *Communications of the ACM* **7** (1964), 134–136.

[26] Robert M. McClure, "TMG — A syntax-directed compiler," *Proceedings of the ACM National Conference* **20** (1965), 262–274.

[27] Peter Naur, editor, "Report on the algorithmic language ALGOL 60," *Communications of the ACM* **3** (1960), 299–314.

[28] Luigi Petrone, "Syntax directed mappings of context-free languages," preprint (Phoenix, Arizona: General Electric Corporation, 1965), 50+7 pages. [A short summary was published in *Information Processing 65*, Proceedings of IFIP Congress 65 (1965), 590–591. See also L. Petrone, "Linguaggi programmativi formali," *Calcolo* **2**, Supplement 2 (1965), 47–68, especially §18–20.]

[29] D. V. Schorre, "META II: A syntax-directed compiler writing language," *Proceedings of the ACM National Conference* **19** (1964), D 1.3.1–D 1.3.11.

[30] T. B. Steel, Jr. (editor), *Formal Language Description Languages for Computer Programming*, Proceedings of an IFIP Working Conference held at Vienna, Austria, 15–18 September 1964 (Amsterdam: North-Holland, 1966).

[31] T. B. Steel, Jr., "A formalization of semantics for programming language description," in [30], 25–36.

[32] Christopher Strachey, comment on paper by J. V. Garwick, "The definition of programming languages by their compilers," in [30], 139–147.

[33] A. van Wijngaarden, "Recursive definition of syntax and semantics," in [30], 13–24.

[34] Wayne Theodore Wilner, *A Declarative Semantic Definition*, report STAN-CS-71-233 (Ph.D. thesis, Stanford University, 1971).

[35] "Burroughs announces B6500," *Communications of the ACM* **9** (1966), 541.

[36] "Salton announces new departments, editors for *Communications*," and "*Journal* changes are outlined by Gotlieb," *Communications of the ACM* **9** (1966), 825.

[37] "On FJCC 66 at the Golden Gate," *Communications of the ACM* **9** (1966), 885.

[38] "ACM National Lecturers 1966–7," *Communications of the ACM* **10** (1967), 68–69.

[39] "SIAM 1967 Fall Meeting," *SIAM Review* **10** (1968), 260–280.

Chapter 20

A History of Writing Compilers

Compilers — their origin, development and operation. The author, the creator of three compilers himself, includes a useful dose of compiler writing "how-to-do-it."

[Based on a talk given at the Annual Meeting of the Association for Computing Machinery, Syracuse, New York, 4–7 September 1962. Originally published in Computers and Automation 11, 12 (December 1962), 8–18.]

In the field of programming for computers, the time seems to be ripe for a look back at the evolution of techniques used in writing algebraic compilers. People with experience writing translators should profit by some reflection on the historical trends; and people who are more accustomed to using compilers than to creating them will perhaps feel more familiar with compilers if they see how such programs evolved. This article therefore attempts to review briefly the history of techniques for writing a compiler.

A great development of compiler *languages* has, of course, taken place as well as of techniques for translating them, but we will concern ourselves primarily with the techniques.

The first compilers came into being about the same time that I myself was becoming exposed to computers. I basically learned about computing by reading a listing, written in the assembly language SOAP (Symbolic Optimum Assembly Program), of the first compiler IT (Internal Translator).[1] An enormous number of compilers have been written since then; I cannot, of course, claim to be familiar with even most of them. I am only vaguely aware of developments in the Soviet Union and in Europe. But I have examined closely the internal workings and

---

[1] *Internal Translator (IT): A Compiler for the 650*, by A. J. Perlis, J. W. Smith, and H. R. Van Zoeren (Pittsburgh, Pennsylvania: Computation Center, Carnegie Institute of Technology, 1957).

machine language code of a large number of American compilers produced by various groups all over the country, and I hope that the ones I have examined represent a good cross-section. I have also written three compilers (in the summers of 1958, 1960, and 1962); each of those three looks quite different from the other two, reflecting the changing times. This experience is the background from which the present article has been written.

A true history gives dates of events and names of people, but I will not do that. In our field there has been an unusual amount of parallel discovery of the same technique by people working independently. Perhaps you remember the time when three different people, in the same month, sent in the same idea to the *Communications of the ACM* for counting binary ones in a computer word.[2] The literature of compiling has many, many accounts of what is essentially the same thing, by people who were obviously unaware that others had made the same discovery. I read somewhere recently that the GAT compiler, written at the University of Michigan, was written using an algorithm due to the Soviet Academician A. P. Ershov, and I'll wager that this comes as quite a surprise to the people at Michigan who weren't consciously borrowing a Russian compiler method. Other references give credit to H. Kanner's algorithm, or that of A. Oettinger, or B. Arden and R. Graham, or K. Samelson and F. L. Bauer, or H. Huskey and W. H. Wattenburg, etc., etc. I know of several other people who invented the same thing and never published it. The question as to who was really the first to discover a certain technique will probably never be answered, but it is not really important.[3] In fact this latter question has very little meaning, since those named above and others discovered to a greater or less degree various aspects of a nice method, and it has been polished up through the years into a very pretty algorithm that none of the originators fully realized. So I cannot give credit to one without giving it to all; let it suffice to say merely that the compiling art has been advanced by many people with many

---

[2] Author's note, December 2002: I must have been thinking about the comments by S. S. Kutler, Howard Frieden, and P. M. Sherman in *Communications of the ACM* **3** (1960), pages 474 and 538, inspired by Peter Wegner's note on page 322. However, all four techniques were different, so my memory of the situation was incorrect.

[3] Author's note, December 2002: Ouch! I'm now dismayed by the cavalier attitude that I once had about the roles of individual contributors. Furthermore I neglected to mention that I myself was *not* one of the people who had discovered the methods described in this article.

ingenious ideas. Of course Dr. Alan Perlis and his co-workers at Purdue and Carnegie deserve credit for showing that compiling is possible in the first place.

Decomposition of Formulas

So much for introductory remarks. Try now for a moment to imagine that nobody has ever written a compiler before, but that somebody has asked you to write one. Chances are that one difficulty will overshadow all the others in your mind, namely how to translate arithmetic expressions. We all recognize algebraic formulas simply by looking at them and reading them off; but how can this be done by a machine, without asking it to be able to "think" first? Take for example $[(Y * Z) + (W * V)] - X$, where '$*$' stands for multiplication; we must systematically begin with the formula and find a way to evaluate it, taking one step at a time.

The first solution to this problem, used in the IT compiler, was based on the concept of parenthesis levels. When I learned algebra, we were taught to use parentheses first, then brackets around the parentheses, then curly braces; and if we had to go farther, we used extra large parentheses or something. I think the first time I was taught that only one kind of parenthesis is really necessary was when I learned a compiler language. (This concept was well known to logicians but I doubt if it was generally known until algebraic compiler languages became popular.)

We can draw a kind of "contour map" of an expression, going up one unit for each left parenthesis, and down one unit for each right parenthesis; the "altitude" thus achieved is the so-called parenthesis level. (See Figure 1.) In the IT compiler a maximum parenthesis level of ten was allowed, and the formulas were processed by breaking them into levels. Precedence or rank of operators was not recognized; for example, $A + B/C$ meant $A + (B/C)$ and $A/B + C$ meant $A/(B + C)$.

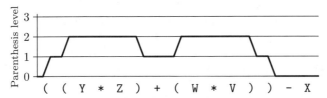

FIGURE 1. "Contour map" of the expression $((Y * Z) + (W * V)) - X$.

In order to see how a translation algorithm might be organized around the concept of parenthesis level, we can investigate the method shown in Figure 2, which shows a grossly simplified version of the IT algorithm. First we need to adopt the convention that a binary operator

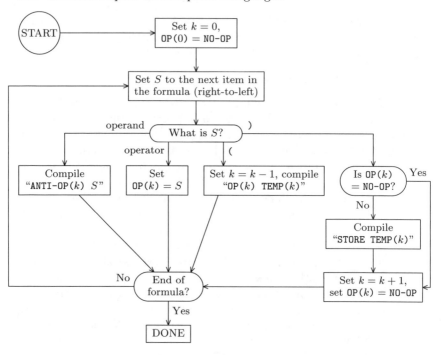

FIGURE 2. Translation based on parenthesis levels,
without considering precedence of operators.

has a corresponding so-called anti-operator such that

$$A \text{ op } B = B \text{ anti-op } A.$$

Since $A + B = B + A$, ADD is its own anti-op; and the anti-op of division
is inverse division. Remington Rand computers tend to have only the
"inverse divide" command in their machine language, and IBM computers tend to have only the "divide" command. But for simplicity we will
assume that both operations are present in our machine, and that there
is even an "inverse subtract" command. We will also think of NO-OP
("no-operation") and LOAD as anti-operators of each other; if you want
some justification for this policy you should ponder over the formulas

$$\text{LOAD}(b) = 0 + b; \qquad \text{NO-OP}(b) = b + 0.$$

With this setup, the compilation algorithm is roughly the following:

Take the next item, from right to left in the formula. Then branch four ways, depending on the type of item:

1. For an operand (a variable or constant), output the machine language code 'ANTI-OP(k) operand'. The counter k represents the parenthesis level, and it starts out at zero; there is a ten-place OP table, OP(0) through OP(9). The meaning of 'ANTI-OP(k)' is, "The anti-operator of OP(k)."

2. For an operator, save this operator in position OP(k) of the OP table.

3. For a left parenthesis, decrease k by 1, then output the machine language code 'OP(k) TEMP(k)'. Here TEMP(k) is the kth temporary storage cell.

4. For a right parenthesis, check first if OP(k) = NO-OP; if not, output the code 'STORE TEMP(k)'. Then increase k by 1, and set OP(k) equal to NO-OP for the new value of k.

Repeat these steps until the end of the formula is reached.

This whole process becomes clear when we look at a play-by-play account of the method as it acts on the formula $((Y * Z) + (W * V)) - X$; see Figure 3.

Item	OP Table			Compiled Code
	NO-OP			
X	NO-OP			LOAD X
−	−			
)	−	NO-OP		STORE TEMP(0)
)	−	NO-OP	NO-OP	
V	−	NO-OP	NO-OP	LOAD V
*	−	NO-OP	*	
W	−	NO-OP	*	MULTIPLY W
(	−	NO-OP		NO-OP TEMP(1)
+	−	+		(note: a NO-OP may be deleted from the code)
)	−	+	NO-OP	STORE TEMP(1)
Z	−	+	NO-OP	LOAD Z
*	−	+	*	
Y	−	+	*	MULTIPLY Y
(	−	+		ADD TEMP(1)
(	−			SUBTRACT TEMP(0)

FIGURE 3. Item by item action produced by the parenthesis-level method of Figure 2 when it is applied to the formula $((Y * Z) + (W * V)) - X$. Notice how the OP-table, if tipped on its side and reflected, corresponds to the contour map in Figure 1.

Interested readers will learn a lot if they try to revise the method so that it works from left to right rather than from right to left. The right-to-left approach has been considered here because compilation was done that way in IT; but an equally simple algorithm can be worked out for the left-to-right direction, and the necessary changes turn out to be quite instructive.

The IT compiler actually treated the formula $A - B + C - D/E$ as if it were $A + (-B) + C + (-D)/E$; our simplified algorithm treats it as $A - (B + (C - D/E))$, which is rather different. Moreover, the basic concept represented in Figure 2 needs to be extended in order to handle negation, subscripting, function calls, constants, mixed floating- and fixed-point arithmetic, and so on.

Operator Precedence

The lack of operator priority (often called precedence or hierarchy) in the IT language was the most frequent single cause of errors by the users of that compiler. So people hunted for ways to supply the hierarchy automatically. The IT parenthesis-level scheme didn't lend itself to precedence very readily. An ingenious idea used in the first FOR-TRAN compiler was to surround binary operators with peculiar-looking parentheses:

> + and − were replaced by)))+(((and)))−(((
> * and / were replaced by))*((and))/((
> ** was replaced by)**(

and then an extra (((was tacked on at the left, and))) at the right. The resulting formula is properly parenthesized, believe it or not: For example, if we consider (X+Y)+W/Z, we get

$$((((X)))+(((Y))))+(((W))/((Z))).$$

The expanded version is, admittedly, highly redundant, and hard for human beings to read; but extra parentheses don't confuse a computer, and they need not affect the resulting machine language code. A parenthesis-level method can be applied to the formulas that result after such replacements have been made.

A close examination of this process showed later that we really don't need to insert the artificial parentheses; the same effect can be achieved by merely comparing *adjacent* operators, and doing first the operation with higher priority. This observation led to another approach to the translation problem, namely to start moving along the statement until finding something that can be done, then going back and doing it, going forward to get more, and so on. In other words we essentially look for an inner pair of parentheses and work outward, instead of using the "outside-in" approach of parenthesis levels mentioned earlier.

The new idea had the advantage that it could easily be adapted to handle operator hierarchies; hence it led directly to the efficient scheme that is often used nowadays (in many equivalent guises).

The modern technique was discovered in several ways. Another way to run across it is to write a program that translates from arithmetic statements to expressions in "Polish notation" — a parenthesis-free way to represent formulas — and then to write a second program that translates from Polish notation to machine language. Each program is rather trivial in itself, and the combination of the two programs gives the same algorithm that was discovered in other ways.

Shortly I will discuss the details of the new algorithm, but first I want to list the main "bright ideas" that went into its discovery:

(1) The first bright idea was the realization that the information needed when translating can conveniently be kept in a *stack* (which is also known as a *nest* or *push-down* or *cellar* or *yo-yo list* or *last-in-first-out* or *first-in-last-out list*, etc.; the number of different names indicates the number of different discoverers of the algorithm). A stack is distinguished from other types of tables by the fact that only the items near the "top" of the stack (namely, the youngest items, those placed on most recently) are actually important at any given time. An example of this phenomenon occurred in the parenthesis-level method, where the OP table was really a stack. With the new method, the height of the stack takes the place of the former parenthesis level.

(2) The second bright idea was that comparison of adjacent operator priorities provides a valuable criterion, and that no further information is needed to interpret a formula properly.

(3) The third bright idea was that parentheses themselves can be treated as operators with priorities, giving a more elegant algorithm.

Now we will study the new algorithm, which is shown in Figure 4. We start by assigning priority numbers to symbols, according to Table 1. Here ':=' stands for the replacement operation, '↑' for exponentiation, '÷' for integer division as in ALGOL, and '@' means beginning-of-formula. Functions of a single variable, like COS (cosine), are unary operators, which have priority 4 in the chart. Notice that '(' and ')' have priority 0; this convention is "bright idea number 3" mentioned above.

Priority	Symbols
0	@ ; := ( )
1	+ −
2	* / ÷
3	↑
4	ABS SQRT COS etc.

TABLE 1. The precedence of various operators.

A rough description of Figure 4 can be given as follows: We "scan" along the expression (left to right this time) until we find some operation that can be performed *regardless* of what will occur in the remainder of the expression. The actual precise conditions for this event appear in boxes 2 and 3 of the flow chart. As soon as we see something that we can definitely do regardless of future input, we do it; meanwhile we save the unused portion of the formula in STACK. The formula ends with a semicolon.

Box 1 starts out by setting the counter i equal to one, and artificially inserts the character '@' at the left of the formula to mark the boundary.

Box 2 tests the current item S; if S is a binary arithmetic operator (+, −, *, /, ÷, or ↑) or a right parenthesis or a semicolon, this may initiate some action. Otherwise S is a variable, a constant, a left parenthesis, the replacement operator :=, the symbol @, or a unary operator such as ABS or negation, in which case we merely go to Box 4 to save S on the stack for future action.

Box 3 is the all-important hierarchy test. The item next to the top of STACK is an operator (if all is working properly); and if it has higher priority in the table than S has, or if they have equal priority, the time has come to initiate compiler action. However, if S has higher priority, we must wait for future developments, so we simply go to Box 4.

Box 4 puts S on top of the STACK to save it for later action.

Box 5 steps along to the next item in the formula.

Box 6 is the entry to various generators; we now branch to the generator for the operator that is next to the top of STACK.

Box 7, the left parenthesis generator, merely removes the left parenthesis from within STACK.

Box 8 is the replacement generator; the top three items of STACK are of the form X := Z. The code for replacement is now generated, and only Z is left on the STACK.

Box 9 is the generator for a unary operator; the top two items of STACK are of the form OP X, and we compile the code for 'T(i) := OP X'. In general, T(i) represents the ith computed result.

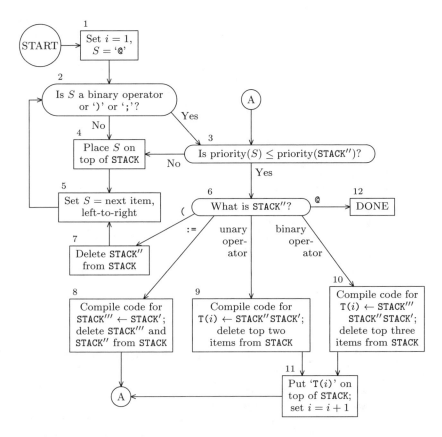

FIGURE 4. A version of the "modern" translation algorithm. The notation STACK′ denotes the top item in STACK, while STACK″ signifies the next from the top, and so on.

Box 10 is the generator for a binary operator; the top three items of STACK are of the form X OP Y, and we compile the code for 'T(i) := X OP Y'.

Box 11 places the result of the previous computation, T(i), as an operand on STACK and advances i by 1, then returns to the priority test.

Box 12 is the generator for the symbol @. We get here when the entire statement has been translated.

Notice that the algorithm given in Figure 4 handles more complex input than the one in Figure 2. The earlier flow chart applied only to formulas with binary operations and parentheses, but the new one can

FIGURE 5. Snapshots of the algorithm of Figure 4 applied to the replacement statement '$U := V := X + \cos(Y*Z)/W;$'.

Stack	S	Input	Code
@	U	:= V := X + COS (Y * Z) / W ;	
@ U	:=	V := X + COS (Y * Z) / W ;	
@ U :=	V	:= X + COS (Y * Z) / W ;	
@ U := V	:=	X + COS (Y * Z) / W ;	
@ U := V :=	X	+ COS (Y * Z) / W ;	
@ U := V := X	+	COS (Y * Z) / W ;	
@ U := V := X +	COS	(Y * Z) / W ;	
@ U := V := X + COS	(	Y * Z) / W ;	
@ U := V := X + COS (	Y	* Z) / W ;	
@ U := V := X + COS (Y	*	Z) / W ;	
@ U := V := X + COS (Y *	Z	) / W ;	*Code*
@ U := V := X + COS (Y * Z	)	/ W ;	
@ U := V := X + COS (T_1	)	/ W ;	T(1) := Y * Z
@ U := V := X + COS T_1	/	W ;	
@ U := V := X + T_2	/	W ;	T(2) := COS(T(1))
@ U := V := X + T_2 / W	;		
@ U := V := X + T_3	;		T(3) := T(2) / W
@ U := V := T_4	;		T(4) := X + T(3)
@ U := T_4	;		V := T(4)
@ T_4	;		U := T(4)

also be used for unary operators and multiple assignment statements, and it treats operator priorities properly.

As an example of the operation of Figure 4 a snapshot description of the method applied to the statement '$U := V := X + \cos(Y * Z)/W;$' is given in Figure 5. This particular statement causes almost all of the input to be put onto the STACK, until the right parenthesis is sensed. The right parenthesis, which has priority 0, forces out the multiplication operator, then it also forces out the matching left parenthesis. Shortly afterwards, the '/' symbol causes COS to be computed. Finally the ending semicolon triggers all of the remaining operators.

Once again, it would be a worthwhile exercise for the reader to try to modify the algorithm, this time to make it go from right to left rather than from left to right. (*Hints:* The test in Box 3 should not branch to Box 6 on equality, lest $X - Y - Z$ be translated incorrectly. It will also be convenient to assign the priority '-1' to each left parenthesis!)

The Object Program Produced

Let us turn back now to our original problem; you are supposed to write a compiler, remember? Your first worry, that of how to systematically decompose formulas, has been pretty well settled by now; the next problem is to generate efficient machine language code. The vast majority of the literature on compilers deals with the analysis of algebraic expressions, and comparatively little has ever been written about generation of the object program (which is the really important part). Syntactic analysis is today the most trivial part of writing a compiler, because of all the research that has gone into recognition of formulas. But a person cannot really begin to write a good compiler until after sitting down and taking a good look at the object computer, figuring out exactly what code should be compiled from any given statement. So far we have just discussed the input to the compiler; but as everyone knows, output is the important thing.

The earliest compilers sometimes turned out shockingly poor machine code. For example, one compiler (which I will not name) would compute

$$A = B + C$$

with the sequence of instructions

```
LOAD    B
STORE   working-storage-1
LOAD    C
STORE   working-storage-2
LOAD    working-storage-1
ADD     working-storage-2
STORE   working-storage-1
LOAD    working-storage-1
STORE   A
```

plus several NO-OP instructions thrown in. This sequence computes the correct answer all right; but another compiler for the same computer later achieved a 7:1 reduction ratio in the number of instructions compiled in a typical program. Of course this is an extreme example; but notice that the IT compiler algorithm turned out the instructions LOAD X, STORE TEMP(0) in Figure 3, and those two instructions are quite unnecessary. Most of the early compilers would do this. (The first FORTRAN compiler, on the other hand, took fairly great care to produce efficient code, although the methods used were quite painful.)

One of the first attempts to eliminate extraneous instructions was to go ahead and compile them as usual, but later to recognize that they were unnecessary and at that point to "decompile" them, removing them from the code. A fairly elaborate algorithm was used, so that from

```
LOAD NEGATIVE ABSOLUTE  A
STORE                   TEMP
LOAD                    B
MULTIPLY                C
ADD                     TEMP
```

the code

```
LOAD               B
MULTIPLY           C
SUBTRACT ABSOLUTE  A
```

would be produced.

With the "modern" algorithm, however, this saving of temporary storage is accomplished so easily that it is virtually a free byproduct of the method.

It is interesting to pursue this matter further, however, and to consider the expression

$$A * B + (C * D + E * F).$$

Suppose we have a fancy machine with two accumulators; the modern algorithm, adapted in a straightforward way, would produce

```
LOAD1   A
MULT1   B
LOAD2   C
MULT2   D
STORE2  TEMP
LOAD2   E
MULT2   F
ADD2    TEMP
ADD1    ACCUMULATOR2
```

The STORE into TEMP could have been saved if $A * B$ had been computed last; in other words, we should prefer the formula

$$(C * D + E * F) + A * B.$$

Our modern algorithm is effectively able to rewrite '$A + B * C$' as '$B * C + A$' but it cannot make the switch on higher order expressions. This observation leads to a generalized modern algorithm for an n-register machine, which scans formulas until it gets to an expression that cannot be computed with fewer than n registers before it starts to produce object code. For $n = 1$ this gives the former algorithm, and for $n > 1$ it gives a small improvement in minimizing temporary storage. The generalized method requires more structure to its list than a simple push-down stack, however.

There is even a generalization to a "zero-register" machine, in which the order of calculation is immaterial. A zero-register machine would be similar to the Burroughs B5000, except that it would have only one fast register at the top of its stack. In general, a Polish-notation machine with $n + 1$ fast registers would use a temporary storage minimization algorithm equivalent to that for a conventional machine with n accumulators, for optimum efficiency.

Many refinements can easily be added to the modern algorithm to help it produce better code. For example, a sign can be attached to each operand, so that computed results can be negated and algebraic identities can be employed. Then $\cos(A - B * C)$ can be calculated by

```
LOAD          B
MULT          C
SUB           A
RETURN JUMP   COS
```

which is the equivalent of $\cos(B * C - A)$.

A similar technique, which I haven't seen published yet although it is fairly old, is to attach an absolute value tag also, so that ADD ABSOLUTE and similar instructions can be utilized on various object machines. Attaching a type indicator (fixed or floating point) to operands and computed partial results is another obvious extension.

A refinement that is only slightly more difficult would be to treat groups of statements together, so that if no labels intervene between statements the compiler can remember what the preceding statement left in the accumulator.

A whole series of interesting techniques has been designed to optimize the use of index registers in loops. Most of these require several passes over the program. I must mention briefly the question of many passes versus one pass, although it is well nigh impossible nowadays to define exactly what a "pass" is. Back in the old days the number of passes was the number of times we took the cards out of the punch hopper, put them in the reader, and perhaps changed plugboards. But now there are so-called one-pass compilers for sequential machines. How many passes is a load-and-go compiler?[4] Probably zero passes, since it takes one less than one pass.

Ignoring the difficulty of defining a pass, however, we can find many arguments pro and con about relative merits. The one-pass compiler is considerably faster, because multipass schemes spend a good deal of time physically generating an intermediate language and later translating it back again. On the other hand, many things cannot be done well in one pass, such as checking for common subexpressions and optimizing loops. Many programmers, however, are not concerned with such refinements; if they want a really good object program they let an expert programmer write it in machine language. I can't settle the argument, but I do think it is a valid point that there should not be n passes if the object programs produced are not noticeably better than could be done in $n - 1$ passes.

Organization of the Compiler

I have tried to point out that most compilers use essentially the same techniques in different guises for formula translation. The real place where they differ is in their organization, in the timing of the basic components and the structure of the programs. I will discuss briefly the principal types of organization.

A. Symbol Pairs. IT and RUNCIBLE and many other compilers were organized around a symbol pair concept. At the close of each operation, a "window" of two symbols L and R was moved; scanning from right to left, L became the new value of R, and the preceding character became the new L. Then the pair LR was looked up in a table, thus giving the entry to a generator program for this case. Any information that was needed for future use was stored in tables. Several push-down lists (stacks) were implicitly present, but nobody realized it at the time.

Beyond this the organization was pretty much of a hodgepodge that couldn't be broken into logical parts. These compilers grew like Topsy and were the result of several years of patching. The program was so interwoven that every time something was changed in RUNCIBLE, six other seemingly unrelated things would fail. And we had the entire compilation process in just as disorganized a fashion in our minds. We more or less knew that it was correct and why, but to explain it to anyone required at least 100 boxes on a horrible flow chart, which actually

---

[4] A *load-and-go compiler* is one in which a person enters as input some algebraic statements, and the compiler translates them into machine language and immediately transfers control to the new program. Thus with a "load and-go compiler" the first output consists of the answers.

couldn't be untangled. That was the algorithm, and it worked, and it fitted onto the IBM 650 drum, but it was a mess. For all anybody knew at that time, however, that was the only way it could be done.

B. Operator Pairs. A next step is to use operator pairs rather than symbol pairs to control the operation. The operands distribute themselves nicely between operators, so an essentially identical plan as the above can be used, except that adjacent operators are used to reference a table of generators. This approach gives some economy over the previous method, since all operands are put into a single class. Operator-pair logic has been used in the Neliac compilers, and the generator tables are called CO-NO or NO-CO tables by the authors.

C. Simple Scan. Further improvement can be gained by lumping *operators* into classes, as well as operands. Only a few classes of operators are actually necessary; with FORTRAN, for example, we would have perhaps four classes of operators:

1) Those that require immediate action when first sensed, such as READ and DO.
2) Those that are placed immediately on the stack when first sensed, such as COS, ABS, and left parenthesis.
3) Those that are not placed on the stack until their priority is more than the preceding operator; for example, binary operators.
4) Those that are never placed on the stack, but their priority is used to force out previous operators; for example, comma and semicolon.

The main control is along the lines of the modern algorithm given in Figure 4, with an input routine to condense identifiers and constants into single items. Usually, however, many stacks are used instead of one, for convenience, typically including some of the following:

1) operand stack;
2) operator stack;
3) mode stack (to specify the meaning of commas);
4) subscript stack (where computed subscripts wait their turn);
5) temp storage stack (a list of locations available for temporary storage cells in the object program);
6) DO stack (for controlling loops);

and so on.

D. Recursive Organization. Some recent compilers are written with generators that work recursively. Typically when a construct (part of a formula) is recognized as being of a certain syntactical type, its generator is brought out. Somehow the end of the construct is detected, and this causes the generator to go into action. For example, there might be a generator for variables. If the variable-handling generator happens to encounter an array variable, the expression generator will be entered for the subscript, and it may call on the variable generator, which may in turn call on the expression generator, etc. Delimiters are used to take generators out of control at the appropriate time. Examples of such compilers are the threaded-list compiler at Carnegie Tech and the B5000 ALGOL compiler at Burroughs.

E. Syntax-Directed Compilers. Another form of recursive compiler is called "syntax-directed," and it is very closely related to the former type. In theory such a compiler is completely general, since it is built to operate from an arbitrary syntax list (description of the language) and an arbitrary semantics list (description of the meaning of the language in terms of the object computer). Such compilers are still in the experimental stages, and with apologies to Ned Irons and the other researchers I must say that they appear to be primarily of theoretical interest at the present time. The syntax of a language has to be carefully rewritten in order to produce efficient object code, and the creation of semantical tables is as cumbersome a job as writing generators for ordinary compilers. Compilers organized along the lines of C or D can easily be modified for all but major language revisions; so no great advantage to syntax-directed compilers has been proved as yet.

I certainly do not want to discourage anyone from working on a syntax-directed compiler, for there is good reason to believe that significant strides forward in this direction are possible and that syntax-directed compilers will be very important in the future. On the contrary, I hope to stimulate more people towards working in this potentially fruitful area, even though it has as yet been unable to compete with handmade compilers. As we have seen, the recognition of syntax is one of the simpler facets of compiling; a good deal of research still needs to be done, in order to simplify the real problem of how to produce efficient code once the syntax has been recognized.

F. Multi-Pass Compilers. A fairly large number of compilers operate in two passes; the first pass is organized something like class C above, and it produces a pseudocode analogous to the 'T(i) := Y * Z' output of

Figure 4. The second pass uses this pseudocode to generate the object program. I would classify such compilers under category C.

Category F of compiler organization is rather for the expensive compilers that consist of *many* separate passes. Such compilers defy simple explanation, and the only way to learn to know them is to spend a good deal of time studying what each pass does and how it fits into the whole scheme. Two such compilers usually have very little in common, and all I can say is that the well-written ones of this type usually are built around some major modification of a one-pass compiler, designed to produce more efficient object programs from a more thorough analysis of the source program.

References

A complete bibliography of the compiler literature is hard to give; you may, in fact, find it quite distressing to try to read many of the articles. This will happen because so many of them are about how a particular author discovered the same thing as other authors (although it may take several hours for you separate what has been discovered from what hasn't). Therefore I will give only a short bibliography, for use by those interested in pursuing the subject further.

The complexity of early translators is indicated in two articles: (a) Donald E. Knuth, "RUNCIBLE — Algebraic translation on a limited computer," *Communications of the ACM* **2**, 11 (November 1959), 18–21. [Reprinted as Chapter 21 of the present volume.] In this article I include a flowchart of a portion of the RUNCIBLE compiler, and also make the untrue statement that such an algorithm may well be the only possible one to use on a small computer such as the IBM 650. (b) Peter Sheridan, "The arithmetic translator-compiler of the IBM FORTRAN automatic coding system," *Communications of the ACM* **2**, 2 (February 1959), 9–21. This article is rather heavy reading, but it will at least impress the reader with the complexity of the algorithm.

Neliac compilers are discussed as the principal subject of the book *Machine-Independent Computer Programming* by Maurice H. Halstead (Washington: Spartan Books, 1962). "NO-CO" is a term used by the authors of Neliac meaning "Next-Operator — Current-Operator."

Excellent introductory expositions of the modern scanning algorithm and its refinements have been written by Robert Floyd: "An algorithm for coding efficient arithmetic operations," *Communications of the ACM* **4** (1961), 42–51, and "A descriptive language for symbol manipulation," *Journal of the Association for Computing Machinery* **8** (1961), 579–584.

Finally, to study the organization of various compilers, the entire January 1961 issue of *Communications of the ACM* is recommended. Of special interest is "The internal organization of the MAD translator," by B. W. Arden, B. A. Galler, and R. M. Graham, on pages 28–31. This is one of the few articles in the literature where general methods for producing the object program are discussed without requiring a separate generator to be written for each special case.

Addendum

When I wrote this article in 1962, I fully believed that working algebraic compilers had not existed until about 1957. But I soon learned that about a dozen compilers or near-compilers had actually been developed before 1954, during an era when few programmers had worried about programming time versus machine time, and before appropriate journals were available to publish the results. Therefore the earliest compilers were all but forgotten by the time my article was written. I eventually gave a series of lectures in order to atone for my earlier ignorance [see *Communications of the ACM* **10** (1967), 68], and went on to "compile" what I believe is a proper history of the subject [see Chapter 1].

Chapter 21

RUNCIBLE — Algebraic Translation on a Limited Computer

[Originally published in Communications of the ACM **2**, *11 (November 1959), 18–21.]*

Introduction

The RUNCIBLE I compiler was developed in 1958 at Case Institute of Technology for a standard 650 computer requiring only an alphabetic device as extra hardware. The main features of this compiler are:

a) Choice of either direct machine instruction output or an optional intervening phase that uses the SOAP assembler. The intermediate phase facilitates alterations to the finished program. Another version of RUNCIBLE ("Runcible Zero"), also operating from a minimum 650, punches the answers immediately from the statements, eliminating all extra passes.

b) Extended IT language. There is no need for users of the original IT compiler to learn another statement form, but additional features allowing more flexible operation and increased use of English words are available in addition.

c) Clocking. At the election of the user, a record of which statement is presently under execution is kept at running time. If the machine stops for some reason, the operator can thus pinpoint where the error occurred. Various forms of tracing may be used as a further aid.

d) Choice of output language. Compiled instructions are normally for a basic machine, but they will utilize core storage and/or floating point instructions and index registers at the user's option.

e) All the features of IT: iteration statements, mixed floating- and fixed-point arithmetic, and matrix notation.

f) Additional matrix variables. Ten matrices are available in addition to the two found in IT.

g) Statistical extensions. A large library of statistical routines has been developed for general use with the Runcible System.

457

Transforming the Statements

In order to produce an efficient output program, the translation techniques used in RUNCIBLE are highly machine-oriented. In a computer with only a limited amount of storage space, the method outlined here may be the only feasible way to fit an efficient compiler into the machine.

The translation approach is quite different from the methods that are most commonly discussed nowadays, but it is presented as a procedure that has proved its usefulness for an intermediate-size computer.*

RUNCIBLE's replacement or substitution statement decomposition procedure is given in Figure 1. The statement is considered to be a string of symbols s_1, s_2, ..., s_m. Blanks do not appear in this string. The program starts at the right-hand symbol s_m and works toward the left; every symbol is "scanned" once and only once. For simplicity, we will consider integers (like 719) and floating-point numbers (like 3.1416) to be condensed into a single symbol of the string, designated generally by n.

The flowchart of Figure 1 does not include the processing of special extensions, matrix notation, or relations. It does, however, handle mixed arithmetic, parenthesis nesting, variable subscripting, the binary operations of addition, subtraction, multiplication, division, substitution, and exponentiation, and the unary operations of absolute value and negation.

The following statement has been chosen to illustrate compilation:

$$C((I1*I4)+I3)\leftarrow((C1+Y1)*Y2)+2.768+((I2-I5)*-I6)/C2$$

This statement is essentially the same as the example that appears in the July *Communications* [1], where it is translated by the GAT compiler. A minus sign has been added before the variable I6 to illustrate a unary operation. This particular statement was chosen since a comparison of the output between the two compilers will be the most instructive.

The output of Figure 1 is the type that utilizes the 650's floating point attachment. RUNCIBLE would make a few changes if only the standard machine instructions were desired.

In RUNCIBLE language, as in IT, all variables belong to one of three arrays, I, Y, or C; I-variables are fixed-point integers, while Y- and C-variables have floating-point values. Floating-point operations are done in the upper accumulator of the 650, while fixed-point calculations are made in the lower accumulator because of the absolute-value commands.

---

*Note added December 2002: The IBM 650 had a total memory capacity of just 2000 words, where each word consisted of a signed 10-digit decimal number. Yet in 1959 we considered it "intermediate" in size, not "small."

The statement is scanned in one pass, and instructions are compiled directly as the symbols are met. There is no intermediate language, although of course the compiled instructions are stored in coded form as ten-digit numbers. Numbering of the operation codes is changed from 650 machine language into a more natural order under the following equivalence:

RAL ↔ 0	ALO ↔ 10	STL ↔ 20
RSL ↔ 1	SLO ↔ 11	MPY ↔ 21
RAU ↔ 2	FAD ↔ 12	STU ↔ 22
RSU ↔ 3	FSB ↔ 13	FMP ↔ 23
RAM ↔ 4	AML ↔ 14	DVR ↔ 24
RSM ↔ 5	SML ↔ 15	FDV ↔ 26
LDD ↔ 8	FAM ↔ 16	STD ↔ 28
RAA ↔ 9	FSM ↔ 17	

These numbers are used interchangeably with the alphabetic codes in the flowchart.

Outline of Decomposition Procedure

A given statement symbol s_i falls into one of five categories, and the routine branches immediately into one of five directions. There are two major sections:

1) If s_i is a number or a right parenthesis, it is the beginning of a new operand; at this point the previous operand, if any, is stored, and it is tested to see whether or not it is simple.

2) If s_i is an operator or a left parenthesis, any outstanding binary operations are completed.

Since the translation proceeds in one pass, and does not know whether or not the symbols it is to meet will be difficult to compile, RUNCIBLE always prepares for the worst. A subsequent complication is thus no longer troublesome; and if the succeeding symbols call for a simple case, the unnecessary instructions are *decompiled*, and they do not clutter up the final output. For example, fixed-point numbers are automatically floated, because they might be used together with a floating-point operation. If no floating-point operation appears, the instruction that floated the original number is erased.

Play-by-Play Account

The reader may now follow the flowchart by hand as we list, for each symbol s_i, all of the changes that appear in the set $\{I_1, I_2, I_3, \ldots\}$ of compiled instructions as RUNCIBLE processes the example statement $s_1 s_2 \ldots s_m$ from right to left.

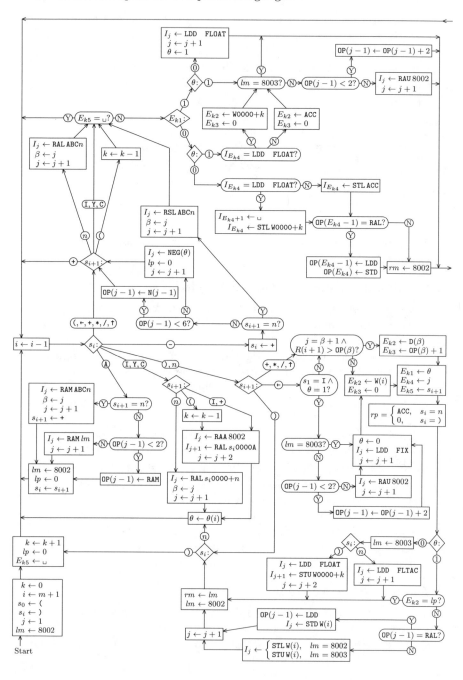

Start

$rp \leftarrow 0$
$lm \leftarrow 8002 + \theta$
$\beta \leftarrow 0$

$I_j \leftarrow (\text{TMP})\, E_{k2}$
$j \leftarrow j + 1$

$I_{E_{k4}} \leftarrow \sqcup$
$I_{E_{k4}-1} \leftarrow \sqcup$

$OP(j-2) \leftarrow OP(j-2) + 2$

$I_j \leftarrow I_{j-1}$
$I_{j-1} \leftarrow RAU\,8002$
$j \leftarrow j + 1$

$E_{k3} = 0?$ $OP(j-1) \leftarrow N(j-1)$ $I_j \leftarrow NEG(\theta)$
$j \leftarrow j + 1$

$OP(j-2) < 2?$

$TMP \leftarrow DVR + 2\theta$ $E_{k3} = 2?$ Y $OP(j-1) < 6?$

$OP(\beta - 1) \leftarrow N(\beta - 1)$ $rm = 8003?$ Y

$TMP \leftarrow MPY + 2\theta$ $OP(j-1) \leftarrow OP(j-1) + 2$

$I_\beta \leftarrow I_\beta$
$I_\beta \leftarrow NEG(\theta)$
$j \leftarrow j + 1$

$I_j \leftarrow RAU\,8002$
$j \leftarrow j + 1$

$OP(\beta - 1) < 6?$

$\theta: 0$ $OP(j-1) < 2?$

$I_{\beta-1} \leftarrow L(\beta - 2)$
$I_{\beta-2} \leftarrow \sqcup$ TMP odd?

$j = \beta + 1 \wedge$
$OP(\beta) < 4?$ $TMP \leftarrow OP(\beta)$
$OP(\beta) \leftarrow MPY + 2\theta$ $OP(\beta - 1) < 10?$

$lp \leftarrow 0$ E_{k5} $+$ $j = \beta + 1?$ $OP(\beta) \leftarrow OP(\beta) + ALO$ $OP(\beta - 1) < 10?$ $\theta: 0$

$j = \beta + 1?$ $E_{k3} = 0?$ $I_{E_{k4}} \leftarrow \sqcup$
$I_{E_{k4}-1} \leftarrow \sqcup$
$E_{k3} \leftarrow E_{k3} - 1$ $I_{\beta-1} \leftarrow L(\beta - 2)$
$I_{\beta-2} \leftarrow \sqcup$

$I_j \leftarrow STD\,D(j-1)$ $OP(\beta - 1) < 10?$ $I_j \leftarrow (ALO + 2\theta + E_{k3})\, E_{k2}$
$j \leftarrow j + 1$

$E_{k3} = 0?$ $I_{\beta-1} \leftarrow L(\beta - 2)$
$I_{\beta-2} \leftarrow \sqcup$ $\theta: 1$ $I_j \leftarrow LDD \quad PFLOT$
$lp \leftarrow ACC$

$I_{E_{k4}} \leftarrow \sqcup$
$I_{E_{k4}-1} \leftarrow \sqcup$ $OP(\beta - 1) = RAL?$ $I_j \leftarrow LDD \quad PFIX$ $I_{j+2} \leftarrow I_j$
$j \leftarrow j + 1$ $rp = ACC?$

$I_{j-1} \leftarrow LDD\, E_{k2}$
$j \leftarrow j + 1$ $OP(\beta) \leftarrow \begin{cases} STL, & rm = 8002 \\ STU, & rm = 8003 \end{cases}$ $OP(\beta - 1) \leftarrow LDD$
$OP(\beta) \leftarrow STD$ $E_{k3} = 0?$

$I_{E_{k4}} \leftarrow \sqcup$
$I_{E_{k4}-1} \leftarrow \sqcup$ $I_{j-1} \leftarrow LDD\, E_{k2}$
$I_j \leftarrow STD\, ACC$
$j \leftarrow j + 2$

Punch out I_1 through I_{j-1}

Stop

FIGURE 1. Compilation by RUNCIBLE. In this diagram, I_j refers to the jth instruction compiled; $OP(j)$ means the operation code of instruction I_j, and $D(j)$ stands for the DATA address. Several functions have been defined to simplify the notation:

$$R(i) = (1, 1, 4, 4, 6), \quad \text{if } s_i = (\leftarrow, \uparrow, *, /, +), \text{ respectively};$$

$$L(j) = RAL\, D(j), \quad \text{if } OP(j) = LDD \text{ and } D(j) \neq \text{ ' ', } \quad \text{otherwise } L(j) = I_j;$$

$$\theta(i) = \begin{cases} 0, & \text{if } s_i = I \text{ or fixed-point } n; \\ 1, & \text{if } s_i = Y,\ C, \text{ or floating-point } n; \end{cases} \qquad W(i) = \begin{cases} W0000 + k, & \text{if } s_i = \text{)}; \\ ACC, & \text{if } s_i = n; \end{cases}$$

$$N(j) = \begin{cases} OP(j) + 1, & \text{if } OP(j) \text{ is even}; \\ OP(j) - 1, & \text{if } OP(j) \text{ is odd}; \end{cases} \qquad NEG(\theta) = \begin{cases} RSL\, 8002, & \text{if } \theta = 0; \\ RSU\, 8003, & \text{if } \theta = 1. \end{cases}$$

The E-matrix is a 10×5 array used for temporary storage of right-hand operands before they have been operated upon: E_{k1} is the type, E_{k2} is a memory address, E_{k3} is nonzero if simplification may be possible, E_{k4} is a location in the compiled program, and E_{k5} is the binary operator. Integer variable k is the number of parentheses that enclose the symbol presently being interrogated, and θ indicates the type of arithmetic (fixed-point or floating-point).

The following output is produced, symbol by symbol s_i:

2 No change. [The program actually sets $k \leftarrow 0$ and initializes a few other variables; then after it sees $s_m = n$ and $s_{m+1} =)$, it sets $\theta \leftarrow 0$, indicating a fixed-point constant. But only changes to the compiled instructions I_j will be mentioned in this abbreviated commentary.]*

C The instruction 1: RAL C0002 is compiled; that is, instruction I_1 is set to RAL C0002. [This instruction, "Reset and add to lower," sets the machine's accumulator to the contents of memory location C0002, which holds the value of variable C_2 in the user's program.]

/ No change.

) Instruction 1 becomes LDD C0002. Then another instruction, 2: STD W0001, is compiled. [The combined effect of LDD C0002 and STD W0001 is to set the "distributor" register to C_2 and to store that value in the working-storage location W0001, without changing the accumulator.] Note: These instructions will both be dropped later when they are found to be unnecessary.

6 No change.

I Instruction 3: RAL I0006 is compiled.

– Instruction 3 becomes RSL I0006. [It sets the accumulator to the *negative* of the value in I0006.]

* No change.

) The fixed-point number [in the lower half of the accumulator] is floated by compiling 4: LDD FLOAT [linking to a subroutine] and 5: STU W0002 [storing the upper half of the accumulator in location W0002].

---

* Note added December 2002: Comments in brackets have been added for the benefit of modern readers. They were unnecessary in 1959, when almost all subscribers to *Communications of the ACM* were familiar with 650 machine language; at that time the IBM 650 was by far the world's most widely used computer. See *Annals of the History of Computing* **8** (1986), 3–88.

5 No change.

I Instruction 6: RAL I0005 is compiled.

- Instruction 6 becomes RSL I0005.

2 The number is floated with 7: LDD   FLTAC. Here FLTAC is the entrance to a subroutine that changes a fixed-point number into floating-point form, placing the answer in the upper accumulator and also into the storage location ACC.

I Instruction 8: RAL I0002 is compiled.

(All of a sudden things start to happen. First, instruction 7 is changed to STL ACC ["Store the lower half of the accumulator in location ACC"]. Instruction 8 becomes ALO I0002 ["Add the value in I0002 to the accumulator"]. Finally instruction 7 is changed to RSL I0005 and instruction 6 is erased.

(Instruction 5 is wiped out and instruction 4 becomes STL W0002. Then 9: RAU 8002 ["Set the upper accumulator to the contents of the lower accumulator (8002), and clear the lower accumulator"] is compiled, and changed to RSU 8002 [thus changing the sign]. Instructions 3 and 4 are blanked out and instruction 10 becomes MPY I0006 ["Multiply the upper accumulator by the value in I0006, obtaining a 20-digit product in the accumulator"]. Notice that the minus sign before I6 was transferred to the other side of the multiplication operation; similarly, the combination '-Y1/-Y2' would have been compiled exactly as if it were written 'Y1/Y2'.

+ First 11: LDD   FLOAT is compiled; then instructions 1 and 2 are erased and 12: FDV C0002 ["Floating-divide the upper accumulator by C_2"] is appended.

2.768 Now comes 13: STU ACC.

+ The instruction 14: RAL ABC00 is compiled; ABC00 is the address of the constant 2.768. Then it is changed to RAU ABC00, and finally to FAD ABC00 [floating-add]. Instruction 13 becomes FDV C0002 and instruction 12 is erased.

) Instruction 15: STU W0001 saves the current result.

2 No change.

Y Instruction 16: RAL Y0002 brings Y_2 into play.

* No change.

) 16 becomes LDD Y0002; then 17: STD W0002.

1 No change.

Y 18: RAL Y0001.

+ No change.

1 18: LDD Y0001;   19: STD ACC.

C 20: RAL C0001.

(20: RAU C0001, becomes FAD C0001. Then 19: RAL Y0001 is compiled, 18 is erased, and 19 becomes RAU Y0001.

(16 and 17 are erased, then 21: FMP Y0002 is compiled.

← 22: FAD W0001.

) 23: STU W0001.

3 No change.

I 24: RAL I0003.

+ No change.

) 25: LDD   FLOAT; 26: STU W0002.

4 No change.

I 27: RAL I0004.

* No change.

1 28: LDD   FLTAC.

I 29: RAL I0001.

(28: STL ACC; 27: LDD I0004, 28: STD ACC; 29: MPY I0001; 28: RAL I0004, then RAU I0004; 27 erased.

(26 erased, 24: LDD I0003, 25: STD W0002. Then 24 and 25 erased, 30: ALO I0003.

C 31: RAA 8002 ["Set index register A to the least significant digits of the accumulator"]; 32: RAL C0000A ["Set the accumulator to the contents of location C0000 + A"].

(32: RAU C0000A, then 33: STD C0000A; 32: LDD W0001. Compilation ends.

Finished Product

The final sequence of machine instructions now appears as follows:

1	RSL	I0005		[accum ← $-I_5$]
	ALO	I0002		[accum ← accum + I_2]
	RSU	8002		[upper ← $-$accum]
	MPY	I0006		[accum ← upper × I_6]
	LDD		FLOAT	[upper ← float(accum)]
	FDV	C0002		[upper ← upper/C_2]
	FAD	ABC00		[upper ← upper + 2.768]
	STU	W0001		[W_1 ← upper]

```
        RAU  Y0001           [upper ← Y₁]
        FAD  C0001           [upper ← upper + C₁]
        FMP  Y0002           [upper ← upper × Y₂]
        FAD  W0001           [upper ← upper + W₁]
        STU  W0001           [W₁ ← upper]
        RAU  I0004           [upper ← I₄]
        MPY  I0001           [accum ← upper × I₁]
        ALO  I0003           [accum ← accum + I₃]
        RAA  8002            [A ← accum]
        LDD  W0001           [distributor ← W₁]
        STD  C0000A    1F    [Cₐ ← distributor]
```

Observe that even though the given statement was a bit more complicated than the example from [1], the finished instruction sequence is two lines shorter than the output quoted there. Thus the translation scheme is entirely adequate to produce output that not only works correctly, but works rapidly.

The flowchart of Figure 1 has been coded into RUNCIBLE language and successfully tested by the author. Nearly 250 statements were required, but the finished program fit comfortably into the machine memory. The compiler thus derived is called DRUNCIBLE, and it will be used to illustrate the internal workings of RUNCIBLE to various computer programming classes.

As a final note, the FLOAT conversion subroutine called for in the preceding sequence is worth recording since it uses the floating-point-multiply operation in an unusual fashion. Input is any ten-digit integer, positive or negative, in the lower accumulator; output is the same number properly rounded into floating-point form in the upper accumulator.

```
FLOAT  STD  EXIT            [save subroutine link]
       NZU  OVFLO           [overflow error if |accum| ≥ 10¹⁰]
       RAB  0196    2F      [B ← 196]
  2    SLT  0002            [accum ← 100 × accum]
       NZU          2F      [forward to 2 if |accum| < 10¹⁰]
  3    AXB  0001            [B ← B + 1]
       SRT  0001            [accum ← accum ÷ 10]
       NZU  3B              [back to 3 if |accum| ≥ 10¹⁰]
       SRD  0002    2B      [accum ← round(accum/100); back to 2]
  2    RAU  8002            [upper ← float(accum × 10⁻⁵⁸)]
       FMP  8006            [upper ← upper × 10^(B−158)]
       FMP          EXIT    [upper ← upper × 10²⁰]
       10   0000    0071    [10²⁰]
```

The instruction 'FMP 8006' works because $196 \leq B \leq 199$.

References

[1] B. Arden and R. Graham, "On GAT and the construction of translators," *Communications of the ACM* **2**, 7 (1959), 24–26.

[2] Computing Center Staff, *RUNCIBLE I*, Computing Center Report, Series 5, Volume 1 (Cleveland, Ohio: Case Institute of Technology, 1959), 67 pages.

Postscript (December 2002)

This article was my first publication about computer science, written during the summer of 1959 as I was about to begin my fourth year of college study. I wrote it on behalf of my coworkers at Case Computing Center, where the enlightened policies of Fred Way had created an environment in which several undergraduates like myself were allowed (and even encouraged) to write software for use by the entire Case Tech community.

Although I was familiar with national magazines like *TIME* and *LIFE*, I had no prior experience reading technical journals, and in my naïveté I blithely assumed that my name as author meant only that I was acting as a technical writer/reporter, not that I was implicitly claiming to have invented any technical ideas. Therefore I was extremely surprised and embarrassed to learn a few months later that people were giving me credit for the algorithm in Figure 1, while in fact the ideas presented there were almost entirely due to Bill Lynch (who had just begun graduate school at the University of Wisconsin). Indeed, the opening pages of [2] state clearly that

> "RUNCIBLE I is a project of such a magnitude that it is impossible to acknowledge everyone who has contributed to the effort. As with Compiler II, the entire blame for the whole operation belongs with Mr. Frederick Way III, Assistant Director of the Computing Center, who with George Haynam made the major decisions on the philosophy to be carried out. Bill Lynch did the greater part of the work of converting the compiler to floating point instructions and expanding the language ... and almost every other member of the staff at the computing center has had his hand in at one time or another. Donald Knuth, author of this manual, added the one-pass feature ..."

My contribution in writing the article for ACM was merely to explain the relevant details of the compiler program, by recasting the method in the form of a flowchart — which at the time was the only acceptable way to present an algorithm. I sketched the flowchart on a blackboard at the lab, and my classmate Carl Opaskar (whose initials 'C. O.' can be seen on the drawing in the original publication) valiantly drafted the illustration that was submitted to ACM's editorial board.

Figure 1 is probably the most complex flowchart ever published — and thank goodness for that! Programmers gradually came to realize that documentation in the form of a flowchart does not scale up well to algorithms of greater complexity. For example, Christopher Strachey made the following remarks in 1967:

> "It is important to realise that diagrams are not suitable for conveying complicated information. They are only suitable for conveying very simple information and we use block diagrams, flow diagrams and so on in order to simplify what we are doing. We do not try to put an entire problem on to one diagram. You cannot see it all at the one time. I think there is a very important way in which we think about complicated things and that is the hierarchical way. If we have got a whole system, we like to think of the overall system to start with and then break that down into smaller sections and consider those one at a time. ...
> It is a great mistake to think that you have got to have access to everything from everything. If you do this you immediately get into a very complicated state and you cannot structure the problem in the way which is necessary to help human thought."

[*Simulation Programming Languages*, edited by J. N. Buxton (Amsterdam: North-Holland, 1968), page 52.]

Nowadays we can point to Figure 1 as an excellent example of how *not* to do things, a specimen of so-called "spaghetti" that is prone to error. But in the 1950s we had no idea that programs might be proved correct; such a concept never entered our heads. We simply followed the conventional wisdom of the time, which was to keep debugging our code until we were no longer able to make it fail.

Shortly after publication of the original article, I noticed a few small errors in the original Figure 1, not present in "DRUNCIBLE," and I noted them on the reprints that were mailed to interested readers. But when I recently redrew the illustration using METAPOST, in order to prepare this chapter for publication, I discovered a few further mistakes, which may or may not have been present in the production version of the RUNCIBLE compiler. I have decided to correct all of the known errors, so that Figure 1 as it now stands represents a correct way to compile reasonably efficient "peephole optimized" code for the IBM 650, as claimed in my article.

But I still haven't constructed a formal proof of correctness. The task of finding such a proof should be quite interesting and instructive, and I hope some reader will rise to the occasion some day. In order to make this task more precise, let me present here a rigorous definition of the RUNCIBLE input language that Figure 1 is supposed to decipher correctly in all cases, using an attribute grammar to specify the semantics:

$$
\begin{aligned}
&S \rightarrow V \leftarrow E && \text{meaning}(S) = \text{set the value of var}(V) \text{ to } v(E) \\
&V \rightarrow \mathtt{I}\, P && \text{var}(V) = I_{v(P)};\ v(P) \text{ must be fixed point} \\
&V \rightarrow \mathtt{Y}\, P && \text{var}(V) = Y_{v(P)};\ v(P) \text{ must be fixed point} \\
&V \rightarrow \mathtt{C}\, P && \text{var}(V) = C_{v(P)};\ v(P) \text{ must be fixed point} \\
&P \rightarrow V && v(P) = \text{value of var}(V) \\
&P \rightarrow n && v(P) = \text{value of the constant } n \\
&P_1 \rightarrow \mathtt{+}\, P_2 && v(P_1) = v(P_2) \\
&P_1 \rightarrow \mathtt{-}\, P_2 && v(P_1) = -v(P_2) \\
&P_1 \rightarrow \mathtt{A}\, P_2 && v(P_1) = |v(P_2)| \\
&P \rightarrow \mathtt{(}\,E\,\mathtt{)} && v(P) = v(E) \\
&E \rightarrow P && v(E) = v(P),\ v'(E) = -v(P) \\
&E_1 \rightarrow P\, \mathtt{+}\, E_2 && v(E_1) = v(P) + v(E_2),\ v'(E_1) = -v(P) + v(E_2) \\
&E_1 \rightarrow P\, \mathtt{-}\, E_2 && v(E_1) = v(P) + v'(E_2),\ v'(E_1) = -v(P) + v'(E_2) \\
&E_1 \rightarrow P\, \mathtt{*}\, E_2 && v(E_1) = v(P) \times v(E_2),\ v'(E_1) = -v(P) \times v(E_2) \\
&E_1 \rightarrow P\, \mathtt{/}\, E_2 && v(E_1) = v(P)/v(E_2),\ v'(E_1) = -v(P)/v(E_2) \\
&E_1 \rightarrow P\, \mathtt{\uparrow}\, E_2 && v(E_1) = v(P)^{v(E_2)},\ v'(E_1) = (-v(P))^{v(E_2)}
\end{aligned}
$$

Notice that, as in IT, binary operators have no precedence and are right-associative, but negation and subtraction are somewhat tricky:

        1*2+3 means the same as 1*(2+3);

        1-2+3 means the same as 1+(-2+3);

        1/2/3 means the same as 1/(2/3);

        1-2↑3 means the same as 1+(-2)↑3.

This semantic definition glosses over the details of fixed-point versus floating-point arithmetic. Constants n may be either fixed or floating. The I variables are fixed, while Y and C variables are floating. If one operand of a binary operator is fixed and the other is not, the fixed operand is first floated and the result is floating.

Readers who study Figure 1 carefully will discover that the elaborate mechanism controlled by the variable called lp has very little effect on the output. Indeed, the test '$E_{k2} = lp$?' will succeed only in unusual cases that involve floating-point exponentiation, when we can have $E_{k2} = lp = $ ACC. The reason is that the runtime subroutine PFLOT, which computes x^y when x is given in the upper half of the accumulator and y is given in memory location ACC, returns its answer in the upper accumulator and also in ACC. No other subroutine that appears in Figure 1 affects ACC, except FLTAC. But in the version of RUNCIBLE that did *not* use the floating-point hardware, the basic arithmetic operations of floating addition, multiplication, and division all were done by subroutines that used ACC heavily, and RUNCIBLE's lp logic was quite important in those cases.

The almost incredible hack in the FLOAT subroutine at the end of the article was probably invented either by George Haynam or by George Petznick, Jr.

Chapter 22

Computer-Drawn Flowcharts

[Originally published in Communications of the ACM 6 (1963), 555–563.]

To meet the need for improved documentation of written computer programs, this paper describes a simple system for effective communication that has shown great promise. The programmer describes a program in a simple format, and the computer prepares flow charts and other cross-referenced listings from this input. The description can be kept up-to-date easily, and the final output clearly explains the original program. The system has also proved to be a valuable debugging and coding aid.

Introduction

Perhaps the greatest problem in computing today, although little has been written about it, is the need for better documentation of programs. This problem arises in many ways, but basically it boils down to the question: "How can a computer programmer write down an algorithm so that somebody else will readily be able to understand it?"

This problem arises at any computer center where the standard programs have to be documented for future reference. It is especially acute when a computer users' group or computer manufacturer distributes programs among installations. It is also important for intercommunication among several programmers working on the same project. Every group of programmers has of course been faced with this problem and has developed some policy designed to circumvent the difficulties. In most cases, each programmer of the group is expected to follow a set of standard rules for documenting all programs; these rules commonly involve preparation of flow charts. Such a system usually works fairly well (at least as far as the manager of the group is concerned!), but people are beginning to realize more and more that there are shortcomings in the traditional flow chart methodology:

471

1. *Obsolescence.* Although a typical flow chart might have described the corresponding computer program at one time, a common comment is, "Any resemblance between our flow charts and the present program is purely coincidental." Another frequent remark: "Some day we will update the flow charts." It is expensive to maintain flow charts, yet every change to a program makes the charts obsolete. In fact, busy programmers often retain only the flow chart they used for coding, without incorporating any of the changes that occurred during the debugging stages.

2. *Lack of readability.* After looking at dozens of sets of flow charts for system programs, I find that I have been able to understand only about 25 percent of them. Apparently brevity is a virtue, and everybody tends to make up their own cryptic notations for writing down the information. Elaborate subscripting, superscripting, and Greek letter conventions are created, which are usually quite useless to anyone but the author. This problem is caused largely by the form of a flow chart itself: There simply isn't room to say very much inside those boxes. Another factor is that flow charts have two purposes: A *creative* flow chart is supposed to help programmers get their thoughts in order, when initially setting up an algorithm, while an *expository* flow chart is intended to elucidate the algorithm to someone else. There is no reason that both types of flow charts should be the same. The problem is that the distinction is not clear, and creative flow charts are often passed off as being expository. One frequently hears of computer programs for which "complete flowcharts" are available; fine, you write for them and receive copies, but they tell you virtually nothing.

3. *Time consumption.* Programmers have spent many hours with template in hand, drawing beautiful charts on vellum. The fact that this process requires a good deal of time tends to provoke a hurried job and a less careful one; thus the obsolescence and lack-of-readability problems are intensified. Even when the charts are drawn by someone else, a great deal of time is required of the programmer, for preparing and proof-reading the copy.

4. *Level of detail.* A wide variation is possible in flow charts. Here, for example, is a flowchart for a compiler, where a lot of the detail has

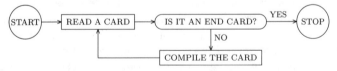

been suppressed. At the other extreme we find a flow chart with approximately as many boxes as machine-language instructions. To present an efficient exposition, several levels of detail are actually necessary; no one level is sufficient for any but the shortest programs.

Many people have felt that problem-oriented languages, such as AL-GOL, COBOL, and FORTRAN, take the place of flow charts. Although programs expressed in this way are somewhat easier to read, it is still a fact that much more information is necessary before someone other than the original programmer is able to understand the method used. For example, several hours of study are typically necessary to discover how some of the published ALGOL algorithms work (see the Algorithms department of the *Communications of the ACM*). This difficulty is not a fault of the ALGOL language; it is due to the fact that compiler languages provide too detailed a level of description for purposes of exposition.

How can we avoid such problems? A logical approach would be to *let the computer help us*. The computer can at least handle the more mechanical, clerical details; only the basic ideas should be required of the programmer.

A simple system along these lines was tried on an experimental basis during the summer of 1962. The ideas used were by no means ingenious or completely new; they were merely a combination of several notions that have already appeared in the literature. However, when the system was put into operation, it seemed to "click," and it was extraordinarily successful — much more useful than expected. Therefore the author and his colleagues feel that it may be the start of something valuable, and the ideas are being published here with the hope that they will stimulate others to try such a system and perhaps to develop it further.

Computers are, of course, widely used today for drawing charts, especially for helping to automate the design of other computers. Circuit diagrams have been prepared by machine for quite a few years [1]. Weather charts, holiday greetings, and similar items are often produced on the printers attached to computers. An application to program-flowcharts was given by Lois Haibt in 1959 [5]; this is an ambitious program that attempts to go from machine language to flow charts automatically, and it is currently in use.

Perhaps the greatest difficulty encountered, if we attempt to have a computer draw flowcharts, is the lack of a large character set. IBM distributes special print wheels designed to help print circuit diagrams (on special order), and other manufacturers may perhaps offer similar devices; but the idea here is to try to do a good job using only equipment that is already available at a typical computer center. Although a more extensive character set would be quite helpful, it has not proved to be necessary. A question mark '?' is an especially useful symbol on flow charts, but techniques to avoid using it are not hard to discover. Today's trend is towards larger and larger character sets on the new output devices, so things will be improving in this area; the system to be described will, however, work satisfactorily on systems with only upper-case letters, numeric digits, and a few special characters usually found in a FORTRAN character set. The original system runs on a UNIVAC Solid State computer, whose character set includes no equal sign, but a colon, semicolon, and apostrophe; those more exotic characters were useful but not essential.

The main part of this paper begins with a discussion of a three-level system for effective documentation, then describes a simple format for writing algorithms such that a computer can do the rest of the work. Two appendices appear at the end of the text, for those interested in pursuing the details further: Appendix 1 is a statement of the precise rules of the original flowcharting system, and Appendix 2 is an algorithm by which readers can set up their own system.

Three Levels of Documentation

Let us try to find a way to present algorithms as effectively as possible. A hint of such an approach appears in a brief article written in 1959, "Flow Outlining — A Substitute for Flow Charting" [4]. The author, W. T. Gant, says that the programmers at Shell Oil Corporation found this system "superior to flowcharting, because it is less time-consuming to prepare, easier to code from, and permits more detailed remarks where needed." A *flow outline* is simply a step-by-step, English language description of the algorithm, where every step is numbered or otherwise named.

The difference between a flow outline and a flow chart is essentially that the flow outline is one-dimensional while the flow chart is two-dimensional. But for some reason, a two-dimensional, graphical presentation greatly helps to clarify an explanation for human readers. "A picture is worth 1000 words." Therefore, although flow outlines obviously have merit, we cannot expect to do away with flow charts entirely, if we are to have the most effective communication.

An interesting method has appeared in some Russian publications (see, for example, [2, page 37]). In this case, the algorithm is explained in a written flow outline, with an accompanying flow chart. The surprising feature is that each box on the flow chart contains nothing but a single number, referring to a step of the same number in the text. No words or other symbols appear in the flow chart; the chart shows the flow, pictorially, nothing more.

Experience has shown that a modification of this method is very effective. In this version, the steps in a flow outline are not only numbered, but a short *title* is also given. This title or headline, which summarizes the basic process described in that step, should be five words or less (preferably less); its purpose is to indicate briefly what happens at this step in general terms.

A flow chart accompanies such a flow outline. On the flow chart, *only the step number and title appear*, and also the conditions for branching that distinguish between different exits of the same block. All other details are suppressed from the flow chart.

Looking at flow charts from this point of view, we see that the graphical, two-dimensional effect is being used to its full advantage; for the effectiveness of charts tends to be inversely proportional to their complexity.

In fact, the reader needs to examine the more lengthy information (given in the flow outline) only once or twice; from then on, the *title* of the step *alone* is enough to signify all the details of each step. The flow chart itself, although only the titles appear, then suffices to illustrate the meaning of the situation.

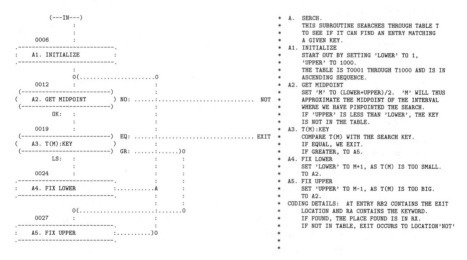

FIGURE 1. Flow chart and flow outline for binary search.

Figure 1 gives an example of such a flow outline, with an accompanying flowchart. The algorithm described is a simple "binary search" of a sorted table. Notice how each step in the flow outline has a few key words serving as the title, and this title appears on the flow chart.

Another important point to consider is the type of description that appears in the flow outline. Because the size limitation imposed by boxes is now gone, a clearer explanation of each step is possible. In the flow outline, the programmer should not specify merely *what* is done at that step; it is highly desirable to have some indication of *why* it is being done. Information relating this step to the program as a whole can be given, as well as a description of the current state of affairs and current subgoals at the time this step is reached. One should not merely say, "J is replaced by $J + 1$," for such a statement does not imply much to a reader who is not keenly aware of what J means at this point. Better, perhaps, would be something like this: "We are finished processing the Jth item of TABLE; therefore J is increased by 1, in preparation for a new item."

A great variation in detail is obviously possible here. In general it is preferable to include several related steps in a single flow-outline step. It is even valuable to include some alternative conditions in a single step, such as, "If N is even then square M, but if N is odd, subtract one from N and double M." The test whether N is even or odd need not appear in the flow chart. Such abbreviations are quite often desirable, because a two-dimensional diagram is not necessary to clarify a simple test that can be described in such plain terms. On the other hand, there are many applications in which a greater level of detail is desirable for the flowchart, and programmers are free to choose what they prefer in each case.

A third level of detail is also necessary in a well-documented program, namely the formal, precise language that was input to the computer. In the author's prototype system, an assembly language serves as this detailed description, although a compiler language or any other well-defined language would serve as well. Figure 2 shows an assembly language program corresponding to the algorithm in Figure 1. (The machine being used in this case is a UNIVAC Solid State computer.)

Notice that the same titles and step numbers appear on the assembly language listing as in the flow chart and flow diagram. Furthermore, the numbers just above each box on the flow chart represent the line number of the same step in the assembly language listing. Thus, complete cross-referencing is automatically provided.

It is unnecessary to specify all details of a program in the flow outline; only the important points need appear there. After all, the assembly listing provides the final level of detail, and the flow outline is an informal description. At the beginning of a fairly complicated program, for example, the title in a flow chart box might say, 'A1. INITIALIZE'. The flow outline might give the additional comment, "Set all pertinent

```
0000                                        FLO               A.  SERCH.
0001                              T0001      BLR   1000  1999
0002                              LOWER      EQU   B01A
0003                              UPPER      EQU   B02A
0004                              KEY        EQU   B03A
0005                                         HHH          H
0006    4006  BBB 0 60  B03A  4010  SERCH    STA   KEY       A1. INITIALIZE
0007    4010  BBB 0 25  4012  4014           LDA#  00000 10000
0008    4014  BBB 0 60  B01A  4018           STA   LOWER
0009    4018  BBB 0 37  0300  4024           SHL   0300  1F
0010    4024  BBB 0 60  B02A  4028   1       STA   UPPER
0011    4028  BBB 0 70  B01A  4033           ADD   LOWER 3F
0012    4033  BBB 0 77  4033  4036   3       ATL             A2. GET MIDPOINT
0013    4036  BBB 0 85  4038  4015           MUL#  00000 000A5
0014    4015  BBB 0 05  000A  4019           LDX   RA
0015    4019  BBB 0 30  B01A  4023           LDL   LOWER
0016    4023  BBB 0 87  4026  4226           TGR   2F
0017    4226  BBB 0 82  4026  4029           TEQ   2F    NOT
0018    4026  BBB 0 70  4228  000A   2       ADD         RA
0019    4228  BBB 0 25  0999  4001           LDA   T0000       A3. T(M):KEY
0020    4001  BBB 0 30  B03A  4005           LDL   KEY
0021    4005  BBB 1 82  0000  4009           TEQ2  0000
0022    4009  BBB 0 87  4212  4412           TGR   2F
0023    4412  BBB 0 25  000C  4016           LDA   RX
0024    4016  BBB 0 70  4218  4021           ADD#  00000 10000 A4. FIX LOWER
0025    4021  BBB 0 60  B01A  4025           STA   LOWER
0026    4025  BBB 0 70  B02A  4033           ADD   UPPER 3B
0027    4212  BBB 0 25  000C  4216   2       LDA   RX          A5. FIX UPPER
0028    4216  BBB 0 75  4418  4024           SUB         1B
0029    4418  BBB 0 00  0001  0000           CON   00000 10000
0030
0031                                         HHH
```

FIGURE 2. Assembly language corresponding to Figure 1.

temporary storage locations and counters to zero." The precise names of all those locations would appear only on the assembly listing.

The example just given should clarify the relationships between the three levels of detail discussed here. Those levels, namely

1) formal language
2) flow outline
3) flow chart

in increasing order of abstraction and generality, work together as a team to provide efficient person-to-person communication of algorithms. Experience has confirmed the practical value of this method.

Programmer's Format

The reader may very well ask how all this is going to save any time, if three levels of documentation are now required rather than the one or two now being used. In this section we describe a simple format for writing flow outlines in such a way that the computer can readily

```
            FLO                    A.    SERCH.
T0001   BLR   1000       1999            THIS SUBROUTINE SEARCHES THROUGH TABLE T
LOWER   EQU   B01A                       TO SEE IF IT CAN FIND AN ENTRY MATCHING
UPPER   EQU   B02A                       A GIVEN KEY.
KEY     EQU   B03A
        HHH         H
SERCH   STA KEY                    A1.   INITIALIZE
        LDA#00000   10000                START OUT BY SETTING 'LOWER' TO 1,
        STA LOWER                        'UPPER' TO 1000.
        SHL   0300     1F                THE TABLE IS T0001 THROUGH T1000 AND IS IN
1       STA UPPER                        ASCENDING SEQUENCE.
        ADD LOWER      3F
3       ATL                        A2.   GET MIDPOINT
        MUL#00000   000A5                SET 'M' TO (LOWER+UPPER)/2.  'M' WILL THUS
        LDX RA                           APPROXIMATE THE MIDPOINT OF THE INTERVAL
        LDL LOWER                        WHERE WE HAVE PINPOINTED THE SEARCH.
        TGR 2F                     NO: IF 'UPPER' IS LESS THAN 'LOWER', THE KEY
        TEQ 2F         NOT             IS#NOT IN THE TABLE.
2       ADD            RA          OK:
        LDA T0000                  A3.   T(M):KEY
        LDL KEY                          COMPARE T(M) WITH THE SEARCH KEY.
        TEQ2 0000                  EQ: IF EQUAL, WE#EXIT.
        TGR 2F                     GR: IF GREATER, TO#A5.
        LDA RX                     LS:
        ADD#00000   10000          A4.   FIX LOWER
        STA LOWER                        SET 'LOWER' TO M+1, AS T(M) IS TOO SMALL.
        ADD UPPER      3B                TO#A2.
2       LDA RX                     A5.   FIX UPPER
        SUB            1B                SET 'UPPER' TO M-1, AS T(M) IS TOO BIG.
        CON 00000   10000                TO#A2.
                                   CODING DETAILS:  AT ENTRY RB2 CONTAINS THE EXIT
                               X   LOCATION AND RA CONTAINS THE KEYWORD.
                               X   IF FOUND, THE PLACE FOUND IS IN RX.
        HHH                            IF NOT IN TABLE, EXIT OCCURS TO LOCATION'NOT'
NOT     HLT            *           T.    TEST.
TEST    LIR1 0000      -T          T1.   SET UP T
-T      IIR1 0001                        FILL UP TABLE T, PUTTING 2I IN T(I).
        ADD   RA
        STA1T0000
        IIR1 0000
        ADD            -T
        CON 99900   00000
&T      LDA#00010   00000          T2.   SERCH 100
        LIR2        SERCH                USE THE SEARCH ROUTINE TO SEE IF 100 IS IN.
        ADD#00000   10000          T3.   SERCH 101
        LIR2&T      SERCH                SEARCH ALSO FOR 101 WHICH IS#NOT IN THE TABLE
        END TEST
        FIN
```

FIGURE 3. Input as punched on cards.

draw the flow diagrams automatically and can also provide the cross-referencing. The net effect is to save considerable time, while greatly increasing the clarity of the final documentation.

FIGURE 4. Another flow chart produced from the input of Figure 3.

The programmer's first step is to divide the program into logical sections; each section will yield one flow chart. A typical way to make such a breakdown is to indicate one section for each subroutine, and one section for each major division of the program. An alphabetic letter is assigned to each section, for reference. (The subroutine in Figure 1 has for example been designated section A.) The steps in section A are labeled A1, A2, ..., A99.

Every section of the program is an independent unit. If the program is large enough to require more than five sections, a special "preamble section" is given, which explains the basic structure of the program, perhaps gives the format of the files and tables, and shows how data is packed into words. Then a table of contents is given, listing the key letter and the name of each section. The flow charts and flow outlines of each section follow the introductory information.

As in Figure 1, each section usually begins with a description of its general function and some of the assumptions made. At the close of each section another explanatory paragraph often appears, in order to clarify the more important coding details.

Figure 3 shows the input as it was punched on cards before feeding it into the present system. Figures 1, 2, and 4 represent part of the output resulting from this input. Only the right-hand side of the input is of concern to us here; the left-hand side is written in assembly language.

There are two fields on the documentation form. The first, consisting of four columns in this case, serves to control the operation, and it is called the "documentation key" field, or DK-field. The remaining field, 45 card columns in this particular implementation, is the "title and remarks" field. In Figure 3, the DK-field can be located as those four columns containing 'A.', 'A2.', 'OK:', etc.

The rules regarding the DK-field are rather simple:

1) At the beginning of each new section, the letter indicating that section, followed by a period, is put in the DK-field, and the remarks field contains the name of the section. (By the way, this section name will appear on all listings. It also causes page ejection on all listings, so that each new section begins at the top of a page.)

2) At the beginning of each step, the step number is given in the DK-field, in the form 'An.' or 'Ann.', where n or nn is a decimal number. Then the remarks field contains the title of that step. This title appears on all listings; in the prototype implementation a title was limited to a maximum of 20 characters, which was always found to be adequate except in a few cases where 21 characters would have been preferable.

3) The DK-field is also used to give names of conditions. Examples of this in Figure 3 are 'NO:', 'OK:', 'EQ:', 'GR:', and 'LS:'. Such conditions are transferred directly to the flowchart (see Figure 1), just as they appear in the DK-field.

The final rule for the formatting is the way in which the *successor* of each step is specified. A special character, in this case the number-sign #, is reserved for this purpose and it may not be used in any other way. This special character is punched just preceding the name of the step following the present one. An arrow leading to that step will be drawn on the flow chart. Examples of this in Figure 3 are '#EXIT' and '#A5' in step A3. Notice that the #-sign has been deleted from the actual listing of the flow outline in Figure 1. The name of a successor begins with the first character after the #-sign and continues until the first character that is not a letter or digit, up to a maximum of five characters.

If the only exit from a step is to the step following, no condition is given and no #-sign is used. (This case occurs, for example, in step A1.) If the only exit from a step is to another place, not to the step following, no condition is given and the #-sign is used to specify the succeeding step. (This case occurs, for example, in steps A4 and A5.) If a step has two or more successors, condition names are given to distinguish between branches, and a special shape of box is generated on the flow chart.

For each condition name, a successor is specified using the #-sign. If no #-sign appears for a condition, the "next step in sequence" is implied. (For example, consider step A3, where three conditions are given; 'EQ:' and 'GR:' have out-of-sequence successors specified, while 'LS:' refers to the next step. Notice the different treatment given to these condition names in Figure 1.)

If the successor name is of the form 'An' or 'Ann', where A is the key letter of the *current section*, the successor is somewhere in the same flow chart, and an internal branch line is drawn in the chart. If the successor name has any other form, it is merely placed at the right with a line leading out to it. For example, 'NOT' and 'EXIT' are such external references in Figure 1, while the references to A2 and other local steps have been drawn with internal branch connections.

To summarize this section, we have discussed two main rules:

1) The DK-field is used for (a) a key letter indicating a new section, (b) a step number, indicating the title line of a new step, or (c) a condition name.

2) Users should place a #-sign in front of the name of the successor to a step, unless the successor is simply the next step.

Conclusions

As stated earlier, the prototype system saved much more time and gave far better results than were anticipated.

One of the greatest triumphs, perhaps, was that one of the users who frankly disliked documenting programs, and who usually did so somewhat grudgingly and cryptically, confessed that it was actually fun to generate program documentation by this new method, and he turned out very readable flow charts (for perhaps the first time in his life).

We used several different approaches while trying the system. In our first experiments, programs were written and checked out first, then the documentation was written and added to the code. This mode of operation was in accord with our original intent — merely to save the labor of drawing flow diagrams and keeping them up to date.

But a surprising feature developed. Although our entire plan was oriented towards the preparation of *expository* flow charts, we found that the computer output actually served many purposes of *creative* flow charts. A large number of bugs in the programs were detected during the documentation process, thus saving check-out time on the computer. Two different methods were both found to be fruitful:

1) First prepare a (sloppy) creative flow chart, then prepare code for the program. Before debugging the program, compose a flow outline description for the final documentation, using the handwritten computer code as the source material. Then run this flow outline through the computer, and *debug the flow charts* produced by the flowcharting program. Nearly all of the mistakes in the program logic are caught in this manner, as it is immediately clear when the flow chart makes no sense. Since automatic flowcharting is designed for effective person-to-person communication, it works very well also for "person-to-self" communication.

2) Alternatively, one can develop the flow outline and debug it (using computer-drawn charts) before writing any of the code, then code from the resulting diagrams.

Clearly a combination of techniques (1) and (2) could also be used.

Thus we found that our program, which was written purely to help solve the documentation problem, gave us unexpected help in another problem area (namely rapid desk-checking of algorithms) as a free bonus.

Another advantage of the system was that it took little time to prepare. Some quantitative time considerations might be of interest in this regard: We had approximately seven person-months in which to write a FORTRAN II compiler and a complete library of arithmetic and input-output subroutines. These were to be fully documented. (Since we actually worked 12–14 hours per day, seven days a week, the time scale given here is somewhat unrealistic, and perhaps 15 months would be a truer figure for the total time in terms of an ordinary working schedule; but the actual time spent will be given here.) Absurd as it may seem, we decided to write a complete assembly program as well, and the assembly program was to include an extra pass for drawing flow diagrams. The times taken for the various stages of the project, including planning, coding and debugging, were approximately:

Card-to-tape and tape-to-tape pass for assembler	2 weeks
Basic assembly features	3 weeks
Flowcharting portion of the assembler (2 passes)	2 weeks
FORTRAN translator	8 weeks
FORTRAN loader and storage allocator	4 weeks
FORTRAN library subroutines	7 weeks
Utility routines for debugging, etc.	2 weeks

Each pass of the flowcharting portion required less than 600 lines of coding.

The two weeks spent preparing the flowchart routine were saved many times over; although we cannot be sure, it is likely that we would never have finished if we had not spent nearly one-third of our allotted time preparing auxiliary programs, and the flowcharter in particular. It was very gratifying to see our flow charts pouring out of the printer at 600 lines per minute. All of the programs in the list above are completely documented; the FORTRAN translator has 26 flow charts with accompanying flow outline descriptions. These charts have been published in limited distribution [3].

Design of the flowcharter changed several times during the course of the summer, until it now has the form indicated in Figures 1 to 4. Since the flow chart program was not our main goal, we did not take the time to dress it up with many frills, or to make any major changes after it began to work.

There is one feature in particular that we would now change, based on experience in use. Notice that the condition names, which are written in the DK-field (Fig. 3), are suppressed on the final flow outline (Fig. 1). This occasionally caused peculiar wording to occur in the resulting flow outline, because the programmer forgot to restate the condition in the text. As the system is now (see, for instance, step A3), each condition must effectively appear twice, once in abbreviated form in the DK-field, and again in the text. It would have been preferable to reproduce the condition names on the final listing, perhaps separated from the text by an additional blank column.

A further suggestion for future systems is that the flow chart language be divorced from the assembly language, and actually punched on separate decks of cards. Only a DK-field, containing the key letter of a new section and the step number of each step in its proper place, would need to appear on the assembly language cards. The flow chart program would carry out the necessary merging process, or could be used independently for preparing the charts and outlines only, with no formal language description.

The only disadvantage of this dichotomy would be a slightly increased tendency to neglect changing the flow description whenever a change is made in the program. However, the advantages are more significant, as the same basic flow charting program can be made to work with assemblers, compilers, and any other formal language system that is present at an installation.

The flow charts produced by our system are, of course, not as beautiful as those done by hand, but they seem to be quite adequate for their purpose. In order not to be accused of putting good draftsmen out of work, however, we should perhaps add that these diagrams are at least suitable for submission to a professional, so that if there is at some point in time very little chance for a flow chart to become obsolete, it can be redrawn in the most beautiful manner.

A very simple-minded scheme was used for drawing the flow charts: All boxes appear in a single column, and all connector lines occur to their right. Actually we found this format to be quite sufficient, but future systems may wish to add some more topological sophistication. In particular, a two-way branch something like (A) below is a fairly common occurrence, and in our system the resulting chart is rather clumsily expressed as in (B). A test for special cases of this type might be desirable, as it has been done in [5]. Such an improvement could be incorporated into the algorithm of Appendix 2 without great difficulty.

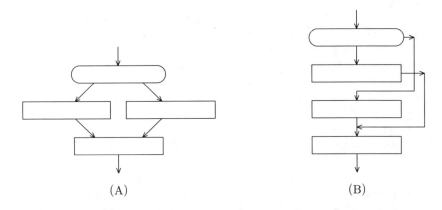

(A)   (B)

Even though an automated system will produce improved documentation, there still is an art to creating an extremely effective presentation. Programmers can certainly do a sloppy job with this system as with any system, if they are so inclined; there is no guarantee of good results. But now that a more effective medium for documentation is available, our experience has indicated that programmers will tend to strive harder to do a better job, thus getting more satisfaction from the result.

Of course we realize that our system is just a first step, but we feel that it has been taken in the right direction. We also realize that such a system will not be *widely* used unless computer manufacturers create and distribute such flowcharting programs to their customers. But we hope that this article will tempt a few groups into trying the ideas on their own; after all, the program is really rather easy to write, and Appendix 2 describes a suitable method. Because of our encouraging success, we are sure that such efforts will go a long way towards relieving the current documentation headaches.

Appendix 1

A few more rules were made regarding the DK-field in our prototype system; they were not sufficiently important to mention in the main text, and they may be improved upon in future versions.

The DK-field in our system is allowed to take the following forms:

1. Blank No special significance.
2. K.   Beginning of a new section, with key letter K.

3. K*n*.   Beginning of a new step, with this step number. Step numbers
   or   within a section must be in ascending order but not necessarily
   K*nn*.   consecutive.

4. X   Same as blank, except that the entire left-hand part of the card is
         deleted from the *assembly* listing. (For example, two lines of Fig-
         ure 3 have been omitted between lines 0030 and 0031 of Figure 2.)

5. G   The remarks in this card are not part of the flow outline; they are
         machine-oriented or coding-oriented details that are supposed to
         appear only on the assembly listing itself.

6. TABL   Treated as blank; these are the first letters of 'TABLE OF CONTENTS'
   or   and 'CODING DETAILS', respectively, and they are allowed in the
   CODI   DK-field primarily for better-looking output.

7. Other A condition name. Although all the condition names in Figure
         1 have colons, special punctuation is by no means a requirement.
         A five-column DK-field would have been somewhat nicer than the
         four columns in our prototype system, because it would have al-
         lowed longer condition names.

Our prototype assembler can be used with or without the flowchart
features. When flowcharting is not being used, the DK-field and remarks
are simply treated as standard comments in an ordinary assembly program listing. On the other hand when flow charts are being drawn,
most of the comments are suppressed from the assembly listing (see Figure 2). This policy makes the assembly listing more readable, but it
also increases the difficulty of making corrections to the sources when
changes are necessary. Therefore we found it wise to assemble both with
and without flowcharting, marking our corrections on the listing that
included all of the punches on the source cards.

Incidentally, the assembly program described here was prepared for
a rather unusual machine configuration (Solid State II-80, with 8800-
word drum, 1280-word core, and 6 tape units); it was designed merely
to help create the FORTRAN II compiler rather than for general use.
Therefore the assembly and flowcharting system are not distributed as
part of the UNIVAC Solid-State Library.

Appendix 2

If this method for explaining algorithms has any merit at all, we should
at least use it in the present article to explain the flowcharting algorithm
itself. Due to lack of space, however, a somewhat abbreviated description
of the algorithm must appear here.

We shall discuss a method that is independent of an assembly program, as suggested in the last portion of the text; the only connection

with other programs is that we assume the existence of a reference number for each step, typically indicating a line number on some other listing.

The algorithm proceeds in two passes. The first pass digests the information and edits it into a convenient form, then the second pass produces the actual listing. In the present system, the listing contains the flow chart at the left; the flow outline is reproduced at the right. For simplicity, we will only describe a program to print the flow charts; the rest of the program, which simply copies the input but suppresses the #-signs, is a straightforward addition (the only complication being to terminate a chart properly when both halves of the listing are finished). A simpler alternative would be to print the flow outline listing during Pass 1, and to print only the flow charts in Pass 2. This was not done in our system since we printed the assembly listing during the first pass.

Some intermediate language must be devised for any two-pass algorithm, in order to communicate the information from one pass to the other. In this case, as in many others, it is convenient to transmit the necessary data in an *interpretive* type of language. The first pass "compiles" into this machine-like pseudocode, and the second pass is merely an *interpretive routine* that executes the pseudocode instructions.

The instructions in our simple pseudocode have the general form

$$(\text{OP}, \text{ADDRESS}),$$

although other information is also intermixed with certain operators, as will be evident in the discussion that follows. Here are the details of the various operators:

$(1, n)$ Prepare a square box for step Kn, where K denotes the key letter of the current section. The next line of code is the line reference number corresponding to the formal language listing. The following five lines contain 25 alphameric characters to insert in the flow chart box.

$(2, n)$ This instruction is exactly the same as $(1, n)$, except that a branch-shaped box is produced rather than a square box.

$(3, 0)$ Terminate this flow chart, and get ready to begin another.

$(4, 0)$ Terminate this flow chart, then stop everything.

$(5, n)$, $(6, n)$, $(7, n)$ Draw a branch to step Kn. The next line contains a five-character condition name to identify the branch. OP $= 7$ is used for the *first* branch if there are more than one; OP $= 5$ is used for the *last* branch, if there are more than one; OP $= 6$ is used for any other branches. If $n = 0$, an extra line of code appears, giving the *name* of the place branched to; in such a case branching occurs to a step external to the present section.

$(8,0)$ Label the branch to the next box. The following line has the condition name to be used as a label.

$(9,n)$ Draw an unconditional branch to step n. If $n = 0$, the next line has the appropriate successor name.

These conventions can be explained most clearly by exhibiting the pseudocode that caused Figure 1 to be drawn:

Location	Instruction	Location	Instruction
01:	$(1,1)$	26:	␣␣␣␣␣
02:	0006	27:	$(7,0)$
03:	␣A1.␣	28:	␣EQ:␣
04:	INITI	29:	␣EXIT
05:	ALIZE	30:	$(5,5)$
06:	␣␣␣␣␣	31:	␣GR:␣
07:	␣␣␣␣␣	32:	$(8,0)$
08:	$(2,2)$	33:	␣LS:␣
09:	0012	34:	$(1,4)$
10:	␣A2.␣	35:	0024
11:	GET␣M	36:	␣A4.␣
12:	IDPOI	37:	FIX␣L
13:	NT␣␣␣	38:	OWER␣
14:	␣␣␣␣␣	39:	␣␣␣␣␣
15:	$(6,0)$	40:	␣␣␣␣␣
16:	␣NO:␣	41:	$(9,2)$
17:	␣␣NOT	42:	$(1,5)$
18:	$(8,0)$	43:	0027
19:	␣OK:␣	44:	␣A5.␣
20:	$(2,3)$	45:	FIX␣U
21:	0019	46:	PPER␣
22:	␣A3.␣	47:	␣␣␣␣␣
23:	T(M):	48:	␣␣␣␣␣
24:	KEY␣␣	49:	$(9,2)$
25:	␣␣␣␣␣	50:	$(3,0)$

In addition to this pseudocode, a table LREF with 99 entries is transmitted to the second pass, where $\text{LREF}(n)$ is zero if no branch lines occur to step Kn, otherwise $\text{LREF}(n)$ is the location of the pseudocode instruction on which the vertical line connecting to box Kn is to be discontinued. In the case of Figure 1 we have $\text{LREF}(n) = 0$ except $\text{LREF}(2) = 49$, $\text{LREF}(5) = 42$.

Armed with this information, the second pass will not need to look ahead, and it can print the information at high speed.

Pass 1. The algorithm for the first pass could use the following flow outline, whose corresponding flow chart is shown in Figure 5.

S1. INPUT NEXT CARD

Read in the next card image. (But if there are no more cards left, compile a $(4, 0)$ instruction, then dump out the LREF table and all the pseudocode for the previous section, and transfer to the second pass of the program.)

S2. WHAT DK-FIELD?

If the DK-field is of the form 'K.', go to step S3; if it has the form 'Kn.' or 'Knn.', go to step S4; if it is blank, go to step S6; otherwise the DK-field is assumed to contain a condition name, and we go to step S5.

S3. FINISH PREV SECTION

Compile a $(3, 0)$ instruction, and dump out the LREF table plus all the pseudocode for the previous section onto tape; this will be sent to the second pass. (This step is bypassed the very first time, since there was no previous section.) Then record the new key letter, set the entire LREF table to zero, and get ready to begin a new section. Go back to step S1.

S4. COMPILE $(1, n)$

We are at the beginning of a new step. If the preceding step had a condition name branching to here (that is, not followed by any successor indication), compile $(8, 0)$ followed by the condition name. In any event, compile a $(1, n)$ operation, followed by the line reference number and the five words of alphabetical information in the title of this step. If LREF(n) is not zero, set LREF(n) equal to the location of this $(1, n)$ operation code. Return to step S1.

S5. COMPILE CONDITION

If a condition preceded and had no named successor, save its condition name (which will be used later to form an $(8, 0)$ operation the next time step S4 occurs). Increase the last operation code by 1; this will change 1 to 2, 5 to 6, or 6 to 7. If the last operation had been a 1, compile $(6, 0)$, otherwise compile $(5, 0)$; then compile the condition name. These manipulations will cause the following sequence of operation codes in the pseudocode:

If there are no conditions:	1;
If there is one condition:	2, 6;
If there are two conditions:	2, 7, 5;
If there are three conditions:	2, 7, 6, 5;
If there are four conditions:	2, 7, 6, 6, 5;

and so on with additional 6s inserted before the 5. (The different numbering of branch operation codes 5, 6, 7 is used by the second pass to control where the condition name is placed on the charts.)

S6. ANY #?

Search the remarks field to see if the character '#' occurs. If not, return to step S1.

S7. COMPILE SUCCESSOR

If the preceding operation code is 1, the '#' that we have just scanned is an unconditional branch, and so a $(9,0)$ instruction should now be compiled. Determine the successor name (the characters following the # sign). If it has the form Kn or Knn, where K is the current key letter, change the address of the previous pseudocode instruction to n, and set $\text{LREF}(n)$ equal to the location of that instruction. Otherwise, compile the successor name into the pseudocode. Return to step S1.

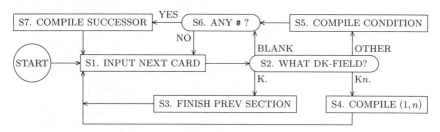

FIGURE 5. Flow diagram for the first pass of the algorithm in Appendix 2.

Pass 2. As mentioned earlier, the second pass is a type of interpretive system. For simplicity, we shall assume that the character set and the line lengths are exactly those used in Figure 1.

The only complexity in this pass consists of controlling the lines to be drawn. This mechanism is handled by considering 15 sets of 2-column pairs, each of which is set to 'ON' or 'OFF' or 'SPECIAL'. The operation of 'ON' and 'OFF' varies depending on whether a horizontal line is crossing this column or not:

	OFF	ON
horizontal line	. .	. :
no horizontal line	⊔⊔	⊔:

The meaning of 'SPECIAL' is that one of the special 2-character pairs

$$)0 \quad .0 \quad .V \quad .A$$

is used, and that a horizontal line is suppressed to the right of this column. Furthermore, a SPECIAL column will be changed to OFF or ON by the time we get to the following line.

Besides the 15 column-pairs, there is a vertical line for connecting a box to the one below it; this line is also said to be either OFF or ON.

A subroutine called ASSIGN is used to handle horizontal lines. If an external reference is to be made (for example, to 'EXIT'), a horizontal line is simply run all across the page. Otherwise an internal reference is being made (for example, to Kn). First the subroutine checks whether one of the 15 columns is already in use for Kn. If not, a new column is chosen (the first available column of the sequence 1, 5, 9, 13, 3, 7, 11, 15, 8, 14, 2, 12, 4, 10, 6, in that order of preference) and it is given the SPECIAL status ')0'. If a column has already been assigned, however, the routine checks LREF(n) to see if we are at the place where the vertical line is to be stopped. If so, the SPECIAL status ')0' is given to this column; otherwise either '.V' or '.A' is given, depending upon whether flow is currently going down or up the line.

The ASSIGN subroutine is used when a condition name is to be processed: A column is ASSIGNed, and a horizontal line is run up to this column. The ASSIGN subroutine is also used when bringing a horizontal line *into* the flow, except here the special status '.0' overrides the status chosen by the algorithm in the preceding paragraph.

The logic of the preceding two paragraphs is hard to explain briefly, but the example of Figure 1 should help to clarify the situation. At the beginning, all 15 columns are in the OFF status. Then at line 9 of that chart, the ASSIGN subroutine is first used to choose a column for step A2. Column 1 is chosen, and it is given the special status ')0', which is later overridden to be '.0' since it is an input line. After line 9, column 1 remains in the ON status. In line 19 the ASSIGN subroutine is used to select a column for step A5. Column 5 is chosen, and given the status ')0', remaining ON afterwards. In line 24 the ASSIGN subroutine is used for step A2; column 1 is already assigned for A2, therefore the status '.A' is given to column 1 at this point (the flow is going upwards). In lines 27 and 30, the ASSIGN subroutine is used again, for steps A5 and A2 respectively, and in both cases the LREF table indicates that the column is to be OFF after that reference.

Here now is a line-by-line description of the procedure followed for the operators $(1, n)$ or $(2, n)$:

First line (input node): If LREF(n) = 0, there are no branch lines leading into this node, and no special action occurs. If LREF(n) $\neq$ 0, the box-connector line is set to ON, and the ASSIGN subroutine is used as described above to run a horizontal line to it.

Second line (cross reference number): On this line the cross-reference number is obtained from the pseudocode and put into the listing.

Third line (top line of box): The top line of a box is created. If the current operation is $(1, n)$, turn ON the box-connector line, and draw a square box; but if the current operation is $(2, n)$, turn OFF the box-connector line, and draw a rounded box. If the next operation in the pseudocode is of the form $(7, n)$, the associated condition name is also processed for the current line.

Fourth line (title of box): The alphameric characters of the title are put into the box. If the next operation in the pseudocode is of the form $(6, n)$, the associated condition name is also processed for the current line. If the next operation is of the form $(9, n)$, an unconditional branch is made (as if the condition name were '. . . . .'), and the box connector line is turned OFF.

Fifth line (bottom line of box): The bottom line of a box is created. If the next operation is of the form $(5, n)$, the associated condition name is processed. If the next operation is of the form $(6, n)$ there were more than four conditions; extra lines are added, one condition per line, until a condition of the form $(5, n)$ is finally processed.

Sixth line (possible label): If the next operator is of the form $(8, 0)$, the label is inserted now and the box connector line is turned ON.

Transfer to next operation: If the bottom of the page is dangerously near, print lines that are blank (except for the vertical lines that are currently ON) until the top of the next page is reached. Then examine the next line of the pseudocode: The operator must be less than or equal to 4, or else an error has occurred. Process the next operator.

Comparison with Figure 1 will illustrate this procedure. The essential feature of the algorithm is that it processes each line by itself and then prints the line, rather than consuming memory space to store a whole flow chart before printing it out.

The preparation of this paper was supported in part by the Burroughs Corporation, and in part by the Evergreen Corporation. The design of the system described was enhanced by discussions with W. C. Lynch and Joseph Speroni.

References

[1] David A. Aaronson and Clarissa J. Kinnaman, "Production of large and variable size logic block diagrams on a high speed digital computer," AIEE conference paper 61-1116 (Murray Hill, New Jersey: Bell Telephone Laboratories, October 1961), ii + 15 + 12 pages. (This paper includes a valuable bibliography of the subject.)

[2] A. P. Ershov, *Programming Programme for the BESM Computer*, translated from the Russian by M. Nadler (London: Pergamon, 1959).

[3] *FORTRAN II Routine Block Chart (Annotated)*, Document UP-3843.1 (Bluebell, Pennsylvania: Univac Division of Sperry Rand Corporation, 1963), 50 pages. (To adequately understand this document, the reader should be familiar with the FORTRAN II input

language of this particular implementation, and with the UNIVAC Solid-State computer machine language.)

[4] W. T. Gant, "Flow outlining — a substitute for flow charting," *Communications of the ACM* **2**, 11 (November 1959), 17.

[5] Lois M. Haibt, "A program to draw multilevel flow charts," *Proceedings of the Western Joint Computer Conference* **15** (1959), 131–137.

[6] *IBM 7090/7094 IBSYS-IOEX Programming System Analysis Guide,* IBM Form C28-6299 (IBM Corporation, 1963). This document, which has just come to the attention of the author, includes flowcharts printed in a pleasing format by computer. Unfortunately no mention is made of the input language for this program.

[7] A. E. Scott, "Automatic preparation of flow chart listings," *Journal of the Association for Computing Machinery* **5** (1958), 57–66.

[8] Victor H. Yngve and Jean E. Sammet, "Toward better documentation of programming languages," a series of eight papers, *Communications of the ACM* **6** (1963), 76–92. These articles are primarily concerned with the documentation of *languages* and computer systems for the user, rather than with the documentation of the *techniques* used in the programs themselves as described here.

Addenda

The IBM flowcharting software mentioned in [6] was known as AUTO-CHART; see *IBM 7070/7074 AUTOCHART Programming System*, IBM Systems Reference Library File 7070/7074-48, Form C28-6772 (Poughkeepsie, New York: Programming Systems Publications, IBM Corporation, October 1963), 58 pages. Another routine called 80FLOW was written for the IBM 7080 by Lou Copits at about the same time, as was FLOWSY for the Burroughs B5000/B5500 by Glyn H. Jones.

A popular system called AUTOFLOW was released in 1965 by Applied Data Research, Inc., under the direction of Martin A. Goetz, who later received U.S. Patent 3533086, "Automatic system for constructing and recording display charts" (6 October 1970), 38 sheets. AUTOFLOW is said to have been the first commercial software product to be sold independent of hardware. The 87-page AUTOFLOW Reference Manual for IBM System/360 was issued by ADR in October 1967.

Modern readers who are curious about the machine-language code shown in Figures 2 and 3 should note the following points about the UNIVAC Solid State computers: (1) Instructions consisted of a two-digit operation code, a four-digit data address (modifiable by index registers rB1, rB2, or rB3), and a four-digit address of the next instruction. (2) Multiplication by a number with fewer than ten digits was accomplished by placing the nondigit 'A' to the left of the multiplier. For example, multiplication by the constant 00000000A5 would put half the contents of register L into register A. (3) There were 5000 addressable locations on the magnetic drum; the address 9001 would be the same as 4001. (4) An address like B01A was in core memory. (5) The command SHL 0n00 shifted register A left by n decimal digits; thus SHL 0300 multiplied by 1000. (6) Arithmetic overflow would cause the next instruction to be taken from an address one greater than usual. A symbolic location like &T was required to be one greater than its mate -T.

Chapter 23

Notes on Avoiding 'go to' Statements

[Written with Robert W. Floyd. Originally published in Information Processing Letters 1 (1971), 23–31, 177.]

The last decade has witnessed a growing sentiment that the use of '**go to**' statements is undesirable, or actually harmful. This attitude is apparently inspired by the idea that programs expressed solely in terms of conventional iterative constructions ('**for**', '**while**', etc.) are more readable and more easily proved correct. In this note we will make a few exploratory observations about the use and disuse of **go to** statements, based on two typical programming examples (from "symbol table searching" and "backtracking").

In the first place let us consider systematic ways for eliminating **go to** statements, without changing the sequence of computations specified by the program. There are two apparent ways to achieve this:

a) *Recursive procedure method.* Suppose that every statement of a program is labeled. Replace each labeled statement

$$L: S$$

by

procedure L; **begin** S; L' **end**

where L' is the static successor of the statement S. A **go to** statement becomes simply a procedure call. The program ends by calling a null procedure. This construction shows that the mere elimination of **go to** statements does not automatically make a program better or easier to follow; '**go to**' is in some sense a special case of the procedure calling mechanism. (It is instructive in fact to consider this construction in reverse, realizing that it is sometimes more efficient to *replace* procedure calls by **go to** statements.)

495

b) *Regular expression method.* For convenience, imagine a program expressed in flowchart form, as a directed graph. It is well known that all paths through this graph can be represented by "regular expressions" involving the operations of concatenation, alternation, and "star"; these latter correspond to familiar programming language constructs that do not depend on **go to** statements. Therefore it appears that 'go to' statements can be eliminated, although it may be necessary to duplicate the code for other statements in several places.

Consider, for example, the following typical programming situation:

> **for** $i := 1$ **step** 1 **until** n **do**
>   **if** $A[i] = x$ **then go to** *found*;
> *not found*: $n := i$; $A[i] := x$; $B[i] := 0$;
> *found*: $B[i] := B[i] + 1$;

(We shall assume, for convenience, that $i = n + 1$ if the **for** loop is exhausted.) It is not obvious that the **go to** statement here is all that unsightly, but let us suppose that we are reactionary enough that we really want to abolish them from programming languages [4, 6]. One way to avoid the **go to** is to use a recursive procedure:

> **procedure** *find*;
>   **if** $i > n$ **then begin** $n := i$; $A[i] := x$; $B[i] := 0$ **end**
>   **else if** $A[i] \neq x$ **then begin** $i := i + 1$; *find* **end**;
> $i := 1$;   *find*; $B[i] := B[i] + 1$;

An optimizing compiler could perhaps produce the same code for both programs, but again it is debatable which of the programs is most readable and simple.

Other solutions change the structure of the program slightly:

a) $i := 1$;
        while $i \leq n$ **and** $A[i] \neq x$ **do** $i := i + 1$;
        if $i > n$ **then begin** $n := i$; $A[i] := x$; $B[i] := 0$ **end**;
        $B[i] := B[i] + 1$;

b) $i := 1$;
        while $A[i] \neq x$ **do**
            begin $i := i + 1$;
                if $i > n$ **then begin** $n := i$; $A[i] := x$; $B[i] := 0$ **end**
            end;
        $B[i] := B[i] + 1$;

Solution (b) assumes that $n > 0$. Both solutions increase the amount of calculation that is specified: Version (a) tests '$i > n$' twice, while (b) tests '$A[i] \neq x$' after n has been increased.

The flowchart of the original program is:

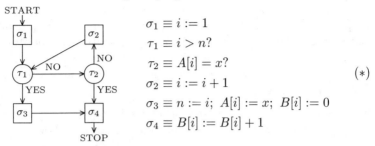

$$\sigma_1 \equiv i := 1$$
$$\tau_1 \equiv i > n?$$
$$\tau_2 \equiv A[i] = x?$$
$$\sigma_2 \equiv i := i + 1$$
$$\sigma_3 \equiv n := i;\ A[i] := x;\ B[i] := 0$$
$$\sigma_4 \equiv B[i] := B[i] + 1$$

$$(*)$$

By a suitable extension of BNF we can write a grammar for all flowcharts producible by a language without procedure calls or **go to** statements:

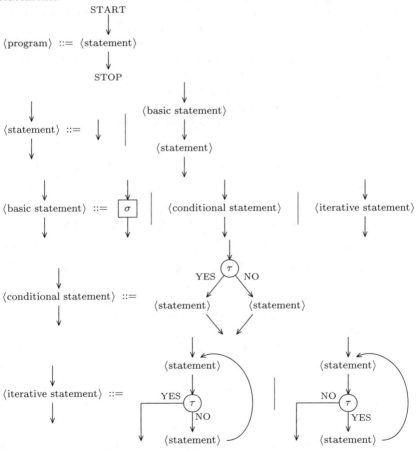

Here σ denotes a "statement" and τ denotes a "test."

The authors have not completely analyzed this grammar, although it appears to be unambiguous; there is probably an efficient parsing algorithm that will decide whether or not a given flowchart is derivable from the grammar, constructing a derivation when one exists. But we can easily prove that the flowchart above is *not* producible by this grammar. In fact, a stronger result is true:

Theorem. *No flowchart producible by the grammar above specifies precisely the computations of the example flowchart* (∗) *above.*

This theorem contradicts the observations that we made about regular expressions being reducible to concatenation, alternation, and iteration; for our flowcharts provide each of these operations, yet they cannot reproduce the computations in (∗). What went wrong? Perhaps the reason is that regular expressions are nondeterministic, while computations are inherently deterministic? But no, it is well known that regular expressions may be considered to be deterministic. The difference really lies in the nature of computational tests.

Thus, let us consider a special class $\mathcal{R}$ of regular expressions; $\mathcal{R}$ describes all computational sequences (paths in the flowchart) producible by flowcharts corresponding to a language without procedures or **go to** statements:

the empty sequence is in $\mathcal{R}$;

$\sigma \in \mathcal{R}$, for all statements σ;

$R_1 R_2 \in \mathcal{R}$, for all $R_1 \in \mathcal{R}$ and $R_2 \in \mathcal{R}$;

$(\tau_Y R_1 \mid \tau_N R_2) \in \mathcal{R}$, for all $R_1 \in \mathcal{R}$, $R_2 \in \mathcal{R}$, and all tests τ;

$(\tau_Y R_1)^* \tau_N \in \mathcal{R}$ and $(\tau_N R_1)^* \tau_Y \in \mathcal{R}$, for all $R_1 \in \mathcal{R}$ and all tests τ.

Here the subscripts Y and N denote the 'YES' or 'NO' branches in the flowchart.

To prove the theorem, consider the computational sequences producible by the flowchart (∗); they may be described by the regular expression

$$\sigma_1 (\tau_{1N} \tau_{2N} \sigma_2)^* (\tau_{1Y} \sigma_3 \mid \tau_{1N} \tau_{2Y}) \sigma_4. \qquad (**)$$

We will show that the corresponding regular event (the sequences defined by this regular expression) cannot be defined by any of the regular expressions in $\mathcal{R}$.

Proof. (Suggested by John Hopcroft.) Every regular expression $R \in \mathcal{R}$ clearly has the property that τ_Y appears in some string of R if and only if

τ_N appears in some string of R, for all tests τ. Since $(**)$ contains strings with arbitrarily many occurrences of τ_{1N} separated by occurrences of τ_{2N}, it must contain a "star" construction including some regular $R \in \mathcal{R}$ in which both τ_{1N} and τ_{2N} appear. But R must also contain a string that includes τ_{1Y} or τ_{2Y}. Hence no regular expression in $\mathcal{R}$ can produce the regular event $(**)$, and the theorem is proved. $\square$

Perhaps the reader feels that the proof just given is too "slick," or that something has been concealed. In fact, this is quite true; we have penalized the class of flowcharts too severely! Compound tests such as 'τ_1 and τ_2' have not been allowed sufficient latitude. Our flowchart grammar should be extended as follows: Replace

in the definitions of ⟨conditional statement⟩ and ⟨iterative statement⟩ by

and add the new definition

The grammar now becomes ambiguous in several cases, although the ambiguity can be removed at the expense of some complications that are irrelevant here. More important is the change to grammar $\mathcal{R}$, where we are allowed to substitute

$$\tau_N' \tau_N'' \quad \text{for} \quad \tau_N, \qquad (\tau_Y' \mid \tau_N' \tau_Y'') \quad \text{for} \quad \tau_Y$$

or

$$\tau_Y' \quad \text{for} \quad \tau_N, \qquad \tau_N' \quad \text{for} \quad \tau_Y$$

whenever τ, τ', and τ'' are tests. Thus since $\sigma_1(\tau_N \sigma_2)^* \tau_Y \sigma_4 \in \mathcal{R}$, so is

$$\sigma_1(\tau_{1N} \tau_{2N} \sigma_2)^*(\tau_{1Y} \mid \tau_{1N} \tau_{2Y})\sigma_4,$$

and this is the same as (**) with σ_3 deleted. The theorem above is almost false! But we can still prove it by an exhaustive case analysis, considering all possible substitutions of compound tests and showing that none are permissible because of the presence of σ_3.

The theorem becomes almost false in another sense too, when compound conditions are considered, since the expression

$$\sigma_1(\tau_{1N}\tau_{2N}\sigma_2)^*(\tau_{1Y} \mid \tau_{1N}\tau_{2Y})(\tau_{1Y}\sigma_3 \mid \tau_{1N})\sigma_4$$

is now in $\mathcal{R}$, and it differs from (**) only in that τ_{1Y} becomes $\tau_{1Y}\tau_{1Y}$ and $\tau_{1N}\tau_{2Y}$ becomes $\tau_{1N}\tau_{2Y}\tau_{1N}$; $\tau_{1Y}\tau_{2Y}$ isn't viable. The sequences are essentially the same except that redundant tests are made.

We could therefore consider equivalence relations on regular expressions, allowing commutativity of successive tests, and the idempotent law $\tau_Y\tau_Y \equiv \tau_Y$. The associative law

$$\big((\alpha \mid \beta) \mid \gamma\big) \equiv \big(\alpha \mid (\beta \mid \gamma)\big)$$

is valid, and so are the distributive laws

$$(\alpha \mid \beta)\gamma \equiv (\alpha\gamma \mid \beta\gamma) \qquad \text{and} \qquad \alpha(\beta \mid \gamma) \equiv (\alpha\beta \mid \alpha\gamma),$$

with the understanding that terms including consecutive tests $\tau_Y\tau_N$ may be dropped.

With respect to such an equivalence relation, our theorem would become false. But we can easily find another flowchart for which the theorem still holds: Simply put another statement box σ_5 between τ_1 and τ_2. Then no two tests are adjacent, and the original "slick" proof immediately shows that the regular event defined by

$$\sigma_1(\tau_{1N}\sigma_5\tau_{2N}\sigma_2)^*(\tau_{1Y}\sigma_3 \mid \tau_{1N}\sigma_5\tau_{2Y})\sigma_4$$

is not equivalent to any regular event definable with the extended flowchart language $\mathcal{R}$. (When no two tests are adjacent, compound conditions cannot appear, nor do any of the equivalences apply, so none of the extensions affect the original proof of the theorem.)

Therefore, the "slick" proof is vindicated, and we have proved the existence of programs whose **go to** statements cannot be eliminated without introducing procedure calls. A somewhat stronger result has recently been obtained by Ashcroft and Manna [1].

Let us now consider a second example program, taken this time from a typical application of "backtracking" or exhaustive enumeration [5]. Most backtrack problems can be abstracted into the following form:

```
start: m[1] := 0;  k := 0;
up: k := k + 1;  list(k);  a[k] := m[k];
try: if a[k] < m[k + 1] then begin move(a[k]);  go to up end;
```

down: $k := k - 1$;
   if $k = 0$ **then go to** *done*;
   unmove$(a[k])$;
   $a[k] := a[k] + 1$; **go to** *try*;
done:

Here the procedures *list*, *move*, and *unmove* may be regarded as manipulating a variable-width stack $s[0]$, $s[1]$, ... of possible choices in this abstracted algorithm. Procedure *list*(k) determines all possible choices at the kth level of backtracking, based on the previously made choices $a[1]$, ..., $a[k - 1]$. If there are c choices now possible, *list*(k) will set $m[k + 1] := m[k] + c$, and it will also set the stack entries $s[m[k]]$, $s[m[k] + 1]$, ..., $s[m[k] + c - 1]$ to identify the choices. (Note that c can be zero. The choices might be, for example, where to place the kth queen on a chessboard, given positions of $k - 1$ other queens, if we are trying to solve the eight-queens problem.) Procedure *move*(t) makes the decision to choose alternative $s[t]$; this usually means that some internal tables need to be updated. Procedure *unmove*(t) reverses the decision made by *move*(t).

It is not necessary to understand the exact mechanism of this construction, although people familiar with backtracking should find the previous paragraph self-explanatory. The main point is that essentially all backtracking programs have the form of the program above, when appropriate sequences of code are substituted for *list*(k), *move*$(a[k])$, and *unmove*$(a[k])$; hence the program is worth considering from the standpoint of **go to** elimination.

First we can eliminate **go to**'s by introducing a procedure:

```
procedure backtrack(k); value k; integer k;
    begin list(k); a[k] := m[k];
        while a[k] < m[k + 1] do
            begin move(a[k]); backtrack(k + 1);
                unmove(a[k]); a[k] := a[k] + 1;
            end
    end backtrack;
m[1] := 0; backtrack(1);
```

This use of recursion is rather clean, so the program above is attractive except for the procedure-calling overhead (which can be significant, because backtrack programs typically involve many millions of iterations). It is an interesting exercise to prove this program equivalent to our first version.

Now let's try to eliminate the **go to** statements without introducing a new procedure. The flowchart is:

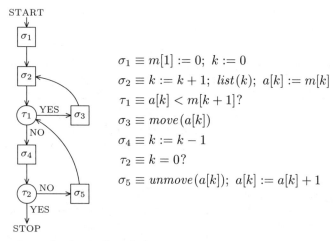

$$\sigma_1 \equiv m[1] := 0; \; k := 0$$
$$\sigma_2 \equiv k := k + 1; \; list(k); \; a[k] := m[k]$$
$$\tau_1 \equiv a[k] < m[k+1]?$$
$$\sigma_3 \equiv move(a[k])$$
$$\sigma_4 \equiv k := k - 1$$
$$\tau_2 \equiv k = 0?$$
$$\sigma_5 \equiv unmove(a[k]); \; a[k] := a[k] + 1$$

Here we have the basic flowchart structure

instead of the previous situation when we had

It turns out that "node splitting" works in this case but not the other: We can make two copies of node σ_2 in the flowchart above and we obtain

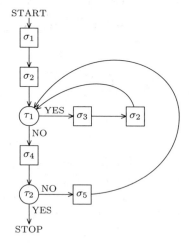

This diagram obviously satisfies the conditions of our flowchart grammar above, so we can avoid the **go to** statements.

What is the resulting program? Our flowchart grammar allows more general iterative statements than present-day programming languages will admit. A general iterative construction might be written

$$\textbf{begin loop } \sigma_1; \textbf{ exit loop if } \tau_1; \; \sigma_2 \textbf{ end loop}; \qquad (***)$$

but today's languages only consider the case that σ_1 is empty:

$$\textbf{while } \neg\tau_1 \textbf{ do } \sigma_2;$$

or if σ_2 is empty:

$$\textbf{do } \sigma_1 \textbf{ until } \tau_1.$$

We can always rewrite $(***)$ in the equivalent form

$$\sigma_1; \; \textbf{while } \neg\tau_1 \textbf{ do begin } \sigma_2; \; \sigma_1 \textbf{ end};$$

but this alternative is quite unattractive when σ_1 is long, so a programmer will certainly prefer to use **go to** statements in that case. If we want to teach programmers to avoid **go to**'s, we must provide them with a sufficiently rich syntax of iterative statements to serve as a substitute.

Using $(***)$ leads to the following program for backtracking without **go to** statements:

```
m[1] := 0;  k := 1;  list(1);  a[1] := 0;
begin loop
   while a[k] < m[k + 1] do
      begin move(a[k]);
         k := k + 1;  list(k);  a[k] := m[k];
      end;
   k := k − 1;
   exit loop if k = 0;
      unmove(a[k]);  a[k] := a[k] + 1;
   end loop.
```

This code, although free of **go to**'s, involves an uncomfortable element that may not make it very palatable: The condition '**while** $a[k] < m[k+1]$' is rather peculiar, since k varies and the test involves different variables each time. The appearance of the same clause in our recursive procedure $backtrack(k)$ did not have the same peculiarity.

Yet we can think of the program in a fairly natural way nevertheless, for example (in tree language) as follows:

> *Start at the root of the search tree*;
> **begin loop**
>   **while** *possible to go down and left in the tree* **do**
>   *Move down and left*;
>   *Move up one level in the tree*;
>   **exit loop if** *at the root*;
>   *Move to the right in the tree*;
> **end loop**.

This code is a typical tree traversal algorithm.

The syntax in $(***)$ is perhaps not the best way to improve iteration statements. An alternative proposal, based on some unpublished ideas of Niklaus Wirth, has just been implemented as an extension to Stanford's ALGOL W compiler: The statement

> **repeat** ⟨block⟩

has the effect of

> L_1: ⟨block⟩; **go to** L_1; L_2:

where L_1 and L_2 are implicit labels; and the statement

> **exit**

has the effect of

> **go to** L_2

where L_2 is the second implicit label corresponding to the smallest repeat block statically enclosing the **exit** statement. Thus, $(***)$ becomes

> **repeat begin** σ_1; **if** τ_1 **then exit**; σ_2 **end**;

and we can even write our symbol table search routine without **go to**:

> $i := 1$;
> **repeat begin**
>   **while** $i \leq n$ **do if** $A[i] = x$ **then exit else** $i := i + 1$;
> $n := i$; $A[i] := x$; $B[i] := 0$; **exit**;
> **end**;
> $B[i] := B[i] + 1$;

Here the "repeat loop" is never repeated, but the desired effect has been achieved. It appears doubtful that Wirth's repeat-exit mechanism will be able to eliminate **go to** statements in general, since it allows only a "one-level exit"; further study of these issues is indicated.

In this paper we have considered only transformations of the program that avoid **go to** statements, without introducing new variables or changing the sequence of computations and tests. Böhm and Jacopini [2] and Cooper [3] have observed that additional Boolean variables can be added in such a way that the program structure becomes very trivial and **go to**'s are obviously unnecessary; but in fact, as Cooper has observed, these Boolean variables essentially simulate a program counter and they contribute nothing to the clarity of the program. Ashcroft and Manna [1] have recently found a more meaningful way to introduce variables into programs so that **go to**'s can be omitted without changing the program's "topology."

The research reported here was supported by IBM Corporation.

References

[1] Edward Ashcroft and Zohar Manna, "The translation of **go to** programs to **while** programs," *Information Processing 71*, Proceedings of IFIP Congress 71 (Amsterdam: North-Holland, 1972), 250–255.

[2] Corrado Böhm and Guiseppe Jacopini, "Flow diagrams, Turing machines and languages with only two formation rules," *Communications of the ACM* **9** (1966), 366–371.

[3] David C. Cooper, "Böhm and Jacopini's reduction of flow charts," *Communications of the ACM* **10** (1967), 463, 473.

[4] Edsger W. Dijkstra, "Go to statement considered harmful," *Communications of the ACM* **11** (1968), 147–148.

[5] Solomon W. Golomb and Leonard D. Baumert, "Backtrack programming," *Journal of the Association for Computing Machinery* **12** (1965), 516–524.

[6] D. V. Schorre, "Improved organization for procedural languages," Technical Memo 3086/002/00 (Santa Monica, California: System Development Corporation, 8 September 1966), 8 pages.

Addendum

Further discussion appears in a subsequent paper by Donald E. Knuth, "Structured programming with **go to** statements," *Computing Surveys* **6** (December 1974), 261–301; reprinted with revisions as Chapter 2 of *Literate Programming*, CSLI Lecture Notes 27 (Stanford, California: Center for the Study of Language and Information, 1992), 17–89.]

Chapter 24

An Empirical Study of FORTRAN Programs

A sample of programs, written in FORTRAN *by a wide variety of people for a wide variety of applications, was chosen "at random" in an attempt to discover quantitatively "what programmers really do." Statistical results of this survey are presented here, together with some of their apparent implications for future work in compiler design. The principal conclusion that may be drawn is the importance of a program "profile," namely a table of frequency counts that record how often each statement is performed in a typical run; there are strong indications that profile-keeping should become a standard practice in all computer systems, for casual users as well as system programmers. This paper is the report of a three-month study undertaken by the author and about a dozen students and representatives of the software industry during the summer of 1970. It is hoped that a reader who studies this report will obtain a fairly clear conception of how* FORTRAN *is being used, and what compilers can do about it.*

[Originally published in Software — Practice & Experience **1** *(1971), 105–133.]*

1. Introduction

Designers of compilers and instructors of computer science usually have comparatively little information about the ways in which programming languages are actually used by typical programmers. We think that we know what programmers generally do, but our notions are rarely based on a representative sample of the programs that are actually being run on computers. Since compiler writers must prepare a system capable of translating a language in all its generality, they can easily fall into the

507

trap of assuming that complicated constructions are the norm, when in fact such constructions are rare. There has been a long history of optimizing the wrong things, using elaborate mechanisms to produce beautiful code in cases that hardly ever arise in practice, while doing nothing about certain frequently occurring situations.

For example, the present author once ascribed great significance to the fact that a certain complicated method was able to translate the statement

$$C[I \times N + J] := ((A + X) \times Y) + 2.768 + ((L - M) \times (-K))/Z$$

into only nineteen machine instructions compared to the twenty-one instructions obtained by a previously published method due to Arden and Graham (see Knuth [12]). The fact that arithmetic expressions usually have an average length of only two operands, in practice, would have been a great shock to the author at that time.

There has been widespread realization that more data about language use is needed; we cannot really compare two different compiler algorithms until we understand the input data they deal with. Of course, the great difficulty is that there is no such thing as a "typical programmer." A tremendous variation exists among programs written by different people with different backgrounds and sympathies, and indeed there is considerable variation even in different programs written by the same person. Therefore we cannot trust any measurements to be very accurate, although we can measure the degree of variation in an attempt to determine how significant it is. Not all properties of programs can be reduced to simple statistics; it is necessary to study selected programs in detail, in order to appreciate their characteristics more clearly. For a survey of early work on performance measurement and evaluation, see Calingaert [2] and Cerf [3].

During the summer of 1970, the author worked together with several other people in order to explore the nature of actual programs, and to consider the corresponding implications both for software design and for computer science education. Our results are by no means a definitive analysis of programming behavior; our goal was to explore the various possibilities, as a group, in order to set the stage for subsequent individual research, rather than to go off in all directions at once. Each week the entire group had an eight-hour meeting in order to discuss what had been learned during the previous week, hoping that by combining our differing points of view we might arrive at something reasonably close to Truth.

A first idea for obtaining "typical" programs was to go to Stanford's Computation Center and rummage in the waste-baskets and the recycling bins. This gave results, but showed immediately what should have been obvious: Waste-baskets usually receive undebugged programs. Furthermore, it seems likely that compilers usually are confronted with undebugged programs, too; so it was necessary for us to choose whether we wanted to study the distributions of syntax errors, etc., or to concentrate on working programs. Some excellent analyses of common errors have already been made (see Freeman [6], Moulton and Muller [14]) and one of our main goals was to study the effects of various types of optimization. Therefore we decided to restrict ourselves to programs that actually run to completion.

The waste-basket method turned up some interesting programs but it was not really satisfactory. If we wanted to automate the process, extensive typing from the listings would have been necessary; so we tried another tack. Our next method of obtaining sample data was to post a student by the card reader at various times; the student would ask for permission to copy decks into a special file. Fifteen programs, totaling about 5,000 cards, were obtained in this way. But the job was very time-consuming, since it was necessary to explain the objectives of our project each time, and to ask embarrassing questions about the status of people's programs.

The next approach was to probe randomly among the semi-protected files stored on disks, looking for source text; this tactic was successful, resulting in thirty-three programs, totaling about 20,000 cards. We added nine programs from the Computer Science Department's subroutine library, and three programs from the "Scientific Subroutine Package," together with some production jobs from the Stanford Linear Accelerator Center. A few classical benchmark programs (nuclear codes, weather codes, and aerospace calculations) were also contributed by IBM representatives. To top things off we threw in some codes of personal interest to members of the group.

All told, we came up with quite a varied collection of programs: some large, some small; some sophisticated, some crude; some important, some trivial; some for production, some for play; some numerical, some combinatorial.

It is well known that different programming languages lead to the evolution of different programming styles, so our study was necessarily language-dependent. For example, one would expect that expressions in APL programs tend to be longer than those in FORTRAN programs. But virtually all of the programs obtained by our sampling procedure were written in FORTRAN (this was the first surprise of the summer), so our main efforts were directed toward the study of FORTRAN programs.*

Was this sample representative? Perhaps the users of Stanford's computers are more sophisticated than the general programmers to be found elsewhere; after all we have such a splendid Computer Science Department! But it is doubtful whether our department had any significant effect on these programs, because for one thing we do not teach FOR-TRAN; indeed, it was distressing to see what little impact our courses seem to be having, since virtually all of the programs we saw were apparently written by people who had learned programming elsewhere.

Furthermore, the general style of programming that we encountered showed very little evidence of "sophistication"; if what we saw was better than average, the average is too horrible to contemplate! (This remark is not intended as an insult to Stanford's programmers; after all, we were invading their privacy, and they would probably have written the programs differently if they had known that the code was to be scrutinized by self-appointed experts like ourselves. Our purposes were purely scientific in an attempt to find out how things are, without moralizing or judging people's competence. The point is that the Stanford sample seems to be reasonably typical of what might be found elsewhere.)

Another reason for believing that our sample was reasonably good is that the programs varied from text-editing and discrete calculations to number-crunching; they were by no means from a homogeneous class of applications. On the other hand, we do have some definite evidence of differences between the Stanford sample and another sample of over 400 programs written at Lockheed (see Section 2 of this paper).

The programs in our sample were analyzed in various ways. First we performed a *static* analysis, simply counting the number of occurrences of easily recognizable syntactic constructions. Statistics of this kind are relevant to the speed of compilation. The results of this static analysis

---

* By contacting known users of ALGOL, it was possible to collect a fairly representative sample of ALGOL W programs as well. The analysis of these programs is still incomplete; preliminary indications are that the increased flexibility of data types in ALGOL W makes for much more variety in the nature of inner loops than was observed in FORTRAN, and that the improved control structures make **go to**'s and labels considerably less frequent. A comprehensive analysis of ALGOL 60 programs has recently been completed by B. Wichmann [19].

We analyzed one PL/I program by hand. COBOL is not used at Stanford's Computation Center, and we have no idea what typical COBOL programs might be like.

are presented in Section 2. Secondly, we selected about 25 programs at random and subjected them to a *dynamic* analysis, taking into account the frequency with which each construction actually occurs during one run of the program; statistics of this kind are presented in Section 3. We also considered the "inner loops" of 17 programs, translating them by hand into machine language using various styles of optimization, in an attempt to weigh the utility of various local and global optimization strategies; results of that study are presented in Section 4.

Section 5 of this paper summarizes the principal conclusions we reached, and lists several areas that appear to be promising for future study.

2. Static Statistics

We examined a large number of FORTRAN programs to see how frequently certain constructions are used in practice. Over 250,000 cards (representing 440 programs) were analyzed by M. Maybury at the computer center of Lockheed Missiles and Space Corporation in Sunnyvale.

Table 1 shows the distribution of statement types. A "typical Lockheed program" consists of 120 comment cards, plus 178 assignment statements, 63.5 IF's, 56 GO TO's, 34 CALL's, 21 CONTINUE's, 18 WRITE's, 18 FORMAT's, 17 DO's, 72 miscellaneous other statements and 31 continuation cards (mostly involving COMMON or DATA). Essentially the same over-all distribution of statement types was obtained when individual groups of about thirty programs were tested, so these statistics tended to be rather stable. We forgot to test how many statements had non-blank labels.

The same test was run on the much smaller but still rather large collection of programs from our "Stanford sample" (about 11,000 cards). Unfortunately the corresponding percentages shown in Table 1 do *not* agree very well with the Lockheed sample; Stanfordites definitely use more assignments and fewer IF's and GO's than Lockheedians. A superficial examination of the programs suggests that Lockheed programmers are perhaps more careful to check for erroneous conditions in their data. Note also that 2.7 times as many comments appear on the Lockheed programs, indicating somewhat more regimentation. The professional programmers at Lockheed have a distinctly different style from Stanford's casual coders.

The 7,933 DO loops were investigated further to determine their length and depth of nesting. About 95 percent of the DO statements used the default increment of one. Most DO loops were quite short,

TABLE 1. Distribution of statement types

	Lockheed		Stanford	
	Number	Percent*	Number	Percent*
Assignment	78,435	41.0	4,869	51.0
IF	27,967	14.5	816	8.5
GO TO	24,942	13.0	777	8.0
CALL	15,125	8.0	339	4.0
CONTINUE	9,165	5.0	309	3.0
WRITE	7,795	4.0	508	5.0
FORMAT	7,685	4.0	380	4.0
DO	7,476	4.0	457	5.0
DATA	4,468	2.0	28	0.3
RETURN	3,639	2.0	186	2.0
DIMENSION	3,492	2.0	141	1.5
COMMON	2,908	1.5	263	3.0
END	2,565	1.0	121	1.0
BUFFER	2,501	1.0	0	
SUBROUTINE	2,001	1.0	93	1.0
REWIND	1,724	1.0	6	
EQUIVALENCE	1,382	0.7	113	1.0
ENDFILE	765	0.4	2	
INTEGER	657	0.3	34	0.3
READ	586	0.3	92	1.0
ENCODE	583	0.3	0	
DECODE	557	0.3	0	
PRINT	345	0.2	5	
ENTRY	279	0.1	15	0.2
STOP	190	0.1	11	0.1
LOGICAL	170	0.1	9	0.1
REAL	147	0.1	3	
IDENT	106	0.1	0	
OVERLAY	82		0	
PAUSE	57		6	0.1
ASSIGN	57		4	
PUNCH	52		5	0.1
EXTERNAL	23		1	
COMPLEX	6		0	
NAMELIST	5		0	
DOUBLE	3		99	1.0
BLOCKDATA	1		2	
IMPLICIT	0		16	1.5
INPUT	0		0	
OUTPUT	0		0	
Comment	52,924	(28)	1,090	(11)
Continuation	13,709	(7)	636	(7)

* Percent of the total number of statements, excluding comments and continuation cards. The construction 'IF (⟨condition⟩) ⟨statement⟩' counts as an IF as well as a statement, so the total is more than 100 percent.

involving only one or two statements:

Length	1	2	3	4	5	> 5
Number	3046	1467	758	576	1043	1043
Percent	39.0	18.5	9.5	7.0	13.0	13.0

The depth of DO nesting was subject to considerable variation; the following totals were obtained:

Depth	1	2	3	4	5	> 5
Number	4211	1853	1194	437	118	120
Percent	53.5	23.0	15.0	5.5	1.5	1.5

Of the 28,783 IF statements scanned, a total of 8,858 (30 percent) were of the "old style" IF $(\ldots)$ n_1, n_2, n_3 or IF $(\ldots)$ n_1, n_2 while the other 19,925 (70 percent) had the form IF $(\ldots)$ $\langle$statement$\rangle$; and 14,258 (71 percent) of the latter were 'IF $(\ldots)$ GO TO', which count also as GO TO statements. Only 1,107 of the 25,719 GO TO statements were computed (runtime-switch) GO's.

An average of about 48 blank columns was found per non-comment card. A compiler's lexical scanner should therefore include a high-speed skip over blanks.

Assignment statements were analyzed in some detail. There were 83,304 assignment statements in all; and 56,751 (68 percent) of them were trivial replacements of the form $A = B$ where no arithmetic operations were present.* The remaining assignments included 10,418 of the form $A = A$ op α; that is, the first operand on the right was the same as the variable on the left.

We attempted to rate the complexity of an assignment statement by counting one point for each + or - sign, five for each *, and eight for each /; the distribution was

Complexity	0	1	2	3	4	5	6	7	8	9
Number	56751	14645	1124	106	267	2436	1988	562	2359	552
Percent	68.0	17.5	1.3	0.1	0.3	3.0	2.0	0.6	3.0	0.6

Occurrences of operators and constants were also tallied:

Operator	+	-	*	/	**	=	standard function	constant
Occurrences	17973	10298	12348	4739	1108	90257	3994	49386

---

* In the Stanford sample the corresponding figures were 2,379 out of 4,869 (49 percent); this was another example of a Lockheed versus Stanford discrepancy.

It is rather surprising to note that 7,200 (40 percent) of the additions had the form $\alpha + 1$; also 349 (3 percent) of the multiplications had the form $\alpha * 2$; 180 (4 percent) of the divisions had the form $\alpha/2$; and 427 (39 percent) of the exponentiations had the form $\alpha**2$. (We forgot to count the fairly common occurrences of expressions like $2 * \alpha$, $2. * \alpha$, $\alpha * 2.$, $\alpha/2.$, $2.0 * \alpha$, etc.)

Our statistics-gathering program analyzed the indices of arrays, although it was unable to distinguish subscripted variables from calls on programmer-defined functions. Of the 166,599 appearances of variables, 97,051 (58 percent) were unindexed, 50,979 (30.5 percent) had one index, 16,181 (9.5 percent) had two, 2,008 (1 percent) had three, and 380 (0.2 percent) had four.

Another type of "static" test on the nature of FORTRAN programs was also made, in an attempt to discover the complexity of *control flow* in the programs. Cocke's "interval reduction" scheme [4] was applied to fifty randomly selected FORTRAN programs and subroutines, and in every case the flow graph was reduced to a single vertex after at most six transformations. The average number of transformations required per program was only 2.75.

The obvious conclusion to draw from all these figures is that compilers spend most of their time doing surprisingly simple things.

3. Dynamic Statistics

The static counts tabulated above are relevant to the speed of compilation, but they do not really have a strong connection with the speed of object program execution. We need to give more weight to statements that are executed more frequently.

Two different approaches to dynamic program analysis were explored in the course of our study: (1) the method of frequency counts or program profiles; and (2) the method of program status sampling. The former method inserts counters at appropriate places of the program in order to determine the number of times each statement was actually performed. The latter method makes use of an independent system program that interrupts the object program periodically and notes where it is currently executing instructions.

Frequency counts were commonly studied in the early days of computers (see Goldstine and von Neumann [8]) and they are now experiencing a long-overdue revival. We made use of a program called FORDAP, which had been developed previously by R. W. Stoltey, Jr., of IBM in connection with some research on compilation. FORDAP takes a FORTRAN program as input, and outputs an equivalent program that also maintains frequency counts and writes them on to a file. When the latter program is compiled and run, its output will include a listing of the executable statements together with their frequency counts. See Figure 1, which illustrates the output corresponding to a short program, using an extension of FORDAP that includes a rough estimate of the relative cost of each statement (see Ingalls [10]). The principles of preparing such a routine were independently developed at UCLA by Russell [15]; Russell's efforts were primarily directed towards a study of potential parallelism in programs, but he also included some serial analyses of large scale routines that exhibit the same phenomena observed in our own studies.

Frequency counts add an important new dimension to the FORTRAN programs; indeed, it is difficult to express in words just how tremendously "eye-opening" they are. Even the small example in Figure 1 has a surprise: The frequency counts reveal that about half the running time is spent in the subroutine linkage of the FUN function. After studying dozens of FORDAPed programs, and after experiencing the reactions of programmers who see the frequency counts of their own programs, our group came to the almost unanimous conclusion that all software systems should provide frequency counts to all programmers, unless specifically told not to do so.

The advantages of frequency counts in debugging have been exploited by Satterthwaite [16] in his extensions to Stanford's ALGOL W compiler. They can be used to govern selective tracing and to locate untested portions of a program. Once the program has been debugged, its frequency counts show where the "bottlenecks" are, and this information often suggests improvements to the algorithm and/or data structures. For example, we applied FORDAP to *itself*, since it was written in FORTRAN, and we immediately found that it was spending about half of its time in two loops that could be greatly simplified; this made it possible to double the speed of FORDAP, after less than an hour's work, without even looking at the rest of the program. (See Example 2 in Section 4.) The same thing happened many times with other programs.

Thus our experience has suggested that frequency counts are so important, they deserve a special name. Let us call the collection of frequency counts the *profile* of a program.

Programs typically have a very jagged profile, with a few sharp peaks. As a very rough approximation, it appears that the nth most important statement of a program from the standpoint of execution time accounts for about $(\alpha - 1)\alpha^{-n}$ of the running time, for some $\alpha > 1$ and for small n. We also found that less than 4 percent of a program generally accounts for more than half of its running time. This observation has

```
        EXECUTABLE STATEMENTS                      EXECUTIONS COST

10 READ (5,1) XO,YO,H,JNT,IENT                         2      100
   IF (IENT) 20,40,20                                  2        4
20 WRITE (6,2) H,XO,YO                                 1       50
   CALL RK2 (FUN,H,XO,YO,JNT,IENT,A)                   1        2
   STEP=FLOAT(JNT)*H                                   1       11
   X=XO                                                1        1
   DO 30 I=1,IENT                                      1        2
   X=X+STEP                                           30       60
30 WRITE (6,3) X,A(I)                                 30     1530
   GO TO 10                                            1        1
40 STOP                                                1        1
   END


   FUNCTION FUN(X,Y)                                1200    18000
   FUN =1./X                                        1200     9600
   RETURN                                           1200     6000
   END


   SUBROUTINE RK2(FUN,H,XI,YI,K,N,VEC)                 1       15
   H2=H/2.                                             1        8
   Y=YI                                                1        1
   X=XI                                                1        1
   DO 2 I=1,N                                          1        2
   DO 1 J=1,K                                         30       60
   T1=H*FUN(X,Y)                                     300     2700
   T2=H*FUN(X+H2,Y+T1/2.)                            300     5400
   T3=H*FUN(X+H2,Y+T2/2.)                            300     5400
   T4=H*FUN(X+H,Y+T3)                                300     3300
   Y= Y+(T1+2.*T2+2.*T3+T4)/6.                       300     6900
 1 X=X+H                                              300      900
 2 VEC(I)=Y                                            30       90
   RETURN                                              1        5
   END
```

FIGURE 1. The profile of a short program.

important consequences, since it means that programmers can make substantial improvements in their own routines by being careful in just a few places. And optimizing compilers can be made to run much faster, since they need not study the whole program with the same amount of concentration.

Table 2 shows how the relative frequency of statement types changes when the counts are dynamic instead of static. This table was compiled from the results of twenty-four FORDAP runs, with the statistics for each program weighted equally. We did not have time to break the statistics down further (to discover, for example, the distribution of operators), except in one respect: 45 percent of the assignment statements were simply replacements of the form $A = B$ (where B is a simple variable or constant), when counting statically, but this figure dropped to 35 percent when counting dynamically. In other words, replacements tend to occur more often outside of loops (in initialization sections, etc.).

TABLE 2. Distribution of executable statements

	Static	(percent)	Dynamic
Assignment	51		67
IF	10		11
GO TO	9		9
DO	9		3
CALL	5		3
WRITE	5		1
CONTINUE	4		7
RETURN	4		3
READ	2		0
STOP	1		0

The other approach to dynamic statistics gathering, based on program status sampling, tends to be less precise but more realistic, in the sense that it shows how much time is actually spent in system subroutines. We used and extended a routine called PROGTIME [11] that was originally developed by Johnston and Johnson to run on System/360 under MVT. PROGTIME spawns the user program as a subtask, then samples its status word at regular intervals, rejecting the datum if the program was dormant since its last interruption. An example of the resulting "histogram" output appears in Figure 2; it is possible (although not especially convenient) to relate the histogram to the FORTRAN source text.

In general, the results obtained from PROGTIME runs were essentially what we would have expected from the FORDAP produced profiles, except for the influence of input/output editing times. The results of FORDAP would have led us to believe that the code between relative locations 015928 and 015A28 in Figure 2 would consume most of the

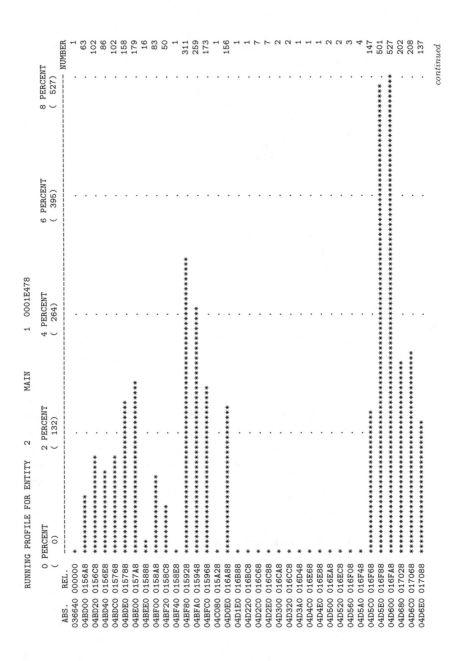

continued

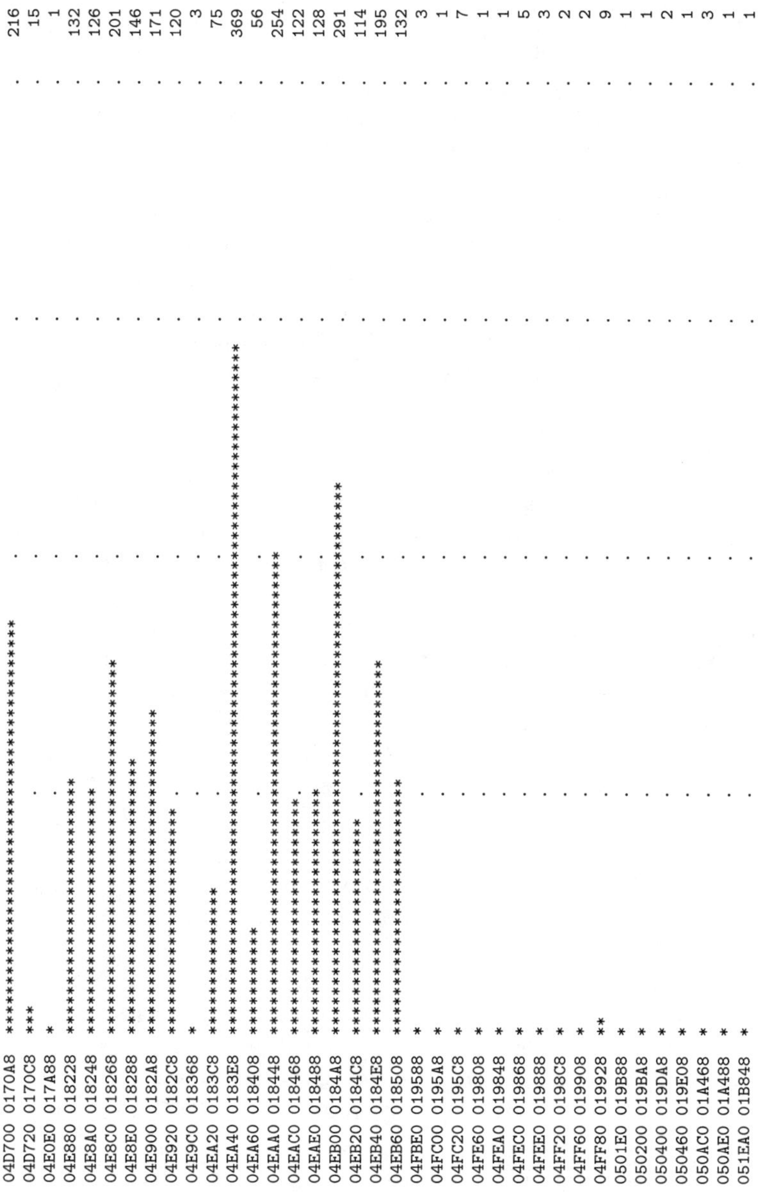

FIGURE 2. Histogram corresponding to a PROGTIME run.

running time; but in fact FORDAP does not give the true over-all picture, since 70 percent of the time was actually spent in those beloved system subroutines IHCECOMH and IHCFCVTH (relative locations 016A88–019080). Roughly half of the programs we studied involved substantial amounts of formatting for output and unformatting for input; this fact led us to believe that considerable gains in efficiency might be achieved if compilers would do such editing in-line wherever possible. It was easy to match up the formats with the quantities to be formatted, in every case we looked at. However, we did not have time to study the problem further to investigate just how much of an improvement in performance could be expected from in-line editing. Clearly the general problem of formatting deserves further attention, since it seems to use up more than 25 percent of the running time of FORTRAN programs in spite of the extremely infrequent occurrence of actual input/output statements reflected in Table 2.

Due to the random nature of the sampling process, two PROGTIMEs of the same program will not give identical results. It is possible to get accurate frequency counts and accurate running times by using the technique of "jump tracing" (see Gaines [7]). A jump trace routine scans a program down to the next branch instruction and executes the intervening code at machine speed; when a branch occurs, the location transferred to is written out on an auxiliary file. Subsequent processing of the file makes it possible to infer the frequency counts. The jump trace approach does not require auxiliary memory for counters and it can be used with arbitrary machine language programs. Unfortunately we were unable to develop such a routine for Stanford's computers during the limited time in which our study was performed.

4. The Inner Loops

We selected seventeen programs at random for closer scrutiny; this section contains a summary of the main features of those programs. (It is worth emphasizing that we did not modify the programs, nor did we discard programs that did not produce results in accordance with our preconceived ideas. We analyzed every routine we met, whether we liked it or not. The result is hopefully a good indication of typical FORTRAN programming practice, and we believe that a reader who scans these programs will obtain a fairly clear conception of how FORTRAN is being used.)

First the program profile was found by running each selected program with FORDAP and PROGTIME. (This policy caused the chief limitation on our selection, because we were unable to study programs for which input data was on inaccessible tapes or otherwise unavailable.) In each case a glance at the profile reduced the program to a comparatively small piece of code that represented the majority of the execution time, exclusive of input/output statements. These "inner loops" of the programs are presented here. The names of identifiers have been changed in order to give some anonymity, but no other changes have been made.

In each case we hand-translated the inner loop into System/360 machine language using five different styles of "optimization":

Level 0. Straight code generation according to classical one-pass compilation techniques.

Level 1. Like level 0, together with local optimizations based on a good knowledge of the machine: Common subexpressions are eliminated; register contents are remembered across statements, if no labels intervene; and so forth. The index of a DO is kept in a register, but no optimizations requiring global flow analysis are made.

Level 2. "Machine-independent" optimizations are applied, based on global flow analysis. Such optimizations include constant folding, invariant expression removal, strength reduction, test replacement, and load-store motion (see Allen [1]).

Level 3. Like level 2, plus machine-dependent optimizations based on the System/360 hardware, such as the use of BXLE and LA, and the possibilities afforded by double indexing.

Level 4. The highest level represents the "best conceivable" code that would be discovered by any compiler imaginable. Anything goes here except a change in the algorithm or its data structures.

These styles of optimization are not extremely well defined, but in each case we produced the finest code we could think of consistent with that level. (In nearly every case this was noticeably better than the optimizations produced by the existing FORTRAN compilers; FORTRAN H OPT 02 would presumably be able to reach level 3 if it were carefully tuned.) Level 4 represents the ultimate achievable, by comparison with what is realized by current techniques, in an attempt to assess whether or not an additional effort would be worthwhile.

These styles of optimization can best be appreciated by studying Example 1, for which our machine language coding appears in the Appendix to this paper. It is appropriate to restrict our attention solely to the inner loop, since the profiles show that the effect of optimization on this small part of the code is very indicative of the total effect of optimization on the program as a whole.

In order to compare one strategy to another, we decided to estimate the quality of each program by hand instead of actually running our codes with a timer, as in Wichmann [18]. We weighted the instructions in a crude but not atypical manner as follows: Each instruction costs one unit, plus one if it fetches or stores an operand from memory or if it is a branch that is taken, plus a penalty for specific slower opcodes:

Floating add/subtract	add 1
Multiply	add 5
Divide	add 8
Multiply double	add 13
Shift	add 1
Load multiple	add $n/2$ (n registers loaded)
Store multiple	add $n/3$ (n registers stored)

This evaluation corresponds roughly to 1 unit per 0.7 microseconds on our model 67 computer. Other machine organizations (with "pipe-lining," etc.) would, of course, behave somewhat differently, but the weights above should give some insight. We also assumed the following additional costs for the time spent in library subroutines (see [9]):

SQRT	85
SIN, COS	110
ALOG	120
ERF	130
Complex multiply	60
Real ** Integer	75

Example 1

The first program we studied involved 140 executable statements, but the following five represented nearly half of the (level 0) running time:

```
      DO 2 J = 1, N
      T = ABS(A(I,J))
      IF (T - S) 2,2,1
    1 S = T
    2 CONTINUE
```

Statement 1 was executed about half as often as the others in the loop. The programs in the Appendix have a "score" of

$$37.5, \quad 28.5, \quad 14.0, \quad 8.0, \quad 7.0$$

per iteration for levels 0, 1, 2, 3, 4 respectively.

The same program also included another time-consuming loop,

```
      DO 3 J = 1,N
    3 A(I,J) = A(I,J) * B
```

for which the respective scores per iteration are

$$51.0, \quad 29.0, \quad 17.0, \quad 12.0, \quad 11.0.$$

In this case, level 0 is penalized for calculating the subscript twice.

Example 2

The next example came from the original FORDAP program itself. Although there were 455 executable statements, more than half of the program time was spent executing two loops like this:

```
      DO 1 J = 38,53
      IF (K(I) .EQ. L(J)) GO TO 3
    1 CONTINUE
    2 ...
```

The value of J is not examined at label 3. The five styles of translation give respective scores of

$$23.0, \quad 19.0, \quad 9.0, \quad 5.0, \quad 3.5.$$

Level 4's score of 3.5 is obtained in an interesting way that applies to several other loops we had examined earlier in the summer; we call it the technique of *combining tests*: The array element L(54) is set equal to K(I), so that the loop involves only one test. Then after reaching L3, if $J = 54$ we go back to L2. The machine language code is

```
Q1   LA    3,8(0,3)      r3 ← r3 + 8.
     C     4,0(0,3)      compare r4 to mem[r3].
     BER   5             to L3 if equal.
     C     4,4(0,3)      compare r4 to mem[r3 + 4].
     BNE   Q1            to Q1 if not equal.
L3   ...
```

(Register r5 contains the address L3.) If necessary, L(54) could be restored.

Of course, in this particular case the loop is executed only sixteen times; hence it could be completely unrolled into 32 instructions

```
C     4,L(38)
BER   5
C     4,L(39)
BER   5
      ⋮
C     4,L(53)
BER   5
```

reducing the score per iteration to 3.0.

But in actual fact the L table was loaded in a DATA statement, and it contained a list of special character codes; a more appropriate program would replace the entire DO loop by a single test

```
IF (LT(K(I))) 1,3,1
```

for a suitable table LT, thereby saving over half the execution time of the program. (Furthermore, the environment of the DO loop shown above was

```
DO 2 I = 7,72
```

so that any assembly language programmer would have reduced the whole business to a single "translate and test.")

Example 3

```
      DOUBLE A,B,D
      DO 1 K = 1,N
      A = T(I-K,1+K)
      B = T(I-K,J+K)
    1 D = D-A*B
```

(This is one of the few times we observed double precision being used, although the numerical analysis professors in our department strongly recommend against the short precision operators of System/360. It serves as another indication that our department seems to have little impact on the users of our computer.) The scores for this loop are

$$89.0, \quad 67.0, \quad 38.0, \quad 13.0, \quad 12.0;$$

here level 2 suffers from some clumsiness in the indexing and a lack of knowledge that an ME instruction (short floating multiply) could be used instead of MD.

Example 4

Here the inner loop is longer and involves a subroutine call. The following code accounted for 70 percent of the running time; the entire program had 214 executable statements.

```
        DO 1 K = M,20
        CALL RAND(R)
        IF (R .GT. .81) N(K) = 1
1       CONTINUE

   . . . . . . . . .
        SUBROUTINE RAND(R)
        COMMON I,K
        J = I*65539
        IF (J) 1,2,2
1       J = J + 2147483647 + 1
2       R = J
        R = R * .4656613E-9
        I = J
        K = K + 1
        RETURN
        END
```

(Here we have a notoriously bad random number generator that the programmer must have found in an obsolete reference book; see [13]. It is *another* example of our failure to educate the community.) Conversion from integer to real is assumed to be done by the sequence

X	r,=XL4'80000000'	$r \leftarrow r \oplus (1000\ldots0)_2$.
ST	r,SPEC+4	$\text{mem}[\text{spec} + 4] \leftarrow r$.
LD	0,SPEC	$\text{rf0} \leftarrow \text{mem}[\text{spec}]$.
AD	0,SPEC1	$\text{rf0} \leftarrow \text{rf0} + \text{mem}[\text{spec1}]$.

for suitable contents of SPEC and SPEC1. By adjusting these constants further the multiplication by $0.4656613 \times 10^{-9} \approx 2^{-31}$ could be avoided; but that observation was felt to be beyond the scope of level 4 optimization, although it would occur naturally to any programmer using assembly language. Indeed, careful FORTRAN programmers would never convert to floating point at all in Example 4; they would simply compare J to the integer constant $1739461754 \approx .81 \times 2^{31}$.

The most interesting thing here, however, is the effect of subroutine linkage, since the long prolog and epilog significantly increase the time of the inner loop. The timings for levels 0–3 assume standard OS subroutine conventions, although levels 2 and 3 are able to shorten the prolog and epilog somewhat because of their knowledge of program flow. For level 4, the subroutine was "opened" and placed in the loop without any linkage, like a macro; hence we obtain the sequence of scores

$$119.9, \quad 105.1, \quad 81.4, \quad 76.2, \quad 27.2.$$

Without subscripting, there is comparatively little difference between levels 0 and 3; this implies that optimization probably has more payoff for FORTRAN than we would find for languages with more flexible data structures.

It would be interesting to know just how many hours each day are spent in prologs and epilogs establishing linkage conventions.

Example 5

The next inner loop is representative of several programs that had to be seen to be believed.

```
     DO 1 K = 1, N
     M = (J-1)*10+K-1
     IF (M.EQ.0) M = 1001
     C1 = C1+A1(M)*(B1**(K-1))*(B2**(J-1))
     C2 = C2+A2(M)*(B1**(K-1))*(B2**(J-1))
     IF ((K-1).EQ.0) T = 0.0
     IF ((K-1).GE.1) T = A1(M)*(K-1)*(B1**(K-2))*(B2**(J-1))
     C3 = C3+T
     IF ((K-1).EQ.0) T = 0.0
     IF ((K-1).GE.1) T = A2(M)*(K-1)*(B1**(K-2))*(B2**(J-1))
     C4 = C4+T
     IF ((J-1).EQ.0) T = 0.0
     IF ((J-1).GE.1) T = A1(M)*(B1**(K-1))*(J-1)*(B2**(J-2))
     C5 = C5+T
     IF ((J-1).EQ.0) T = 0.0
     IF ((J-1).GE.1) T = A2(M)*(B1**(K-1))*(J-1)*(B2**(J-2))
     C6 = C6+T
   1 CONTINUE
```

After staring at this for several minutes our group decided that it did not deserve to be optimized. But after two weeks' rest we looked at it again and found interesting applications of "strength reduction," both for the exponentiations and for the conversion of K to real. (The latter applies only in level 4, which knows that K does not get too large.) The scores were

$$1367.0, \quad 545.0, \quad 159.0, \quad 145.0, \quad 104.0.$$

Level 1 optimization finds common subexpressions and level 2 finds the reductions in strength. Level 4 removes nearly all the IF tests and rearranges the code so that C1 and C2 are updated last; thus only B1**(K-1) is a necessary auxiliary variable, not both it and B1**(K-2).

Example 6

In this case the inner loop involves subroutine calls instead of a DO loop:

```
      SUBROUTINE S(A,B,X)                            9
      DIMENSION A(2),B(2)                            9
      X = 0                                          9
      Y = (B(2)-A(2))*12+B(1)-A(1)                   9
      IF (Y.LT.0) GO TO 1                            9
      X = Y                                          5
    1 RETURN                                         9
      END                                            9
      SUBROUTINE W(A,B,C,D,X)                        4
      DIMENSION A(2),B(2),C(2),D(2),U(2),V(2)        4
      X = 0                                          4
      CALL S(A,D,X)                                  4
      IF (X.EQ.0) GO TO 3                            4
      CALL S(C,B,X)                                  2
      IF (X.EQ.0) GO TO 3                            2
      CALL S(C,A,X)                                  1
      U(1) = A(1)                                    1
      U(2) = A(2)                                    1
      IF (X.NE.0) GO TO 1                            1
      U(1) = C(1)                                    0
      U(2) = C(2)                                    0
    1 CONTINUE                                       1
      CALL S(B,D,X)                                  1
      V(1) = B(1)                                    1
      V(2) = B(2)                                    1
      IF (X.NE.0) GO TO 2                            1
      V(1) = D(1)                                    0
      V(2) = D(2)                                    0
    2 CALL S(U,V,X)                                  1
    3 CONTINUE                                       4
      RETURN                                         4
      END                                            4
```

The numbers at the right of this code show the approximate relative frequency of occurrence of each statement; calls on the W subroutine accounted for 60 percent of the execution time of the program. The scores for various optimization styles are

$$1545.5, \quad 1037.5, \quad 753.3, \quad 736.3, \quad 289.0.$$

Here 270 of the 1545.5 units for level 0 are due to repeated conversions of the constant 0 from integer to real. Levels 2 and 3 move the first statement 'X = 0' out of the main loop, performing it only if 'Y.LT.0'. The big improvement in level 4 comes from inserting the code for subroutine S in-line and making the corresponding simplifications. Statements like U(1)=A(1) and U(2)=A(2) become simply a change in base register. Perhaps further reductions would be possible if the context of subroutine W were examined, since if we denote 12*A(1)+A(2) by A and 12*B(1)+B(2) by B, etc., the subroutine computes $\max\bigl(0, \min(B, D) - \max(A, C)\bigr)$.

Example 7

In this program virtually all of the time exclusive of input/output editing was spent in the two loops

```
      DO 1 I = 1, N
      A = X**2+Y**2-2.*X*Y*C(I)
      B = SQRT(A)
      K = 100.*B+1.5
    1 D(I) = S(I)*T(K)
      Q = D(1)-D(N)
      DO 2 I = 2,N,2
    2 Q = Q+4.*D(I)+2.*D(I+1)
```

where array D was not used subsequently. The scores are

$$744.0, \quad 387.0, \quad 316.0, \quad 292.0, \quad 256.0.$$

Here level 1 computes X**2 by 'MER 0,0' instead of a subroutine call, and it computes 2.*D(I+1) by 'AER 0,0' instead of multiplying. Level 4 combines the two DO loops into one and eliminates array D entirely. (Such savings in storage space were present in quite a few of the programs we looked at; some matrices could be reduced to vectors, and some vectors could be reduced to scalars, due to the nature of the calculations. A quantitative estimate of how much space could be saved by such optimization would be interesting.)

Example 8

Ninety percent of the running time of the next program was spent in the following subroutine:

```
SUBROUTINE COMPUTE
COMMON ...
COMPLEX Y(10), Z(10)
R = REAL(Y(N))
P = SIN(R)
Q = COS(R)
S = C*6.*(P/3.-Q*Q*P)
T = 1.414214*P*P*Q*C*6.
U = T/2.
V = -2.*C*6.*(P/3.-Q*Q*P/2.)
Z(1) = (0.,-1.)*(S*Y(1)+T*Y(2))
Z(2) = (0.,-1.)*(U*Y(1)+V*Y(2))
RETURN
END
```

This was the only example of complex arithmetic that we observed in our study. The scores

$$841.5, \quad 735.5, \quad 336.0, \quad 336.0, \quad 249.0$$

reflect the fact that levels 0 and 1 make six calls on the complex-multiply subroutine, while levels 2 and 3 expand complex multiplication into a sequence of real operations (with obvious simplifications). Level 4 in this analysis makes free use of the distributive law, for example by setting $S=C*P*(2.-6.*Q*Q)$, although this may not be numerically justified. Furthermore level 4 assumes the existence of a single subroutine 'SINCOS(R)' that computes both the sine and cosine of its argument in 165 units of time; programmers who calculate the sine of an angle usually want to know its cosine too and vice versa, and it is possible to calculate both in somewhat less time than would be required to compute them individually.

Example 9

A program with 245 executable statements spent 70% of its time in

```
DO 2 K = 1, M
DO 2 J = 1, M
```

```
            X = 0.
            Y = 0.
            DO 1 I = 1, M
            N = (J+J+(I-1)*M2)
            B = A(K,I)
            X = X+B*Z(N)
          1 Y = Y+B*Z(N-1)
            DY(L) = W*X
            DY(L+1) = -W*Y
          2 L = L+2
```

when M was only 3. Scores (for the innermost I loop only) are

$$84.0, \quad 69.0, \quad 30.0, \quad 24.0, \quad 24.0,$$

reflecting the fact that level 4 cannot do anything for this case.

Example 10

In this excerpt from a contour plot routine, the CALL is done only rarely:

```
DO 1 I = L, M
1 IF(X(I-1,J).LT.Q.AND.X(I,J).GE.Q) CALL S(A1,A2,A3,A4,7,A5)
```

The scores, assuming that X(I).LT.Q about half the time, are

$$40.0, \quad 31.5, \quad 14.5, \quad 7.5, \quad 5.0.$$

Level 3 keeps Q in a register, while level 2 does not. Level 4 is especially interesting since it avoids testing X(I-1,J).LT.Q in those cases where the result is known to be true from the previous loop. We had noticed similar situations in other routines.

Example 11

This 'fast Fourier transform' example shows that inner loops are not always signaled by the word 'DO'.

```
          1   K = K+1
              A1 = A(K)*C(J)+A1
              B1 = B(K)*C(J)+B1
              K = K+1
              A2 = A(K)*S(J)+A2
              B2 = B(K)*S(J)+B2
              J = J+I
              IF (J.GT.M) J = J-M
              IF (K.LT.M) GO TO 1
```

The scores are

$$118.0, \quad 91.0, \quad 60.0, \quad 54.0, \quad 50.0.$$

Level 4 is able to omit the second 'K=K+1', and to use a BXLE command for 'J=J+I'.

Example 12

Unfortunately an inner loop is not always as short as we had hoped. This rather long program (1,300 executable statements) spent about half of its time in the following rather horrible loop:

```
      DO 3 I = 1,M
      J0 = J1
      IF (J0.EQ.0) J0 = J2
      J1 = J1+1
      J3 = J3+1
      J4 = J4+1
      IF (J4.EQ.(L(J-1)+1)) J4 = 1
      J5 = J1+1
      IF (J5.EQ.(J2+1)) J5 = 1
      U1 = U(J1,K1,K2)
      V1 = V(J1,K1,K2)
      W1 = W(J1,K1,K2)
      P(J1) = .25*(Q1(I)*(V1+V(J3,K3,K2))*(W1+W(J3,K3,K2))
     +Q2(I)*(V1+V(J3+1,K3,K2))*(W1+W(J3+1,K3,K2))
     -Q3(I)*(V1+V(J4,K4,K2))*(W1+W(J4,K4,K2))
     +D*((U1+U(J5,K1,K2))*(W1+W(J5,K1,K2))
      - (U1+U(J0,K1,K2))*(W1+W(J0,K1,K2))))
     +R1(J1,K1)*R2(K2)*(S(J1,K2+1)*(W1+W(J1,K1,K2+1))
         - S(J1,K2)*(W1+W(J1,K1,K2-1)))
      IF (I.EQ.1) GO TO 1
      J6 = J4-1
      IF (J6.EQ.0) J6 = L(J-1)
      P(J1) = P(J1)-.25*Q4(I)*(V1+V(J6,K4,K2))*(W1+W(J6,K4,K2))
      GO TO 3
    1 IF (M.EQ.1) GO TO 2
      P(J1) = P(J1)+.25*Q4(I)*(V1+V(J3-1,K3,K2))*(W1+W(J3-1,K3,K2))
      GO TO 3
    2 P(J1) = P(J1)+.25*Q4(I)*(V1+V(J2+4,K3,K2))*(W1+W(J2+4,K3,K2))
    3 CONTINUE
```

Here levels 2 and 3 have just enough registers to maintain all the necessary index variables. The scores are

$$792.0, \quad 368.0, \quad 242.0, \quad 238.0, \quad 207.0.$$

Level 4 observes that J6 can more easily be computed by 'J6=J4' before J4 is changed; and the Q4(I) terms are included as if they were conditional expressions within the big formula for P(J1).

Example 13

Here is a standard "binary search" loop:

```
      I = 0
      K = N+1
 1    J = (I+K)/2
      IF (J.EQ.I) GO TO 5
      IF (X(J) - X0) 2,4,3
 2    I = J
      GO TO 1
 3    K = J
      GO TO 1
 4    ...
 5    ...
```

The scores
$$38.5, \quad 33.0, \quad 27.0, \quad 21.0, \quad 10.0$$

for the inner loop are of interest primarily because level 4 was able to beat level 3 by a larger factor than in any other example (except where subroutines were expanded in-line). The coding for level 4 in this case consisted of six packets of eight lines each, one for each permutation of the three registers α, β, and γ:

L1$\alpha\beta\gamma$	LA	$\gamma,0(\alpha,\beta)$	r$\gamma \leftarrow$ r$\alpha +$ rβ.
	SRL	$\gamma,1$	r$\gamma \leftarrow \lfloor$r$\gamma/2\rfloor$.
	NR	$\gamma,8$	r$\gamma \leftarrow$ r$\gamma \wedge$ r8.
	CR	γ,α	compare rγ to rα.
	BE	L5α	to L5α if equal.
	CE	$0,X(\gamma)$	compare rf0 to mem$[$x0 $+ \gamma]$.
	BL	L1$\gamma\beta\alpha$	to L1$\gamma\beta\alpha$ if less.
	BE	L4γ	to L4γ if greater.
L1$\alpha\gamma\beta$	...		

Here 4I, 4J and 4K are respectively assumed to be in registers α, γ, and β; register r8 contains -4. Division by 2 can be reduced to a shift, since it is possible to prove that I, J, and K are nonnegative. Half of the instructions 'CR γ,α; BE L5α' could have been removed if X(0) were somehow set to $-\infty$; this would save another 10 percent.

Actually the binary search was *not* the inner loop in the program we analyzed, although the programmer (one of our group) had originally thought it would be! The frequency counts showed that his program was actually spending most of its time *moving* entries in the X table, to keep the table in order when new elements were inserted. This was one of many cases we observed where a knowledge of frequency counts immediately suggested vital improvements by directing a programmer's attention to the real bottlenecks. Changing to a hash-coding scheme made this particular program run about twice as fast.

Examples 14–17

From this point on, the programs we looked at began to seem rather repetitious. We worked out four more examples, summarized here with their scores:

```
      DO 1 I = 1,N
      C = C/D*R
      R = R+1.
    1 D = D-1.                    [45.0, 42.0, 27.0, 21.0, 20.0]

      DO 1 J = I,N
      H(I,J) = H(I,J)+S(I)*S(J)/D1-S(K+I)*S(K+J)/D2
    1 H(J,I) = H(I,J)             [136.0, 103.0, 58.0, 49.0, 41.5]

      REAL FUNCTION F(X)
      Y = X*.7071068
      IF (Y.LT.0.0) GO TO 1
      F = 0.5*(1.0+ERF(Y))    ⎫  low frequency
      RETURN                  ⎭
    1 F = 1.0-0.5*(1.0+ERF(-Y))
      RETURN
      END                         [219.5, 208.5, 191.3, 191.3, 151.0]

      DO 1 I = 1,N
    1 A = A+B(I)+C(K,I)           [41.0, 31.0, 14.0, 9.0, 8.0]
```

(The final example is the loop from 015928 to 015A28 in Figure 2.)

Cursory examination of other programs led us to believe that the seventeen examples above are fairly representative of the programs now being written in FORTRAN, and that they indicate the approximate effects achievable with different styles of optimization (on our computer).

Only one of the other programs we looked at showed essentially different characteristics, and this one was truly remarkable. It contained more than 700 lines of straight calculation (see the excerpts in Figure 3), involving no loops, IF's or GO's! (Idiosyncrasies of spacing indicate that it was generated by hand, not by program.) This must be some sort of record for the length of program text without intervening labeled statements, and we did not believe it could possibly be considered typical.

All but one of the DO loops in the examples above apparently have variable bounds, but in fact the compiler could deduce that the bounds are actually constant in most cases. For instance, in Example 17, the variable N is set equal to 805 at the beginning of the program and never changed thereafter.

Table 3 summarizes the score ratios obtained in these examples; 0/1 denotes the ratio of the score for level 0 to the score for level 1, etc.

It may be objected that measurement of the effects of optimization is impossible, since programmers tend to change the style of their FORTRAN programs when they know what kind of optimizations are being done for them. However, the programs we examined showed no evidence that the programmers had any idea what the compiler does, except perhaps the knowledge that '1' is or is not converted to '1.0' at compile time when appropriate. Therefore we expect that such feedback effects are very limited.

Notice that level 3 and level 4 programs ran four or more times as fast as level 0 programs, in about half of the cases. Level 3 was not too far from level 4 except in Examples 4 and 6, where short subroutine code was expanded in-line; by incorporating this technique and the idea of replicating short loops, level 3 would come very close indeed to the "ultimate" performance of level 4 optimization. (Before conducting this study, the author had expected a much greater difference between levels 3 and 4, and had been experimenting with some more elaborate schemes for optimization, capable of coming close to the level 4 code in the binary search example above. But the sample programs seem to show that existing optimization techniques are good enough, on our computer at least.)

5. Summary and Conclusions

Compiler writers should be familiar with the nature of the programs that their compiler will have to handle. Besides constructing "best cases"

$\vdots$ $\qquad\qquad\qquad\qquad\qquad\qquad\qquad\qquad\qquad\qquad\qquad$ $\vdots$

```
U23 =-ES12T*SETN + ES12B*SEBN                                      264.
U24 =-ES22T*SETN + ES22B*SEBN                                      265.
U30 = ES66T*SETN + ES66B*SEBN                                      266.
U31 =-ES66T*SETN + ES66B*SEBN                                      267.
V3T =-2.*((ES11T+M*ES12T)*SXT+(M*ES22T+ES12T)*SYT)*C2XC2Y          268.
1     -2.*DSQRT(M)*TT*ES66T*S2XS2Y                                 269.
V3B =-2.*((ES11B+M*ES12B)*SXB+(M*ES22B+ES12B)*SYB)*C2XC2Y          270.
1     -2.*DSQRT(M)*TB*ES66B*S2XS2Y                                 271.
V4T =-8.*((ES11T+M*ES12T)*SXT+(M*ES22T+ES12T)*SYT)*C4XC4Y          272.
1     -8.*DSQRT(M)*TT*ES66T*S4XS4Y                                 273.
V4B =-8.*((ES11B+M*ES12B)*SXB+(M*ES22B+ES12B)*SYB)*C4XC4Y          274.
1     -8.*DSQRT(M)*TB*ES66B*S4XS4Y                                 275.
V5T =-2.*((9.*ES11T+M*ES12T)*SXT+(M*ES22T+9.*ES12T)*SYT)*C2XC6Y    276.
1     -6.*DSQRT(M)*TT*ES66T*S2XS6Y                                 277.
```

$\vdots$ $\qquad\qquad\qquad\qquad\qquad\qquad\qquad\qquad\qquad\qquad\qquad$ $\vdots$

```
A(3) = -A11*ML2*2.*XI1 - 4.*A22*ML2*4.*XI2 - A13*ML2*2.*XI1        604.
1      +T1*64.*XI3                                                 605.
2      -TML20*(A11 + 2.*A22 + A13)                                 606.
3      -4.*HY*SB02*ML2                                             607.
A(4) = -ML2*(2.*XI1*(XI2+XI3)-BETA*XI1/LSQ )-A11*Q2S              608.
1      -TML20*(XI1/4. +XI2 + XI3)                                  609.
2      +(HX*(K11B+M*K12BX)*SA11+M*HY*(M*K22B+K12BY)*SB11           610.
3       +HXY*M*K66H*SC11)/2.                                       611.
4      +Y3                                                         612.
A(5) = -ML2*XI23*16. - A22*Q2S*I6.                                 613.
1      - TML20*2.*XI3                                              614.
2      +Y4                                                         615.
```

$\vdots$ $\qquad\qquad\qquad\qquad\qquad\qquad\qquad\qquad\qquad\qquad\qquad$ $\vdots$

```
B(14,16)= +Y1315                                                  959.
B(14,17)= +Y1316                                                  960.
B(15,14)= B(14,15)                                                961.
B(16,14)= B(14,16)                                                962.
B(17,14)= B(14,17)                                                963.
B(15,1) = 0.                                                      964.
B(15,2) = 0.                                                      965.
B(15,3) = -4.*ML2*HY                                              966.
B(15,15) = -HY*HY*MSQ*D11B/(2.*DB) + Y1414                        967.
B(15,16)=  Y1415                                                  968.
B(15,17)=  Y1416                                                  969.
B(16,15)= B(15,16)                                                970.
B(17,15)= B(15,17)                                                971.
B(16,1)= +ML2*HXY                                                 972.
B(16,2) = 0.                                                      973.
B(16,3) = 0.                                                      974.
B(16,16) = -HXY*HXY*M/(4.*D66B) + Y1515                           975.
```

$\vdots$ $\qquad\qquad\qquad\qquad\qquad\qquad\qquad\qquad\qquad\qquad\qquad$ $\vdots$

FIGURE 3. Excerpts from a remarkable program.

TABLE 3. Execution speed ratios with various types of optimization

Example	0/1	0/2	0/3	0/4	1/4	2/4	3/4
1a	1.3	2.7	4.7	5.4	4.1	2.0	1.1
1b	1.8	3.0	4.3	4.8	2.7	1.5	1.1
2	1.2	2.6	4.6	6.6	5.4	2.6	1.4
3	1.3	2.3	6.8	7.4	5.6	3.2	1.1
4	1.1	1.5	1.6	4.4	3.9	3.0	2.8
5	2.5	9.0	9.4	13.1	5.2	1.5	1.4
6	1.5	2.0	2.1	5.4	3.6	2.6	2.5
7	1.9	2.4	2.5	2.9	1.5	1.2	1.1
8	1.1	2.5	2.5	3.4	3.0	1.3	1.3
9	1.2	2.8	3.5	3.5	2.9	1.3	1.0
10	1.3	2.8	5.3	8.0	6.3	2.9	1.5
11	1.3	2.0	2.2	2.4	1.8	1.2	1.1
12	2.2	3.3	3.3	3.8	1.8	1.1	1.1
13	1.2	1.4	1.8	3.9	3.3	2.7	2.1
14	1.1	1.6	2.1	2.3	2.1	1.4	1.1
15	1.3	2.3	2.8	3.3	2.5	1.4	1.1
16	1.1	1.1	1.1	1.5	1.4	1.3	1.3
17	1.3	2.9	4.6	5.1	3.9	1.8	1.1

and "worst cases" it is a good idea to have some conception of "average cases." We hope that the data presented in this paper will help to give a reasonably balanced impression of the programs that are actually being written today.

Of course every individual program is atypical in some sense, yet our study showed that a small number of basic patterns account for most of the programming constructions in use. Perhaps these programs can be used to make a more realistic comparison of compiler and machine speeds than is obtained with the "GAMM test" [17]. See also P. Bryant's comparison of FORTRAN compilers summarized in [4, pages 764–767].

Our sample may not be typical, so we hope that people in other parts of the world will conduct similar experiments in order to see if independent studies yield comparable results.

While gathering these statistics we became convinced that a comparatively simple change to the present method of program preparation can make substantial improvements in the efficiency of computer usage. The program profiles (namely collections of frequency counts) that we used in our analyses turned out to be so helpful that we believe profiles should be made available routinely to all programmers by all of the principal software systems.

The "ideal system of the future" will keep profiles associated with source programs, using the frequency counts in virtually all phases of a program's life. During the debugging stage the profiles can be quite useful, for selective tracing as well as for inner-loop detection. Statements with zero frequency indicate untested sections of the program. After the program has been debugged, the profile may already have served its purpose; but if the program is to be used frequently, the high counts in its profile often suggest basic improvements that can be made. An optimizing compiler can also make very effective use of the profile, since time-consuming optimization often needs to be done on only one-tenth or one-twentieth of a program. The profile can also be used effectively in storage management schemes.

In early days of computing, machine time was king, and people worked hard to get extremely efficient programs. Eventually machines got larger and faster, and the payoff for writing fast programs was measured in minutes or seconds instead of hours. Moreover, in considering the total cost of computing, people began to observe that program development and maintenance costs often overshadowed the actual cost of running the programs. Therefore most of the emphasis in software development has been in making programs easier to write, easier to understand, and easier to change. There is no doubt that this emphasis has reduced total system costs in many installations; but there also is little doubt that the corresponding lack of emphasis on efficient code has resulted in systems that can be greatly improved, and it seems to be time to right the balance.

Frequency counts give an important dimension to programs, showing programmers how to make their routines more efficient with comparatively little effort. A recent study [5] showed that this approach led to an elevenfold increase in a particular compiler's speed. It appears useful to develop interactive systems that tell programmers the most costly parts of their programs, and that give positive reinforcement for improvements, so that programmers might actually *enjoy* making the changes. For most of the examples studied in the previous section we found that it was possible to obtain noticeably better performance by making straightforward modifications to the inner loop of a FORTRAN source language program.

In these remarks we have implicitly assumed that the design of compilers should be strongly influenced by what *programmers* do. An alternative point of view is that programmers should be strongly influenced by what their *compilers* do; compiler writers in their infinite wisdom may in fact know what is really good for programmers and would like to steer them towards a proper course. This viewpoint has some merit, although it has often been carried to extremes in which programmers have to work harder and make unnatural constructions just so that the compiler writer has an easier job. When weighted frequency counts are supplied routinely, it will become clear to a programmer just which aspects of a language the implementor has chosen to treat most efficiently; the reporting of this information seems to be the best way to exert a positive influence on the users of a language.

The results of our study suggest several avenues for further research. For example, additional static and dynamic statistics should be gathered that are more meaningful with respect to local optimizations. A more sophisticated study of these statistics would also be desirable.

Our survey seems to have given a reasonably clear picture of FOR-TRAN as it is now used. Other languages should be studied in a similar way, so that software designers can conceptualize the notion of "typical" programs in COBOL, ALGOL, PL/I, LISP, APL, SNOBOL, etc.

We found that well-done optimization leads to at least a four- or five-fold increase in program speed (exclusive of input/output formatting) over straight translation in about half of the programs we analyzed. This figure is based on a computer such as the 360/67 at Stanford, and it may prove to be somewhat different on other configurations; we would like to see how much different the results turn out to be if the seventeen examples are worked out carefully for other types of computers. Furthermore, a study of the performance gain that would be achieved by in-line formatting is definitely called for.

As our group discussed the example programs, we ran into many instances where it would have been natural for compiler optimization to be done interactively. The programmer could perhaps be asked in Example 11 whether or not J will be nonnegative and less than 2^{24} throughout the loop (so that J=J+1 can be done with a "load address" instruction). In Example 8 we wished we could ask whether the distributive law could be used on the formulas. In Example 7 the programmer might be asked if the subexpression

$$X**2 + Y**2$$

can ever overflow — if not, this calculation may be taken out of the loop. And so on.

As the reader can see, considerable work remains to be done on empirical studies of programming, much more than we could achieve in one summer.

Acknowledgments

This study would not have been successful without the many hours of volunteer work contributed by members of the group who were not supported by research funds. Members of the group included G. Autrey, D. Brown, I. Fang, D. Ingalls, J. Low, F. Maginnis, M. Maybury, D. McNabb, E. Satterthwaite, R. Sites, R. Sweet, and J. Walters; these people did all of the hard work that led to the results reported here. We are also grateful for computer time contributed by the Stanford Linear Accelerator Center, IBM Corporation, and Lockheed Missiles and Space Corporation.

This research was supported, in part, by IBM Corporation, by Xerox Corporation, and by the Advanced Research Projects Agency of the Office of the Department of Defense (SD-183).

Appendix: Examples of Hand Translation

The following code was produced from

```
DO 2 J = 1, N
  T = ABS(A(I,J))
  IF (T-S) 2,2,1
1 S = T
2 CONTINUE
```

using the various styles of hand translation described in Section 4. Only the inner loop is shown, not the initialization.

Level 0

			Cost	
Q1	ST	5,J	2	$J \leftarrow$ r5.
	L	3,J	2	r3 $\leftarrow J$.
	M	2,=A(AROWS)	7	(r2, r3) $\leftarrow$ r3 × arows.
	A	3,I	2	r3 $\leftarrow$ r3 $+ I$.
	SLL	3,2	2	r3 $\leftarrow$ 4r3.
	LE	0,A(3)	2	rf0 $\leftarrow$ mem[a0 + r3].
	LPER	0,0	1	rf0 $\leftarrow$ |rf0|.
	STE	0,T	2	$T \leftarrow$ rf0.
	LE	0,T	2	rf0 $\leftarrow T$.
	SE	0,S	3	rf0 $\leftarrow$ rf0 $- S$.
	BNH	L2	1.5	to L2 if not positive.
	B	L1	2 × 0.5	to L1.
L1	LE	0,T	2 × 0.5	rf0 $\leftarrow T$.
	STE	0,S	2 × 0.5	$S \leftarrow$ rf0.

```
L2  L     5,J          2      r5 ← J.
    A     5,=F'1'      2      r5 ← r5 + 1.
    C     5,N          2      compare r5 to N.
    BNH   Q1           2      to Q1 if not greater.
```

A "dedicated" use of registers, and a straightforward statement-by-statement approach, are typical of level 0.

Level 1

$$Cost$$

```
Q1  ST    5,J          2           J ← r5.
    LA    3,AROWS      1           r3 ← arows.
    MR    2,5          6           (r2,r3) ← r3 × r5.
    A     3,I          2           r3 ← r3 + I.
    SLL   3,2          2           r3 ← 4r3.
    LE    0,A(3)       2           rf0 ← mem[a0 + r3].
    LPER  0,0          1           rf0 ← |rf0|.
    STE   0,T          2           T ← rf0.
    CE    0,S          2           compare rf0 to S.
    BNH   L2           1.5         to L2 if not greater.
L1  LE    0,T          2 × 0.5     rf0 ← T.
    STE   0,S          2 × 0.5     S ← rf0.
L2  LA    5,1(0,5)     1           2r5 ← r5 + 1.
    C     5,N          2           compare r5 to N.
    BNH   Q1           2           to Q1 if not greater.
```

Note the uses of LA and CE, the knowledge of register contents, and the removal of the redundant branch. The redundant LE in location L1 is still present because the occurrence of a label potentially destroys the register contents.

Level 2

$$Cost$$

```
Q1  LE    0,0(0,3)       2           rf0 ← mem[r3].
    LPER  0,0            1           rf0 ← |rf0|.
    LER   4,0            1           rf4 ← rf0.
    SER   4,2            2           rf4 ← rf4 − rf2.
    BNH   L2             1.5         to L2 if not positive.
L1  LER   2,0            1 × 0.5     rf2 ← rf0.
L2  A     3,=A(AROWS*4)  2           r3 ← r3 + 4arows.
    C     3,SPEC         2           compare r3 to SPEC.
    BNH   Q1             2           to Q1 if not greater.
```

Here SPEC contains the precomputed address of A(I,N); the variable S is maintained in floating-point register rf2.

Level 3   *Cost*

Q1	LE	0,0(0,3)	2	rf0 ← mem[r3].
	LPER	0,0	1	rf0 ← |rf0|.
	CER	0,2	1	compare rf0 to rf2.
	BNHR	2	1.5	to L2 if not greater.
L1	LER	2,0	1 × 0.5	rf2 ← rf0.
L2	BXLE	3,4,Q1	2	r3 ← r3 + r4, to Q1 if r3 ≤ r5.

Here register r2 is preloaded with the address of L2 (for a microscopic improvement); registers r4 and r5 are preloaded with appropriate values governing the BXLE.

Level 4   *Cost*

Q1	LE	0,0(0,3)	2 × 0.5	rf0 ← mem[r3].
	LPER	0,0	1 × 0.5	rf0 ← |rf0|.
	CER	0,2	1 × 0.5	compare rf0 to rf2.
	BNHR	2	1.5 × 0.5	to L2.1 if not greater.
L1.1	LER	2,0	1 × 0.25	rf2 ← rf0.
L2.1	LE	0,4(0,3)	2 × 0.5	rf0 ← mem[r3 + 4].
	LPER	0,0	1 × 0.5	rf0 ← |rf0|.
	CER	0,2	1 × 0.5	compare rf0 to rf2.
	BNHR	6	1.5 × 0.5	to L2.2 if not greater.
L1.2	LER	2,0	1 × 0.25	rf2 ← rf0.
L2.2	BXLE	3,4,Q1	2 × 0.5	r3 ← r3 + r4, to Q1 if r3 ≤ r5.

Since the loop program is so short it has been duplicated, saving half of the BXLE's, when proper initialization and termination routines are appended. (The code would have been written

Q1	LE	0,0(0,3)	rf0 ← mem[r3].
	LPER	0,0	rf0 ← |rf0|.
	CER	0,2	compare rf0 to rf2.
	BHR	2	to L1.1 if greater.
L2.1	LE	0,4(0,3)	rf0 ← mem[r3 + 4].
	LPER	0,0	rf0 ← |rf0|.
	CER	0,2	compare rf0 to rf2.
	BHR	6	to L1.2 if greater.
L2.2	BXLE	3,4,Q1	r3 ← r3 + r4, to Q1 if r3 ≤ r5.
	. . .		
L1.1	LER	2,0	rf2 ← rf0.
	B	L2.1	to L2.1.
L1.2	LER	2,0	rf2 ← rf0.
	B	L2.2	to L2.2.

if the profile of this program had given less weight to statement 1.)

The FORTRAN convention of storing arrays by columns would make these loops rather inefficient in a paging environment. A compiler should make appropriate changes to the storage mapping function for arrays in such a case.

References

[1] F. E. Allen, "Program optimization," *Annual Review in Automatic Programming* **5** (1969), 239–307.

[2] Peter Calingaert, "System performance evaluation: Survey and appraisal," *Communications of the ACM* **10** (1967), 12–18, 224.

[3] Vinton G. Cerf, *Measurement of Recursive Programs*, Report 70-43 (M.S. thesis, School of Engineering and Applied Science, University of California, Los Angeles, California, 1970). [See also Vinton G. Cerf and Gerald Estrin, "Measurement of recursive programs," *Information Processing 71*, Proceedings of IFIP Congress 71 (Amsterdam: North-Holland, 1972), 314–319.]

[4] John Cocke and J. T. Schwartz, *Programming Languages and Their Compilers*, 2nd edition (New York: Courant Institute of Mathematical Sciences, New York University, 1970).

[5] Stephen C. Darden and Steven B. Heller, "Streamline your software development," *Computer Decisions* **2**, 10 (October 1970), 29–33.

[6] D. N. Freeman, "Error correction in CORC, The Cornell computing language," *Proceedings of the AFIPS Fall Joint Computer Conference* **26** (1964), 15–34.

[7] R. Stockton Gaines, *The Debugging of Computer Programs* (Ph.D. thesis, Princeton University, 1969), Chapter 3.

[8] Herman H. Goldstine and John von Neumann, *Planning and Coding of Problems for an Electronic Computing Instrument*, 3 volumes (Princeton, New Jersey: Institute for Advanced Study, 1947–1948). Reprinted in von Neumann's *Collected Works* **5**, edited by A. H. Taub (Oxford: Pergamon, 1963), 80–235.

[9] IBM System/360 FORTRAN IV Library: Mathematical and Service Subprograms, File number S360-25, Form C28-6818-0, Table 13, Model 65 (IBM Corporation, 1969).

[10] D. Ingalls, *FETE — a FORTRAN Execution Time Estimator*, Stanford Computer Science report STAN-CS-71-204 (Stanford, California: 1971).

[11] T. Y. Johnston and R. H. Johnson, *Program Performance Measurement*, SLAC User Note 33, Revision 1 (Stanford, California: Stanford University, 1970).

[12] Donald E. Knuth, "RUNCIBLE — Algebraic translation on a limited computer," *Communications of the ACM* **2**, 11 (November 1959), 18–21. [Reprinted as Chapter 21 of the present volume.]

[13] Donald E. Knuth, "The dangers of computer science theory," in *Logic, Methodology and Philosophy of Science* **4** (Amsterdam: North-Holland, 1973), 189–195. [Reprinted as Chapter 2 of *Selected Papers on Analysis of Algorithms*, CSLI Lecture Notes 102 (Stanford, California: Center for the Study of Language and Information, 2000), 19–26.] See also the discussion of RANDU in *Seminumerical Algorithms*, Volume 2 of *The Art of Computer Programming*, third edition (Reading, Massachusetts: Addison–Wesley, 1997).

[14] P. G. Moulton and M. E. Muller, "DITRAN — A compiler emphasizing diagnostics," *Communications of the ACM* **10** (1967), 45–52.

[15] Edward Charles Russell, Jr., *Automatic Program Analysis*, Report 69-12 (Ph.D. thesis, School of Engineering and Applied Science, University of California, Los Angeles, California, 1969).

[16] E. Satterthwaite, "Debugging tools for high level languages," *Software — Practice & Experience* **2** (1972), 197–217. See also Edwin Hallowell Satterthwaite, Jr., *Source Language Debugging Tools*, report STAN-CS-75-494 (Ph.D. thesis, Stanford University, 1975).

[17] E. Schmid, "Rechenzeitenvergleich bei Digitalrechnern," *Computing* **5** (1970), 163–177.

[18] B. A. Wichmann, *A Comparison of ALGOL 60 Execution Speeds*, Report 3 (Teddington, Middlesex, United Kingdom: National Physical Laboratory, Central Computer Unit, 1969).

[19] B. A. Wichmann, *Some Statistics from ALGOL Programs* (Teddington, Middlesex, United Kingdom: National Physical Laboratory, Central Computer Unit, 1970).

Addenda

The following references summarize some of the subsequent story:

Jon Louis Bentley, *Writing Efficient Programs* (Englewood Cliffs, New Jersey: Prentice–Hall, 1982).

David W. Wall, "Predicting program behavior using real or estimated profiles," *SIGPLAN Notices* **26**, 6 (June 1991), 59–70.

Rafael H. Saavedra and Alan J. Smith, "Performance characterization of optimizing compilers," *IEEE Transactions on Software Engineering* **SE-21** (1995), 615–628.

Chapter 25

Efficient Coroutine Generation of Constrained Gray Sequences

An interesting family of cooperating coroutines is able to generate all patterns of bits that satisfy certain fairly general ordering constraints, changing only one bit at a time. (More precisely, the directed graph of constraints is required to be cycle-free when it is regarded as an undirected graph.) If the coroutines are implemented carefully, they yield an algorithm that needs only a bounded amount of computation per bit change, thereby solving an open problem in the field of combinatorial pattern generation.

[To Ole-Johan Dahl on his 70th birthday, 12 October 2001. Written with Frank Ruskey. Originally published in From Object-Orientation to Formal Methods: Dedicated to the Memory of Ole-Johan Dahl, edited by O. Owe, S. Krogdahl, and T. Lyche, Lecture Notes in Computer Science 2635 (Heidelberg: Springer-Verlag, 2003).]

Much has been written about the transformation of procedures from recursive to iterative form, but little is known about the more general problem of transforming *coroutines* into equivalent programs that avoid unnecessary overhead. The present paper attempts to take a step in that direction by focusing on a reasonably simple yet nontrivial family of cooperating coroutines for which significant improvements in efficiency are possible when appropriate transformations are applied. The authors hope that this example will inspire other researchers to develop and explore the potentially rich field of coroutine transformation.

Coroutines, originally introduced by M. E. Conway [2], are analogous to subroutines, but they are symmetrical with respect to caller and callee: When coroutine A invokes coroutine B, the action of A is temporarily suspended and the action of B resumes where B had most recently left off. Coroutines arise naturally in producer/consumer situations or multipass processes, analogous to the "pipes" of UNIX, when each coroutine transforms an input stream to an output stream; a sequence of such processes can be controlled in such a way that their intermediate data files need not be written in memory. (See, for example, Section 1.4.2 of [9].)

The programming language SIMULA 67 [3] introduced support for coroutines in terms of fundamental operations named **call, detach,** and **resume.** Arne Wang and Ole-Johan Dahl subsequently discovered [20] that an extremely simple computational model is able to accommodate these primitive operations. Dahl published several examples to demonstrate their usefulness in his chapter of the book *Structured Programming* [4]; then M. Clint [1] and O.-J. Dahl [6] began to develop theoretical tools for formal proofs of coroutine correctness.

Another significant early work appeared in R. W. Floyd's general top-down parsing algorithm for context-free languages [8], an algorithm that involved "imaginary men who are assumed to automatically appear when hired, disappear when fired, remember the names of their subordinates and superiors, and so on." Floyd's imaginary men were essentially carrying out coroutines; but their actions could not be described naturally in any programming languages that were available to Floyd when he wrote about the subject in 1964, so he presented the algorithm as a flow chart. Ole-Johan Dahl later gave an elegant implementation of Floyd's algorithm using the features of SIMULA 67, in §2.1.2 of [5].

The coroutine concept was refined further during the 1970s; see, for example, [19] and the references cited therein. But today's programming languages have replaced those ideas with more modern notions such as "threads" and "closures," which (while admirable in themselves) support coroutines only in a rather awkward and cumbersome manner. The simple principles of old-style coroutines, which Dahl called *quasi-parallel processes*, deserve to be resurrected again and given better treatment by the programming languages of tomorrow.

In this paper we will study examples for which a well-designed compiler could transform certain families of coroutines into optimized code, just as compilers can often transform recursive procedures into iterative routines that require less space and/or time.

The ideas presented below were motivated by applications to the exhaustive generation of combinatorial objects. For example, consider a coroutine that wants to look at all permutations of n elements; it can call repeatedly on a permutation-generation coroutine to produce the successive arrangements. The latter coroutine repeatedly forms a new permutation and calls on the former coroutine to inspect the result. The permutation coroutine has its own internal state — its own local variables and its current location in an ongoing computational process — so it does not consider itself to be a "subroutine" of the inspection coroutine. The permutation coroutine might also invoke other coroutines, which in turn are computational objects with their own internal states.

We shall consider the problem of generating all n-tuples $a_1 a_2 \ldots a_n$ of 0s and 1s with the property that $a_j \leq a_k$ whenever $j \to k$ is an arc in a given directed graph. Thus $a_j = 1$ implies that a_k must also be 1; if $a_k = 0$, so is a_j. These n-tuples are supposed to form a "Gray path," in the sense that only one bit a_j should change at each step. For example, if $n = 3$ and if we require $a_1 \leq a_3$ and $a_2 \leq a_3$, five binary strings $a_1 a_2 a_3$ satisfy the inequalities, and one such Gray path is

$$000, \ 001, \ 011, \ 111, \ 101.$$

The general problem just stated does not always have a solution. For example, suppose the given digraph is

so that the inequalities are $a_1 \leq a_2$ and $a_2 \leq a_1$; then we are asking for a way to generate the tuples 00 and 11 by changing only one bit at a time, and this is clearly impossible. Even if we stipulate that the digraph of inequalities should contain no directed cycles, we might encounter an example like

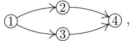

in which the Gray constraint cannot be achieved; here the corresponding 4-tuples

$$0000, 0001, 0011, 0101, 0111, 1111$$

include four of even weight and two of odd weight, but a Gray path must alternate between even and odd. Reasonably efficient methods for solving the problem without Grayness are known [17, 18], but we want to insist on single-bit changes.

We will prove constructively that Gray paths always do exist if we restrict consideration to directed graphs that are *totally acyclic*, in the sense that they contain no cycles even if the directions of the arcs are ignored. Every component of such a graph is a free tree in which a direction has been assigned to each branch between two vertices. Such digraphs are called *spiders*, because of their resemblance to arachnids:

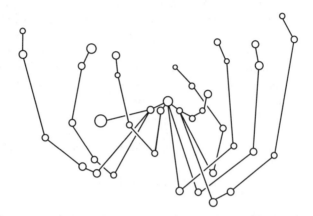

(In this diagram, as in others below, we assume that all arcs are directed upwards. More complicated graph-theoretical spiders have legs that change directions many more times than real spider legs do.) The general problem of finding all $a_1 \ldots a_n$ such that $a_j \le a_k$ when $j \to k$ in such a digraph is formally called the task of "generating the order ideals of an acyclic poset"; it also is called, informally, "spider squishing."

Sections 1–3 of this paper discuss simple examples of the problem in preparation for Section 4, which presents a constructive proof that suitable Gray paths always exist. The proof of Section 4 is implemented with coroutines in Section 5, and Section 6 discusses the nontrivial task of getting all the coroutines properly launched.

Section 7 describes a simple technique that is often able to improve the running time. A generalization of that technique leads in Section 8 to an efficient coroutine-free implementation. Additional optimizations, which can be used to construct an algorithm for the spider-squishing problem that is actually *loopless*, are discussed in Section 9. (A loopless algorithm needs only constant time to change each n-tuple to its successor.)

Section 10 concludes the paper and mentions several open problems connected to related work.

1. The Unrestricted Case

Let's begin by imagining an array of friendly trolls called $T_1, T_2, \ldots, T_n$. Each troll carries a lamp that is either off or on; he also can be either awake or asleep. Initially all the trolls are awake, and all their lamps are off.

Changes occur to the system when a troll is "poked," according to the following simple rules: If T_k is poked when he is awake, he changes the state of his lamp from off to on or vice versa; then he becomes tired and goes to sleep. Later, when the sleeping T_k is poked again, he wakes up and pokes his left neighbor T_{k-1}, without making any change to his own lamp. (The leftmost troll T_1 has no left neighbor, so he simply awakens when poked.)

At periodic intervals an external driving force D pokes the rightmost troll T_n, initiating a chain of events that culminates in one lamp changing its state. The process begins as follows, if we use the digits 0 and 1 to represent lamps that are respectively off or on, and if we underline the digit of a sleeping troll:

$\quad$ ...0000   Initial state
$\quad$ ...000$\underline{1}$ D pokes T_n
$\quad$ ...00$\underline{11}$ D pokes T_n, who wakes up and pokes T_{n-1}
$\quad$ ...00$\underline{1}$0 D pokes T_n
$\quad$ ...0$\underline{1}$10 D pokes T_n, who pokes T_{n-1}, who pokes T_{n-2}
$\quad$ ...0$\underline{1}$11 D pokes T_n
$\quad$ ...0$\underline{1}$0$\underline{1}$ D pokes T_n, who pokes T_{n-1}

The sequence of underlined versus not-underlined digits acts essentially as a binary counter. And the sequence of digit patterns, in which exactly one bit changes at each step, is a *Gray binary* counter, which follows the well-known Gray binary code; it also corresponds to the process of replacing rings in the classic Chinese ring puzzle [12]. Therefore the array of trolls solves our problem of generating all n-tuples $a_1 a_2 \ldots a_n$, in the special case when the spider digraph has no arcs. (This troll-oriented way to generate Gray binary code was presented in a lecture at the University of Oslo in October, 1972 [10].)

During the first 2^n steps of the process just described, troll T_n is poked 2^n times, troll T_{n-1} is poked 2^{n-1} times, ..., and troll T_1 is poked twice. The last step is special because T_1 has no left neighbor; when he is poked the second time, all the trolls wake up, but no lamps change. The driver D would like to know about this exceptional case, so we will assume that T_n sends a message to D after being poked, saying '*true*' if one of the lamps has changed, otherwise saying '*false*'. Similarly, if $1 \le k < n$, T_k will send a message to T_{k+1} after being poked, saying '*true*' if and only if one of the first k lamps has just changed state.

These hypothetical trolls T_1, ..., T_n correspond to n almost-identical coroutines $poke[1]$, ..., $poke[n]$, whose actions can be expressed in an ad hoc ALGOL-like language as follows:

> **Boolean coroutine** $poke[k]$;
> **while** *true* **do begin**
> awake: $a[k] := 1 - a[k]$; **return** *true*;
> asleep: **if** $k > 1$ **then return** $poke[k-1]$ **else return** *false*;
> **end**.

Coroutine $poke[k]$ describes the action of T_k, implicitly retaining its own state of wakefulness: When $poke[k]$ is next activated after having executed the statement '**return** *true*', it will resume its program at label 'asleep'; and it will resume at label 'awake' when it is next activated after '**return** $poke[k-1]$' or '**return** *false*'.

In this example and in all the coroutine programs below, the enclosing '**while** *true* **do begin** $\langle P \rangle$ **end**' merely says that program $\langle P \rangle$ should be repeated endlessly; all coroutines that we shall encounter in this paper are immortal. (This is fortunate, because Dahl [6] has observed that proofs of correctness tend to be much simpler in such cases.)

Our coroutines will also always be "ultra-lightweight" processes, in the sense that they need no internal stack. They need only remember their current positions within their respective programs, along with a few local variables in some cases, together with the global "lamp" variables $a[1]$, ..., $a[n]$. We can implement them using a single stack, essentially as if we were implementing recursive procedures in the normal way, pushing the address of a return point within A onto the stack when coroutine A invokes coroutine B, and resuming A after B executes a **return**. (Wang and Dahl [20] used the term "semicoroutine" for this special case. We are, however, using **return** statements to return a value, instead of using global variables for communication and saying '**detach**' as Wang and Dahl did.) The only difference between our coroutine conventions and ordinary subroutine actions is that a newly invoked coroutine always begins at the point following its most recent **return**, regardless of who had previously invoked it. No coroutine will appear on the execution stack more than once at any time.

Thus, for example, the coroutines $poke[1]$ and $poke[2]$ behave as follows when $n = 2$:

$$
\begin{array}{ll}
00 & \text{Initial state} \\
0\underline{1} & poke[2] = true \\
\underline{1}1 & poke[2] = poke[1] = true \\
\underline{1}0 & poke[2] = true
\end{array}
$$

$$10 \quad poke\,[2] = poke\,[1] = false$$
$$11 \quad poke\,[2] = true$$
$$01 \quad poke\,[2] = poke\,[1] = true$$
$$00 \quad poke\,[2] = true$$
$$00 \quad poke\,[2] = poke\,[1] = false$$

The same cycle will repeat indefinitely, because everything has returned to its initial state.

Notice that the repeating cycle in this example consists of two distinct parts. The first half cycle, before *false* is returned, generates all two-bit patterns in Gray binary order $(00, 01, 11, 10)$; the other half generates those patterns again, but in the *reverse* order $(10, 11, 01, 00)$. Such behavior will be characteristic of all the coroutines that we shall consider for the spider-squishing problem: Their task will be to run through all n-tuples $a_1 \ldots a_n$ such that $a_j \le a_k$ for certain given pairs (j, k), always returning *true* until all permissible patterns have been generated; then they are supposed to run through those n-tuples again in reverse order, and to repeat the process ad infinitum.

Under these conventions, a driver program of the following form will cycle through the answers, printing a line of dashes between each complete listing:

⟨ Create all the coroutines ⟩;
⟨ Put each lamp and each coroutine into the proper initial state ⟩;
while *true* **do begin**
    for $k := 1$ **step** 1 **until** n **do** $write\,(a[k])$;
    $write\,(newline)$;
    if not *root* **then** $write\,(\texttt{"-----"}, newline)$;
    end.

Here *root* denotes a coroutine that can potentially activate all the others; for example, *root* is $poke\,[n]$ in the particular case that we've been considering. In practice, of course, the driver would normally carry out some interesting process on the bits $a_1 \ldots a_n$, instead of merely outputting them to a file.

The fact that coroutines $poke\,[1]$, $\ldots$, $poke\,[n]$ do indeed generate Gray binary code is easy to verify by induction on n. The case $n = 1$ is trivial, because the outputs will clearly be

```
0
1
-----
1
0
-----
```

and so on. On the other hand if $n > 1$, assume that the successive contents of $a_1 \ldots a_{n-1}$ are α_0, α_1, α_2, ... when we repeatedly invoke $poke[n-1]$, assuming that $\alpha_0 = 0 \ldots 0$ and that all coroutines are initially at the label 'awake'; assume further that *false* is returned just before α_m when m is a multiple of 2^{n-1}, otherwise the returned value is *true*. Then repeated invocations of $poke[n]$ will lead to the successive lamp patterns

$$\alpha_0 0, \ \alpha_0 1, \ \alpha_1 1, \ \alpha_1 0, \ \alpha_2 0, \ \alpha_2 1, \ \ldots,$$

and *false* will be returned after every sequence of 2^n outputs. These are precisely the patterns of n-bit Gray binary code, alternately in forward order and reverse order.

2. Chains

Now let's go to the opposite extreme and suppose that the digraph of constraints is an oriented path or chain,

$$1 \to 2 \to \cdots \to n.$$

In other words, we want now to generate all n-tuples $a_1 a_2 \ldots a_n$ such that

$$0 \leq a_1 \leq a_2 \leq \cdots \leq a_n \leq 1,$$

proceeding alternately forward and backward in Gray order. Of course this problem is trivial, but we want to do it with coroutines so that we'll be able to tackle more difficult problems later.

Here are some coroutines that do the new job, if the driver program initiates action by invoking the root coroutine $bump[1]$:

> **Boolean coroutine** $bump[k]$;
>   **while** *true* **do begin**
>
> awake0: **if** $k < n$ **then while** $bump[k+1]$ **do return** *true*;
> $a[k] := 1$;   **return** *true*;
>
> asleep1: **return** *false*;   **comment** $a_k \ldots a_n = 1 \ldots 1$;
>
> awake1: $a[k] := 0$;   **return** *true*;
>
> asleep0: **if** $k < n$ **then while** $bump[k+1]$ **do return** *true*;
>   **return** *false*;   **comment** $a_k \ldots a_n = 0 \ldots 0$;
>   **end.**

For example, the process plays out as follows when $n = 3$:

000	Initial state	123
00$\underline{1}$	$bump[1] = bump[2] = bump[3] = true$	12$\underline{3}$
0$\underline{1}$1	$bump[1] = bump[2] = true,\ bump[3] = false$	1$\underline{2}$
$\underline{1}$11	$bump[1] = true,\ bump[2] = false$	$\underline{1}$
111	$bump[1] = false$	1
$\underline{0}$11	$bump[1] = true$	1$\underline{2}$
$\underline{0}$01	$bump[1] = bump[2] = true$	12$\underline{3}$
$\underline{0}$00	$bump[1] = bump[2] = bump[3] = true$	12$\underline{3}$
000	$bump[1] = bump[2] = bump[3] = false$	123

Each troll's action now depends on whether his lamp is lit as well as on his state of wakefulness. A troll with an unlighted lamp always passes each bump to the right, without taking any notice unless a *false* reply comes back. In the latter case, he acts as if his lamp had been lit — namely, he either returns *false* (if just awakened), or he changes the lamp, returns *true*, and nods off. The Boolean value returned in each case is *true* if and only if a lamp has changed its state during the current invocation of $bump[k]$.

(*Note:* The numbers '123', '12$\underline{3}$', ... at the right of this example correspond to an encoding that will be explained in Section 8 below. A similar column of somewhat inscrutable figures will be given with other examples we will see later, so that the principles of Section 8 will be easier to understand when we reach that part of the story. There is no need to decipher such notations until then; all will be revealed eventually.)

The dual situation, in which all inequalities are reversed so that we generate all $a_1 a_2 \ldots a_n$ with

$$1 \geq a_1 \geq a_2 \geq \cdots \geq a_n \geq 0,$$

can be implemented by interchanging the roles of 0 and 1 and starting the previous sequence in the midpoint of its period:

> **Boolean coroutine** $cobump[k]$;
> $\qquad$ **while** *true* **do begin**
> awake0: $a[k] := 1$; **return** *true*;
> asleep1: **if** $k < n$ **then while** $cobump[k+1]$ **do return** *true*;
> $\qquad$ **return** *false*; **comment** $a_k \ldots a_n = 1 \ldots 1$;
> awake1: **if** $k < n$ **then while** $cobump[k+1]$ **do return** *true*;
> $\qquad$ $a[k] := 0$; **return** *true*;
> asleep0: **return** *false*; **comment** $a_k \ldots a_n = 0 \ldots 0$;
> $\qquad$ **end.**

A mixed situation in which the constraints are

$$0 \le a_n \le a_{n-1} \le \cdots \le a_{m+1} \le a_1 \le a_2 \le \cdots \le a_m \le 1$$

is also worthy of note. Again the underlying digraph is a chain, and the driver repeatedly bumps troll T_1; but when $1 < m < n$, the coroutines are a mixture of those we've just seen:

> **Boolean coroutine** *mbump*$[k]$;
>   **while** *true* **do begin**

awake0: **if** $k < m$ **then while** *mbump*$[k+1]$ **do return** *true*;
   $a[k] := 1$;   **return** *true*;

asleep1: **if** $m < k \,\wedge\, k < n$ **then while** *mbump*$[k+1]$ **do return** *true*;
   if $k = 1 \,\wedge\, m < n$ **then while** *mbump*$[m+1]$ **do return** *true*;
   return *false*;

awake1: **if** $m < k \,\wedge\, k < n$ **then while** *mbump*$[k+1]$ **do return** *true*;
   if $k = 1 \,\wedge\, m < n$ **then while** *mbump*$[m+1]$ **do return** *true*;
   $a[k] := 0$;   **return** *true*;

asleep0: **if** $k < m$ **then while** *mbump*$[k+1]$ **do return** *true*;
   return *false*;
   end.

The reader is encouraged to simulate the *mbump* coroutines by hand when, say, $m = 2$ and $n = 4$, in order to develop a better intuition about coroutine behavior. Notice that when $m \approx \frac{1}{2}n$, signals need to propagate only about half as far as they do when $m = 1$ or $m = n$.

Still another simple but significant variant arises when several separate chains are present. The digraph might, for example, be

in which case we want all 6-tuples of bits $a_1 \ldots a_6$ with $a_1 \le a_2$ and $a_4 \le a_5 \le a_6$. In general, suppose there is a set of endpoints $E = \{e_1, \ldots, e_m\}$ such that

$$1 = e_1 < \cdots < e_m \le n,$$

and we want

$$a_k \in \{0, 1\} \quad \text{for } 1 \le k \le n; \qquad a_{k-1} \le a_k \quad \text{for } k \notin E.$$

(The set E is $\{1, 3, 4\}$ in the example shown.) The following coroutines $ebump[k]$, for $1 \leq k \leq n$, generate all such n-tuples if the driver invokes $ebump[e_m]$:

> **Boolean coroutine** $ebump[k]$;
> > **while** *true* **do begin**
>
> awake0: **if** $k + 1 \notin E \cup \{n + 1\}$ **then**
> > **while** $ebump[k + 1]$ **do return** *true*;
> > $a[k] := 1$; **return** *true*;
>
> asleep1: **if** $k \in E \setminus \{1\}$ **then return** $ebump[k']$ **else return** *false*;
> awake1: $a[k] := 0$; **return** *true*;
> asleep0: **if** $k + 1 \notin E \cup \{n + 1\}$ **then**
> > **while** $ebump[k + 1]$ **do return** *true*;
> > **if** $k \in E \setminus \{1\}$ **then return** $ebump[k']$ **else return** *false*;
> > **end**.

Here k' stands for e_{j-1} when $k = e_j$ and $j > 1$. These routines reduce to *poke* when $E = \{1, 2, \ldots, n\}$ and to *bump* when $E = \{1\}$. If $E = \{1, 3, 4\}$, they will generate all 24 bit patterns such that $a_1 \leq a_2$ and $a_4 \leq a_5 \leq a_6$ in the order

000000, 000001, 000011, 000111, 001111, 001011, 001001, 001000,
011000, 011001, 011011, 011111, 010111, 010011, 010001, 010000,
110000, 110001, 110011, 110111, 111111, 111011, 111001, 111000;

then the sequence will reverse itself:

111000, 111001, 111011, 111111, 110111, 110011, 110001, 110000,
010000, 010001, 010011, 010111, 011111, 011011, 011001, 011000,
001000, 001001, 001011, 001111, 000111, 000011, 000001, 000000.

In our examples so far we have discussed several families of cooperating coroutines and claimed that they generate certain n-tuples, but we haven't proved anything rigorously. A formal theory of coroutine semantics is beyond the scope of this paper, but we should at least try to construct a semi-formal demonstration that *ebump* is correct.

The proof is by induction on $|E|$, the number of chains. If $|E| = 1$, $ebump[k]$ reduces to $bump[k]$, and we can argue by induction on n. The result is obvious when $n = 1$. If $n > 1$, suppose repeated calls on

$bump[2]$ cause $a_2 \ldots a_n$ to run through the $(n-1)$-tuples α_0, α_1, α_2, ..., where $bump[2]$ is *false* when it produces $\alpha_t = \alpha_{t-1}$. Such a repetition will occur if and only if t is a multiple of n, because n is the number of distinct $(n-1)$-tuples with $a_2 \leq \cdots \leq a_n$. We know by induction that the sequence has reflective symmetry: $\alpha_j = \alpha_{2n-1-j}$ for $0 \leq j < n$. Furthermore, $\alpha_{j+2n} = \alpha_j$ for all $j \geq 0$. To complete the proof we observe that repeated calls on $bump[1]$ will produce the n-tuples

$$0\alpha_0, \ 0\alpha_1, \ \ldots, \ 0\alpha_{n-1}, \ 1\alpha_n,$$
$$1\alpha_n, \ 0\alpha_n, \ 0\alpha_{n+1}, \ \ldots, \ 0\alpha_{2n-1},$$
$$0\alpha_{2n}, \ 0\alpha_{2n+1}, \ \ldots, \ 0\alpha_{3n-1}, \ 1\alpha_{3n},$$

and so on, returning *false* every $(n+1)^{\text{st}}$ step as desired.

If $|E| > 1$, let $E = \{e_1, \ldots, e_m\}$, so that $e'_m = e_{m-1}$, and suppose that repeated calls on $ebump[e_{m-1}]$ produce the $(e_m - 1)$-tuples α_0, α_1, α_2, ... Also suppose that calls on $ebump[e_m]$ would set the remaining bits $a_{e_m} \ldots a_n$ to the $(n+1-e_m)$-tuples β_0, β_1, β_2, ..., if E were empty instead of $\{e_1, \ldots, e_m\}$; this sequence β_0, β_1, β_2, ... is like the output of $bump$. The α and β sequences are periodic, with respective periods of length $2M$ and $2N$ for some M and N; they also have reflective symmetry $\alpha_j = \alpha_{2M-1-j}$, $\beta_k = \beta_{2N-1-k}$. It follows that $ebump[e_m]$ is correct, because it produces the sequence

$$\gamma_0, \gamma_1, \ldots = \alpha_0\beta_0, \ \alpha_0\beta_1, \ \ldots, \ \alpha_0\beta_{N-1},$$
$$\alpha_1\beta_N, \ \alpha_1\beta_{N+1}, \ \ldots, \ \alpha_1\beta_{2N-1},$$
$$\vdots$$
$$\alpha_{M-1}\beta_{(M-1)N}, \ \alpha_{M-1}\beta_{(M-1)N+1}, \ \ldots, \ \alpha_{M-1}\beta_{MN-1},$$
$$\alpha_M\beta_{MN}, \ \alpha_M\beta_{MN+1}, \ \ldots, \ \alpha_M\beta_{(M+1)N-1},$$
$$\vdots$$
$$\alpha_{2M-1}\beta_{(2M-1)N}, \ \alpha_{2M-1}\beta_{(2M-1)N+1}, \ \ldots, \ \alpha_{2M-1}\beta_{2MN-1}, \ \ldots$$

which has period length $2MN$ and satisfies

$$\gamma_{Nj+k} = \alpha_j\beta_{Nj+k} = \alpha_{2M-1-j}\beta_{2MN-1-Nj-k} = \gamma_{2MN-1-Nj-k}$$

for $0 \leq j < M$ and $0 \leq k < N$.

The patterns output by $ebump$ are therefore easily seen to be essentially the same as the so-called *reflected Gray paths* for radices $e_2 + 1 - e_1$, ..., $e_m + 1 - e_{m-1}$, $n + 2 - e_m$ (see [12]); the total number of outputs is

$$(e_2 + 1 - e_1) \ldots (e_m + 1 - e_{m-1})(n + 2 - e_m).$$

3. Ups and Downs

Let's turn now to a "fence" digraph

which leads to n-tuples that satisfy the up-down constraints

$$a_1 \leq a_2 \geq a_3 \leq a_4 \geq \cdots.$$

A reasonably simple set of coroutines can be shown to handle this case, rooted at $nudge[1]$:

> **Boolean coroutine** $nudge[k]$;
>   **while** $true$ **do begin**
>
> awake0: **if** $k' \leq n$ **then**
>   **while** $nudge[k']$ **do return** $true$;
> $a[k] := 1$; **return** $true$;
>
> asleep1: **if** $k'' \leq n$ **then**
>   **while** $nudge[k'']$ **do return** $true$;
>   **return** $false$;
>
> awake1: **if** $k'' \leq n$ **then**
>   **while** $nudge[k'']$ **do return** $true$;
> $a[k] := 0$; **return** $true$;
>
> asleep0: **if** $k' \leq n$ **then**
>   **while** $nudge[k']$ **do return** $true$;
>   **return** $false$;
>   **end**.

Here $(k', k'') = (k+1, k+2)$ when k is odd, $(k+2, k+1)$ when k is even.

But these coroutines do *not* work when they all begin at 'awake0' with $a_1 a_2 \ldots a_n = 00 \ldots 0$; they need to be initialized carefully. For example, when $n = 6$ it turns out that exactly eleven patterns of odd weight need to be generated, and exactly ten patterns of even weight, so a Gray path cannot begin or end with an even-weight pattern such as 000000 or 111111.

One proper starting configuration is obtained if we set $a_1 \ldots a_n$ to the first n bits of the infinite string $000111000111\ldots$, and if we start coroutine *nudge*[k] at 'awake0' if $a_k = 0$, at 'awake1' if $a_k = 1$. For example, the sequence of results when $n = 4$ is

0001	Initial configuration	124
000<u>0</u>	*nudge*[1] = *nudge*[2] = *nudge*[4] = *true*	12<u>4</u>
0<u>1</u>00	*nudge*[1] = *nudge*[2] = *true*, *nudge*[4] = *false*	12<u>3</u>4
0<u>1</u>0<u>1</u>	*nudge*[1] = *nudge*[2] = *nudge*[3] = *nudge*[4] = *true*	12<u>3</u>4
0<u>1</u>11	*nudge*[1] = *nudge*[2] = *nudge*[3] = *true*, *nudge*[4] = *false*	12<u>3</u>
<u>1</u>111	*nudge*[1] = *true*, *nudge*[2] = *nudge*[3] = *false*	13
<u>1</u>1<u>0</u>1	*nudge*[1] = *nudge*[3] = *true*	1<u>3</u>4
<u>1</u>1<u>00</u>	*nudge*[1] = *nudge*[3] = *nudge*[4] = *true*	1<u>3</u>4
1100	*nudge*[1] = *nudge*[3] = *nudge*[4] = *false*	134
110<u>1</u>	*nudge*[1] = *nudge*[3] = *nudge*[4] = *true*	134
11<u>1</u>1	*nudge*[1] = *nudge*[3] = *true*, *nudge*[4] = *false*	1<u>3</u>
<u>0</u>111	*nudge*[1] = *true*, *nudge*[3] = *false*	1<u>2</u>3
<u>0</u>1<u>0</u>1	*nudge*[1] = *nudge*[2] = *nudge*[3] = *true*	12<u>3</u>4
<u>0</u>1<u>0</u>0	*nudge*[1] = *nudge*[2] = *nudge*[3] = *nudge*[4] = *true*	12<u>3</u>4
<u>0</u><u>0</u>00	*nudge*[1] = *nudge*[2] = *true*, *nudge*[3] = *nudge*[4] = *false*	12<u>4</u>
<u>0</u><u>0</u>01	*nudge*[1] = *nudge*[2] = *nudge*[4] = *true*	12<u>4</u>
0001	*nudge*[1] = *nudge*[2] = *nudge*[4] = *false*	124

Again the cycle repeats with reflective symmetry; and again, some cryptic notations appear that will be explained in Section 8. The correctness of *nudge* will follow from results we shall prove later.

4. The General Case

We have seen that cleverly constructed coroutines are able to generate Gray paths for several rather different special cases of the spider-squishing problem; thus it is natural to hope that similar techniques will work in the general case when an arbitrary totally acyclic digraph is given. The spider

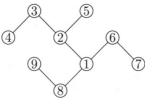

illustrates most of the complications that might face us, so we shall use it as a running example. In general we shall assume that the vertices have been numbered in *preorder*, as defined in [9, Section 2.3.2], when the digraph is considered to be a forest (ignoring the arc directions). This means that the smallest vertex in each component is the root of that component, and that all vertex numbers of a component are consecutive. Furthermore, the children of each node are immediately followed in the ordering by their descendants. The descendants of each node k form a subspider consisting of nodes k through scope(k), inclusive; we shall call this "spider k." For example, spider 2 consists of nodes $\{2,3,4,5\}$, and scope(2) = 5. Our sample spider has indeed been numbered in preorder, because it can be drawn as a properly numbered tree with directed branches:

The same spider could also have been numbered in many other ways, because any vertex of the digraph could have been chosen to be the root, and because the resulting trees can be embedded several ways into the plane by permuting the children of each family.

Assume for the moment that the digraph is connected; thus it is a tree with root 1. A nonroot vertex x is called *positive* if the path from 1 to x ends with an arc directed towards x, *negative* if that path ends with an arc directed away from x. Thus the example spider has positive vertices $\{2,3,5,6,9\}$ and negative vertices $\{4,7,8\}$.

Let us write $x \to^* y$ if there is a directed path from x to y in the digraph. Removing all vertices x such that $x \to^* 1$ disconnects the graph into a number of pieces having positive roots; in our example, the removal of $\{1,8\}$ leaves three components rooted at $\{2,6,9\}$. We call these roots the *positive vertices near* 1, and we denote that set by U_1. Similarly, the *negative vertices near* 1 are obtained when we remove all vertices y such that $1 \to^* y$; the set of resulting roots, denoted by V_1, is $\{4,7,8\}$ in our example, because we remove $\{1,2,3,5,6\}$.

The relevant bit patterns $a_1 \ldots a_n$ for which $a_1 = 0$ are precisely those that we obtain if we set $a_j = 0$ whenever $j \to^* 1$ and if we supply bit patterns for each subspider rooted at a vertex of U_1. Similarly, the bit patterns for which $a_1 = 1$ are precisely those we obtain by setting $a_k = 1$ whenever $1 \to^* k$ and by supplying patterns for each subspider rooted at a vertex of V_1. Thus if n_k denotes the number of bit patterns for spider k, the total number of suitable patterns $a_1 \ldots a_n$ is $\prod_{u \in U_1} n_u + \prod_{v \in V_1} n_v$.

The sets U_k and V_k of positive and negative vertices near k are defined in the same way for each spider k.

Every positive child of k appears in U_k, and every negative child appears in V_k. These are called the *principal* elements of U_k and V_k. Every nonprincipal member of U_k is a member of U_v for some unique principal vertex v of V_k. Similarly, every nonprincipal member of V_k is a member of V_u for some unique principal vertex u of U_k. For example, the principal members of U_1 are 2 and 6; the other member, 9, belongs to U_8, where 8 is a principal member of V_1.

We will prove that the bit patterns $a_1 \ldots a_n$ can always be arranged in a Gray path such that bit a_1 begins at 0 and ends at 1, changing exactly once. By induction, such paths exist for the n_u patterns in each spider u for $u \in U_1$. And we can combine such paths into a single path that passes through all of the $\prod_{u \in U_1} n_u$ ways to combine those patterns, using a reflected Gray code analogous to the output of *ebump* in Section 3 above. Thus, if we set $a_k = 0$ for all k such that $k \to^* 1$, we get a Gray path P_1 for all suitable patterns with $a_1 = 0$. Similarly we can construct a Gray path Q_1 for the $\prod_{v \in V_1} n_v$ suitable patterns with $a_1 = 1$. Thus, all we need to do is prove that it is possible to construct P_1 and Q_1 in such a way that the last pattern in P_1 differs from the first pattern of Q_1 only in bit a_1. Then $G_1 = (P_1, Q_1)$ will be a suitable Gray path that solves our problem.

For example, consider the subspiders for $U_1 = \{2, 6, 9\}$ in the example spider. An inductive construction shows that they have respectively $(n_2, n_6, n_9) = (8, 3, 2)$ patterns, with corresponding Gray paths

$$G_2 = 0000, 0001, 0101, 0100, 0110, 0111, 1111, 1101;$$
$$G_6 = 00, 10, 11;$$
$$G_9 = 0, 1.$$

We obtain 48 patterns P_1 by setting $a_1 = a_8 = 0$ and using G_2 for $a_2 a_3 a_4 a_5$, G_6 for $a_6 a_7$, and G_9 for a_9, taking care to end with $a_2 = a_6 = 1$. Similarly, the subspiders for $V_1 = \{4, 7, 8\}$ have $(n_4, n_7, n_8) = (2, 2, 3)$ patterns, and paths

$$G_4 = 0, 1;$$
$$G_7 = 0, 1;$$
$$G_8 = 00, 01, 11.$$

We obtain 12 patterns Q_1 by setting $a_1 = a_2 = a_3 = a_5 = a_6 = 1$ and using G_4 for a_4, G_7 for a_7, and G_8 for $a_8 a_9$, taking care to begin with $a_8 = 0$. Combining these observations, we see that P_1 should end with 011011100, and Q_1 should begin with 111011100.

In general, the last element of P_k and the first element of Q_k can be determined as follows: For all children j of k, set $a_j \ldots a_{\text{scope}(j)}$ to the last element of the previously computed Gray path G_j if j is positive, or to the first element of G_j if j is negative. Then set $a_k = 0$ in P_k, $a_k = 1$ in Q_k. It is easy to verify that these rules make $a_j = 0$ whenever $j \to^* k$, and $a_j = 1$ whenever $k \to^* j$, for all j such that $k < j \leq \text{scope}(k)$. A reflected Gray code based on the paths G_u for $u \in U_k$ can be used to construct P_k ending at the transition values, having $a_k = 0$; and Q_k can be constructed from those starting values based on the paths G_v for $v \in V_k$, having $a_k = 1$. Thus we obtain a Gray path $G_k = (P_k, Q_k)$.

We have therefore constructed a Gray path for spider 1, proving that the spider-squishing problem has a solution when the underlying digraph is connected. To complete the construction for the general case, we can artificially ensure that the graph is connected by introducing a new vertex 0, with arcs from 0 to the roots of the components. Then P_0 will be the desired Gray path, if we suppress bit a_0 (which is zero throughout P_0).

5. Implementation via Coroutines

By constructing families of sets U_k and V_k and identifying principal vertices in those sets, we have shown the existence of a Gray path for any given spider-squishing problem. Now we want to make the proof explicit by constructing a family of coroutines that will generate the successive patterns $a_1 \ldots a_n$ dynamically, as in the examples worked out in Sections 1–3 above.

First let's consider a basic substitution or "plug-in" operation that applies to coroutines of the type we are using. Consider the following coroutines X and Y:

> **Boolean coroutine** X;
>   **while** *true* **do begin**
>   **while** A **do return** *true*;
>   **return** *false*;
>   **while** B **do return** *false*;
>   **if** C **then return** *true*;
>   **end**;
>
> **Boolean coroutine** Y;
>   **while** *true* **do begin**
>   **while** X **do return** *true*;
>   **return** Z;
>   **end**.

Here X is a more-or-less random coroutine that invokes three coroutines A, B, C; coroutine Y has a special structure that invokes X and an arbitrary coroutine $Z \neq X, Y$. Clearly Y carries out essentially the same actions as the slightly faster coroutine XZ that we get from X by substituting Z wherever X returns *false*:

> **Boolean coroutine** XZ;
>   **while** *true* **do begin**
>   **while** A **do return** *true*;
>   **return** Z;
>   **while** B **do return** Z;
>   **if** C **then return** *true*;
>   **end**.

This plug-in principle applies in the same way whenever all **return** statements of X are either 'return *true*' or 'return *false*'. And we could cast XZ into this same mold, if desired, by writing 'if Z then return *true* else return *false*' in place of 'return Z'.

In general we want to work with coroutines whose actions produce infinite sequences of patterns $\alpha_1, \alpha_2, \ldots$ having period length $2M$, where $(\alpha_M, \ldots, \alpha_{2M-1})$ is the reverse of $(\alpha_0, \ldots, \alpha_{M-1})$, and where the coroutine returns *false* after producing α_t if and only if t is a multiple of M. The proof at the end of Section 2 shows that a construction like coroutine Y above, namely

> **Boolean coroutine** *AtimesB*;
>   **while** *true* **do begin**
>   **while** B **do return** *true*;
>   **return** A;
>   **end**

yields a coroutine that produces such sequences of period length $2MN$ from coroutines A and B of period lengths $2M$ and $2N$, when A and B affect disjoint bit positions of the output sequences.

The following somewhat analogous coroutine produces such sequences of period length $2(M + N)$:

> **Boolean coroutine** *AplusB*;
>   **while** *true* **do begin**
>   **while** A **do return** *true*;
> $a[1] := 1$; **return** *true*;
>   **while** B **do return** *true*;
>   **return** *false*;

```
        while B do return true;
        a[1] := 0;  return true;
        while A do return true;
        return false;
    end.
```

This construction assumes that A and B individually generate reflective periodic sequences α and β on bits $a_2 \ldots a_n$, and that $\alpha_M = \beta_0$. The first half of *AplusB* produces

$$0\alpha_0, \ \ldots, \ 0\alpha_{M-1}, \ 1\beta_0, \ \ldots, \ 1\beta_{N-1},$$

and returns *false* after forming $1\beta_N$ (which equals $1\beta_{N-1}$). The second half produces the n-tuples

$$1\beta_N, \ \ldots, \ 1\beta_{2N-1}, \ 0\alpha_M, \ \ldots, \ 0\alpha_{2M-1},$$

which are the first $M + N$ outputs in reverse; then it returns *false*, after forming $0\alpha_{2M}$ (which equals $0\alpha_0$).

The coroutines that we need to implement spider squishing can be built up from variants of the primitive constructions for product and sum just mentioned. Consider the following coroutines $gen[1], \ldots, gen[n]$, each of which receives an integer parameter l whenever being invoked:

```
        Boolean coroutine gen[k](l);  integer l;
            while true do begin
    awake0:  if maxu[k] ≠ 0 then
                    while gen[maxu[k]](k) do return true;
                a[k] := 1;  return true;
    asleep1: if maxv[k] ≠ 0 then
                    while gen[maxv[k]](k) do return true;
                if prev[k] > l then return gen[prev[k]](l)
                else return false;
    awake1:  if maxv[k] ≠ 0 then
                    while gen[maxv[k]](k) do return true;
                a[k] := 0;  return true;
    asleep0: if maxu[k] ≠ 0 then
                    while gen[maxu[k]](k) do return true;
                if prev[k] > l then return gen[prev[k]](l)
                else return false;
    end.
```

Here $maxu[k]$ denotes the largest element of $U_k \cup \{0\}$, and $prev[k]$ is a function that we shall define momentarily. This function, like the sets U_k and V_k, is statically determined from the given totally acyclic digraph.

The idea of '$prev$' is that all elements of U_l can be listed as u, $prev[u]$, $prev[prev[u]]$, ..., until reaching an element $\leq l$, if we start with $u = maxu[l]$. Similarly, all elements of V_l can be listed as v, $prev[v]$, $prev[prev[v]]$, ..., while those elements exceed l, starting with $v = maxv[l]$. The basic meaning of $gen[k]$ with parameter l is to run through all bit patterns for the spiders $u \leq k$ in U_l, if k is a positive vertex, or for the spiders $v \leq k$ in V_l, if vertex k is negative.

The example spider of Section 4 will help clarify the situation. The following table shows the sets U_k, V_k, and a suitable function $prev[k]$, together with some auxiliary functions by which $prev[k]$ can be determined in general:

k	scope(k)	U_k	V_k	$prev[k]$	ppro(k)	npro(k)
1	9	$\{2,6,9\}$	$\{4,7,8\}$	0	1	0
2	5	$\{3,5\}$	$\{4\}$	0	2	0
3	4	$\emptyset$	$\{4\}$	0	3	0
4	4	$\emptyset$	$\emptyset$	0	3	4
5	5	$\emptyset$	$\emptyset$	3	5	0
6	7	$\emptyset$	$\{7\}$	2	6	0
7	7	$\emptyset$	$\emptyset$	4	6	7
8	9	$\{9\}$	$\emptyset$	7	1	8
9	9	$\emptyset$	$\emptyset$	6	9	8

If u is a positive vertex, not a root, let v_1 be the parent of u. Then if v_1 is negative, let v_2 be the parent of v_1, and continue in this manner until reaching a positive vertex v_t, the nearest positive ancestor of v_1. We call v_t the *positive progenitor* of v_1, denoted ppro(v_1). The main point of this construction is that $u \in U_k$ if and only if k is one of the vertices $\{v_1, v_2, \ldots, v_t\}$. Consequently

$$U_k = U_l \cap \{k, k+1, \ldots, \text{scope}(k)\}$$

if l is the positive progenitor of k. Furthermore U_k and $U_{k'}$ are disjoint whenever k and k' are distinct positive vertices. Therefore we can define $prev[u]$ for all positive nonroots u as the largest element less than u in the set $U_k \cup \{0\}$, where $k = \text{ppro}(\text{parent}(u))$ is the positive progenitor of u's parent.

Every element also has a negative progenitor, if we regard the dummy vertex 0 as a negative vertex that is parent to all the roots of the digraph. Thus we define $prev[v]$ for all negative v as the largest element less than v in the set $V_k \cup \{0\}$, where $k = \text{npro}(\text{parent}(v))$.

Notice that 9 is an element of both U_1 and U_8 in the example spider, so both $gen[9](1)$ and $gen[9](8)$ will be invoked at various times. The former will invoke $gen[6](1)$, which will invoke $gen[2](1)$; the latter, however, will merely flip bit a_9 on and off, because $prev[9]$ does not exceed 8. There is only one coroutine $gen[9]$; its parameter l is reassigned each time $gen[9]$ is invoked. (The two usages do not conflict, because $gen[9](1)$ is invoked only when $a_1 = 0$, in which case $a_8 = 0$ and $gen[8]$ cannot be active.) Similarly, $gen[4]$ can be invoked with $l = 1$, 2, or 3; but in this case there is no difference in behavior because $prev[4] = 0$.

In order to see why $gen[k]$ works, let's consider first what would happen if its parameter l were ∞, so that the test '$prev[k] > l$' would always be false. In such a case $gen[k]$ is simply the $AplusB$ construction applied to $A = gen[maxu[k]](k)$ and $B = gen[maxv[k]](k)$.

On the other hand when l is set to a number such that $k \in U_l$ or $k \in V_l$, the coroutine $gen[k]$ is essentially the $AtimesB$ construction, because it results when $Z = gen[prev[k]](l)$ is plugged in to the instance of $AplusB$ that we've just discussed. The effect is to obtain the Cartesian product of the sequence generated with $l = \infty$ and the sequence generated by $gen[prev[k]](l)$.

Thus we see that 'if $maxu[k] \neq 0$ then while $gen[maxu[k]](k)$ do return $true$' generates the sequence P_k described in Section 4, and 'if $maxv[k] \neq 0$ then while $gen[maxv[k]](k)$ do return $true$' generates Q_k. Therefore $gen[k](\infty)$ generates the Gray path G_k. We get the overall solution, path P_0, by invoking the root coroutine $gen[maxu[0]](0)$.

Well, there is one hitch: Every time the $AplusB$ construction is used, we must be sure that coroutines A and B have been set up so that the last pattern of A equals the first pattern of B. We shall deal with that problem in Section 6.

In the unconstrained case, when the given digraph has no arcs whatsoever, we have $U_0 = \{1, \ldots, n\}$ and all other U's and V's are empty. Thus $prev[k] = k - 1$ for $1 \leq k \leq n$, and $gen[k](0)$ reduces to the coroutine $poke[k]$ of Section 1.

If the given digraph is the chain $1 \to 2 \to \cdots \to n$, the nonempty U's and V's are $U_k = \{k + 1\}$ for $0 \leq k < n$. Thus $prev[k] = 0$ for all k, and $gen[k](l)$ reduces to the coroutine $bump[k]$ of Section 2. Similar remarks apply to $cobump$, $mbump$, and $ebump$.

If the given digraph is the fence $1 \to 2 \leftarrow 3 \to 4 \leftarrow \cdots$, we have $U_k = \{k'\}$ and $V_k = \{k''\}$ for $1 \leq k < n$, where $(k', k'') = (k + 1, k + 2)$ if k is odd, $(k + 2, k + 1)$ if k is even, except that $U_{n-1} = \emptyset$ if n is odd, $V_{n-1} = \emptyset$ if n is even. Also $U_0 = \{1\}$. Therefore $prev[k] = 0$ for all k, and $gen[k](l)$ reduces to the coroutine $nudge[k]$ of Section 3.

6. Launching

Ever since 1968, Section 1.4.2 of *The Art of Computer Programming* [9] has contained the following remark: "Initialization of coroutines tends to be a little tricky, although not really difficult." Perhaps that statement needs to be amended, from the standpoint of the coroutines considered here. We need to decide at which label each coroutine $gen[k]$ should begin execution when it is first invoked: awake0, asleep1, awake1, or asleep0. And our discussion in Sections 3 and 4 shows that we also need to choose the initial setting of $a_1 \ldots a_n$ very carefully.

Let's consider the initialization of $a_1 \ldots a_n$ first. The reflected Gray path mechanism that we use to construct the paths P_k and Q_k, as explained in Section 4, complements some of the bits. If, for example, $U_k = \{u_1, u_2, \ldots, u_m\}$, where $u_1 < u_2 < \cdots < u_m$, path P_k will contain $n_{u_1} n_{u_2} \ldots n_{u_m}$ bit patterns, and the value of bit a_{u_i} at the end of P_k will equal the value it had at the beginning if and only if $n_{u_1} n_{u_2} \ldots n_{u_{i-1}}$ is even. The reason is that subpath G_{u_i} is traversed $n_{u_1} n_{u_2} \ldots n_{u_{i-1}}$ times, alternately forward and backward.

In general, let

$$\delta_{jk} = \prod_{\substack{u<j \\ u \in U_k}} n_u, \text{ if } j \in U_k; \qquad \delta_{jk} = \prod_{\substack{v<j \\ v \in V_k}} n_v, \text{ if } j \in V_k.$$

Let α_{jk} and ω_{jk} be the initial and final values of bit a_j in the Gray path G_k for spider k, and let τ_{jk} be the value of a_j at the transition point (the end of P_k and the beginning of Q_k). Then $\alpha_{kk} = 0$, $\omega_{kk} = 1$, and the construction in Section 4 defines the values of α_{ik}, τ_{ik}, and ω_{ik} for $k < i \le \text{scope}(k)$ as follows: Suppose i belongs to spider j, where j is a child of k.

- If j is positive, so that j is a principal element of U_k, we have $\tau_{ik} = \omega_{ij}$, since P_k ends with $a_j = 1$. Also $\alpha_{ik} = \omega_{ij}$ if δ_{jk} is even, $\alpha_{ik} = \alpha_{ij}$ if δ_{jk} is odd. If $k \to^* i$ we have $\omega_{ik} = 1$; otherwise i belongs to spider j', where j' is a nonprincipal element of V_k. In the latter case $\omega_{ik} = \alpha_{ij'}$ if $\omega_{j'j} + \delta_{j'k}$ is even, otherwise $\omega_{ik} = \omega_{ij'}$. (This follows because $\omega_{j'j} = \tau_{j'k}$ and $\omega_{j'k} = (\tau_{j'k} + \delta_{j'k}) \bmod 2$.)

- If j is negative, so that j is a principal element of V_k, we have $\tau_{ik} = \alpha_{ij}$, since Q_k begins with $a_j = 0$. Also $\omega_{ik} = \alpha_{ij}$ if δ_{jk} is even, $\omega_{ik} = \omega_{ij}$ if δ_{jk} is odd. If $i \to^* k$ we have $\alpha_{ik} = 0$; otherwise i belongs to spider j', where j' is a nonprincipal element of U_k. In the latter case $\alpha_{ik} = \alpha_{ij'}$ if $\alpha_{j'j} + \delta_{j'k}$ is even, otherwise $\alpha_{ik} = \omega_{ij'}$.

For example, when the digraph is the spider of Section 4, these formulas yield

k	n_k	Initial bits α_{jk}	Transition bits τ_{jk}	Final bits ω_{jk}
9	2	$a_9 = 0$	$*$	1
8	3	$a_8 a_9 = 00$	$*1$	11
7	2	$a_7 = 0$	$*$	1
6	3	$a_6 a_7 = 00$	$*0$	11
5	2	$a_5 = 0$	$*$	1
4	2	$a_4 = 0$	$*$	1
3	3	$a_3 a_4 = 00$	$*0$	11
2	8	$a_2 a_3 a_4 a_5 = 0000$	$*111$	1101
1	60	$a_1 a_2 \ldots a_9 = 000001100$	$*11011100$	111111100

Suppose j is a negative child of k. If n_u is odd for all elements u of U_k that are less than j, then $\delta_{ij} + \delta_{ik}$ is even for all $i \in U_j$, and it follows that $\alpha_{ik} = \tau_{ij}$ for $j < i \leq \text{scope}(j)$. (If i is in spider j', where $j' \in U_j \subseteq U_k$, then α_{ik} is $\alpha_{ij'}$ or $\omega_{ij'}$ according as $\alpha_{j'j} + \delta_{j'k}$ is even or odd, and τ_{ij} is $\alpha_{ij'}$ or $\omega_{ij'}$ according as $\alpha_{j'j} + \delta_{j'j}$ is even or odd; and we have $\delta_{j'k} \equiv \delta_{j'j} \bmod 2$.) On the other hand, if n_u is even for some $u \in U_k$ with $u < j$, then δ_{ik} is even for all $i \in U_j$, and we have $\alpha_{ik} = \alpha_{ij}$ for $j < i \leq \text{scope}(j)$. This observation makes it possible to compute the initial bits $a_1 \ldots a_n$ in $O(n)$ steps (see [13]).

The special nature of vertex 0 suggests that we define $\delta_{j0} = 1$ for $1 \leq j \leq n$, because we use path P_0 but not Q_0. This convention makes each component of the digraph essentially independent. (Otherwise, for example, the initial setting of $a_1 \ldots a_n$ would be $01 \ldots 1$ in the trivial "poke" case when the digraph has no arcs.)

Once we know the initial bits, we start $gen[k]$ at label awake0 if $a_k = 0$, at label awake1 if $a_k = 1$.

7. Optimization

The coroutines $gen[1]$, $\ldots$, $gen[n]$ solve the general spider-squishing problem, but they might not run very fast. For example, the *bump* routine in Section 2 takes an average of about $n/2$ steps to decide which bit should be changed. We would much prefer to use only a bounded amount of time per bit change, on the average, and this goal turns out to be achievable if we optimize the coroutine implementation.

A brute-force implementation of the *gen* coroutines, using only standard features of ALGOL, can readily be written down based on an explicit stack and a switch declaration:

> **Boolean** *val*;   **comment** the current value being returned;
> **integer array** *stack* [0 : 2 ∗ *n*];   **comment** saved values of *k* and *l*;
> **integer** *k*, *l*;   **comment** the current coroutine and parameter;
> **integer** *s*;   **comment** the current stack height;
> **switch** *sw* := p1, p2, p3, p4, p5, p6, p7, p8, p9, p10, p11;
> **integer array** *pos* [0 : *n*];   **comment** coroutine positions;

⟨Initialize everything⟩;

p1: **if** *maxu*[*k*] ≠ 0 **then begin**
        invoke(*maxu*[*k*], *k*, 2);
   p2: **if** *val* **then** *ret*(1);
       end;
    a[*k*] := 1;   *val* := *true*;   *ret*(3);
p3: **if** *maxv*[*k*] ≠ 0 **then begin**
        invoke(*maxv*[*k*], *k*, 4);
   p4: **if** *val* **then** *ret*(3);
       end;
    if *prev*[*k*] > *l* **then begin**
        invoke(*prev*[*k*], *l*, 5);
   p5: *ret*(6);
       end
    else begin *val* := *false*;   *ret*(6);   **end**;
p6: **if** *maxv*[*k*] ≠ 0 **then begin**
        invoke(*maxv*[*k*], *k*, 7);
   p7: **if** *val* **then** *ret*(6);
       end;
    a[*k*] := 0;   *val* := *true*;   *ret*(8);
p8: **if** *maxu*[*k*] ≠ 0 **then begin**
        invoke(*maxu*[*k*], *k*, 9);
   p9: **if** *val* **then** *ret*(8);
       end;
    if *prev*[*k*] > *l* **then begin**
        invoke(*prev*[*k*], *l*, 10);
   p10: *ret*(1);
       end
    else begin *val* := *false*;   *ret*(1);   **end**;
p11: ⟨Actions of the driver program when *k* = 0⟩;

Here $invoke(newk, newl, j)$ is an abbreviation for

$$pos[k] := j; \quad stack[s] := k; \quad stack[s+1] := l; \quad s := s + 2;$$
$$k := newk; \quad l := newl; \quad \textbf{go to } sw[pos[k]]$$

and $ret(j)$ is an abbreviation for

$$pos[k] := j; \quad s := s - 2;$$
$$l := stack[s+1]; \quad k := stack[s]; \quad \textbf{go to } sw[pos[k]].$$

This brute-force implementation can be streamlined in several straightforward ways. First we can use a well-known technique to simplify the "tail recursion" that occurs when $invoke$ is immediately followed by ret (see [11, example 6a]): The statements '$invoke(prev[k], l, 5)$; p5: $ret(6)$' can, for example, be replaced by

$$pos[k] := 6; \quad k := prev[k]; \quad \textbf{go to } sw[pos[k]].$$

An analogous simplification is possible for the constructions of the form 'while A do return $true$' that occur in $gen[k]$. For example, we could set things up so that coroutine A removes two pairs of items from the stack when it returns with $val = true$, if we first set $pos[k]$ to the index of a label that follows the while statement. More generally, if coroutine A itself is also performing such a while statement, we could allow return statements to remove even more than two pairs of stack items at a time. Details are left to the reader.

8. The Active List

The gen coroutines of Section 5 perform $O(n)$ operations per bit change, as they pass signals back and forth, because each coroutine carries out at most two lines of its program. This upper bound on the running time cannot be substantially improved, in general. For example, the $bump$ coroutines of Section 2 typically need to interrogate about $\frac{1}{2}n$ trolls per step; and it can be shown that the $nudge$ coroutines of Section 3 typically involve action by about cn trolls per step, where $c = (5 + \sqrt{5})/10 \approx 0.724$. (See [9, exercise 1.2.8–12].)

Using techniques like those of Section 7, however, the gen coroutines can always be transformed into a procedure that performs only $O(1)$ operations per bit change, amortized over all the changes. A formal derivation of such a transformation is beyond the scope of the present paper, but we will be able to envision it by considering an informal description of the algorithm that results.

The key idea is the concept of an *active list*, which encapsulates a given stage of the computation. The active list is a sequence of nodes that are either awake or asleep. If j is a positive child of k, node j is in the active list if and only if $k = 0$ or $a_k = 0$; if j is a negative child of k, it is in the active list if and only if $a_k = 1$.

Examples of the active list in special cases have appeared in the tables illustrating *bump* in Section 2 and *nudge* in Section 3. Readers who wish to review those examples will find that the numbers listed there do indeed satisfy these criteria. Furthermore, a node number has been underlined when that node is asleep; bit a_j has been underlined if and only if j is asleep and in the active list.

Initially $a_1 \ldots a_n$ is set to its starting pattern as defined in Section 6, and all elements of the corresponding active list are awake. To get to the next bit pattern, we perform the following actions:

1) Let k be the largest nonsleeping node on the active list, and wake up all nodes that are larger. (If all elements of the active list are asleep, they all wake up and no bit change is made; this case corresponds to *gen*[*maxu*[0]](0) returning *false*.)

2) If $a_k = 0$, set a_k to 1, delete k's positive children from the active list, and insert k's negative children. Otherwise set a_k to 0, insert the positive children, and delete the negative ones. (Newly inserted nodes are awake.)

3) Put node k to sleep.

Again the reader will find that the *bump* and *nudge* examples adhere to this discipline.

If we maintain the active list in order of its nodes, the amortized cost of these three operations is $O(1)$, because we can charge the cost of inserting, deleting, and awakening node k to the time when bit a_k changes. Steps (1) and (2) might occasionally need to do a lot of work, but this argument proves that such difficult transitions must be rare.

Let's consider the spider of Section 4 one last time. The sixty bit patterns that satisfy its constraints are generated by starting with $a_1 \ldots a_9 = 000001100$, as we observed in Section 6, and the Gray path G_1 begins as follows according to the active list protocol:

000001100	1235679
00000110$\underline{1}$	123567$\underline{9}$
000001$\underline{0}$01	12356$\underline{7}$$\underline{9}$
000001$\underline{0}$0$\underline{0}$	12356$\underline{7}$$\underline{9}$
00000$\underline{0}$000	12356$\underline{9}$

$$
\begin{array}{ll}
000000\underline{001} & 1235\underline{69} \\
0000\underline{1}0001 & 123\underline{5}69 \\
00001000\underline{0} & 123\underline{5}69 \\
000011000 & 123\underline{5}679
\end{array}
$$

(Notice how node 7 becomes temporarily inactive when a_6 becomes 0.) The most dramatic change will occur after the first $n_2 n_6 n_9 = 48$ patterns, when bit a_1 changes as we proceed from path P_1 to path Q_1:

$$
\begin{array}{ll}
0\underline{11011100} & 1\underline{24679} \\
\underline{1}11011100 & \underline{1}4789
\end{array}
$$

(The positive children 2 and 6 have been replaced by the negative child 8.) Finally, after all 60 patterns have been generated, the active list will be $1\underline{4789}$ and $a_1 \ldots a_9$ will be $1111111\underline{00}$. All active nodes will be napping, but when we wake them up they will be ready to regenerate the 60 patterns in reverse order.

It should be clear from these examples, and from a careful examination of the *gen* coroutines, that steps (1), (2), and (3) faithfully implement those coroutines in an efficient iterative manner.

9. Additional Optimizations

The algorithm of Section 8 can often be streamlined further. For example, if j and j' are consecutive positive children of k and if V_j is empty, then j and j' will be adjacent in the active list whenever they are inserted or deleted. We can therefore insert or delete an entire family en masse, in the special case that all nodes are positive, if the active list is doubly linked. This important special case was first considered by Koda and Ruskey [14]; see also [12, Algorithm 7.2.1.1K].

Further tricks can in fact be employed to make the active list algorithm entirely *loopless*, in the sense that $O(1)$ operations are performed between successive bit changes in *all* cases — not only in an average, amortized sense. One idea, used by Koda and Ruskey in the special case just mentioned, is to use "focus pointers" to identify the largest nonsleeping node (see [7] and [12, Algorithm 7.2.1.1L]). Another idea, which appears to be necessary when both positive and negative nodes appear in a complex family, is to perform lazy updates to the active list, changing links only gradually but before they are actually needed. Such a loopless implementation, which moreover needs only $O(n)$ steps to initialize all the data structures, is described fully in [13]. It does not necessarily run faster than a more straightforward amortized $O(1)$ algorithm, from the standpoint of total time on a sequential computer; but it does prove that a strong performance guarantee is achievable, given any totally acyclic digraph.

10. Conclusions and Acknowledgments

We have seen that a systematic use of cooperating coroutines leads to a generalized Gray code for generating all bit patterns that satisfy the ordering constraints of any totally acyclic digraph. Furthermore those coroutines can be implemented efficiently, yielding an algorithm that is faster than previously known methods for that problem. Indeed, the algorithm is optimum, in the sense that its running time is linear in the number of outputs.

Further work is clearly suggested in the heretofore neglected area of coroutine transformation. For example, we have not discussed the implementation of coroutines such as

> **Boolean coroutine** *copoke*[k];
>   **while** *true* **do begin**
>   **if** $k < n$ **then while** *copoke*[$k + 1$] **do return** *true*;
> $a[k] := 1 - a[k]$;   **return** *true*;
>   **if** $k < n$ **then while** *copoke*[$k + 1$] **do return** *true*;
>   **return** *false*;
>   **end**.

These coroutines, which are to be driven by repeatedly calling *copoke*[1], generate Gray binary code, so their effect is identical to repeated calls on the coroutine *poke*[n] in Section 2. But *copoke* is much less efficient, since *copoke*[1] always invokes *copoke*[2], ..., *copoke*[n] before returning a result. Although these *copoke* coroutines look superficially similar to *gen*, they are not actually a special case of that construction. A rather large family of coroutine optimizations seems to be waiting to be discovered and to be treated formally.

Another important open problem is to discover a method that generates the bit patterns corresponding to an *arbitrary* acyclic digraph, with an amortized cost of only $O(1)$ per pattern. The best currently known bound is $O(\log n)$, due to M. B. Squire [17]; see also [16, Section 4.11.2]. There is always a listing of the relevant bit patterns in which at most two bits change from one pattern to the next [15, Corollary 1].

Donald E. Knuth thanks Ole-Johan Dahl for fruitful collaboration at the University of Oslo during 1972–1973 and at Stanford University during 1977–1978; also for sharing profound insights into the science of programming and for countless hours of delightful four-hands piano music over a period of more than 30 years. Frank Ruskey thanks Malcolm

Smith and Gang (Kenny) Li for their help in devising early versions of algorithms for spider-squishing during 1991 and 1995, respectively. Both authors are grateful to Stein Krogdahl and to an anonymous referee, whose comments on a previous draft of this paper have led to substantial improvements.

References

[1] M. Clint, "Program proving: Coroutines," *Acta Informatica* **2** (1977), 50–63.

[2] Melvin E. Conway, "Design of a separable transition-diagram compiler," *Communications of the ACM* **6** (1963), 396–408.

[3] Ole-Johan Dahl, Bjørn Myhrhaug, and Kristen Nygaard, *SIMULA-67 Common Base Language*, Publication S-2 (Oslo: Norwegian Computing Center, 1968), 141 pages. Revised edition, Publication S-22 (1970), 145 pages. Third revised edition, Report number 725 (1982), 127 pages.

[4] Ole-Johan Dahl and C. A. R. Hoare, "Hierarchical program structures," in *Structured Programming* (Academic Press, 1972), 175–220.

[5] Ole-Johan Dahl, *Syntaks og Semantikk i Programmeringsspråk* (Lund: Studentlitteratur, 1972), 103 pages.

[6] Ole-Johan Dahl, "An approach to correctness proofs of semi-coroutines," Research Report in Informatics, Number 13 (Blindern, Norway: University of Oslo, 1977), 20 pages.

[7] Gideon Ehrlich, "Loopless algorithms for generating permutations, combinations and other combinatorial configurations," *Journal of the Association for Computing Machinery* **20** (1973), 500–513.

[8] Robert W. Floyd, "The syntax of programming languages — A survey," *IEEE Transactions on Electronic Computers* **EC-13** (1964), 346–353.

[9] Donald E. Knuth, *Fundamental Algorithms*, Volume 1 of *The Art of Computer Programming* (Reading, Massachusetts: Addison–Wesley, 1968). Third edition, 1997.

[10] Donald E. Knuth, *Selected Topics in Computer Science, Part II*, Lecture Note Series, Number 2 (Blindern, Norway: University of Oslo, Institute of Mathematics, August 1973). See page 3 of the notes entitled "Generation of combinatorial patterns: Gray codes."

[11] Donald E. Knuth, "Structured programming with **go to** statements," *Computing Surveys* **6** (1974), 261–301. [Reprinted with

revisions as Chapter 2 of *Literate Programming*, CSLI Lecture Notes 27 (Stanford, California: Center for the Study of Language and Information, 1992), 17–89.]

[12] Donald E. Knuth, "Generating all *n*-tuples," Section 7.2.1.1 of *The Art of Computer Programming*, Volume 4 (Addison–Wesley), in preparation.

[13] Donald E. Knuth, SPIDERS, a CWEB program downloadable from `http://www-cs-faculty.stanford.edu/~knuth/programs.html`.

[14] Yasunori Koda and Frank Ruskey, "A Gray code for the ideals of a forest poset," *Journal of Algorithms* **15** (1993), 324–340.

[15] Gara Pruesse and Frank Ruskey, "Gray codes from antimatroids," *Order* **10** (1993), 239–252.

[16] Frank Ruskey, *Combinatorial Generation* [preliminary working draft] (Victoria, British Columbia: Department of Computer Science, University of Victoria, 1996).

[17] Matthew Blaze Squire, *Gray Codes and Efficient Generation of Combinatorial Structures* (Ph.D. thesis, North Carolina State University, 1995), x + 145 pages.

[18] George Steiner, "An algorithm to generate the ideals of a partial order," *Operations Research Letters* **5** (1986), 317–320.

[19] Leonard I. Vanek and Rudolf Marty, "Hierarchical coroutines: A method for improved program structure," *Proceedings of the 4th International Conference on Software Engineering* (Munich: 1979), 274–285.

[20] Arne Wang and Ole-Johan Dahl, "Coroutine sequencing in a block-structured environment," *BIT* **11** (1971), 425–449.

Index